Frommer's

W9-BWS-947

India
1st Edition

by Pippa de Bruyn & Dr. Keith Bain

Here's what the critics say about Frommer's:

"Amazingly easy to use. Very portable, very complete."
—*Booklist*

"Detailed, accurate, and easy-to-read information for all price ranges."
—*Glamour Magazine*

"Hotel information is close to encyclopedic."
—*Des Moines Sunday Register*

"Frommer's Guides have a way of giving you a real feel for a place."
—*Knight Ridder Newspapers*

WILEY
Wiley Publishing, Inc.

About the Authors

Pippa de Bruyn is an award-winning journalist, travel writer (author of *Frommer's South Africa*), and freelance editor. She spent almost 2 years researching, writing, and editing this first edition, and says she wouldn't dream of returning to India without it. **Dr. Keith Bain** has a doctoral degree in cinema. When he's not traveling the world in search of fantastic experiences, he spends his time writing and lecturing about film, media, theater, and contemporary culture. Having written and performed in several plays, he is currently turning his attention to writing for the big screen.

Published by:

Wiley Publishing, Inc.

111 River St.
Hoboken, NJ 07030-5744

ISBN 0-7645-6727-6

Editor: Alexis Lipsitz Flippin
Production Editor: Ian Skinnari
Cartographer: Roberta Stockwell
Photo Editor: Richard Fox
Production by Wiley Indianapolis Composition Services

Front cover photo: A visitor dips her hand into the reflecting pool at the Taj Mahal
Back cover photo: An Indian tiger in the wild

For information on our other products and services or to obtain technical support, please contact our Customer Care Department within the U.S. at 800/762-2974, outside the U.S. at 317/572-3993 or fax 317/572-4002.

Wiley also publishes its books in a variety of electronic formats. Some content that appears in print may not be available in electronic formats.

Manufactured in the United States of America

5 4 3 2

Contents

9 Rajasthan: Land of Princes 305

10 Himachal Pradesh: On Top of the World 382

11 Uttaranchal: Sacred Source of the Ganges 420

List of Maps

An Invitation to the Reader

In researching this book, we discovered many wonderful places—hotels, restaurants, shops, and more. We're sure you'll find others. Please tell us about them, so we can share the information with your fellow travelers in upcoming editions. If you were disappointed with a recommendation, we'd love to know that, too. Please write to:

Frommer's India, 1st Edition
Wiley Publishing, Inc. • 111 River St. • Hoboken, NJ 07030-5744

An Additional Note

Please be advised that travel information is subject to change at any time—and this is especially true of prices. We therefore suggest that you write or call ahead for confirmation when making your travel plans. The authors, editors, and publisher cannot be held responsible for the experiences of readers while traveling. Your safety is important to us, however, so we encourage you to stay alert and be aware of your surroundings. Keep a close eye on cameras, purses, and wallets, all favorite targets of thieves and pickpockets.

Other Great Guides for Your Trip:

Frommer's Southeast Asia

Frommer's Star Ratings, Icons & Abbreviations

Every hotel, restaurant, and attraction listing in this guide has been ranked for quality, value, service, amenities, and special features using a **star-rating system.** In country, state, and regional guides, we also rate towns and regions to help you narrow down your choices and budget your time accordingly. Hotels and restaurants are rated on a scale of zero (recommended) to three stars (exceptional). Attractions, shopping, nightlife, towns, and regions are rated according to the following scale: zero stars (recommended), one star (highly recommended), two stars (very highly recommended), and three stars (must-see).

In addition to the star-rating system, we also use **seven feature icons** that point you to the great deals, in-the-know advice, and unique experiences that separate travelers from tourists. Throughout the book, look for:

Finds	Special finds—those places only insiders know about
Fun Fact	Fun facts—details that make travelers more informed and their trips more fun
Kids	Best bets for kids, and advice for the whole family
Moments	Special moments—those experiences that memories are made of
Overrated	Places or experiences not worth your time or money
Tips	Insider tips—great ways to save time and money
Value	Great values—where to get the best deals

The following **abbreviations** are used for credit cards:

AE	American Express	DISC	Discover	V	Visa
DC	Diners Club	MC	MasterCard		

Frommers.com

Now that you have the guidebook to a great trip, visit our website at **www.frommers.com** for travel information on more than 3,000 destinations. With features updated regularly, we give you instant access to the most current trip-planning information available. At Frommers.com, you'll also find the best prices on airfares, accommodations, and car rentals—and you can even book travel online through our travel booking partners. At Frommers.com, you'll also find the following:

- Online updates to our most popular guidebooks
- Vacation sweepstakes and contest giveaways
- Newsletter highlighting the hottest travel trends
- Online travel message boards with featured travel discussions

The Best of India

India will humble, awe, frustrate, amaze, and intimidate—all in the same day. Home to the world's most spectacular medieval architecture and largest slums; sacred rivers and filth-strewn streets; religious rituals and endless traffic jams; aristocratic tigers and casteless untouchables; jewel-encrusted tombs and pavement-bound beggars; ancient traditions and modern-day scams—there is so much to take in. Whether you're here to soak up India's spirituality, chill out on the beaches, rejuvenate at an Ayurvedic spa, or live like a king in the land of princes, this chapter will help you experience the very best India has to offer.

1 Experiencing Spiritual India

Visiting temples that pulsate with devotion will evoke a sense of the sacred, but even in India, where religion is such an intricate part of daily life, spiritual experiences come when you least expect them.

- **Hop on a Motorbike and Head for the Drumbeat** (Goa): Once capital of the global beach party, Goa may be past its prime, but when rumors start that an event is in the making at a to-be-announced venue, keep your ear to the ground. Why? Because only in some deserted clearing near a golden Goan beach can you trance out with the nations of the world, then find solace in the serenity of a rural villager's smile as she hands over cups of comforting *chai* for the duration of the party. See chapter 4.

- **Worship the Sunrise as It Touches the Southernmost Tip** (Kanniyakumari, Tamil Nadu): You can't help but be moved by a sense of the miraculous when a simple daily occurrence is venerated by thousands of pilgrims who plunge themselves in the turbulent swell, believing that the tri-oceanic

waters at India's southernmost tip are holy, while others delight in the glorious spectacle as though it were a major Bollywood (the nickname for India's booming film industry) premiere. See chapter 5.

- **Lose All Sense of Reality in the City of Light** (Varanasi, Uttar Pradesh): Drifting at dawn on a boat along Varanasi's bathing *ghats* (steps leading down to the river), against a backdrop of 18th- and 19th-century temples and palaces, you will witness some surreal sights—hundreds of pilgrims waist-deep in the Ganges cleansing their souls in its holy waters, while others pound laundry, meditate by staring into the sun, or limber up to wrestle. All the while, bodies burn on the sacred banks, thereby achieving *moksha*—liberation from the eternal cycle of rebirth. See chapter 8.

- **Purchase a Pushkar Passport** (Pushkar, Rajasthan): As you wander around the ghats of Pushkar, the beautifully serene temple town on the edge of the Thar Desert, you will almost certainly be approached by a Brahmin priest to offer *puja* (prayers) at the sacred lake; in exchange for a "donation" he will then tie a red thread around your wrist—the "passport" you can brandish at the next priest who approaches. This is the commercial side of India's spirituality, and one you need to be aware of. See chapter 9.

- **Count Time at the Tomb of a Sufi Saint** (Ajmer, Rajasthan): The great Sufi saint Khwaja Muin-ud-Dir Chisti was known as the "protector of the poor," and his tomb is said to possess the power to grant the wishes of all those who visit. His Dargah Sharif is the most sacred Islamic shrine in India, second in importance only to Mecca. The atmosphere of pure devotion is both ancient and surreal, as is the sight of a long line of men who sit silently counting huge mounds of beads heaped before them—apparently keeping track of time. See chapter 9.

- **Carry the Holy *Granth Sahib* to its Evening Resting Place** (Amritsar, Punjab): In Sikh temples, the *Granth Sahib*—holy book of the Sikhs—is an object of devotion in its own right, and nowhere is this more evocative than at the Golden Temple, the most tangibly spiritual destination in the country. In the evenings men line up to carry the precious *Granth Sahib* from its gold sanctuary at the center of the Amrit Sarovar ("Pool of Nectar"), crossing the **Guru's Bridge,** which symbolizes the journey of the soul

after death, to the **Akal Takht,** where the Holy Book rests for the night. You can take part in this ceremony by joining the line that forms behind and ahead of the heavy palanquin. Being part of this ancient tradition is a deeply moving experience and indicative of the embracing atmosphere you'll find in Sikh temples throughout India. See chapter 10.

- **Look into the Eyes of the Dalai Lama** (Dharamsala, Himachal Pradesh): There's a good chance you'll meet the Dalai Lama in person if you visit Dharamsala, home to the exiled Tibetan government, which fled its homeland in 1959. Arranging a private audience isn't easy (unless you're Richard Gere), but if you attend one of his public appearances, you will—like everyone else in the audience—receive a personal blessing. And whatever your convictions, when you look into the eyes of His Holiness, you know you are in the presence of pure energy. See chapter 10.

- **Witness a Thousand Prayers Take Flight on the Wind** (Leh, Ladakh): Take the overland journey from Manali to Leh and enter the stark world of the trans-Himalayas—a breathtakingly beautiful yet desolate lunar-like landscape, with arid peaks and ancient Buddhist monasteries perched on rocky crags. Here prayer flags flutter against an impossibly blue sky, sending their silent prayers to the heavens. See chapter 10.

2 The Best Temples, Monuments & Lost Cities

- **Cave Temples at Ajanta & Ellora** (Aurangabad, Maharashtra): Fashioned out of rock by little more than simple hand-held tools, the cave temples at Ajanta (created by Buddhist monks between the 2nd

and 7th c.) and Ellora (a marriage of Buddhist, Hindu, and Jain temples, created between the 4th and 9th c.) are the finest examples of rock-cut architecture in India, and deserving of their World Heritage status. The zenith is **Kailashanath Temple,** effectively a mountain whittled down to a free-standing temple. See "Aurangabad & the Ellora and Ajanta Caves" in chapter 3.

- **Lord Gomateswara Monolith** (Sravanabelagola, Karnataka): One of the oldest (ca. A.D. 918) and most important Jain pilgrimage sites, this 18m (60-ft.) statue of the naked Lord Gomateswara—a representation of Bahubali, son of the first Jain *tirthankara,* said to have sought enlightenment by standing naked and motionless for an entire year—is the tallest monolithic statue on earth. (Don't miss the 2005 ceremony, when pilgrims will bathe the giant monolith with bucketfuls of milk and honey.) See "Exploring the Hoysala Heartland: Belur, Halebid & Sravanabelagola" in chapter 7.

- **Hampi** (Karnataka): Scattered among the Henri Moore–like boulders in the heart of Karnataka's rural interior, Hampi was once the royal seat of the powerful Vijayanagar kingdom, its size and wealth drawing comparisons with imperial Rome. Today, the city has crumbled away to just a few starkly beautiful leftovers, but the remote setting couldn't be more romantic. See "Hampi & the Ruined City of Vijayanagar" in chapter 7.

- **The Temples of Mamallapuram** (Tamil Nadu): A visit to this once-thriving port city of the Pallavas dynasty, who ruled much of South India between the 4th and 9th centuries A.D., is an essential stop on Tamil's temple tour. The earliest examples of monumental architecture in southern India (the celebrated **Arjuna's Penance** is the largest relief-carving on earth), these rock-cut shrines are best explored in the morning, leaving you time to unwind on the pleasant beach and dine on succulent seafood at village cafes for a song. See "Mamallapuram (Mahabalipurum)" in chapter 6.

- **Shri Meenakshi-Sundareshwarar Temple** (Madurai, Tamil Nadu): Alive with prayers, processions, garland-makers, and joyous devotees who celebrate the mythological romance between the beautiful three-breasted goddess and her mighty Lord Shiva, this colorful and lively complex of shrines, halls, and market stalls is almost Disneyesque, marked as it is by numerous entrance towers tangled with colorful stucco gods, demons, beasts, and mythological heroes. It truly embodies the spirit of Tamil Nadu's deeply embedded temple culture. See "Madurai" in chapter 6.

- **Taj Mahal** (Agra, Uttar Pradesh): Nothing can prepare you for the beauty of the Taj. The perfect symmetry, the ethereal luminescence, the wonderful proportions, the sheer scale—virtually impossible to imagine from staring at its oft-reproduced image—and the exquisite detailing make this bejeweled monument to love a justifiable wonder of the world. See "Agra" in chapter 8.

- **Fatehpur Sikri** (near Agra, Uttar Pradesh): From the intricacy of the glittering white marble screens that surround the *dargah* (tomb) of Salim Chisti to Pachisi Court, where the emperor played a ludo-like game using the ladies of his harem as live pieces, this magnificent ghost city—built almost entirely from red sandstone in 1571 and deserted only 14 years later—is a testament to the secular vision of Akbar, one of the great players in India's most dynamic dynasty. See "Agra" in chapter 8.

- **The Temples of Khajuraho** (Khajuraho, Madhya Pradesh): Built between the 10th and 12th centuries by the Chandela Rajputs, these World Heritage monuments are most famous for the erotic sculptures that writhe across the interiors and exteriors. But even the temple designs—their soaring *shikharas* (spires) serving as metaphoric "stairways to heaven"—are striking, and are considered the apotheosis of medieval Hindu architecture. See "Khajuraho" in chapter 8.

- **Meherangarh Fort** (Jodhpur, Rajasthan): The impenetrable walls of this 15th-century edifice to Rajput valor rise seamlessly from the rocky outcrop on which they were built, literally dwarfing the labyrinthine city at its base; from its crenelated ramparts you enjoy postcard views of the "Blue City" below. In the distance is the grand silhouette of the Umaid Bhawan Palace, heritage hotel and residence of the current maharaja. Within the fort is one of the best palace museums in India. See "Jodhpur" in chapter 9.

- **Jain Temples of Rajasthan & Gujarat** (Ranakpur & Mount Abu, near Udaipur, Rajasthan, and Palitana, Gujarat): The Jain put all their devotional passion (and not inconsiderable wealth) into the creation of the most ornate marble temples; with exquisitely detailed relief carvings covering every inch, they are all simply jaw-droppingly beautiful. Make sure you visit at least one while you're in India, preferably either the Ranakpur or Dilwara temples in Rajasthan. Or head for Palitana, in Gujarat, where 850 Jain temples and 1,000 shrines top sacred Mount Satrunjaya, "the hill that conquers enemies." See chapter 9.

- **Golden Temple** (Amritsar, Punjab): Arguably the greatest spiritual monument in India. The name derives from the central gold-plated Hari Mandir—the inner sanctuary featuring gold-plated copper cupolas and white marble walls inlaid with precious stones—which sits at the center of the "Pool of Nectar." Every day thousands of disciplined devotees pay their respects, touching their heads to the glistening marble floor while singing devotional songs continuously—a wonderful, welcoming, and humbling experience. See "The Golden Temple in Amritsar" in chapter 10.

- **The Sun Temple at Konark** (near Bhubaneswar, Orissa): An enormous war chariot carved from a massive chunk of rock during the 13th century, this masterpiece of Indian temple art is covered with detailed sculpted scenes, from the erotic to the mythological. Guarded by stone elephants and lions, the immense structure is seen as the gigantic chariot of the sun god emerging from the ocean, not far from Orissa's 500km (300-mile) beach. See "Orissa's Golden Temple Triangle" in chapter 12.

- **Tabo** (Spiti Valley, Himachal Pradesh): This 1,005-year-old Buddhist complex houses magnificent frescoes and brilliant stucco and relief figures that recount ancient myths and celebrate the deities and demons that make up the Buddhist pantheon. You'll need a torch to adequately explore the dark, smoldering halls and shrines lit only by thin shafts of natural light, and brought to life by the resonant chants and ringing of bells by the monks and nuns who populate this sacred center of Tibetan Buddhism. See "Exploring Kinnaur & Spiti" in chapter 10.

3 Unique Places to Stay

Not surprisingly, most of these are in Rajasthan, which has almost 80 heritage properties—castles, palaces, forts, and ornate *havelis* (traditional mansions), now hotels with varying degrees of comfort.

- **Taj Mahal Hotel** (Mumbai): George Bernard Shaw famously claimed that after staying here, he no longer had any need to visit the real Taj Mahal in Agra. Built just over a century ago by an Indian industrialist to avenge the whites-only policy of Watson's, then the city's poshest hotel, the Taj remains the most celebrated address in Mumbai, with a seemingly endless stream of Bombabes and playboy millionaires vamping their way through the lobby toward the popular restaurants, shops, and watering holes. See p. 79.

- **Nilaya Hermitage** (Goa): Parisian fashion stylist Claudia Derain and her husband, Hari Ajwani, came to Goa on vacation and—like so many—never left. Together with Goan architect Dean D'Cruz, they've created an *Arabian Nights* fantasy, with only 12 "cosmic-themed" guest suites and gorgeously informal public spaces overlooking paddy fields and coconut-palm groves. Despite being 6km (4 miles) from the nearest beach, Nilaya is one of Goa's most perfect getaways. See p. 115.

- **Surya Samudra Beach Garden** (near Kovalam, Kerala): A small collection of traditional cottages on a terraced hillside overlooking the sea, with direct access to two picture-perfect beaches, Surya Samudra is quite simply the most paradisiacal destination on the Malabar coast. Gazing over the Arabian Sea from your private deck (ask for a cottage near the beach), you will no doubt wish you'd spent your entire vacation here. See p. 162.

- **Green Magic Nature Resort** (Calicut, Northern Kerala): If you've always dreamed of sleeping in a treehouse in the heart of a dense forest, this is the place to do it. Getting to your room is a heart-stopping experience (one treehouse requires climbing into a pulley-rigged bamboo cage and being hoisted 26m/85 ft. up in the air), but once inside the canopy, you luxuriate in plenty of living space, private wraparound balconies, and attached bathrooms, watched only by your neighbors: giant Malabar squirrels. See p. 175.

- **Amarvilas** (Agra, Uttar Pradesh): If you've always dreamed of seeing the Taj Mahal, this is the place to celebrate your achievement. Built within the green belt that surrounds the monument, you can literally see the Taj from your bed, but you'll probably spend just as much time gazing at your immediate surroundings. With its huge reflecting pools, colonnaded courts, terraced lawns, inlaid murals, and pillowed pavilions, this palatial hotel is worth every cent. See p. 271.

- **Rajvilas** (near Jaipur, Rajasthan): This is arguably the best of the Oberoi's flagship Vilas properties. Built like a traditional fortified Rajasthani palace, Rajvilas may not have the history of an authentic heritage hotel, but it offers a level of comfort, luxury, and service these properties simply cannot match, enabling even the most world-weary guest (Bill Clinton loved it) to "live in the princely style of Rajasthan." See p. 321.

- **Deogarh Mahal** (Deogarh, Rajasthan): An ornate 17th-century fort-palace with domed turrets and balconies, personally managed by the charming Thakur of Deogarh, this is one of the most authentic and best-value heritage hotels in Rajasthan. Book the aptly named "Royal" suite, and it's not hard to feel that all you survey from your private balcony is yours. See p. 347.
- **Lake Palace Hotel** (Udaipur, Rajasthan): Built on an island by the maharana in 1740 as a cool summer retreat (swimming distance from his palace), this is perhaps the most romantic—certainly the most photographed—hotel in India. Whizzing across the waters to your private palace, you'll feel you've finally arrived—and if you've booked one of the heritage suites, you have. Floating like a beautiful white ship on the waters of Lake Pichola, the hotel offers good service, comfortable lodging, and picture-perfect 360-degree views—from Udaipur's statuesque City Palace and the surrounding whitewashed havelis, lit by the first rays of dawn, to the Aravalli Hills, behind which the sun sets. See p. 361.
- **Kankarwa** (Udaipur, Rajasthan): A short stroll from the City Palace, this ancient haveli right on the shores of Lake Pichola is the best budget heritage option in Rajasthan. Run by a family who have resided here for 200 years, rooms cost a mere Rs 650 to Rs 1,200 ($14–$26). Book room no. 204—a cool whitewashed room with white bedding, perfectly offset by two touches of color: the blue waters of the lake reflected outside the *jarokha* (window seat), and a red lamp. See p. 363.
- **Devi Garh** (near Udaipur, Rajasthan): If you're a modern-design enthusiast, this hotel will simply blow you away. An 18th-century Rajput palace-fort, its formidable exterior, towering over the tiny village at its base, remains unchanged. But step inside and you find a totally reinvented minimalist interior, with 14 floors transformed into 23 chic suites that have clearly utilized the talents of the best young Indian designers—all of whom laid to rest the perception that design here reached its apotheosis with the Mughals. It's an unparalleled modern Indian masterpiece, and a destination in its own right. See p. 365.
- **Umaid Bhawan Palace** (Jodhpur, Rajasthan): Commissioned in the 1930s by Maharaja Umaid Singh (father of the current maharaja, who still resides in the palace) as a poverty-relief exercise to aid his drought-stricken subjects, this cathedral-like palace took some 3,000 laborers 13 years to complete. At the time the largest private residence in the world, the palace remains one of the best examples of the Indo-Saracenic Art Deco style, one of Jodhpur's top attractions, and a wonderful heritage hotel (soon to be taken over by Aman resorts). See p. 373.
- **Killa Bhawan** (Jaisalmer, Rajasthan): Built entirely from yellow sandstone, **Sonar Qila** ("Golden Fort") rises like a giant sandcastle from its desert surrounds—this is the world's only living medieval fort, inhabited by families who have been here for more than 8 centuries. Within the ramparts, Killa Bhawan is a charming five-room guesthouse with rather basic facilities (only two rooms are en-suite) but lovely furnishings and stunning views,

best enjoyed from the rooftop, which is comfortably furnished with mattresses and bolsters. See p. 379.

- **Gangeshwari Suite at the Glasshouse on the Ganges** (Garhwal, Uttaranchal): Just steps away from the raging Ganges River, this thoroughly inventive suite oozes style. The immaculately laid-out sleeping area has a four-poster canopy bed and antique furniture, while the alfresco bathroom features a tub carved into the rock, with greenery spilling down the walls. You can relax on your private balcony and watch India's holiest river gushing by, or head for a hammock strung between the mango, lychee, and citrus trees. See p. 430.

4 Most Memorable Moments

- **Sharing a Cup of *Chai* with a Perfect Stranger:** You will typically be asked to sit and share a cup of *chai* (tea) a dozen times a day, usually by merchants keen to keep you browsing. Although you may at first be nervous of what this may entail, don't hesitate to accept when you're feeling more comfortable, for while sipping the milky sweet brew (flavored with ginger and cardamom), conversation will flow, and you might find yourself discussing anything from women's rights in India to the individualism that marks Western society.

- **Helping Lord Venkateshwara Repay His Debt to the God of Wealth** (Tirupati, Andhra Pradesh): Tirupati, the richest temple in India, is the most active religious pilgrimage destination on earth, drawing more than 10 million devoted pilgrims every year (more than either Jerusalem or Rome!) who line up for hours, even days, to see the diamond-decorated black stone idol Lord Venkateshwara (aka Vishnu) for just a few seconds. Afterward, you stare in disbelief as vast piles of cash and other contributions are counted by scores of clerks behind a wall of glass. See chapter 6.

- **Watching the *Mela* Moon Rise from Pushkar Palace** (Pushkar, Rajasthan): The sunset is a spectacular sight on any given evening, but on the evening of the full *mela* moon, hundreds of Hindu pilgrims, accompanied by temple bells and drums, wade into the lake—believed to miraculously cleanse the soul—before lighting clay lamps and setting them afloat on its holy waters, the twinkling lights a surreal reflection of the desert night sky. If you're lucky enough to have bagged a room at Pushkar Palace, you can watch this ancient ritual from a deck chair on the terrace on the banks of the lake. See chapter 9.

- **Gawking and Being Gawked At** (Dungarpur, near Udaipur, Rajasthan): As a woman, you may attract uncomfortably long stares (particularly on public transport), but there are a few moments that you will recall with a wry smile, like the gimlet eye of the toothless old royal retainer as he shows you the explicit Kama Sutra paintings in the hidden cupboard of the 13th-century Juna Mahal—one of Rajasthan's undiscovered gems. See chapter 9.

- **Playing Chicken with a Tata Truck:** The rules of the road (which is almost always single-laned, potholed, and unmarked) are hard to understand, but it would seem that (after the cow, which is of course sacred) the tinsel-covered Tata trucks rule the road, an assumption your hired driver is likely to test—and you will, more than once, find yourself involuntarily closing your eyes as destiny appears to race toward you, blaring its horn.

• **Meeting a Maharajah** (Rajasthan): India must be the only place in the world where you can, armed with a credit card, find yourself sleeping in a king's bed, having dined with the aristocrat whose forebears built, and quite often died for, the castle or palace walls that surround it. While most heritage properties are still owned by India's oldest monarchies, and many still live there, only some (like Mandawa Castle and Deogarh Mahal in Rajasthan, and Nilambagh Palace in Gujarat) are personally managed by these urbane aristocrats. See chapter 9.

• **Unraveling the Intricacies of Hinduism** (Master Paying Guest House, Delhi): Staying here is not only the best-value deal in town, but the sophisticated, charming, and extremely knowledgeable Avnish Puri will take you on a "Hidden Delhi" tour, showing you a world not seen by many outsiders, during which he will unravel Hinduism's spiritual tenets in a profoundly logical way—no mean feat! See chapter 8.

• **Dancing Down the Aisle to a Bollywood Blockbuster:** When the buxom, bee-stung-lipped heroine gyrates to a high-pitched Hindi melody as her strapping stud thrusts his groin across the screen, the movie audience around you is likely to break out in cheers and whistles, even dancing down the aisles, singing along to the banal-and-breezy lyrics. These wonderful, predictable melodramas, in which the hero is always valiant and virile, and the girl always voluptuous and virtuous, are best enjoyed in the high-energy atmosphere of a local cinema (though single females should be wary of going alone).

• **Setting a Candle Adrift on the Sacred Ganges** (Rishikesh, Uttaranchal): By day, Rishikesh is like a spiritual Disneyland, where the commercial excesses of packaged meditation and two-for-one tantric yoga hang heavily about the concrete ashrams, bedecked with gaudy statues of Vishnu and Shiva. But at night, to the accompaniment of hypnotic prayers and harmonious singing, the town undergoes a magical transformation, when thousands of golden marigolds and devotional candles mounted on banana leaves are set adrift on the river, a gloriously simple spectacle that reminds all that this really is a spiritual retreat. See chapter 11.

5 Exploring Natural India

• **Watch Cows Sunbathing with Tourists on the Beach** (Goa): While there's plenty of marijuana doing the rounds in Goa, you don't need to smoke a thing to be amused by the mellow cows that wander onto the beach and chill out among the tourists and hawkers. Chewing their cud while seemingly gazing out to sea, these cows really take the Goan motto, *"Sossegarde"* ("Take it easy"), to heart. See chapter 4.

• **Ply the Backwaters on a** *Kettuvallam* (Alleppey & Kumarakom, Kerala): Aboard your private houseboat you aimlessly drift past villages, temples, and churches, watching as village children, unperturbed by your drifting presence, play at the water's edge while elephants and water buffalo wade at will. Though the facilities might strike the well-heeled as basic, you're looked after by a private team (guide, cook, and pilot) who manage to be both discreetly invisible and at your beck and call. See chapter 5.

• **Quench Your Thirst with Fresh Coconut Juice on an Uninhabited Island** (Lakshadweep): One of India's best-kept secrets, the 36 atolls and coral reefs that make up the remote union territory of Lakshadweep (an extension of the better-known Maldives) are rated among the best diving destinations in Asia. Only 10 of the islands are populated, almost exclusively by Malayalam-speaking Muslims who make their living from fishing and harvesting coconut coir. These relaxed islanders seldom see outsiders but are supremely welcoming, happily climbing a towering coconut tree to help you quench your thirst. See chapter 5.

• **Wake to Hear a Herd of Elephants Approaching** (Periyar Wildlife Sanctuary, Kerala): The best way to experience this park—famous for its herds of wild elephants—is with the privately run Periyar Tiger Trail. Accompanied by a naturalist and a game ranger armed with a rifle, you are taken farther into the tourist zone than any other operator is allowed to penetrate. What's more, you are looked after by a team of reformed poachers, who skillfully track and spot animals, carry all the gear, strike camp, cook, clean and—most important—stand sentinel throughout the night when the danger of being trampled by elephants becomes a serious risk. See chapter 5.

• **Immortalize a Wild Tiger from the Back of an Elephant** (Bandhavgarh National Park, Madhya Pradesh): With the densest population of tigers of any park in India, you are practically guaranteed a sighting at this relatively low-key, remote part of Madhya Pradesh. But it's the approach that's so exciting—elephant *mahouts* set off at dawn to track the royal cats. As soon as they've spotted one, you rendezvous with your pachyderm, who then takes you within striking distance of this most royal of cats. The tiger—unperturbed by the presence of an elephant—will then strike a pose of utter indifference for your camera. See chapter 8.

• **Pick a Picture-Perfect Beach** (Goa, Kerala): India has some of the world's best beaches, most of them on the Malabar Coast. Easily accessed, **Asvem** (northern Goa) is an idyllic haven that's drawn Olive Ridley turtles for centuries, yet remains off the well-beaten tourist track. **Palolem** (southern Goa), a gorgeous crescent of sand backed by coconut palms and a handful of laid-back shacks where you can feast on fresh fish and bottles of cold beer, is deservedly India's most photographed beach. From here, time allowing, you should head over the border to beautiful and remote **Ohm** beach (Gokam, Karnataka). In Kerala, the competition is equally stiff, but we award the picture-perfect prize to the resort beaches at **Marari** and **Surya Samudra**. See chapters 4 and 5.

• **Find Divinity in *Devbhumi*, "Land of the Gods"** (Spiti to Kinnaur, Himachal Pradesh): The stark rust-colored snowcapped slopes in the Indo-Tibetan regions of Kinnaur, Spiti, and Lahaul are the stuff adventurers' dreams are made of, offering sublime mountainscapes, flower-filled valleys, terrifying roads, atmospheric Tibetan Buddhist *gompas* (monasteries), and high-altitude villages that seem to cling to the mountainsides. Only recently opened to visitors, the region is one of the most profoundly beautiful in the world, but the drive is not for the fainthearted. See chapter 10.

6 The Best Ayurvedic Pampering

- **Pousada Touma** (Goa): Loved by top Indian director Mira Nair as well as jet-setting French designer Michéle Klein, this intimate 12-suite resort, fashioned entirely from distinctively Goan laterite stone, offers a small, exclusive Ayurvedic center—the ideal place to finish off a day spent on the beach, with a professional doctor, two excellent treatment rooms, and an exhaustive range of Ayurvedic packages. An excellent in-house restaurant offers tailor-made Ayurvedic meals. See p. 116.
- **The Marari Beach** (Mararikulam, Kerala): Ayurveda is taken very seriously at this attractive beach resort in South India, not far from Kerala's tantalizing backwaters. The well-stocked Ayurvedic center is run by two physicians, who dispense sound medical advice as well as treatments, and your program is backed up with special Ayurvedic meals at the resort's restaurant. Or forgo the rules and just head for the beach, cocktail in hand. See p. 148.
- **Kumarakom Lake Resort** (Kumarakom, Kerala): The swankiest of Kumarakom's retreats, this has an extensive Ayurvedic spa—one of Kerala's most sophisticated, catering primarily to the well-heeled globe-trotter—but there's more besides, like the exquisite traditionally styled teak-and-rosewood houses with open-air garden bathrooms, a fabulous restaurant, and super-slick service. See p. 145.
- **Somatheeram** (Southern Kerala): This shabby-chic center, carved out of red sandy soil and perched on a terraced cliff overlooking a beach, is more hospital than hotel, but it has been inundated with awards for "Best Ayurvedic Centre" (mostly from Kerala's Tourism Department). Ayurvedic therapy is the primary reason to book here, joining the many European "patients" who shuffle around in pastel dressing gowns, serene expressions on their tanned faces. See p. 161.
- **Poovar Island Resort** (Southern Kerala): It's the location as much as anything that sets this stylish resort apart. Set amid dense coconut groves and banana trees, this island resort is only accessible by boat, and you can elect to stay on a floating cottage built of Malaysian teak and coconut timber. There's not much to do but idle away your time watching fishermen from your private veranda or pool, and entrust yourself to the excellent bamboo-walled Ayurvedic center, staffed by two doctors and a handful of top-notch no-nonsense masseurs. See p. 161.
- **Shalimar Spice Garden Resort** (Kerala): Not far from Periyar Tiger Reserve, this lovely inland resort occupies a 2.4-hectare (6-acre) plantation scented by exotic

spices. Over and above the enchanting Euro-chic accommodations designed by Italian owner-architect Maria Angela Fernhof is an intimate Ayurvedic center drawing a regular European clientele. Built according to traditional specifications, with a stone floor, handmade brick walls, and an open fire for heating the medicated oils, the small space is always filled with the aroma of coconut oil. See p. 170.

- **Wildflower Hall, Mashobra** (near Shimla, Himachal Pradesh): The *pièce de résistance* at what once was the mountain retreat of Lord Kitchener and is today the most beautiful resort in the Himalayas is the spa—not only because the highly trained therapists offer the ultimate rub-down (Balinese, Thai, Swedish, Ayurvedic—and

that's just for starters), but it takes place while you stare out blissfully at snowcapped peaks and a magnificent deodar valley, swirling with mists. See p. 399.

- **Ananda-in-the-Himalayas** (near Rishikesh, Uttaranchal): The 1,951-sq.-m (21,000-sq.-ft.) Wellness Center at this destination spa resort, located high above the Ganges, is rated one of the best in the world. This reputation is well-earned—thanks not only to its ultra-efficient team of therapists, masseuses, and yoga instructors, but also because you are totally pampered from the moment you wake (to a steaming cup of honey, lemon, and ginger) until you retire to a bath (where a pre-lit candle heats fragrant essential oils) and a bed (warmed by a hot-water bottle). See p. 429.

7 The Best Eating & Drinking Experiences

- **Bumping into a Bollywood Idol** (Mumbai): Nowhere in India is dining more rewarding than in Mumbai, where there are literally thousands of restaurants representing every kind of Indian cuisine. But if it's star-gazing you're after, head for places like the **Olive Bar and Kitchen** or **Shatranj Napoli.** Alternatively, hang out at **Leopold Café;** casting agents looking for foreigners to work as extras frequently scan the clientele at this favored travelers' hangout. See chapter 3.

- **Eating a Piping-Hot *Sev Puri* on Chowpatty Beach** (Mumbai): Mumbai is famous for its delicious street food, but every city has street-side vendors that tempt you with tantalizing smells. It's not always easy to figure out which street foods are safe, however (outlets with huge lines are a good bet)—if you don't feel secure about it, it's better to forgo this

particular experience or opt for restaurants that offer a safer version of "street" food. See chapter 3.

- **Dining with Ancient Delhi at Your Feet** (Delhi, Uttar Pradesh): Head for **Thai Wok,** the designer-chic rooftop restaurant with great views of the ancient Qutb Minar—the sandstone Victory Tower built by Qutbuddin Aiback in 1193. Reached via an ancient elevator and a short set of stairs, the artful alfresco setting includes a walled area with cushioned seating under wind-blown canopies; reserve well ahead to sit here. Seafood dishes are exceptional; try red snapper in chili-sour sauce, or prawns stir-fried with fresh green chilies and sweet basil. See p. 258.

- **Eating with Your Hands:** Though it may initially go against the grain, there's something immensely rewarding about digging into a delicious meal with your hands. Indians generally do, and—at least once—you should follow suit. Note that ideally you only use your right hand, and in the North, where the food is "drier," you are traditionally not supposed to dirty more than the first two digits; in the South you may use the whole hand. See the appendix.

- **Sipping a *Lassi* Thick with Chunks of Banana:** A delicious drink of liquefied sweetened yogurt, this is almost a meal in a glass and should definitely be sampled (some of the best we've tried were in Goa and Jaipur). Do, however, make sure that no water has been added (including ice), and beware the *bhang lassi*—spiced with marijuana, it can make the usually surreal scenes of India a little too out of this world.
- **Sitting Around a Bonfire under a Desert Sky** (Rajasthan): There's nothing quite like eating a superb meal around a raging campfire in the peace of the desert night. Camel and horseback safaris are run out of the Shekawati, Bikaner, Pushkar, and Jaisalmer. If you opt for the latter, the **Royal Desert camp,** a permanent tented camp with en-suite tents near Sam's Dunes, is run by Fort Rajwada, with food supplied by the team of chefs that cooks up a storm at Trio, Jaisalmer's best restaurant. See chapter 9.
- **Sampling Tibetan Butter Tea with a Buddhist Lama** (Leh, Ladakh): Many people gag at the taste of butter tea, made with salt and—you guessed it—a good dollop of the clarified butter known as ghee. It's an acquired taste, but if you get the hang of it, sipping the buttery concoction with a friendly Buddhist monk when you visit one of the many monasteries tucked in the lunar landscapes around Leh is a truly memorable experience. See chapter 10.

8 The Best Savvy Traveler Tips

- **"You pay what you like":** This rather annoying response from guides, drivers, and rickshaw-*wallahs* to the question "How much will it cost?" will no doubt end with at least one of you feeling very disappointed. Try to find out how much something should cost *before* you enter into this dialogue (we've tried to advise this wherever possible), and always negotiate the fare or rate upfront. (Note that "I come later" is another irritating response, this time to your declining a service, and you will need to remain firm or prepare to go through the entire experience again.)
- **"Just look, no buy":** You will be urged to enter shops from all corners in both explicit and less obvious ways—your driver, guide, even the seemingly innocent bystander offering assistance, are almost all operating on the ubiquitous commission system, and whatever they make on the deal is added to the quoted price. Note that to avoid this kind of hassle, look for the fixed-rate shops or those that mark their wares with prices. But beware of government emporiums with fixed rates—these are sadly often outrageously expensive.
- **"We look; we look":** This response from a rickshaw-*wallah* or driver usually means that the person either doesn't know where you've asked him to take you, or you'll end up somewhere with a similar name but nothing else to recommend it (Hotel *Chandra,* for example, rather than Hotel

Chand). Prebook your accommodations whenever you can so that you don't have to deal with touts and hawkers when you arrive. And be aware that a hotel or guesthouse that is successful will often have a rival opening within the year with a confusingly similar name.

- **"So where are you from, good gentleman?"** (or more commonly, "Coming from?"): You will be asked this often, so prepare yourself. One of the possible reasons Indians kick-start conversations this way is that it may in the past have indicated caste or social position; whatever the reason, engage in the opener—it's far preferable to living in a five-star hotel cocoon.

- **"Hashish, taxi, guide, young girls?":** In the well-traveled parts of India, you will be inundated with offers of assistance; again, the best response is to doggedly desist in what is essentially a game of endurance, and certainly ignore those unsolicited offers that are illicit—these can carry a hefty penalty, including a lengthy jail sentence.

- **"Cof-fay, chai; cof-fay, chai; cof-fay, chai?":** This incessant call given by the *chai-wallah* wandering the corridors of your train will put to rest any romantic notions about the relaxation of train travel. Note that you will be most comfortable aboard the overnight **Rajdhani Express,** which connects all the major cities, while the best daytime train is the **Shatabdi Express** (book Chair Class). Time allowing, you should definitely book a "toy train" to the hill stations of Shimla and Darjeeling—the latter approach is so spectacular it has been named a World Heritage Site.

- **"You wait, no problem":** Finally, we can't emphasize enough how important it is to simply relax and accept whatever's going on around you. Many Indians subscribe to the philosophy that life is destiny, and getting uptight or flying into a rage usually won't solve much. You'll have a far better vacation if you simply give in to the moment and enjoy the experience; after all, the only aspect you have control over is your response.

2

Planning Your Trip to India

Once the playing fields of only die-hard budget New Age travelers, India has in the past decade come into its own for top-end travelers who need to be pampered and rejuvenated as well as spiritually and culturally challenged. Given its vast size, it is remarkably easy to get to the majority of its top attractions, using a clever combination of internal flights or long-haul train journeys and chauffeur-driven cars (no sane traveler would self-drive). Hotels, particularly in the heritage category, offer excellent value-for-money in Western terms, and despite a number of potential health concerns, sensible travelers will enjoy their sojourn with little more than a brief tummy upset. It is, however, very important to plot out your itinerary and make reservations well in advance. Finally, though India has definite Third World elements—infrastructure and service levels leave much to be desired—you'll find almost everything you need here, particularly if you're armed with a credit card and *Frommer's India, 1st Edition,* of course.

1 The Regions in Brief

India is a vast country, roughly divided—for the purposes of this book—into North, East, and South.

The South (again, for the purposes of this book), accessed most conveniently via **Mumbai** (state capital of **Maharashtra**) refers to **Goa, Karnataka** (with an excursion to **Hyderabad,** capital of Andhra Pradesh), **Kerala,** and **Tamil Nadu.**

The North refers to **Rajasthan** (and its southern neighbor **Gujarat**) in the west; **Delhi, Uttar Pradesh,** and **Madhya Pradesh** in the center (only **Bodhgaya** in **Bihar** is covered in brief). Northeast of Delhi lie the largely unvisited states of **Haryana** and **Punjab** (with the exception of the Golden Temple at Amritsar, one of India's most wonderful attractions), and—moving even farther north—**Uttaranchal** and **Himachal Pradesh** (with references to **Jammu** and **Kashmir**) in the Himalayas.

The East refers to Jarkhand (not a tourist destination), West Bengal (centered around **Kolkata,** or Calcutta), **Orissa** (with top attraction Konark) and, moving north into the Himalayas again, **Sikkim.** Seven more states lie farther east (north and east of Bangladesh); the infrastructure here is virtually nonexistent, and with travel considered less than safe, these areas are not covered here.

The largest differences lie between the northern and southern regions. The former offers predominantly a plethora of medieval Mughal and Rajput architecture, ancient cities, deserts and camel safaris, heritage accommodations, tiger parks, Buddhism, and the snowcapped peaks of the Himalayas. The latter is rich in beautiful beaches, Ayurvedic spas, ancient Dravidian/ Hindu temples, cosmopolitan colonial coastal towns, and a generally more laid-back atmosphere. We suggest that rather than try to cover both, concentrate your energies on either the North or the South. If you do decide to combine the two, stick to two states, or you'll find yourself exhausted at the end of your vacation.

MUMBAI (BOMBAY) & MAHARASHTRA   Teetering on the edge of the Arabian Sea, its heaving population barely contained by palm-fringed beaches, India's sexiest city is a vibrant, confident metropolis that's tangibly high in energy. The state capital of Maharashtra, this is home to many of the subcontinent's best restaurants and great (but pricey) hotels. It's also the ideal starting point for a tour northwest to **Gujarat,** or south along the Konkan railway to **Goa** and beyond. Whichever you choose, consider a jaunt to the ancient rock-cut caves of **Ajanta** and **Ellora,** Maharashtra's startling World Heritage sites.

GOA   Nirvana for flower children since the late 1960s, Goa still attracts a cosmopolitan mix of youngsters who cruise from beach to beach, looking for action. But Goa is more than a party in paradise. A Portuguese colonial heritage has left an indelible mark on this tiny enclave (India's smallest state), from cuisine to architecture, with plenty to see. And if the crowded beaches and vibrant markets leave you gasping for solitude, you can still find the original Goan paradise on far-flung beaches, reviewed in detail here.

KARNATAKA & KERALA   Traveling south along India's west coast, you will pass through untouched Karnataka, possibly overnighting in the hip city of **Bangalore.** From there you can head to **Hyderabad,** the 400-year-old capital of Andhra Pradesh, as famous for its minarets as for its burgeoning software industry, or south to **Mysore,** "City of Incense." Whatever you do, set aside time to explore the lost city of **Hampi,** arguably Karnataka's most evocative attraction, or to join the Jain pilgrimage to anoint the giant feet of **Lord Gomateswara,** said to be the largest monolith in the world. There's more besides, but who

can tarry long when Kerala, "God's own country," awaits? South India's top destination, particularly for the well-heeled traveler in search of pampering and relaxation, Kerala offers ancient backwaters plied by houseboats, herds of wild elephant, coconut-lined beaches and, of course, the ancient healing art of Ayurveda.

TAMIL NADU   Occupying a long stretch of the eastern Indian Ocean coastline, India's southernmost state seems little touched by the cocktail of foreign influences that contributed to the cultural developments in the North. This is where you'll find India's most superb Dravidian temples, from **Mamallapuram** (7th c. A.D.) to the **Madurai temple complex** (16th c. A.D.). When you're all templed out, there's always **Pondicherry,** the former French coastal town where traditional Indian snack joints feature signs proclaiming MEALS READY—BIEN VENUE and loincloth-clad locals converse in flawless French.

DELHI, MADHYA & UTTAR PRADESH   Entered through Delhi, capital of the largest democracy in the world, the central states of Madhya and Uttar Pradesh are the real heart of India, where great rulers battled for power over vast swaths of India, and where you'll find arguably the densest concentration of top attractions on the subcontinent. From the "seven cities" of Delhi, it's a short train or road journey to **Agra,** home to the Taj Mahal and other superb examples of medieval Mughal architecture. From there you can either head west to Rajasthan, or east—via the erotic temples of **Kajuraho,** considered the pinnacle of Hindu medieval architecture—to the ancient city of **Varanasi,** India's holiest pilgrimage, where the faithful come to die on the banks of the sacred Ganges to achieve *moksha*—liberation from earthly life. To escape the well-beaten tourist

India

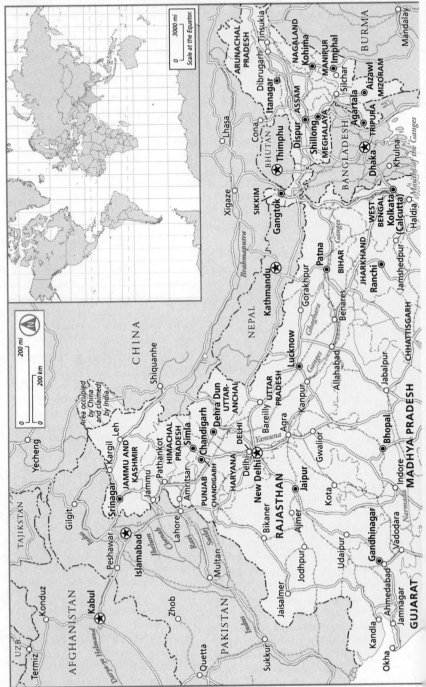

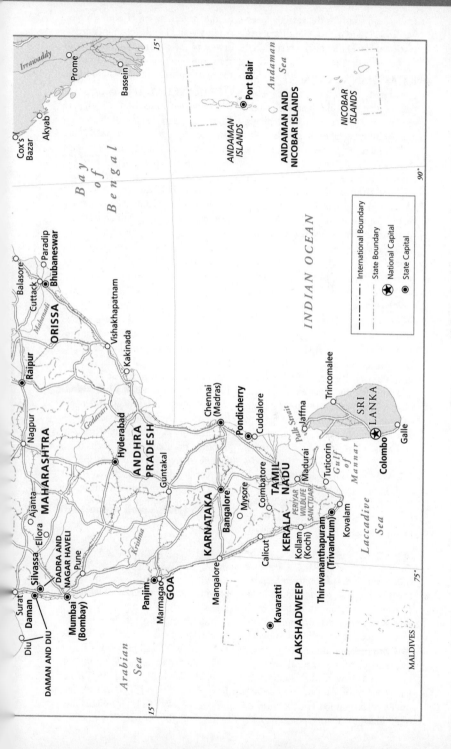

track, head south to the vast plains of Madhya Pradesh, to **Bandhavgarh National Park,** one of the best places to see tigers in Asia.

RAJASTHAN & GUJARAT With crenelated forts and impregnable palaces that rise like giant fairy-tale sets above dusty sun-scorched plains and shimmering lakes, Rajasthan—literally "land of princes"—epitomizes the romance of India. Whether you choose to linger in the untainted medieval atmosphere of little towns like **Bundi,** browse the bumper-to-bumper shops in **Jaipur,** track tigers in **Ranthambhore,** overnight on the lake at the beautiful city of **Udaipur,** or explore the world's only living fort in **Jaisalmer,** you will want to see it all. South lies the less-traveled state of Gujarat, filled with hidden gems and lacking the touts and hawkers of more heavily traveled sites.

HIMACHAL PRADESH & LADAKH Bordered by Tibet to the east, Himachal Pradesh incorporates great topographic diversity, from vast, bleak tracts of the rust-colored high-altitude trans-Himalayan desert to dense green deodar forests, apple orchards, and cultivated terraces. Together with **Ladakh** (known as "Little Tibet"), this is also where you'll find India's largest concentration of Buddhists, their atmospheric *gompas* (temples, including **Tabo,** the World Heritage Site in Spiti) a total contrast

to the pageantry of Hindu temples. An easy—and highly recommended—detour to the region is via Amritsar to view the **Golden Temple,** arguably the most spiritual destination in India.

UTTARANCHAL Comprising the pre-Vedic territories of Garhwal and Kumaon, the mountains of the central Himalayan state of Uttaranchal are riven with ancient Hindu pilgrimage routes, and offer wonderful trekking routes. Non-hikers come here to practice yoga at **Rishikesh** on the banks of the holy river Ganges, or to take a road trip through the **Kumaon,** possibly ending their sojourn looking for tigers in **Corbett National Park,** which vies with Ranthambhore for ease of accessibility from Delhi.

KOLKATA (CALCUTTA) & THE EAST Kolkata, the much-maligned capital of West Bengal, never fails to surprise the visitor with its beautiful albeit crumbling colonial architecture, sophisticated Bengali culture, and wonderful restaurants and hotels. From here you can either head north to the cooling breezes of West Bengal's hill station, **Darjeeling,** famous for its tea, and on to the Buddhist state of **Sikkim** (in many ways even more remote than Himachal Pradesh); or you can head south to Orissa to visit the monolithic **Sun Temple** at Konark, yet another of India's awesome array of World Heritage sites.

2 Visitor Information

India's **Tourism Information Department** is going all out to seduce international visitors, and has fairly extensive representation around the globe. Access one of its **websites** (www.tourisminindia.com or www.tourindia.com) for general information, but be aware that some pages may be out of date or permanently under construction. The websites do offer links to all of India's regional

tourism departments, some of which provide fantastic coverage of what's on offer.

Indian tourism offices may be found worldwide as follows. In the **U.S.:** 3550 Wilshire Blvd., Room 204, Los Angeles, CA 90010; ✆ **0213/380-8855;** and 30 Rockefeller Plaza, Suite 15, N. Mezzanine, New York, NY 10112; ✆ **0212/586-4903.** In the **U.K.:** 7 Cork St.,

Tips Visa Savvy

Travelers to India can apply for a tourist visa from their nearest Indian Consulate or High Commission. This is valid for multiple entries for 6 months from the date of issue. Given the nature of India's bureaucracy, rules and fees for application change regularly, so it's best to check with your travel agent or with the relevant authority for the latest visa information. Accurately completed visa application forms must be accompanied by three passport-size photographs and the appropriate processing fee; apply well in advance to avoid unforeseeable delays. You won't be admitted to India unless your passport is valid for at least 6 months after your entry, and it should typically also be valid for at least 3 months beyond the period of your intended stay.

In the U.S., the **Indian Embassy** is at 2107 Massachusetts Ave., Washington, DC 20008 (*© 0202/939-7000*), and there are consulates in Houston, New Orleans, New York, San Francisco, and Chicago. In the U.K., **India House** is in Aldwych, London WC2B 4NA (*© 020/7836-8484*). If you're applying for a visa in a country where India does not have a representative, make inquiries at the nearest British authority.

A **special permit** is required for foreigners wishing to visit the Lakshadweep Islands, as well as remote areas such as Sikkim and Ladakh. For Lakshadweep, your permit will be arranged when your accommodations are reserved. Permits for the other restricted regions can be obtained in India; specific details are given in the appropriate chapters. Carry a number of passport-size photographs and copies of the personal particulars and Indian visa pages of your passport in order to apply for these permits.

London W1X 2LW; *© 0207/437-3677.* In **Canada:** 60 Bloor St. (West), Suite 1003, Toronto, Ontario M4W 3B8; *© 0416/962-3787.* In **Australia:** Level 1, 17 Castlereagh St., Sydney, NSW 2000; *© 02/232-1600.*

Websites You can access up-to-the-minute news and stories through the websites of some of the country's largest English dailies, including **www.timesofindia.com**, **www.hindustan** **times.com**, and **www.thehindu** **online.com.** For up-to-date news, gossip, and tourism-related information, visit **www.indiawww.com**, which covers everything from Bollywood happenings to currency conversion and current weather conditions. Travel Spirit International (**www.tsi** **india.com**) has a wide range of links as well as easy access to sites where you can book reduced-price accommodations and travel.

3 Entry Requirements & Customs

ENTRY REQUIREMENTS

For information on how to get a passport, go to the "Fast Facts" section of this chapter. The websites listed there provide downloadable passport applications as well as the current fees for processing passport applications. For an up-to-date country-by-country listing of passport requirements around the world, go the "Foreign

Entry Requirement" Web page of the U.S. State Department at **http://travel.state.gov/foreignentryreqs.html**.

CUSTOMS
WHAT YOU CAN BRING INTO INDIA

You can bring as much foreign currency into India as you like; if you have over $10,000 in cash or traveler's checks, however, you should complete a declaration form. You may not import Indian currency into India. In addition to your personal effects, you are allowed .95 liters of alcohol, and 200 cigarettes or 50 cigars. (Know that foreign liquors and imported cigarettes are very heavily taxed and in some areas difficult to come by.) You may carry a camera and pair of binoculars, but officially you may have only five rolls of film. You must complete a special Tourist Baggage Re-Export Form if you are carrying valuables such as a laptop computer, video equipment, special camera gear, or jewelry. Although there is a strong possibility that you may encounter difficulties upon leaving if these forms are not completed, you'll discover a general malaise among Customs officials, who seldom hassle foreign visitors on international flights. Also, much of the bureaucratic heavy-handedness has eased off in recent years, and there is less suspicion of foreign travelers.

WHAT YOU CAN TAKE HOME FROM INDIA

You may not export Indian currency. Exchange all notes at the airport before you depart. Note that airport money-changers frequently run out of certain currencies, so you might want to complete any exchange before you go to the airport. There is a restriction on the exportation of anything over 100 years old, particularly works of art and items of cultural significance. It is illegal to export animal or snake skins, ivory, *toosh* wool, or anything that has been produced using these items. Generally, jewelry valued under Rs 10,000 ($218) may be exported, while gold jewelry valued only up to Rs 2,000 ($44) is allowed.

Returning **U.S. citizens** who have been away for at least 48 hours are allowed to bring back, once every 30 days, $400 worth of merchandise duty-free. You'll be charged a flat rate of 4% duty on the next $1,000 worth of purchases. Be sure to have your receipts handy. On mailed gifts, the duty-free limit is $100. With some exceptions, you cannot bring fresh fruits and vegetables into the United States. For specifics on what you can bring back, download the invaluable free pamphlet *Know Before You Go* online at **www.customs.gov**. (Click on "Travel," then "Know Before You Go Online Brochure.") Or contact the **U.S. Customs Service,** 1300 Pennsylvania Ave. NW, Washington, DC 20229 (© **877/287-8867**), and request the pamphlet.

For a clear summary of **Canadian** rules, write for the booklet *I Declare,* issued by the **Canada Customs and Revenue Agency** (© **800/461-9999** in Canada, or 204/983-3500; www.ccra-adrc.gc.ca). Canada allows its citizens a C$750 exemption, and you're allowed to bring back, duty-free, one carton of cigarettes, one can of tobacco, 40 imperial ounces of liquor, and 50 cigars. In addition, you're allowed to mail gifts to Canada valued at less than C$60 a day, provided they're unsolicited and don't contain alcohol or tobacco (write on the package "Unsolicited gift, under $60 value"). You should declare all valuables on the Y-38 form before your departure from Canada, including serial numbers of valuables you already own, such as foreign cameras. *Note:* The $750 exemption can only be used once a year and only after an absence of 7 days.

Citizens of the U.K. returning from a non-EU country have a Customs allowance of: 200 cigarettes; 50 cigars; 250 grams of smoking tobacco; 2 liters of still table wine; 1 liter of spirits or strong liqueurs (over 22% volume); 2 liters of fortified wine, sparkling wine or other liqueurs; 60cc (ml) of perfume; 250cc (ml) of toilet water; and £145 worth of all other goods, including gifts and souvenirs. People under 17 cannot have the tobacco or alcohol allowance. For more information, contact **HM Customs & Excise** at ℭ **0845/010-9000** (from outside the U.K., 020/8929-0152), or consult their website at www.hmce.gov.uk.

The duty-free allowance in **Australia** is A$400 or, for those under 18, A$200. Citizens can bring in 250 cigarettes or 250 grams of loose tobacco, and 1,125 milliliters of alcohol. If you're returning with valuables you already own, such as foreign-made cameras, you should file Form B263. A helpful brochure available from Australian consulates or Customs offices is *Know Before You Go.* For more information, call the **Australian Customs Service** at ℭ **1300/363-263,** or log on to www.customs.gov.au.

The duty-free allowance for **New Zealand** is NZ$700. Citizens over 17 can bring in 200 cigarettes, 50 cigars, or 250 grams of tobacco (or a mixture of all three if their combined weight doesn't exceed 250g); plus 4.5 liters of wine and beer, or 1.125 liters of liquor. New Zealand currency does not carry import or export restrictions. Fill out a certificate of export, listing the valuables you are taking out of the country; that way, you can bring them back without paying duty. Most questions are answered in a free pamphlet available at New Zealand consulates and Customs offices: *New Zealand Customs Guide for Travellers, Notice no. 4.* For more information, contact **New Zealand Customs,** The Customhouse, 1721 Whitmore St., Box 2218, Wellington (ℭ **04/473-6099** or 0800/428-786; www.customs.govt.nz).

4 Money

CURRENCY

The Indian rupee (Rs) is available in denominations of Rs 1,000, Rs 500, Rs 100, Rs 50, Rs 20, Rs 10, Rs 5, and Rs 2 notes. You will occasionally come across an Rs 1 note—treat this as a souvenir. Minted coins come in denominations of Rs 5, Rs 2, and Rs 1, as well as 50, 25, 20, 10, and 5 paise. There are 100 paise in a rupee.

Note: Badly damaged or torn rupee notes (of which there are many) may be refused, particularly in some small towns. Check the change you are given and try to avoid accepting these.

EXCHANGE RATES

Exchange rates fluctuate dramatically. At press time, US$1 bought you around Rs 45, while £1 was worth around Rs 72. Bear in mind that a few dollars, pounds, or euros go a very long way in India. You will enjoy your vacation a whole lot more if you don't sweat the small stuff: A difference of a couple of rupees will hardly show up on your bank statement. For up-to-the-minute **currency conversions,** log on to www.oanda.com/convert/classic.

You cannot obtain Indian currency anywhere outside India, and you may not carry rupees beyond India's borders. You may have to exchange at least some money at the airport upon your arrival; change just enough to cover airport incidentals and transportation to your hotel, since the rate will be quite unfavorable.

Tip: India is one destination in which it is really worthwhile to arrange an airport transfer with your hotel so

What Things Cost in India

This is a sampling of *average* prices you're likely to pay in India. Bear in mind that big cities generally have much higher prices than smaller towns, and that any place that attracts tourists inevitably attracts rip-off artists.

	Rupees	U.S. Dollar	British Pound
Luxury hotel room	Rs 3,500–Rs 21,000	$77–$450	£48.54–£714
Budget–moderate hotel room	Rs 100–Rs 2,000	$2.20–$43.90	£1.39–£27.76
Cup of tea from a stall	Rs 2–Rs 12	5¢–26¢	£0.03–£.17
Cup of tea at a hotel	Rs 30–Rs 50	66¢–$3.30	£.42–£2.08
Newspaper	Rs 15	33¢	£.21
Weekly magazine	Rs 50	$1.10	£.69
Taxi for the day	Rs 600–Rs 1,400	$13.10-$30.56	£8.34–£19.46
1km by auto-rickshaw	Rs 4–Rs 12	9¢–26¢	£.06–£.17
A meal at a local diner *(dhaba)*	Rs 30–Rs 100	66¢–$2.20	£.42–£1.39
Main course in a luxury restaurant	Rs 150–Rs 800	$3.30–$7.47	£2.08–£11.12

that you can avoid waiting in long lines at the airport money-changer, dealing with prepaid booths, or negotiating fees with drivers and touts. After a good night's rest, head to the nearest bank or ATM for a cash infusion.

Banks offer the best exchange rates, but they tend to be inefficient and the staff lethargic about tending to foreigners' needs. You run the risk of being ripped off by using **unauthorized money-changers;** the most convenient option is to avail yourself of ATMs while you're in the big cities. Always ask for an encashment receipt when you change cash—you will need this when you use local currency to pay for major expenses (such as accommodations and transport, though you should use a credit card wherever possible). You will also be asked to produce this receipt when you re-exchange your rupees before you leave India.

ATMS (AUTOMATED TELLER MACHINES)

Getting cash from your checking account (or cash advances on your credit card) at an ATM is by far the easiest way to get money. These 24-hour machines are readily available in most Indian cities and larger towns and at large commercial banks such as Citibank, Standard Chartered BNP, Bank of America, and Hong Kong Bank. **Cirrus** (© 800/424-7787; www.mastercard.com) and **PLUS** (© 800/843-7587; www.visa.com) networks span the globe; call or check online for ATM locations at your destination. Be sure to find out your daily withdrawal limit before you depart. Also keep in mind that many banks impose a fee every time a card is used at a different bank's ATM, and that fee can be higher for international transactions (up to $5 or more). On top of this, the bank from which you withdraw cash likely charges its own fee. To find out what these international withdrawal fees are, ask your bank.

Keep in mind that credit card companies try to protect themselves from theft by limiting the funds you can withdraw outside your home country, so call your credit card company before you leave home. You should have no problem withdrawing Rs 10,000 (almost $200) at a time from an ATM (which goes a long way in

---

Tips   The Battle of the Haggle

Sure, things are cheap to begin with and you may feel silly haggling over a few rupees, but keep in mind that if you're given a verbal quote for an unmarked item, it's probably twice the realistic asking price. To haggle effectively, make a counter-offer under half price, and don't get emotional. Protests and adamant assertions ("This is less than it cost me to buy!") will follow. Stick to your guns until you've reached a price you can live with. Remember that once the haggle is on, a challenge has been initiated, and it's fun to regard your opponent's act of salesmanship as an artistic endeavor. Let your guard slip, and he will empty your wallet. Take into account the disposition and situation of the merchant; you don't want to haggle a genuinely poor man into deeper poverty! And if you've been taken (and we all have), see it as a small contribution to a family that lives on a great deal less than you do.

India), although some may have slightly lower limits.

TRAVELER'S CHECKS

Traveler's checks are useful in that, unlike cash, they can be replaced if lost or stolen, but they are far less popular now that most cities have 24-hour ATMs that allow you to withdraw small amounts of cash as needed. If you want to avoid the high withdrawal fees most ATMS impose, you might be better off using traveler's checks—but know that you may not get the best exchange rate in the process. Keep a record of their serial numbers separate from your checks in the event that they are stolen or lost.

You can get traveler's checks at almost any bank. **American Express** offers denominations of $20, $50, $100, $500, and (for cardholders only) $1,000. You'll pay a service charge ranging from 1% to 4%. You can also get American Express traveler's checks over the phone by calling *C* **800/221-7282;** Amex gold and platinum cardholders who use this number are exempt from the 1% fee. AAA members can obtain checks without a fee at most AAA offices. **Visa** offers traveler's checks at Citibank locations nationwide, as well as at several other banks. The service charge ranges between 1.5% and 2%; checks come in denominations of $20, $50, $100, $500, and $1,000. Call *C* **800/732-1322** for information. **MasterCard** also offers traveler's checks; call *C* **800/223-9920** for a location near you.

CREDIT CARDS

Credit cards are a safe way to carry money, they provide a convenient record of all your expenses, and they generally offer good exchange rates. You can also withdraw cash advances

---

Tips   Small Change

When you change money, ask for some small bills (a wad of Rs 10 and Rs 20s) for tipping or *baksheesh* (see "Tipping" under "Fast Facts," later in this chapter). At smaller outlets and vendors, you'll frequently be told that there is no change for your Rs 500 note! Keep your smaller bills separate from the larger ones, so that they're readily accessible and you'll be less of a target for theft.

from your credit card at banks or ATMs, provided you know your PIN (personal identification number). If you've forgotten your PIN or didn't even know you have one, call the phone number on the back of your credit card and ask the bank to send it to you. It usually takes 5 to 7 business days, though some banks will provide the number over the phone if you provide personal information. Your credit card company will likely charge a commission (1% or 2%) on every foreign purchase, but you'll still get the best deal with credit cards when you factor in things like ATM fees and traveler's check exchange rates. MasterCard and Visa are commonly accepted throughout India. American Express is accepted by most major hotels and restaurants; Diners Club has a much smaller following.

5 When to Go

Your choice of where and when to go will be determined primarily by the weather. India's vastness means that the climate varies greatly from region to region, and sometimes even just from day to night, as in the desert regions. The Indian year features six seasons: spring, summer, the rainy season, early and late autumn, and winter, but from the visitor's perspective, there are but three—summer, winter, and monsoon.

You'll be better off visiting during the **high-season winter** months (Nov–Mar), when most of the country experiences pleasant, moderate temperatures (still hot enough to luxuriate in the pool), though cities in the North get chillier days as snow falls in the Himalayas. As a rule, always be prepared for warm to hot days, with the possibility of cooler weather at night. (If this has you worrying about how to pack, remember that you can pick up the most wonderful throwaway cotton garments for next to nothing and a real Pashmina scarf in every color to ward off an unexpected chill.) As with all season-driven destinations, there is a downside to traveling during peak months: From December to January, for example, Goa swells to bursting point with foreigners and city folk who arrive for the sensational beaches and parties. Lodging rates often soar during these periods, so you may want to wait until the **shoulder season** (Apr, Sept, Oct, Mar, Apr) when there are fewer people and rates are very negotiable.

Summer (generally Apr–June) sees little traffic, and for good reason—the daytime heat, particularly in India's north-central regions, is debilitating, even for the locals. This is the time to plan your trip to the Himalayas instead, particularly to the Himachal Pradesh region. Ladakh, a magical region in the far north of the country, can only be visited July through September—the rest of the year it remains cut off by cold and snow.

The **monsoon** drenches much of the country between June (sometimes as early as Apr) and September, usually starting its season in Kerala and Karnataka. In Tamil Nadu and parts of Andhra Pradesh, a second monsoon hits around mid-October and runs through December. In Rajasthan, central India, and the northern plains, the rains typically arrive by July and fall until early September. Some of the regions are at their most beautiful during the monsoon, but it can be difficult to move around, and there is a higher risk of exposure to diseases like malaria. Flooding, power failures, and natural destruction are also not uncommon.

INDIA'S WEATHER MONTH BY MONTH

The following charts indicate the average maximum and minimum temperatures for each month of the year, as well as the average rainfall, in major tourist destination cities and towns.

THE HIMALAYA
SHIMLA

	Jan	Feb	Mar	Apr	May	Jun	Jul	Aug	Sept	Oct	Nov	Dec
Temp (°F)	48/36	50/37	57/45	66/52	73/59	75/61	70/61	68/59	68/57	64/52	59/45	52/39
Temp (°C)	9/2	10/3	14/7	19/11	23/15	24/16	21/16	20/15	20/14	18/11	15/7	11/4
Rainfall (mm)	50	50	50	25	50	150	400	375	200	50	0	25

MAHARASHTRA
MUMBAI

	Jan	Feb	Mar	Apr	May	Jun	Jul	Aug	Sept	Oct	Nov	Dec
Temp (°F)	88/61	90/63	91/68	92/75	90/79	90/79	86/79	84/79	86/79	90/75	91/64	90/55
Temp (°C)	31/16	32/17	33/20	33/24	33/26	32/26	30/26	29/26	30/26	32/24	33/18	32/13
Rainfall (mm)	0	1	0	0	20	647	945	660	309	117	7	1

SOUTH INDIA
PANJIM, GOA

	Jan	Feb	Mar	Apr	May	Jun	Jul	Aug	Sept	Oct	Nov	Dec
Temp (°F)	88/70	90/63	90/68	91/75	91/81	88/75	84/73	84/75	84/75	88/75	91/73	91/70
Temp (°C)	31/21	32/17	32/20	33/24	33/27	31/24	29/23	29/24	29/24	31/24	33/23	33/21
Rainfall (mm)	2	0	4	17	18	580	892	341	277	122	20	37

COCHIN, KERALA

	Jan	Feb	Mar	Apr	May	Jun	Jul	Aug	Sept	Oct	Nov	Dec
Temp (°F)	88/73	88/75	88/79	88/79	88/79	84/75	82/75	82/75	82/75	84/75	86/75	86/73
Temp (°C)	31/23	31/24	31/26	31/26	31/26	29/24	28/24	28/24	28/24	29/24	30/24	30/23
Rainfall (mm)	9	34	50	139	364	756	572	386	235	333	184	37

MADURAI

	Jan	Feb	Mar	Apr	May	Jun	Jul	Aug	Sept	Oct	Nov	Dec
Temp (°F)	86/70	90/72	95/73	97/77	99/79	99/79	97/79	95/77	95/77	91/75	88/73	86/72
Temp (°C)	30/21	32/22	35/23	36/25	37/26	37/26	36/26	35/25	35/25	33/24	31/23	30/22
Rainfall (mm)	26	16	21	81	59	31	48	117	123	179	161	43

HYDERABAD

	Jan	Feb	Mar	Apr	May	Jun	Jul	Aug	Sept	Oct	Nov	Dec
Temp (°F)	86/59	90/63	88/73	100/75	102/81	95/75	88/73	86/72	86/72	88/68	84/68	84/55
Temp (°C)	30/15	32/17	31/23	38/24	39/27	35/24	31/23	30/22	30/22	31/20	29/20	29/13
Rainfall (mm)	8	10	14	30	28	110	140	133	163	63	28	8

DELHI, RAJASTHAN & CENTRAL INDIA
DELHI/AGRA

	Jan	Feb	Mar	Apr	May	Jun	Jul	Aug	Sept	Oct	Nov	Dec
Temp (°F)	70/45	75/50	86/59	97/70	106/81	104/84	95/81	93/79	93/77	95/66	84/54	73/46
Temp (°C)	21/7	24/10	30/15	36/21	41/27	40/29	35/27	34/26	34/25	35/19	29/12	23/8
Rainfall (mm)	25	22	17	7	8	65	211	173	150	31	1	5

JAIPUR

	Jan	Feb	Mar	Apr	May	Jun	Jul	Aug	Sept	Oct	Nov	Dec
Temp (°F)	72/46	77/52	88/59	99/70	106/79	102/81	93/79	90/75	91/73	91/64	84/54	75/48
Temp (°C)	22/8	25/11	31/15	37/21	41/26	39/27	34/26	32/24	33/23	33/18	29/12	24/9
Rainfall (mm)	14	8	9	4	10	54	193	239	90	19	3	4

EAST INDIA
KOLKATA

	Jan	Feb	Mar	Apr	May	Jun	Jul	Aug	Sept	Oct	Nov	Dec
Temp (°F)	79/54	84/59	93/68	97/75	97/79	93/79	90/79	90/79	90/79	88/75	84/64	81/55
Temp (°C)	26/12	29/15	34/20	36/24	36/26	34/26	32/26	32/26	32/26	31/24	29/18	27/13
Rainfall (mm)	13	22	30	50	135	263	320	318	253	134	29	4

EVENTS, HAPPENINGS & FESTIVALS

Indians love to celebrate, and there is no end to the list of festivals that are held in honor of the gods, gurus, and historical figures that make this such a colorful destination. Festivals usually coincide with the Indian lunar calendar, with dates only published a year in advance, so check with the local tourism office about exact dates (some may move into another month). India has relatively few national holidays when attractions, government offices, and banks are closed: Republic Day, January 26; Independence Day, August 15; Gandhi's Birthday, October 2; and Christmas.

February

Vasant Festival, countrywide. The onset of spring *(vasant)* is marked by various celebrations. Citrus-colored clothes are worn, and there is a profusion of dancing and singing coupled with great dinner spreads and feasts to mark the season of agricultural plenty.

Holi, northern India. Celebrated predominantly in the North, this joyous Hindu festival is held during the full moon—expect to be bombarded with colored water and powder.

Desert Festival, Rajasthan. This festival takes place in Jaisalmer.

March

Carnival, Goa. It may not be on quite the same level as celebrations in Rio, but the riot of colorful costumes and processions, as well as the exuberant dancing and music, make this an especially fun time to visit the tiny state and its beautiful beaches.

Ellora Festival of Classical Dance and Music, Maharashtran interior. This festival draws some of the country's top artists to the ancient caves at this World Heritage Site.

International Yoga Festival, Rishikesh. Spiritually inclined visitors head here to take classes with *Yogacharyas* from all over the world teaching a variety of yogic disciplines.

Khajuraho Dance Festival, Madhya Pradesh. Get a glimpse of all of India's great classical dance forms.

April/May

Muharram. Best experienced in the city of Lucknow, the 10-day Shi'ite festival commemorates the martyrdom of the grandson of the Prophet, Mohammed; during a parade of religious fervor, penitents scourge themselves with whips—often with nails or blades attached.

June/July

Rath Yatra, Puri. In the Orissan seaside temple town of Puri, this is one of the largest annual gatherings of humanity; thousands of devotees come together to help pull the Lord of the Universe and his two siblings through the streets on massive cars.

Hemis Tsechu, Ladakh. The town's most impressive monastic celebration happens from July 24 to July 27, 2004, when the birthday of the founder of Tibetan Buddhism is celebrated with lamastic masked dances *(chaams)*, chanting, and music at Hemis Monastery. The 2004 celebration is destined to be especially magnificent—the unfurling of the monastery's massive sacred *thangka* (tantric wall hanging) occurs only every 12 years.

August/September

Nehru Cup Snake Boat Races, Alleppey. Kerala's backwaters come alive with these renowned snake boat races. Second Saturday of August.

Independence Day, countrywide. Indians unite to celebrate independence. August 15.

Ganesh Chhaturthi, countrywide. This 5-day celebration of Ganesha, the elephant-headed god, is popular across India, but Mumbai is arguably the best place to experience this vibrant event, celebrated with fireworks and the construction of special shrines. At the end of the festival, clay images of the god are immersed in the sea.

September/October

Kullu Dussehra. Head for the Kullu Valley in Himachal Pradesh, where you can join the crowds when idols of Hindu deities from around the region are brought together in a colorful Festival of the Gods. Similarly ecstatic revelry occurs in Mysore (Karnataka) and Ahmedabad (Gujarat).

October/November

Diwali (Festival of Light; also **Deepavali**), countrywide. This huge celebration among Hindu Indians is best experienced on the lawns of the Umaid Bhawan Palace in Jodhpur, at a wonderful party hosted by the maharajah (which hotel guests are invited to attend). Note, however, that just as Christmas has been exploited commercially in the West, Diwali has become a time of excessive noise, increased alcohol consumption, and all-night fireworks.

Mela (Cattle Fair), Pushkar, Rajasthan. The annual cattle fair in Pushkar, Rajasthan, is the biggest of its kind in Asia. Traders, pilgrims, and tourists from all over the world turn this tiny temple town into a huge tented city, with camel races, cattle auctions, huge bonfires, traditional dances, and the like.

December/January

Christmas, New Year, countrywide. Prepare for increased hotel prices as wealthy Indians celebrate both Christmas and New Year, often by taking the entire family on an extravagant vacation. New Year, in particular, may be marked by compulsory hidden extras such as special entertainment and celebratory meals. Christmas is celebrated with as much fervor, if not more, as it is in the West. City hotels take great advantage of the situation, while in certain areas, such as Goa, midnight Mass and other traditions are observed.

6 Travel Insurance

Check your existing insurance policies and credit card coverage before you buy travel insurance. You may already be covered for lost luggage, canceled tickets, or medical expenses. The cost of travel insurance varies widely, depending on the cost and length of your trip, your age, your health, and the type of trip you're taking.

TRIP-CANCELLATION INSURANCE Trip-cancellation insurance helps you get your money back if you have to back out of a trip, if you have to go home early, or if your travel supplier goes bankrupt. Allowed reasons for cancellation can range from sickness to natural disaster to the State Department declaring your destination unsafe for travel. (Insurers usually won't cover vague fears, though, as many travelers discovered when they tried to cancel their trips in Oct 2001 because they were wary of flying.) In this unstable world, trip-cancellation insurance is a good buy if you're getting tickets well in advance. Insurance policy details vary, so read the fine print and make sure that your airline or cruise line is on the list of carriers covered in case of **bankruptcy** (note that purchasing with a credit card is often a good insurance against the carrier going bankrupt, if you request the refund within 60 days of the bankruptcy). For information, contact one of the following insurers: **Access America** (✆ 866/807-3982; www.accessamerica.com); **Travel Guard International** (✆ 800/826-4919; www.travelguard.com); **Travel Insured International** (✆ 800/243-3174; www.travelinsured.com); and **Travelex Insurance Services** (✆ 888/457-4602; www.travelex-insurance. com).

MEDICAL INSURANCE Most health insurance policies cover you if you get sick away from home. However, do check, particularly if you're insured by an HMO. With the exception of certain HMOs and Medicare/Medicaid, your medical insurance should cover medical treatment and even hospital care overseas. However, most out-of-country hospitals make you pay your bills upfront, and send you a refund after you've returned home and filed the necessary paperwork. And in a worst-case scenario, there's the high cost of emergency evacuation. If you require additional medical insurance, try **MEDEX International** (✆ 800/527-0218 or 410/453-6300; www. medexassist.com) or **Travel Assistance International** (✆ 800/821-2828; www.travelassistance.com). For general information on services, call the latter company's **Worldwide Assistance Services, Inc.,** at ✆ 800/777-8710.

LOST-LUGGAGE INSURANCE On international flights (including U.S. portions of international trips), baggage is limited to approximately $9.07 per pound, up to approximately $635 per checked bag. If you plan to check items more valuable than the standard liability, see if your valuables are covered by your homeowner's policy, get baggage insurance as part of your comprehensive travel-insurance package, or buy Travel Guard's "Bag-Trak" product. Don't buy insurance at the airport—it's usually overpriced. Put any valuables or irreplaceable items in your carry-on luggage—many items (including books, money, and electronics) aren't covered by airline policies.

Tip: It's a good idea to arrive in India with as little luggage as possible—you can buy cheap clothes when you arrive and you don't have to worry about losing them or about laundry mishaps (which can happen even in five-star hotels in India).

7 Health & Safety

STAYING HEALTHY

Consult your doctor or local travel clinic concerning precautions against diseases that are prevalent in India. The following cautionary list may have you wondering whether travel is advisable at all; don't be alarmed, however: Millions of travelers leave India having suffered nothing more than an upset stomach—even this small inconvenience should settle within a few days, your system all the stronger for it.

VACCINATIONS You will almost certainly be advised to be vaccinated against **hepatitis A, cholera, tetanus,** and **typhoid;** also make sure your polio immunization is up to date.

Longer-stay visitors should consider getting the hepatitis B and meningitis vaccinations as well. Note that travelers arriving from yellow fever–infected areas must have a yellow fever vaccination certificate.

MALARIA   Most doctors will advise you to take a course of malarial tablets, but as is the case elsewhere, the best prevention is not to get bitten. Malaria is a parasitic infection borne by mosquitoes, and risks are greater in warm, wet areas (particularly during monsoon) and at night, when mosquitoes are at their most active. Cover all exposed skin with anti-mosquito creams or sprays as evening approaches, and use repellent coils as a preventive measure at night, particularly in hotel rooms without air-conditioning. It may even be worthwhile to pack a mosquito net, though how to hang it can cause more headaches than necessary. Wear loose, floppy clothes that cover as much skin as possible.

TROPICAL ILLNESSES   India's mosquitoes are also responsible for spreading untreatable dengue fever and virulent Japanese encephalitis. Again, the best advice it to avoid getting bitten in the first place (see above).

PACKING A FIRST-AID KIT Besides anti-diarrheal medication, of which the most important are rehydration salts, it may be worthwhile to carry a course of antibiotics for **stomach-related illnesses.** It's also worthwhile to take an antiseptic cream, and possibly an antibacterial soap (though the type of soap used matters less than vigilance: Wash your hands regularly, particularly before eating). Pack **prescription medications** in your carry-on luggage in their original containers with pharmacy labels, so they'll make it through airport security. Also bring along copies of your prescriptions in case you lose your pills or run out (include the generic name, in the event that a local pharmacist is unfamiliar with the brand name). Don't forget an extra pair of contact lenses or prescription glasses or an extra inhaler.

SEXUALLY TRANSMITTED DISEASES & BLOOD INFECTIONS Keep in mind that HIV and hepatitis B are transmitted not only through sexual contact, but by infected blood. This means that any procedure involving a used needle or a blade can be hazardous. Avoid getting tattoos or piercings, and steer clear of roadside barbers offering shaves. For haircuts and procedures such as manicures and pedicures, stick to salons in upmarket hotels. Take the usual precautions if you are about to engage in any sexual activities—AIDS numbers are not well publicized, but this is a huge and growing problem.

DIETARY RED FLAGS & TUMMY TROUBLES   Many visitors to India fall victim to the ubiquitous "Delhi belly," an unfortunate reaction to unfamiliar rich and spicy foodstuffs that can overwhelm the system and cause symptoms ranging from slight discomfort and "the runs" to extreme cases of nausea, fever, and delirium. To avoid this, simply be sensible. Adjust slowly; move on to spicy foods in small doses. You should also be on your guard about *where* you eat; if you have any fears at all, stick to the upmarket restaurants, usually those in five-star hotels—but do venture out to those recommended in this guide. Remember that uncooked vegetables or fruit can be hazardous if washed in water that has not been boiled, so peel all your own fresh fruit and avoid salads. Unless you're in an upmarket hotel, don't eat fruit that has already been cut—any water on the knife or on the skin of the fruit is likely to seep into the flesh. Be wary of undercooked meats—they may harbor intestinal worms—and stay away from pork unless you're in a five-star hotel. (For more tips and guidelines, see the appendix: "India in Depth.")

The first thing to bear in mind when diarrhea or nausea strike is that your body is trying to cleanse itself, so only use an anti-diarrhea medication (like Imodium) if you are desperate—about to embark on a long train journey, for example. Ideally, you should plan a few days of rest and cut back on all food except plain basics (a diet of boiled rice and bananas is ideal), and drink plenty of boiled water (or black tea) or bottled water with rehydration salts. If your tummy trouble doesn't clear up after 3 to 4 days, consult a physician—you may be suffering from something more serious: a protozoa (amoeba or giardia) or a viral or bacterial infection.

WATER CONCERNS   More than anything else in India, it is the water that is likely to make you ill. For this reason, you should not only avoid untreated drinking water, but be on your guard against any food product that is washed with water or has had water added to it. When buying tea (or *chai*) on the streets, for example, check that the cup is washed with hot water and even ask to dry it yourself—carry a small cloth or napkins so that you can remove any and all water from anything that is going to go into your mouth. Use bottled water when you brush your teeth, and do not open your mouth in the shower. Do not have ice added to your drink unless you've been assured that it's purified. If purchasing bottled water from roadside stalls, dodgy-looking shops, or small towns, check the seal on the cap and investigate the bottle for any signs of tampering. Also try to determine the age of the packaged water; if it looks like it's been sitting on the shelf for too long, give it a miss. The only exception to the bottled water rule may be in very upmarket hotels and restaurants that purify their water in-house; always ask the manager or

maitre d' if the water has been purified. Remember not to clean wounds, cuts, or sores with tap water. Instead, douse and cleanse any open wound with antiseptic solution, cover it with an adhesive bandage, and consult a doctor if it doesn't heal soon.

BUGS, BITES & OTHER WILDLIFE CONCERNS   Remote areas are alive with insects and creepy-crawlies, but the greatest risk is malaria (see above). Wear shoes when trekking or in wet areas; you can be contaminated from worm-infested soil or mud, which can also be a source of microbial, bacterial, or hookworm infection. Leeches are a common problem in the rainforest regions. Do not try to pull them off your skin; salt usually does the trick. It's possible to prevent this nasty experience by wearing special anti-leech "socks" and dousing your shoes with lime powder. You're more likely to be bitten by a rabid dog or monkey than by a snake, spider, centipede, or sea creature, but it does occur: Wear thick trousers and boots when hiking, tread carefully, keep your eyes peeled, and in the unlikely event that you are bitten, try to get a good look at the animal so that medical staff know what antivenin to use. And yes, get to a doctor or hospital as soon as possible. Animals are seldom treated as pets in India—as a general rule, steer clear of them, and should you be bitten, use antiseptic and consult a physician immediately.

SUN/ELEMENTS/EXTREME WEATHER EXPOSURE   Carry high-SPF sunscreen and use it liberally. It's also advisable to wear a hat or cap during the day, and try to avoid midday sun wherever possible. In the cities, pollution often cloaks the high-level exposure, so keep that hat on. Remember that in the high-altitude Himalayan regions, you can experience cold weather and chilly winds while being burnt to a cinder. During the monsoons, certain regions can become impossible to traverse because of flooding. Orissa, Tamil Nadu, and Andhra Pradesh are prone to cyclones in November and December. Keep abreast of conditions by following weather reports.

WHAT TO DO IF YOU GET SICK IN INDIA

Don't panic. Medicines are widely and easily available in India. You can even describe your problem to your hotel concierge or receptionist and he or she will arrange for the necessary medication to be dropped off, doing away with possible translation problems. Pharmacies and chemists hand out pills and antibacterial medication upon request—even those that would require a prescription back home. (This is not always a good thing; if possible, consult a physician before resorting to over-the-counter drugs. Also beware of being given incomplete courses of antibiotics.) There are hospital listings for major cities in each chapter, but it's best to consult your hotel concierge regarding the best medical attention in town, particularly if you're in a more remote area. In fact, *do not solicit the assistance of anyone who is unknown to your hotel.* Well-documented scams operating in certain tourist destinations involve prolonging your illness in order to attract large payouts from your insurance company. If you or someone you are traveling with needs hospitalization, shell out for a private one, and if you're able to travel, head for the nearest big city. Advise your consulate and your medical insurance company as soon as possible.

In most cases, your existing health plan will provide the coverage you need. Double-check—you may want to buy **travel medical insurance** (see "Travel Insurance," above.) Bring your insurance ID card with you when you travel.

The United States **Centers for Disease Control and Prevention** (℃ **800/ 311-3435;** www.cdc.gov) provides up-to-date information on necessary vaccines and health hazards by region or country.

STAYING SAFE

Considering its poverty and population size, India enjoys an amazingly low incidence of violent crime, and the vast majority of visits to India tend to be trouble-free. That said, the usual rules apply—no wandering around back alleys at night, for example, no flashing of valuables or wads of cash. Foreign visitors may be targeted by corrupt cops looking to get a handsome bribe or payoff, so you'd best steer clear of any suspicious behavior such as purchasing illegal drugs. If you're caught, even with marijuana, there is a good chance that you could be thrown in prison. If you're involved in a car accident, have your hotel manager report the incident immediately. Avoid provocative debates and arguments where alcohol may be involved. Exercise caution during festivals and religious processions, where crowds are usually overwhelming and can become unruly.

TERRORISM & CIVIL UNREST

Avoid political demonstrations—these occasionally erupt into violence. Election rallies frequently turn bitter, and you don't want to be caught in the middle of an angry mob. In recent years, there have been incidents of terrorist bombings, kidnapping, and murder in various parts of India, particularly in the northernmost state of Jammu and Kashmir. With the exception of the eastern district of Ladakh, avoid travel in this volatile and unsafe war-torn region, no matter what tour operators and tourist offices have to say; more than 1,000 civilians were killed by terrorists in the region in 2002 alone. In 1999, the terrorist organization Harakat Ul Mujahideen

Surviving Scams & Con Artists

In India, scamming is an art form—and you, the tourist, are a prime target for scam artists. The best defense against the regular plague of touts and con men, who will try to tap into your supply of foreign currency by calling themselves "guides" or representatives of a local temple, is a combination of awareness, common sense, and fortitude. Scammers rely largely on **human psychology** to either win your confidence or tap into your irrational sense of guilt. Although it's okay to have a heart, don't fall into the costly pit of naiveté. **Politeness is likely to be your enemy.** Stick to your guns when you're approached by anyone offering to get you something "cheap," "quality," or "easy" by firmly declining. In fact, get used to shaking your head and saying "no" three to four times without losing your temper, which only serves to make you feel guilty while the perpetrator looks hurt and violated. If someone tells you upfront that they're not interested in your money, the warning bells should begin to sound; 9 times out of 10, a casual conversation or unintentional sightseeing trip will end with a suggestion that you hand over a token of your appreciation. Remember: **Don't pay for services you have not requested.** And when you do ask for help, ask if there's going to be a demand for money at the end, and decide on a price upfront. Here, then, is a guide to handling India's touts, hucksters, scam artists, and general wheeling and dealing.

- **Street touts** Touts operate under guises of initial friendship, wanting to practice their English or making promises of cheap accommodations or shopping. Often (but not always), the initial kindness turns sour when you don't comply with a suggestion that you buy something or check in at a crummy hotel. When browsing a street or market, you will be accosted by what appears to be the owner of the shop but is in fact one of a host of men to whom shopkeepers pay a commission to bring you inside—"to look, no buy, madam." Since scam artists know that foreigners rely on hired transport, you also need to be particularly wary when considering car hire, taxis, guides, sightseeing tours, or travel agents. The rule is: Never jump into a deal.
- **"Official" unofficial operators** Even more annoying than the slippery-tongued con artists of the street are those who operate under the guise of perceived legitimacy by calling themselves "travel agents" or "tour operators"—and a sign saying "government-approved" often means anything but. Before purchasing anything, you need to know in advance what the going rate is, and preferably deal with someone who comes recommended by this book or a reputable operator recommended by your hotel. Time allowing, shop around.
- **Dealing with drivers** Taxi drivers are notorious for telling passengers that their hotel does not exist or has closed for some reason. Never allow yourself to be taken to a hotel or restaurant unless it is the one you've asked to be taken to (specified by exact name and address). Note that any successful establishment will soon have competition opening with a similar name. Drivers also moonlight as restaurant and shop touts and receive a commission for getting you through the door (see the next bullet). If a taxi driver is very persuasive about

taking you to a particular shop, this is a sure sign that you're about to be taken for a ride. Taxi drivers often have meters that have been tampered with, or refuse to use fare-conversion charts issued by the city authority. Whenever you're suspicious about a driver's conduct, ask to be let out of the vehicle immediately, or seek the assistance of your hotel manager before paying the cab fare. When arriving at major airports and train stations, make use of **prepaid taxis** (the booths are clearly marked) whenever possible.

- **The commission system**   Try to establish the commission fee upfront. It's not just street touts you need to be wary of, but even your rickshaw-*wallah*, guide, or driver (hotels are surrounded by taxis that work on a commission basis), who without fail are out to earn commission from the shops they suggest you visit. Then this gets added to the price you're quoted—as much as 50%.
- **Bargains**   *Beware of unmarked wares*—this means the goods are priced according to the salesman's projection of your ability to pay. Also beware of the ultimate "bargain." Any deal that seems too good to be true, is. If this all sounds too tedious, head for the government shops, where goods are sold at fixed prices. Know that these prices are not negotiable and are usually a great deal heftier than elsewhere (see "The Battle of the Haggle," under "Money," above).
- **Credit card fraud**   Beware of unscrupulous traders who run off extra dockets, then forge your signature. Never let your credit card out of sight.
- **Getting the goods on precious goods**   If you're shopping for **silk carpets**, ask the salesman to razor a small sample and light it with a match. Unlike wool, silk does not burn, it smolders. Tricksters will mix silk and wool—which is why you'll need to ask for a sample across the whole color range. And don't fall for anyone who tries to persuade you to purchase **precious stones** on the premise that you can resell them at a profit to a company they supposedly know back home (a Jaipur scam). Note that **gold** is imported and therefore hugely overpriced, so cheap gold jewelry is exactly that.
- **Scam doctors**   Be wary when offered food or drink by a stranger—it's better to be offered food by a family rather than by a lone male or group or men. There have been isolated incidences of travelers being drugged or poisoned in order to rob them. Worse still, there are well-documented (though again isolated) accounts of these kinds of scammers in cahoots with doctors. Once you are ill, they will recommend a doctor, and after you're admitted into the care of the fraudulent physician, your medical insurance is contacted, and you're kept ill until a substantial medical bill has been run up.
- **Surviving the scam**   Frankly, it's unlikely that you'll leave India without having been the victim of at least one minor scam—either accept your loss and humiliation as a lesson in local custom (and good dinner-party fodder) or, as the scam unfolds, insist on being taken to a police station, the threat of which alone might force a con man's hand. Whatever happens, don't let it ruin your holiday!

issued a ban on Americans, including tourists, visiting Kashmir. Travelers should also exercise extreme caution when undertaking treks and travel to remote parts of Ladakh, where solo travelers can potentially be targeted by terrorist factions; in isolated cases, unaccompanied trekkers have been kidnapped or simply disappear. Trekkers in Himachal Pradesh should stay clear of any drug-related activity—the trade has begun to attract nasty criminal elements. Travel to the northeastern states of Assam, Manipur, Nagaland, Tripura, and Meghalaya remains risky due to sporadic incidents of ethnic insurgent violence. These areas—and Kashmir—have not been included in this guide.

Bomb blasts believed to be connected with the unrest in Jammu and Kashmir have also occurred in public places in other parts of the country. Incidents include a bomb blast at Delhi's Red Fort in December 2000, leaving three Indians dead, and at the Indian Parliament in December 2001, while civil unrest between Hindus and Muslims plagued the state of Gujarat throughout 2002. The motive for several bomb blasts in Mumbai in 2002 and 2003 has yet to be established. Communal violence can occur without advance warning, but such incidents rarely involve foreigners, and thus far there have been no attacks directed against Americans or other foreigners. That said, the threat—as anywhere in the world—should not be ignored completely: Exercise vigilance and caution if you find yourself near any government installations or tourist attractions that might be regarded as potential terrorist targets; read the local papers, heeding any relevant reports and travel advisories. Access up-to-the-minute travel warnings at **http://travel.state.gov**. U.S. citizens should contact the U.S. Embassy (**http://usembassy.state.gov/posts/in**) or the nearest U.S. Consulate for more information about the current situation in areas you plan to visit.

CRIME Yes, India is one of the safest destinations in the world when it comes to violent assault or threat, but petty crime, like pickpocketing, can be a problem. Apply common sense at all times. Don't carry wallets and keep a firm hand on purses (women have reported having their purse straps cut or purse bottoms slit), and don't wear jewelry or carry around other valuables. Most hotels have in-room electronic safes where you should stash valuables, including passports and most of your cash. Be discreet about your money, and never take out large wads of cash in public; exercise modesty at all times. Solo travelers are at greater risk of becoming victims of crime; unless you're relatively streetwise, don't tour India alone. And know that it is as a victim of a scam that you are most at risk, which at least hurts nothing but your pocket and your pride; see "Surviving Scams & Con Artists," above.

8 Etiquette & Customs

As a rule of thumb, pay attention to what local people are doing, and try to blend in as much as possible.

APPROPRIATE ATTIRE In India, your attire will often signal your status, and casual dress will make it more difficult for you to elicit respect. Women should wear loose, cool clothing that covers up as much as possible. Exposed flesh suggests that you're too poor to dress properly, or that you're shameless about flaunting your body. Tight clothes are also considered shameless; the more you can disguise your shape, the better. Men should avoid shorts, which are considered bizarre. Women visiting public beaches should be as discreet as possible and avoid sunbathing on empty beaches. In mosques you need to make sure your shoulders are covered—it's worth purchasing a scarf for this and keeping it in your bag at all times—and in Sikh *gurudwaras* you need to keep your head covered. In certain Hindu temples—particularly in South India—a man may be required to wear a *lungi* (a long piece of cloth worn like a kilt) and remove his shirt. Always check what others are wearing before venturing in, and approach slowly so that someone can intervene before you offend the sanctity of the holy sanctuary.

SHOES Shoes are never worn in places of worship—you are even required to remove your shoes when entering certain churches. It makes good sense to wear a pair of comfortable, cool, and cheap sandals, like flip-flops—they're easy to remove and unlikely to be stolen; leaving a pair of expensive shoes outside a temple or mosque is not a good idea. Some museums and historical monuments may also require you to remove your shoes, and you should extend a similar courtesy when entering someone's home. In Sikh *gurudwaras* you are expected to wash your feet after removing your shoes.

TOUCHING Public physical contact between men and women is far less acceptable in India than in other parts of the world. Some Indians—particularly those who live in the larger cities and have traveled—understand that Western men and women may shake hands (or even kiss) as expressions of social friendship, but you should be cautious of casually touching an Indian woman in small towns and villages. Even the slightest touch can have a sexual connotation. Remember that it is not unusual to encounter someone who has never seen a foreign face; attempting to shake hands with such a person may prove overwhelming. Traditionally, Indian people use the left hand as part of their toilet routine. Consequently, the left hand is considered unclean, and you should only offer your right hand when greeting someone. Don't touch a religious object with your feet or left hand.

AVOIDING OFFENSE Indians love to discuss all manner of subjects, and more educated individuals will readily get into a wonderfully heated debate—which may be one of your most memorable moments in India. Do exercise discretion, however, when trying to understand the enigma of India's overwhelming poverty and the caste system. Don't harshly judge or criticize things you don't understand fully; Indians can be quite passionate about their nation and will defend it unequivocally. Words are seldom enough to offend an Indian, but avoid strong swear words in the context of an argument or insult. And always be considerate and humble when entering a place of worship.

EATING & DRINKING When eating at someone's home, remember that it is not unusual for the woman to cook and spend the entire evening serving. Don't interfere with this custom, and don't try to lend a hand by venturing into the kitchen—especially if you're a man. Foreign women will generally be treated as "honorary men" and should dine at the table unless an alternative suggestion is made. Use only your right hand when eating (unless knives and forks are used), and follow the lead of your host when you're unsure. Don't be afraid to ask about the food, but you must be quite firm about not drinking water (unless it's bottled) and being mindful of salads and cut fruit (see above). Consider bringing your own bottled water with you.

MIND YOUR TEMPER When confronted with bureaucracy and IST

(Indian "Stretchable" Time), maintain your cool. Schedules are bound to go awry and government offices are notoriously inefficient, so there's simply no point in losing your temper. You'd be well advised to adopt a similar attitude with wealthy and "important" Indian men who, as a matter of course, jump the line. Rather than fly into a rage, point out the lack of consideration firmly and earnestly, or better still, smile beatifically and practice a meditation technique.

PHOTOGRAPHY Photography at airports or military installations is strictly forbidden, as it is at all burning *ghats* (crematorium sites) in Varanasi. Note that carrying a camera to attractions throughout India will add significantly to your entry fee.

9 Specialized Travel Resources

TRAVELERS WITH DISABILITIES

Disabilities shouldn't stop anyone from traveling, but it must be noted that India—despite the fact that it has such a high disabled population—is not well geared for travelers with disabilities. Destinations are far from wheelchair friendly, and it is hard enough for an able-bodied person to negotiate the crowded, filth-strewn, and potholed streets, where cars, animals, and rickshaws drive at will. Access to historical monuments is also difficult (though you will have the small reward of free access). Certainly you would need to be accompanied by a traveler familiar with the destination, and you must carefully sift through the accommodations options, almost none of which are specifically geared to travelers with disabilities. For more information, contact ny@itony.com (www.tourismindia.com).

GAY & LESBIAN TRAVELERS

Homosexuality remains frowned upon in India, and the law actively outlaws sexual acts between men (although gay women do not attract this prejudicial legislation). On the other hand, Indian men are a great deal more affectionate with one another than they are with women in public, and you'll frequently see men walking hand-in-hand, arm-in-arm, and embracing, though this is said to be an act of "brotherliness" without any sexual connotation. Recent high-profile cases have brought the issue of gay and lesbian rights into the social and political sphere, and there is increased awareness in this regard. Nevertheless, discretion is probably best observed outside your hotel room (note that no one questions the same sex sharing a room).

A useful website is **www.gay bombay.com**, which offers information on gay venues in Mumbai.

For more information and gay- and lesbian-friendly contacts nationwide, write to **Bombay Dost** (105A Veena-Beena Shopping Centre, Bandra Station Rd., Bandra, Mumbai, 400 050) or to the **Gay Info Centre** (P.O. Box 1662 Secunderabad HPO 500 003, Andhra Pradesh).

SENIOR TRAVEL

India is not for the fainthearted, and this is definitely the one place senior travelers should utilize the services of a reliable agency and organization that targets the 50-plus market. **Elderhostel** (© 877/426-8056; www.elderhostel. org) arranges study programs for those ages 55 and over (and a spouse or companion of any age) in India. Most courses last 15 to 21 days and include airfare, accommodations, meals, and tuition.

FAMILY TRAVEL

Just reading the list of inoculations and possible diseases in "Staying Safe" will probably have you thinking twice about taking your kids to India. But many do, and if the color and pageantry of India amaze adults, they will absolutely delight smaller eyes, opening them to the rich cultural texture of the world at large. What's more, children receive the most wonderful attention, and can do no wrong in Indian eyes—for instance, restaurants are a nightmare for those who don't like children, as kids are allowed to run roughshod and make as much noise as they want while parents look on benignly. All hotels are geared toward kids (Indian parents always travel with their kids), and babysitting is generally available everywhere. On the downside are the extreme heat, the likelihood of tummy trouble from the water (it's very hard to totally avoid ingesting a single molecule), and the unavailability of suitable foodstuffs outside the big cities.

WOMEN TRAVELERS

Foreign women will almost certainly experience India as sexist, but if you are confident, relaxed, and assertive, you are unlikely to experience any serious hassles. That said, traveling solo is only for the very brave and thick-skinned, unless of course you're traveling in comfort (using the accommodations selected in this book) and have hired a car and driver for the duration (using public transport is when you are at your most vulnerable). At best, you will experience being stared at intensely for an unbearable length of time, at worst you may be groped—some men are convinced that all Western women are loose and slutty. To a great extent, Western cinema and fashion trends have helped fuel the legend that women from abroad welcome these attentions, and you'd do well to take precautions, like wearing appropriate attire (see "Etiquette & Customs," above). On trains, on buses, and in other public places,

you are best off ignoring advances or questions from suspicious-looking men. You should have little difficulty determining when a line of questioning is likely to lead to problems. In particular, steer clear of men who have been drinking alcohol. "Eve-teasing" (the word denoting public "flirtation" by men) is an offense is certain parts of India, and you are within your rights to report inappropriate advances or remarks to the police—the easiest response, however, is to simply loudly tell the offender off, even striking him—you will almost certainly be supported by those around you. You may want to ask whether or not your hotel offers a special room for solo women travelers; these are now offered in a few upmarket hotels in the larger cities, and include special privacy/security features.

Note that women are excluded from certain religious sites and attractions (which we have pointed out wherever relevant), but this is unlikely to impact too strongly on your plans. Menstruating women are, technically, not entitled to enter Jain temples.

SINGLE TRAVELERS

Many people prefer traveling alone, and solo journeys in India certainly offer infinite opportunities to meet locals who are notoriously curious and keen to make friends. Indians are profoundly curious about visitors to their country, and their seemingly nosy line of questioning (opening conversations with lines like "So what is your line of service?" are simply their way of getting to know you) can spark a connection that will aid you throughout your trip.

You will be approached everywhere by people (almost always men) keen to strike up conversations (though see the tips in "Surviving Scams & Con Artists" earlier in this chapter, to help you distinguish between a genuine encounter and a con game). Single women should also be wary and on guard. This, together with the fact that a high proportion of Indians are remarkably fluent in English, means you are more likely to engage in lively discussions with total strangers in India than almost anywhere else. Be aware again, though, that you need to be as curious about their country as they are about yours, and voice judgmental or critical questions in discreet terms.

Unfortunately, single travelers are always at an economic disadvantage. Single occupancy in guest rooms costs almost as much as double occupancy, and only a select number of hotels in India have specifically designated "single rooms." Single travelers can avoid this disadvantage, of course, by agreeing to room with other single travelers on the trip.

10 Planning Your Trip Online

SURFING FOR AIRFARES

The "big three" online travel agencies, **Expedia.com, Travelocity.com,** and **Orbitz.com,** sell most of the air tickets bought on the Internet. (Canadian travelers should try Expedia.ca and Travelocity.ca; U.K. residents can go for Expedia.co.uk.) Each website has different business deals with the airlines and may offer different fares for the same flights, so it's wise to shop around. Travelocity.com has a section devoted specifically to India, so you may want to begin your search there.

For savvy air-travel tips and advice, pick up a copy of *Frommer's Fly Safe, Fly Smart* (Wiley Publishing, Inc.).

SURFING FOR HOTELS

Most of the budget or moderate hotel recommendations do not have websites, and many hotel websites are poorly maintained, which means you may come across tariffs and information dating as far back as the previous decade. Smaller hotels change e-mail service providers almost as often as they change sheets. For basic but up-to-the-minute information about practically every hotel in India, the website for the **Federation of Hotel and Restaurant Associations of India** (www.fhrai. com) can be a useful resource.

You'll also come up against a plethora of accommodations booking

Frommers.com: The Complete Travel Resource

For an excellent travel-planning resource, we highly recommend Frommers.com (www.frommers.com). We're a little biased, of course, but we guarantee that you'll find the travel tips, reviews, monthly vacation giveaways, and online-booking capabilities indispensable. Among the special features are our popular **Message Boards,** where Frommer's readers post queries and share advice (sometimes we authors even show up to answer questions); **Frommers.com Newsletter,** for the latest travel bargains and insider travel secrets; and **Frommer's Destinations Section,** where you'll get expert travel tips, hotel and dining recommendations, and advice on the sights to see for more than 3,000 destinations around the globe. When your research is done, the **Online Reservations System** (www.frommers.com/book_a_trip) takes you to Frommer's preferred online partners to book your vacation at affordable prices.

services that presume to be direct representatives of the hotel you're searching for, but that actually hike up the lowest available tariff considerably, which may leave you feeling ripped off before you even bed down. Always compare the website rate with the cheapest rate offered directly by the hotel before making a reservation. On the upside, several hotel networks offer unbelievable Internet discounts that simply can't be ignored.

For recommended hotel groups and websites and essential lodging advice, see "Tips on Accommodations," later in this chapter.

SURFING FOR RENTAL CARS

It is not advisable to hire a rented car without a driver in India. Driving is the most dangerous activity you can undertake, with the rules of the road (which are usually in an awful state) totally incomprehensible to an outsider, and no sign of law enforcement. To hire a car and driver, you're best off dealing directly with the local tourism office, or contacting the recommended operators or drivers listed in relevant "Getting Around" sections in each chapter.

11 The 21st-Century Traveler

INTERNET ACCESS AWAY FROM HOME

Travelers have any number of ways to check their e-mail and access the Internet on the road. Of course, using your own laptop or even a PDA (personal digital assistant) or electronic organizer with a modem gives you the most flexibility, but you run the risk of having it stolen or lost. Best to access your e-mail from cybercafes or your hotel. All big cities in India have a host of cybercafes.

Hotels Dataports (and well-equipped business centers) are available in all luxury city hotels in India (as well as many outside of cities). Note that the electric current is 220 to 240 volts AC, and that different socket and plug standards are used in different parts of the country. Although good hotels usually have multi-socket units, you should consider bringing a universal adaptor (if you're unsure, call your hotel in advance to find out what the options are). Note that power outages are regular, as are variations in voltage, so be prepared for any eventuality.

USING A CELLPHONE

The three letters that define much of the world's **wireless capabilities** are GSM (Global System for Mobiles), a big, seamless network that makes for easy cross-border cellphones. If your cellphone is on a GSM system and you have a world-capable phone such as many (but not all) Sony, Ericsson, Motorola, or Samsung models, you can make and receive calls across much of the globe. Just call your wireless operator and ask for "international roaming" to be activated on your account. Unfortunately, per-minute charges can be high—up to $5.

World-phone owners can bring down their per-minute charges with a bit of trickery. Call up your cellular operator and say you'll be going abroad for several months and want to "unlock" your phone to use it with a local provider. Usually, they'll oblige. Then, in your destination country, pick up a cheap, prepaid phone chip at a mobile phone store and slip it into your phone. (Show your phone to the salesperson, as not all phones work on all networks.) You'll get a local phone number in your destination country, and much, much lower calling rates.

Otherwise, you could **rent** a phone in India—but due to security reasons, mobile phone rental is not easy or widely available in India at present, and you'll need copies of passport and other security checks. If Delhi is your gateway, the easiest place to stop at is **Airtel,** which has counters at both international and domestic terminals in the arrivals hall in New Delhi; or call © **981/001-234** or 981/015-2345. You'll pay about Rs 150 ($3.15) for the SIM card rental and Rs 250 ($5.35) for the handset rental plus actual calls made. A service charge of 10% is levied on local calls and 25% on "roaming" calls. For trips of more than a few weeks, **buying a phone** becomes economically attractive, with a cheap, no-questions-asked prepaid phone system the best option.

12 Getting There

BY PLANE

Most major airline carriers have flights to India. It's a good idea to shop around for fares or make use of a consolidator that hunts for the cheapest available seats on your travel dates.

From North America Count on spending between 18 and 22 hours traveling if you fly directly to India; you'll have to touch down at least once in Europe, the Gulf, or an Asian destination. With flights from the U.S. or Canada, the following airlines all offer service to India:

British Airways (© 800/247-9297; www.british-airways.com); **Virgin Atlantic** (© 800/862-8621; www.virgin-atlantic.com); **Air-India** (© 212/751-6200; www.airindia.com); **United** (© 800/328-6877; www.unitedairlines.com); **KLM/Northwest** (© 800/447-4747; www.nwa.com); **Lufthansa** (© 800/645-3880 in the U.S., 800/563-5954 in Canada; www.lufthansa.com); and **Air France** (© 800/237-2747 in the U.S., 800/667-2747 in Canada; www.airfrance.fr). **Air Canada** (© 800/776-3000 in the U.S., 800/263-0882 in Canada) flies directly from Vancouver to Delhi with a touchdown in London. From other Canadian hubs, you'll fly to London or Zurich, where you pick up the connecting flight to Delhi.

From the U.K. Flights are usually cheaper if you're prepared to change to a connecting flight in continental Europe or in the Middle East; a number of European airlines (such as KLM and Alitalia) will get you there affordably if you don't mind a change of planes.

British Airways (© 0345/22-2111; www.ba.com) has daily direct flights to both Delhi and Mumbai, and occasional direct flights to Kolkata and Chennai. **Air-India** (© 01753/68-4828 or 020/8560-9996; www.airindia.com) is the national carrier operating regular non-stop flights to Delhi and Mumbai. **Emirates** (© 0870/243-2222; www.emirates.com) flies to Mumbai, Delhi, and Kerala, via Dubai. **KLM UK** (© 08705/07-4074; www.klmuk.com) operates flights from all over Britain to Amsterdam, where you pick up your connection with **KLM Royal Dutch Airlines** (www.klm.com) to Delhi, Mumbai, or Calcutta.

Lufthansa (© 0845/773-7747; www.lufthansa.co.uk) has flights to Delhi and Mumbai, through Frankfurt. **United Airlines** (© 0845/844-4777; www.unitedairlines.co.uk) flies to Delhi each day out of Heathrow. **Singapore Airlines** (© 0870/608-8886; www.singaporeair.co.uk) flies nonstop from Manchester twice a week.

From Australia & New Zealand You can't fly directly to India from either Australia or New Zealand, and you will more than likely be offered a flight package that incorporates more than one airline. The majority of touchdowns and changeovers are in Malaysia, Thailand, and Singapore.

The following airlines offer service to India: **British Airways** (© 02/8904-8800 in Australia, 09/356-8690 in New Zealand; www.british-airways.com); **Air-India** (© 02/9299-2022 in Australia, 09/303-1301 in New Zealand; www.airindia.com); **Air New Zealand** (© 0800/73-7000 in New Zealand, 13-2476 in Australia; www.airnewzealand.com); **Ansett Australia** (© 13-1414 in Australia, 09/336-2364 in New Zealand; www.ansett.com.au); **Singapore Airlines** (© 13-1011 or 02/9350-0262 in Australia, 0800/80-8909; www.singaporean.com); and **Qantas** (© 13-1313 in Australia, 0800/80-8767 or 09/375-8900 in New Zealand; www.qantas.com).

From South Africa: South African Airways (© 011/978-1763) flies nonstop to Mumbai several times a week.

INTERNATIONAL AIRPORTS

India has five designated international airports: **Mumbai, Delhi, Kolkata (Calcutta), Chennai** (Tamil Nadu), and **Trivandrum** (Kerala). Mumbai (Bombay) receives the greatest amount of international traffic and is the best point of arrival for onward travel to Goa, South India, or Gujarat. Be warned, however, that Mumbai airport facilities are poor. Most Mumbai flights arrive late at night, so you need to be wary of booking "immediate" onward domestic flights; you don't want to spend any significant amount of time waiting at the airport. Delhi's international airport—the principal starting point for journeys throughout North India, including the Himalayan regions and Rajasthan as well as east India—is substantially better. Only fly in to Kolkata (Calcutta) if you plan to explore east India exclusively.

13 Customized Tours for the Independent Traveler

PACKAGE TOURS Before you start your search for the lowest airfare, consider booking your flight as part of a travel package. Package tours (not to be confused with escorted tours) are simply a way to buy the airfare, accommodations, and other elements of your trip (such as car rentals, airport transfers, and sometimes activities) at the same time and often at discounted prices—one-stop shopping that saves you money but allows for independent travel.

RECOMMENDED OPERATORS FOR CUSTOMIZED PACKAGE & ADVENTURE TOURS

If you're happy to pay good money for a very well-organized deluxe tailored tour, **Abercrombie & Kent** (www.abercrombiekent.com) are the masters, not only choosing the most expensive accommodations options, but the best (there is often a difference!). The company also specializes in putting together trekking trips and

packages that tap into India's great wildlife resources—in comfort, of course. The only drawback is that always traveling in style can cocoon you from the raw experiences that make India such a memorable experience. For this, consider a tour that includes houseboat and private homestays in Kerala, Tamil Nadu, and Haryana on tours organized by **Colours of India** (www.partnership travel.co.uk); the selection is very exciting. Another Indian stalwart is **Cox & Kings** (www.coxandkings.com), who, like Abercrombie & Kent, work hard to create a really relaxing top-end holiday (rather than the hard work that India can be), tailor-made to personal preferences. Another good upmarket agency, specializing in customized travel itineraries, is **Western & Oriental** (www.westernoriental.com).

A highly recommended option if you're traveling on a budget (or even if you have money to burn) is Raj Singh,

Discovering Spiritual India

Many visitors come to India to experience some sort of spiritual transformation, and the increasing plethora of First World hotels, English-speaking guides, and Western-style food options are making it easier than ever (and in some ways more difficult, by cocooning travelers from unvarnished India). Indeed, you are likely to find a moment of enlightenment in the most unexpected places, such as engaging in conversation with a shopkeeper over a cup of *chai*. However you choose to spend your time, you are unlikely to return home unaffected by your sojourn here. That said, a few destinations are worth highlighting for those travelers intent on working on their dharma and kharma. **Varanasi** (Uttar Pradesh) and **Bodhgaya** (Bihar) are particularly worthwhile spots, as is (to a lesser extent) **Rishikesh** (Uttaranchal). Whether you want to learn how to meditate or improve your current abilities, **www.dhamma.org** is an excellent resource for courses in Vipassana meditation (originally taught by Buddhists but today a largely secular form, immensely popular throughout the world)—these are short, very rewarding retreats, and highly recommended as an entry into meditation. Alternatively, browse **www.sivananda.org** for yoga-based ashrams in Kerala (or the original **www.sivanandadlshq. org** in Rishikesh), **www.rootinstitute.com** for 7- to 10-day meditation retreats in Bodghaya, and **www.osho.com,** a healing and meditation center near Mumbai.

proprietor of **Indian Experience,** who arranges tailor-made tours throughout India—you can literally contact him and tell him your area of interest and a daily limit and he will come up with the goods (2 weeks in Rajasthan, Agra, Delhi: Rs 1,200–Rs 1,800/$26–$40 per person per day including accommodations, entry fees, and private car and driver!). Contact him at Rajsingh53@aol.com.

Reliable operators **Sita World Travel** and **Thomas Cook** offer both individually tailored and escorted tours; see contact details for both under "Escorted Tours," below. **Audley Travel** (www.audleytravel.com,) is a recommended U.K.–based outfit. If you're specifically looking for an agent for trekking, try **Trans Indus Travel** (www.transindus.co.uk), although their itineraries are not limited to outdoor excursions. **Steppes East Ltd.** (www.steppeseast.co.uk) is another reputable option; they let you conveniently create your personal itinerary online. **Wilderness Travel** (www. wildernesstravel.com) specializes in Rajasthan camel safaris and elephant expeditions. Other Himalayan trekking outfits are **Mountain Travel/ Sobek** (www.mtsobek.com), **Geographic Expeditions** (www.geoex. com), and **Adventure Center** (www. adventurecenter.com); the latter two also have general adventure expeditions.

14 Escorted Tours

Escorted tours are structured group tours with a group leader. The price usually includes everything from airfare to hotels, meals, tours, admission costs, and local transportation.

Many people (particularly those with limited mobility) derive a certain ease and security from escorted trips, and many tours let you see the maximum number of sights in the minimum amount of time with the least amount of hassle or worry. On the downside, an escorted tour often requires a big deposit upfront, and lodging and dining choices are predetermined. As part of a cloud of tourists, you'll get little opportunity for serendipitous interactions with locals. The tours can be jam-packed with activities, leaving little room for individual sightseeing, whim, or adventure—plus they often focus only on the heavily touristed sites, so you miss out on the lesser-known gems.

Before you invest in an escorted tour, ask about the **cancellation policy** and think strongly about purchasing trip-cancellation insurance, especially if the tour operator asks you to pay upfront. See the section on "Travel Insurance," earlier in this chapter. You'll also want to get a complete **schedule** of the trip to find out how much sightseeing is planned each day and whether enough time has been allotted for relaxing or wandering solo. The **size** and **demographics** of the group is also important to know upfront. Generally, the smaller the group, the more flexible the itinerary, and the less time you'll spend waiting for people to get on and off the bus. Discuss what is included and excluded in the **price.** Also check the **accommodations choices** by looking up the reviews in a Frommer's guide (and do check rates to see if you're getting good value).

For small, high-end, exotic birdwatching tours of India, look no further than **Victor Emanuel Nature Tours** (www.ventbird.com), based in Austin, Texas; the tours are usually sold out as soon as they come online. Victor often includes the "Palace on Wheels," a weeklong journey through Rajasthan (including Agra) in a luxury train; for standard Palace on Wheels tours, see "Getting Around India," below. **Dagmar von Harryegg** is based in Australia but is passionate about India, particularly the desert states of Rajasthan and Gujarat, where she has developed an extensive network of contacts and friends, from elephant *mahouts* to reclusive princes. She offers twice-yearly 18-day trips for a maximum of eight travelers— thereby ensuring a flexible timetable "cruising in wonderfully old-fashioned Ambassador limousines with overnight stays in off-the-beaten-track palaces, forts, and havelis." Trips take off in Delhi and include a visit to the Taj Mahal. For information, contact Dagmar at maharani_travels@ iprimus.com.au.

One of India's foremost tourism operators, **Sita World Travel** is represented throughout the length and breadth of India. Sita offers a wide range of tours (7–22 days) to cover a range of budgets and interests. These include sightseeing trips and excursions to India's top attractions, as well as soft-adventure and special-interest tours that can really get you off the beaten track (www.sitaindia.com; or contact Mr. Ashok Sultan in New Jersey at indrama@worldnet.att.net or © 973/ 758-0385). **Thomas Cook** also has a range of individual and group packages; e-mail them at holidays@ in.thomascook.com or inbound@in. thomascook.com, or check out www. thomascook.co.in. Note that many of the recommended individual and adventure operators listed above offer escorted group tours.

Animal lovers beware: India will horrify you if you have a real soft spot for animals. You will feel particularly sickened by the "dancing bears" in North India—sloth bears cruelly tethered and forced to perform for tourists—as well as severely malnourished dogs, feral cats, diseased pigs, and even cows, considered sacred, emaciated and chewing on plastic bags and cardboard for sustenance. If you can see someone to rant at, do, but for the most part you just have to bear it.

15 Getting Around India

BY CAR

India's roads are statistically the most dangerous in the world; renting your own car and attempting to traverse the chaos that passes for traffic is simply suicidal. That said, having your own vehicle—and a driver who knows the roads, can read road signs when they're present, and can communicate with locals—is in many ways the best way to get around. You can set your own pace, without having to worry about making public-transport connections (a major headache taken care of), and you can see the sights and experience many of the attractions without feeling anxious (your driver will be a huge help in providing advice on customs and pricing), as well as experience off-the-beaten-track towns and rural scenes that give you the only sense of real India. And by American and European standards, the luxury of being chauffeured around the country—not necessarily in a high-end luxury vehicle, keep in mind—is ridiculously cheap. Certainly this is the way to go to concentrate on certain parts of India, such as Rajasthan, but it's not advisable as a way to cover long-distance journeys—aim to spend no more than 3 to 4 hours a day in the car (there will be, of course, exceptions). *Note:* Whatever you do, make sure your plan does not include traveling at night.

What kind of car? Standard cars are often antique-looking and very romantic Ambassadors, tough cars despite their appearance, but sometimes unpredictable; don't rely on them for long out-of-town journeys—better perhaps to opt for a modern vehicle like the little Indica. A vehicle with off-road capabilities is essential in some of the more remote and hilly regions, including eastern Himachal Pradesh, Ladakh, Sikkim, and parts of Uttaranchal; it is also recommended for some of the awful road conditions in Madhya Pradesh and Karnataka, for example, where there may be more potholes than patches of tarmac. Air-conditioned vehicles cost more but are always recommended because you may want to keep windows closed in order to shut out the endless traffic noise and pollution.

How much will it cost? Charges for this sort of car hire vary considerably. Use a hotel rental service, and you stand the chance of forking out exorbitant fees—although the vehicle and quality of service will generally be top-notch. At the other end of the scale, you can walk up to a driver in the street, negotiate an excellent deal, and spend the rest of your vacation watching the tires being changed. It's always a good idea to start by contacting the Tourist Development Corporation in whatever state you wish to hire a car (contact details are in individual chapters). Their rates are reasonable and fixed; you'll be spared the battle of the haggle; and you won't have to live with the misery of being overcharged (we provide price indications in individual chapters). Each chapter lists travel agencies that can assist you with car hire; but remember that you'll also have to pay a commission to the agency, so shop around.

Note: If you are involved in an accident, get out of your vehicle and get away from the scene without delay. An accident involving the injury or death of a cow or person may result in a mob assault on all occupants of the offending vehicle as well as its incineration.

Taxis & auto-rickshaws These modes of transportation are the ways to go when getting around in your chosen city or town. Auto-rickshaws are best for short journeys only, being slow, bumpy, and open-air—in other words, open to pollution. Always, always (unless the driver is using a "meter reading chart," in which case check it carefully, and make sure he is not using the night 11pm–5am chart, when charges are higher) negotiate the rate upfront, having established (with this book or your hotel) the average going rate. To get from the station or airport to your hotel, use the prepaid taxi booths; remember to hand over your receipt only *after* reaching your destination.

Remember: Carry your passport at all times—many of the borders between states have checkpoints where passports may be checked.

BY PLANE

Because train travel is time-consuming (and amenities like clean toilets are totally lacking) and roads generally appalling, the best way to cover distances is by air, and the best airline by far is **Jet Airways** (www.jetairways. com), with its fleet of new planes, First-World service, and good connections (it's rapidly on track in its goal to link almost every significant destination in the country). If you have to use the state-run carrier, **Indian Airlines** (http://indian-airlines.nic.in), you will find that it leaves much to be desired in terms of reliability, cleanliness, and service, but it does get you where you want to go, with the subcontinent's most extensive network. Of the

smaller carriers, **Air Sahara** (www.air sahara.net) is the best established and often offers excellent deals despite the fact that it doesn't cover all major destinations.

Both Jet Airways and Indian Airlines offer special **unlimited travel programs** that allow multiple flights over a certain period of time. These cost $500 for 15 days, and $750 for 21 days; backtracking is not permitted. A similar package costing $300 covers a week's worth of travel but only within particular regional zones. Children under 12 pay half, while those under 2 pay only 10% of the dollar fare.

Passengers between ages 12 and 30 can receive a 25% **youth discount** on dollar fares; you are required to submit a copy of the main page of your passport when paying in order to qualify.

India's **domestic and international check-in and preboarding procedure** may be one of the most rigorous in the world. Technically, check-in will start 150 minutes prior to international departure, and you need to produce a ticket before being allowed access to the airport building (if you plan to purchase your ticket inside the airport, speak to a security officer, who will escort you to the appropriate ticket counter). Arriving less than 75 minutes prior to domestic departure is *definitely* not recommended. You need to have your checked baggage scanned and sealed before reporting to the check-in counter. The list of dangerous items not permitted in your carry-on bags is fairly extensive; you will be asked to remove batteries from your camera, and these will be stowed by

---

Tips **Ticket Reconfirmation**

Always have your concierge (or yourself to be sure) reconfirm your flight at least 72 hours before departure to save yourself the frustration of arriving only to find that your name has been deleted from the computer.

security until you reach your destination. Check-in closes 30 minutes prior to departure. After check-in, you should immediately head for the first security check, which will involve a body pat-down and a scan of your carry-on luggage. Boarding gates close 15 minutes prior to scheduled departure (although delays are fairly frequent), and there will be second body and carry-on checks before you are permitted to board the plane. In some instances, you will be asked to identify your checked luggage on the tarmac. Also note that, even if you've checked your luggage through to a final destination, you will be required to identify your checked luggage at each transit point, as well as pass through security procedures.

While frequent travelers may be irritated by these ungainly, time-consuming methods, others find the process provides peace of mind.

BY TRAIN

India's rail network is the second largest in the world, and you can pretty much get anywhere in the country by train. That said, train journeys between major destinations can consume massive amounts of time (often more than car travel); and the network, tiers (A/C class may, for instance, be better than 1st class), and connections can be confusing. It's best to determine well in advance whether or not your destination is accessible from your point of origin and which tier is the most comfortable, and then factor in delays; some slow trains stop at every two-hut village along the way, and this can extend traveling time by hours. Generally, you should only consider long-distance train travel if you are assured of exotic scenery (like the **Konkan Railway,** which connects Mumbai with Goa, Karnataka, and Kerala, running along the Arabian coast), or if the journey is overnight (like Delhi to Varanasi) and you have

reserved a **first-class air-conditioned sleeper** berth. (Never book **2nd class,** which can be torturous, claustrophobic, and distressing if you are at all intimidated by crowds.) You will be particularly comfortable aboard the overnight **Rajdhani Express**—the superfast train connects Delhi to Mumbai for Rs 2,405 ($53) or to Kolkata for Rs 2,480 ($55); it also connects Delhi with Chennai, Bangalore, Bhubaneswar, Thruvananthapuram, Abu Road, Ahmedabad, and Ajmer. The best daytime travel train is the **Shatabdi Express,** an intercity train that has several routes between important tourist destinations in North India (Delhi to Amritsar: Rs 645/$14; Mumbai to Vadodra: Rs 545/$12; Chennai to Mysore: Rs 630/$14). Book a seat in the air-conditioned **Chair Car** class; small meals, tea, coffee, and bottled water are included in the ticket, and seats are comfortable and clean.

For extensive railway information, log on to **www.indianrail.gov.in** or **www.indianrail.com**, which show routes, availability, and prices. The website **www.indiatravelinfo.com/railway.html** lists departure and arrival times for all Indian trains. Purchasing first-class tickets usually requires some advance planning, and it's a good idea to make all-important train reservations (particularly for overnight travel) through an agent before you leave for India. Alternatively, speak to your hotel travel desk as soon as you arrive.

Ticket reservations should be made through your hotel or an agent (usually for a relatively small fee), or you can brave the possibility of long lines and silly form-filling; if so, check if there's a special counter for foreigners before joining a queue. In fact, it's wise to double-check that you're in the appropriate queue; some counters may be set up specifically for politicians or women or military personnel,

The Romance of Rail: India's Special Train Journeys

India's most famous luxury train, **Palace on Wheels,** currently operates in Rajasthan, and has 14 elegantly furnished en-suite saloons, a bar, and two restaurants (www.palaceonwheelsindia.com; www.inetindia. com.rajasthan; jaipur.rtdc@axcess.net.in; $700 double per night). Alternatively, you can tour Rajasthan and Gujarat with **Royal Orient,** each carriage with its own lounge minibar, kitchenette, and toilets (www. gujarattourism.com). Getting to the hill stations of Shimla (Himachal Pradesh), Darjeeling (West Bengal), and Ooty (Tamil Nadu) can be a scenic novelty if you don't mind spending long hours traveling in the atmospheric **"toy trains"** that chug their way along narrow-gauge tracks to high altitudes by way of an endless series of hairpin loops—fabulous views are guaranteed. And then, of course, there is the **Konkan Railway,** which runs along the Malabar coast and has truly wonderful scenery almost every click-clack of the way.

excluding you. Note that the **Indian Railways Indrail Pass** is a "discount" ticket for unlimited travel over a specific number of days (for example, A/C class: 1 day $95, 2 days $160, 4 days $220, 7 days $270), but these are only likely to benefit travelers who are spending their entire vacation onboard a train.

Tip: To avoid unnecessary stress while traveling by train (particularly on overnight journeys), use a chain and padlock to secure your luggage and fasten it to some part of your berth or cabin. Be sensible, and don't leave valuables lying around while you sleep.

BY BUS

Unless you are on a serious budget and traveling India for months, we recommend you avoid all forms of bus travel.

Often crammed full of commuters, state-operated buses are driven at blood-curdling speeds along dangerous and punishing roads. Numerous so-called deluxe or luxury buses, operated by private companies, often ply similarly dangerous routes overnight. You may be tempted to save time and money with this option, but be aware that safety is never a priority, and sleeping is almost impossible thanks to generally uncomfortable seating and/or noise. Regular stops at roadside truck stops along the way will have you arriving at your destination bleary-eyed and exhausted, wondering why you've opted for a holiday in hell. One of the few exceptions is the Manali-to-Leh route, where the trans-Himalayan scenery is jaw-droppingly awesome, and an overnight stop in tents is part of the deal (see chapter 10).

16 Tips on Accommodations

One of the best developments in the past decade has been the increase in **luxury boutique-type options** offering international standards of service and comfort, and flavored with Indian accents—like beautiful craftsmanship

and ancient traditions (we're talking Ayurvedic masseurs on tap)—which means that the subcontinent is now a very desirable destination for the visitor wanting relaxation and pampering. A few independent hotels have sprung up, such as **Nilaya Hermitage** (Goa) and **Devi Garh** (outside Udaipur)— even **Aman** is due to open a resort on the edges of Ranthambhore National Park by early 2004—but the pace has been set by the **Villas** properties, owned by India's very own, very fabulous **Oberoi** chain. Besides the Villas properties (the best of which are **Amarvilas** in Agra, and **Rajvilas** in Jaipur), Oberoi runs some of the very best city hotels, as well as several spa resorts in key tourist destinations. You will pay top dollar (though these still represent good value), but you can generally count on superb service and attention to detail. Best of all, you can often get great discounts on room rates by reserving in advance over the Internet (**www.oberoihotels.com**). Note that Oberoi also operates a tier of smaller, less opulent hotels under the **Trident** banner, aimed principally at business and/or family travelers.

India's other famous hotel chain is the **Taj Group** (**www.tajhotels.com**), with an enormous inventory of properties, particularly in South India, where Oberoi is largely absent. Quality varies somewhat, but comfort is generally guaranteed, particularly in big cities and resort destinations—the best properties are the **Taj Mahal** in Mumbai and the **Lake Palace Hotel** in Udaipur.

Tip: Be aware that any hovel will attach "palace" to its name in the hopes that this may attract more customers. This is often amusing if you're walking past, but disastrous if you're checking in.

HERITAGE HOTELS   Staying in a medieval palace or fort is a unique and wonderful aspect of India's accommodations options (particularly in Rajasthan), especially when your host is the aristocrat whose forebears built the palace or fort in which you're overnighting; the best are discussed in detail in relevant sections/chapters throughout this guide. Many were built centuries ago, so it's not surprising that heritage hotels are seldom the most luxurious option, with the possibilities of many stairs, dodgy plumbing, low ceilings, strange room layouts, and other eccentricities. Acting principally as marketing agencies for privately owned palaces, forts, and *havelis* (Indian mansions) as well as a number of small resorts around the country (primarily North India), two websites worth checking out are **www.indianheritagehotels.com** and **www.heritagehotels.com**.

The **Neemrana group** (**www.neemranahotels.com**) includes a select collection of lovely boutique heritage hotels, often located in off-the-beaten-track destinations; rates generally represent excellent value.

BEST OF KERALA   In Kerala, the **Casino** group of hotels (**www.casinogroup.com**) is committed to investing in ecologically sound resorts that combine great comfort, friendly and professional service, unpretentious charm, and beautiful natural settings. Also based in Kerala, **TourIndia** (**www.tourindia.com**) is run by India's principal ecotourism entrepreneur, Babu Varghese, who came up with the popular "backwater houseboat" concept. Also offered by TourIndia are the opportunities to sleep in a rainforest treehouse with a functioning bathroom, and to overnight in a tent in the heart of a tiger reserve.

CITY HOTELS   The biggest problem in big cities and popular tourist areas is that the good hotels are often priced way out of reach, while moderate options are thin on the ground. **Midrange hotels** are sub-standard, by Western standards, though considerably cheaper. Wherever possible, we've also provided budget options that are scrupulously clean and moderately comfortable. Most of the top-of-the-range city hotels are operated by major international chains, including many of the usual suspects: **Sheraton** (www.starwoodhotels.com), **Hyatt** (www.hyatt.com), **Radisson** (www.radisson.com), **Le Meridien** (www.lemeridien.com), **Nikko Hotels** (www.nikkohotels.com), and **Marriott** (www.marriott.com).

THE RATING SYSTEM India's hotel rating system refers to size and facilities on offer, not to the potential quality of your stay. Often the best hotels have no rating because they are heritage properties and—despite their overwhelming loveliness—just don't conform to the norms laid down by India's tourism department.

Tip: One hotel chain to avoid is the so-called "five-star deluxe" government-operated **Ashok group.** Most of its properties have "five-star facilities" and an inventory of hundreds of rooms but are often decaying concrete blocks manned by disinterested staff. In fact, as a general rule of thumb, government-run properties are best avoided throughout.

BARGAINING In India, even hotel rates are up for a bit of hard-core bargaining, particularly given the current low-traffic state of the industry. If you're thin-skinned, bargain online (many hotels offer Internet-only discounts); alternatively, show up and stay tough—when you hear the rate quoted, brazenly pretend to walk out; there's no shame in India in turning back and accepting the rate.

In remote areas, small towns and villages, and many places in the Himalayan foothills, you can find good (basic but clean) budget accommodations at unbelievable prices. The same cannot generally be said of the major cities, and a cheap, dingy hotel may expose you to bedbugs and despair; stick to the budget recommendations in this book.

Note: Prices in a number of the hotel listings throughout the book are stated in U.S. dollars—this is, in fact, the way many hotels targeting foreign markets quote their rates.

Wherever you stay, you will be asked to complete a foreign tourist information form, so have your passport ready in order to complete the details; the best hotels will complete the form on your behalf so that you only have to sign. Also note that top-range hotels (usually the options listed that only quote their rates in dollars) require payment in foreign currency; this is when a credit card is invaluable.

LANDING THE BEST ROOM
Somebody has to get the best room in the house. It might as well be you. Make sure your room has air-conditioning (ask for a split-air-conditioned room, as they're far less noisy—and ugly—than a room with window air-conditioner). If it doesn't, ask whether there is a ceiling fan or a water-cooling system. Ask about nonsmoking rooms, rooms with views (though many hotel staff don't understand this concept in India, so it's best to look around on arrival), showers or tubs (tubs in medium or budget category are usually old and stained, so don't

---

Of Hotels & Taxes
Almost every hotel in India (the exception being the flea pits aimed at serious budget travelers) will quote a rate to which an additional state and/or luxury tax will be added. This figure changes from state to state and from tariff to tariff but is usually about 10% to 12%—though be warned that in certain states, such as Tamil Nadu, it's an astronomical 35%. *Always* check whether the tax has been included in the rate you've been quoted and, if not, exactly how much it is.

shy away from shower-only options), and bed size. Ask for one of the most recently renovated or redecorated rooms—bathrooms in particular seem to suffer heavy wear and tear in India. If you aren't happy with your room when you arrive, say so and look around. If another room is available, most lodgings will be willing to accommodate you.

17 Suggested Itineraries

India is such a vast country and has so much to see that the temptation for visitors is to pack in as much as possible. But despite the improved range of accommodations and transportation, it is still a challenging destination, and you shouldn't tear your hair out because of a late plane or slow check-in, or find yourself on a long-distance train with an upset tummy. Set aside time to acclimatize and simply unwind—this is, after all, a holiday.

The range of possible itineraries is endless; what we've suggested below is a very full program covering either North or South India over a **2-week period.** If possible, you should extend your time—2 weeks is not really enough time to come to grips with India—or cut out some of the destinations suggested. Ideally, you should use this book's "Best of" chapter to work out a route that covers those experiences or sights that really appeal to you. You could, of course, combine a trip to the North and the South, but then you really should stick to one state (even one hotel!) in each area. Whatever you finally decide to do, we highly recommend that you end your holiday in one of India's natural paradises, not least to recover from the sensual assault that you'll experience exploring the crowded and often polluted urban areas—these oases include the beaches on the Malabar coast, the backwaters of Kerala, the lunar landscapes of the Himalayas, and Udaipur, Rajasthan's city of lakes.

Important: Should limited time force you to include only the most obvious stops in your itinerary, you will invariably only make contact with those locals who depend on you to make a living, which regrettably could leave you with a frustrated sense that many of India's inhabitants are grasping, manipulative, or downright pushy. This is why it is so important to *get off the beaten tourist track,* to experience the warmth, hospitality, and generosity of Indian culture, which celebrates an ancient philosophy of the guest as god.

CENTRAL/NORTH INDIA

Two Weeks

Day 1–2   After arriving in Delhi, allow yourself a full day to recover and possibly see a few of the top attractions. Spend the night in the hotel **Imperial.**

Day 3   Fly to **Varanasi** and watch the sunset on the Ganges. Spend the night in the **Ganga View Guest House.**

Day 4   Take a dawn cruise along the *ghats* (steps; here along the waterfront). That afternoon, fly to **Agra;** time allowing, visit **Agra Fort** or **Itimad-ud-Daulah's tomb.** Stay in the hotel Amarvilas. **Alternative to Varanasi:** Catch a train to Amritsar to visit the **Golden Temple,** returning the following day to Delhi, from where you can catch the superfast Shatarbi Express to Agra.

Day 5   See the **Taj** at dawn, then head for the lost city of **Fatehpur Sikri.** Catch a train or hire a car and driver to get to **Ranthambhore**

National Park. Spend the night in the **Sher Bagh camp** or the new **Aman tented camp.**

Day 6 Go **tiger tracking;** unwind around a campfire. Or take an overnight excursion to **Bundi.**

Day 7 Catch a train to **Jaipur** and meet your driver there. Explore the **City Palace.** Spend the night in the **Rajvilas** hotel.

Day 8 Spend the day **bargain-hunting,** visit **Amber fort,** or unwind around the pool.

Day 9 Head for the temple town of **Pushkar,** stopping to view the top attractions of **Ajmer** along the way. Spend the night in the **Pushkar Palace.**

Day 10 Spend the morning browsing the **market;** then either head for **Deogarh** or **Jodhpur.**

Day 11 Explore Jodhpur's **magnificent fort.** Spend the night in the **Umaid Bhawan Palace.**

Day 12 Explore the **fort.** Spend another night in Jodhpur (or drive to **Jaisalmer**). Or consider a 2-night excursion to Jaisalmer.

Day 13 Drive to **Udaipur.** Stay in either the **Lake Palace Hotel** or **Devi Gahr.** Explore the **City Palace** and old markets, or do the **Ranakpur-Kumbhulgarh** excursion.

Day 14 Fly out to **Delhi** or **Mumbai.**

SOUTH INDIA

Two Weeks

Day 1–2 After you arrive in Mumbai, allow yourself a full day to recover, and dine out at night at one of the city's top restaurants.

Spend the night in the heritage wing of the **Taj Mahal.**

Day 3 Fly to **Bangalore** (or Mangalore, if you'd prefer to explore the palaces of **Mysore**). Catch the overnight train to the lost city of **Hampi;** spend the night in the **Hampi Boulders** hotel.

Day 4–5 Overnight in Hampi. Then catch the train back to Bangalore.

Day 6 Fly to **Chennai.** Hire a car and driver through your hotel or use our recommendations. Spend the night at **Fisherman's Cove.**

Day 7 Head for **Pondicherry,** the French colonial town on the Indian Ocean's coast.

Day 8 Spend the day exploring Pondicherry. Overnight in the **Hotel de l'Orient.**

Day 9 Spend the day traveling to **Madurai.** Overnight at the **Taj Garden Retreat.**

Day 10 Either fly to **Trivandrum** to overnight at **Surya Samudra** (where you can stay for the day's duration or head north to the backwaters); or drive over the **Cardamom Hills** to **Shalimar Spice Village** for a bit of Ayurvedic pampering.

Day 11–12 Head to **Alleppey** (or **Fort Cochin**). Spend the next day cruising the backwaters on a **houseboat,** or overnight at Kumarakom in the **Kumarakom Lake Resort hotel.**

Day 13 Drive to **Trivandrum,** to Surya Samudra.

Day 14 Spend the day wishing you had come here in the first place, and figuring out how soon you can return.

FAST FACTS: **India**

American Express Report lost or stolen cards by calling ℰ **011/2687-5050** (all hours) or 011/2614-5920. Individual branches are listed in the "Fast Facts" sections of individual chapters.

Area Codes The international telephone access code for India is **91**. Area codes for principal cities and towns are listed in the "Fast Facts" sections in each chapter. All numbers listed in this guide include the local area code (which you would dial from another Indian town or city); this is separated from the actual telephone number by a forward slash (/).

Business Hours Banks open weekdays from 10am to 2pm and Saturday from 10am to noon. Most museums are closed Monday. Hours of retail outlets vary depending on where you are, but many close Sunday.

Cameras & Film You can purchase film just about anywhere in India, but it's best to buy it from high-traffic areas. Remember to store your film in transparent baggies, so you can remove it easily before you go through airport scanners. Always place your loaded camcorder on the screening conveyor belt or have it hand-inspected. Be sure your batteries are charged, as you will probably be required to turn the device on to ensure that it's what it appears to be. **Film Safety for Traveling on Planes, FSTOP** (ℰ **888/301-2665**; www.f-stop.org), can provide additional tips for traveling with film and equipment.

Electricity 220 to 240 volts AC.

Embassies & Consulates Embassies of major English-speaking countries are listed in the "Fast Facts" section for New Delhi; see chapter 8. For quick reference: **Australia** ℰ **011/2688-8223** or 011/2688-5556; **Canada** ℰ **011/2687-6500; New Zealand** ℰ **011/2688-3170**; and the **U.K.** ℰ **011/ 2687-2161**. The U.S. State Department encourages American citizens visiting India to register at the **U.S. Embassy** in New Delhi (Shantipath, Chanakyapuri; ℰ **011/2419-8000**; fax 011/2419-0017; http://usembassy. state.gov/delhi.htm) or at one of the U.S. consulates in India; a booklet entitled "Guidelines for American Travelers in India" is available. The U.S. Consulate General in Mumbai is located at Lincoln House, 78 Bhulabhai Desai Rd., 400 026 (ℰ **022/2363-3611**; fax 022/2363-0350; http://mumbai. usconsulate.gov). The U.S. Consulate General in Kolkata is at 5/1 Ho Chi Minh Sarani, 700 071 (ℰ **033/2282-3611/2/3/4/5**; fax 033/2282-2335; http://calcutta.usconsulate.gov). The U.S. Consulate General in Chennai is at 220 Anna Salai, Gemini Circle, 600 006 (ℰ **044/2811-2000**; fax 044/ 2811-2027; http://chennai.usconsulate.gov).

Emergencies Refer to "Fast Facts" sections in individual chapters for police, ambulance, and emergency contact numbers.

Internet Access Although they're not always fantastic in terms of connection speed (or cleanliness), cybercafes are a roaring trade, and usually cheap. To minimize frustration, it's generally recommended that you only check your e-mail in large towns and cities; there's simply no point in spending hours behind a computer screen in Darjeeling trying to send a single message when you could be admiring Mount Everest. *Note:* Avoid the ridiculous prices charged by business centers at luxury hotels; there's often Internet connection for 10% of the cost just around the corner.

Language You shouldn't have to battle too much if you speak English with a clear accent. Do not assume that everyone in India understands or speaks English, however. Also don't feel affronted when you run into locals who seem to smile in acknowledgement, only to reveal much later that they haven't the foggiest notion what you're talking about; they are simply trying to make you feel more at home. Hindi is widely spoken throughout North India, while many of the states are divided linguistically; for example, Tamil is spoken in Tamil Nadu, Kannada in Karnataka, Telugu in Andhra Pradesh, Malayalam in Kerala, Gujarati in Gujarat, and Konkani in Goa; and there are literally hundreds of local dialects.

Liquor Laws Attitudes toward alcohol vary considerably. In Gujarat, prohibition is in force and liquor can only be obtained from the permit rooms of luxury hotels, a concession made principally for foreigners and out-of-state businesspeople. In most other non-Muslim areas, alcohol is freely available and exceedingly popular. In top hotels, you'll find a full range of imported liquor, available to those who can afford the extravagance.

Lost & Found Be sure to contact your credit card companies the minute you discover that your wallet has been lost or stolen. Also file a report at the nearest police precinct, because your credit card company or insurer may require a police report number. Most credit card companies have an emergency number to call if your card is lost or stolen. They may be able to wire you a cash advance immediately or deliver an emergency credit card in a day or two. **Visa**'s U.S. emergency number is ✆ **800/847-2911** or 410/581-9994. **American Express** cardholders and traveler's check holders should call ✆ **800/221-7282**. **MasterCard** holders should call ✆ **800/307-7309** or 636/722-7111. If you need emergency cash over the weekend when all banks and American Express offices are closed, you can have money wired to you via **Western Union** (✆ **800/325-6000**; www.western union.com).

Mail Buy stamps for letters and postcards from your hotel, and have your concierge post them for you. International postage is extremely affordable (under Rs 12/25¢ per item), and the Indian postal service is generally efficient. However, sending a package or parcel abroad involves a tedious process of wrapping it in cloth and sealing it with string and wax (again, ask your concierge); you'll also have to complete a Customs declaration form. All this may have you spending a great deal of time at the post office (typically open 9am–5pm). Also, bear in mind that surface mail runs the risk of spending months in the system, or of never arriving at all. You can spare yourself a great deal of torment by having a local or international courier company deliver any important packages.

Newspapers & Magazines Major English dailies include *The Hindu* (www.thehinduonline.com), *The New Indian Express, The Times of India* (www.timeofindia.com), *Hindustan Times* (www.hindustantimes.com), and Kolkata's *The Statesman.* These make for interesting reading and will keep you up-to-date on local and international events. You may find that much of the writing assumes a great deal on your part, however. If you haven't been following certain stories for some time, the latest update may be impossible to fathom. For our money, *The Economic Times* provides the most news-intensive articles, written in a language that's less colorful but easier to follow. Each week you can pick up fresh issues of *The Week, India Today,* and *Outlook,* which provide quite venomous analyses of the nation's social, political, and economic situations. These are available at railway stations and not only help pass travel time but add immensely to your understanding of India. If you're looking specifically for travel information, the monthly *Outlook Traveller* (www.outlook traveller.com) features tourist information and colorful articles from an Indian perspective.

Passports For residents of the **United States:** Whether you're applying in person or by mail, you can download passport applications from the U.S. State Department website at **http://travel.state.gov**. For general information, call the **National Passport Agency** (✆ **202/647-0518**). To find your regional passport office, either check the U.S. State Department website or call the **National Passport Information Center** (✆ **900/225-5674**); the fee is 55¢ per minute for automated information and $1.50 per minute for operator-assisted calls.

For residents of **Canada:** Passport applications are available at travel agencies throughout Canada or from the central **Passport Office,** Department of Foreign Affairs and International Trade, Ottawa, ON K1A 0G3 (✆ **800/567-6868**; www.dfait-maeci.gc.ca/passport).

For residents of the **United Kingdom:** To pick up an application for a standard 10-year passport (5-year passport for children under 16), visit your nearest passport office, major post office, or travel agency; or contact the **United Kingdom Passport Service** at ✆ **0870/521-0410**; www. ukpa.gov.uk.

For residents of **Ireland:** You can apply for a 10-year passport at the **Passport Office,** Setanta Centre, Molesworth Street, Dublin 2 (✆ **01/671-1633**; www.irlgov.ie/iveagh). Those under age 18 and over 65 must apply for a 3-year passport. You can also apply at 1A South Mall, Cork (✆ **021/272-525**) or at most main post offices.

For residents of **Australia:** You can pick up an application from your local post office or any branch of Passports Australia, but you must schedule an interview at the passport office to present your application materials. Call the **Australian Passport Information Service** at ✆ **131-232,** or visit the government website at www.passports.gov.au.

For residents of **New Zealand:** You can pick up a passport application at any New Zealand Passports Office or download it from their website. Contact the **Passports Office** at ✆ **0800/225-050** in New Zealand or ✆ **04/474-8100**; or log on to www.passports.govt.nz.

Police Emergency and police contact numbers are listed in individual "Fast Facts" sections.

Restrooms Avoid public restrooms in India, and always carry toilet paper with you, since it's not always provided.

Smoking Whatever curbs the government has tried to place on cigarette usage, there are no signs of society giving in to concerns about the hazards of smoking. Nearly every male in India seems to smoke something. Most luxury hotels have introduced nonsmoking rooms; request one when you book your reservation.

Taxes Levies on luxuries such as hotel accommodations and alcohol vary from state to state. In Tamil Nadu, for example, a night in a luxury hotel will attract 35% in government-imposed taxes on the published room tariff. Even if you pay a discounted rate on the room, you will cough up a hefty additional fee. Imported liquors attract a similarly disagreeable sin tax, making local brands far more attractive than their quality might suggest. Restaurant bills often include additional charges that usually account for between 10% and 15% of the total cost of your meal.

Telephones Phone numbers in India change at the drop of a hat, and businesses are slow in updating contact information, including websites.

To call India:

1. Dial the international access code: 011 (from the U.S. and Canada); 00 (from the U.K., Ireland, or New Zealand); or 0011 (from Australia).

2. Dial the country code **91.**

3. Dial the city code (these are provided in the relevant chapters), omitting the first zero.

4. Dial the telephone number.

Making calls within India: Hotel telephone costs are exorbitant, even when you're making a domestic long-distance call. All over India, you'll see illuminated yellow **ISD/STD** signs indicating a privately operated "International Subscriber Dialing" and "Standard Trunk Dialing" facility; these are very reasonably priced. Your call is monitored by a computer system, and you pay at the end of your session. Make sure you have the correct phone number with you, and check that the phone is in a quiet spot or you run the risk of not hearing a word during your conversation.

To make international calls: Dial 00 and then the country code (U.S. or Canada 1, U.K. 44, Ireland 353, Australia 61, New Zealand 64). Next, dial the area code and number. For example, if you want to call the British Embassy in Washington, D.C., dial ✆ **00-1-202-588-7800.**

For directory assistance: Dial **197** if you're looking for a local number within India, and dial **183** for long-distance numbers within India. Don't hold your breath for accurate or up-to-date assistance, and speak slowly and clearly. There's every chance your request will be ignored.

For operator assistance: If the phone you're using is not an International Subscriber Dialing (ISD) facility, you'll need operator assistance; dial **186.** Using an ISD facility without the need for an operator will save you a great deal of time. **Toll-free numbers:** Calling a 1-800 number in the U.S. from India is not toll-free. In fact, it costs the same as an overseas call.

Time Zone Despite India's vastness, the entire country operates according to the same time zone, 5½ hours ahead of Greenwich mean time and 10½ hours ahead of Eastern Standard Time (New York). There is no daylight savings time. *Note:* You may find your sense of time threatened while you're in India; the rule of thumb is *don't panic.* Remember that there's simply no point in getting worked up about delayed trains and such. In fact, when you arrive on time or ahead of schedule, be thankful. Use "wasted time" to chat with locals.

Tipping Tipping in India is an industry unto itself, and it's a relief to find yourself in an environment like the Oberoi, where individual tipping is not encouraged, for this very reason. Money certainly speeds up most processes, and you're treated with a certain degree of dignity and respect the moment you produce a wad of cash—don't tip and you'll more than likely have to deal with a disgruntled and/or depressed porter/driver/ guide. Bear in mind that many of the people who serve you are possibly living on the bread line, and your monetary contribution will be greatly appreciated; handing over a Rs10 (20¢) or R20 (40¢) note will hardly dent your pocket. Obviously it's not worthwhile to tip someone who hasn't eased your journey, but do reward those drivers, guides, and hotel staff who go out of their way to make your stay an enjoyable one. A driver or guide who's been with you an entire day will be most grateful for an extra Rs 100 ($2.10).

Tipping is but one strain of India's all-pervasive **baksheesh** system, which is apparently an accepted means of distributing wealth to the lower echelons of society. As a foreigner, you will be regarded as wealthy, and your endless charity is almost expected by those who are less fortunate. It's therefore an excellent idea to always keep a stash of Rs 10 (20¢) notes in an easy-to-access pocket, so that you can hand cash to the person who has just carried your bags or given you an unsolicited tour or looked after your shoes (the list is endless), and is now hanging around hopefully. Occasionally, someone will bluntly make demands for *baksheesh,* and this is the same term that may be used by beggars, religious mendicants, and bare-foot children looking for a handout. You are not obliged to pay anything, of course, but your conscience and irritation level will probably sway you either way. *Tip:* In Hindu temples, priests will happily encourage you to hand over huge sums of cash, often insisting that the money is for the poor. Be wary of such scams, and bear in mind that many temple officials have grown wealthy on the charity of the poor.

3

Mumbai: City of Dreamers

India's biggest, fastest, richest city will bowl you over. Teetering on the edge of the Arabian Sea, its heaving population barely contained by palm-fringed beaches, India's commercial capital, formerly known as Bombay, is a vibrant, confident metropolis that's tangibly high in energy.

Originally home to Koli fisherfolk, the seven swampy islands that today comprise Mumbai originally commanded little significance. The largest of the islands was part of a dowry given by Portugal to England, which promptly took control of the six remaining islands and then leased the lot to the East India Company for a paltry £10. Massive land-reclamation projects followed, and by the 19th century all seven islands had been fused to form one narrow promontory and India's principal port.

Today the city continues to draw fortune-seekers from all over India. More than a thousand newcomers squeeze their way in every day, adding to the coffers of greedy slumlords and placing the city, which already has a population density four times greater than New York City's, on target for a population of 28 million by 2015.

A city with a dual identity, Mumbai is as flamboyantly materialistic as it is downright choked by squalor and social drudgery. The citizens of Mumbai pay almost 40% of India's taxes, yet half of its 15 million people are homeless. While the moneyed groovers and label-conscious shakers retire in luxury behind the security gates of their Malabar Hill mansions,

emaciated survivors stumble home to cardboard shacks in congested shanty-towns or onto tiny patches of open pavement. At every intersection you are accosted by these destitute hopefuls, framed against a backdrop of Bollywood vanity boards and massive advertisements promoting provocative underwear and sleek mobile-phone technology. Feeding into this social schizophrenia are the one-dollar whores, half-naked fakirs, underworld gunmen, bearded sadhus, Bhangra VJs and, of course, movie moguls and cell-phone-clutching starlets.

It is not just the economic disparities that bewilder: Looking down from the Hanging Gardens on Malabar Hill, you see the assertively modern metropolis of Nariman Point, but just a little farther south, on Malabar Point, is the Banganga Tank, one of the city's holiest sights, where apartment blocks overlook pilgrims who come to cleanse their souls by bathing in its mossy waters. Twenty-first-century Mumbai is brassy and vital, yet it can also transport you to another epoch. It is, in this sense, a quintessentially Indian city, encapsulating the raw paradoxes of the entire subcontinent.

You will almost certainly touch down in Mumbai—it's the most common point of arrival for visitors, and well connected to the rest of the country (including the UNESCO World Heritage sites of Ajanta and Ellora, also located in Maharashtra, and described at the end of the chapter). If you're looking for peace and quiet in meditative surroundings, move on as

> **_Fun Fact_ You Say Mumbai, I Say Bombay**
>
> In 1995, Bombay, the name the British bestowed upon the city, was renamed in honor of the local incarnation of the Hindu goddess Parvati, "Mumba Devi." The city's name change (along with a host of others that hark back to its colonial past) was enforced by the ruling Shiv Sena, a Hindu fundamentalist party that eschews the presence of any other than the Marathi people, a glaring irony given that this is a city of immigrants; a cocktail influenced as much by the grand Gothic monuments left by the British as it is by the many cultures who've set up shop here. Although it's difficult to understand how goodwill can prevail in a city led by politicians bred on xenophobia, Mumbai's well-intentioned optimism and its social cosmopolitanism prevail, and most of Mumbai's English-speaking inhabitants still refer to it as Bombay.

fast as jet lag and arrival times dictate. But if you want to experience modern India at its vibrant best, and dine at what are arguably some of the finest restaurants on the globe, tarry for at least 2 days. You may arrive appalled by the pitiful faces of the poor, shocked by the paradox of such wealth and poverty, and overcome by the heavy, heady stench and toxic pollution. But give India's dream factory a little time, and you'll discover it has a sexy, smoldering soul.

1 Arrival & Orientation

ARRIVING

BY PLANE   Most Westerners experience moderate shock when they arrive at Mumbai's sprawling **Chhatrapati Shivaji International Airport** (© 022/2836-6700), which wears its years of wear and tear with the indifference characteristic of much of India. The airport is located in Sahar, 30km (19 miles) north of the center. Most flights arrive and depart between midnight and dawn, which can make finding your feet difficult. A **Government of India Tourist Office** (© 022/2832-5331) at the airport should be open 24 hours but—as is the case in most of India's tourist offices—it's certainly not the best place to obtain advice; you'll find the contents of this book far more useful.

Because you will no doubt have to wait in line for foreign exchange (there is only one small booth), it is advisable that you arrange an **airport transfer** to meet you—important, too, because you will be accosted by a loud, expectant mass of touts and taxi drivers the minute you exit the terminal doors, all of whom need to be treated with a degree of caution. If you are expecting a pickup, don't get sidetracked or deterred from boarding the correct hotel shuttle—ignore strangers offering help.

Should you need to hire a taxi, make use of the overpriced but reliable **prepaid taxi** service; a trip to a city-center hotel should cost Rs 400 to Rs 500 ($8.75–$11) but may depend on the amount of luggage you're carrying. (Expect to pay well over double these rates for a hotel airport transfer.) Alternatively, having ascertained the prepaid rate, you can negotiate a lower rate with an **independent taxi** outside the terminal. Always agree on the final cost in advance, and do not allow your driver to take you *anywhere* other than your desired destination. If the driver seems unable to understand your English, do not get into his vehicle.

Metered taxis (where you don't bargain upfront but pay a rate dependent on mileage predetermined by a structured fare card—see "Getting Around," below) also cost less than prepaid services, but these are not usually available at the international airport. *Note:* **Auto-rickshaws** are banned from the city's center, so don't rely on these unless your hotel is located in the immediate vicinity of the airport.

Because most international flights arrive late at night, traffic delays are not usually a problem, and you should be at your hotel within an hour even if you're staying downtown.

DOMESTIC AIRPORT If you are flying direct from Mumbai's international airport on to the next destination, note that you will have to transfer (there is a free bus; make sure you get on it) to the **Santa Cruz Domestic Airport** (© 022/ 2615-6500; 4km (2½ miles) from Saha International and 26km (16 miles) north of the city), where you will have to spend the rest of the night in a very uncomfortable seat. If you have arrived at Santa Cruz and plan to spend some time in the city, you can catch a metered taxi from the airport, which should set you back about Rs 300 ($6.50) for a trip to a hotel in the city center. Since domestic flights are likely to arrive during the day, be prepared for a long, congested, frustrating journey into the city.

BY TRAIN If you are traveling from Central, South, or East India, you will no doubt arrive at "VT," Victoria Station (or Chatrapathi Shivaji Terminus). A taxi ride farther downtown, to Colaba, should take about 10 to 15 minutes. From the north, you'll arrive at Mumbai Central; from here you can either cross a footbridge to the local platform and catch another train to Churchgate Station, Colaba, or you can brave the traffic and take a taxi.

WHEN TO GO Mumbai's humidity—even in the small hours of the morning—is felt instantly, and the sun shines year-round. You always seem drenched in warm sweat, and the heat can be terribly cruel, making sightseeing far less agreeable than a tour of the city's wonderful restaurants and drinking holes. Winter (Nov–Feb) is still hot, although not so entirely unpleasant; the sultry sea air sets the tone for an adventure in exotic dining and an intoxicating jaunt through lively, Victorian-era streets that are constantly crammed with people. The only real relief from the heat comes midyear, when the annual monsoon drenches the city with heavy, nonstop tropical rains.

CITY LAYOUT

Mumbai city lies on the western coast of India, on a thin peninsula that extends southward almost parallel to the mainland. At the southern end of this peninsula are the Colaba and adjoining Fort area. West of Fort, hugging the Asiatic Sea, is the popular promenade Marine Drive, which terminates at Chowpatty Beach and Malabar Hill. These are the focal nodes for tourists, who, unlike the locals, often refer to the area as downtown. In fact, locals say they are going uptown, or "into town," by which they mean they are going toward South Mumbai, the area stretching south from Mahim Creek to Colaba. South Mumbai is where most tourists choose to base themselves. It is the historic heart of the city, with attractions like the Gateway of India and the Prince of Wales Museum, and the widest selection of restaurants and accommodations options. The South Mumbai neighborhoods are described in detail below, but to see where most Mumbaiikers live, including the jet-set stars, it may be worth taking a trip into one of the suburbs. Of these, the most interesting option (and a good alternative to South Mumbai if you're just staying over 1 night—it's a great deal closer to the airport) is Juhu Beach.

Mumbai

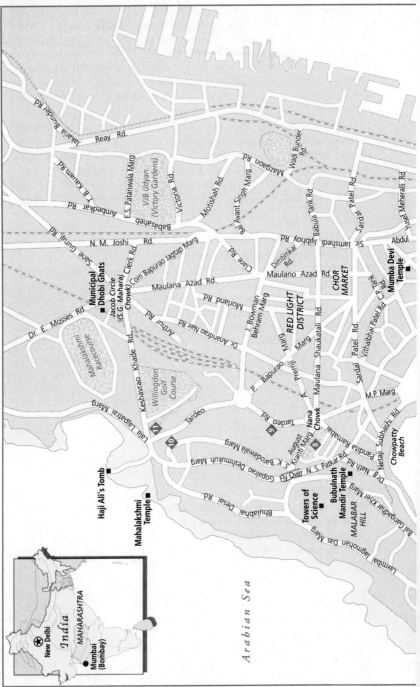

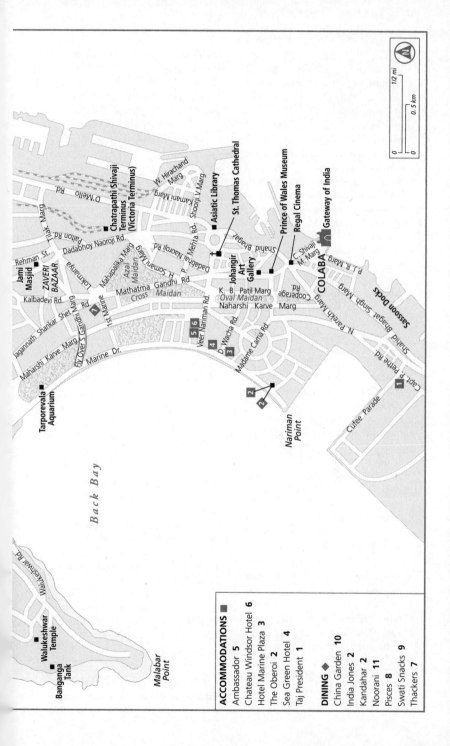

ACCOMMODATIONS ■
Ambassador **5**
Chateau Windsor Hotel **6**
Hotel Marine Plaza **3**
The Oberoi **2**
Sea Green Hotel **4**
Taj President **1**

DINING ◆
China Garden **10**
India Jones **2**
Kandahar **2**
Noorani **11**
Pisces **8**
Swati Snacks **9**
Thackers **7**

NEIGHBORHOODS IN BRIEF

COLABA

Because of its proximity to most of Mumbai's landmarks and colonial buildings, this, the southern tip of Mumbai, is the real tourist hub. In many ways this has also contributed to giving Colaba a seedy side, though certain areas are showing signs of rejuvenation. Many of the city's budget accommodations are situated along **Colaba Causeway,** punctuated by (at the southernmost end) the **Taj Mahal,** Mumbai's most famous hotel, which is located opposite the **Gateway of India,** Mumbai's most famous marker (both were slightly damaged in an Aug 2003 bombing that killed 45 people). **Apollo Bunder** refers to the area around the Gateway of India, though the easiest way to get there is to ask for directions to the Taj. West of this is **Cuffe Parade,** an upmarket residential neighborhood, and farther south, the restricted navy cantonment area.

If you travel west from Colaba to the other end of the narrow peninsula until you hit the sea, you'll arrive at **Nariman Point,** starting point of Marine Drive. Nariman Point was once Mumbai's most bustling business district but is now facing decline (though most airline offices and several foreign embassies are still situated here).

FORT

North from Colaba is the business neighborhood called Fort. By day the area comprising **Fort, Fountain, Ballard Estate,** and **VT** (or **CST) Station** is an extremely busy commercial district, but at night the neighborhood is rather forlorn, with many of the large parks *(maidans)* now empty. Just beyond VT Station is **Crawford Market,** which leads to the heart of Mumbai's congested markets.

Just west of the Fort area is **Churchgate Station. Veer Nariman Road,** the street leading from Churchgate Station to Marine Drive, is lined with restaurants.

MARINE DRIVE/CHOWPATTY BEACH

Marine Drive stretches from Nariman Point in the south to Malabar Hill in the north. Edged by a broad promenade that follows the curve of the seafront, this is a very popular place to take a morning or evening walk. At night the streetlights along this drive accentuate the dramatic arch of the bay, giving it the name **Queen's Necklace,** a term that has become less frequently used in recent years. Marine Drive is a long arterial road that runs along the curve of Back Bay. This road ends at **Chowpatty Beach** and then climbs uphill toward the very expensive and prestigious neighborhood of **Malabar Hill.**

MALABAR HILL/BREACH CANDY/PEDDAR ROAD

Malabar Hill connects to Napean Sea Road and beyond to **Breach Candy, Kemps Corner,** and **Peddar Road**—all upmarket residential areas. This is mostly a residential neighborhood, but it's got plenty of restaurants and stores, many open quite late. Several hotels in this area and particularly along Kemps Corner are good options for tourists who want to avoid the heavily touristy parts of Colaba and Churchgate.

CENTRAL MUMBAI

Central Mumbai extends beyond Crawford Market through **Mohammedali Road** and **Kalbadevi** to

Colaba

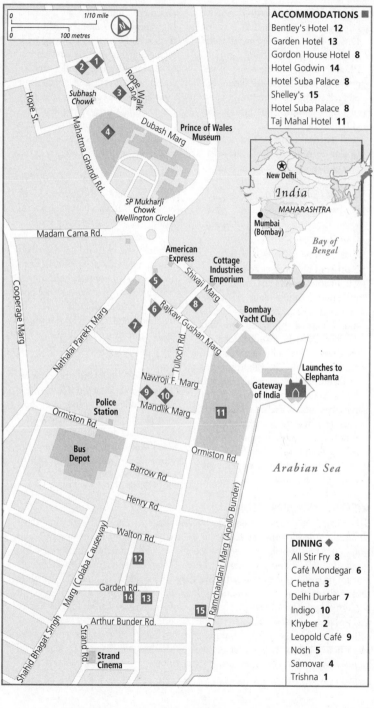

ACCOMMODATIONS ■
Bentley's Hotel **12**
Garden Hotel **13**
Gordon House Hotel **8**
Hotel Godwin **14**
Hotel Suba Palace **8**
Shelley's **15**
Hotel Suba Palace **8**
Taj Mahal Hotel **11**

DINING ◆
All Stir Fry **8**
Café Mondegar **6**
Chetna **3**
Delhi Durbar **7**
Indigo **10**
Khyber **2**
Leopold Café **9**
Nosh **5**
Samovar **4**
Trishna **1**

Mumbai Central Station and the fast-growing commercial areas of **Lower Parel.** The greatest developments are occurring around **Phoenix Mills,** where some of the erstwhile mill buildings have been converted into shopping complexes, restaurants, and gaming and entertainment spots.

West from Mumbai Central Station are **Tardeo** and **Haji Ali,** where you drive along yet another of Mumbai's bays. Extending northward of Parel along the western side of the city is the Western Railway local train line; traveling northeast is the Central Railway network.

SUBURBS (BANDRA & JUHU)

North of Mahim Creek extend Mumbai's vast suburbs, from where millions commute daily. First up, just across the creek, in fact, is Bandra, which, along with Juhu and Andheri (West), just north of it, is the place where Bollywood stars live and hang out. Although it's not really on the tourist circuit, Bandra, being home to a sizeable portion of the city's elite, is packed with uppercrust restaurants, steamy clubs, and trendy bars. At night young people gather along Carter Road to drink, smoke (cigarettes or dope), and chill out before making their way to expensive clubs. The area around Juhu Beach is where many of the city's wealthy escape; crowded with picnicking bourgeoisie and a host of vendors flogging popular eats, ice cream, coconuts, and fresh fruit juice, it's worth coming here to soak up Mumbai's carnivalesque atmosphere rather than contemplate sunbathing on the beach, which is filthy, or venturing into the even dirtier seawater. It does, however, have some fine hotels, restaurants, and nightclubs—Enigma at Juhu's new JW Marriott Hotel is one of Mumbai's most happening spots.

Just east of Juhu lie the city's two airports and a host of upmarket hotels. The area of **Andheri (East)** around the international airport has become a crowded (and rather polluted) commercial and residential neighborhood. Yet many business visitors prefer to stay in this part of town if their business lies there, to avoid the stressful commute. Farther north in the suburbs is **Goregaon,** home to Film City, where many Bollywood films are shot; past that is **Borivali,** where Mumbai's most popular theme park, EsselWorld, is situated. Beyond, the city goes on (and on), with little to tempt the visitor.

VISITOR INFORMATION

Technically, there are tourist information desks at both airports, and these should be open for the arrivals of all flights. Don't count on it, however, and don't expect a lot of help, other than being handed a brochure or booklet and given some bland details of available hotels. That said, an excellent source of visitor information is the comprehensive *City Info* booklet, published fortnightly and available at tourist information offices, as well as upmarket hotels and even certain pubs and restaurants. The main **Government of India Tourist Office** (123 Maharishi Karve Rd., Churchgate; ℭ **022/2207-4333** or -4334) is where to head for general tourist-related information, but if you're staying at one of the city's better hotels, your concierge will be the best source of information on sightseeing, performances, events, and activities.

FAST FACTS: Mumbai

Airlines Domestic airlines connect Mumbai to nearly every corner of the subcontinent. For the best service, try **Jet Airways, Amarchand Mansion, Madame Cama Road** (© 022/2285-5788). It's open Monday to Friday 9am to 7pm; Saturday 9am to 5:30pm; Sunday 9:30am to 1:30pm. Its **check-in/reservations desk** (© 022/2615-6666) is open round-the-clock. **Indian Airlines** (© 022/2202-3031 or -5654) is the state-owned carrier, while **Sahara Airlines** (© 022/2283-5671, -5672, or -5673) flies to considerably fewer destinations.

Ambulance Dial **102.** You can also contact **Bombay Hospital,** 12 New Marine Lines (© 022/2206-7676); or try **Swati Ambulance** (© 022/2387-1215), which has 24-hour service.

American Express The office is at the Regal Cinema Building on Wellington Circle, Chhatrapati Shivaji Maharaj Road, Colaba (© 022/2204-8291). Open Monday to Friday 9:30am to 6:30pm; Saturday 9:30am to 2:30pm.

Area Code The area code for **Mumbai** is **022.**

ATMs Undoubtedly the most convenient way to get local currency, ATMs are to be found throughout the city, and 24-hour security guards man many of them. Your best bet for a quick transaction is to head for an ATM machine belonging to either the UTI or HDFC banking system; note that ATMs in the ICICI network are frequently unreliable.

Bookstores **Crossword Bookstore** (22 Mahalakshmi Chambers, 26 Bhulabhai Desai Rd., Breach Candy; © 022/2498-5801) has a Western ambience and Mumbai's largest selection of books. Alternatively, head for **Shankar's Bookstore** (© 022/2204-7491) just outside Café Mondegar, Colaba Causeway, or **Strand Book Stall** (Sir PM Rd., Fort; © 022/2266-1994 or -1917).

Car Hires See "Getting Around," below.

Consulates **U.S.:** Lincoln House, 78 Bhulabhai Desai Rd., Breach Candy (© 022/2363-3611 or -3617); Monday to Friday 8:30am to 1pm and 2 to 3:45pm. **U.K.:** 1st and 2nd floors, Maker Chambers IV, J. B. Marg, 521 Nariman Point (© 022/2283-3602 or -0517); Monday to Friday 8am to 4pm. **Australia:** 16th floor, Maker Towers East, Cuffe Parade (© 022/2218-1071); Monday to Friday 9am to 5pm. **Canada:** 41/42 Maker Chambers VI, Nariman Point (© 022/2287-6027); Monday to Thursday 9am to 5:30pm; Friday 9am to 3pm. **South Africa:** Gandhi Mansion, Altamount Road, near Kemp's Corner (© 022/2389-3725); Monday to Friday 9am to 5pm.

Currency Exchange **Thomas Cook India** is located in the Thomas Cook Building, Dr. D. Naoroji Road, Fort (© 022/2204-8556), and is open 9:30am to 6:30pm weekdays and 9:30am to 6pm on Saturday. For those willing to wait in line and put up with annoying service, the **State Bank of India** is on Madame Cama Road, Fort (© 022/2202-2426).

Drugstores The Apollo Pharmacy is in Kala Ghoda (© 022/2282-9707).

Emergencies See "Police," below.

Hospitals **Breach Candy Hospital,** 60 Warden Rd., Breach Candy (© 022/2363-3651, 022/2367-1888, or 022/2367-2888) is open 24 hours and is one of the most advanced and reliable hospitals in Mumbai. **Bombay Hospital,**

12 New Marine Lines (✆ **022/2206-7676**) is more centrally located and has a 24-hour ambulance service.

Internet Access For a cheap (around Rs 30/60¢ per hour), reliable connection, pop into **Waghela**, 23-B Nowroji Furdunji Rd., Colaba (✆ **022/2204-8718**). Open daily 8:30am to midnight, it's just around the corner from Leopold's Café.

Newspapers/Magazines For the scoop on day-to-day city news, buy a copy of the local rag *Mid Day,* sold on street corners and at intersections from around noon. *The Indian Express* and *The Sunday Express* are both good national dailies that provide the lowdown on current and social events. **Outlook Traveller** (www.outlooktraveller.com) is a top-quality, locally produced travel magazine.

Police Colaba 022/2285-6817; Cuffe Parade 022/2218-8009; Juhu 022/2618-4368; Khar 022/2649-6030; Malabar Hill 022/2363-7571; Sahar 022/2822-1748.

Post Office You'll find the **General Post Office** near Victoria Terminus, off Nagar Chowk (✆ **022/2262-4343** or -0956). It's open Monday to Saturday 9am to 8pm; Sunday 10am to 5pm.

Restrooms Make full use of your bathroom facilities *before* you head out for a day of sightseeing. Use only restrooms in hotels and upmarket restaurants.

Taxis See "Getting Around," below.

Travel Agencies Contact IATA-affiliated **NAC Travels Pvt Ltd,** 412 Raheja Centre, Nariman Point (✆ **022/2202-8810;** nactravels@yahoo.com).

2 Getting Around

Mumbai is a city on the go—but don't expect to get anywhere fast, because traffic is lousy at the best of times. Already, close to a million vehicles crowd the streets, and each week another 1,400 scooters and cars join the congestion caused by battered black-and-yellow taxis, Marutis, Indigos, leftover red double-decker Routemaster buses, and the occasional cow. You will certainly need to take a taxi to get around (or, if you're arriving from the airport, arrange a transfer with your hotel; see "Arriving," earlier in this chapter), but if you're overnighting in the Colaba-Fort area, you will, for the most part, be able to get around on foot.

Finding (and Losing) Your Way . . .

It soon becomes apparent that Mumbai is not a planned city but has mushroomed according to the needs, wisdom, and follies of its citizens and administrators. Street names in particular can be confusing to first-time visitors; street signs, when they exist, are often ignored—many people continue to use the old colonial names instead. Colaba Causeway, for example, is the colloquial name for Shahid Bhagat Singh Road; Breach Candy for Bhulabhai Desai Road; and Peddar Road for Deshmukh Marg. In times of confusion, refer to a landmark (or hotel); for example, if you're trying to find Veer Nariman Road and no one understands you, ask for Churchgate Station instead.

Moments **Mumbai Diary: Lessons from My Taxi Driver**

I've just disembarked from a 10-hour flight, and my taxi driver, Ramon, insists on showing me the city. Looming over the wheel, he steers his tiny, disheveled vehicle from one unmarked lane to another, tearing through red traffic lights, and racing so close to the bumpers of slower cars you'd swear each was a bitch in heat. All the while, he calmly honks his horn (every truck has a signboard that reads: HORN PLEASE, an invitation to help alert the driver to your presence in this stomach-churning game of chicken) and supplies delightful (and, as he chews on betel nut, at times incomprehensible) anecdotes. En route, he points out the endless lines of taxis waiting at various CNG (compressed natural gas) stations; at one, the stream of cars is backed up for over a mile. According to Ramon, there are approximately 50,000 taxis in Mumbai, and most of them now use CNG. "But when they run out, they have no choice but to queue," he says resignedly. It's only just after one in the morning, but I will be Ramon's last fare. While I'm checking into my hotel, he'll search for a CNG queue and turn off his engine, waiting in line until the sun comes up. I feel a touch guilty about convincing him to lower his initial fee for the 40-minute journey from Rs 350 to Rs 250 ($7.60 to $5.35). But this is Mumbai, and somehow it felt right.

PUBLIC TRANSPORTATION

BY TAXI   You can pick up a cab almost anywhere, simply by looking as if you're about to start walking. Typically, the taxi meters in Mumbai are mounted on the hood of the vehicle, and taxi drivers are required to carry a conversion chart that tells passengers how much they owe, based on the original fare displayed on the ludicrously old-fashioned meters. Do not start the journey before checking to see if the driver is carrying the correct chart; these are often tampered with, with vital information missing—for example, the part of the chart informing you that the rates quoted are for nighttime travel, which are higher. If you're in any doubt, ask a policeman or your hotel doorman to decipher the fare for you.

If you're looking for a vehicle for the day, you can strike a deal with a private taxi driver directly, but again, do negotiate the deal upfront—you should pay around Rs 700 to Rs 800 ($16–$18), plus a tip, for an 8-hour (or 80km/50-mile) stint. Note that it's worth shelling out extra for an air-conditioned cab—you're likely to spend long stretches waiting in traffic jams at overcrowded intersections. To rent an air-conditioned car and an English-speaking driver privately (which will cost a bit more but may take out the hassle of haggling), the following operators are recommended: **Cool Cabs** (52 Andheri; ✆ **022/2490-5151,** 022/2822-7006, or 022/2824-6216); **Car Hirers** (1403 Arcadia, Nariman Point; ✆ **022/2283-4689;** www.carhirers.com); **Euro Cars** (Kinis Causeway, 526 A.S.V. Rd., Bandra W.; ✆ **022/2655-2424;** euro_cars@vsnl.net); and **Ketan Travels Pvt. Ltd.** (R.T. Building, P.M. Rd., Ville Parle E.; ✆ **022/2614-0554;** www.ketancars.com). Hertz (✆ **022/5691-0908;** mumbai@carzonrent.com) has cars throughout the subcontinent, but unless you're suicidal, do not attempt to self-drive.

Hiring a taxi through your hotel can get very pricey, but the fleet of cars maintained by some of the upmarket hotels is unlikely to be matched in quality by

---

> **Tips**   **Dealing with Beggars**
>
> As a first-time visitor, you will no doubt be struck first and foremost by the seemingly endless ordeal of the impoverished masses. Families of beggars will twist and weave their way around the cars at traffic lights, hopping and even crawling to your window with displays of open wounds, diseased sores, crushed limbs, and starving babies, their hollow eyes imploring you for a few life-saving rupees. Locals will tell you that these poverty performances are Mafia-style rackets, with protection money going to gangs, and sickly babies being passed around to gain more sympathy for their "parents." In the worst of these tales of horror, children are maimed to up the ante by making them appear more pathetic. The choice is stark: Either lower the window and risk having a sea of unwelcome faces descend on you, or stare ahead and ignore them. To salve your conscience, tip generously those who have made it onto the first rung of employment.

---

anyone in the city, and it may be convenient to have taxi charges added to your hotel bill. Do, however, remember to tip your driver directly.

BY TRAIN   Train travel in the city is strictly for the adventurous, but then again, joining the peak-hour commuters gives you the opportunity to see how the other half lives, as the tracks wend their way through some of the city's most squalid slums. A first-class return ticket from Victoria Terminus to the suburb of Thane costs about Rs 210 ($4.50). Leave luggage and valuables in your hotel room.

ORGANIZED TOURS & TRIPS

You will be offered tours of various descriptions by at least half the people you meet on the streets of Mumbai; everyone from your taxi driver to the guy who asks you for the time will have a contact in the tourism industry who'll be more than happy to take you sightseeing. Use your discretion, watch your wallet, and remember that Mumbai's traffic makes it impossible to see everything in 1 day.

To arrange a legitimate tour of the city, set it up through your hotel, which should have access to the best guides (from an English and knowledge point of view). Or contact the **Maharashtra Tourist Development Corporation** (Madame Cama Rd., opposite L.I.C. Building; © **022/2202-6713** or -7762) or any **Government of India Tourist Office** (© **022/2203-3144**).

Bear in mind that there's little point in seeing Mumbai only from the back-seat of a chauffeur-driven taxi; leave time to explore the city on foot. If you're keen on architecture, a group of young architects conduct **Bombay Heritage Walks** on weekends (© **022/2834-4627;** Oct–May; by prior arrangement only)—these tours take in various fascinating parts of the city.

Note: One of the best organized trips in the city is the boat trip departing half-hourly from the Gateway to Elephanta Island (see "What to See & Do," below).

3 What to See & Do

Mumbai doesn't have the wealth of historical attractions of, say, Kolkata or Delhi. Rather, it is a city that revolves around its manic pace and the head-spin energy exuded by the millions of diverse people that have settled here. This is a city you *experience* rather than sightsee, and sampling from the fantastic restaurants described later in the chapter should be highest on your must-do list. That said, Mumbai does have a few attractions you should make time for; and be sure to set aside some time to explore at least part of the **Colaba/Fort area,** described below, on foot—do this at the beginning of the day before the heat becomes suffocating. Another good area to explore on foot is the **Marine Drive/Chowpatty Beach stretch,** possibly after a boat trip to **Elephanta Island.** Finally, you may wish to visit **Malabar Hill,** also in the South Mumbai area and home to two top attractions (see below), as well as the **Hanging Gardens** (also known as Ferozeshah Mehta Gardens). Laid out in the early 1880s, the terraced park at the top of Malabar Hill covers (or "hangs over") the city's main water reservoir, but unfortunately it fails to live up to its spectacular-sounding name. The best reason to visit here is to wander over to the **Kamala Nehru Park** (across the road from the Hanging Gardens), from where you have a great view of Nariman's skyscrapers and the sumptuous curve of Marine Drive.

EXPLORING COLABA & FORT

If you're at all inspired by Gothic Victorian architecture, then a jaunt through Mumbai's older districts is essential. Most tours kick off at the **Gateway of India** (see below), but a more authentic place to start, given Mumbai's origins, is **Sassoon Docks** ★★ (aka the Fisherman's Market), which lies just south of the Gateway, off Shahid Bhagat Singh Marg (near Colaba Bus Station). Most of the delicious seafood dishes in the city's finest establishments start out here, where Koli women in rainbow-colored saris whip the shells off prawns while others gut and sort fish. Get here early, when the boats return with their first catch, for the vibrant, communal spirit as baskets full of fish are moved around the dock through various stages of processing. It makes for absorbing viewing.

From here, catch a cab or walk to the Gateway, possibly stopping for a refresher at the Taj Mahal Hotel, situated directly opposite. From here it's a 15-minute walk north to Fort, Mumbai's cultural center, where you will find the superb **Prince of Wales Museum** (see below), the nearby **Jehangir Art Gallery,** and the rather mediocre **National Gallery of Modern Art,** as well as a host of Raj-era Gothic architectural highlights. From the museum you can either head north along M. Gandhi Road to Flora Fountain, hub of downtown Mumbai, or travel southwest down the famous Colaba Causeway.

Surrounded by colonial buildings that testify to the solid architecture of a bygone era, **Flora Fountain** has, since 1960, had to compete for attention with a **Martyrs' Memorial** that honors those who died in the creation of the state of Maharashtra. As you head toward the fountain, take in the impressive **High Court** building (which overlooks the Oval Maidan, where aspiring cricketers practice their paces), the neoclassical **Army & Navy Building,** and the 78m (256-ft.) **Rajabai Clock Tower,** which towers over the Bombay University complex. East of the fountain lies **Horniman Circle,** where you will find the **Town Hall,** a regal colonnaded building with original parquet wood floors, wrought-iron loggias, spiral staircases, and marble statues of leaders associated with Mumbai's history. The major drawing card here is the **Asiatic Society Library,** which has a collection of around 800,000 valuable texts. You can join the seniors and students who fill the library's popular reading room to peruse local newspapers and check out the public book collection, but you'll need special permission if you're interested in looking at some of the priceless treasures.

Also facing the Horniman Circle is the late-19th-century Gothic Venetian **Elphinstone Building** and, opposite it, on Veer Nariman Road, **St. Thomas'**

Cathedral, thought to be the oldest colonial structure in Mumbai. (Note that if you head west along Veer Nariman Rd., known for its many good restaurants, you will come to Marine Dr.) St. Thomas' Cathedral is a stark contrast to the pink and blue neoclassical **Kenneth Eliyahoo Synagogue,** Mumbai's oldest and loveliest Sephardic synagogue, located off K. Dubash Marg, in Forbes Street. North of Flora Fountain, up Dr. Dadabhai Naoroji Road, is the Art Deco–style Parsi fire temple, **Watcha Agiary.** Built in 1881, it features carvings in a distinctly Assyrian style.

If you prefer shopping (albeit of a tourist-trap nature) to architecture, opt instead for the famous **Causeway** (now officially renamed **Shahid Bhagat Singh Marg,** though, thankfully, no one refers to it as such). Budget travelers have long been drawn to this vibrant street, but in recent years Colaba and its seedy side streets have begun to slip into an increasingly urbane and upmarket second skin. Hip bars, swinging clubs, and tasteful restaurants are drawing the smart crowd, and the Taj Mahal is no longer the only reason for chauffeured luxury cars to make the rather lengthy trip from Bandra, Juhu, and Malabar Hill. Anything and everything seems to be available from the peddlers *(wallahs)* on Colaba's sidewalks and back alleys, whether it's fruit, cheap cigarettes, currency, or hashish. Shop in exclusive boutiques or rummage through heaps of cheap trinkets sold on the sidewalks, where you can bargain for everything from imitation perfume to piles of cheap, tasteless T-shirts, all the while avoiding the advances of streetwise beggars and con artists sporting half-moon smiles and incongruous American accents.

At the southernmost end of the Causeway (that's if you manage to get this far south before grabbing a taxi and heading for the peace of your hotel room!) you will see the neo-Gothic **Afghan Memorial Church of St. John the Evangelist.** Dating back to 1858, it memorializes those who fell in the First Afghan War—proof yet again of Mumbai's mosaic past.

TOP ATTRACTIONS: DOWNTOWN

Gateway of India & Taj Mahal Hotel ★★★   Easily the most recognizable remnant of the British Raj, the Gateway was designed by George Wittet (also responsible for the Prince of Wales Museum). The Gujarati-inspired yellow

---

Need a Break?

Besides the options listed under "Where to Dine," below, the following are pleasant places to pop in for a snack or drink if you don't feel like having a full meal. **Stadium** ★ (© 022/2204-6819) is an unpretentious Irani restaurant outside Churchgate Station. Sip a beer at **New York** ★ (© 022/2363-2876) on Hughes Road—not to be mistaken for New Yorker or New York, New York, both of which are in Chowpatty nearby; it's one of the few places in the city with a jukebox. At the upmarket end is **Shamiana** ★ (© 022/2202-3366), the Taj hotel's 24-hour coffee shop; **Gallops** ★ (© 022/2307-1448), a colonial-style restaurant at the racecourse; **Geoffrey's** ★ (© 022/2285-1212), at the Marine Plaza Hotel; or the very pleasant **Café Bascilico** ★★, at Colaba (Azmi St., near the old Strand cinema), where you get great breakfasts, deli-style sandwiches, juices, and more. If you're near the American Consulate, stop off at the cafe/bistro **Sin** ★ (© 022/236-7564), which is furnished in 1970s retro style. The deli-style sandwiches, coffees, and wines are good, but avoid the mediocre starters. The grilled rockfish entree is quite popular if you want something more substantial.

basalt structure was supposed to commemorate the visit of King George V and Queen Mary, who arrived in 1911 to find a fake cardboard structure instead; the Gateway was eventually completed in 1924 and was the final departure point for the British when they left Indian soil in 1947. It is the most obvious starting point for any tour of Mumbai (and is where the boats to Elephanta are launched), and to this end it draws large numbers of visitors as well as hordes of locals keen to take money off unsuspecting foreigners. The area makes for a quick-fix introduction to Mumbai tout dynamics; expect to be offered everything from photographs of yourself posing here to hashish and even young girls. Opposite the Gateway is an equestrian statue of Chhatrapati Shivaji, the Indian hero who gives his name to several renamed Mumbai institutions.

More impressive—in beauty and size—is the hotel behind the Gateway, which in many ways symbolizes Mumbaiikers' determined and enterprising attitudes. Inspired by its namesake in Agra, the **Taj Mahal Hotel** (see "Where to Stay," below) was built just over a century ago by an industrialist named Jamshedji Tata, who wanted to avenge the whites-only policy of Watson's, then the city's poshest hotel—today the Taj Mahal is legendary, while Watson's is a run-down dump. Designed by a European architect who mailed the plans to India, the hotel was mistakenly constructed back-to-front, so what was meant to be a fantastic seafacing facade actually overlooks a side street. The blunder makes not a jot of difference, and the palatial edifice remains a dominant feature of Colaba's waterfront, its six-story domed structure best viewed from an offshore boat. For a great view of the Gateway, head inside the Taj and make for the **Apollo Bar.**

Chhatrapati Shivaji Maharaj Marg. Gateway information: 𝄢 022/2202-3585 or -6364. Half-hour harbor cruise Rs 30 (60¢) deluxe.

Elephanta Island Caves ⋘   For a taste of Mumbai's early history and an opportunity to view the city's skyline from the water (not to mention escape from the tumult of the streets), grab a ferry and head out to Elephanta Island, declared a UNESCO World Heritage Site in 1987. The hour-long trip also provides a good introduction to Hinduism; the guides on board describe the religious significance of what you're about to see, though the origins of the Shiva temple caves—thought to date from the revivalist Hindu movement between A.D. 450 and 750—remain obscure.

Entry is via the main northern entrance to a massive hall, supported by large pillars, where the enormous Mahesamurti statue is housed. At 6.3m (18 ft.), the remarkable sculpture depicts Shiva in his three-headed aspect: as Creator (facing right), Protector (the crowned face at the center), and Destroyer (facing left, with serpents for hair). Left of the Mahesamurti is Shiva as both male and female, Ardhanarishvara, an aspect suggesting the unity of all opposites. Other sculptures refer to specific actions of the god and events in Hindu mythology, but many were damaged or destroyed by the Portuguese, who apparently used the Hindu gods for target practice.

Tip: Plan your trip so that you can witness sunset over the Mumbai skyline on your return journey, then pop into the Taj Mahal Hotel for a post-culture cocktail. Note that a music and dance festival is held at Elephanta every February.

9km (5½ miles) from Mumbai. Tickets and ferries from the Gateway of India. Admission $5. Boats depart from the Gateway of India every half-hour Wed–Mon 10am–4:30pm or 9am–2:30pm depending on season.

Prince of Wales Museum ⋘   Renamed the Chhatrapati Shivaji Maharaj Vastu Sangrahalaya, but thankfully also still known by its colonial name, this is Mumbai's top museum and arguably the best in India, providing an extensive and accessible introduction to Indian history and culture. The Indo-Saracenic building itself is rather lovely, but it is the collection that is outstanding, not least because it is well laid out (unlike the collections of most museums throughout the subcontinent) and aided by a useful audio guide highlighting "curator's choice" exhibits. The central hall features a "précis" of the collection, but don't stop here—from sculptures of Hindu deities to beautiful temple art, Buddhist *thangkas* from Nepal and Tibet to gruesome Maratha weaponry, there is much to see. Highlights are found on the first floor: Among them are the spectacular collection of more than 2,000 miniature paintings representing India's various schools of art (look for the portrait of Shah Jahan, creator of the Taj Mahal), and the exhibit relating to the Indus Valley Civilization (which is remarkably civilized considering that it dates from 3500 B.C.). Least impressive is the natural history section with its collection of stuffed animals.

Note: Art lovers may wish to include a visit to the **Jehangir,** Mumbai's foremost art gallery, part of the complex but located a little farther along M Gandhi Road, and open daily from 11am to 7pm, free of charge. The work is mediocre— or perhaps so to the Western-trained eye—but the gallery is worth popping into even if it's just to grab something to drink at the Samovar cafe (see full review under "Where to Dine," later in this chapter). For reviews of current art exhibitions, consult "The List," the entertainment supplement in the local rag *Mid Day.*

159/161 Mahatma Gandhi Rd., Fort. powm@vsnl.com. Rs 300 ($6.50), includes audio guide. Tues–Sun 10:30am–6pm.

Victoria Terminus (Chhatrapati Shivaji Terminus) ★★★

Also rechristened as part of Mumbai's nationalist-inspired anti-Raj drive, but more often than not referred to as "VT," this baroque, cathedral-like building must rank as Mumbai's most marvelous Raj-era monument. India's very first steam engine left this station when it was completed in 1887; today at least a thousand trains leave every day, carrying some 2.5 million commuters in and out of the city. With its vaulted roofs, arches, Gothic spires, flying buttresses, gables crowned by neoclassical sculptures, stone carvings, and exquisite friezes, the terminus is an architectural gem, worth entering to see the massive ribbed Central Dome (topped by a statue of the torch-wielding "Progress") that caps an octagonal tower featuring beautiful stained-glass windows with colorful images of trains and floral patterns. But come, too, for the spectacle of the disparate people, from sari-clad beauties to half-naked fakirs, that makes up Mumbai. Get here just before lunch to watch the famous *dabbah-wallahs* stream out into the city: A vast network of dabbah-wallahs transfer some 10,000 cooked lunches, prepared by housewives and kept warm in identical metal tiffin containers, from the suburbs to a central sorting house before redistribution to office workers. The success of this system (almost no one gets the wrong lunch) is proof of how well India works, despite its reputation for obstructive bureaucracy.

Dr. Dadabhai Naoroji Rd., Fort. ✆ 022/2269-5959.

Marine Drive & Chowpatty Beach ★★★

Marine Drive (renamed Netaji Subhash Chandra Marg) follows the sweeping curve of sea that stretches north from Nariman Point's high-rise buildings to infamous Chowpatty Beach, located at the foot of Malabar Hill. It's the ultimate seaside promenade, where Mumbaiikers come to escape the claustrophobia of central Mumbai, gratefully eyeing an endless horizon while strolling or jogging along the broad windswept promenade. In the evenings, casual stalls are set up for brisk trade when families go for a relaxed jaunt or a ride on a rickety fly-by-night Ferris wheel. This is the city's ultimate sunset spot, when—having watched the orange globe sink into the Arabian Sea—you can witness the street lights transform Marine Drive into the aptly named Queen's Necklace, a choker-length of twinkling jewels adorning Back Bay. The scene is perhaps best enjoyed with cocktail in hand at one of Marine Drive's classier establishments: either the revolving rooftop restaurant at the **Ambassador,** or the Oberoi's **Bayview Bar,** which also offers jazz music and cigars.

Once the sun has set, catch a ride (or walk) north along Marine Drive to Chowpatty, Bombay's oldest seafront. Chowpatty is no longer the filth-ridden extravaganza its long-acquired reputation suggests (though it's still not in any state for sunbathing or swimming), and at night it assumes the demeanor of a colorful fair, with children of all ages flocking to ride the ancient Ferris wheels and tacky merry-go-rounds, and fly-by-night astrologers, self-styled contortionists, snake charmers, and trained monkeys providing the flavor of the bazaar— and bizarre—especially on weekends. This is a great place to try some of Mumbai's famous street snacks, especially *bhelpuri:* crisp puffed rice, vegetables, and fried noodles doused in a pungent chutney of chili, mint, and tamarind, and then scooped up with a flat *puri* (puffy deep-fried bread). Chowpatty bhelpuri is renowned throughout India, sold here by the eponymous *bhelwallahs,* who now ply their trade in the recently constructed Bhel Plaza, where other traditional treats like *kulfi* are on offer at dirt-cheap prices. *Note:* Ensure that water and ice aren't used in anything you eat or drink. Another excellent option is the **Cream Centre** (25 Fulchand Niwas, Chowpatty Beach; © **022/2363-2414** or 022/2369-2025; all credit cards accepted; open 11am–11:30pm). For close to half a century this vegetarian snack place has been serving up delicious food— so good, in fact, that whenever you pass Chowpatty Beach in the evening, you'll see a queue of people waiting to get in. Make a meal of the signature *chole bhature* (spiced chickpeas and a large puri), a typical Punjabi dish that is made everywhere but rarely so well as here.

Jain Temple   This is arguably the prettiest temple in Mumbai (indeed, Jain temples are generally the prettiest in India)—if your itinerary does not include a visit to one elsewhere (the most famous being in Rajasthan), do make the time to visit Mumbai's. Members of the peace-loving Jain community (the Jains will not tread on an ant, and at their most extreme wear masks to avoid breathing in even tiny insects) are known to be exceptional in the world of business, and although they believe in self-restraint and aestheticism, they pour large sums into the construction and maintenance of their places of worship. Officially called **Babu Amichand Panalal Adishwarji Jain Temple,** this beautifully

---

Moments **Dunking Ganesh**

To experience Mumbai at its most exuberant, get to Chowpatty Beach for the culmination of **Ganesh Chaturthi** , the city's biggest and most explosive celebration. Held in honor of the much-loved elephant-headed god (here called Ganapati), the 11-day festival culminates on the last day when a jubilant procession is held and Ganapati is dunked in the sea. Ganesh Chaturthi is held in August and September; for exact dates contact the Government of India Tourist Office.

decorated and adorned temple has an entrance flanked by two stone elephants. The downstairs area houses an array of deities and saints, including an image of Ganesh that recalls historical links between Jainism and Hinduism.

Ridge Rd., Walkeshwar (Malabar Hill). ✆ 022/2369-2727.

Mani Bhavan Gandhi Museum ★★★   Mahatma Gandhi lived in this quaint Gujarati-style house from 1917 to 1934, and it was here in November 1921 that he conducted a 4-day fast in order to restore peace to the city. This quiet three-story home now preserves the spirit of the man who selflessly put his nation before himself. There's a library of Gandhi-related works, as well as displays of photographs, posters, slogans, and other items that document and explain Gandhi's legendary life; dioramas depicting major events and turning points in his fight for the nation's freedom draw particular attention to his devotion to the poor. You can see Gandhi's old *charkha* (spinning wheel), which in many ways symbolized the struggle for independence, and which now appears on the Indian flag. A visit to this tranquil spot makes a welcome change from the continuous hubbub of life in Mumbai—go up to the roof to really appreciate the relative stillness of the surrounding Parsi neighborhood.

19 Laburnam Rd., near Malabar Hill. ✆ 022/2380-5864. www.gandhi-manibhavan.org. Donations appreciated. Daily 10am–5:30pm.

Banganga Tank ★★   Here the paradox of traditional life coexisting with unbridled modernization is all too vivid. Near the edge of the Arabian Sea at the southern tip of Malabar Hill, several small crumbling stone-turreted temples and flower-garlanded shrines surround a rectangular pool of holy water in an area of looming modern-day skyscrapers and encroaching urbanization. Ritual bathers who come here believe the mossy waters have healing powers and originated from a natural spring created by an arrow shot by Rama (the hero of the *Ramayana*), who rested here while on a mission to rescue his beloved Sita from the demon king's abode in Lanka. The source of the spring is said to be an underground offshoot of the Ganga, and the waters are considered just as sacred as those of the great river itself. In the shadow of one of present-day Mumbai's most prosperous neighborhoods, Banganga continues to function as an out-of-time devotional hub, its tolling bells and mantra-chanting *pujaris* drawing devotees to worship the divine.

Walkeshwar Rd., Malabar Hill.

TOP ATTRACTIONS OUTSIDE DOWNTOWN MUMBAI

Dhobi Ghats ★★   It's a fascinating spectacle, looking down on row upon row of open-air concrete wash pens, each fitted with its own flogging stone, while Bombay's *dhobis* (around 200 dhobi families work together here) relentlessly pound the dirt from the city's garments in a timeless tradition. Known as the world's largest outdoor laundry, Dhobi Ghats is where Mumbai's traditional launderers—or dhobis—provide a wonderful service, collecting dirty laundry, washing it, and returning it neatly pressed, all for a very small fee. Stubborn stains are removed by soaking garments in a boiling vat of caustic soda; drying takes place on long, brightly colored lines; and heavy wood-burning irons are used for pressing. At the very least, it's a great photo opportunity. (Note that there is another Dhobi Ghat off Capt. Prakash Petha Marg, Colaba, which may be more accessible.)

Dr. E. Moses Rd. (near Mahalakshmi Station).

Bollywood Celebrity: High-Octane Overdrive

It's inevitable that the world's biggest film industry (twice as many films are made here as in Hollywood) would produce a host of celebrities, but in India stars are worshipped with the fervor usually reserved for gods and goddesses, not least because these are often the roles they play. Sadly, the virtues associated with religious idols often do not apply to the stars themselves. In 2002, when one of Bollywood's high-octane celebrities, 37-year-old Salman Khan, got slam-drunk and skidded onto a sidewalk, killing a man who—like so many of Mumbai's citizens—lived on the pavement outside the laundry where he worked, it turned out to be one of the media events of the decade, with arresting officers ordering prints of the front-page photos of themselves "posing" with the superstar, and readers rallying behind the "unfair" treatment of their hero. Khan's stardom proved to be his "get-out-of-jail-quick" card; he spent a mere 17 days in prison, claiming that it was his chauffeur who had been behind the wheel, and that the experience had taught him "to trust no one."

Film City ⋆   These are the largest film studios in Asia, but don't expect Universal Studios or Disneyland—there are no rides or queues at ticket turnstiles. That said, this 140-hectare (350-acre) Bollywood back-lot with dozens of film sets will interest film fanatics and those keen to get out of central Mumbai for the day. Highlights include a fake slum, a replicated hill station and, of course, the chance to spot the likes of Aamir Khan (the star of internationally acclaimed *Lagaan*) or Bipasha Basu—or a local Mafia boss. Most sets are heavily booked throughout the year, and Film City is not officially open to visitors; phone ahead and make arrangements to secure entry.

Goregaon E. ✆ 022/2840-1533. Admission by prior arrangement.

MARKETS

Mumbai has more than 70 markets, and it's worthwhile to spend a couple of hours exploring at least one, not so much for the shopping (for that, see "Shopping," later in this chapter) but for the human spectacle of it all. Flowers are an intrinsic part of Indian culture, and **Bhuleshwar Wholesale Flower Market** ⋆⋆ (CP Tank Circle) is the best place in the city to witness the Indian romance with color and fragrance. Note that according to Hindu beliefs, if you touch or sniff the flowers, you'll ruin them—so don't. **Chor Bazaar (Thieves' Market)** ⋆⋆ (Mutton St., off Sardar Vallabhbhai Patel Rd.; Sat–Thurs 11am–7pm) conjures up *Arabian Nights'* cloak-and-dagger intrigue and precious rings sold with the finger of the former owner still attached, but in reality this is just a fun place to rummage through an extravagant assortment of antiques, fakes, and junk and get into the rhythm of that favorite Indian pastime: bargaining.

If you visit only one market, make it **Crawford Market** ⋆⋆⋆ (Lokmanya Tilak Marg and Dr. Dadabhai Naoroji Rd.; Mon–Sat 11:30am–8pm), Mumbai's quintessential fresh-produce shopping experience, now officially known as **Mahatma Jyotiba Phule Market.** Dating back to the 1860s, it combines the traditional Indian bazaar experience with both Norman and Flemish architecture. (*Note:* Above the main entrance is a bas-relief frieze designed by Rudyard Kipling's father.) Admire the colorful pyramids of heavenly mangoes and ripe bananas, but steer clear of the disturbing pet stalls.

Moments **Catch a Bollywood Blockbuster**

You can't say you've properly done the biggest film-producing city on earth if you haven't gone to the cinema to catch a blockbuster, or tried to, as the crowds clap, cheer, jeer, and—when the song-and-dance numbers crop up—even dance in the aisles. Listings are found in daily newspapers, where you can also determine quality and even figure out the storyline by reading reviews from contenders for the world's bitchiest critic; alternatively, ask your hotel concierge for recommendations. Of course, you can always get completely into the swing of things by picking up a copy of one of Bollywood's gossip magazines. *Filmfare* and *Stardust* not only fill you in on what's hot or not, but are crammed with glossy airbrushed close-ups of silver-screen idols. Cinemas that also offer historic Art Deco appeal include the famous **Eros Cinema** (Cambatta Building, opposite Railway Station, Churchgate; ✆ **022/2282-2335**) and the **Metro** (Dhobi Talao; ✆ **022/2203-0303**); there, good seats cost as little as Rs 100 ($2.10), a pittance considering that you're also privy to a rather spectacular live show from the audience. *Warning:* Women traveling alone are advised to avoid attending theaters (or any event where you're likely to be sitting in the dark)—there's a good chance you'll end up receiving more attention than the movie.

Clothing is one of Mumbai's major exports, and at **Fashion Street** ✪ (Mahatma Gandhi Rd., across the road from Bombay Gymkhana), a motley collection of shops and stalls, you will pay a fraction of the price asked in foreign stores. Much of what is here is surplus stock; other garments have been rejected by quality controllers. Start your haggling at half the quoted price.

Taxi drivers get nervous when you tell them you want to visit the **Zaveri Bazaar** ✪✪ (Sheik Memon St.; Mon–Sat 11am–7pm). You'll soon discover why. Shoppers and space-fillers shuffle and push their way endlessly through narrow gaps in this cluttered, heaving market, and it's often impossible to inch forward by car—or even on foot. Behind the street stalls and milling masses, glittering jewels are sold from family shops. If the glitzy accessories don't fascinate you, perhaps you'll be drawn to the packed **Mumbadevi Temple,** where the city's namesake deity is housed. Activity around the temple is chaotic, with devotees splurging to prove their devotion to the powerful goddess. *Note:* The bazaar may still be recovering from a devastating August 2003 bombing at the time of your visit. Ask your concierge or taxi driver if the market is open.

CRICKET

Although hockey is India's official national sport, cricket is by far the best-loved game, and even watching a group of schoolboys practicing in a field is an experience unto itself. Mumbaiikers play the game with an enthusiasm that's quite intoxicating—almost as if it provides some measure of relief from the hardships of daily life. In India, the stars of the game are worshiped like gods, and Indian spectators at international games have the ability to transform even the blandest match into an exciting event.

During the season (Oct–Mar), several matches are held each week at **Wankhede Stadium** (Churchgate), which is where Mumbai's big national and international games are hosted. Tickets are sold by the **Bombay Cricket Association** (© **022/2281-9910** or 022/2281-2714), but it's worth asking your concierge to arrange good seats for you at a decent price (top-tier tickets can go for as much as $100).

4 Where to Stay

Be prepared to spend more on lodging in Mumbai than in any other city on the subcontinent; standards at the low end can be difficult to stomach, so you're better off forking out a little more for a decent place to stay. Remember to ask for discounts, which are common (sometimes as much as 50%), and cruise the Internet for bargains—it's not uncommon to find ridiculously cheap deals, available even during the popular winter season.

Marine Drive is a great option if you want a prime view of the Asiatic sea, but it's pricey. With a variety of options to suit every budget (top choice obviously being the Taj Mahal Hotel, reviewed below), Colaba-Fort is where most tourists end up. If you are on a really tight budget, a cheap, decent option worth noting is **Bentley's Hotel** (17 Oliver Rd., Colaba; © **022/2284-1474** or -1733; bentleys hotel@hotmail.com), which has old, threadbare accommodations with enough character and antique furniture to make it livable. You can get a room with wooden floors, a balcony, and an attached bathroom for under Rs 1,200 ($26); be warned that at least several days' advance reservation might be necessary. If you are literally overnighting and have no desire to spend time in Mumbai, a number of options are located close to the international airport, but these are pricey. A good compromise is Juhu Beach, which has cheaper choices and a great nighttime atmosphere, and is only a 20-minute drive from the airport.

Note: The prices below are sometimes given in rupees, with U.S. dollar conversions; others are stated in U.S. dollars only, which is how many hotels targeting foreign markets quote their rates.

MARINE DRIVE

Within walking distance of the city's commercial center, Marine Drive is a great place to base yourself, not least for the sea views and sense of space these provide—offering a relief from the hustling, bustling streets that lie east. Expect to pay for the privilege, however. If your budget can't stretch to pay for the suggestions below, check out **Sea Green Hotel** (© **022/5633-6525** or 022/2282-2294; www.seagreenhotel.com). This is the best budget option on Marine Drive, where relatively large guest rooms with French doors (with flaking paint) open onto balconies overlooking Back Bay. The furnishings are quite awful, and mattresses are wafer-thin and without sheets (blankets are provided), but the attached shower-toilets are large and clean, and there's TV, air-conditioning, and minibar. You can bed down for Rs 1,975 ($45) double.

VERY EXPENSIVE

Hotel Marine Plaza ★★   Any address along Marine Drive is highly sought after, and the blue-mirrored glass facade of this self-styled "fashionably small" upmarket establishment is no exception, though it's not in the same class as the Oberoi. Like the hotel, the marble lobby is small, its main stairway concealing a quaint lounge from where you can stare up at people swimming in the glass-bottom pool on the fifth floor. Behind the lobby lounge, a waterfall resembling a giant clam is flanked by two capsule elevators that whisk you up to your room. Most of the accommodations are suites, some of which are relatively well-priced but require neck-straining to get a look at the view; make sure to specify a room with a direct sea view. Besides swimming, the pool deck affords wonderful views over Back Bay and the entire Queen's Necklace strip. Like many other upscale hotels in Mumbai, Marine Plaza gets busy at weekends, especially for Sunday lunch, when the popular **Oriental Blossom** restaurant is filled with locals.

29 Marine Dr., Mumbai 400 020. ℂ 022/2285-1212. Fax 022/2282-8585. www.sarovarparkplaza.com. hotelmarineplaza@vsnl.com. 68 units. Doubles: $275 superior room; $300 executive suite; $400 deluxe suite; $575 special suite. AE, DC, MC, V. **Amenities:** 2 restaurants; bar; pool with Jacuzzi; gym; business center; shop; 24-hr. room service; laundry; doctor-on-call. *In room:* A/C, TV, dataport, minibar, tea- and coffee-making facility, electronic safe, scale.

The Oberoi ★★★   What do Richard Gere, Michael Jackson, Rupert Murdoch, Liz Hurley, and the leaders or the heads of state of the United States, Russia, Greece, China, Indonesia, and Iceland all have in common? Yes, they've all stayed at the best hotel on Marine Drive, and arguably (at least tying with the Taj) the best in all of Mumbai. It's particularly from a service point of view that the Oberoi wins hands-down; touches like a personal butler on each floor and genuflecting staff members who go out of their way to make you feel revered are always welcome. And the genteel atmosphere is a relief—tranquil, sophisticated, and relaxed, this is where you want to retreat after spending a few hours out on the street. You can head for the top-rated **Banyan Tree spa,** or for the second-floor pool where you can soak up the Mumbai sun next to a dramatic faux-rock waterfall. Accommodations are spacious, with tasteful decor and all the amenities you'd expect from a five-star hotel; opt for one of the upper-floor sea-facing rooms for dramatic views of Back Bay and, at night, the lighting up of the Queen's Necklace—a dazzling pre-dinner spectacle. Bathrooms are great, with separate showers and tub, and a neatly proportioned dressing room offers ample cupboard space. If you can afford to really splurge, choose the immaculate Kohinoor Suite, which covers 152 sq. m (1,634 sq. ft.) on a corner with smashing 270-degree views of Marine Drive and the bay.

Note: If the rates are a tad stiff for your budget, you can choose to overnight in the adjoining Oberoi Towers. Though a stay here is by no means as relaxing as what's on offer at its more exclusive neighbor, this is still an excellent hotel, with a constant stream of people wanting to see and be seen—plus you'll have access to all the facilities next door. Rates start from $255 double.

Nariman Point, Mumbai 400 021. ℂ 022/5632-5757; reservations 022/5632-6887. Fax 022/5632-4142. www.oberoi.com. 337 units. Doubles: $295 superior city-facing; $315 premium bay-view; $355 deluxe ocean-view; $670 executive ocean-view suite; $900 deluxe ocean-view suite; Kohinoor suite tariff on request. Airport transfers and breakfast included. Weekend rates offer considerable savings. AE, DC, MC, V. **Amenities:** 3 restaurants; bar; pool; spa; salon and health club; concierge; sightseeing, travel, and limousine service; business center; currency exchange; shopping arcade; bookshop; 24-hr. room service; babysitting; laundry and dry cleaning; doctor-on-call; floor butler. *In room:* A/C, TV, fax machine, dataport, minibar, hair dryer, electronic safe, scale. Sea-facing rooms and suites have DVD players; suites and deluxe rooms include CD players.

EXPENSIVE

Ambassador ★   Capped by the city's only revolving restaurant, this kitsch 1940s hotel welcomes you with a baroque-inspired marble lobby adorned with cheap cherub statues, giant decorative vases, and an eclectic, extravagant mix of furniture, all under a gold-painted molded ceiling dripping with chandeliers. If you want a sea view (and that's why you're on the Drive), opt for one of the "superior" guest rooms: Clean, neat and functional, these occupy the second, third, and fourth floors and have carpeted passages decorated with Mughlai miniatures. Expect pink wall panels, pink carpets, pink marble, and bedspreads featuring pink flowers. The slightly cheaper "executive" rooms on the upper floors include some units with partial sea views: ask for room no. 8, 9, or 10. On the plus side, executive rooms are reasonably sized and have a slightly less overwhelming white, cream, and blue decor; roomy white-and-gray marble bathrooms feature large tubs. Apart from the enthusiastic turbaned doorman and the dedicated restaurant staff, service here is unexceptional, with some irritating heel-dragging that's particularly evident behind the crowded reception counter.

Veer Nariman Rd., off Marine Dr., Churchgate 400 020. ✆ 022/2204-1131. Fax 022/2204-0004. www. ambassadorindia.com. 123 units. Doubles: $200 executive room; $220 superior room; $240 premier room; $400 suite; $25 extra bed; no charge for children under 12 sharing parent's room. AE, DC, MC, V. **Amenities:** 3 restaurants; bar; health club and sports activities by arrangement; travel assistance and car hires; business center; currency exchange; florist; 24-hr. room service; laundry and dry cleaning; doctor-on-call. *In room:* A/C, TV, bedside console, minibar, hair dryer, electronic safe.

COLABA

With the city's densest concentration of sights, hotels, and restaurants (of which the best are reviewed below), Colaba is an ideal location. The Taj Mahal is here, as is the excellent-value Gordon's House, a personal favorite.

VERY EXPENSIVE

The Taj Mahal Hotel ★★★   George Bernard Shaw famously claimed that after staying here, he no longer had any need to visit the original Taj Mahal in Agra. Despite some stiff competition from relative newcomer the Oberoi, it remains *the* most celebrated address in Mumbai (see "Top Attractions: Downtown," earlier in this chapter), with a seemingly endless stream of Bombabes and playboy millionaires emerging from limos and vamping their way through the lavish lobby toward the popular restaurants and watering holes. You'll want to wallow in the luxurious old-world splendor of the Heritage Wing, where individually themed high-ceilinged suites transport you to another era, when the likes of Somerset Maugham and Duke Ellington bedded down in the city's best hotel. The history here is tangible: Public areas are decorated with carefully chosen antiques and vintage artworks. For a view of the Gateway, book a luxury sea-view room, but if money is no object, nothing less than the Rajput Suite will do. The looming Intercontinental arm of the hotel (or Tower Wing) is more business-oriented, and a letdown if you've explored the original, but service and attention to detail are fabulous no matter which part of the hotel you occupy. Bombay's very first licensed drinking establishment, **Harbour Bar,** is found here, as is the still trendy **Insomnia** nightclub. As the crowning glory of one of India's most prominent hotel chains, the Taj Mahal may well double as the nerve center for moneyed mischief, but it remains a great blend of old-world charm and modern conveniences.

Apollo Bunder, Mumbai 400 001. ✆ 022/202-3366. Fax 022/287-2711. www.tajhotels.com. mahal.mumbai@ tajhotels.com. 582 units. Tower Wing doubles: $300 superior city-view; $315 superior sea-view; $315 deluxe city-view; $330 deluxe sea-view. Heritage Wing doubles: $335 luxury city/pool-view; $350 luxury sea-view; $395 Taj Club (includes limousine airport transfer, club floor check-in, breakfast, personal valet, and cocktail hour). Heritage suites: $450 junior; $600 executive; $750 luxury; $1,000 grand luxury; $1,500 presidential. AE, DC, MC, V. **Amenities:** 5 restaurants; 3 bars; nightclub; swimming pool; sports arrangements on request (golf, badminton, squash, billiards, tennis, table tennis); fitness center; concierge; travel desk; car hires; business center; currency exchange; shopping arcade; pastry shop; salon; babysitting; laundry; doctor-on-call; valet service; personal valet service for Grand Luxe and Presidential Suite guests. *In room:* A/C, TV (some with DVD), fax machine, dataport and modem, minibar, hair dryer, personal safe.

EXPENSIVE

Taj President ★★   It may not be the most beautiful or luxurious hotel in Mumbai, but this classy business property offers ultra-efficient service, excellent

Five-Star Dining: The Foodies' Choice

If your choice of hotels is based on the quality of the in-house dining, here's a review of the best of the five-star hotels' restaurants.

On Marine Drive, the Oberoi wins first prize with **Kandahar** ★★★, **India Jones** ★★★ (see both in "Where to Dine," below), and **Frangipani** ★, a Mediterranean/Italian option that's ideal if your stomach can't take the spiciness and richness of Asian cuisine (all © 022/2232-6310). Farther along Marine Drive, at the Hotel Marine Plaza, are **Oriental Blossom** ★★, one of Mumbai's best Chinese restaurants, serving both Szechuan and Cantonese cuisine under the able direction of Chef Huang; and **Bayview** ★ (both © 022/2285-1212), which provides lunch, dinner, and midnight buffets that are great value for money; for about Rs 300 ($6.50) you can eat to your heart's delight and enjoy a great view. For an elegant evening, **Pearl of the Orient** ★ (© 022/2204-1131), the revolving restaurant at the top of the Ambassador Hotel, will please you not only with the best view of Mumbai but also with its good service and satisfying food. It has Korean barbecue, not very authentic Japanese food, and a sprinkling of Thai and Chinese dishes. **Dome** ★ (© 022/5639-9999), at the spanking-new Intercontinental Hotel on Marine Drive, is a stylish terrace lounge where you can sip wine, smoke a stogie, and snack on kebabs from the open grill while you watch the sun sink into the Arabian Sea.

The Taj Mahal Hotel's best restaurants are **Golden Dragon** ★★ (© 022/2202-3366), a Szechuan Chinese eatery with a huge menu (try the Peking duck or lobster in black-bean sauce); and the more formal **Zodiac Grill** ★★ (both © 022/2202-3366). The latter is widely regarded as Mumbai's most exclusive restaurant, with legendary service, food, and ambience. It is also requires deep pockets—an average meal here will set you back at least Rs 2,500 ($55) per head. Perched atop the Taj Mahal Hotel and providing a fantastic view of the harbor is **Souk** ★

restaurants, and a convenient location in a smart neighborhood not too far from the maelstrom of busy Colaba. Shades of purple combine with marble, wood, and metal, and are playfully offset by elegant bonsai trees in a brand-new lobby that pays homage to the 1970s. Standard rooms are decently sized, with solid wooden furniture, brown-red carpets, and an emphasis on paisley fabrics. It's worth paying a little extra for a room on the Executive Floor, which has received an ultra-contemporary makeover by one of Bombay's leading designers; pale tones and modern works of art combine to make this, the 17th floor, quite different from the other, old-fashioned floors.

90 Cuffe Parade, Mumbai 400 005, Maharashtra. © 022/2215-0808. Fax 022/2215-1201. www.tajhotels. com. president.mumbai@tajhotels.com. 300 units. Doubles: $225 standard city-facing; $240 standard sea-facing; $255 executive room; $295 executive suite. Executive rooms and suites include breakfast. AE, DC, MC, V. **Amenities:** 3 restaurants; bar; pool; fitness center (gym, steam, massage); concierge; travel desk; car hires; business center; currency exchange; bookshop; pastry shop; salon; 24-hr. room service; babysitting; laundry service; safe deposit lockers; doctor-on-call. *In room:* A/C, TV (satellite), dataport. Fax machines in some rooms.

(© 022/2202-3366), a West Asian restaurant that offers food from Iran, Turkey, Lebanon, Egypt, Greece, and Morocco. Also in the Taj is **Sea Lounge** ✦ (© 022/2202-3366), a renowned coffee shop where you can unhurriedly sip tea and nibble on cucumber sandwiches while you watch the little boats float by. Of course, you don't have to stay here to dine here, but do note that your manner of dress directly affects how well you are treated.

Moving deeper into Colaba, the Taj President offers **Thai Pavillion** ✦✦ (© 022/2215-0808), perhaps the most authentic Thai restaurant in the city, as well as the **Konkan Café** ✦✦ (see review later in this chapter).

In Bandra, the Taj Land's End Hotel offers **Ming Yang** ✦ (© 022/2644-1234), a Szechuan Chinese eatery that gives diners a fine view of the Arabian Sea and the Portuguese Fort. If you are in the suburbs, Juhu has several options. At the JW Marriott you'll have your choice of places to eat: **Lotus Café** ✦✦ (© 022/5693-3000), **Mezzo Mezzo** ✦✦ (see review later in this chapter), and the brilliant **Saffron** ✦✦ (© 022/5693-3000), with its kebab counter and superb Hyderabadi cuisine. The poolside **Kabab Hut** ✦ (© 022/2624-2983) at the Sun 'n' Sand Hotel is another outstanding showcase of fabulous kebabs. Also on Juhu Beach is the open-air seaside restaurant at the **Juhu Hotel** (© 022/2618-4013), serving regular Punjabi fare in a tranquil setting.

Of the airport hotels, it's worth noting that **Vindhyas** ✦✦ (Orchid Hotel, near Santacruz airport; © 022/2616-4040) offers a brilliant way to get a feel for the eight different cuisines of peninsular India, while at **Dum Pukht** ✦✦ (ITC Grand Maratha Sheraton Hotel; © 022/2830-3030), you can enjoy a truly remarkable traditional Indian meal slow-cooked in sealed vessels topped with coals.

MODERATE

The Gordon House Hotel ✦✦   Set among a rash of rather ordinary old-fashioned hotels, Colaba's sexiest lodging option and Mumbai's only boutique-style hotel is perfect for those raring to have a good time. Originally owned by Arthur Gordon, an early-20th-century trader who made his fortune in Bombay, and now the pride of Sanjay Narang, one of Mumbai's most high-profile restaurateurs, this trendy pad with its toothpaste-white interiors comes as a breath of fresh air, as does the slick, attentive service that starts with the super-fast check-in. There are three themed guest-room floors: The Scandinavian level offers smart, contemporary rooms with parquet floors and sleek Ikea-style furniture, timber blinds, and large Euro-themed black-and-white photographs. Mediterranean rooms are also charming, with bright blues and yellows, tiled floors, cane chairs, John Miller posters, and cool aqua-toned bathrooms. Rooms on the feminine Country Floor are strictly for floral, patchwork, and pastel fans. Accommodations are small but well proportioned, with comfortable beds and extras like a stereo system with VCD (video compact disc; a media format popular in

Asia that never really caught on in the west) and CD player so you can rent a movie or request complimentary music from the hotel's library. A selection of magazines, bowls of sweets, designer toiletries, free Internet access, and complimentary ironing are more thoughtful touches. The bathrooms may be tiny but they offer great walk-in showers. Opulent and over the top, the one and only suite has been themed on the Sun King's palace at Versailles, complete with crystal chandeliers and lavish gilded furniture. Sadly, the place has one drawback: The nonstop thumping from the in-house nightclub can seriously impact your sleep, especially on weekends.

5 Battery St., Apollo Bunder, Colaba, Mumbai 400 039. ✆ 022/2287-1122. Fax 022/2287-2026. www.gh hotel.com. rooms@ghhotel.com. 29 units. Doubles: Rs 5,000 ($110); Rs 10,000 ($218) Versailles Suite. Tariff includes American breakfast. AE, MC, V. **Amenities:** 2 restaurants; bar; nightclub; health club privileges; exercise equipment; concierge; travel, transport, and sightseeing arrangements; 24-hr. room service; laundry and dry cleaning; complimentary ironing; doctor-on-call; express check-out; outdoor banqueting terrace. *In room:* A/C, TV, bedside console, minibar, tea- and coffee-making facility, hair dryer, iron and ironing board on request, electronic safe, CD and VCD player (CDs on request).

INEXPENSIVE

Chateau Windsor Hotel   Clean, very basic rooms on the fifth floor of an apartment block, this "hotel" is approached via an ancient elevator that may have you panicking even before check-in. It may be unspectacular but it's cheap, and you get to hang out with real Mumbaiikers. Do specify that you want an air-conditioned room with attached bathroom; these units have small balconies, stone tile floors, and thin mattresses with clean white sheets and towels. The simple furnishings include an armless "sofa," a linoleum-topped table, and a small, narrow cupboard. Management is rather helpful, and although there is no dining facility, room service is available, and a large number of excellent restaurants are in the neighborhood. The kitchen is also available for you to do your own cooking—as long as it's vegetarian.

86 Veer Nariman Rd., Churchgate, Mumbai 400 020. ✆ 022/2204-4455. Fax 022/2202-6459. info@ ChateauWindsor.com. 40 units. Doubles: Rs 1,590 ($35) small non-A/C room; Rs 1,890 ($41) standard non-A/C room; Rs 2,190 ($48) standard A/C room; Rs 300 ($6.50) extra person; Rs 150 ($3.15) children ages 3–12 sharing parent's room. MC, V. **Amenities:** Travel assistance; 24-hr. room service; laundry; doctor-on-call. *In room:* A/C, TV.

Hotel Godwin   The facade of this nine-story budget hotel harks back to the 1930s and suggests a faded grandeur that is sadly not realized in most of the rooms. Because the range of accommodations varies a lot here, you should specifically request a centrally air-conditioned deluxe room that has been refurbished. Also insist that it's one of the 8th-floor units that are blessed with a view (distant as it is) of the Taj Mahal Hotel. On the top floor is **Cloud 9,** a restaurant with a fabulous view that transports you well away from the otherwise mediocre environment.

Note: Guest rooms at the Godwin's sister establishment, the **Garden Hotel** (✆ **022/2284-1476;** gardenhotel@mail.com), immediately next door, are slightly cheaper, but rooms are cluttered and a bit grubby.

Jasmine Building, 41 Garden Rd., Colaba, Mumbai 400 039. ✆ 022/2287-2050. Fax 022/2287-1592. www. cybersols.com/godwin. 52 units. Doubles: Rs 2,482 ($54) standard; Rs 2,650 ($58) deluxe; Rs 2,893 ($63) suite. AE, MC, V. **Amenities:** 2 restaurants; bar; taxi service; currency exchange; room service; laundry; doctor-on-call. *In room:* A/C, TV, minibar.

Hotel Suba Palace ⭑   A friendly doorman sporting an elaborate moustache welcomes you politely to this small, rather nondescript hotel not far from the Gateway of India. Despite the side-street location and total absence of views, a full upgrade in 2001 has rendered it bright and spotless, with brand-new fittings and a focus on service (such as 24-hr. room service—always useful). Accommodations are on the small side, and there are no bedside lamps, but Suba will suit the traveler looking for a smart option (as opposed to character-filled, like Shelleys) that offers good value.

Near Gateway of India, Apollo Bunder, Mumbai 400 039. (*) **022/2202-0636** or 022/22885444. Fax 022/22020812. www.hotelsubapalace.com. info@hotelsubapalace.com. 50 units. Doubles: Rs 2,350 ($52), breakfast included. AE, MC, V. **Amenities:** Restaurant; travel assistance; foreign exchange; 24-hr. room service; laundry; doctor-on-call. *In room:* A/C, TV.

Shelleys ☆ *Value* Ignore the gruff bloke at reception; for this type of money you won't find a better location (on the waterfront and near the Gateway) with the same degree of comfort, a fact that makes up for the lack of facilities. Shelleys has, for instance, no restaurant, but there is no shortage of options in the neighborhood. Try to book one of the four sea-facing rooms; each features dark carpets and orange bedcovers, earthy-red drapes over shallow bay windows, large dark wood cupboards, a desk, and—inexplicably—a big, fake orange-painted "oak" tree. The large, clean bathrooms have tubs and natural light, and there's even a small dressing area. Public sea-facing terraces with deep, black leatherette sofas catch the sea breeze and afford lovely views. Budget rates mean putting up with wall-attached air-conditioning units and ancient elevators, but many find the old-fashioned ambience very agreeable.

30 P.J. Ramchandani Marg (opposite Radio Club), Colaba, Mumbai 400 039. (*) **022/2284-0229** or 022/2284-0270. Fax 022/2284-0385. www.shelleyshotel.com. shelleyshotel@vsnl.com. 17 units. Doubles: Rs 1,935 ($40) sea-facing; Rs 1,622 ($200) non-sea-facing. AE, DC, MC, V. **Amenities:** Tea-cum-waiting room; laundry. *In room:* A/C, TV, fridge.

JUHU & BANDRA

About a 30-minute (to an hour) drive from the heavily touristed downtown area, the seaside suburb of Juhu attracts a predominantly local, moneyed crowd, and as such affords in many ways a truly genuine introduction to Mumbai. Juhu's relative proximity to the airport (it's a 20-min. drive) makes it the ideal stopover if you have no strong desire to engage with the historical side of the city, or if you need to recover from jet lag before moving on, but aren't keen to fork over the exorbitant rates demanded by the airport hotels.

VERY EXPENSIVE

JW Marriott Hotel ☆ Designed by the renowned architect Bill Bensley, the opulent JW opened in 2002 and is currently Juhu's most luxurious hotel. Its massive, sprawling coffee shop at the bottom of the split-level lobby is already a popular hangout with the local trendy crowd. Set over five floors, guest rooms are comfortable, with modern, albeit rather predictable, decor and amenities. The best aspect of the hotel, aside from its many extras, is the expansive tropical seaside garden, which features naturalistic waterfalls, torch-lit pathways, a lotus pond, and Indian sandstone sculptures crafted by artisans from Rajasthan.

Juhu Tara Rd., Juhu Beach, Mumbai 400 099. (*) **022/5693-3000.** Fax 022/5693-3100. 358 units. Doubles: $315 superior; $335 deluxe; $550 suite. AE, DC, MC, V. **Amenities:** 4 restaurants; 2 bars; nightclub; 2 pools; fitness center/spa; personal trainer; game room and video games; concierge; business center; gift shop; 24-hr. room service; babysitting with advance notice; laundry and dry cleaning; doctor-on-call. *In room:* A/C, TV, dataport, minibar, tea- and coffee-making facility, hair dryer, electronic safe.

EXPENSIVE

Holiday Inn Until the JW opened, this rather anonymous hotel was Juhu's best, no doubt because of its beachfront location and extensive facilities. The standard rooms—called "superior deluxe"—feature pale-blue partially wallpapered walls and marble floors covered with floral carpets that match the curtains; beds are comfortable, if a little low. More expensive (and spacious) are the Club Select rooms on the sixth and seventh floors, which have a breezier feel, with bright blue carpets and bedcovers in pink, beige, and blue; guests here have access to an exclusive lounge. Direct sea views are only available from the suites.

Balraj Sahani Marg, Juhu Beach, Mumbai 400 049. ✆ 022/5693-4444. Fax 022/5693-4455 or -4466. www. holidayinnbombay.com. hib@holidayinnbombay.com. 191 units. Doubles: $220 superior deluxe; $290 Club Select; $400 special suite; $450 deluxe suite; $500 superior deluxe suite; $750 presidential suite. AE, DC, MC, V. **Amenities:** 3 restaurants; pub; pool; health club; travel agency; car hires; shopping arcade; salon; 24-hr. room service; laundry and dry cleaning. *In room:* A/C, TV, bedside panel, minibar, tea- and coffee-making facility, hair dryer, safe, scale. Suites include stereo system and kitchenette with microwave and fridge.

Taj Lands End ★★   Location, location, location! It may be away from the central tourist area of Colaba, but this hotel enjoys a lovely seaside setting in one of Mumbai's hippest suburbs. It originally opened in 1999 as the Regent, but in 2002 the Taj Group took it over and it is one of the city's finest hotels, with each and every guest room affording views of the Arabian Sea through palm trees. Plush and slightly over the top, the carpeted guest rooms feature wonderful, solid king-size mattresses covered in soft, cool white linen. Pale pink or darker maroon walls are decorated with contemporary prints and watercolors, and the rooms feature quality embroidered fabrics and plenty of wood—only the slightly ruddy carpets could do with a makeover. At press time, all the upper floors were being completely overhauled to create more suites. (Ask about special promotions, which the hotel has been using to entice new visitors.)

Land's End, Bandstand, Bandra (West), Mumbai 400 050. ✆ 022/2655-1234. Fax 022/2644-1229. www. tajhotels.com. landsend.mumbai@tajhotels.com. 508 units. Doubles: $240 standard; $265 deluxe; $500 suite. AE, DC, MC, V. **Amenities:** 4 restaurants; 2 bars; pool; fitness center; concierge; travel desk; car hires; business center; currency exchange; bookshop; salon; 24-hr. room service; laundry and dry cleaning; doctor-on-call; butler. *In room:* A/C, TV, electronic bedside console, dataport, minibar, hair dryer, electronic safe.

MODERATE

Sun-n-Sand ★ (Value)   This small, old-fashioned beachfront hotel is showing a few signs of wear and tear but still has a charming air; it's Juhu's best lodging in its price category. Specify a sea-facing standard double room: Breakfast, cocktail hour, and airport transfers are included in the rate. The luxury suites are done in various themes—"Galleria" is apparently inspired by a contemporary art gallery, with mod lights, curved wall paneling, and a Jacuzzi bath and exercise area—but for the same rate you might as well be at the JW Marriott. Service borders on the adequate, with staff a little too lethargic.

39 Juhu Beach, Mumbai 400 049. ✆ 022/5693-8888. Fax 022/2620-2170. www.sunnsandhotel.com. reservations@sunnsandhotel.com. 120 units. Doubles: $160 superior; $190 executive; $260 deluxe suite; $300 luxury suite; $380 presidential suite; $12 extra person. Rates include breakfast, airport transfers, and cocktail hours. AE, DC, MC, V. **Amenities:** 3 restaurants; bar; pool; health and fitness center; travel desk; business center; shops; salon; babysitting; laundry; house doctor. *In room:* A/C, TV, dataport, minibar, tea- and coffee-making facility, hair dryer, electronic safe.

NEAR THE AIRPORT

The reasons for staying here are obvious, but with the exception of the Hyatt, it seems a pity to pay these kinds of rates when the lovely Taj Mahal and Oberoi beckon from Colaba. Cheaper airport options are less than salubrious. An airport choice you may come across, but one that's not in the same league as those described below, is the **Leela** (✆ **800/426-3135** or 022/5691-1234; fax 022/5691-1212; www.theleela.com; mumbaisales@theleela.com). A stalwart of

Mumbai's hospitality industry (and favored by the Dalai Lama), the Leela is chillingly expensive for an airport hotel ($375–$1,330 double) and—relative to the new competitors—rather old-fashioned. Still, it's a good hotel, and you may want to check it out.

Hyatt Regency ✦✦✦   With all the dramatic design-intensive joie de vivre of a modern art gallery, this is the latest newcomer to vie for the tourist and businessperson's buck, and we think it wins hands-down (especially if the tariff remains so low!). Stacked glass walls, brilliant mood lighting, floating ebony ceiling effects, and Italian marble are offset by marigolds in tailored cube bouquets—and that's just the lobby. Sleek and stylish, guest rooms deliver great comfort. The ultra-contemporary design-conscious accommodations ignore typical hotel-room configurations, the dramatic interiors enhanced by the judicious use of space, imaginative lighting concepts, and elegant fittings. One entire wall is a mirror, floors are Malaysian teakwood, desks are swivel-top slabs of glass, and the televisions are flat-screen. White-marble bathrooms offer a choice between large rain showers or separate step-down bathtubs—a welcome treat after a long plane journey or a day in Mumbai. Among the various classy dining venues is a fantastic restaurant with a fun, interactive kitchen, and the **Club Prana spa** is destined to be a big pre- and post-flight hit.

Sahar Airport Rd., Mumbai 400 099. ✆ **022/5696-1234.** Fax 022/5696-1235. www.hyatt.com. 408 units. Rates on day-to-day basis. Special introductory tariff: $120 standard double; $140 Regency Club room. Rates include breakfast and airport transfers. Club rate includes use of private lounge, dedicated concierge, complimentary use of meeting room, all-day tea and coffee service, and evening cocktails and canapés. AE, DC, MC, V. **Amenities:** 3 restaurants; bar; pool; tennis and squash courts; spa and fitness center; 24-hr. room service; laundry; doctor-on-call. *In room:* A/C, TV, dataport, minibar, tea- and coffee-making facility, electronic safe.

ITC Hotel Grand Maratha Sheraton & Towers ✦✦   Having opened in 2001, the Grand Maratha has already been recognized with at least one award as the country's best hotel. An imposing pink sandstone neoclassical building topped by a futuristic dome, the Sheraton recalls elements of India's rich architectural legacy: thick columns, imposing contours, arches, a cobbled entrance flanked by two wooden horses and, in the porte-cochere, a Goan-inspired coffered ceiling. Rooms don't disappoint: Beds are fabulously comfy, London-based interior designer Francesca Basu has captured the local love of bright colors, and the garden views in some rooms (ask for one) are lovely. Five different restaurants of excellent quality offer cuisines ranging from Lebanese (complete with belly dancing) to Northwest Frontier.

Sahar, Mumbai 400 099. ✆ **022/2830-3030.** Fax 022/2830-3131. www.welcomgroup.com. Delhi Reservations: ✆ 011/2614-1821. 386 units. Doubles: $205 Executive Club; $240 Sheraton Towers; $250 ITC One. AE, DC, MC, V. **Amenities:** 5 restaurants; bar; pool; golf by arrangement; wellness center with gym, steam, sauna, Jacuzzi, massage and spa treatments; concierge; travel and tour desk; car hires; business center; currency exchange; shops and boutiques; salon; 24-hr. room service; babysitting; laundry and valet service; doctor-on-call. *In room:* A/C, TV, minibar, tea- and coffee-making facility, hair dryer, electronic safe, scale. Sheraton Towers rooms include fax machine, butler service. ITC One rooms include step machine, hand-held massager, massage chair.

Le Royal Meridien ✦   Wrapped in wall-to-wall marble and dripping with chandeliers, the small lobby of this lavish baroque-style hotel sports a winter garden off the atrium balconies and a wood-paneled cigar-and-brandy bar near the lobby; at night live jazz replaces the daytime piped harpsichord-inspired Western classical music and keeps the lobby abuzz. Ask for a corner room—these are larger. If it's views you're after, ask for a room on the first, second, or third floor. Royal Club rooms have wooden floors and include playfully eccentric touches like plastic ducks in the bathrooms and teddy bears on the canopied king-size poster beds; dark wooden chests with inlaid metalwork, beautiful glassware bedside lamps, and wall prints and photos reflecting local history create a strong sense of luxury. Standard rooms are less spacious but no less luxurious.

Sahar Airport Rd. © 022/2838-0000. Fax 022/2838-0101. lmmumbai@vsnl.com. 171 units. Doubles (includes airport pickup): $270 standard; $280 deluxe; $305 Royal Club (includes airport drop and other club perks); $400 suite; $500 presidential suite. AE, DC, MC, V. **Amenities:** 3 restaurants; 2 bars; pool; health club with steam, sauna, and massage; business center; salon. *In room:* A/C, TV, fax machine, DVD player, minibar, tea- and coffee-making facility.

The Orchid 🏆   In a city this polluted, a stay at this multiple-award-winning eco-friendly hotel at least serves to relieve some tourist guilt. But that's not the only reason to stay here: Thankfully, the hotel's commitment to preserving the environment is combined with reasonably good taste and impressive service. Environment-friendly considerations include solar-powered terrace lights, wastewater treatment technology, in-room recycle bins, and a UV-treated chlorine-free swimming pool. You'll find plants in all the rooms (which are comfortable) and understated furniture made from Nuwud Medium Density Fibre "wood," the eco-conscious alternative to ripping down entire forests. Emphasizing the eco-theme, paintings and prints of orchids and flowers are found throughout the hotel, and the lobby features a six-story water curtain—recycled water, of course. The rooftop pool with its Mexican hacienda–style barbecue restaurant offers interesting views—particularly if you enjoy watching Mumbai's heavy air traffic come and go.

Adjacent Domestic Airport, Nehru Rd., Vile Parle (East), Mumbai 400 099. © 022/616-4040. Toll-free 1-600-115432. Fax 022/616-4141. www.orchidhotel.com. info@orchidhotel.com. 245 units. Doubles: $270 deluxe room; $285 executive suite; $310 Club Privé room; $325 Club Privé suite; $435 Orchid suite; $800 presidential suite; $40 extra bed; children under 12 stay free in parent's room. AE, DC, MC, V. **Amenities:** 3 restaurants; bar; pool; fitness center; travel desk; airport transfers; business center; foreign exchange; gourmet shop; 24-hr. room service; laundry and dry cleaning. *In room:* A/C, TV, minibar.

5 Where to Dine

by Niloufer Venkatraman
Mumbai resident and dedicated foodie

Nowhere in India is dining more rewarding than in Mumbai. The city literally holds thousands of restaurants, and being a city of migrants, every kind of Indian cuisine is represented. But it is Konkan, or coastal food, that is considered the local specialty. You can mingle with the city's crème de la crème at fine-dining or hip venues, or choose from a vast array of inexpensive eating places. Udipi restaurants serving South Indian fast food can be found on every street, but if you sample only one, make it **A. Ramanayak Udipi Shri Krishna Boarding** 🏆 (Main Market Building, 1st floor, near Matunga Railway Station; © 022/2414-2422). Its authentic Madras-style meal is served on a banana leaf (Rs 45/95¢), and you eat with your hands. Other Indian cuisines you will come across everywhere are neighborhood kebab places (**Noorani** 🏆, Haji Ali, © 022/2492-0957, serves good kebabs and even delivers to your hotel); restaurants specializing in local favorites like *pau bhaji* (mixed vegetables and bread); Irani restaurants serving fresh inexpensive breads and pastries; and Chinese restaurants offering "Indianized Chinese." Not surprisingly, vegetarians are particularly well catered for, even in specialty seafood restaurants.

Seafood Thrillers

Anyone with a penchant for seafood will love dining in Mumbai—whether it's Coastal, Konkani, Manglorean, or Malvani cuisine, you are in for a treat. Besides Mahesh Lunch Home and Trishna (see reviews below), you can try **Apoorva** ✿ (© 022/2287-0335 or 022/2288-1457), which has similar Manglorean fare, as does **Excellensea** ✿ (© 022/261-8991). The latter is on the first floor above **Bharat Restaurant** ✿, a non-air-conditioned economy version of Excellensea serving the same food. Note that if you are in a Konkan restaurant, you may want to try the *soul kadi*, a slightly pungent coconut milk drink and a great appetizer, and fresh *appams* and *neer dosas*—both these Southern breads make an excellent accompaniment to your seafood. Closer to central Mumbai is **Pisces** ✿✿ (© 022/2380-5886 or -4367), done up in the standard fish-themed decor but offering more variety in cooking styles. You haven't lived until you've tried the tamarind prawns (not on the menu; they can be requested)—these alone a worth the trip. Also try the *malai chingri* (a cashew nut–based coconut curry with prawns) or the Bengali *sorso batta mach* (fatty fish cooked in a mustard sauce). Manohar Shetty, the owner of Pisces, believes patrons should know exactly what they are getting, so the uncooked fish, prawns, and crab are paraded before you before they are transformed into one of these delectable dishes. In the suburbs, you'll get real value for money at **Gajalee** ✿✿, Vile Parle (E) (© 022/2838-8093 or 022/2822-6470). This Malwani-style seafood eatery has fantastic tandoori prawns, pomfret *kapri*, and *bombil* (Bombay duck; actually a dried fish) fry. **Soul Fry** ✿ (© 022/2604-6892) in Bandra makes great flaky stuffed grilled *rawas* (a local fish), and on weekends live music often accompanies the home-style Goan dishes.

Tip: Bear in mind that Mumbaiikers usually venture out to eat late, around 9pm, so if you're intent on eating at a popular fine-dining restaurant and don't have a reservation, ask if you can arrive at 7:30pm.

COLABA (INCLUDING MARINE DRIVE) & FORT
EXPENSIVE

Athena ✿✿✿ INTERNATIONAL   Not just a restaurant, Athena is also a vodka bar (serving some 70 varieties), champagne cigar lounge, and nightclub, and—because this is part of the growing number of Chateau Indage Winery restaurants—a local wine bar. In the chic white restaurant section, chefs Nitya and Gautam (who change the menu every 6 months) start you off with a delicious complimentary bread basket. Recommended appetizers include chargrilled cottage-cheese bruschetta with different toppings; baked Gouda and tomato on toasted walnut bread; or the crispy *rawas* (a local fish) in Thai basil sauce. Not-to-be-missed mains are the chargrilled rawas drizzled with gremolata; and the lamb Penang or lamb peri-peri, equally succulent.

41/44 Minoo Desai Marg, Colaba, Mumbai. © 022/2202-8699. Main courses Rs 350 ($7.60). AE, MC, V. Daily 12.30–2:45pm and 7.30pm–12.30am (to 4am on Wed, Fri, and Sat).

India Jones ✿✿✿ ASIAN   The menu comes in the form of a "diary," and is a treasure trove of exciting Asian dishes. Start by sharing an appetizer platter: prawn mousse on sugarcane, satay chicken, chicken dumplings, vegetable spring rolls, and cucumber salad with lime, mint, and basil, served with a selection of dips. Or two of you can share the platter of spring rolls from across Southeast Asia: Singapore vegetable spring rolls; deep-fried mango and prawn rolls, bean-curd and chicken rolls; steamed prawn and Chinese cabbage rolls—you name it, they roll it. But the hands-down favorite, certainly with locals, is "a grand sampler," which is exactly that: an appetizer platter, then *tom yam,* or crab and asparagus soup, followed by a platter of green chicken curry, wok-fried prawns marinated with turmeric and lemon grass, pomfret in black pepper, pork with honey, Penang vegetable curry, wok-fried mixed vegetables, steamed rice, Singapore noodles, and steamed Chinese buns—plus a dessert of your choice. At Rs 1,200 ($26) for two, it's quite a bargain.

The Oberoi, Nariman Point. ℂ 022/2232-6210. Main courses Rs 295–Rs 900 ($6.50–$20). AE, DC, MC, V. Daily 12:30–2:45pm and 7:30–11:30pm.

Indigo ⭐⭐⭐ INTERNATIONAL Well-known restaurateur Rahul Akerkar has created a restaurant that tops every food critic's A-list and has been listed by *Condé Nast Traveler* as one of the 60 best restaurants in the world. Credit for the tasteful understated elegance of this bi-level restaurant goes to co-owner Malini Akerkar, who has a keen interest in art and uses the restaurant as an informal exhibition space. Its chic ambience is enhanced by the clientele: By 9:30pm the entire place is heaving with the city's Beautiful People. The international/fusion menu is not extensive, changing once a year, but specials are also on offer, with something for every appetite. Tuna lovers will be hard pressed to choose between the carpaccio of house-cured tuna or the rare, pepper-crusted tuna medallions served with parsley potatoes, arugula beans, peppers, and a vinaigrette—what the heck, order both. Also recommended is the chargrilled cumin-rubbed beef tenderloin, served with a whole roasted garlic head and a peppery Madeira sauce. End the meal with the unique chocolate fondant with jalapeño peppers, made by pastry chef Conrad D'Souza. Naturally all of this comes at a cost, but if it's good enough for the Clintons . . .

4, Mandlik House, Colaba, Mumbai 400 001. ℂ 022/2285-6316 or 022/2202-3592. Reservations essential. Main courses Rs 285–Rs 445 ($6.10–$9.70). AE, DC, MC, V. Daily 12:30–3pm and 7:30–11:45pm.

Kandahar ⭐⭐⭐ NORTHWEST FRONTIER This classy, well-appointed restaurant located in the upmarket Oberoi hotel is a great place to experiment with what will no doubt be new cuisine flavors (though expect to pay five-star prices). With items like salmon *ka tikka* (to die for), created by famous food expert Jiggs Kalra, it's hard to go wrong here. You can watch succulent kebabs being prepared in the glass-front kitchen. Order one, or consider the Kandahar *ki khaas seekh:* Bite into the red meat exterior and you're in for a surprise—it's stuffed with crab and prawns and simply melts in your mouth. For the main course, go for Champ e Kandhari, a robust lamb chop that is flavored with basil, clove, and cardamom, or the Kabuli *raan* (leg of lamb). Wash it all down with smooth *chaas* (a yogurt drink), flavored with roasted cumin and ginger. If you're around during one of its food festivals, don't miss it—you're sure to sample some unrivalled delights.

The Oberoi, Nariman Point. ℂ 022/2232-6210. Meal that includes kebabs, a main course, and *naan* or *roomali roti:* Rs 1,000 ($22) per person. MC, V. Daily 12:30–2:45pm and 7:30–11pm.

Khyber ⭐⭐⭐ NORTH INDIAN Khyber has been going strong for decades now, and its classic Mughlai cuisine and tender kebabs remain outstanding. Start with the *kali mirch rawas* (fish seasoned in black pepper), so firm and yet so meltingly good, and the *paneer shashlik* (Indian cottage cheese, spices, and vegetables). Follow those with Khyber *raan* (lamb) or mutton *chaap* Mughlai and piping hot *naan* bread. To cleanse the palate (Mughlai cuisine is very rich), order the fresh seasonal fruit or a *mishty doi* (Bengali-style sweetened yogurt). Besides the great food, Khyber is an experience in royal dining: The opulent decor includes original paintings by some of India's most famous artists (like M. F. Hussain and Anjolie Ela Menon). Seating is also intimate and maximizes privacy—perfect for a romantic dinner.

154 MG Rd., Kala Ghoda. © 022/2267-3227 or -3229. Main courses Rs 225–Rs 250 ($4.80–$5.35). MC, V. Reservations usually required on weekends. Daily 12:30–3:30pm and 7:30–11:45pm.

Trishna ★★★ SEAFOOD   Another restaurant frequented by the who's who of Mumbai, Trishna, presided over by owner Ravi Anchan, is one of Mumbai's seafood legends and is considered one of the best in the world. Butter pepper garlic king crab is Trishna's signature dish, but you'll also find jumbo pomfrets and tiger prawns (done in any style) cooked to perfection. Despite its reputation as a somewhat snobbish restaurant, Trishna isn't about ambience (the decor in fact is somewhat tacky and, yes, staff do have a reputation for surliness); everyone is here for the food. Recommended dishes include the pomfret Hyderabadi— barbecued with black pepper, it's a true masterpiece; the stuffed pomfret in green masala; fish *sholay* kebab; Kolhapuri prawns (spicy, so order a drink); or squid expertly prepared with butter, pepper, and garlic. Don't expect to get in any night without a reservation.

Birla Mansion, Sai Baba Marg (next to Commerce House), Kala Ghoda, Fort. © 022/267-2176 or 022/2270-1623. Main courses Rs 295–Rs 695 ($6.50–$15) depending on fish size. Crab/lobster Rs 500–Rs 1,000 ($11–$22). Reservations essential. AE, DC, MC, V. Daily noon–3:45pm and 6pm–12:30am (from 7pm on weekends and holidays).

MODERATE/INEXPENSIVE

All Stir Fry ★★ STIR-FRY   Here you choose an assortment of meats, vegetables, and noodles from a noodle bar, then take it to a live cooking counter where you choose the flavoring/sauce you want, with which it is stir-fried in a wok by chefs right in front of you. It also has an a la carte menu (Thai, Chinese, Japanese) for those who don't want to walk to and fro for your meal. The downside of this otherwise good restaurant is that the seating is on Chinese-street-style wooden benches that can get quite uncomfortable after a while, and some of the managing staff is occasionally snobbish and affected.

The Gordon House Hotel, 5 Battery St., Apollo Bunder, Colaba, Mumbai 400 039. © 022/2287-1122. Reservations recommended for dinner, especially on weekends. All you can eat Rs 275 ($5.85) plus taxes; a la carte main courses Rs 165–Rs 300 ($3.45–$6.50). All credit cards accepted. Daily noon–3pm and 7pm–midnight.

Delhi Darbar ★ PUNJABI/MUGHLAI   This 25-year-old restaurant is a Mumbai institution serving authentic Mughlai food. It has four branches in Mumbai, the best one at Colaba. No one comes here for the ambience or service—the only attraction is the food. Start your meal with some of their signature kebabs—the chicken *malai* (cream) kebab and the *seekh* kebab (finely minced lamb kebab) are always a good bet. For the main meal, the mild cardamom-flavored chicken and the *salli boti* (pieces of tender meat cooked in spices and beaten egg) are great with any of the delicious breads. Get the butter *naan* or *roomali roti* (thin bread) if you are unfamiliar with Indian breads—they are excellent here. Even if you are stuffed, you can't leave without trying the delicious (if a trifle oily) mutton or chicken *biryani* (elaborate rice dish). Ignore the Chinese menu. No alcohol is served or allowed.

> ### ⌒Tips   The Skinny on Street Food
>
> Street food is something you should be careful about experimenting with, although there are spots we recommend. One place where you can safely try street food, while you sip on chilled beer, is **Vithal Bhelwala** ✮, near the Excelsior Theatre, Fort (ℂ **022/22074673; daily 10am–11pm**). You get to eat real Mumbai street food under very sanitary (if noisy) conditions at **Swati Snacks** ✮✮, in Tardeo (ℂ **022/24920994; 11am–11pm**). This is the best street food that's not actually on the street. Try the *sev puri, bhel, dahi batata puri* (Rs 30/60¢ each), or any of the numerous snack items that are served topped with delicious sweet, sour, and spicy chutneys and sauces (ask for milder sauces if you prefer). Round out your meal with homemade fruit-flavored ice creams.

Colaba (ℂ **022/2202-0235**): daily 11:30am–midnight. Grant Rd. (ℂ **022/382-7767**): daily 8:30am–3am; Versova (ℂ **022/2634-3352**): daily noon–midnight. MC, V. Kebabs Rs 35–Rs 110 (75¢–$2.30); main courses Rs 55–Rs 75 ($1.15–$1.60); biryanis Rs 42/90¢ (half portion), Rs 72/$1.50 (full).

Konkan Café ✮✮ KONKAN   Chef Ananda Solomon has earned an enviable reputation for his inspired specialties, garnered from up and down the Konkan coast and served with style. Although the menu is constantly being reinvented, look for winter specialties like *moong dal khichdi* (sticky rice and lentils); red snapper cooked in a spicy tomato-onion sauce and baked in banana leaves; and the heavenly *sukha* mutton. You can wash down your Goan chicken *cafreal* (chicken marinated with chilies and spices and roasted or barbecued) or pomfret *recheado* (a hot and spicy masala) with *feni* (the Goan liquor distilled from coconuts or cashews), or savor the spectacular crab cakes with a fine bottle of wine if needed.
Taj President hotel (see "Where to Stay," earlier in this chapter). ℂ **022/22150808**. Thali Rs 375 ($8). A la carte Rs 400–Rs 500 ($9.75–$11) per person. AE, DC, MC, V. Daily 12:30–2:45pm and 7–11:45pm.

Leopold Café ✮✮ CONTINENTAL/INDIAN/CHINESE   It's not uncommon to walk into this Colaba institution and not see a single Indian face around. Why it's such a hit with foreigners is a mystery, since the food is good but not exceptional, and the atmosphere can be noisy and rather smoky. All the same, it is consistent, and because it's one of those popular places where tourists like to share stories with other tourists over a beer, it deserves mention. It caters to Western tastes by providing items like cereals, eggs and toast, fish and chips, and club sandwiches side by side with chicken *biryani* and Indian-Chinese fare. The fresh fruit juices and *lassis* (yogurt drinks) are always a good bet if you're looking for a light pick-me-up during shopping forays on the causeway. *Tip:* If you're keen to get the inside scoop on how Bollywood films are made, hang out here; casting agents looking for foreigners to work as extras on current productions frequently scan the clientele for able bodies at this favored travelers' hangout.
Colaba Causeway, Mumbai 400 005. ℂ **022/2287-3362**. Lassis/juices/milkshakes Rs 50 ($1.05); Mughlai main courses Rs 75 ($1.60); Chinese main courses Rs 100 ($2.10). AE, DC, MC, V. Daily 8am–midnight.

Mahesh Lunch Home ✮✮✮ SEAFOOD   The ceiling may be too low and the tables too close together, but this Manglorean seafood restaurant should not be missed if you love fish—it's consistently pleasing. Everything is incredibly fresh, but favorites include surmai fry, pomfret curry, and tandoori pomfret—all outstanding. The latter (listed as a starter, but you can order it as a main) is served flawlessly moist; eaten with butter *naan*, it provides the most heavenly gastronomic experience imaginable. Also try the scrumptious prawns Koliwada, the crab tandoori, the pomfret in green masala, or any of the fish curries or *gassis*, all first-rate. (Note that *gassi* refers to the thick coconut-based Manglorean curry, while the "curries" on the menu are a thinner version of the same.) Mahesh also serves meat, chicken, and Chinese dishes, but only the misguided would come here and skip the sensational seafood.

8D Cowasji Patel St., off Pherozeshah Mehta Rd., Fort, Mumbai 400 001. © 022/2287-0938. Fish fry/curry/ gassi Rs 85–Rs 140 ($1.75–$2.95); jumbo pomfret/crab/lobster Rs 500–Rs 1,000 ($11–$22); other main courses Rs 200–Rs 325 ($4.30–$7). MC, V. Daily 11:30am–3:30pm and 6–11:30pm.

Nosh ★★ VEGETARIAN/INTERNATIONAL   Owner Czaee Shah has based the menu of this centrally located restaurant on her dining experiences around the world. Kick off your meal with a refreshing sugar-cane juice, then opt for Chiang Mai wontons or Lavoche crispbread with *labneh* (yogurt cheese) and *zhoug* (hot pepper sauce). Indonesian gado-gado salad is made with warm vegetables, fresh fruit, and a peanut sauce. All are delicious, but leave plenty of room for the main course. Arabic *rishta* (pasta) with mint-flavored lentil stew is outstanding, as is the asparagus risotto and the Afghani curry with *naan* bread. If you have a sweet tooth, try the very unusual *kheer kadom* (a Bengali-style dessert served with ice cream) or the heavenly tiramisu. Most portions aren't very large, so if you're hungry, order several starters before your main meal.

Regal Cinema Bldg., Colaba Causeway. © 022/5639-6688. Reservations essential, especially after 9pm. Main courses Rs 175–Rs 210 ($3.60–$4.40). MC, V. Daily 11am–1:30am.

Samovar ★★ INDIAN   This long, narrow restaurant inside the Jehangir Art Gallery is a South Mumbai institution that has retained its charm and low prices in spite of its popularity. With quick, efficient service and a policy of not hurrying diners even if others are waiting, this is the perfect stopover after a day roaming the Prince of Wales museum and other local landmarks. Start with a delicious seasonal fruit juice—the guava juice is the best when it's in season. *Boti* rolls (spiced meat wrapped in flatbreads called *chapatis*) rival with *parathas* (fried breads with a great assortment of stuffings) to satiate the taste buds along with the yummy bean-sprout salad. A stop here is a must: This is as close to home cooking as you are likely to get on a short visit to Mumbai.

Jehangir Art Gallery, Kala Ghoda, Fort, Mumbai 400 023. © 022/2284-8000. No credit cards. Mon–Sat 11am–7pm. Closed Sun.

BEYOND DOWNTOWN: CHOWPATTY TO WORLI

China Garden ★★ CHINESE   Owner-chef Nelson Wang has created waves from the time he opened his celebrated restaurant, considered one of the most authentic in the city. The Mongolian steamboat soup is a great way to start your meal. Order the Peking chicken to follow as well as soy and chili-wine fish—all so very different from the Indo-Chinese food found everywhere in Mumbai. The ambience is classy, but don't expect a quiet meal: The rich and famous have always patronized this award-winning restaurant, and by 9:30pm it's packed and very noisy.

Crossroads, Tardeo, Haji Ali, Mumbai 400 034. © 022/2495-5588 or -5589. Reservations essential. MC, V. Main courses Rs 180–Rs 250 ($3.80–$5.35); crab Rs 1,000 ($22). Daily 12:30–3pm and 7:30pm–midnight.

Copper Chimney ★★★ KEBABS/MUGHLAI   For more than 23 years, Copper Chimney has delighted those looking for the perfect kebabs. To this end, two pages of the menu are dedicated to kebabs, from the popular *reshmi* kebab (chicken) to the *jhinga nisha* (prawn) and tandoori prawn kebabs. These tender, creamy, smoky-flavored, melt-in-your-mouth kebabs can be followed by traditional Dum Pukht specialties such as chicken *makhani* (butter chicken) or the even more exquisite Peshawari lamb. No matter what you pick, you will leave satisfied.

Dr. Annie Besant Rd., Worli, Mumbai 400 018. ℭ 022/2850-5607, -3094, -9233. Also at 1111 Kalpak Corner Guru Nanak Rd., Bandra 400 050. ℭ 022/2644-3131, 022/2643-9191. Main courses Rs 165 ($3.45). MC, V. Open 11:30am–3:30pm and 7:30pm–midnight.

SUBURBS—BANDRA TO JUHU

For prime people-watching, spend some time at the **Prithvi Café** ★★ (ℭ 022/2617-4118) in the compound of the Prithvi theater in Juhu. This pleasant, unpretentious cafe is where many of Mumbai's up-and-coming and/or struggling *artistes* come to nosh and discuss their art. The cafe serves great fresh *parathas* and a variety of teas and coffees with which you can linger undisturbed. If it's stargazing you're after, the restaurant that currently takes the prize is the **Olive Bar and Kitchen** ★ (Pali Hill Tourist Hotel, 14 Union Park Khar [W]; ℭ 022/605-8228), the trendiest restaurant in town. This Mediterranean restaurant is also rather expensive and the food inconsistent, but it's the place to see and be seen. At the other end of the spectrum is **Govinda** ★ (ℭ 022/2620-0337), at the Hare Krishna Temple in Juhu, where you can gorge from a 56-item all-vegetarian buffet (no onions or garlic either). Everything is cooked in pure ghee (clarified butter), however, so expect the meal to be extremely heavy.

EXPENSIVE

Mezzo Mezzo ★★★ ITALIAN   Chef Danio Galli serves up the most authentic Italian cuisine (from Tuscany, Sicily, and Sardinia) in India. He describes his food as no-frills and places great emphasis on fresh ingredients. The menu changes every 3 months, but the delicious pizzas, baked in a wood-fired oven, are always available. The service here is friendly and impeccable, and the chef takes great care of guests, especially if you go on a night when it's not very busy (try Thurs, Tues, or Sun, but make a reservation anyway). If you want to experiment and price is not an issue, let Chef Danio order for you. He'll ask you a few questions about preferences, and then delight you with the most artistic Italian meal on the subcontinent. A fresh buffet lunch with wine on Sunday afternoons is priced at Rs 850 ($19). *Tip:* The best tables by far are those set against the windows; request one when you make reservations.

JW Marriott, Juhu Tara Rd., Juhu Beach, Mumbai 400 049. ℭ 022/5693-3000. Reservations recommended. Rs 800–Rs 1,000 ($18–$22) per person for dinner with an Indian wine. AE, DC, MC, V. Tues–Sun 12:30–2:30pm and 6:30pm–closing.

Papa Päncho ★★ *Finds* PUNJABI   Done up in honor of the thousands of truck drivers who seem to be endlessly careering around the roads of India, this gorgeously atmospheric restaurant is a faux take on the ubiquitous roadside *dhaba* (all-night cafe). Outside, beautiful Mumbaiikers sit or lie on traditional *manjis* (beds), often whiling away the entire afternoon; you can join them, or sit indoors at copper-covered tables. A recent extension has added a larger section in which you can imagine yourself escaping to the peace and quiet of a Punjabi village, with Phulkari embroidery and handicrafts displayed on the stucco walls and dangling from the ceiling, along with old Punjabi folk music albums. The kitchen churns out authentic home-style dishes but with a health-conscious emphasis on using less butter and cream, making the food lighter than you'd find in a real village. Ask the charming hostess-cum-co-owner, "Mamta" Sekhri,

The Thali: Gujarati & Rajasthani Cuisine at its Best

You can't leave this city without consuming at least one *thali,* the meal that really tests the size of your appetite! It works like this: Sit down, and in less than a minute you're expected to declare which thali you want— ordinary, special, and so on. Seconds later, a large stainless-steel plate *(thali)* arrives along with six to eight small bowls *(katoris)* that rest on your plate. The waiters then fill every one of the multiple katoris as well as the rest of the plate with a great assortment of steaming hot, spiced vegetables, savories, *dals,* beans, *rotis, puris,* and so on. To wash it down, you're served water and a glass of delicious super-thin cumin-flavored buttermilk *(chaas).* As you eat, your katoris will be topped up, so indicate what you want for seconds, thirds, fourths . . . Then it's a round of rice or *khichdi* (a mixture of rice and dal) and, in some restaurants, dessert. Not only are thalis a great value (you pay from Rs 50–Rs 250/$1.05–$5.35), but it comes pretty close to the home cooking of the country's Gujarati population. A personal favorite is **Panchvati Gaurav** ★★ ((℃ **022/22084877,** opposite Bombay Hospital, Marine Lines; Tues–Sun 11am–3pm and 7–10:30pm), where you'll pay Rs 105 to Rs 150 ($2.15–$3.15) for an excellent meal. Alternatively, try **Thackers** ★★ ((℃ **022/2205-3641;** 116 Marine St., Marine Lines; daily 12:30–3pm and 7:30–11pm), for a Surat-style Gujarati meal served on silver plates at perhaps a more relaxed pace. **Chetna Restaurant and Bar** ★ ((℃ **022/2284-4968,** Fort; daily 12:30– 3:30pm, 4:30–6:30pm, and 7–11pm) even serves a diet thali (Chetna Lite)—but isn't that missing the point?

about any specials, and insist that she bring you at least one *chaat* (snack) to whet your appetite. *Papdi chaat* is topped with yogurt and is cool, fresh, and delicately spiced—simply wonderful.

Shop no. 12, Gaspar Enclave, Dr. Ambedkar Rd., near Rupee Bank, Bandra W. ℃ **022/2651-8732** or -8733. Main courses Rs 85–Rs 175 ($1.75–$3.70). MC, V. Daily 12:30pm–midnight.

Shatranj Napoli ★ INDIAN/ITALIAN   Owned by Ashok Datwani, one of Mumbai's major young players, Shatranj is done up in chic 1970s retro style, with large statues and a leather-and-steel look. It serves Indian and Italian—though the Italian is really Indo-Italian and you'll probably find chilies in your pasta sauce. Service is good, the food is fine, but what you really go here for is the people-watching—Pierce Brosnan was here for the premiere party of the latest Bond movie, and Bollywood stars love the place, so you're likely to see a celeb on any given night. If you want to order from the Indian menu, try the *murgh ghosht hyderabadi* (Hyderabad-style seasoned chicken) or the *raan e peshwari* (Peshwar-style lamb). Alternatively, try the *gamberetti napoli,* a good choice if you like the combination of prawns and mushrooms in a cheese, tomato, and spinach sauce.

The Palace, 12 Union Park, Khar W. ℃ **022/2649-8458.** Main courses Rs 125–Rs 425 ($2.60–$9). All credit cards accepted. Daily 12:30–3:30pm and 7pm–12:30am.

6 Shopping

From internationally renowned *haute couture* to dirt-cheap one-season wonders, intricate jewelry and unique antiques to tawdry gifts and fabulous textiles, Mumbai is known as a shopper's paradise, and you'll find pretty much everything the country has to offer here. If you're shopping on the street or in the markets (see "Markets," earlier in this chapter), take your time, sift and sort, establish authenticity and, if necessary, don't be afraid to bargain hard. That said, bear in mind that (as elsewhere in India) a "bargain," particularly when it comes to jewelry and antiques, is probably just a cheap bauble or reproduction—fakes are a dime a dozen, as are the con men who sell them.

Central Cottage Industries Emporium (34 Chhatrapati Shivaji Maharaj Marg; © **022/2202-6564** or -7537) is a typical tourist trap with well-crafted but fairly tacky souvenirs at high prices. Established during the 1950s in an attempt to sustain traditional handicrafts, the massive showroom is crammed full of everything and anything that's likely to remind you of India: hand-painted wooden figurines, inlaid wooden items, teakwood elephants, carved stone gods, gold and silver jewelry, precious stones, and a wide range of carpets and rugs from Kashmir—the selection seems endless. A better shopping experience, at least from a store and design point of view, is the **Bombay Store** (Sir P.M. Rd., Fort; © **022/2288-5048**, -5049, or -5052), where you'll find every imaginable Indian handicraft and design, from bed linens and crockery to aromatherapy oils. And if you're looking for another reason to book into either of Mumbai's two top hotels—the **Taj Mahal Hotel** and the **Oberoi**—it's worth knowing that their in-house shops are stocked with some of India's most sought-after brands and products, though obviously you pay a price for the convenience of location, and it's a relatively sterile shopping experience. If you're a serious shopper and are determined to take something of value home with you, you might want to check out some of the following.

CLOTHING & FABRICS

Having created garments for Hillary Clinton, Demi Moore, and Liza Minneli, and earned the accolades "Crystal King" and "Czar of Embroidery," Azeem Khan is one of Mumbai's best-known designers. To find your very own slice of Indian haute couture, visit **Azeem Khan Couture** in Colaba (1 Usha Sadan; © **022/2215-1028;** www.azeemkhan.com). Another famous Indian designer, Ritu Kumar, has two outlets specializing in silk and cotton designer-ethnic wear, much of it a blend of Western and Indian influences. **Ritu's Boutique** can be found on Warden Road (© **022/2367-8593** or -2947) or at the Oberoi Towers Shopping Centre (© **022/2284-6995** or 022/2202-8109). Other boutiques that are a must-see for fashionistas are **Malabar** (© **022/2202-9703**), for embroidered silk jackets, *salwar-kameezes,* kaftans, stoles, and silk saris (various branches, including in the Taj Mahal Hotel), and—if you're not planning to visit Jaipur— **Anokhi** (6 Pandey House, Kemps Corner; © **022/2382-0636**), for its East-meets-England garments (the owner is U.K.–born), accessories, and housewares. **Mélange** (33 Altamount Rd., Kemps Corner; © **022/2385-4492** or 022/2386-5466) is known for its ultra-feminine designer dresses, made from delicate chiffon, while Sangita Kathiwada's trendy store is ideal for hip saris, evening bags, accessories, and stoles. **Ensemble** (Great Western Building, 130/132 Shahid Bhagat Singh Marg, Kala Ghoda/Fort; © **022/2287-2882** or 022/2284-3229) is the boutique where you will find the greatest variety in East-meets-West evening wear; prominent designers to look for here include Shahab Durazi, Tarun Tahiliani, Rajesh Pratap, Monisha Jaisingh, Tarana Rajpal, Abhishek Gupta, and Sunita Shankar.

At **Indian Textiles** (Taj Mahal Hotel; © **022/2202-8783** or 022/2204-9278), you'll find some of the best Benaresi woven silks and brocades in the country, sold by the yard, as well as authentic Pashmina shawls. Also look for hand-dyed silk stoles by **Jamnadas Khatri** (℃ 022/2242-5711 or 022/2374-0947), made with vegetable dyes using the Rajasthani tie-and-dye technique. Hand-loomed products are found in great abundance at the fabulous **Fab India,** which has separate outlets for garments (2&4 Navroze, Pali Hill, Bandra W.; ℃ **022/2646-5286**) and furnishings (junction of Khar Danda and 18th Rd., Khar W.; ℃ **022/2605-7780** or 022/605-8622).

JEWELRY

Tribhovandas Bhimji Zaveri (241–43 Zaveri Bazaar; ℃ **022/2363-3060** or 022/2342-5001), stretching over five separate floors, has a reputation for exceptional gold and diamond jewelry that dates back to 1865. It's very popular with Mumbai's wealthier crowd, so don't expect exceptionally good prices. **Gazdar** (Taj Mahal Hotel shopping arcade; ℃ **022/2202-3666**) has been selling Indian, Western, antique, and contemporary jewelry for more than 70 years; again, the prices go with the territory. Serious buyers looking for one-of-a-kind pieces should consider contacting master craftspeople **Viren Bhagat** (℃ **022/2361-1171** or -1172), or **Panna J. Jhaveri** (℃ **022/2369-0751**), both by appointment only. And prices aren't that ridiculous; you can pick up a pair of diamond earrings from Panna J. Jhaveri for under $100.

HOUSEWARES

Yamini (President House, Wodehouse Rd., Colaba; ℃ **022/2218-4143** or -4145) stocks designer linen, tablecloths, bolsters, curtains, pelmet covers, napkins, and even lampshades, under the local Kahini label. Mumbaiiker Reva Sethi is the fashion designer responsible for the collection, and her designs have even been used on board Prime Minister Atal Behari Vajpayee's private jet. Sethi is particularly adept at combining materials to create new fabrics and fascinating textures, and you can even consult her to design new fabrics for your entire home. There's a second branch in Bandra (34 Turner Rd., Patkars Bungalow; ℃ **022/2643-7667** or 022/2640-4375).

India's most famous dhurrie maker is **Shyam Ahuja** (Crossroads Mall; ℃ **022/2460-3077**, -3078, or -3079), known for outstanding handcrafted products. Besides gorgeous home furnishings, table linen, bathrobes, and towels, you can purchase authentic Pashmina shawls here. **Ravissant** (Taj Mahal Hotel; ℃ **022/2281-5229**) has a selection of sterling-silver teapots, vases, photo frames, and assorted bric-a-brac that sport clean modern lines and hark back to the Deco period. From the studio of Ravi Chawla, you'll find embroidered quilts, cushions, and comforters.

ANTIQUES, ART & FURNITURE

Natesan's Antiquarts, conveniently located at the Jehangir Art Gallery, deals principally in stone, wood, and bronze items. Whether you pick up an ornate teak and sandalwood carving, a bronze created using the 4,500-year-old lost-wax process, or a refurbished antique, Natesan's will arrange shipment. The nearby **Phillips Antiques** (opposite Prince of Wales Museum, Colaba; ℃ **022/2202-0564** or 022/2282-0782; www.phillipsantiques.com) offers a similar service; besides four-poster beds, armchairs, writing tables, and hat stands, you'll find gorgeous porcelain and pottery, brass and silverware, and a range of marble features for the home, not to mention ornamental pieces, antiquarian maps, lithographs, engravings, old photographs, and lovely lamps. Filled with beautiful

> ## Tips Leaving Mumbai
>
> The trip from central Mumbai to either of the airports can take far longer than expected—even outside peak traffic hours. Because most international flights are scheduled at similar, unusual hours, you will not be the only traveler racing to catch a plane. For international flights, you'll also need 3 hours at the airport to negotiate the endless security checks and long waits at passport control. If you're flying out after midnight, plan to leave the city at least 4 hours ahead of your flight. For daytime and earlier evening flights, you may want to add another hour to contend with the slow-moving traffic.
>
> To cut down on time spent in traffic, you can catch a train from Churchgate station to Vile Parle (around Rs 80/$1.70 for a 1st-class ticket) and then take an auto-rickshaw (also Rs 80/$1.70) or taxi to the airport.

objects, **Heeramaneck** (Readymoney Building, Battery St., Colaba; © 022/2202-1694) is another essential pit stop for antiques lovers. It has an especially good collection of Victorian and India silverware, including tea sets, candle stands, and cutlery.

7 Mumbai After Dark

BARS & CAFES

Join the backpackers and other Western tourists for a cold Kingfisher beer at **Leopold's Café** (© 022/2236-8999) on Colaba Causeway, or step into the smoky, popular **Café Mondegar** (near Regal Cinema; © 022/2202-0591), where the atmosphere is always lively, the jukebox firing up popular Western music. For über-trendy, you can't beat **Indigo** (© 022/2236-8999; see "Where To Dine," earlier in this chapter), Colaba's hippest joint, where low tables with flickering candles light up the who's who of Mumbai.

Hidden behind two massive glass doors, the **Library Bar** at the Taj President Hotel is a classy watering hole aimed at businesspeople and high rollers. Despite the plush, sophisticated decor, the atmosphere is pleasantly laid-back. There's live music from Tuesday to Sunday.

At Hotel Marine Plaza, you can enjoy a quiet drink at **Geoffrey's** (29 Marine Dr.; © 022/2285-1212), but better still, slip up to the pool deck and drink in the deep curve of Back Bay. Alternatively, get right on the bay by catching a boat from the H2O Water Sports Complex (toward the top of Marine Dr.) and heading for Mumbai's only floating bar, **Suzie Wong** (© 022/2367-1211).

In Bandra, head for **Restopub Onyx** (Om Palace, Dr. Embedkar Rd. junction, © 022/2605-8802), a seriously stylish drinking-eating-partying venue that puts the glam into the city's glitterati.

MUSIC, THEATER & CINEMA

"The List" supplement in the Friday and Saturday issues of Mumbai's *Mid Day* carries extensive listings of live music events, stage productions, and film screenings. *The Times of India* features an extensive "Bombay Times" section that lists and advertises cultural activities, entertainment happenings, and movies.

Mumbai has numerous performance spaces, including its premier **National Centre for the Performing Arts** (Nariman Point; © 022/2283-3737). The

NCPA houses several stages, including the city's "first opera theater," the Jamshed Bhabha Theatre, which saw its first operatic production in 2003. English dramas and lavish musical concerts are held in the Tata Theatre; the aptly named Little Theatre features work of a more intimate scale; while for offbeat dramas, student work, and small-scale music and dance, the Experimental Theatre is worth a look. The NCPA may occasionally host special film events and festivals, so keep a lookout for posters and newspaper listings.

Not far from Juhu Beach is one of Mumbai's best-known theaters, the **Prithvi** (Janki-Kutir, Juhu-Church Rd.; © **022/2614-9546;** www.prithvitheatre.org), which is owned by Bollywood's founding family, the Kapoors. The country's best plays are staged here during an annual drama festival, and the garden cafe outside is popular with the city's culturati. Over the first weekend of every month, free play readings and other performances are held in the gardens at **Horniman Circle;** contact the Prithvi for details.

Both Indian and Western theater and music performances are staged in the main auditorium of the **Nehru Centre** (Dr. Annie Besant Rd., near Mahalashmi Race Course, Worli; © **022/2492-0510**). There's also a smaller stage for experimental work. The Nehru Centre also houses the **Nehru Science Museum** and a **Planetarium,** with shows Tuesday through Sunday at 3pm and 6pm.

NIGHTCLUBS

You could spend your entire stay in Mumbai partying in fantastic clubs and then recovering in your hotel room the following day—this is one Indian city that really never sleeps. Although Western music is popular and has the buff and the gorgeous strutting their stuff every night of the week, Mumbaiikers (thankfully) have a deep passion for contemporary Hindi songs as well, and it's not unusual to spot young studs demonstrating the choreographed rhythms of *MTV India's* latest local video, much to the delight of their female companions. There are literally dozens of nightspots in the city, the most attractive being in the five-star hotels or in Colaba, Bandra, or Juhu. For the most up-to-date news on what's hot and what's not, talk to your concierge, because the nightclub scene changes rapidly. Here's a list of some of the most popular watering holes in early 2003—and the ones most likely to continue to stay in top gear.

Note: Entry fees differ depending on the night, and prices are often per (heterosexual) couple; usually this entitles you to coupons that can be exchanged for overpriced drinks of the same value. Closing times vary each night and there are "official" and unofficial hours—which essentially means that most clubs stay open later than the time stipulated by law.

Athena Athena is a lounge, restaurant, nightclub, and bar all in one, and the younger generation of Bollywood celebrities and models love to hang out here, so this is the place to hang with Mumbai's trendiest. The place is often packed on Wednesday's theme night. The entry fee is Rs 1,000 ($22) on Wednesday, Friday, and Saturday, when the real party starts at 11pm. Come ready to spend—you'll pay about Rs 500 ($11) for an alcoholic drink and Rs 430 ($9.50) for the midnight buffet. 41/44 Minoo Desai Marg, Colaba. © **022/2202 8699.**

Enigma Ever since this nightclub opened up at the JW Marriott in early 2002, it has become a hot favorite. It's open only on Thursday, Friday, and Saturday nights, when it's packed to the hilt and a long queue of people wait outside to pay an entry fee of Rs 1,000 ($22) per couple. The music here is very modern—a combination of Western music and Hindi pop. Celebrities, models, and Bollywood stars can all be spotted at this friendly but trendy nightspot. JW Marriott, Juhu Tara Rd. ℂ 022/5693 3000.

Fire & Ice Though this nightclub has been around for years, it's still very popular among all age groups and is one of Mumbai's bigger clubs. The music, cocktails, and decor are all as stylish as those who frequent the place. A cover charge of Rs 800 ($18) on weekend nights and half that on weekdays is charged per couple. No singles are permitted. Gala no. 5 Phoenix Mills, Lower Parel. ℂ 022/2498-0555.

Insomnia Although this Taj Mahal club is for members only, it's worth mentioning because it's so popular. Taj guests automatically become members; alternatively, hang around outside to find a member willing to sign you in (which is often not very difficult). Like elsewhere, the crowd that comes to this upmarket, multi-level, multi-space club is here to see and be seen, and the funky lighting, theme bars, and private zones are all wrapped in an air of exclusivity that is comparable to those of some of the most fashionable nightclubs in the world. Taj Mahal Hotel, Colaba. ℂ 022/2202 3366.

Razzberry Rhinocerous Dedicated to rock, this spot provides a regular forum for Mumbai's local rock bands, which play anything from standard 1980s rock 'n' roll to modern heavy metal, and the crowd here is definitely not comprised of teenyboppers. Entry charges are usually Rs 100 ($2.10) for men; women get in free. Juhu Hotel (near JW Marriott), Juhu Tara Rd. ℂ 022/2618-4012.

Velocity This nightclub has several different rooms, all of which are packed on Wednesday (salsa night), Friday, and Saturday. So whether you're in for trance or retro or a combination of the hottest, hippest beats, head here. *Note:* This club tends to attract the younger generation of nightclub goers. Entry is about Rs 800 ($18) per couple. Film Centre, Tardeo, near Crossroads Mall. ℂ 022/2491-2313.

8 Aurangabad & the Ellora and Ajanta Caves

The ancient cave temples at Ellora and Ajanta are among the finest historical sites India has to offer, and a detour to this far-flung region of Maharashtra to view these World Heritage sites is well worth the effort. You can cover both Ellora and Ajanta comfortably in 2 days, but for those who are truly pressed for time it is possible to see both sets of caves in a single (long, tiring) day. To do this you'll need to ask your hotel to prepare a packed lunch, and take plenty of bottled water along. Set out for Ajanta at about 7am, reaching the ticket office as it opens (recommended for the tranquillity of the experience, even if you're not trying to cover both in a day). Spend no more than 3 hours exploring Ajanta, then head for Ellora; your driver should be aware of the detour along the Ajanta-Aurangabad road that will get you here much faster. The caves at Ellora are spread out, so don't drag your heels, and be sure not to miss the ultimate jaw-dropper, known as "Cave 16": the Kailashanath temple complex is more carved mountain than cave, and is the world's largest monolithic structure—twice the size of the Parthenon.

ESSENTIALS
GETTING THERE The quickest, most sensible way to get here is to fly to Aurangabad's airport (in Chikalthana, Jalna Rd., just 10km/6¼ miles from the city center) with **Jet Airways** (ℂ 022/2285-5788 in Mumbai; ℂ 0240/244-1770 in Aurangabad). The flight from Mumbai lasts a mere 45 minutes and

costs around $75. **Indian Airlines** (© **0240/248-5421** or -3392) flies once a day from Mumbai and Delhi; the flight lasts 3 hours and costs around $175.

VISITOR INFORMATION   You'll find a tourist information booth at the airport arrivals hall where you can pick up brochures on Aurangabad, Ajanta, and Ellora. The **MTDC Holiday Resort** (Station Rd., Aurangabad 431 001; © **0240/233-1198**) doubles as a booking office for government-operated guided tours to both sets of caves. You can also book a **private guide** for the caves here, although it'll work out cheaper to pick one up at the caves themselves.

GETTING AROUND   Taxis and **auto-rickshaws** are widely available in Aurangabad, and you'll be approached at the airport by the usual touts offering you a "good deal." As always, arrange the fare upfront; a taxi from the airport into the city should cost about Rs 100 ($2.10). **Classic Travel Related Services** (at the MTDC Holiday Resort; see above; © **0240/233-7788** or -5598; ravindra@ bom4.vsnl.net.in) lives up to its name, and will arrange just about any type of transport—for travel within Aurangabad and environs (count on around Rs 1,200 ($26) for a full day with a car and driver; less if you're only going to Ellora), and beyond.

AJANTA TRAVEL ADVISORY   The drive from Aurangabad to Ajanta takes between 2 and 3 hours, so you're advised to set off early in the day to avoid as much of the midday heat as possible. There are two ways of getting to the caves. Generally, visitors are dropped off in the public parking lot, several kilometers from the caves themselves; here you'll find stalls selling awful souvenirs, snacks, and tourist paraphernalia, and "guides" flogging their services. You'll also find green, eco-friendly buses that are the only vehicles allowed in the vicinity of the caves. Purchase a ticket and hop aboard for the short drive to the Ajanta ticket office.

A far more rigorous but rewarding alternative is to have your driver drop you at the "Viewpoint," reached via a turnoff some distance before the official parking facility. From here you can take in a panoramic view of the site across the river, then make your way down the rather difficult pathway (don't attempt this route if you're unsteady on your feet) and eventually to a footbridge that spans the Waghora River. Make for the ticket booth and proceed to the caves. Be sure to arrange to have your driver collect you from the parking lot when you're done.

ELLORA TRAVEL ADVISORY   These caves are only 30km (19 miles) from Aurangabad, but you should rent a car and driver for the day for transfers between certain caves. Starting at **Cave 1,** visit as many of the principal caves as you have time for, until you reach **Cave 16,** where you should arrange for your driver to pick you up and then drive you to **Cave 21,** which is worth investigating. Having seen this cave, again have your driver take you to **Cave 29,** located alongside a waterfall, reachable via a rather dangerous pathway. Another short drive will take you to the **Jain Group** of temples, of which **Cave 32** is the best example.

Be warned that Ellora is enormously popular—especially during weekends and school vacations. Time your visit accordingly, or get here as soon as it opens. Ellora can be explored independently or with a guide (who may or may not understand English and who may sound rather like a prerecorded message); currently the official rate is Rs 255 ($5.45) for the first 4 hours, or—if you're really enthusiastic—Rs 380 ($8.20) for up to 8 hours.

AURANGABAD

388km (240 miles) E of Mumbai; 30km (19 miles) SE of Ellora; 106km (66 miles) SW of Ajanta

Aurangabad takes its name from the last of the great Moghul emperors, the hard-edged Aurangzeb, who enacted an almost Shakespearean drama in the 17th century when he took control of the empire by murdering his siblings and imprisoning his father, Shah Jahan (see chapter 9), before leaving Delhi in 1693 to make this city his base. Today the sprawling city of Aurangabad is the fastest-growing industrial city in India, and not a destination in its own right, but—time allowing—it has a few attractions worth noting. Best known is **Bibi-ka-Maqbara,** the "Mini-Taj," a mausoleum built for Aurangzeb's empress by his son, Azam Shah, and a supposed replica of the more famous mausoleum built by his grandfather in Agra. Set amid large landscaped gardens and surrounded by high walls, it's primarily interesting from a historical point of view, lacking as it does the fine detail and white marble of its inspiration (the builders were forced to complete the project in stone and plaster because of financial constraints). Although you can't enter the tomb itself, an amble through the grounds affords the opportunity to compare this project with the original Agra masterpiece (daily sunrise–10pm; admission $5). If you follow the dirt road that leads past Bibi-ka-Maqbara up into the hills for some 2km (1¼ miles)—a stiff climb—you will come across the **Aurangabad Buddhist Caves** (Rs 250/$5.35), a series of nine man-made caves dating back to the 6th to 8th centuries. Similar to the Buddhist Caves at Ajanta (but not in the same class), they feature some original painting fragments and offer spectacular views of the city and the landscape beyond.

On the way to Ellora is the **Daulatabad Fort** (Rs 100/$2.10). Built by the Yadavas between the 10th and 11th centuries A.D., it comprises an elaborate system of mazelike tunnels that served as an ingenious defense system: Once intruders were holed up deep within the tunnels, guards would welcome them with flaming torches, hot oil, or burning coals, effectively grilling them alive.

A place largely untouched by tourism is **Lonar Crater**—created some 50,000 years ago when a meteorite careered into the basalt rock, it has a diameter of 1,800m (5,760 ft.), making it the largest crater in the world. Water has filled the bottom of the crater, and Ram and Sita are believed to have bathed in this lake while they were exiled from Ayodhya; temple ruins lie at the water's edge. Tranquil and remote, the crater is around 150km (93 miles) east of Aurangabad.

Tips The Finest of Fabrics

Aurangabad is the only place in the world where *himroo* is still practiced, a millennia-old weaving craft that transforms silk and cotton into an almost satinlike fabric. Weavers spend around 2 to 3 months working on a single sari, even longer on more intricate and detailed designs. A custom-woven sari featuring a design based on one of the Ajanta murals takes a year to produce and costs about Rs 90,000 ($1,964)—which makes a beautiful himroo shawl with gold-plated silver thread for Rs 2,300 ($50) seem like a real bargain. Head for the **Paithani Silk Weaving Centre,** 54 P1 Town Center, behind Indian Airlines Booking Office, opposite M.G.M. College (© **0240/248-2811**).

THE BUDDHIST CAVES OF AJANTA ✬✬✬

During the 2nd century B.C., a long, curving swath of rock at a sharp hairpin bend in the Waghora River was chosen as the site for one of the most significant chapters in the creative history of Buddhism. Buddhist monks spent the next 700 years carving out prayer halls for worship *(chaitya grihas)* and monasteries *(viharas)* using little more than simple hand-held tools, natural pigments, and oil lamps and natural light reflected off bits of metal or pools of water. They decorated the caves with sculptures and magnificent murals that depict the life of the Buddha as well as everyday life.

The caves were abandoned rather abruptly after almost 9 centuries of activity and were only rediscovered in 1819 (by a British cavalryman out terrorizing wild boars). Time has taken its toll on many of the murals, and modern-day restoration projects have even contributed to the near-ruin of some of the work. Despite this, the paintings continue to enthrall, and it's hard to imagine the patience and profound sense of spiritual duty and devotion that led to the creation of this, arguably the best Buddhist site in India.

It takes some time to explore all 29 caves (which are numbered from east to west), and the sensory overload can prove exhausting; try at least to see the eight described below. It's a good idea to make your way to the last cave, then view the caves in reverse numerical order—in this way you won't be running with the masses, and you won't have a long walk back to the exit when you're done.

Richly decorated with carved Buddha figures, **Cave 26** is a *chaitya* hall featuring a stupa (dome-shaped shrine) on which an image of the Master seated in a pavilion appears. In the left-hand wall is a huge carved figure of the reclining Buddha—a depiction of the *Mahaparinirvana,* his final salvation from the cycle of life and death. Beneath him, his disciples mourn his passing; above, the celestial beings rejoice. Featuring the greatest profusion of well-preserved paintings is **Cave 17,** where maidens float overhead, accompanied by celestial musicians, and the doorway is adorned with Buddhas, female guardians, river goddesses, lotus petals, and scroll work. One celebrated mural here depicts Prince Simhala's encounter with the man-eating ogresses of Ceylon, where he'd been shipwrecked.

Cave 16 has a rather lovely painting of the princess Sundari fainting upon hearing that her husband—the Buddha's half-brother, Nanda—has decided to become a monk, while **Cave 10** is thought to be the oldest Ajanta temple, dating from around the 2nd century B.C. Dating to the 1st century B.C., **Cave 9** is one of the earliest chaitya grihas, and is renowned for the elegant arched windows carved into the facade that allow soft diffused light into the atmospheric prayer hall. A large stupa is found at the rear end of the prayer hall.

Cave 4 is incomplete, but its grandiose design makes it the largest of the Ajanta monasteries; take a quick look, then head for **Cave 2.** The facade features images of Naga kings and their entourage, while inside the sanctum a glorious mandala dominates the ceiling amid a profusion of beautiful floral designs, concentric circles, and abstract geometric designs with fantastic arrangements of flying figures, beasts, birds, flowers, and fruits. On the walls, well-preserved panels relate the birth of the Buddha.

Cave 1 is one of the finest and most popular of the viharas at Ajanta, especially renowned for the fantastic murals of two bodhisattvas (saintly beings destined to become the Buddha) that flank the doorway of the antechamber. To the right, holding a thunderbolt, is Avalokitesvara (or Vajrapani), the most significant bodhisattva in Mahayana Buddhism. To the left is the bejeweled Padmapani, his eyes cast humbly downward, with a water lily in his hand. Within the antechamber is a huge seated Buddha with the Wheel of Dharma (or life) beneath his throne—his hands are in the *Dharmachakra pravartana mudra,* the gesture that initiates the motion of the wheel. On the wall to the right of the Buddha is an image of the dark princess being offered lotuses by another damsel.

Last but not least, for a magnificent view of the entire Ajanta site and an idea of just why this particular spot was chosen, visit the viewing platforms on the opposite side of the river; the natural beauty of this horseshoe-shaped cliff is the perfect setting for a project so singularly inspired by spiritual fervor. It may even be the ideal starting point for your exploration (see "Aurangabad & the Ellora and Ajanta Caves," above).

Note: You will be required to remove your shoes before entering many of the caves, so take comfortable (and cheap) footwear that slips on and off easily.

Rs 500 ($11). Tues–Sun 9am–5:30pm; closed national holidays. No photography inside caves.

EXPLORING ELLORA ✶✶✶

Ellora's 34 rock-sculpted temples, created sometime between the 4th and 9th centuries, were chiseled out of the hillside by Buddhists, Hindus, and Jains, and a visit here allows for an excellent comparison of the stylistic features and narrative concerns of three distinct but compatible spiritual streams.

Of the 12 Buddhist cave-temples, carved between the 6th and 8th centuries, the largest is **Cave 5.** The "cave of the celestial carpenter, Vishwakarma" **(Cave 10),** is acknowledged to be most beautiful of the Buddhist group. A large ribbed, vaulted chamber, it houses a large figure of the Teaching Buddha, while smaller figures look down from panels above. The atmosphere here is chilling, a place for the suspension of worldly realities and for complete focus on things divine. In the three-story *vihara* (monks' domicile) of **Cave 12,** note the monks' beds and pillows carved out of rock. **Cave 13** marks the first of those carved by the Hindus which, when viewed in combination, offer a wealth of dynamic, exuberant representations of the colorful Hindu pantheon: Shiva as Natraj performs the dance of creation in **Cave 14** (where he is also seen playing dice with his wife Parvati and piercing the blind demon Andhaka with a spear); and in **Cave 15,** the manifold avatars of Vishnu tell numerous tales while Shiva rides the divine chariot and prepares to destroy the palaces of the demons.

Created over 150 years by 800 artisans, the **Kailashanath Temple (Cave 16)** is the zenith of rock-cut Deccan architecture, and Ellora's star attraction. A dazzling visualization of Mount Kailash, the mythical sacred abode of Shiva in the Tibetan Himalayas, it is unlike the other caves at Ellora, which were excavated into the hillside—it is effectively a mountain that has been whittled down to a free-standing temple, measuring 1,700 sq. m (18,299 sq. ft.). The intricacy of detail is remarkable; the temple basement, for example, consists of a row of mythical elephants carrying lotuses in their trunks as they appear to support the entire structure on their backs. Sculpted detail abounds in the temple and its excavated courtyard, with hardly an inch of wall space left unadorned—demons, dwarfs, deities, humans, celestial *asparas,* and animals occur in abundance. In the Nandi Pavilion facing the entrance is a beautiful carving of Laxshmi surrounded by adoring figures; seated in a pond, she is being bathed by attendant elephants carrying pots in their trunks. Also be on the lookout for *mithunas*—male and female figures in erotic situations.

Entry to Cave 16 is $5, free for children under 15. No filming of interiors. Closed Tues.

Ambient Dining

For a pleasant lunch en route back from Ellora, try the **Ambience,** which belongs to the same group that owns the excellent Tandoor restaurant in Aurangabad (see review below). Recently opened, it is situated 12km (7½ miles) outside the city, in the vicinity of Daulatabad Fort, and is set in pleasant gardens. It's also a lovely, atmospheric venue for dinner. Contact Ranjit (© **98/2243-6988**), or inquire at Tandoor about recent developments.

WHERE TO STAY

If you want ultra-cheap and functional and intend on eating out, then by all means endure a night or two at the government-run **MTDC Holiday Resort** (Station Rd., Aurangabad 431 001; © **0240/233-1513**), which offers relatively clean rooms in a central location (near restaurants, the taxi hub, and travel agencies) but little else. Insist on an air-conditioned unit; standard rooms are Rs 700 to Rs 850 ($15–$19) and family rooms are Rs 700 to Rs 900 ($15–$20).

The Ambassador Ajanta ⭐︎   Set amid lovely lawns with fountains and well-maintained flower beds, the Ambassador offers good facilities and a comfortable environment—ideal for relaxing after a hectic day of cave exploration. Moghul artworks fill the white-and-beige marble lobby, setting a pleasant atmosphere (if not as stylish as at the Taj), and the public spaces are decorated with statues and objets d'art that reflect the creative spirit of Ellora and Ajanta. The best units overlook the swimming pool (ask for room nos. 201–204 or 220–225). Service here is personal and attentive but certainly not up to the standards set in larger cities.

Jalna Rd., CIDCO, Aurangabad. © 0240/248-5211, -5212, -5213, or -5214. Fax 0240/248-4367. www. ambassadorindia.com. amau@vsnl.com. 92 units. Doubles: Rs 2,500 ($55) executive room; Rs 2,750 ($60) superior room; Rs 3,000 ($66) duplex suite; Ajanta and presidential suite tariffs on request. AE, DC, MC, V. **Amenities:** Restaurant; 2 bars; pool; putting green; tennis court; badminton court; squash court; jogging track; health spa; travel assistance and car hires; business center; currency exchange; shopping arcade; 24-hr. room service; babysitting on request; laundry and dry cleaning; doctor-on-call. *In room:* A/C, TV, electronic bedside console, minibar, hair dryer, safe.

Quality Inn The Meadows ⭐︎ *(Kids*   Surrounded by 5.2 hectares (13 acres) of pleasant gardens, this small resort—built in 1996—is great if you'd rather stay out of town. Accommodations are in a variety of simple cottages, the size and level of privacy varying according to price. Deluxe cottages are very basic and badly in need of attention (like a lick of paint), so opt for the superior category (ask for G1), with white marble flooring, stiff cane chairs, and tiled bathrooms with drench showers. There's plenty here to keep young children occupied (including rabbits, parrots, and ducks) while you relax in a quiet corner after sightseeing under the Maharashtran sun. Breakfast is served poolside, under large umbrella-like canopies; exotic birds, wild parrots, and busy butterflies provide the entertainment. Service tends to be a tad amateurish when guest numbers are down, so you may need to exercise patience.

Gat no. 135 and 136, Village Mitmita, Mumbai-Nasik Hwy., Aurangabad 431 002. © 0240/267-7412, -7413, or -7414. Fax 0240/267-7416. Reservations (Mumbai): © 022/2822-5653 or -5654, or 022/5692-2962. Fax 022/2825-1450. meadows@gnbom.global.net.in. 48 units. Doubles: Rs 2,400 ($50) deluxe cottage; Rs 2,850 ($62) superior cottage; Rs 4,400 ($47) 1-bedroom suite; Rs 7,150 ($156) 2-bedroom suite; Rs 450 ($9.80) extra bed. Rates include airport/station transfers and breakfast. AE, MC, V. **Amenities:** 2 restaurants; bar; pool; health club; skating rink; children's playground; petting zoo. *In room:* A/C, TV, minibar in suites.

Taj Residency ★★   This is the best hotel in town, catering to Aurangabad's high society crowd as well as to business and leisure travelers. Located away from the center, it's a tranquil retreat, surrounded by verdant gardens that guest rooms either overlook or lead out to; ground-floor patios also have swings. Don't expect the type of ultra-luxurious decor you'll find in major city hotels (the mattresses are foam and the carpeting slightly tatty in places), but accommodations are reasonably spacious, with teak furniture, Mughal arched-shaped mirrors, and miniature paintings on the walls. Ask for one of the corner units (no. 201 or 221)—these have extra balcony space. Suites, which include all meals, are large and plush and have wonderful private terraces.

8-N-12 CIDCO, Aurangabad 431 003. ☎ **0240/238-1106,** -1107, -1108, or -1109. Fax 0240/238-1053. www. tajhotels.com. residency.aurangabad@tajhotels.com. 40 units. Doubles: $75 standard; $85 executive (includes breakfast); $125 executive suite (includes all meals). AE, DC, MC, V. **Amenities:** 2 restaurants; bar; pool; fitness center; travel assistance and car hires; banqueting; business center; currency exchange; 24-hr. room service; babysitting on request; laundry and dry cleaning; doctor-on-call. *In room:* A/C, TV, minibar.

WHERE TO DINE

Most foreign visitors end up at **Food Lovers** (Station Rd. E., MTDC Holiday Resort), a palace of kitsch done in bamboo and fish tanks, with a separate entrance for "Families, Foreigners and Non-drinking Gents." Backpackers swear by the food (the Chinese is actually better than the Indian), and prices are very reasonable. Our money's on Tandoor, however (see review below). Another spot worth noting is **Angeethi Restaurant & Bar** (Jalna Rd.; ☎ **0240/244-1988**), one of Aurangabad's most popular restaurants, particularly with the business set. Try the Afghani chicken masala (pieces of boneless chicken cooked in a cashew-nut gravy), or the popular—and spicy—tandoori chicken masala. For something authentically Maharashtran, order chicken *kola ha puri* (not on the menu, but ask for it anyway), a spicy-hot chicken dish with a sharp chili, onion, and garlic base; if you can handle the sting, it's delicious. But if it's real authenticity you're looking for, head to **Thaliwala's Bhoj** (Bhau Phatak Smruti Kamgar Bhavan, opposite Hotel Kartiki; ☎ **0240/232-9915**) and order a *thali* (see "The Thali: Gujarati & Rajasthani Cuisine at its Best," earlier in this chapter). Waiters (who generally don't speak a syllable of English) will fill your platter with wonderful concoctions—mop it all up with savory, freshly prepared *naan* (flour bread).

Tandoor ★★★ INDIAN/MUGHLAI/CHINESE   A large square door swings open to reveal a stylish eatery with walls of clay face-brick, tiled flooring, and a bold collection of Egyptian figures (King Tut's head emerges incongruously from the brickwork). A hot favorite since 1988, this is our choice for Aurangabad's best eating experience. It's greatly enhanced by wonderful service and welcoming management. You could spend ages pondering the extensive menu, or simply ask the manager, Mr. Hussain, for his choices. Okra (or *bindi*) is a house specialty. The basil-flavored *kasturi kebab* (barbecue chicken) and *kabuli* tandoori chicken (marinated in a creamy yogurt and flavored with ginger, garlic, turmeric, and white pepper) are both outstanding. If you're looking for a mild curry that's been delicately prepared to bring out the most subtle flavors, ask for chicken *korma*—the sauce is made from cashew nuts, poppy seeds, sweet-melon seeds, and white sesame seeds.

Shyam Chambers, Station Rd. ☎ 0240/232-8481. Main courses Rs 35–Rs 320 (75¢–$6.90). MC, V. Daily 11am–4pm and 6:30–11pm.

4

Goa: Party in Paradise

Nirvana for dropouts, flower children, and New Age travelers since the late 1960s, Goa's hippie invasion peaked in the '70s, when Anjuna Beach became a rocking venue for party demons and naturalists who would sell their last piece of clothing at the local flea market for just enough cash to buy more dope and extend their stay. For many, Goa still conjures up images of all-night parties and tripping hippies sauntering along sun-soaked beaches. But there is more to the tiny western state than sea and sand, coconut palms, and hedonists. A living museum of colonization, Goa is a rich amalgam of Portuguese and Indian influences. The Portuguese arrived in 1498 and stayed for almost 500 years (kicked out, finally, in 1961—the last Europeans to withdraw from the subcontinent), leaving an indelible impression on the local population and landscape. One in every three Goans is Catholic, and you'll meet Portuguese-speaking Mirandas, da Sousas, and Braganzas, their ancestors renamed by the colonial priests who converted them, often by force. Garden Hindu shrines stand cheek-by-jowl with holy crosses, and the local *vindaloo* (curry) is made with pork. Dotted among the palm groves and rice fields are dainty villas bearing European coats of arms and imposing mansions with wrought-iron gates—built not only for European gentry but for the Brahmins who, by converting, earned the right to own land.

Today, Goa is colonized every winter by white-skinned tourists here to indulge in the rather commercialized trance culture, joined increasingly by loud middle-class puppies (children of yuppies) from Mumbai, Delhi, and Bangalore. While local farmers still plough their mud-soaked paddy fields with water buffalo, hip youngsters cruise from beach to beach, legs wrapped around cheap motorbikes, credit cards tucked into their Diesel jeans. Goa is very much "India Light," a cosmopolitan tourist-oriented place of five-star resorts, and in many ways this is the perfect introduction to a country that, elsewhere, can be very challenging indeed. Of course, when the crowds arrive, Goa's beaches and markets are anything but tranquil. Sun beds and shacks line the most commercial beaches, and hawkers haggle ceaselessly with droves of fresh-off-the-charter-plane Europeans here to sample paradise at bargain prices. If it's action you're after, you will run into endless opportunities for all-night partying and reckless abandonment, but Goa's true pleasures are found away from the crowds, on the more remote beaches to the far north and south, or on the beaches adjoining expensive luxury resorts. Come for at least 3 days, and you may end up staying for a lifetime—as a number of very content expats from around the world have done. However you decide to play it, live the local motto—*"Sossegarde":* "Take it easy."

1 Arrival & Orientation

ESSENTIALS

GETTING THERE   By Air   The state capital is Panjim (also called Panaji), which is pretty much centrally located; **Dabolim Airport** lies 29km (18 miles) south. Many travelers to Goa arrive on charter flights as part of ever-popular package deals direct from the U.K., and **Air-India** has direct flights from London once a week. Or you can fly in from Mumbai (around $85; four flights per day) or Delhi ($167; one flight per day), as well as from Kolkata, Chennai, Cochin, Hyderabad, Bangalore (via Mumbai), and Ahmedabad. The flight from Mumbai is a mere 40 minutes, and the best service is offered by **Jet Airways** (© 022/2285-5788 in Mumbai); ask about discounts for travelers under 30. A helpful government **tourist desk** (© 0832/251-2644) is in the baggage-claim hall. If you have a hotel or resort reservation, a **courtesy bus** will probably be waiting for you. If not, use a **prepaid taxi** (see chapter 2) or bargain directly with a driver; the trip to Panjim should cost Rs 500 ($11). As is the case everywhere, prebook your accommodations, and don't fall for a tout's offer of "discount" lodging.

By Train   Several trains travel daily from Mumbai to Goa along the **Konkan Railway;** these take a good 10 to 12 hours, so it's best to book the overnight **Mumbai-Madgaon Konkan Express,** which leaves at 10:40pm. Otherwise, you need to be up early for the 5:15am **Mumbai-Madgaoan Mandari Express.** If you're traveling from the south, catch the 7am train from Mangalore to Margao (6½ hr.); the trip offers mesmerizing views along the Konkan coast. Goa's three main jumping-off points are at **Thivim** in the north (20km/12 miles inland from Vagator), **Karmali** (12km/7½ miles from Panjim), and **Margao** (in the south). If you're going straight to Palolem in the far south (almost on the border with Karnataka, where the fabulous Ohm Beach is), jump off at **Canacona.** For onward transportation, taxis and auto-rickshaws are always available at stations. *Tip:* Try to book your train reservation in your home country, especially if you plan on moving to Goa soon after your arrival in India or in peak season when trains between Mumbai and Goa are often fully booked.

VISITOR INFORMATION   For general information on the state, visit the 24-hour **Government of Goa Department of Tourism office** in Panjim (Patto Tourist Home; © 0832/222-5583; http://goatourism.nic.in). Branch offices are in **Mapusa** (Mapusa Residency; © 0832/226-2390) and **Margao** (Margao Residency; © 0834/271-5204). Information counters can be found at the **Konkan Railway Station** in Margao (© 0834/270-2298) and at Panjim's **Bus Terminus** (© 0832/222-5620).

GETTING AROUND   Note that it shouldn't take much longer than 3 hours to cruise the entire coastline, so everything in this chapter is within easy reach.

By Motorbike   Motorbikes are *très* cool in Goa, and you'll encounter an endless barrage of young backpackers and old hippies zipping around Goa's roads on two-wheelers—*sans* helmets. Hiring a bike gives you absolute freedom to move from beach to beach, village to village, shack to all-night party. Have your international driver's license handy (just in case), and check the bike thoroughly before handing over any cash; bank on paying around Rs 300 ($6.50) a day. You can find motorbikes practically everywhere; in Panjim, try across the road from the post office. Riding on the back of on someone else's motorbike is another popular way to get around; this can be both invigorating and terrifying. When

Goa

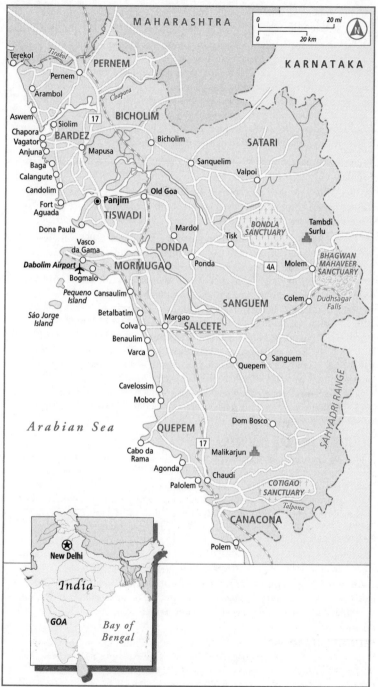

someone stops to ask if you need a lift (and they will), negotiate a price in advance. And, if you don't like the pace or style of driving, say something immediately.

By Taxi & Auto-Rickshaw   Negotiate privately with one of the many taxi-drivers that you'll find around tourist areas—including those near your hotel entranceway (you can of course get one through your hotel, but this will cost at least double). Figure on spending Rs 600 to Rs 750 ($13–$17) for a 6-hour outing, or agree to pay Rs 8 (15¢) per kilometer. Auto-rickshaws are considerably cheaper than taxis, but you'll have to fight to ensure that the meter is used, or agree on a price upfront. Remember that if you need a one-way lift to a more remote region, you'll be asked to pay for the return journey.

By Jeep   Arrange transport through the **Choco Marie shack** (© 98-2216-2772).

By Bus   Buses ply their way up and down the state, stopping in a rather chaotic fashion whenever someone needs to get on or off. If you're in a hurry, try for an express bus; otherwise you could be in for an endless series of stop-starts.

By Boat   Andy of **Marin Boat Trip** (stationed at Reggie's Café) will organize sea-going excursions anywhere in Goa. For trips to Terakol (Goa's northernmost point), he charges Rs 900 to Rs 1,000 ($20–$22) each, including refreshments, for a minimum of seven passengers. **Goan Bananas** (© 0832/227-6362 or -6739) organizes backwater cruises, spice plantation excursions, and island trips to nearby Bat Island. You'll find this outfit located along the beach at Calangute. Also on Calangute Beach is **Cats Cruise Boats** (© 0832/227-7000). At Kenilworth Beach Resort in south Goa, **Sea Adventure** (Utorda; © 98-2216-1712 or 0832/288-1289) organizes dolphin cruises, snorkeling trips to Paradise and Libiza islands, and a backwater cruise that takes in basking river crocodiles. The operation runs from late October until the end of April.

The *Precious Dragon,* a Chinese junk that now finds itself in Goa, is available for chartered trips and half-day cruises. Contact **Maneck Contractor** (© 0832/227-9894) for details.

TOURS & TRAVEL AGENTS

The **Goa Tourism Development Corporation** (Trionara Apartments, Dr. Alvares Costa Rd., Panjim; © 0832/222-6515, -4132, or -6728; www.goacom.com/goatourism) has full-day tours, aimed primarily at domestic tourists, of the north and the south. For personalized adventure expeditions to any number of Goan destinations, try **Kennedy's Adventure Tours and Travels** (© 0832/227-6493, -9381, -5076, or 98-2327-6520; kennedy@goatelecom.com).

MGM International Travels has offices in both Panjim (Navelcar Trade Centre, opposite Azad Maidan; © 0832/222-5150) and Calangute (Simplex Chambers, Umtavaddo; © 0832/227-6073). Other reliable travel agents include **Trade Wings** (6 Mascarenhas Building, Mahatma Gandhi Rd., Panjim; © 0832/243-2430); **Goa Sea Travels Agency** (opposite the Tourist Hotel in Panjim; © 0832/242-5925); and **Coastal Tours and Travels** (31st January Rd., Panjim; © 0832/242-3072).

BUNGEE-JUMPING   Almost as exciting as an Indian bus journey, seasonal bungee-jumping is offered at Anjuna's **Gravity Zone.** Contact Kaushik Suchak (© 0832/227-3897 or -3685) for details.

SCUBA DIVING   **Barracuda Diving India** (Goa Marriott Resort, Miramar, Panaji; © 0832/243-7001, ext. 6807 or 98-2218-2402; fax 0832/243-7020;

barracuda@vsnl.com; www.barracudadiving.com) is a PADI–recognized dive center where you can rent equipment or take diving courses and get certified (from beginner to advanced levels). Venkatesh Charloo and Karen Gregory, both master diver-trainers, also offer dive safaris south, in Karnataka, where visibility can reach up to 30m (100 ft.). Bookings can also be made through **Atlantis Water Sports** (see below).

WATERSPORTS   Most of the upmarket resorts offer a range of watersports facilities. Goa's best-established watersports company is **Atlantis Water Sports** (℃ **98-2212-2060**). Jet-skiing, parasailing, windsurfing, wakeboarding, scuba diving, and other ocean-going pastimes are available from a makeshift structure roughly halfway along the beach between Baga and Aguada (at the foot of Vila Goesa Rd., Cobra Vaddo, Calangute).

FAST FACTS: Goa

Airlines Even the smallest hotels are able to make air travel arrangements for you, and usually charge a small fee to process tickets for you, which saves you the hassle of having to travel all the way to Panjim. **Jet Airways,** the best domestic airline, is open Monday to Friday 9:30am to 1pm and 2 to 5pm (Patto Plaza, near the Patto Tourist Hotel and the bus stand, Panjim; ℃ **0832/243-1472** or **-7497**). You can usually purchase Jet Airways tickets an hour before the flight, at the airport.

Ambulance Dial ℃ **102,** or you can call the **Red Cross** (Panjim; ℃ **0832/222-4601**). In Margao, call the local **Ambulance Trust** (℃ **0834/274-0886** or 0834/273-0953). In Mapusa, call ℃ **0832/226-2372.**

American Express Call **Menezes Air Travel** (℃ **0832/222-5081**) in Panjim.

Area Code For most of **Goa** dial **0832.** In **Margao,** dial **0834.**

ATMs Ask your hotel for the nearest ATM with credit card facilities. In Panjim, there's an HDFC machine on 18th June Road, and a UTI machine in the Atmaram Commercial Complex, Dr. Atmaram Borkar Rd.

Banks & Currency Exchange For the best rates, you can exchange cash and traveler's checks at **Thomas Cook** in Panjim (8 Alcon Chambers, D.B. Marg; ℃ **0832/222-1312**; open Mon–Sat 9:30am–6pm and in winter also Sun 10am–5pm), or between Baga and Calangute, alongside the road, near the Hotel Ofrill building (℃ **0832/227-5693**).

Car Rentals Try **Sita World Travel** (101 Rizvi Chamber, Caetano Albu-querque Rd., Panjim; ℃ **0832/222-0476,** -0477, -3134, -6477, or 0832/242-3552).

Drugstores Try **Farmacia Salcete** (18th June Rd., Panjim; ℃ **0832/222-5959**; Mon–Sat 9am–7:30pm).

Emergencies In Panjim, dial ℃ **102** for an ambulance, and ℃ **101** in case of fire. See "Police," below.

Hospital **Dr. Bhandari Hospital** (℃ **0832/222-4966** or **-5602**) is in Panjim's Fontainhas area. For hospital emergencies in Margao, call ℃ **0834/270-5664.**

Internet Access High numbers of backpackers mean plenty of Internet facilities, particularly in tourist areas. In Panjim, head for **Cybercafé 2000**

(Shop no. 1, Sapana Centre; © 0832/223-1892); or **Cosy Nook** (18th June Rd.; daily 8:30am–8:30pm).

Police Dial © **100**. **Panjim Police Headquarters** (© **0832/222-4488** or -3400) is on Malaca Road, at the western edge of Azad Maidan.

Post Office Panjim's **General Post Office** (© **0832/222-3706**) is at Patto Bridge and is open Monday to Friday 9:30am to 5:30pm.

GOA'S BEST BEACHES

Goa's reputation for having some of the world's best beaches is well-deserved, but inevitable commercialization has taken its toll, with the infamous **Baga to Calangute** area (north of Panjim) now part of a tourist-infested strip of sun loungers, backed by beach shacks serving beer, cocktails, and fresh seafood—the sort of packaged beach experience we feel is best avoided. A little north of Baga, **Anjuna** comes alive with parties and trance music during the winter, when full-moon festivals get the crowds howling, and it also has a fabulous Wednesday market. But the real northern paradise starts at **Asvem** ☆☆☆, which has somehow managed to remain off the beaten tourist road. A little north of Asvem, **Arambol** ☆☆☆, seductively far away from the package-tour masses, is one of the last refuges of hard-core hippies. The southern beaches are generally the private domain of the five-star resorts fronting them, but in the far south, gorgeous **Palolem** ☆☆☆ is mercifully free of large resorts and gets our vote for the best beach in Goa—although it's become increasingly popular in the high season and is home to a sizable hippie community, it has yet to be overwhelmed by day-trippers. Just 7km (4 miles) north of Palolem, **Agonda** ☆☆☆ is even more isolated and peaceful, while to the south, **Galgibaba** ☆☆☆ is another remote haven with eucalyptus trees and empty stretches of sand. And then, of course, there's the incomparable **Om** ☆☆☆ beach, just over the border, an hour into neighboring state of Karnataka, considered the best beach in India and one of the most beautiful in the world.

2 Panjim (Panaji) & Old Goa

Located at the mouth of the Mandovi River (which you can explore by boat if you wish), the state capital of Panjim, moved here from Old Goa in 1759, is a breezy, laid-back town that lends itself to easy exploration. The chief attraction is the wonderful colonial Portuguese architecture, particularly in the eastern neighborhoods of Fontainhas and San Taome, where the atmospheric cobbled streets are lined with old mansions and churches dating as far back as the mid-1700s—look for Fontainhas's **Chapel of St. Sebastian,** where the crucifix from Old Goa's "Palace of the Inquisition" is now kept.

Dominating Panjim's town center is the imposing **Church of the Immaculate Conception,** built in the Portuguese baroque style in 1541. Nearer the water's edge is the **Secretariat**—an old palace of Adil Shah of Bijapur, this became the Portuguese viceroy's residence when the colonial administration moved here.

Wandering around Panjim on foot shouldn't take more than a few hours; if you're pushed for time, skip this and hop on an auto-rickshaw or on the back of a bike to **Old Goa** (30 min. from Panjim), reviewed in detail below. From Old Goa, it's a short trip (and a great contrast) to view the popular Hindu temples

(*Moments* **Carnival!**

Each year in February, during the festivities leading up to Lent, the people of Goa get down for 3 days and nights of hedonistic revelry as King Momo commands them to party hard. Goa's most famous festival—a Latin-inspired extravaganza of drinking and dancing—traces its roots to ancient Roman and Grecian ritual feasts. Cities and towns come under the spell of colorful parades, dances, floats, balls, and bands, concluding with the red-and-black dance at Panjim's Club National.

that lie north of the dull town of Ponda, on National Highway 4. Very few Hindu temples dating back earlier than the 19th century still exist (affronted by the Hindus' "pagan" practices, the Portuguese tore them down). The **Sri Mangeshi Temple** was built specifically as a refuge for icons of deities smuggled away from the coast during the violent years of the 16th-century Inquisition. A path lined with palm trees leads to a colorful entranceway, behind which the tiled steep-roofed temple exemplifies a fusion of Hindu and Christian architectural styles, hardly surprising considering that it was constructed by Goan craftsmen weaned on 200 years of Portuguese church-building. Walking distance from here (15 min. south) is the slightly less commercial (no temple "guides") **Sri Mahalsa Temple.**

EXPLORING OLD GOA ON FOOT ★★

The once-bustling Goan capital is said to have been the richest and most splendid city in Asia during the late 16th and early 17th centuries, before a spate of cholera and malaria epidemics forced a move in 1759; today this World Heritage Site is tepid testament to the splendor it once enjoyed. The tranquillity behind this well-preserved tourist site (barring the grubby stands selling refreshments and hideous souvenirs) belies the fact that it was built on plunder and forced conversions, though you'll see little evidence (like the basalt architraves) of the mass destruction of the Hindu temples initiated by the fervent colonialists.

The entire area can easily be explored on foot because the most interesting buildings are clustered together. To the northwest is the **Arch of the Viceroys,** built in 1597 in commemoration of the arrival of Vasco da Gama in India. Nearby, the Corinthian-styled **Church of St. Cajetan** (1651) was built by Italian friars of the Theatine order, who modeled it after St. Peter's in Rome. Under the church is a crypt in which embalmed Portuguese governors were kept before being shipped back to Lisbon—in 1992 three forgotten cadavers were removed. St. Cajetan's is a short walk down the lane from **Adil Shah's Gate,** a simple lintel supported by two black basalt columns.

Southwest of St. Cajetan's are the highlights of Old Goa: the splendid **St. Catherine's Cathedral (Sé)** ★, which took nearly 80 years to build and is said to be larger than any church in Portugal; and the **Basilica of Bom Jesus (Cathedal of the Good Jesus)** ★. The so-called Miraculous Cross, housed in a box in a chapel behind a decorative screen, was brought here from a Goan village after a vision of Christ was seen on it—apparently a single touch (there is a hole in the glass for just this purpose) will cure the sick. The surviving tower of the Sé's whitewashed Tuscan exterior houses the Golden Bell—the tolling of the bell indicated the commencement of the *auto da fés,* brutal public spectacles in which suspected heretics were tortured and burnt at the stake. Nearby, the

Hindu Christians

In 1623 the Pope agreed to tolerate converted Brahmin Catholics, who were then allowed to wear their sacred thread and the marks of their Hindu caste. This extraordinary concession played its part in allowing Goa to ultimately adopt a practice of syncretism that embraced Hindus and Christians alike, though it drew its fair share of criticism from the more narrow-minded: The British adventurer Sir Richard Burton once noted that the "good" Hindus converted to Catholicism by the Portuguese were simply "bad" Christians.

Convent and Church of St. Francis of Assisi (now an unimpressive archaeological museum) has a floor of gravestones and coats of arms; note that the images of Mary and Christ are darker-skinned than usual.

Opposite the Sé, the **Basilica of Bom** was built between 1594 and 1605 as a resting place for the remains of the so-called saint Francis Xavier (he was responsible for most of the conversions); the withered body of the venerated saint lies in a silver casket to the right of the altar, his corpse surprisingly well-preserved (although one arm is on display in Rome).

Up the hill from the Basilica are the ruins of the **Church of St. Augustine;** below is the **Church and Convent of St. Monica Christon,** where a miraculous image of the crucified Christ once regularly bled, spoke, and opened its eyes.

Basilica de Bom Jesus: Mon–Sat 9am–6:30pm, Sun 10:30am–6:30pm. Sé Cathedral: Daily 8:30am–5:30pm. Archaeological Museum: Sat–Thurs 10am–5pm; admission Rs 5 (10¢). Convent and Church of St. Francis of Assisi: daily 8:30am–5:30pm. Church of St. Cajetan: daily 8:30am–12:30pm and 3–5:30pm.

WHERE TO STAY & DINE

In the unlikely event that you will be staying this close to the capital, there are two good dining options, both reviewed below. The **Marriott** is an upmarket resort situated on the outskirts of the city (avoid **Cidade de Goa,** which is looking tired and is overpriced), while **Panjim Pousada,** situated in the heart of the Fontainhas neighborhood, has more character and is very affordable.

Panjim is filled with shabby-looking "pure veg" *udipi* eating halls. If you're in the mood for an Indian snack or a quick, cheap dish, aren't afraid to get your hands dirty, and feel like hanging with the locals, try one out; **Vihar** (31 Janeiro Rd.) is a good option. Opposite the Church of Our Lady of Immaculate Conception, **George Restaurant** (order Goan sausage) is convenient. For more atmosphere, head for Luiz D'Souza's **Hospedaria Venite** ⚸ (31st January Rd., Fontainhas; ✆ **0832/242-5537**), a tiny upstairs restaurant in a 200-year-old building where you can sit on the balcony and order wonderful Goan specialties. **Goenchin** ⚸ (Mandovi Apartments, Dr. Dada Vaidya Rd.; ✆ **0832/222-7614** or 0832/243-4877), located along a grisly side street, is *the* place to enjoy quality Chinese dishes prepared by a talented Tibetan chef.

Catering to a steady stream of tourists who are told that it's the best restaurant in town for North Indian cuisine, **Delhi Darbar** (M.G. Rd.; ✆ **0832/222-2544**) turns a heavy trade, but it's an unexciting experience.

Down the road from the **Goa Marriott Resort** (which, incidentally, has three good restaurants, particularly **Simply Fish,** an outdoor venue overlooking the bay) is **Mum's Kitchen** (Martin's Building, D.B. Marg, Miramar; ✆ **0832/222-9220** or 0832/242-8282; daily noon–5pm and 7pm–midnight), which has a laid-back Mediterranean atmosphere and does wonderful crab *xec-xec* (cooked in coconut gravy) and pomfret *recheado* (fish stuffed with hot spices and pan-fried).

To sample traditional Goan sweets while wandering Fontainhas, pop into **Confeitaria 31 de Janueiro,** one of the oldest bakeries in the state (31 Janeiro Rd.; © **0832/222-5792**).

Goa Marriott Resort ⊛   With its gorgeous rim-flow pool (and swim-up bar) situated as near as possible to the edge of riverside Miramar Beach, this stylish business hotel claims to have the only PADI-recognized diving center on the subcontinent. The road leading to the resort is somewhat neglected, but don't let this deter you, since this—the capital's smartest hotel, with great facilities— is conveniently within walking distance of Panjim. Guest rooms are tastefully furnished if a little cramped. Each one has its own tiny balcony; however, be sure to book a sea-facing executive room. Airport transfers are included.

Miramar, Goa 403 001. © **0832/243-7001.** Fax 0832/243-7020. www.marriott.com. 165 units. Doubles (Oct 15–Mar 31, excluding Dec 23–Jan 6): $98 executive; $90 bay-view; $80 garden-view; AE, MC, V. **Amenities:** 3 restaurants; 3 bars; dance club; health club (including Ayurveda); tennis courts; squash; table tennis; watersports; dive center; tours and travel desk; vehicle rental with chauffeur and taxi hire; boutique; salon; room service; babysitting; laundry; house doctor; on-site astrologer. *In room:* A/C, TV, dataport, minibar, tea- and coffee-making facilities, hair dryer.

Panjim Pousada & Inn ⊛   Situated in Panjim's historic Fontainhas district, these are the only authentically Goan guesthouses in Panjim. There's nothing luxurious about the restored colonial-era Hindu Pousada, but it offers a taste of Panjim's 19th-century upper-class lifestyle (along with hot water). The simple rooms are furnished with antiques (including four-poster beds) arranged around an empty courtyard. Windows and balconies look out onto the back streets and backyards of Panjim's old "Latin Quarter." Together with its older Catholic sister, Panjim Inn (incidentally listed as one of *The Independent*'s 50 best budget hotels in the world), the Pousada is owned by retired engineer Ajit Sukhija, who will obligingly regale you with accounts of the local history while proudly pointing out family photographs. The Panjim Inn is an old family property dating back to 1880. If you opt to stay here, ask for the room where Ajit's mother was born; it contains a lovely rosewood four-poster. Rooms vary in size and price, so ask if it's okay to look around before deciding.

House no. 156, Circle no. 5, Cunha Gonsalves Rd., Fontainhas. © **0832/222-8136** or -6523. Panjim Inn reception: E-212, 31st January/31 Janeiro Rd., Fontainhas. © 0832/222-8136 or -6523. www.panjiminn.com. panjimin@goatelecom.com. Pousada: 9 units. Doubles: Rs 540–Rs 1,220 ($12–$27); Rs 720–Rs-1,575 ($16–$35) A/C; Rs 50-Rs 360 ($1.05–$7.75) extra person. Panjim Inn: 13 units. Doubles slightly more expensive than Pousada's. MC, V. **Amenities:** Restaurant; foreign exchange; room service; laundry; doctor-on-call. *In room:* A/C in some.

The Unique Flavors of Goa

If you don't know your *xacuti* from your *baboti,* here's a short guide: *Cafreal* is chicken marinated in mint masala and then fried. *Vindaloo* is a curry usually made with pork and marinated in vinegar, garlic, and chilies. *Balchao* is fish cooked in shrimp preserve and coconut *feni. Ambot-tik* is baby shark in a hot sour tamarind and chili curry. The state's favorite fish, pomfret *recheado,* is stuffed with chilies and spices. *Xacutti* is chicken in a coconut-based masala. *Bebinca* is the traditional layered sweet pancake dessert made with coconut milk. And *feni* is the strong alcoholic spirit distilled from cashew nuts or coconut; try it, but be wary.

3 North of Panjim

Goa's reputation as a hangout for hippies during the '60s and '70s was made on the northern beaches of **Calangute, Baga,** and **Anjuna.** Along with the relaxed lifestyle and good times came busloads of Indian men keen to observe free-spirited foreigners and, finally, a crackdown by local government. This forced fun-loving hippies to head to more remote tracts of coastline, leaving the door open to backpackers and package tourists. Thus were the north's most famous beaches transformed into tanning lots for the masses— even Anjuna has become an Ibiza-like experience—and today no card-carrying hippie would deign to set foot on the beach that stretches between Calangute and Baga (defined by resort-centered **Sinquerim** in the south to **Vagator** in the north). That said, you can't deny the beauty of the beaches (to the south of Vagator, **Ozran** beach is peaceful and beautiful, with relaxed swimming in a bay at its southernmost end)— certainly this is where you'll want to be if you're here to party during the season. Baga is the smaller, slightly less-developed area of activity, where shacks like **Britto's** and **St. Anthony's** are crowded with beer-quaffing visitors recovering from the previous night's adventure at the legendary bar-cum-nightclub, **Tito's.** (Be warned that the "special *lassis*" served at these classic Goan beach shacks will dramatically increase your amusement at the cows sunbathing alongside the tourists on Baga Beach.)

For a sense of Goa's hippie origins, head for **Arambol,** Goa's most northerly beach (36km/22 miles northwest of Mapusa). It also offers better bodysurfing— the water's a little more turbulent. It draws quite a crowd during the season (you arrive through a lane crammed with stalls selling CDs and T-shirts, and laid-back restaurants playing competing brands of music), but the setting is nevertheless lovely, with a hill looming over a small freshwater lake fed by a spring. The farther north you walk, the more solitude you enjoy. Besides looking at beautiful bodies, you can spend hours watching the surf glide, or check out **Dreamcatcher Shack,** started in 2002 by well-known Bollywood producers Shahnaab and Bhavna. Or head a little farther south from Arambol for **Asvem** Beach, more popular with the Olive Ridley turtles who have been coming here for centuries than with either package tourists or hippies.

Shopping in the Global Village Markets

Anjuna is the site of Goa's wonderful **Wednesday market** ★★, where a nonstop trance soundtrack sets the scene, and a thousand stalls sell everything from futuristic rave gear to hammocks that you can string up between two palm trees on the nearby beach. It's a wonderful place to meet people from all over the world as well as Rajasthanis, Gujaratis, Tibetans—even drought-impoverished Karnataka farmers with "fortune-telling" cows; it's a bit like London's Camden, but everyone's tanned and the weather's almost always wonderful. When the crowd gets too much, pull up a chair at **Mango Shade,** an outdoor family-run restaurant at the edge of the market. Come the weekend, Goa's global residents head for **Ingo's Saturday Night Bazaar,** where most of the spending seems to involve liquor and food, and scores of happy-go-lucky revelers dance and cruise around exchanging plans for the remainder of the evening.

WHERE TO STAY

Naturally, Goa offers a wide range of accommodations options, but the luxury resorts tend to offer the best proximity to secluded beaches. If you're design-conscious and keen on a "non-hotel" experience, Goa's best options by far are Nilaya Hermitage or Pousada Touma, both reviewed below, or—if you're on a budget—Siolim House. Even more affordable are the two suites (Rs 1,000–Rs 2,000/$22–$44) at **Hotel Bougainvillea** (© **0832/227-3270** or -3271); book the one with its own garden. Inherited by Betina Faria, it was built by her grandfather and is consequently also known as Grandpa's Inn. It's small, and accommodations are quiet and cool, with a lovely garden and swimming pool, and an old pool table.

Fort Aguada Beach Resort & Hermitage ★★   Situated on the short peninsula upon which the Portuguese built their defensive Fortress of Aguada, this resort complex (comprising the Beach Resort, Hermitage, and Taj Holiday Village) has one of the most spectacular locations in all of Goa, with picture-postcard views of the beach, which stretches all the way to Baga, 8km (5 miles) away. Behind the main Beach Resort block are 42 new cottages tucked almost invisibly among groves of lantana, cashew, and bougainvillea bush; these are the best places to stay at the Beach Resort. Alternatively, for absolute privacy (ideal for groups or families), consider one of the 15 top-end Hermitage cottages, built as a retreat for delegates during the 1983 meeting of the Commonwealth heads of government. The cottages are set among terraced gardens of exotic orchids, bougainvilleas, cashew trees, jasmine, and Krishna fichus, and each villa has a separate living room; a dining area; one, two, or three bedrooms; two bathrooms; a *balcao* (balcony); and a private garden. Interiors are luxurious and include all modern amenities; request a villa near Sunset Point, where cocktails are served while the sun descends over the Arabian Sea. It's quite a stiff climb between the cottages and the hotel lobby (shared with the Beach Resort); courtesy vehicles are available for the short transfer. Also sharing the facilities offered by Fort Aguada Resort is Taj Holiday Village, fronted by Sinquerim Beach, with cottages and villas scattered among towering coconut trees and lush vegetation. Accommodations at this resort vary considerably, ranging from lavish sea-facing villas to less desirable suites in clustered or duplex cottages.

Sinquerim, Bardez, Goa 403 519. © **0832/479123-136**. Fax 0832/479200. www.tajhotels.com. fortaguada. goa@tajhotels.com. 130 units. Doubles (Oct 1–Apr 15/Apr 16–Sept 30/Dec 23–Jan 5): $150/$75/$250 standard; $160/$75/$260 deluxe; $170/$80/$290 cottage; $190/$83/$350 deluxe sea-view with terrace; $210/$83/$400 junior suite with terrace; $20 extra bed. Rate per Hermitage villa (Oct 1–Apr 15/Apr 16–Sept 30/Dec 23–Jan 5): $225/$83/$475 1-bedroom; $325/$166/$575 2-bedroom; $500/$249/$675 3-bedroom. Taj Holiday Village doubles (Oct 1–Apr 15/Apr 16–Sept 30/Dec 23–Jan 5): $140/$75/$250 standard; $160/$80/$275 cottage; $190/$83/$320 villa; $280/$83/$400 sea-view villa; $20 extra bed. AE, DC, MC, V. **Amenities:** 3 restaurants; 2 bars; pool; tennis; volleyball; squash; badminton; billiards; table tennis; adventure activities (trekking, rock climbing, rappelling); cycling; watersports; fitness center; spa; activity center; airport transfers; currency exchange; shop; salon; room service; babysitting; laundry; house doctor. *In room:* A/C, TV, minibar, tea- and coffee-making facilities, hair dryer, safe.

Nilaya Hermitage ★★★   From the moment you arrive at this place, you know you're going to be very comfortable indeed (though perhaps it's not suited for the over-55 market). Parisian fashion stylist Claudia Derain and her Indian husband, Hari Ajwani, started this exclusive hillside resort when they fell in love with Goa during a vacation from Europe. Together with Goan architect Dean D'Cruz, they have created something out of *Arabian Nights,* with 12 cosmic-themed guest suites featuring vibrant colors, terrazzo flooring, and minimalist decor. Giant mosquito nets hang from a high-beamed ceilings, and sweeping archways lead off to open-plan bathrooms with views of the tropical garden. Like a chic harem, the split-level, saffron-colored "Music Room" is where guests unwind on sprawling mattresses, or meditate while soothing music plays beneath a high blue-domed ceiling. Overlooking paddy fields and coconut palm groves, the setting is romantic and classy, and despite being 6km (4 miles) from the nearest beach, Nilaya is one of Goa's most perfect getaways, as regular guest Demi Moore no doubt agrees.

Arpora Bhati, Goa 403 518. ℂ **0832/227-6793**, -6794, -5187, or -5188. Fax 0832/227-6792. www.nilaya hermitage.com. 12 units. Doubles: $140 low season; $280 high season; $400 Dec.20–Jan 10. Rates include breakfast, dinner, and airport transfers. MC, V. **Amenities:** Restaurant; breakfast area; bar; cultural performances; pool; tennis court; Ayurvedic center; spa; travel assistance; room service; laundry; doctor-on-call; meditation room. *In room:* Some have A/C; TV and DVD players can be organized.

Pousada Touma 𝄖𝄖𝄖 This is Goa's top Ayurvedic retreat (a professional doctor presides over two excellent treatment rooms), and even though it's located in the heart of a bustling tourist center (a 10-min. walk from popular Calangute Beach), it is sheltered from the high-season madness by thick, verdant vegetation. Neville Proenca, the charming owner-manager, takes a hands-on approach—a far cry from the package-mentality tourism that's swept through the state. Working with award-winning architect Dean de Cruz, it took Neville 3½ years to create his retreat, fashioned entirely out of distinctively Goan laterite stone and set around a pool with cascading water. Each suite has its own balcony, overlooking either the garden or pool, and is uniquely themed with eccentric pieces (a cradle-turned-table; dentist chair–turned–recliner). The stylish bathrooms are done in shattered tile mosaics. Pousada is the perfect getaway for artists and sophisticated socialites—filmmaker Mira Nair stayed in the Mountain Suite after filming *Monsoon Wedding,* while French designer Michéle Klein enjoys the deluxe Castle Suite, which has two living rooms leading off a single bedroom, all within a fairy-tale tower. In addition to its Goan menu, the excellent **Copper Bowl Restaurant** offers special Ayurvedic meals.

Porba Vaddo, Calangute, Bardez. ℂ **0832/227-9061.** Fax 0832/227-9064. www.pousada-tauma.com. 12 units. Doubles: $95–$390. MC, V. No children. **Amenities:** Restaurant; bar; pool; gym; Ayurvedic center; travel services, airport transfers; room service (until 11pm); Internet facility. *In room:* A/C, TV, minibar, hair dryer on request.

Siolim House 𝄖𝄖 Leafy Siolim village (30 min. from the busy market town of Mapusa—delightfully far from the maddening crowd) is where you will find the wonderful 300-year-old former residence of a governor of Macau, which has been wonderfully restored by London-based investment banker Varun Sood (who, incidentally, designed the wrought-iron furniture mixed in with the antiques). Located around an open courtyard with a lovely blue-tiled fountain, guest rooms feature whitewashed walls with hand-painted friezes, solid wood-beamed ceilings, decorative terra-cotta tile floors, mother-of-pearl windowpanes, and wonderful open-plan showers. Staff will gladly arrange trips to beaches up and down the coast. Meals are prepared according to personal requests, so let your imagination wander.

Waddi (opposite Wadi Chapel), Siolim, Bardez. ℂ **0832/227-2138.** Fax 0832/27-2941. www.siolimhouse. com. info@siolimhouse.com. 7 units. Doubles: $100; $125 honeymoon suite; $125 family suite; children under 12 free. Rates include breakfast. 25% extra during peak season (Dec 16–Jan 9); 35% discount in low season (May–Aug). MC, V. **Amenities:** Restaurant; pool; bicycles; airport transfers; car and motorbike hire; room service; Ayurvedic massage; babysitting; laundry; doctor-on-call; Internet; television lounge, library.

WHERE TO DINE

Beach-shack dining is one of the essential Goa experiences—sipping *feni* while you feast on grilled tiger prawns or masala shark at unbelievable prices is a must. With at least 200 licensed seasonal shacks between Candolim and Baga, you certainly won't go hungry, but with names like Lover's Corner, Fawlty Towers, and Goan Waves, don't expect culinary magic. And if you don't like the look of the kitchen (ask where the dishes are washed), opt for the following.

While in Baga, check out **Casa Portuguesa** (Baga Beach; ℂ **0832/227-7024;** closed May–Oct), set in a charming old bungalow near the beach; the chicken *cafreal* is highly recommended.

A number of decent restaurants can also be found along the stretch of road between Arpora Hill and Baga Creek, leading inland from Baga Beach. When Indian spices begin to take their toll, **Lila Café** (Baga River)—Goa's number-one breakfast and lunch cafe (and apparently where Gregory Peck, David Niven, and Roger Moore hung out when filming *Sea of Wolves*)—is the perfect place to enjoy a decent breakfast: muesli and cereals, along with a selection of breads and croissants served with a variety of toppings. Enjoy views of paddy fields and coconut groves as you dine. The fresh salads are also good, as is the catch of the day and the goulash with spaetzle. Alternatively, famous **J & A's Little Italy** (℃ **0832/228-2364** or 98-2313-9488) is where Jamshed and Ayesha Madon serve fantastic pastas and wood-fired pizzas. Nearby, in an unusual orange house, is **Moon Crest Restaurant** (℃ **0832/2275790**), a popular hangout where hip locals enjoy the casual atmosphere and the friendly vibe conjured up by the personable host, David Gonzavez. You can sit outside, and on Tuesday a live jazz band entertains. Choices range from chateaubriand to chicken stuffed with crabmeat, but it's the seafood that you simply must try; the spicy prawn curry is superb.

Axirvaad ☆☆ NEW-WORLD FUSION   The name means "blessing," and that's exactly what this fashionable "lounge groove space temple" is. Deepti Datt (a Bombay-based filmmaker) and her husband (a DJ and model) came to Goa to raise their daughter away from the hectic city and established a gorgeous, sophisticated restaurant in a 150-year-old Portuguese mansion, transforming the spacious high-ceilinged interiors into a triumph of cool, with Latino lounge music and designer crockery. The menu changes weekly and is driven by what Arnold, the Texan chef-cum-jewelry-designer, finds fresh and exciting at the market. Dishes combine local and international tastes like cashew-crusted kingfish drizzled with chili syrup, served with mixed vegetables in basil butter. Ask about specials, and let the waiter in on any taste preferences; Arnold is always willing to oblige. Deepti is also a wonderful source of knowledge regarding Indian cinema, local parties, and Goa's latest social intrigue.

Rua de Boa Vista, 483 Bouta Vaddo, Assagao, (Mapusa-Anjuna Main Rd.). ℂ **0832/226-8949.** sybarite@ vsnl.com. Main courses Rs 150–Rs 330 ($3.15–$7). AE, MC, V. Open mid-Sept to mid-Apr, Thurs–Sat 6–11pm (last orders).

Banyan Tree ☆☆☆ THAI   Each year since 1988, a different Thai chef is imported from Thailand to spruce up the menu and add a personal touch. Set back from the main road behind a 320-year-old banyan tree within the gardens of the Taj Holiday Village, this upmarket Asian eatery is proud of its own private herb garden where essential Thai ingredients like lemon grass, *kha* (Siamese) ginger, pandanus leaves, *kachai* (a peppery ginger), and bird chilies are grown.

Start with spicy *talle tom yam* seafood soup, a hot-and-sour concoction of mushrooms, calamari, chili, and ginger, not for the faint-hearted; or try the very tangy *som tham* papaya salad, which comes with a peanut sauce. This being Goa, the seafood creations are a must; try the tasty *poo gathi*—a curry-sauce infusion of river crabmeat that's spicy yet flavorful—or the rather pricey *choo chi goong mangkon* (diced lobster in a *makrut* [lime] infused red-curry sauce). If you've overdone the chili and spice, spoil yourself with refreshing *tab tim grob*—water chestnuts soaked in rose syrup and dusted with tapioca flour—with or without coconut-flavored ice cream.

Taj Holiday Village, Sinquerim, Bardez. © **0832/247-9123**; 866/235-9330 in U.S. Main courses Rs 115–Rs 850 ($2.40–$18). AE, DC, MC, V. Daily 12:30–2:30pm and 7:30–10:30pm.

Copper Bowl ★★★ GOAN/ECLECTIC   It's not just the setting that makes dining here so pleasurable, it's the food, which is sensational. Graciously served from quaint copper pots, the typically Goan dishes are exquisite; try coconut-based chicken *xacutti* (pronounced cha-*cooty*), or fragrant prawn *balchao*, a mouth-watering combination of crispy unshelled prawns, aromatic spices, chili, onion, and prawn powder. If your taste leans more toward non-spicy cuisine, try the seafood in coconut milk soup, followed by the seafood treasure—baby lobster, prawns, and two kinds of fish served in a banana leaf. Guests at the Pousada are even allowed to take over the kitchen and prepare their own specialties, but nothing will be served unless it's fresh.

Pousada Touma, Porba Vaddo, Calangute. © **0832/227-9061**. Main courses Rs 190–Rs 400 ($4.25–$8.75). MC, V. Open all day, but reservations are essential if you're not a resident.

Le Restaurant Français ★★★ FRENCH   Lit by the moon, the stars, and a number of old chandeliers dangling from the branches of surrounding trees, this charming slice of Gaul shares the same magical garden venue as the daytime eatery, **Milky Way,** where Janis Joplin and The Beatles once hung out. Those erstwhile pop stars would have loved the elegantly laid-back atmosphere that fun-loving accidental restaurateurs Morgan, Florence, and Serge brought with them from the Continent. The menu (beautifully handwritten by Florence in French, with lively English translations) features imaginatively innovative dishes concocted by Morgan, who likes to "escape" (read: "experiment"), so dishes change regularly, along with the decor. Must-tries include the baby calamari stuffed with a ratatouille of prawns, and the filet of sardines on phyllo pastry with basil coulis. This is also the only place in Goa where rabbit is served, and the fresh (nonfrozen) beef is specially flown in from Bangalore. Be sure to leave space for the addictive chocolate cake, whose recipe Morgan once used as *baksheesh* (tip/bribe) at airport Customs while bringing essential cooking ingredients back from the Continent.

Baga Rd., Calangute. © **98-2212-1712**. frenchfoodindia@hotmail.com. Main courses Rs 140–Rs 390 ($3.10–$8.50). No credit cards. Late Nov to mid-Apr, Thurs–Tues 7:30pm–late.

Maya ★ *Finds* NORTH INDIAN   Sanjay Nagpal wanted to get away from his hectic business life, so he enlisted Mumbai-based designer Jangu Sethna to help him convert a Portuguese house built in 1937 into a stylish eatery, one of the very few places in Goa that specializes in North Indian cuisine. Sethna used eco-friendly natural materials and ultra-modern lighting designs to create a quaint, quietly magical outdoor restaurant. You can spend the entire evening sampling a huge variety of starters, or go for the selection of tandoori items; again, focus on the fresh seafood.

Casa Lemos, House no. 1932, next to Santiago Resorts, Calangute Baga Rd. ℂ **0832/227-6497**. Main courses Rs 90–Rs 250 ($1.90–$5.35). AE, DC, MC, V. Daily 6–11pm year-round. Also open for lunch Dec–Feb; call for hours.

Olive Ridley Beach Restaurant 🄰 *Finds* FUSION   A smart upgrade of the archetypal Goan beach shack, this simple outdoor restaurant on the edge of Asvem Beach was set up by a Belgian-Swiss couple, Loulou and Francis, in 2000. It now attracts diners from all over north Goa. Unlike most shacks, which have plastic seats and serve food from a loosely defined "kitchen," here you can relax on comfortable cane chairs with your feet on the sand. Expect fresh seafood— especially crab, lobster, rockfish, and tiger prawns—bought from the local fishermen and prepared with a French-Italian touch, as well as fresh salads and organic vegetables brought in from Maharashtra. Besides serving delicious dishes at excellent prices, the owners contribute to the welfare of the diminishing Olive Ridley turtle population by signposting the area and helping to ensure that the animals are not disturbed during their most vulnerable time—when they lay their eggs on the beach from November to March.

Vithaldas Vaddo, Morjim. ℂ **0832/224-6732**. ridley@goatelecom.com. Main courses Rs 100–Rs 290 ($2.10–$6.25). No credit cards. Daily Oct 15–May 15 breakfast to dinner; hours fluctuate, so call ahead.

St. Anthony's *Moments* GOAN BEACH SHACK   People come here for the atmosphere and the "special *lassis*" rather than the food, but that doesn't mean you'll starve. You can have crab, baby kingfish, or pomfret, all prepared in the tandoor oven, or go for vinegar-spicy chicken *xacuti*, pork *vindaloo*, or *sorpotel*. Besides the laced *lassis* (yogurt drinks), you can try papaya and banana flavors, and cold bottles of Kingfisher are always available.

Baga Beach. ℂ **0832/227-6121** or 0832/228-1150. migeul@goa1.dot.net.in. Main courses Rs 50–Rs 150 ($1.05–$3.15). No credit cards. Daily mid-Oct to mid-May, early–late; call for hours.

SHOPPING

Besides the vibrant markets (see "Shopping in the Global Village Markets" box, above), Calangute has a variety of options worth checking out. **Casa Goa** is a stylish boutique featuring designer wear by celebrated Goan designer Wendell Rodericks, as well as local artwork, silk drapes, and a variety of antiques (Baga Rd.). Then take a look at **Leela Art Palace** (Khobro Waddo; ℂ **98-2213-5370**); with any luck, proprietor Ravi will be in. You might find yourself agreeing to accompany him on an exotic journey into some of the country's remotest regions, where he regularly treks to source tribal art. Also in Calangute, **Subodh Kerkar Art Gallery,** run by Goa's well-known watercolorist, showcases contemporary Indian art including ceramics, hand-painted chests, and Rajasthani sculptures (Gaurowaddo; ℂ **0832/227-6017**). Based in a 200-year-old Portuguese mansion, **Sangolda** is the housewares boutique venture by the dynamic duo behind the boutique hotel Nilaya Hermitage; here you can shop for unusual home accessories and furniture sourced from all over India—from Keralan rattan loungers to Rajasthani chests. Attached is a gallery-cum-coffee shop (Chogm Rd., Sangolda; ℂ **0832/227-6793**). If you're not traveling north, Kashmir House is another must. Known for its fabulous collection of jewelry, gems, leather goods, "Ardebil" carpets, marble artifacts, sterling silver, papier-mâché trinkets, and 100% Pashmina shawls, it's located in both north Goa (opposite Taj Holiday Village; ℂ **0832/227-6072**) and south Goa (Carpet House, Goa Renaissance Resort; ℂ **0832/274-5201**).

WHERE'S THE PARTY?

Your best bet for finding a good party is to hang out around whatever appears to be the most popular beach shack of the season, and to get chatting with the locals (but be wary of getting lifts to unknown venues with strangers). Other excellent spots for picking up the scent of out-of-the-way parties are **Ingo's Saturday Night Bazaar,** the **Wednesday Market** in Anjuna, or the ever-popular **Tito's**—this local institution has been going for years and attracts anyone and everyone who's up for a party. Or check out **Kamaki,** up the road from Tito's (stay clear of karaoke nights, however). Better by far is **Nine Bar** ✪, the quintessential Goan sundowner hangout (above Ozran Beach; closes 9pm), where delicious trance accompanies the scene as the sun plunges exotically behind palm fronds and the horizon. On Thursday nights, **Axirvaad** ✪ (see "Where to Dine," above) transforms into an "ethnofunky groove" space where edgy tunes are spun by well-known Mumbai model Ranjeev Mulchandani or touring guest artists.

4 South of Panjim

Compared with the beach playgrounds of north Goa, the south is more about solitude and stretches of virgin sand (with the north only a short ride away). For the most part, you'll be sunning yourself on whatever beach is slap-bang in front of your resort hotel—each with its own idyllic setting, these stretches of private, largely untouched beaches are paradise. If you're on a tighter budget or simply want a bit more atmosphere, head farther south to picturesque **Palolem** ✪✪✪. Remote and tranquil (yet only 40km/25 miles from Margao), this is one of Goa's most beautiful stretches of coastline, a gorgeous sandy crescent cove lined with coconut palms and a few shacks and stalls. Although it's becoming increasingly popular over the high season, it remains free of sun beds, day-trippers, and large resorts, with accommodations options limited to thatched treehouses or wooden houses on stilts. At sunset, Palolem becomes a natural meditation spot; the sun disappearing slowly behind the beach's northernmost promontory casts a shadow over local fishing boats, swimmers, joggers, and cavorting dogs, as the rusticated bars come to life with pleasant lounge music. Just 7km (4½ miles) north of Palolem, **Agonda** is even more isolated and peaceful, while to the south, **Galgibaba** is another remote haven with eucalyptus trees and empty stretches of sand.

Getting There   From Panjim you can travel direct to your beachfront resort by taxi or motorbike (the latter should take no more than 2–3 hr.), possibly stopping off for a swim at **Bogmalo,** one of the quietest of south Goa's popular beaches, with quaint shacks (as well as a number of ugly concrete buildings), fishing boats, and a view of two small islands some distance out to sea—ask about trips to the islands at the **Watersports Goa** shack, which also has equipment for activities like windsurfing and water-skiing. Farther south, you can stop for lunch at **Martin's Corner** (✆ **0832/288-0061;** follow the back road between Majorda and Colva), where Martin Pereira's widow, Carafina, runs the kitchen with an iron fist. She began cooking wonderful dishes for this family restaurant back in 1994, when it opened with only two tables. Now Martin's sons operate a successful and extremely popular courtyard establishment, surrounded by mango, coconut, and jackfruit groves (it's cricket star Sachin Tendulkar's favorite Goan restaurant). Order snapper *recheado,* prawns with either butter or garlic, or pomfret *caldin,* made with a coconut milk curry. Carafina makes a mean homemade masala, prepared according to a secret family recipe with fresh Goan spices.

Travel Tip: He who finds the best hotel deal has more to spend on facials involving knobbly vegetables.

Hello, the Roaming Gnome here. I've been nabbed from the garden and taken round the world. The people who took me are so terribly clever. They find the best offerings on Travelocity. For very little cha-ching. And that means I get to be pampered and exfoliated till I'm pink as a bunny's doodah.

travelocity®

1-888-TRAVELOCITY / travelocity.com / America Online Keyword: Travel

travel • news • classifieds • health • personals • maps • autos • sp

Plan your vacation

- flights, hotels, car rentals
- cruises & vacation packages
- destination guides
- fare alerts
- go to yahoo.com, click travel

Om Beach: Escape to Paradise

Often cited as the top beach in India and one of the best in the world, paradisiacal **Om Beach** ★★★ lies south in Gokarna, an hour across the border into Karnataka. Black rocks divide the superb white sand into three interconnected bays that more or less resemble the Sanskrit "om" symbol, the invocation that created the universe. Infrastructure here remains practically nonexistent, but the tranquil **Devbagh Beach** resort (© 08382/21603, 080/558-3276, or 080/559-7021, -7024, or -7025; www.junglelodges.com) in Karwar, slightly north of Gokarna, makes for a pleasant getaway. Guests stay in log cabins on stilts among groves of casuarina trees—spend your days scuba diving (with PADI-affiliated instructors) or lazing in your hammock.

Alternatively, consider a meandering trip via the Goan interior, traveling past Ponda to the Bhagwan Mahaveer Sanctuary to view Goa's oldest Hindu temple, **Mahadeva Temple** in Tambdi Surla, and the 600m (190-ft.) high **Dudhsagar** ("Sea of Milk") **Falls.** Constructed from slabs of black basalt, the 11th-century Mahadeva Temple is one of the few to have survived the Portuguese, thanks largely to its distance from the coast (some 75km/46 miles from Panjim). To reach the falls, you will need a jeep, so either set off with one from the outset (see "Arrival & Orientation," earlier in this chapter), or hire one in nearby Collem. Take lunch (look out for greedy monkeys) and a costume in which to swim in the deep, icy pool surrounded by rocks and wild greenery. There is no reason to stop in Goa's second city, **Margao,** which has little more to offer than a stroll through the sprawling spice-scented town market—a maze of covered stalls selling everything from garlands of flowers and peeled prawns to sacks bursting with turmeric, chilies, and tamarind—but two worthwhile house museums are nearby. In Loutolim (10km/6¼ miles north of Margao), you can tour the Miranda family home, **Casa Araujo Alvares** (arrangements through Loutolim's Ancestral Goa Museum; © 0832/277-7034; daily 9am–6pm), while 13km (8 miles) west lies the old Portuguese village of Chandor and the impressive **Casa de Braganza** ★, Goa's largest residence. The two-story facade of this Indo-Portuguese mansion—which practically takes up an entire street—features 28 balconies fronted by a lush, narrow garden. The land-owning Braganzas rose to prominence during the 17th century and today are divided into two clans, the Pereira-Braganzas and the Menenzes-Braganzas, who occupy separate wings of the house. The large, high-ceilinged rooms (including a 250-year-old library) are filled with original antiques, rosewood four-poster beds, mosaic floors, and Belgian glass chandeliers. Sunlit galleries and parlors are filled with bric-a-brac, and French windows open onto an interior garden. You can arrange (© 0832/278-4201) to have a private tour conducted by one of the duke's descendents; concentrate on the west wing, which is in the best condition.

WHERE TO STAY & DINE

South Goa has more five-star resorts than north Goa, and the number is added to annually (raising the hackles of eco-watchdogs). Two upmarket newcomers are the **Hyatt Regency Goa Resort and Spa** (© 0832/272-1234; www.hyatt.com; from $190)—sprawled over 18 hectares (45 acres), on the virgin beach of Arrossim—and the **Radisson White Sands Resort** (© 0832/272-7272) at

Varca Beach. Note that all of these resorts are very child-friendly, often with separate pools and activities, and babysitters are always available.

The southernmost beach of Palolem is one of the last areas of south Goa that is free of resorts; here you'll have to venture back to nature at one of many budget options, or cozy up at the wonderful **Bhakti Kutir** eco-resort, reviewed below. Even if you've just come for the day, dine at **Aahar,** where you're served delicious organic health food under a giant cloth draped from the surrounding trees—try the dal and red spinach, served with organic rice, coconut chutney, and fresh, nutty hummus. The fish curry is light and not too spicy, made with coconut gravy and served with coconut chutney. The salad is made with sprouts, steamed spinach, and toasted nuts and seeds marinated with tofu, and is served with homemade whole-wheat, rice-bread, or millet crackers.

Bhakti Kutir ✿ *(Value)*   This is by far Palolem's most atmospheric and comfortable option, though don't expect any real luxury. It's the brainchild of Panta Ferrao, a Goan lawyer who (aided by his German wife) dropped out to start an ecologically sensitive resort that would empower local people with skills and provide comfortable accommodations in a fantastic location. Bhakti Kutir offers a selection of lime-plastered bamboo "cottages" made entirely from natural materials, with en-suite ablution facilities—squat toilets (organic, of course) and bucket showers. Windows are ingeniously crafted from seashells, while the cushions, fabrics, beds, and even mattresses (some comfortable, others hard) are all made by locals. Try to book room no. 6, which is built on different levels; no. 8, a double-story unit with an upstairs balcony; or the "stone house" (built with Panta's German in-laws in mind) with more traditionally Western facilities (like a toilet). Come prepared for mosquitoes, dark pathways, and plenty of back-to-nature experiences. Set a short distance from the beach, the resort features a health-conscious restaurant, a bar serving beer and wine, and an assortment of esoteric activities like Ayurvedic treatments, yoga, and meditation. Workshops and cooking classes are also held for those wishing to extend their knowledge of local culture. It's very popular, so reserve well in advance.

Palolem. ✆ **0832/264-3460.** bhaktikutir@yahoo.com. 40 units. Doubles (Dec 15–Jan 15): Rs 3,000 ($65) stone house; Rs 1,200–Rs 1,250 ($26–$27) cabana; Rs 2,000–Rs 2,500 ($44–$55) 2-bedroom cabana; Rs 350 ($7.60) off-season discount; rates are flexible. No credit cards. **Amenities:** Restaurant; bar; amphitheater; Ayurvedic and healing center, massage, yoga, meditation, mud baths, cooling baths; pool table; airport transfers; boutique; babysitting; laundry; kitchen; tailor. *In room:* Mosquito net.

The Kenilworth Beach Resort ✿   A charming hotel with an immaculate beach, this also boasts Goa's largest swimming pool—a split-level work of liquid art surrounded by beautiful Rajasthani tiles. The enormous pool occupies most of the area between the salmon-pink doubloon-style hotel building and peaceful Utorda Beach. All guest rooms enjoy either full or partial views of the pool and the beach from their private, enclosed balconies—it's worth requesting one with a full beach view. Offering good service, and all the amenities you could want from a beach resort, the Kenilworth received a complete overhaul and refurbishment after its acquisition by new owners.

Utorda, P.O. Marjorda, Salcete, Goa 403 713. ✆ **0832/275-4180.** Fax 0832/275-4183. www.kenilworth hotels.com. kenilworthgoa@kenilworthhotels.com. 91 units. Doubles (Jan 3–Apr 15/Apr 16–Oct 31/Nov 1– Dec 22/Dec 23–Dec 28/Dec 29–Jan 2): $118/$78/$123/$188/$223 superior; $124/$88/$138/$203/$238 deluxe. AE, DC, MC, V. **Amenities:** 4 restaurants; 2 bars; patisserie; ice-cream parlor; pool; putting green; minigolf; 2 tennis courts; health club; Jacuzzi; sauna; Ayurvedic spa; watersports; card room; pool table; video games; travel desk, airport transfers; business center; foreign exchange; conferencing; 24-hr. room service; babysitting (24-hr. notice); laundry; library. *In room:* A/C, TV, minibar, tea- and coffee-making facilities.

The Leela ★★   Spectacularly positioned on the edge of the bleached-white sands of a near-private stretch of beach with scattered coconut palms, the resort—fashioned after the palaces of the great 14th-century Hindu kingdom of Vijayanagar—straddles the slender Mobor peninsula where the Sal River flows into the sea. It was recently refurbished and is under new management. Most of the accommodations are now in expansive "lagoon" suites, all with views overlooking the lagoon—an unfortunate use of the superb location. No doubt you'd much rather face the Arabian Sea (as you can at nearly all accommodations at the Taj Exotica do; see below).

Cavelossim, Mobor, Goa 403 731. © **0832/287-1234.** Fax 0832/287-1352. www.ghmhotels.com. 137 units. Doubles (Apr 1–Sept 30/Oct 1–Dec 27/Dec 28–Jan 2/Jan 3–Mar 31): $130/$260/$350/$260 pavilion room; $210/$400/$580/$400 lagoon suite; $275/$475/$750/$475 lagoon deluxe suite; $500/$950/$1,650/$950 royal villa; $1,300/$1,800/$2,750/$1,800 presidential villa. AE, MC, V. **Amenities:** 4 restaurants; 4 bars; pool; children's pool; 9-hole golf course; tennis courts; health club; Ayurvedic spa; watersports; children's activity center; travel desk; airport transfers; casino; shopping arcade; salon; 24-hr. room service; laundry; dry cleaning; doctor-on-call; valet. *In room:* A/C, TV, VCR, hi-fi with CD player, dataport, tea- and coffee-making facilities, hair dryer.

Taj Exotica Goa ★★   Packing much the same punch as the Leela, this resort features lovely surrounds (18 hectares/46 acres of landscaped gardens with 36 varieties of hibiscus trees), great accommodations, warm service, and a kick-ass beach that might as well be private. It's more affordable than the Leela, however, and even the cheapest "deluxe" guest rooms are spacious, with large picture windows and private patios or balconies. Ask for one on the ground floor—these are accessed via their own garden area. The private villas are ideal if you don't want to be in the main block, which looks something like a large Portuguese hacienda—specify a "sunset villa" for a sea view (the cheaper villas have garden views). Another good reason to book here is **Alegria,** where the most delicious home-cooked Goan, Portuguese, and Hindu Goan Saraswat meals are prepared by Goa's only female executive chef, Julia de Sa. Mainstay dishes include *komdechem lomin* (gently spiced grilled chicken), *sungtachi koddi* (prawns in a fragrant gravy of coconut milk and mild spices), *galinha cafreal* (chicken in garlic, fresh coriander, and ginger), and authentic Goan *sorpotel* (a spicy pork stew). Upstairs at **Miguel Arcanjo** is where de Sa prepares the best pizza in Goa.

Calwaddo, Benaulim, Salcete, Goa 403 716. © **0832/277-1234.** Fax 0832/277-1515. www.tajhotels.com. exotica.goa@tajhotels.com. 140 units. Doubles (Oct 1–Apr 15/Apr 16–Sept 30/Dec 23–Jan 1): $180/$110/$290 deluxe room; $190/$120/$310 villa room; $220/$135/$350 sunset villa room; $250/$150/$400 luxury room; $400/$250/$500 luxury suite; $20 extra bed. AE, MC, V. **Amenities:** 5 restaurants; 4 bars; pool with Jacuzzi; kids' pool; 9-hole pitch and putt golf course; 2 tennis courts; beach volleyball; jogging track; table tennis; pool tables; watersports; fitness center, Ayurvedic treatments, yoga, aerobics; children's activity center; travel desk, car rental; airport transfers; helipad; shop; salon; 24-hr. room service; babysitting; doctor-on-call. *In room:* A/C, TV, minibar, tea- and coffee-making facilities, hair dryer.

5

God's Own Country:
Kerala & Lakshadweep

The god who made Kerala, according to a popular Malayali saying, had a green thumb. Indeed, India's most verdant state—rated by *National Geographic Traveler* as one of the world's 50 must-see destinations—is a paradisiacal landscape of palm-lined beaches, steamy jungles, plantation-covered hills, and tropical rivers and lakes. Visitors come here primarily to unwind and indulge; this is, after all, where succumbing to a therapeutic Ayurvedic massage is as mandatory as idling away an afternoon aboard a slowly drifting *kettuvallam,* or sipping coconut juice under a tropical sun before taking in a wonderfully ritualized Kathakali dance. Eastward, the spice-scented Cardamom Hills and wild elephants of Periyar beckon, while a short flight west takes you to the little-known but sublime tropical reefs off the Lakshadweep islands. All of which make Kerala not just a must-see on your India itinerary, but a major destination in its own right.

A thin strip on the southwest coastline, sandwiched between the Lakshadweep Sea and the forested Western Ghats that define its border with Tamil Nadu to the east, Kerala covers a mere 1.3% of the country's total land area, yet its rich resources have long attracted visitors from across the oceans—it is in fact here that the first seafarers set foot on Indian soil. Legend has it that King Solomon's ships traded off the Malabar coast between 972 and 932 B.C., followed by the Phoenicians, Romans, Christians, Arabs, and Chinese, all of whom came to stock up on Malabar's monkeys, tigers, parrots, timber, and, of course, the abundance of spices that were literally worth their weight in gold. Seafarers not only brought trade but built synagogues and churches in the emerging port cities, while an entirely Muslim population set up shop on the islands of Lakshadweep. Despite its religious cosmopolitanism (many locals will tell you they subscribe to both Hinduism and Christianity), Kerala's Hindu tradition is deeply engrained in daily life. Most temples do not permit non-Hindus to enter, but almost every month brings magnificent temple processions involving chanting devotees and squadrons of elephants adorned in flamboyant caparisons.

Contemporary Kerala was created in 1956 from the former princely states of Travancore, Kochi, and Malabar. Largely ruled by benevolent maharajas who introduced social reforms emphasizing the provision of education and basic services, Kerala remains one of the most progressive, literate, and educated states in post-independence India. In 1957, it became the first place in the world to democratically elect a Communist government, and the first Indian state to introduce a family-planning program. Despite its high population density, Keralites have the country's highest life expectancy and the lowest

Ayurveda: Kerala's Healing Balm

An ancient healing tradition that draws on 3,000 years of Vedic culture, Ayurveda is the subcontinent's traditional science of "life, vitality, health, and longevity" or, to tap into a more contemporary buzzphrase, "the science of well-being." Kerala has long been considered the home of Ayurveda, no doubt due to the abundance of herbal and medicinal plants that thrive in its tropical environment. You will find therapists, physicians, and commercial Ayurvedic shops selling roots, herbs, and bark throughout the state.

Renowned for its curative and rejuvenating powers (and a gift from no other than Lord Brahma), Ayurveda works on your physical, mental, and emotional well-being by rectifying any imbalances in the three *doshas*—*vata* (air), *pitta* (fire), and *kapha* (water)—that are believed to make up the human constitution. In fact, in one ancient tome on Ayurveda, the *Caraka Samhita*, it is stated that the mind, body, and soul are like a tripod, and that the world's continued existence relies on their combination.

It takes 5½ years of training to qualify as an Ayurvedic doctor, who is then able to prescribe the herbal remedies and related therapies. While much of what is practiced in Ayurvedic medicine has similarities to Western medical practice (the first 3 years of training in anatomy are basically the same), the most significant difference lies in the area of pharmacology, since Ayurvedic medicines are all natural. Some may scoff, but no one can deny the sheer pleasure of the treatments—Ayurveda will suit those skeptics who merely seek the ultimate in pampering, whether you opt for a soothing facial treatment, where the face is massaged and steamed with herbal oils, or for an energizing full body massage performed with hands and feet (and often by several masseuses simultaneously). Skeptics take note: To truly experience the strange bliss and resultant high of Ayurveda, book a *sirodhara* treatment, wherein 5 to 6 liters of warm herbal oil (selected according to the body constitution) are poured steadily onto your "third eye" (the forehead) for the better part of an hour while (or after which) you are massaged—this is said to retard the aging process (by arresting the degeneration of cells) and to relieve the body of all stress.

No matter which balm you choose, you'll find that the well-practiced masseuses of Kerala will treat your body like a temple; for them, the massage or treatment is a spiritual exercise. Of course, it helps to know that your body is being worshipped when you're lying there in your birthday suit (note that in strict accordance with Indian piety, you will be assigned a same-sex therapist). Whatever its purported virtues and pleasures, Ayurveda lures thousands of Westerners to Kerala, which in turn sustains a thriving industry that puts food on the table for many people. For our selection of the best Ayurvedic resorts, see chapter 1.

infant mortality rates. Kerala is considered one of the cleanest and most peaceful parts of India, a claim substantiated by its prosperity—the state remains a major source of India's bananas, rubber, coconuts, cashews, and ginger. While much of Kerala retains an untouched charm, this prosperity has a downside: A highly educated population has meant that many are unwilling to do menial jobs, creating extensive unemployment. Others head for the Gulf to seek their fortunes, returning with sufficient cash to tear down the traditional carved wood dwellings that so greatly characterize the region and replace them with "modern" status symbols. Many of these traditional homes have been bought and reassembled in top-notch resorts like Coconut Lagoon and Surya Samudra, a practice vilified as exploitative by Kerala native Arundhati Roy in her Booker Prize–winning *The God of Small Things*. Others applaud their preservation, and for visitors a stay in these *tharavadu* cottages is one of the most charming aspects of a trip to Kerala.

If you're interested in ancient history and grand temples, you'll need to include a visit to neighboring Tamil Nadu or Karnataka, but if all you need is to rejuvenate, head straight for Fort Cochin, then head south to cruise the backwaters and wash up on some of the world's most beautiful beaches. "God's Own Country" is one tourist slogan that really does deliver.

1 Cochin (Kochi)

1,080km (670 miles) S of Mumbai

Cochin is not the capital of Kerala, but it is its most charming city, blessed with its own international airport and a relatively good infrastructure, making it the ideal gateway to the state. This has been the case since 1341, the year nature carved out Cochin's harbor with a massive flood. As a result, Cochin became the first port of call for Arabs, Chinese and, finally, European sea merchants, who sailed for barter into what came to be known as the "Queen of the Arabian Sea."

Lured by the promise of pepper, the Portuguese under Vasco da Gama arrived in 1500, and the Franciscan friars who accompanied the explorer Pedro Alvarez Cabral established a church and set about converting the locals. By 1553, the Maharajah of Cochin had granted permission for the construction of the first European fort in India, and what had been an obscure fishing hamlet became India's first European settlement. In 1663, Cochin fell to the Dutch, and then to the British in 1795. Each of these foreign influences left their mark, resulting in a distinctly Indo-European culture, most evident in the architecture.

Today, Cochin (or Kochi, as it has been renamed) comprises three distinct areas. Down at heel, but wonderfully atmospheric, the historic districts of Mattancherry and Fort Cochin lie on one of two peninsular arms that shield the Kochi harbor—this is where you should try to find accommodations and spend most of your time. Opposite it, on the mainland that creates the eastern peninsula, lies modern Ernakulam, and in between, the islands, well connected to the mainland by bridges.

Fort Cochin, the oldest European settlement in India, retains an old-world charm; its battlements no longer stand, but the combination of Portuguese, Dutch, British, and local influences is evident in the tiled, steep-roofed bungalows that line its quaint streets. Fort Cochin's oldest section, still referred to as Jew Town, is home to the oldest synagogue in the Commonwealth. Plan to spend at least 2 nights in Cochin, enjoying its charming atmosphere and low-key sights at

Kerala

a lazy, relaxed pace. Take in a Kathakali performance, enjoy a romantic sunset cruise around the harbor and, if you're at all interested in antiques bargains, get ready to wade through stores packed with unexpected curiosities.

ESSENTIALS

VISITOR INFORMATION   Kerala has perhaps the best tourism bureaus in India, and Cochin is no exception. In Ernakulam and on Willingdon Island, you will find the surprisingly helpful **Kerala Tourism Development Corporation** (**KTDC,** Shanmugham Rd., Ernakulam; © **0484/235-3234;** Willingdon Island branch is near the Taj Malabar Hotel). The best one-stop shop is probably the privately run **Tourist Desk Information Counter** (© **0484/237-1761**), located at Ernakulam's Main Boat Jetty. Be sure to pick up *Hello Cochin,* a free booklet published every couple of months and filled with useful contacts and information. If you're traveling farther afield and need general information, visit the **Government of India Tourist Office** (Malabar Rd., Willingdon Island; © **0484/266-8352;** Mon–Fri 9am–5:30pm, Sat 9am–1pm). A **Tourism Information Counter** (© **0484/261-0113,** ext. 2105) at the airport is usually open for all arrivals.

GETTING THERE & AWAY   By Air   Kochi International Airport (© **0484/ 261-0115** or -0116, or 0484/261-0126) is one of India's best. It's located alongside National Highway 47, in Nedumbassery, which is 42km (26 miles) from the historic heart of Fort Cochin. There are flights to and from Mumbai, Delhi, Chennai, Goa, Lakshadweep, Kozhikode, Tiruchirappalli, Thiruvananthapuram, and Bangalore; international flights are mostly through the Middle East, with flights also arriving from Singapore, the Maldives, and Sri Lanka.

A prepaid taxi service into the city is available at the airport; transfers to Fort Cochin cost between Rs 400 and Rs 500 ($9 and $11). **Air Dash Travel Services** (Mather Sq.; © **0484/236-2309** or 98/4607-5277) operate a round-the-clock share-taxi service between the city and the airport; you can also arrange to be picked up from your hotel.

By Train   Cochin is well connected by rail to almost every part of India. Some of the journeys can be long and grueling, however, so check on times, or opt for train travel only within Kerala. Departing from Delhi, the **Trivandrum Rajdhani Express** makes its way to Calicut, Cochin, and Trivandrum; this is one of the best connections in Kerala—much of the journey involves the scenic Konkan Railway.

Cochin has three principal railway stations: **Ernakulam Town Station** (© **0484/235-3920**), **Ernakulam Junction** (© **131** or 132, which are also the numbers to call for general train information), and Willingdon Island's **Cochin Harbour Railway Station** (© **0484/266-6050**). The **computerized reservations office** is at the Junction Railway Station (open Mon–Sat 8am–2pm and 2:15–8pm; Sun 8am–2pm).

By Road   Traveling around Kerala with a rented car and driver can be wonderful and exhilarating; there's plenty of natural beauty worth taking in. Compared with roads in other parts of India, Kerala's roads are in good shape. North of Cochin, the coast-hugging National Highway 17 passes through Calicut and runs all the way to Mangalore in Karnataka. Traveling south between Cochin and the capital Trivandrum (a 6-hr. journey), the NH 47 has been resurfaced in recent years, and the highway really spreads out for the popular segment between Cochin and the backwater town of Alleppey. For journeys between

Tamil Nadu and Kerala, you can expect long but beautiful stretches along the NH 47, which traverses hairpin mountain passes. Private and state buses connect Cochin with many cities and towns throughout South India; these provide something bordering on a theme-park experience, however, and have a reputation for thrill-ride speeds.

GETTING AROUND   By Taxi & Auto-Rickshaw   Speak to your hotel management about the most up-to-date rates. For the most part, it's best to negotiate a mutually agreeable fare before starting off; auto-rickshaws should charge around Rs 6 (13¢) for the first kilometer, with the rate dropping to Rs 2 (2¢) for each additional kilometer. For longer journeys, you'll be asked to pay for the return trip. Many auto-rickshaws will refuse to travel between Ernakulam and Fort Cochin; some even pretend they've never heard of it. Taxicabs are reasonable, charging around double the auto-rickshaw rates: A one-way trip between Fort Cochin and Ernakulam should cost in the region of Rs 175 ($4).

Note that the New Mattancherry Bridge between Fort Cochin and Willingdon, built in 2001, charges a tiny toll for cars, jeeps, and vans.

By Ferry   The ferry is a quick, convenient, and cheap way to get between any of Kochi's main areas and to travel to any of the islands. Ernakulam's two most important jetties are the **Main Jetty** off Fore Shore Road, for services to Willingdon Island (about 15 min.), Fort Cochin (about 30 min.), and Vypeen; and **High Court Jetty** off Shanmugham Road, from which you can get to Bolgatty Island. Ferry services begin at 6am and continue until 9:30pm; fares are nominal.

GUIDED TOURS   Kerala Tourism Development Corporation (KTDC, Shanmugham Rd., Ernakulam; © **0484/235-3234**) and the privately run **Tourist Desk** (Main Boat Jetty, Ernakulam; © **0484/237-1761**) offer half-day boat cruises of Cochin as well as daily tours and longer *kettuvallam* houseboat cruises of the backwaters near Cochin. **Sita Travels** (Tharakan Building, M.G. Rd., Ravipuram, Ernakulam; © **0484/236-3801;** cok@sitaincoming.com) is useful for private tours of the entire state; they can also help with booking arrangements. You can also tailor splendid packages to destinations all over Kerala through **Cox & Kings** (www.coxandkings.co.uk). The same company can arrange tours by train or with car and driver, as well as trips of varying duration on Kerala's famous backwater houseboats. The **Kerala Tourism Development Corporation Limited** (KTDC) offers a wide range of tours and packages to suit different budgets, but be aware that most of these will include accommodations at state-run hotels, which are of varying standards. For details and bookings, contact their central reservations in Trivandrum, the capital (Mascot Sq.; © **0471/231-6736;** fax 0471/231-4406; www.ktdc.com; ktdc@vsnl.com; open Mon–Sat 8am–8pm, Sun and public holidays 10am–4pm).

If you're keen to do your own deep-sea fishing off the Malabar Coast, contact **TourIndia** (31/670 Narayani Nivas, Sahodaran Ayyappan Rd., Vyttila, Kochi; © **0484/238-9862;** fax 0484/238-9029; tourindiakochi@eth.net). This innovative company introduced marine sports fishing to the area, and takes clients out in canopied twin-engine boats modeled on traditional fishing boats. All fishing gear is provided.

WHEN TO GO   The best time to visit Kerala is between mid-October and April, with December and January the most pleasant months, though many resorts charge accordingly, some even doubling their rates. The backwaters are best visited from mid-November to February, when the muggy heat and mosquitoes are less bothersome. From about August to May, caparisoned elephants take to the streets in spectacular festivals; by far the biggest festival takes place in April in Thrissur (Trichur), 74km (46 miles) north of Cochin. Contact the tour offices in Cochin (from where you can reach almost any of the festivals) for exact dates.

FAST FACTS: Cochin

Airlines For the **Jet Airways city office** (B.A.B. Chambers, Atlantis Junction, M.G. Rd., Ravipuram, Ernakulam), call ℂ **0484/236-9423** or -9212; for the **airport counter,** call ℂ **0484/261-0037** or -0038. The **Indian Airlines city office** (Durbar Hall Rd., Ernakulam; ℂ **0484/235-2065**) is open daily 10am to 5pm; or call the **airport** (ℂ **0484/261-0101** or 0484/261-0041).

Ambulance Dial **101.**

Area Code The area code for **Cochin** is ℂ **0484.**

ATMs Always the best way to get instant cash in Indian cities. Cochin now has several ATMs where you can use your Visa or MasterCard, if it has been encoded in your home country.

Banks See "Currency Exchange," below.

Bookstores Both branches of **Idiom Books** are wonderful for a wide variety of books on India, its culture, and its literature. In Fort Cochin, the store is at the corner of Bastion and Quirose streets, and is open Monday to Saturday noon to 9pm. In Mattancherry, it's opposite the Pardesi Synagogue, and is open daily 10am to 6pm.

Car Hires/Taxis On average, you can expect to pay around Rs 5 to Rs 10 (10¢–20¢) per kilometer for a car and driver; more expensive cars will include air-conditioning, which will prove invaluable in Kerala's sultry climate. Also count on paying a small overnight fee for each stopover. The **Government of India Tourist Office** (Malabar Rd., Willingdon Island; ℂ **0484/266-8352**; Mon–Fri 9am–5:30pm, Sat 9am–1pm) has a fleet of vehicles. Also try: **Sita Travels** (Tharakan Building, M.G. Rd., Ernakulam; ℂ **0484/236-1101**) and the **Great India Tour Company** (Pithura Smarana, 1st Floor, Srikandath Rd., Ravipuram, Cochin; ℂ **0484/237-4109**). The city **taxi stand** (ℂ **0484/ 222-9020**) is situated near the Corporation Office.

Currency Exchange Your best option is **Thomas Cook** (M.G. Rd., Ernakulam; ℂ **0484/236-9729**; Mon–Sat 9:30am–6pm), which also has a branch at the airport (ℂ **0484/261-0052**). **Canara Bank** in Fort Cochin (Kunnumpuram Junction, T.M. Mohammed Rd.; ℂ **0484/222-4812**; Mon–Fri 10am–2pm, Sat 10am–noon) can exchange traveler's checks and give cash advances against your credit card. Also try **ANZ Grindlays** (M.G. Rd., Ernakulam; ℂ **0484/ 237-2086**).

Drugstores **Jeny Medicals** (corner of T.M. Mohammed and Bastion roads, Kunnumpuram Junction, Fort Cochin; ℂ **0484/222-4253**) is open from 8:15am to 10pm. In Ernakulam, the pharmacy at **Medical Trust Hospital** (M.G. Rd.; ℂ **0484/237-1852**) is open around the clock.

Emergencies For fires and other emergencies, including medical services, call **101.**

Hospitals In Ernakulam, head for **Medical Trust Hospital** (M.G. Rd.; © 0484/237-1852) or **Lissy Hospital** (Lissy Junction; © 0484/235-2006). If you have a medical emergency in Fort Cochin, your hotel should be able to organize good medical assistance.

Internet Access Cochin has plenty of Internet cafes, and these generally charge more than any of the options in Ernakulam. **Call'n'Fax/Shop'n'Save** (Princess St.; © 0484/222-3438; Mon–Sat 8am–11pm, Sun 5–11pm) charges Rs 60 ($1.25) per hour.

Police Dial © **100.**

Post Office In Ernakulam, use the **General Post Office** (Hospital Rd.; © 0484/222-4661; Mon–Fri 8:30am–8pm, Sat 9:30am–8pm, Sun 10am–5pm). **Kochi Head Post Office** in Fort Cochin is open Monday to Saturday 9am to 5pm.

Website Visit **www.keralatourism.org** for up-to-date information.

WHAT TO SEE & DO

Lazy and laid-back, Fort Cochin offers a tranquillity that is in complete contrast to the heaving city experience of Ernakulam, which is ultimately missable. Comprising **Mattancherry** and **Jew Town,** Fort Cochin has a historic atmosphere—in a town where 14 different languages are spoken, tumbled-down mansions line narrow ancient lanes. Near the water's edge, old warehouses (or *godowns*) are filled with the state's treasured cash crops—pepper, tea, Ayurvedic roots, whole ginger, and betel nuts—being dried, sorted, and prepared for direct sale or auction. The area is wonderful for historic walks, particularly into Jew Town, which hosts a community that dates back to the 1st century A.D. and was augmented during the 16th century when the Inquisition brought a fresh wave of Jewish immigrants here. Today only a handful of aging "white Jewish" families remain in Cochin, but their residential quarter retains a charming ambience, with cobbled streets and fascinating antiques shops and spice markets.

The man-made **Willingdon Island,** a short ferry ride or bridge journey away, was created in the 20th century by large-scale dredging. There are several good hotels here, but the island is primarily concerned with naval and commercial port activity and is not worth visiting unless you're based here. **Bolgatty Island,** reached by ferry, is of no interest other than the rather lovely palace, which has been converted into a government-run hotel.

EXPLORING FORT COCHIN ON FOOT

Start your tour at the harbor near Vasco da Gama Square, where you can watch fishermen hoisting their catch from the cantilevered **Chinese fishing nets** that line the shore, then head along Church Road to **St. Francis Church.** Keep going toward Parade Road (near the Malabar House Residency; see "Where to Stay," below), making your way to **Peter Celli Street** to explore a few local shops before you drift down Bastion Street, in the direction of **Santa Cruz Cathedral.** Then head back toward Princess Street, where you can see **Koder House.** Built in 1808 by Jewish patriarch Samuel Koder, this is a good example of the hybrid Indo-European style that developed in Cochin. It's still occupied, so you'll have to appreciate it from the sidewalk. In the same road, the **Pierce Leslie Bungalow** is a charming 19th-century mansion reflecting Portuguese and Dutch influences on local architecture. Take a break at **Kashi Art Café** (Burgher St.; ✆ **0484/276-9215**), where the food and service are uninspired but the contemporary art and vibrant atmosphere provide a colorful contrast to the historic surroundings. Afterward, catch an auto-rickshaw to Mattancherry, where you should visit the **Dutch Palace** and the **Paradesi Synagogue** (see below) before discovering the fragrant scents of Kerala's **spice warehouses.** Make time to visit a few of the antiques warehouses, and don't be put off by the layers of dust and grime—there are some real treasures to be found. End your day full circle with a **sunset cruise** ✸✸✸ around the harbor; this is the best way to enjoy the most-photographed of Cochin's historic sights, the Chinese fishing nets that form wonderful silhouettes against a red- and orange-hued sky.

Chinese Fishing Nets ✸✸✸   Said to have been introduced by traders from the court of Kublai Khan, these cantilevered nets, set up on teak and bamboo poles, are physical remnants of Fort Cochin's ancient trade with the Far East. Fishermen work the nets all day long, lowering them into the water and then hauling them up using a remarkably efficient pulley system. The best place to watch them at work is from **Vasco da Gama Square** or from a boat at sunset. Nearby, the Indo-European **Bastion Bungalow** (now the official residence of the Sub Collector) dates back to 1667; built on the site of the old Dutch Fort's Stromberg Bastion, it is believed to stand above a network of secret tunnels.

Vasco da Gama Sq. is on the water's edge along River Rd.

Mattancherry Palace ✸✸   Also known as the Dutch Palace, this large two-story 16th-century building was actually built by the Portuguese, who gave it to the Raja of Cochin as thanks for trading rights and favors granted to them. When the Dutch claimed Cochin in 1663, they took control of the palace and gave it a makeover. The large two-story building has sloping roofs and pale walls, and is a shadow of what it must have once been. Part of it is open to visitors, and displays include a collection of coronation robes, palanquins, and royal family portraits. Don't miss the bedroom chamber where vibrant murals executed in vivid red, green, and yellow ochre are the main attraction. Particularly notable are erotic scenes of the divine lover, Krishna, surrounded by enraptured female figures. Vishnu, Shiva, and various Hindu deities fill the large walls, their eyes wide and bodies full; these are among the first examples of a school of painting specific to Kerala.

Palace Rd., Mattancherry. Admission Rs 2 (2¢). Sat–Thurs 10am–5pm.

Paradesi Synagogue ✸✸✸   Cochin's first Jewish settlers arrived from Yemen and Babylon as early as A.D. 52; this—the oldest synagogue in the Commonwealth—was originally built 1,500 years later. Set in a corner of Jew Town and rather hemmed in by other buildings, with only the 18th-century clock-tower visible from the outside, it now supports just a handful of Jewish families; many migrated to Israel over the years. Inside, individually hand-painted blue and white Cantonese ceramic floor tiles are its most interesting feature. Above, glorious Belgian chandeliers dangle from the ceiling. At one end of the hall, old Torah scrolls are kept behind the gilded doors of the holy tabernacle.

At press time, only 18 Jews were still living in Cochin, belonging to a mere five families that uphold the traditions of their ancestors. This is not enough to form a *minyan* (the number of men needed to sustain a synagogue), so Jews from outlying areas travel to Cochin to worship in this historic Judaic monument.

The synagogue elders are understandably concerned about tourist numbers, and numerous signs warn that NO ONE IS ALLOWED UPSTAIRS, NO ONE IS ALLOWED INSIDE THE PULPIT, and NO ONE IS ALLOWED TO TOUCH ANYTHING.

Jew Town Rd., Mattancherry. Admission Rs 2 (2¢). Sun–Fri 10am–noon and 3–5pm; closed for Jewish holidays.

St. Francis Church ★★   India's earliest European church was originally constructed in wood, but this was replaced by a stone structure in 1546. It was also originally Roman Catholic, but under the British it became Anglican. Vasco da Gama was originally buried here when he died in Cochin on Christmas Eve, 1524; although his body was later moved to Lisbon, he is still memorialized here with a tombstone. Having passed through the hands of Franciscan friars, Dutch Protestants, and Anglicans, the presiding Church of South India continues to hold its services here every morning at 8am. Note that, as with Hindu temples and Muslim mosques, you are required to remove your shoes before entering.

Church St., Fort Cochin. Mon–Sat, sunrise–sunset.

Santa Cruz Basilica ★   Pope Paul IV elevated this Portuguese church to a cathedral in 1558, but the original building was destroyed by the British in 1795. A new building was commissioned on the same site in 1887; it was declared a basilica in 1984 by Pope John Paul II.

Parade Rd. and K.B. Jacob Rd., near Bastion St., Fort Cochin. Daily, sunrise–sunset.

WHERE TO STAY

The best area to stay is Fort Cochin. Alternatively, opt for Willingdon Island, just across the bay. Ernakulam is a busy, rather ugly city but has more affordable accommodations options, and Fort Cochin is a short, pleasant ferry journey away. *A general note of caution:* If you plan to be in Cochin in December or January, be sure to book well in advance.

If you don't mind being quite far from the ambience of Fort Cochin and the harbor, a truly upscale option is the new **Le Meridien** (NH 47 Bypass, Kundannur Junction, Kochi 682 304; © **0484/270-5777** or -5451). Guests have access to a superb range of resort facilities and services, including a top-rated Ayurvedic spa—check it out on www.lemeridien-hotels.com.

Note: The prices below are sometimes given in rupees, with U.S. dollar conversions; others are in U.S. dollars only, which is how many hotels targeting foreign markets quote their rates.

Black Gold

In Kerala, pepper is still referred to as *karuthu ponnu,* or "black gold," and represents the backbone of the state's international spice trade. Although the furious trade around spices has subsided considerably these days, the sorting houses, warehouses, and auction houses from which these valuable products find their way to the rest of the world still operate in much the same way they have for centuries (though given the current crises surrounding many of the traditional cash crops, there is a possibility that these side-street sights will not be around forever). Ask your guide or auto-rickshaw driver to take you to the ginger, black pepper, betel nut, and Ayurvedic medicine warehouses; or head for the **Kochi International Pepper Exchange** (Jew Town Rd., Mattancherry), which you can visit from Monday to Saturday to see Kerala's black gold being furiously sold off to the highest bidder. Call © **0484/222-4263** to organize a pass.

FORT COCHIN

If you're on a budget, consider **Spencer's Tourist Home** (Parade St.; (C) **0484/222-5049**), which has rooms with attached bathrooms for as little as Rs 200 ($4.30). Located in a lovely old house with a shared sitting room and a garden, its guest rooms are clean and spacious, and the beds are comfortable.

The Brunton Boatyard Hotel ☆☆☆
Situated at the water's edge on the site of a bustling boatyard, this is considered by many to be Fort Cochin's most elegant hotel. A smart whitewashed colonial warehouse-style building with sloping tiled roofs, deep verandas, and terra-cotta floors set around a large open grassy courtyard, Brunton captures the gracious ambience of a bygone era. An open-plan lobby—decked out with a billiards table, antique furniture, and overhead *punkha* fans—spills into spacious passages that lead to the guest rooms, all of which overlook the busy harbor. Each room has its own balcony from which to enjoy views of the fishing boats and ferries that cruise between the islands; those on the second floor are better for views. Original and reproduction antiques include typical Keralan four-poster beds, high enough off the ground to make the footstools a necessity. A sunset cruise from the hotel's own jetty is a great way to kick off the evening. The only possible drawback to staying here is the hotel's proximity to the boatyard—you are literally berthed only steps from the very active waterways, though others may argue that the low-level soundtrack lends an air of authenticity.

1/498 Fort Cochin, Kochi 682 001. (C) **0484/221-5461**, -5462, -5463, -5464, or –5465, or 0484/221-5557. Fax 0484/221-5562. brunton@vsnl.net. Reservations: Casino Hotel, Willingdon Island, Kochi 682 003. (C) 0484/266-8221 or -8421. Fax 0484/266-8001. www.casinogroup.com. 26 units. Doubles: $180 sea-facing room, $190 Dec 21–Jan 20; $250 deluxe suite; $30 extra person. Rates include breakfast. AE, DC, MC, V. **Amenities:** 3 restaurants; bar; tea lounge; pool; Ayurvedic center; sunset cruise; boat rental; car hires; business facilities; shop; room service; laundry; doctor-on-call; pharmacy service. *In room:* A/C, TV, minibar, hair dryer. Suites include personal butler, kitchenette, electronic safe.

Fort Heritage
This small heritage hotel, built by the Dutch East India Company in 1668, features huge, airy, simple guest rooms. The rooms have teak ceilings and floors and both traditional and antique furniture, as well as attached bathrooms and modern amenities. Ask for an upstairs room, preferably with air-conditioning and a private balcony. There are two double suites in a newer building, but avoid these—they lack atmosphere and are rather dowdy. After a full day of sightseeing, you can return for a wonderful Ayurvedic massage and steam bath, or relax in the lovely upstairs lounge, where there's a romantic swing and chaise lounge in which you can curl up with a book from the small library. Fresh, local seafood is served in the **Heritage Zone** restaurant. Service is patchy, but the rates are great.

1/283 Napier St., Elphinstone Rd., Fort Cochin 682 001. (C) **0484/221-5333**, -6901, or -5455. Fax 0484/221-5333. www.fortheritage.com. 12 units. Doubles: $65 heritage room; $95 A/C deluxe suite; $10 extra bed. Rates include breakfast and taxes. AE, DC, MC, V. **Amenities:** Restaurant; steam; travel assistance; sightseeing arrangements; car hires; Ayurvedic massage; laundry; doctor-on-call. *In room:* TV. A/C in some rooms.

Malabar House Residency ☆☆☆
Bright, vibrant colors infuse this 18th-century mansion with a contemporary edge, creating a boutique hotel that is charmingly arty without being pretentious. Conceived, converted, and run by Joerg Drechsel and his Basque wife, Txuku, Malabar House is a chunky white colonial British bungalow at the edge of the Parade Maiden, a grassy expanse for schoolboy cricketers and frolicking goats. Its *tharavadu*-style sloping terra-cotta roof is typically Keralan, while the tropical inner courtyard (trees, potted shrubs,

and stone pathways) features a lovely plunge pool, wooden foldaway chairs, a small open-air theater area, and a covered restaurant. Rooms feature waxed black Kadapa stone floors offset by bright red or yellow walls and, in some rooms, a hint of turquoise. Each guest room contains a selection of paintings, sculptures, and period furniture reflecting the cultural heritage of Kerala, while the beds, solid in every sense, are made from carved teak and rosewood. Discarded pillars from traditional 18th-century Tamil Nadu houses up the atmosphere ante and dramatically enhance the use of space in the generous suites. Three of the (marginally more) expensive guest suites have private roof gardens—these are the best on offer; alternatively, book room no. 4. Although you don't have views of the harbor, this is a cheaper option than Brunton and scores high on privacy, class, and tranquillity.

1/268, 1/269 Parade Rd., Fort Cochin 682 001. ℂ 0484/221-6666. Fax 0484/221-7777. www.malabarhouse. com. 17 units. Doubles: $140 deluxe; $160 suite; $180 roof garden suite. Rates include breakfast. AE, DC, MC, V. **Amenities:** Restaurant; pool; Ayurvedic spa; bicycle rental; boat rental; airline bookings; car hires; currency exchange; boutique; salon; room service (6am–midnight); babysitting (with prior notice); laundry; doctor-on-call; tailor. *In room:* A/C, TV, mosquito net.

The Old Courtyard ⭐ *Value*   A recent overhaul and refurbishment has greatly improved this pleasant, intimate heritage hotel, located in the heart of Fort Cochin's quiet back streets. Each of the eight guest rooms in the 200-year-old Portuguese mansion is different, but all have wooden floors and high beamed ceilings, and most are furnished largely with antique furniture. The rooms are located in wings that lead off a central cobblestone courtyard, which has its own working well. Adjacent to the courtyard is a semi-enclosed restaurant serving a wide range of cuisines; traditional dances are performed here during the season. Accommodations are generally well-priced. Premium rooms and suites have lovely original Portuguese four-poster beds and large, clean bathrooms (the cheapest room is strictly for bargain-hunters). The hotel is the best lodging option in this price range, but then again, service is a drawback.

1/371–372 Princess St., Fort Cochin 682 001. ℂ 0484/221-6302. www.oldcourtyard.com. 8 units. Doubles: Rs 1,000 ($22) regular non-A/C; Rs 1,500 ($33) superior non-A/C; Rs 2,000 ($44) premium non-A/C; Rs 2,500 ($55) queen suite non-A/C; Rs 3,500 ($77) king suite non-A/C; Rs 3,000 ($66) premium A/C; Rs 350 ($7.60) extra bed; children under 12 free in parent's room. MC, V. **Amenities:** Restaurant; cultural performances; travel assistance; airport transfers; currency exchange; laundry; doctor-on-call; small library.

WILLINGDON ISLAND

A good option if those hotels below or in Fort Cochin are full is Willingdon's **Casino Hotel** (ℂ 0484/266-8221 or -8421; www.casinogroup.com; from $82 double). The name may set off alarm bells, suggesting as it does Las Vegas–style showgirls, but the atmosphere of this 1950s hotel is decidedly tame. The Casino has good facilities, staff are hospitable, and accommodations, though nothing to write home about, are clean, relatively spacious, and convenient—the nearest jetty for the harbor ferry to either Fort Cochin or Ernakulam is just over 1km (a half mile) away.

Taj Malabar ⭐⭐   A hostel built for those traveling by steamship from England is today the Heritage Wing of Willingdon's only waterfront hotel, an elegant property that includes a more contemporary (and less desirable) pagoda-style low-rise Tower Wing. Refurbished in 2001, the generously proportioned heritage rooms are the ones to book, and feature wood floors, period-style furniture, and assorted knick-knacks—no doubt plundered from the very "antiques" stores you may cruise in Fort Cochin. Make sure to book a heritage room with a view of the channel. A recent addition is the chic Ayurvedic center in the Tamara spa, which occupies its own traditional-style building overlooking the rather gorgeous rim-flow pool. Enjoy sunset drinks on the pool deck or one of the hotel's daily harbor cruises. Or—for those who prefer privacy—book the private yacht that's available for hire. Note that the Taj Malabar has two excellent restaurants (see "Where to Dine," below).

Willingdon Island, Cochin 682 009. ℃ 0484/266-6811 or -8010. Fax 0484/266-8297. www.tajhotels.com. malabar.cochin@tajhotels.com. 96 units. Doubles in Tower Wing: $140 harbor view; $170 sea view; $185 superior sunset view; $250 executive suite. Doubles in Heritage Wing: $160 superior; $185 sea view; $300 deluxe suite. AE, MC, V. **Amenities:** 4 restaurants; 2 bars; pool; gym; Jacuzzi; Ayurvedic center; boat rental; travel desk; sightseeing; car hires; business center; currency exchange; shop; 24-hr. room service; babysitting; laundry; doctor-on-call; valet service. *In room:* A/C, TV, minibar, tea- and coffee-making facility, hair dryer, electronic safe.

The Trident ⨁ This upmarket business hotel (owned by the Oberoi Group) is quiet, tasteful, and replete with modern conveniences. Conceived by a Thai architect, the design blends Keralan and Thai elements, and the hotel has the ambience of a large villa. Accommodations surround a pleasant courtyard where you can swim in the pool and dine alfresco. Traditional artifacts and ornaments have been used to capture the ethos of Kerala; wooden cooking implements and earthenware pots converted into lamps adorn the walls, while the entrance is dominated by a giant *urli* cooking pot mounted on old black and gold snake-boat prows. The modestly sized guest rooms have functional decor and furnishings; bathrooms are small with marble surfaces. Executive rooms include perks like breakfast, one-way airport transfers, free laundry service, and a free drink—which may or may not be useful, depending on how long you've been in India.

Bristow Rd., Willingdon Island, Cochin 682 003, Kerala. ℃ 0484/266-9595 or -6816. Fax 0484/266-9393. frontoffice@tridentcochin.com. 96 units. Doubles: $100 superior; $115 executive; $200 suite; $20 extra bed. AE, DC, MC, V. **Amenities:** Restaurant; bar; pool; exercise room; travel desk; car hires; business center; gift shop; book shop; salon; 24-hr. room service; laundry. *In room:* A/C, TV, dataport, minibar, tea- and coffee-making facility, hair dryer, electronic safe.

ERNAKULAM

If you can't get a room on Fort Cochin or Willingdon Island, or a room in the hotels reviewed below, the following Ernakulam options are worth considering, particularly if you're on a budget. **Avenue Regent** (39/2026 Mahatma Gandhi Rd.; ℃ **0484/237-2660;** www.avenueregent.com; from Rs 2,100/$46 double) is a spruce six-floor business hotel, but located on a busy, noisy main road. Guest rooms are fairly large, with dull Western-style decor, potted palm trees, an abundance of floral fabric, and rather soft mattresses. That said, the reasonable tariff includes breakfast. Note that the same owners have opened the smart new **Avenue Center Hotel** in an attractive white neo-colonial building (Panampilly Ave., Panampilly Nagar, Ernakulam; ℃ 0484/231-5301 or -5302; fax 0484/ 231-5304; www.avenuecenter.com); at press time, opening promo rates were attractive. **The Woods Manor** (Woodlands Junction, Mahatma Gandhi Rd.; ℃ **0484/238-2055,** -2056, -2057, -2058, or -2059; www.thewoodsmanor.com; Rs 1,500–Rs 2,200/$33–$48 double) is another neat, clean hotel. Set in the center of Ernakulam on a busy street, it has no views (but a great rooftop pool). The sixth-floor "Kerala" guest rooms are centrally air-conditioned and have firm mattresses and small tubs in smallish attached bathrooms. The hotel is well-located for the railway station and has a 24-hour check-out policy. The **Grand** (Mahatma Gandhi Rd., Ernakulam 682 011; ℃ **0484/238-2061** or 0484/ 236-6833; www.grandhotelkerala.com; Rs 1,300–Rs 1,950/$28–$43 double) is

Ernakulam's oldest hotel, but ongoing renovations (begun in 1998) have slowly brought improvements. Deluxe rooms have balconies and large black marble bathrooms. Popular with the locals, the Grandeura Bar gets busy in the evenings.

Taj Residency ⍟   If you are going to stay in Ernakulam, this luxury business hotel, which sits right on the harbor's edge and has its own jetty, is by far the best option. Standard guest rooms are comfortable, with high ceilings and firm mattresses; bathrooms feature showers instead of tubs. For an extra $10, you get a view of the harbor, so make sure you do. Also overlooking Cochin's busy port is the popular Bubble Café, a cheerful eatery in a glass-enclosed terrace with tables arranged around a brightly tiled fountain mosaic.

Marine Dr., Ernakulam, Cochin 682 011. © **0484/37-1471** or -3500. Fax 0484/37-1481. www.tajhotel.com. residency.ernakulam@tajhotels.com. 108 units. Doubles: $100 standard; $110 standard sea view; $125 residency (includes breakfast); $150 executive suite (includes breakfast). AE, DC, MC, V. **Amenities:** 2 restaurants; patisserie; bar; fitness center; boat rental; sunset cruises; travel desk; car hires; business center; currency exchange; 24-hr. room service; babysitting; laundry; dry-cleaning; doctor-on-call. *In room:* A/C, TV, minibar.

BOLGATTY ISLAND

Bolgatty Palace ⍟   Built in 1744 by a Dutch trader and later used as the British Residency, this government-run hotel occupies 6 hectares (15 acres) of the southern tip of Bolgatty Island. Accessible only by ferry, the setting here is quite lovely, if a little inconvenient for sightseeing and exploring. Most guest rooms are situated in the Keralan courtyard-style Nalukettu Wing, pleasantly refurbished in 2001, and blending rather well with the original palace. Accommodations are spacious, with high ceilings, wood furniture, bathtubs, and balconies with sea views. Rather pretentiously named after Dutch master painters—Vermeer, van Gogh, Rembrandt, and others—the massive suites in the original palace mansion have dark teak ceiling beams, reproduction period furniture, large beds, and thick drapery; bathrooms are enormous and have bidet, tub, and separate glass-encased shower. Avoid the "honeymoon cottages" which stand on stilts at the edge of the water; these show signs of damp and disrepair. Kathakali performances, presented by the Bolgatty Performing Arts Centre, are held each night.

Bolgatty Island, Kochi, Kerala. Reservations: Bolgatty Palace, Mulavukadu, Kochi 682 504, Kerala. © **0484/ 235-5003.** Fax 0484/354879. www.ktdc.com. 26 units. Doubles: Rs 4,385 ($96) palace suites; Rs 3,390 ($74) executive suites; Rs 2,390 ($52) deluxe rooms; Rs 1,890 ($41) waterfront cottages. Rates include breakfast. AE, DC, MC, V. **Amenities:** Restaurant; beer parlor; pool; golf course; indoor recreation room; Ayurvedic center; travel assistance; conferencing; board room; currency exchange; 24-hr. room service. *In room:* A/C, TV.

WHERE TO DINE

Kochi's best eating establishments are located in the hotels at Fort Cochin and Willingdon. Seafood is always fresh and wonderful; this is generally what you should order. Have protection against mosquitoes ready, particularly in outdoor restaurants, where nighttime attacks can be incessant.

Fort Cochin ⍟⍟⍟ SEAFOOD   Considered one of the state's (if not Asia's) best seafood restaurants, this casual catch-of-the-day semi-alfresco pad is something of a Keralite institution. The atmosphere is charmingly rustic: The excellent food is prepared at an open grill adjacent to a large waist-level fish tank filled with Chinese carp. Tables are set around a huge banyan tree and under light shades made from Chinese fishing baskets. Choose from a range of freshly caught seafood displayed on a cart that makes its way from table to table, and decide how you would like it prepared—grilled whole with heaps of spices, or

---

A Traditional Keralite Feast

Don't pass up the opportunity to enjoy a traditional *saapadu* meal while in Kerala. This five-course feast served on a plantain leaf will give you a very good overview of the state's cuisine. Expect rice and ghee (clarified butter), served with various stews and curries with names like *sambar, rasam, kootu, pacchadi, appalam,* and *payasam,* all of which will be heaped endlessly upon your "plate." Seafood in Kerala is exquisite and plentiful. A popular dish is *meen moilee,* a delicate fish curry tempered with fresh coconut milk. Coconut is used in many dishes: *Avial* is a mixed vegetable curry prepared with coconut, cumin, and turmeric; and *aadu olathiayathu* is a coconut-based curry made with cubes of fried mutton. A steamed rice pancake known as *appam* is very popular and is served with stew.

---

delicately sliced with gentle herbs; the obliging maitre d' will help you make up your mind. The mixed seafood platter is a popular favorite, giving you a selection of fish cutlets, tiger prawns, and other shellfish. Call ahead after 4pm to hear what's on the evening cart.

Casino Hotel, K.P.K. Menon Rd., Willingdon Island. © **0484/266-8221** or -8421. Prices determined on the day and by weight. Mixed seafood platter Rs 675 ($15). AE, DC, MC, V. Daily 7–10:30pm.

The History and Terrace Grill ★★★ KERALITE   The Terrace Grill is the alfresco section of the superb upstairs restaurant at the Brunton Boatyard; inside, the History shares the same menu, and air-conditioning keeps the heat (and mosquitoes) at bay. Most of the recipes are local, many borrowed from the kitchens of Cochin families. Start with mildly spiced and steamed tiger prawns served with mango chutney. Kerala *meen* kebab is the catch of the day marinated in coconut paste, then spit-roasted in a clay oven. Another lovely fish dish is *chuttulli meen,* marinated according to a local Jewish recipe in pearl onions and green spices. You can also have fish flavored with local spices and then grilled in banana leaves. If you've had your fill of seafood, try the First Class Railway lamb curry, which is made with coconut milk and is not overly spicy. Another specialty is *Chuttirachi,* chunks of lamb cooked in a mixture of shallots and spices; it was first prepared by Jew Town's Hallegua family.

The Brunton Boatyard Hotel, 1/498 Fort Cochin, Kochi 682 001. © **0484/221-5461,** -5462, -5463, -5464, -5465, or -5557. Main courses Rs 180–Rs 400 ($3.80–$8.75). AE, DC, MC, V. Daily 7–10:30pm.

Malabar Junction ★★ MALABAR-MEDITERRANEAN FUSION Cochin's Malabar House Residency is the setting for this fine, sophisticated alfresco restaurant where guests sit in a small area covered by a ceiling of traditional Kerala woodwork, watching (at night) a performance on the adjacent stage. Start off with crispy fried prawns tempura, then have fish curry Fort Cochin, which is rather mild for local tastes (if you prefer it spicy, say so). Unfortunately, service can be slow; call to check if the owners are in town, since their presence usually ensures that the staff is a little more on the ball.

Malabar House Residency, 1/268–1/269 Parade Rd., Fort Cochin. © **0484/221-6666.** Menu changes regularly, but expect to pay Rs 90–Rs 370 ($1.90–$8) for a main course. AE, DC, MC, V. Daily 7–10am, 12:30–3pm, and 7–11pm.

Pandhal ★ (Value) ECLECTIC   Run by the same people who own Kerala's dynamic Casino Hotel chain, this pleasant family restaurant is popular with the city's middle class. A cubist "fantasy" in shades of orange and brown with textured white walls, the decor is a bad reminder of the 1970s, but the seafood is fantastically fresh and prepared to exacting standards, particularly the tiger prawns. Vegetarian and *tandoori* items are also available, and there's a pastry shop attached.

Mahatma Gandhi Rd., Ernakulam. ℭ **0484/236-7759.** Dinner reservations recommended. Main courses Rs 70–Rs 285 ($1.50–$6). AE, DC, MC, V. Daily 11am–midnight. Pastry shop open daily 9am–midnight.

Rice Boat ★★★ KERALITE/SEAFOOD   One of *the* places to dine in India, Rice Boat is a small specialty restaurant where guests sit in, well, a rice boat. It's an excellent place to indulge in fresh seafood, including prawns, lobster, and crab. Find out what the catch of the day is, and have the chef add a touch of Kerala with a spicy, coconut-based gravy. Whatever you order, leave room for one of the house-specialty spice ice creams; the Green Pepper Gelato is not to be missed.

Taj Malabar, Willingdon Island. ℭ **0484/266-6811** or -8010. Prices follow market trends. AE, DC, MC, V. Daily 7:30–11:30pm.

Thai Pavilion ★ THAI   Dishes here not only taste wonderful, they look fabulous, too. *Kai haw bai toey* is a starter of marinated chicken pieces wrapped in pandanus (a type of pine) leaves and deep-fried. Vegetarians should try *man jian*—potatoes flavored with ginger, mushroom, pimento, and a light soy sauce—or *fok thong kapprao,* a delightful combination of pumpkin and basil chilies. For something really out of the ordinary, order *phad boong fai daeng,* stir-fried morning glories prepared in yellow bean paste! Here, the spiciness of traditional Thai red curry *(gaeng phed)* is toned down with coconut milk and fragrant lemon grass; served in a small earthenware bowl, it is prepared with your choice of meat, vegetables, or seafood. There's a number of stir-fried prawn dishes, each prepared with a delicate blend of spices and herbs—try *koong phad kapprao,* a hot combination of garlic, chili, and holy basil leaves.

Taj Malabar, Willingdon Island. ℭ **0484/266-6811** or -8010. Main courses Rs 175–Rs 450 ($3.70–$9.80). AE, DC, MC, V. Daily 7:30–11:30pm.

SHOPPING

Ernakulam has scores of shops trading in Indian artifacts and treasures. However, you'll have far more fun exploring the antiques dealerships in Mattancherry and Jew Town, most of which are jam-packed with weird, wonderful, and genuine pieces from Kerala's multifangled past.

Cinnamon ★★★   Don't be fooled by the gallery-like ambience; the lovely furniture and fashions available here are entirely homegrown. Find fishing nets made into pillowcases, vintage prints of Hindu deities, silk caftans, and designer tunics that are ideal for the Indian heat. This new addition is Cochin's most fashionable outlet, and at press time there were plans to add a courtyard cafe. 1/658 Ridsdale Rd. ℭ **0484/221-7124.**

Crafters   In the heart of historic Mattanchery's Jew Town, Crafters is an antiques fetishist's dream come true. A huge selection of antiques ranging from religious curiosities to that perfect doorway are displayed in three different outlets and piled up in massive warehouses that will leave your jaw hanging open. After you've had a really good poke around, you can have your purchase shipped abroad. American Express, Diners Club, MasterCard, and Visa are accepted. VI/141, Jew Town. ℭ **0484/222-3346** or -7652, or 0484/221-2210. Fax 0484/222-3346. www.crafters antique.com.

Galleria Synagogue Art Gallery   Local artists are well represented at this Jew Town art gallery, where you can purchase works by some of Cochin's most celebrated artists, including the much-liked Shakuntala. Near Pradesi Synagogue, Jew Town Rd. ✆ **0484/222-1387** or -1458. fatima2001@alibaba.com.

COCHIN AFTER DARK

When the sun starts to sink, you should be on a harbor cruise or watching the boats from either the **Taj Malabar** on Willingdon Island or the **Taj Residency** in Ernakulam—both sit more or less on the water's edge and offer different venues where you can order a cocktail. After this, a Kathakali or Kalaripayattu demonstration (see below) can easily fill the gap before a fine seafood dinner.

KATHAKALI PERFORMANCES

In Fort Cochin, **Kerala Kathakali** ₳₳₳ (River Rd.; ✆ **0484/221-5827**) hosts the best Kathakali demonstration in the city (see "Kathakali & Kalaripayattu: Kerala's Colorful Art Forms," below). This rustic, atmospheric "theater" also hosts occasional cultural events showcasing diverse dance forms and Karnatic music (the classical music of southern India). Performances are held daily 6:30

Kathakali & Kalaripayattu: Kerala's Colorful Art Forms

A stay in Cochin affords you the opportunity to sample Kerala's best-known classical art form—Kathakali, a performance style that delves into the world of demons, deities, soldiers, sages, and satyrs, taken from Indian epics such as the *Mahabharata*. Combining various theatrical and performance elements, it is said to have developed during the 16th century under the auspices of the Raja of Kottaraka, and today the best Kathakali school is in Kalamandalam, founded by a poet named Vallathol Narayan Menon in 1930. Here, students undergo a rigorous training program that lasts 6 years and includes massage techniques, extensive makeup training, and knowledge of the precise and subtle finger, body, and eye movements that constitute the language and grand emotions of Kathakali. There is also a host of instruments that may be mastered, as no performance is without musical accompaniment. So striking are the costumes, makeup, and jewelry associated with this form of dance-theater, that the image of the elaborately adorned, heavily made-up, and almost mask-like face of the Kathakali performer has become the state's most recognizable icon. Performers employ exaggerated facial expressions (only enhanced by the makeup—bright paint applied thickly to the face) and a highly technical set of symbolic hand gestures (known as *mudras*). Vocalists and musicians help set the mood, utilizing the *chengila* (gong), *elathalam* (small cymbals), and *chenda* and *maddalam* (drums). Traditionally, Kathakali performances are held for entire nights, often as part of festival events. In Cochin, however, a number of Kathakali groups stage short extracts of the longer pieces specifically for tourist consumption. Kerala is also renowned for its unique martial arts form: the supremely acrobatic Kalaripayattu, believed to be the oldest defense-combat system in the world. Apparently discovered in ancient times by traveling Buddhist monks who needed to protect themselves against marauding bandits, Kalaripayattu is believed to predate more recognizable forms, like kung-fu, that emerged further east. For demonstrations of Kathakali and Kalaripayattu, see recommendations above and below.

to 8pm, with makeup demonstrations from 5pm; admission is Rs 100 ($2.10). Note that alongside the theater is the **Old Port Restaurant** (© **0484/221-5341**), a good venue for pre- or post-show meals; fresh fish dishes and various Keralite specialties are served right near the water's edge (bring mosquito repellent for both the show and the restaurant). If you're interested in attending a proper all-night Kathakali performance at a temple, speak to one of the organizers at Kerala Kathakali; some of their top performers are often involved in real ritual events.

Other Kathakali venues worth noting are Fort Cochin's (air-conditioned) **Cochin Cultural Centre** (CC 2/10–A, near Seagull Hotel, Calvetty Rd.; © **0484/221-6911** or -5391), which has daily shows from 6:30pm; and **See India Foundation** (Kalthil Parambil Lane; © **0484/236-9471** or 0484/237-1576) in Ernakulam. The latter has nightly performances, but note that the performances are rather unexceptional.

Music, dance, and other performances are sometimes held at **Draavidia Performance Studio** (1/2002, YMCA Rd., Fort Cochin; © **0484/221-7025**); contact Helen Muir (© **98/4608-5639**) for information.

KALARIPAYATTU PERFORMANCES

While there is a number of dedicated training schools *(kalaris)* where Kerala's traditional martial arts form, Kalaripayattu, is taught for its intended purpose, it is usually performed in a staged environment for tourists. **Shiva Shakti Kalari Kshetram** (Kaloor, Ernakulam; © **0484/253-9453** or 98/4615-0282) holds daily demonstrations of Kalaripayattu; the institute also provides training and Ayurvedic massage based on principles derived from the art of Kalari.

2 The Backwaters

Alleppey is 1,150km (713 miles) SE of Mumbai

Kerala's backwaters comprise a web of waterways that forms a natural inland transport network stretching from **Cochin,** the northern gateway, to **Kollam** (or Quilon), the backwaters' southernmost town. At its heart is Vembanad Lake, on the shores of which lie the top-notch resorts of **Kumarakom** and nearby Bird Sanctuary. Inland, just 12km (7½ miles) east of Kumarakom, is **Kottayam,** a bustling, ugly little town at the foot of the Western Ghats with two historically significant (but ultimately missable) early Syrian Christian churches.

Kumarakom has by far the best accommodations, but unless you're a keen birder, there's not a great deal to do here. Idle away the hours on a houseboat cruise, indulge in Ayurvedic therapies, and laze under the tropical sun—that's about as busy as your day is likely to get. Between November and March, the local **Bird Sanctuary** becomes home to numerous migratory flocks, many of which fly in from Siberia. Regularly seen here are little cormorants, darters (or snake birds), night herons, golden-backed woodpeckers, tree pies, and crow pheasants. Given its exclusivity and sublime setting, Kumarakom does not offer accommodations for budget-oriented travelers; for that you'll need to look farther south to **Alleppey** (or Alappuzha).

Home to the coir (fibers made from coconut husks) industry, Alleppey once bore the nickname "Venice of the East" because of its famed palm-fringed canal network, the intricate byways and narrow streams that allow boats to transport huge bales of coconut fibers. Of the many **snake boat races** (see "Snake Boat Races," below) that take place in the backwaters throughout the year, Alleppey's

Snake Boat Races

Every year Kerala's backwater canals host the world's largest team sport, when scores of streamlined *chundan vallams,* the ram-snouted boats commonly known as snake boats, are propelled across the waters at impressive speeds, cheered on by an exuberant audience. Typically, snake boats are manned by four helmsmen, 25 singers, and 100 oarsmen rowing in unison to the terrific rhythm of the *vanchipattu,* or "song of the boatman." The oldest and most popular event is the **Champakulam Moolam Boat Race,** held in monsoon-soaked July, but the most famous water battle is undoubtedly the **Nehru Trophy Boat Race,** held on the second Saturday of August on the backwaters of Alleppey in conjunction with Kerala's important *Onam* harvest festival. Tickets for the event, which features at least 16 competing *chundan vallams* and attracts thousands of excited supporters, are available from the **District Tourism Promotion Council office** (see "Visitor Information," below).

Nehru Trophy event is the most significant. If you're keen to witness the event, it may be useful to find accommodations in close proximity to the town.

The entire backwaters region is a tranquil paradise, and sustains a delightfully laid-back way of life that has endured for centuries—perfect for sultry, languid, do-nothing houseboat adventures that take you into the heart of Keralan country life. Besides booking into one of the resorts recommended below, a trip on a specially converted *kettuvallam* is a must (see "Hiring a Houseboat," below).

ESSENTIALS

VISITOR INFORMATION   The authority responsible for dishing out information to visitors is the **District Tourism Promotion Council,** which has various offices in the different backwaters towns. In **Alleppey,** it's on Boat Jetty Road (⊘ **0477/225-3308**). In **Kollam,** there are tourism centers at the bus stand and at the railway station. In **Kottayam,** you can contact the state government's **Tourist Information Office** (⊘ **0481/258-4303**). If your main interest is houseboats, contact TourIndia (see "Hiring a Houseboat," below).

GETTING THERE   By Road   Taxis are easily available in all major towns and cities.

By Air   For the northern backwater towns, the nearest airport is at Cochin (Kochi); to save time you'll probably want to head down the 76km (47-mile) road by car to Kottayam (for Kumarakom). For Kollam, at the backwaters' southern end, Thiruvananthapuram Airport is 66km (40 miles) away.

By Train   There are railheads in Kottyam (for Kumarakom), Alleppey, and Kollam. In Alleppey, call ⊘ **477/225-3965** for information regarding train services; in Kollam, dial ⊘ **131.**

GETTING AROUND   By Water-Taxi & Ferry   Kottayam, Alleppey, and Kollam are all connected by ferries. State-run double-decker cruisers ply the route between Alleppey and Kollam daily, departing from the Kollam boat jetty at 10:30am and arriving in Alleppey around 6:30pm. Times are the same for cruises out of Alleppey. State Water Transport Department ferries between Alleppey and Kottyam take 2½ hours.

GUIDED TOURS & CRUISES   Alleppey's **District Tourism Promotion Council** (Boat Jetty; © **0477/225-3308**) has a daily backwater cruise to Kumarakom and back. The 6-hour trip departs at 10am and costs Rs 75 ($1.60). See "Hiring a Houseboat," below, for guided overnight trips on traditional houseboats.

CRUISING THE BACKWATERS

Reset your watch to a rhythm of life that has gone unchanged for centuries by boarding a *kettuvallam,* the long, beautifully crafted cargo boats that ply the waterways with cargo (if you don't mind being referred to as such). An engineering feat, a *kettuvallam* is made from lengths of ironwood, anjeli, or jackwood, and not a single nail is used in the construction—it's joined together with thick coir ropes. The boat is then sealed with fish oil and coated with a black caustic resin produced by boiling cashew kernels.

Today, numerous houseboat operators work out of the Alleppey area, but the original concept of turning cargo boats into tourist cruise vessels was the brainchild of Babu Varghese of TourIndia, an outfit that remains the top operator on the backwaters, with excellent guides and innovative boat designs that are upgraded annually. Varghese transformed the *kettuvallam* into a livable houseboat by expanding the original size to include two or three rooms, a flushing toilet, a functioning shower, and a small viewing or sunbathing platform. Bamboo scaffolding is constructed over the hull, and a thatch roof of plaited palm leaves and walls of bamboo matting are added to create a rustic but very comfortable floating dwelling. With designs that owe some allegiance to the Chinese junk but that more closely resemble a small Sydney Opera House, these beautiful crafts may be propelled by pole (if you're in no particular hurry) or by a small, quiet motor.

The houseboat experience allows you to aimlessly drift past villages, temples, and churches and be thoroughly exposed to the rural lifestyle of the backwaters. Like being on the very large set of a reality TV show, you can watch as women, unperturbed by your drifting presence, wash their long ebony tresses or pound away at laundry, while children play at the water's edge and men dive for mussels, and elephants and water buffalo wade at will. Fishermen suavely holding umbrellas above their head suddenly drift by, their nets at the ready, while floating vendors using single-log canoes and other modest craft deliver commodities such as rice and coir fiber. On the shore, toddy tappers whisk up palm trees (note that you can ask to stop off at a village to buy unforeseen necessities like beer or coconut toddy); see "Toddy Tappers," below. And when the sun sets, the sky lights up in magnificent shades of orange and red. Gliding past the rural communities that cling to the banks is without a doubt one of the most relaxing and romantic ways to witness a timeless lifestyle, where people rely on impossibly tiny tracts of land to cultivate subsistence crops and keep handfuls of animals, using slender jackfruit wood canoes to get around, deliver goods, and do a spot of fishing.

Toddy Tappers

For generations, agile young village men have been clambering up palm trees to tap into the sweet sap known as toddy. Like their fathers and their fathers' fathers, these "toddy tappers" have made a good living over the years harvesting the sap to drink right away (sweet and refreshing) or distill into a popular (and potent) hard liquor known as coconut *feni.*

Mohiniattam: The Dance of the Enchantress

Mohiniattam is another classical dance form, and one of the few performed by a woman. Dressed in white and gold, with her hair gathered and adorned with jasmine, the dancer performs graceful, gliding movements together with elaborate *mudras* and exaggerated facial expressions. Any resort promising evening shows that showcase the region's performance arts (like Coconut Lagoon and Spice Village) will include at least one act of Mohiniattam.

Kettuvallam houseboats are available at various levels of luxury, and may be rented for short trips or for sleep-in journeys of several days. Try to spend at least 1 night on board, since the major attractions are watching the setting sun and witnessing the lakeside activities of various households at dawn and dusk. A great plan is to have a houseboat collect you from one resort (we suggest Coconut Lagoon or Kumarokum) and drop you off at your next destination (say, Kayaloram Lake Resort or—if your budget won't stretch that far—Keraleeyam Lake Resort).

While the general idea is to wind your way aimlessly through the waterways, one of the most popular stop-off points for visitors is the **Mata Amrithanandamayi Ashram** (℃ 0476/262-1279), home of a female guru endearingly known as Amma, the Hugging Mother. Another possible stop is **Champakulam,** where the 150-year-old **St. Mary's Forane Church** shows definite traces of Hindu influence, particularly in a small statue of Christ assuming a pose typical of Krishna.

HIRING A HOUSEBOAT

TourIndia ⭐⭐⭐ (Karukapparambil, Zillah Court Ward, Nehru Trophy Race Finishing Point, Thattampally P.O., Alappuzha; ℃ 0477/226-4961) has a number of houseboats in a range of designs and accommodations to suit your requirements. These feature solar-panel power and heating, bio-toilets, and an average cruising speed of 8km to 10km (5–6 miles) per hour. Although the facilities might strike some as rather basic, you'll be spoiled rotten by your private team—a guide, a cook, and a pilot—who work hard to make your experience unique and exceptional (and discreetly manage to leave you to experience the backwaters in peace). Meals are authentic Keralan fare—served on a plantain leaf and eaten with your fingers. Bring your own drinks if you want something other than mineral water. And if you're curious about Keralan cuisine, you're welcome to observe proceedings in the tiny kitchen at the rear end of the boat. For reservations, contact TourIndia at Post Box no. 163, Mahatma Gandhi Road, Trivandrum 695 001; ℃ 0471/233-0437 or -1507; fax 0471/233-1407; www.richsoft.com/tourindia.

Other reliable houseboat operators are **Spice Coast Cruises** ⭐⭐⭐ (℃ 0484/266-8221; casino@vsnl.com), run by the excellent Kerala-based Casino Hotel group; and **Soma Houseboats** (Nehru Trophy Finishing Point, Thathampally P.O., Alleppey; ℃ 0477/226-4112; reservations: Chowara P.O. Trivandrum 695 501; ℃ 0471/268-0601; www.somahouseboats.com). Expect to pay between $90 and $225 for a one-bedroom houseboat, per night.

WHERE TO STAY ON LAND
KUMARAKOM

Coconut Lagoon Heritage Resort ★★★ *(Kids)*   If private alfresco showers and hammocks rather than room service and television are your idea of bliss, then this is your kind of lakeside idyll (and one that delighted Paul McCartney on a recent visit). Comprising reassembled wooden *tharavads* (traditional Keralan houses) set among coconut trees, hibiscus flowers, and specially grafted orchids, and boasting quite splendid views of Lake Vembanad and the Kavanar River, this family-friendly resort is one of the most popular in Kerala. Most accommodations are in the traditional *tharavads*—choose between duplex-style mansions (nos. 201–204 have views of the lake) or simpler heritage bungalows (nos. 219–221, 223, and 225–228 face the river). Some of the homes here date back to the early 1700s, and each historic teak, anjili, or jackfruit building has been reassembled according to ancient carpentry rules known as *thachu shashtra*. The emphasis here is on providing an authentic Keralan feel and having as little impact as possible on the natural environment. Indeed, much of the resort's rustic charm lies in its simplicity; guest rooms are uncluttered and furnished with traditional Keralan cane and teak pieces, and have neither TVs nor (less satisfactorily) room service. At press time, renovations were underway, so be sure to ask for a recently refurbished room. Better still, splurge on a pool cottage, which (you guessed it) has its own private pool and is situated right on the river's edge.

Kumarakom, Kerala. Communications c/o Casino Hotel, Willingdon Island, Cochin 682 003, Kerala. (C) **0481/ 252-4491** or -4373. Fax 0481/252-4495. www.casinogroup.com. casino@vsnl.com. 14 mansions, 28 bungalows, and 8 private pool villas. Doubles: $143 bungalow, $160 peak season (Dec 21–Jan 20); $154 mansion, $171 peak season; $275 pool villa, $319 peak season; $35 extra person. Rates include breakfast. AE, DC, MC, V. **Amenities:** 2 restaurants; bar; traditional performances; pool (cottages also have private pools); Ayurvedic center; houseboat; boat shuttle service; sunset cruise; hamper service; butterfly garden; village walks; bird-sanctuary visits; cooking demonstrations; shop; 48-hr. external laundry service. *In room:* A/C, minibar, tea- and coffee-making facility.

Kumarakom Lake Resort ★★★   Situated on the edge of Vembanad Lake, in a remote, tranquil location, this is the swankiest of Kumarakom's backwater resorts. Like so many of these resorts, it comprises exquisite *tharavadu*-style carved teak and rosewood houses with curved terra-cotta tiled roofs, many of them reassembled originals salvaged from Keralan villages. The interiors are decidedly more luxurious than those of their neighbors, however, with exquisite antiques and lovely examples of temple mural art. Each room has a beautiful, private small garden into which an open-to-the-air sunken bathtub and granite-floored drench showers have been installed. The cheaper lake-facing cottages

---

Dining-Room Murder

The beautiful dining room at the Coconut Lagoon is apparently part of the house where the awful murder in Arundhati Roy's *The God of Small Things* actually occurred. The acclaimed writer has been very critical of the removal and reassembly of Kerala's traditional homes in what she calls "theme park" resorts, but resort owners argue that they have saved these historic properties from certain destruction. (The dining room at the Coconut Lagoon is not haunted, by the way, but the food is awfully good.)

offer the best value for money—they have a truly authentic heritage feel and are perfect for enjoying the setting sun (standard villas face a canal that reaches all the way to the lobby). In the resort's newest section, a second meandering fresh-water pool snakes its way past the private balconies of luxurious cottages—which means you can swim around the property directly from your back door (which may compromise your privacy, however, because others can choose to do the same). Should you fancy a night or two on the lake, the resort has two of its own fully equipped houseboats. The resort is also home to an excellent restaurant and an extensive Ayurvedic spa—one of Kerala's best, offering a wide range of treatments. And if that isn't enough to persuade you, staff are wonderfully efficient and go all out to make you feel like royalty.

Kumarakom N., Kottayam 686 566. ℂ 0481/252-4900, -4501, or -5020, -5021. Fax 0481/252-4987. www.klresort.com. klresort@vsnl.com. 50 units plus 2 houseboats. Doubles (Apr 1–Sept 30/Oct 1–Mar 31): $135/$180 heritage canal-view villa; $145 heritage lake-view villa; $175 meandering pool villa; $225 meandering pool duplex villa; $315 presidential suite with private pool; $15 extra bed. Tariffs increase Dec 10–Jan 10. Meal plans available. AE, DC, MC, V. **Amenities:** 3 restaurants; 2 pools; gymnasium; Jacuzzi; Ayurvedic center; yoga; billiards; table tennis; children's play area; activity room; travel desk; sightseeing; business center; currency exchange; curio shop; salon; limited room service; babysitting; laundry; computer rentals. In room: A/C, TV, minibar, electronic safe.

Taj Garden Retreat Kumarakom 🏵🏵 This charming resort sits around the edges of a lagoon linked to Vembanad Lake by a narrow channel, just moments away from the Kumarakom Bird Sanctuary. It's in much the same price range as the buzzier Coconut Lagoon, but the advantage here is near-absolute peace and privacy (no doubt the reason it's the preferred retreat for the likes of India's prime minister). Built in the late 1800s, Baker Bungalow was home to four generations of the Baker missionary family before the Taj group converted it into a tranquil resort. Lake-facing guest cottages (nos. 7–17 have the best views) have spacious bedrooms and small private patios that look directly onto the resort's private lake—even the lovely bathrooms have views, albeit of a tiny paved court-yard decorated with tall, narrow clay pots. For a few dollars more, the three cottages situated at the pool have slightly bigger bedrooms; ask for no. 18, since it overlooks the length of the lake. If it's colonial history you want, reserve one of the five massive rooms in the original Baker Bungalow; furnished with antiques, these, too, have their own romantic atmosphere. Alternatively, you can stay in one of two air-conditioned, permanently moored houseboats, each with two roomy bedrooms, bathroom with tub, and attached private deck.

1/404, Kumarakom, Kotyam 686 563. ℂ 0481/252-4377 or 0481/252-5711 or -5712 through -5716. Fax 0481/252-4371. www.tajhotels.com. retreat.kumarakom@tajhotels.com. 23 units. Doubles: $140 ($75 May–Sept) standard lake-view and houseboat; $150 cottage lake-view ($80 May–Sept); $160 deluxe lake- and pool-view ($85 May–Sept). AE, DC, MC, V. **Amenities:** Restaurant; 2 bars; pool; Ayurvedic center; bicycle rentals; backwater cruises; watersports (wind sailing, water skiing); boating (speedboat, kayaking, canoeing, banana boat rides, water scooters); fishing; bird-watching; cultural performances; indoor games; travel desk; gift shop; currency exchange; 24-hr. room service; laundry; doctor-on-call. In room: A/C, TV, minibar, hair dryer on request.

KOTTAYAM

Lake Village Heritage Resort 🏵 This is far from the best lagoon resort, but the rates aren't bad (they include all meals), and if you get the room choice right, you can literally fish from your balcony. The resort is set amid banana trees and manicured lawns, and its best accommodations are (predictably) in a series of reconstructed traditional Keralan mansions that have been converted to include indoor/outdoor bathrooms—book no. 104 or 105 for the balconies that project over the river, or no. 117 or 118, which create the impression of being surrounded by water. Cottages are on two levels, with bedrooms on the upper floor; room interiors are a little dark and uninspiring. An open-air Keralan cuisine eatery, cultural performances at the *mandapam*, boat rides in *chundan vallams*, and an Ayurvedic center make up for views of the adjoining Windsor "Castle" Hotel—this is, incidentally, where you have to check in. *Note:* Don't confuse Lake Village Heritage Resort with the super-kitsch and awful **Vembanad Lake Resort** next door.

Kottayam 686 039. ✆ **0481/236-3637** or -3638. Fax 0481/236-3738. www.thewindsorcastle.net. 31 units, 17 cottages. Doubles: $100; $6.50 extra bed. Rates include all meals. AE, MC, V. **Amenities:** 2 restaurants; bar; 2 pools; Ayurvedic center; car hires; boat rental; boat jetty; currency exchange; pastry shop; salon; 24-hr. room service; doctor-on-call. *In room:* A/C, TV, minibar.

Philipkutty's Farm ★★ *(Kids) (Value)*   This is a real gem, ideal for those who find the whole resort experience a little pretentious. Here you get to experience firsthand the hospitality of a local farming family, albeit in the privacy of your very own waterfront cottage, surrounded by 18 hectares (45 acres) that include banana, mango, nutmeg, coconut, and pepper plantations. The first cottage (two new ones have recently been added) was designed by Karl Damschen, a Swiss architect who combined traditional Keralite design—open-plan living, carved wooden doors, and a veranda—with personal touches. The breezy, homey cottages are filled with antiques, and the en-suite bathrooms are modern and lovely. Hosts Vinod and Anu Mathew treat guests as part of the family yet allow you significant privacy (they stay in a separate house) and time to soak up the tranquillity. Vinod's mother is the kitchen genie; she prepares three marvelous feasts a day, and welcomes you to observe her talents. The only real drawback is that there's no pool, but some guests do venture into the waters of Vembanad Lake, and you're taken on informative excursions of the plantations and get to enjoy a free backwater cruise on a canoe. Children are warmly welcomed.

Pallivathukal, Ambika Market P.O., Vechoor, Kottayam. ✆ **0482/927-6529** or -6530. www.philipkuttysfarm. com. 3 units. Doubles: $90; children under 5 free in parent's room; $15 children 5–12; $30 children over 12. Rates include all meals, tea and coffee, sunset cruise, and farm excursions. 20% discount June–Sept. Credit cards for overseas bank deposits only. **Amenities:** Dining facilities.

IN & AROUND ALLEPPEY (ALAPPUZHA)

Kayaloram Lake Resort ★★★   A scenic 15-minute boat ride from Alleppey's jetty brings you to one of the best resorts the backwaters have to offer: Kayaloram is a relatively intimate and very private lakeside resort, with watery views that seem to stretch forever (or at the very least to distant Kumarakom and Kollam). Guest rooms are in four transplanted and remodeled 75-year-old *tharavads* with wraparound teak verandas and intricately patterned gables. Rooms are uncluttered and feature the de rigueur high-beamed ceilings, bamboo blinds, coir carpets, terracotta tiled floors, and paneled walls of dark jackfruit wood. Outdoor bathrooms with open-air showers are glorious. The best views are from room nos. 2, 3, and 5, which face the lake, less than 10m (30 ft.) away, and allow you to watch the prawn fishermen's lights twinkling on the lake at night. During the day, the continuously changing spectacle of passing boats, canoes, and *vallams* (snake boats) is equally magical. In keeping with the personalized service, individual lunch and dinner orders are taken a few hours in advance (Ayurvedic cuisine is available) to ensure that tastes, needs, and moods are adequately met. The manager is fond of taking guests on walking tours through some of the backwater villages located near the resort; and the Ayurvedic treatments, while not extensive, are considered some of the best in India.

Punnamada, Alleppey 688 006. ✆ **0477/226-2931**, 0477/223-2040, or -1573. Fax 0477/225-2918. www. kayaloram.com. kayaloram@vsnl.com or kayaloram@satyam.net.in. 12 units. $50–$80 double. AE, DC, MC, V. **Amenities:** Restaurant; beer available; pool; Ayurvedic treatments; doctor-on-call. *In room:* A/C.

Keraleeyam Lake Resort 🐟 *Value*   This 70-year-old Kerala home is one of the best-value deals on the backwaters, and unbeatable if you want to experience the heritage atmosphere of the top-notch resorts at budget rates. Set on the water's edge, it includes five rooms and nine cottages. The guest rooms in *tharavad* houses feature high-beamed ceilings, wooden shutters, and small doorways with traditional thick wooden *saksha* locks. Each cottage (without A/C, but naturally cooled by the thatch roofs) has a direct lake view with a private balcony, a personal coconut palm, and an open-to-the-sky shower in a lovely indoor-outdoor bathroom. Air-conditioned cottages, while made entirely of teak, have very standard bathrooms and a shared balcony. Pleasures include backwater cruises and a visit to a living village, as well as Ayurvedic massage facilities.

Thathampally, Alappuzha 688 006. © **0477/223-1468** or -6950. Fax 0477/225-1068. www.keraleeyam.com. 5 units, 9 cottages. Doubles: $25 for 2- and 3-bedrooms; $40 A/C cottage; $30 non-A/C cottage; child under 12 sharing parent's room $5. Food tariff of $15 includes all meals. AE, DC, MC, V. **Amenities:** Restaurant; Ayurvedic center; tours and sightseeing; boat cruises; canoeing; elephant rides; fortune teller; cultural performances; limited room service. *In room:* Some have A/C.

The Marari Beach 🐟🐟🐟 *Kids*   This is without a doubt one of the best beach resorts in Kerala (if not India), with a superb beachfront location. It's also a good choice if you have neither the time nor the inclination to travel farther south to the better-known beach resorts. That said, it's a pretty mellow, down-to-earth place (in other words, not in the same class as the heritage-soaked Surya Samudra or the Poovar Island resort, the best beachfront resorts south of Trivandrum). The Marari Beach features comfortable and spacious (but relatively basic) stand-alone thatched cottages, spread over 12 hectares (30 acres) of lawns and pathways enveloped by coconut groves. The best rooms are nos. 19 and 20, as these are conveniently located near the beach, bar, restaurants, and pool. Marari's laid-back charms are complemented by its eco-friendly undertakings, which include a water-recycling plant, an organic vegetable garden, and a solar-heated hot-water project. The extensive Ayurvedic center is considered one of Kerala's best, serviced by two dedicated doctors and backed up by therapists and special dietary options from the restaurant. But the best aspect is the resort's *au naturelle* setting, with a 25km (15-mile) beach shared only with fellow guests, local fishermen, and a Laurel-and-Hardy duo who serve as the resort's lifeguards.

Mararikulam, Alleppey 688 549, Kerala. © **0478/286-3801,** -3802, -3803, -3804, -3805, -3806, -3807, -3808, or -3809. Fax 0478/286-3810. 58 units. Doubles: $154 garden villa, $171 peak season (Dec 21–Jan 20); $275 pool villa, $319 peak season; $35 extra person. Rates include breakfast. AE, DC, MC, V. **Amenities:** 2 restaurants; 2 bars; pool; 2 tennis courts; volleyball; badminton; bicycles; Ayurvedic center; car hires; currency exchange; shop; laundry; doctor-on-call. *In room:* A/C, minibar, tea- and coffee-making facility, safe.

Privacy 🐟🐟   A secluded bungalow with two en-suite rooms and a central dining/reception room situated at the edge of Vembanad Lake, this lodging option really does live up to its name. Privacy was converted from a workshop-cum-shack into a private resort by a Cochin-based architect; the interiors were designed by owner Joerg Dreschel, who incorporated local skills and elements with his personal take on Keralan style. Polished black oxide flooring contrasts with blue and mustard-yellow fabrics in the bedrooms; latticed walls, large mirrors framed in teakwood, antiques, and traditional masks complete the picture. On the porch, wooden rocking chairs with extendable leg rests invite hours of relaxation. The front door is just steps from the lake, upon which *kettuvallams* idle and birds swoop down to catch fish. Completing the idyll, guests enjoy the personal attention of a dedicated chef and housekeeper. Although Privacy feels like it's a million miles from anywhere, it's only 45km (28 miles) from Cochin and 15km (9⅓ miles) from the backwater-access town of Alleppey.

Reservations through the Malabar House Residency, 1/268–1/269 Parade Rd., Fort Cochin 682 001. ⓒ 0484/ 221-6666. Fax 0484/221-7777. www.malabarhouse.com. Bungalow: $130–$180 with 2-bedroom capacity; $110–$160 with 1-bedroom capacity. Extra bed $20. Meal package $30 per person. MC, V. *In room:* TV, fax machine, kitchenette with tea- and coffee-making facility.

KOLLAM
1,220km (756 miles) S of Mumbai

There is no reason to spend any time in what is the official southern point of Kerala's backwaters, but two accommodations options on the outskirts of town are worth considering, particularly if you plan to head north in a houseboat to Alleppey or beyond. Budget travelers can get a taste of history in a British mansion that's been converted into the **Tourist Bungalow,** which functions primarily as a Government Guest House (Tourist Bungalow Rd.; ⓒ **0474/274-3620**). Located a short distance out of town, the mansion isn't in the best shape, with neglected antiques and aging facilities, but the guest rooms (with attached bathrooms) have a faded grandeur and cost less than $4 per night. A better option, not least because it's on the water, is the rather pompously named **Aquaserene,** a quiet resort with a number of facilities (Ayurvedic center, 24-hr. room service, guided tours) and set on a promontory that's almost entirely bordered by water. A network of canals and concrete pathways links the collection of cottages with various parts of the resort, and coconut palms and watery rockeries set a tropical mood. The Lake Heritage Villas are duplex guest rooms in red-tile-roof *kettuvallam*-style cottages that make use of restored teak pieces and feature indoor-outdoor bathrooms. The upstairs bedroom has a balcony with cane chairs to take in the lovely watery views. Only five have double beds, so book one of these in advance. Doubles cost Rs 7,500 ($164), including all meals and taxes. Contact the resort at ⓒ **0474/251-2410** or check it out at www.aquasereneindia.com.

3 Thiruvananthapuram (Trivandrum) & Varkala
1,200km (756 miles) S of Mumbai

"Thiruvananthapuram" is the mouthful of a name given to Kerala's seaside state capital, but thankfully almost everyone calls it Trivandrum. Although the city has some interesting museums and a temple that's of great significance to Hindus (and off-limits to non-Hindus), the only reason to find yourself here is to utilize the city's excellent transport connections and head for the beautiful beaches that lie north, at Varkala, or south, at Kovalam. Yes, Varkala has certainly been "discovered," but it's a more laid-back alternative to Kovalam, which—no doubt due to its proximity to Trivandrum (a mere 10- to 20-min. drive south)—has been a popular seaside vacation spot for more than 70 years, and as a result has become overcommercialized and saturated with tourist-hungry businesses. If you're looking for Kerala's most stunning, upmarket seaside options, many with more-or-less private beaches, you'll have to travel south of Kovalam (see "From Kovalam to the Tip of India," later in this chapter).

ESSENTIALS
VISITOR INFORMATION   As the state capital, Trivandrum has plenty of outlets for tourist information. There are two **Tourist Information Counters** at the airport; one is run by the Government of India (ⓒ **0471/245-1498**) and

the other by the Government of Kerala (© **0471/250-1085;** open during flight times); the latter also has counters at the Central Bus Station in Thampanoor (© **0471/232-7224**) and at the Railway Station (© **0471/233-4470**), both of which are open daily from 8am to 8pm. Kerala's **Department of Tourism** operates a 24-hour toll-free information line (© **1600/44-4747**). The following offices also provide tourist information: **Kerala Tourism** (Park View, Museum Rd., opposite the museum complex; © **0471/232-1132;** daily 10am–5pm) and the **DTPC Tourist Information Office** (Thampanoor Overbridge, near Central Bus Stand; © **0471/233-0820;** daily 8am–8pm). For local tour information, go to the **Kerala Tourism Development Corporation** or KTDC (at the Chaitram Hotel, adjacent Central Bus Station in Thampanoor; © **0471/233-0031;** Mon–Sat 6:30am–9:30pm).

In Kovalam, visit the **Tourist Facilitation Centre** (© **0471/248-0085**) at the ITDC compound; it's open every day between 10am and 5pm. Besides giving information, the center assists with tour bookings, car hires, boat rides, and lodging. Consider any government-owned accommodations carefully.

GETTING THERE & AWAY   By Road   As mentioned earlier, Kerala is ideal for exploration with a hired car and driver; roads are relatively good, and the countryside is spectacular. See "Guided Tours," below. Trivandrum is connected by principal roads and highways with all parts of the country. Super Deluxe bus services are operated by the **Kerala State Road Transport Corporation** (© **0471/232-3886** for the Central Bus Station in Thampanoor; © **0471/246-3029** for the City Bus Stand in Fort). Private operators run so-called deluxe coaches to more distant towns and cities in south India, but note that overnight buses stop regularly, making sleep quite impossible.

By Air   Trivandrum is connected by air to Delhi, Mumbai, Kochi, Chennai, Bangalore, Hyderabad, and Tiruchirapali. The **international airport** (© **0471/250-1537** for domestic information; © **0471/250-1542** for international flight information) is served by **Jet Airways, Air-India,** and **Indian Airlines** (for details, see "Airlines" under "Fast Facts," below). There are also international flights from various Asian cities, including Dubai, Abu Dhabi, and nearby Malé in the Maldives. The airport is 8km (5 miles) from the city center, and you can pick up taxis and auto-rickshaws for the journey into town.

Buses for the airport depart from the city bus station.

By Train   There are regular trains between Trivandrum and other important destinations in Kerala, including Cochin (5 hr.), Alleppey (3½ hr.), Kollam (1½ hr.), and Varkala (1 hr.). If you're coming from Chennai in Tamil Nadu, the **Thiruvananthapuram Mail** is convenient. Trains also reach India's southernmost point, Kanyakumari; the journey is around 2½ hours.

Thiruvananthapuram Central Railway Station is just east of M.G. Road, on Station Road; for general railway inquiries, call © **131.** For reservations, call © **132,** or you can access the **Interactive Voice Response** service by calling © **1361.**

GETTING AROUND   By Taxi & Auto-Rickshaw   Metered rickshaws charge upwards of Rs 6 (13¢) per kilometer, but you'll more than likely find yourself haggling over a predetermined price, particularly in the resort areas around Kovalam. For auto-rickshaw trips between Trivandrum and Kovalam, expect to pay Rs 100. Between the airport and Kovalam, taxis charge around Rs 250 one-way. From Kovalam north to Varkala, taxis should charge Rs 800. To hire a car and driver, see "Guided Tours," below.

Fun Fact **Women's Lib, Kerala-Style**

For centuries Kerala enjoyed its own complicated caste system. Alone at the top of the social hierarchy were the Namboodiris, who believed they would be atmospherically polluted if they so much as saw a slave at a distance of 100 yards—such a traumatic event would necessitate elaborate purification rites. As a result, the Namboodiris lived isolated lives, in huge, high-walled houses, or *illams,* made of wood, thatch, and tile. Within their highly restrictive system, only the eldest son was encouraged to marry, while all daughters were expected to remain virgins; accordingly, the Namboodiri population experienced continual decline. In Kerala, the Nair warrior caste was, unlike elsewhere in India, near the bottom of the caste hierarchy (though not quite as low as the "polluting" classes who tended the coconut palms). Unusual in India, the Nairs followed a matrilineal system whereby property was common and inherited through the female line. All the members of a single *tharavad* (the traditional Keralan family home) were descended from a single female ancestor. Astonishingly, the Nair women also enjoyed immense sexual freedom and were able to form multiple sexual partnerships. Traditionally, the first such liaison would be with a Namboodiri, then with a Nair of similar status, and then with members of other non-polluting castes. Nair marriages were entered into and ended with ease; the husband was simply not a part of the wife's *tharavad*—he was expected to turn up after dinner and return to his mother's home before breakfast.

By Motorcycle & Scooter   You can rent an Enfield or Honda on a daily basis from **Voyager Travels** (© **0471/248-1993**) in Kovalam. Expect to pay between Rs 200 ($4.30) and Rs 350 ($7.60) per day.

GUIDED TOURS   KTDC (Hotel Chaithram, adjacent Central Bus Station, Thampanoor; © **0471/233-0031;** Mon–Sat 6:30am–9:30pm) organizes sightseeing tours in and around the city. These are cheap (Rs 190/$4 full day) but are aimed primarily at domestic tourists, so they are not recommended. A far better option is to hire a private car and driver and plan a personalized trip. Arrange this through your hotel, or contact **Sita World Travel** (G-2, P.R.S. Court, Ambujavilasam Rd., off G.P.O. Junction; © **0471/247-0921** or 0471/247-1064; fax 0471/245-0851; trv@sitaincoming.com).

FAST FACTS: **Trivandrum**

Airlines As ever, your best option is **Jet Airways** (Sasthamangalam; © **0471/232-5267,** 0471/232-8864, or 0471/232-1018); you can also contact Jet at the airport (© **0471/250-0710** or 0471/250-0860). Other options are **Indian Airlines** (Mascot Sq., M.G. Rd.; © **140** or 141, 0471/231-8288 or -6870; airport location © **142** or 143 or 0471/250-1537); or **Air-India** (Vellayambalam; © **0471/231-4837** or -0310; airport location © **0471/250-1426**).

Ambulance Dial © **102.** Also see "Hospitals," below.

Area Code The area code for **Trivandrum** is **0471.**

ATMs Several ATMs in Trivandrum accept Visa and MasterCard; there are no such facilities south of the capital, however.

Banks You can exchange currency and traveler's checks at **Canara Bank** (Spencer Junction, M.G. Rd.; ✆ **0471/233-1536**; Mon–Fri 10am–2pm and 2:30–3:30pm, Sat 10am–noon); you can also get cash advances against certain credit cards. Currency exchanges only at **Central Bank of India** (Chaitram Hotel lobby, Central Station Rd.; ✆ **0471/233-0359**; Mon–Fri 10am–2pm, Sat 10am–noon).

Car Hires See "Guided Tours," above.

Currency Exchange Most hotels will exchange your dollars, pounds, or euros; also see "Banks," above.

Drugstores Try **Darsana Medicals** (Station Rd.; ✆ **0471/233-1398**; daily 8am–9:30pm).

Emergencies For fires and other emergencies, including medical services, call ✆ **101.**

Hospitals You'll get good care at **Sree Uthradon Thirunal Hospital** (Pattom; ✆ **0471/244-6220**), which is privately run. Also try **Cosmopolitan Hospital** (Maurinja Palayam, Trivandrum; ✆ **0471/244-8182**).

Internet Access Expect to pay around Rs 60 ($1.25) per hour. In Trivandrum, visit **Starnet Communications** (Old Sreekanteswaram Rd.; ✆ **0471/246-4550**) or **Orbit Cybercafé** (Vasantham Chambers, S.S. Coil Rd.; daily 9:30am–10pm). Kovalam has many cyber dens.

Police Dial ✆ **100.** Thampanoor Police Station (✆ **0471/232-6543**) is on Station Road.

Post Office The **General Post Office** (✆ **0471/247-3071**; Mon–Sat 8am–8pm, Sun 10am–4pm) is along M.G. Road.

Travel Agents IATA-affiliated **Altima Tours & Travels** (Corporation Golden Jubilee Building, opposite SMV High School, M.G. Rd., Trivandrum 1; ✆ **0471/246-0807**, -1212, or -3569, or 0471/247-0524, or 0471/47-1383; fax 0471/245-3769; trv@altimaindia.net) is reliable, and foreign clients get instant service.

Visa Extensions Contact the **Office of the Commissioner of Police** (✆ **0471/232-0555**).

WHAT TO SEE & DO IN TRIVANDRUM

Trivandrum, to put it bluntly, is a dump, but it has a number of interesting buildings, including the stately **Secretariat and Legislative Assembly,** situated along Mahatma Gandhi Road, which is the main boulevard and center of activity through town. M.G. Road runs more or less north to south and links the two most significant areas of tourist interest: the **Museum Complex,** to the north of the city; and the Fort area, which houses the **Sree Padmanabhaswamy Temple** and **Puthen Malika Palace Museum,** to the south. It is possible to walk from one area to the other (about 45 min.), and there are numerous shops en route. Alternatively, auto-rickshaws continuously buzz along the road's length, and you will have no trouble catching a ride from one area to the other. Aside from the attractions reviewed below, the **Chacha Nehru Children's Museum** is sure to draw parents traveling with children with its collection of nearly 2,000 dolls.

Shri Padmanabhaswamy Temple ⍟   This Dravidian-style Vishnu temple, said to be the largest in Kerala, may be off-limits to non-Hindus, but the "temple guides" manage to target foreigners with great ease, leading them to the obligatory spots from which to photograph the seven-story-high entrance tower, or *gopuram,* which is pretty much all that can be viewed from the outside. Because the temple is located in the heart of the Trivandrum, it is likely that the city was built around it. The temple is believed to have come into existence on the first day of the Kaliyuga era (Dec 28, 3101 B.C.)—legend has it that the temple "materialized" after a sage prayed to Vishnu asking him to appear in a form that he could comprehend with his limited human vision—but the greater part of the complex was built during the 18th century. The temple is fronted by a massive tank, where devotees take ritual dips. Alongside a promenade are stalls selling ritual items, religious souvenirs, and flowers for use inside the temple.

Fort, Trivandrum. ⓒ 0471/245-0233. Closed to non-Hindus. Strict dress code: Hindu men must wear a white *dhoti* and no upper body covering; women must wear a sari and blouse. Varying hours, generally 4:30am–noon and 5:30–7:30pm.

Puthenmalika (Kuthiramalika) Palace Museum ⍟⍟   A secret, private passage is believed to connect Padmanabhaswamy Temple with this Travancore-style palace, built in the early 18th century by the social reformer Maharajah Swathi Thirunal Balarama Varma, a poet and distinguished musician. Known as the Horse Palace because of the 122 carved horse brackets that buttress the exterior walls, the buildings include some elaborate carvings, among them two extravagant thrones—one made from 25 elephant tusks, another made entirely from Bohemian crystal. Visitors are also allowed into the Maharajah's music room, from where you get the same view of the temple that was apparently a source of inspiration to the erstwhile ruler. Despite the value of much of the collection, the buildings are in need of renovation; the beauty of the carved teakwood ceilings and collected objets d'art are sometimes disguised by insufficient lighting and neglectful curatorship. You'll be taken around by an "official" guide—obviously he'll require a small tip.

100m (328 ft.) from the temple, Fort. ⓒ 0471/247-3952. Entrance Rs 20 (40¢). Tues–Sun 8:30am–1pm and 3–5:30pm.

Museum Complex ⍟   Mercifully, the remainder of Trivandrum's cultural sites are clustered in a huge formal public garden at the northern end of the city. **The Napier Museum** occupies an early Indo-Saracenic building, created in 1880 in honor of the governor of Madras, Lord Napier. This priceless collection includes some excellent 12th-century Chola bronzes, wood carvings, stone idols, and fascinating musical instruments, while more unique pieces include a temple chariot, a 400-year-old clock, and a royal cot made from herbal wood. Fine-art enthusiasts should visit the **Sri Chitra Art Gallery,** which holds an assortment of miniature paintings from the Rajput, Moghul, and Tanjore schools, as well as more exotic works from Japan, China, Bali, and Tibet. One of the country's foremost artists, Raja Ravi Varma (1848–1905), whose oil paintings explore Hindu mythological themes, is represented here. The **K.C.S. Paniker Gallery** is a wholly unnecessary diversion, as is the **Natural History Museum** (unless you want to see stuffed animals and dolls in traditional costumes)—the anthropological exhibit at Kolkata's Indian Museum is far superior. And stay away from the **zoo,** particularly if you're an animal lover—like most zoos in India, it lacks the funding to build bigger, more humane habitats for its animals.

Museum Rd. Purchase tickets for all museums at the ticket booth. Admission Rs 5 (10¢) for each. Thurs–Sun and Tues 10am–4:45pm; Wed 1–4:45pm.

ARTS & ENTERTAINMENT

The **Shree Karthika Thirunal Theatre** (alongside Lucia Continental Hotel; ✆ **0471/247-1335;** fax 0471/246-1248), in Trivandrum's Fort district, holds regular classical dance-theater performances (mostly Karnatic, but also Hindustani) throughout the year. The theater has its own company but hosts outside groups showcasing various genres, including Kathakali, Mohiniattam, and Bharatanatyam. It's worth contacting the secretary, Mr. Sreekumar (✆ **984/7144-1335**), for information about what's on and to find out about any special programs (but find out exactly how "special" the program is before you buy tickets).

You can observe **Kalaripayattu** martial arts classes, and even arrange for special performances or lecture demonstrations, through **C.V.N. Kalari Sangham** (Fort, Trivandrum; ✆ **0471/247-4182;** fax 0471/245-8996; www.cvnkalari.com; sathyacvn@vsnl.com). Established in 1956, this institution has represented India at numerous international festivals.

NORTH OF TRIVANDRUM: THE RED CLIFFS OF VARKALA

A 55km (34-mile) drive north of Trivandrum (and an hour by train), the seaside resort of Varkala draws numerous Hindu pilgrims who come to worship in the 2,000-year-old **Sri Janardhana Swami Temple** and ritualistically cleanse themselves in the mineral spring waters that gush from Varkala's ruby-red laterite cliffs. The cliffs also overlook the rather aptly named "Beach of Redemption." Varkala attracts scores of backpackers searching for an untouched beach paradise—and several years ago, they might have found just that. Today, hawkers and shack-dwellers

---

A Cultural Rendezvous

Backed by UNESCO, the **Vijnana Kala Vedi Cultural Centre** charitable trust was founded in 1977 by a French artist named Louba Schild, who has been living in Kerala since the late 1960s. The center endeavors to preserve traditional Keralite arts and crafts, and to nurture the potential of young artists. The center also runs programs concerned with teaching such diverse cultural traditions as Ayurvedic medicine, local architecture, languages like Sanskrit, Indian cooking, and mural painting, as well as training in classical performance styles such as Mohiniattam, Bharatanatyam, and Karnatic vocal music. Around 200 foreign artists, researchers, and cultural tourists attend the center to learn about local arts and culture, and you are invited to enroll in short- or long-term programs. Vijnana Kala Vedi is situated 3 hours from both Trivandrum and Kochi; the center will gladly make all arrangements for pickups from either airport. Six of the guest rooms have en-suite Western-style bathrooms, but hot water must be ordered by the bucket. Accommodations are simple but lovely, with ceiling fans and mosquito nets. The traditional Keralite meals are strictly vegetarian. For more information, contact the **Vijnana Kala Vedi Cultural Centre** (Tharayil Mukku, Aranmula 689 533; ✆ **0468/221-4483** or -3308; www.vijnanakalavedi.org; $200 all-inclusive tariff per person for the 1st week, with a 10% discount for the 2nd week; $630 1-month stay; a maximum of 3 nights costs $32 per night per person; for accommodations only for a maximum of 1 week, $15 per person per night).

have drifted in and set up shop along the tops of the cliffs; the coconut palms have been replaced by cheap guesthouses and open-air cafes; and children flog cheap jewelry, yards of cloth, and back-to-nature hippie gear.

Nonetheless, being a holy beach, the sand at the base of the cliffs stays relatively free of human pollution—it's neither a convenient public ablution facility nor a waste-dumping ground. Instead, devotees of Vishnu attend to earnest *puja* sessions, offering banana leaves piled with boiled rice and brightly colored marigolds to be carried away by the ocean. Usually, the sand is soft and lovely, and you can find a quiet cove for sunbathing without the crowds that are inescapable in Kovalam. In fact, you can find relative peace and calm if you restrict your beach activities to the morning; by lunchtime the gawkers (female bathers are advised to be discreet), hawkers, and dreadlocked Europeans start to file in, and it's time to venture back to the pool—with any luck, at the Taj Garden Retreat.

Other activities for visitors here include Kathakali demonstrations, elephant rides, village tours, and backwater trips.

WHERE TO STAY & DINE
TRIVANDRAM

Walk up the spiraling incline of the **Indian Coffee House** (between the Tourist Reception Centre and KSRTC bus stand; daily 7:30am–10pm), if only to say you've dined in one of the world's oddest restaurants. Located diagonally opposite the railway station, this unique coffeehouse was designed by Laurie Baker, an English architect who now lives in Kerala, and resembles a squat ochre-colored version of Pisa's leaning tower. It's a favorite hangout for the locals, and an interesting spot in which to spend some time rubbing shoulders with the groundlings and businesspeople who come here for their *iddlis, dosas,* and *chai* or coffee (you can purchase beans here, too). If you're exploring the Secretariat, head across the road to **Arul Jyothi** (Mahatma Gandhi Rd.; © 0471/246-0497; daily 6:30am–10pm). The capital's civil servants pile in here at lunchtime, when there's much ordering of *thalis* (platters featuring Indian breads and various curries and chutneys) and wonderful *masala dosas.*

For more salubrious surrounds (not to mention delicious Malabar fish curry and melt-in-your-mouth chicken masala), the smart **Regency Restaurant** at the South Park Hotel is the place to be (Spencer Junction, Mahatma Gandhi Rd.; © 0471/233-3333; daily 12:30–3pm and 7:30–11:30pm).

There is little reason not to head south before nightfall, but if you really must stay in the city, the **Muthoot Plaza** is Trivandrum's swankiest hotel (© 0471/233-7733; www.themuthootplaza.com; $65–$88 double including breakfast). A seven-story steel-and-glass hangout for foreign visitors and businesspeople who come to the state capital to pay *baksheesh* to various government representatives, Muthoot is functional, with good service and a convenient location, but it has no pool (though staff can arrange access to one). If you need a daily dip (and the best in-house restaurant), the **South Park** (© 0471/233-3333; www.thesouthpark.com; $60–$100 double) is another good choice, especially since the guest rooms benefited from a much-needed refurbishment in 2002.

Budget travelers (or those who'd rather save your cash for the gorgeous resorts that lie south) should head either for **Hotel Saj Lucia** or **Ariya Nivaas.** Hotel Saj Lucia (© 0471/246-3443; www.sajlucia.com; doubles from Rs 2,150/$47) is within strolling distance of Padmanabhaswamy Temple and the Palace Museum, two of the city's more interesting sights. Even better value, **Ariya Nivaas Hotel** (© 0471/330789; www.ariyanivaas.com) is an office-block-style hotel that offers good, clean lodging conveniently located near the Central Railway Station. Deluxe doubles go for Rs 1,000 ($22), and rooms without air-conditioning cost as little as Rs 600 ($13). Staff can help with travel arrangements. The hotel has a decent restaurant and a useful 24-hour check-out policy. It's often full, so book in advance.

VARKALA

Taj Garden Retreat Varkala ★★   Neatly set on the slopes of Varkala's red cliffs and overlooking a beautiful length of coastline, the Garden Retreat is hemmed in by verdant paddy fields and dense groves of coconut palms. It is simply the best address in town; this is definitely where you'll want to head when the crowds get irritating. That said, it's not in the same class as some of the resorts that lie south of Kovalam—while the building is inspired by elements of traditional Keralite architecture, it's essentially a modern concrete hotel with pretty pastel interiors. Reserve a sea-facing superior room; units aren't particularly large but are comfortable, with great views. Alternatively, you can head for the lobby's **Sunset Bar**—the view over the kidney-shaped pool toward the terraced paddy fields and the ocean below is intoxicating. *Note:* Some of the pathways leading down from the hotel toward the beach can be treacherous.

Janardhana Puram, Varkala 695 141. (C) **0472/260-3000**. Fax 0472/260-2296. www.tajhotels.com. retreat. varkala@tajhotels.com. 30 units. Doubles (Oct–Apr/May–Sept/Dec 20–Jan 5): $105/$90/$130 standard; $110/$95/$135 superior sea-view; $110/$110/$138 executive suite sea-view; $20 extra bed. Rates include breakfast and 1 other meal. Christmas/New Year's rate includes all meals. AE, DC, MC, V. **Amenities:** Restaurant; bar; cultural performances on request; pool with swim-up bar; children's wading pool; tennis; badminton; volleyball; fitness center with gymnasium, Jacuzzi, sauna; Ayurvedic center; children's garden; indoor games; travel desk; car hire service; meeting room; currency exchange; salon; 24-hr. room service; laundry; doctor-on-call; library. *In room:* A/C, TV, minibar, hair dryer.

4 From Kovalam to the Tip of India

1,216km (754 miles) S of Mumbai

A mere 16km (10 miles) south of Trivandrum, Kovalam has been a haunt for beach tourism since the 1930s, but its fame as a coastal idyll has wrought the inevitable. Discovered by hippies and then by charter tour groups, it is now a swinging holiday resort, its once-virgin charm plundered by low-rise concrete hotels that have all but totally replaced the coconut palm groves. Even so, Kovalam's three crescent-shaped sandy beaches, flanked by rocky promontories, remain quite impressive, and you can still watch fisherman ply the waters in catamarans (derived from the local word *kattu-maram*) as they have for centuries, at night assisted by the red-and-white lighthouse that beams from Kovalam's southernmost beach.

Lighthouse Beach is in fact where you'll find the bulk of cheap hotels, restaurants, and bars, with fishing-net-strewn Hawah Beach and less-crowded Samudra Beach lying to the north. After the rigors of India's crowded cities and comfort-free public transport, budget travelers are lured by the easy, comfortable (and high) life offered here, often staying until money (or good weather) runs out. You can rent beach umbrellas and watersports equipment along the beach, or hop aboard a fishing boat for a cruise out to sea. Stalls sell colorful fabrics, pseudo-ethnic hippie trinkets, and fresh fruit, fish, and coconut juice; music wafts from shack-style cafes, and unofficial bars survive strict liquor laws by serving beer in ceramic mugs and teapots. (Party animals note, however: The vibe at Kovalam is still far tamer than that found at Goa.)

Moments   Watching the Sun Rise from the Subcontinent's Southernmost Tip

Just 87km (54 miles) southeast of Trivandrum, across the border with Tamil Nadu, **Kanniyakumari** (also known as Cape Comorin) is not only India's southernmost tip but the much-venerated confluence of the Arabian Sea, the Bay of Bengal, and the Indian Ocean. **Watching the sun rise from the subcontinent's southernmost point** 🔥🔥 is an age-old ritual that attracts both thousands of Indian pilgrims each morning—who gather to plunge themselves in the turbulent swell, believing that the tri-oceanic waters are holy—and those who revel in the glorious spectacle as though it were a major Bollywood premiere. Nature's daily show here becomes something akin to a miniature festival, with excited pilgrims besieged by *chai-*, coffee-, and souvenir-*wallahs* selling everything from kitschy crafts (how else to describe conch shells with plastic flower bouquets glued to the top?) to ancient postcards and outdated booklets. Believe me, this is *the* place from which you don't want to receive gifts. But it's all part of the experience, which is quite wonderful; you can't help but be moved by the mass of people who gaze on a natural daily occurrence with such childlike wonder, effectively bestowing upon the event the spiritual significance that draws the crowds in the first place.

To get here you need to arrange for an early-morning wake-up call and have your hotel organize a taxi; you should reach Kanniyakumari at least half an hour before sunrise in order to take in the mounting excitement as the crowds prepare to greet the new day. (*Note:* **Kanniyakumari sunsets,** which are obviously more convenient to reach, also draw a crowd but are only visible mid-Oct to mid-Mar and are not quite as atmospheric, except perhaps for the full-moon evening in Apr, when the sunset and moonrise can be viewed simultaneously along the same horizon.)

Immediately south of Kovalam is **Vizhinjim Beach,** the site of the erstwhile capital of southern Kerala's first dynastic rulers and, between the 8th and 13th centuries, a major natural port for local kingdoms. Now a poor fishing hamlet of thatched huts overlooked by a pink mosque, Vizhinjim is an interesting contrast to the tourist hubbub of Kovalam; swimming here, however, is dangerous, no doubt the reason for its relatively untouched atmosphere. A number of shrines are found in Vizhinjim, including a rock-cut cave enclosing a single-celled shrine with a sculpture of Dakshinamurthy; the outer wall of the cave includes a half-complete relief depicting Lord Shiva and his consort, Parvathi.

Farther south, the Ayurvedic resorts that can still lay claim to the beach idyll that put Kovalam on the map dot the coast (see "Where To Stay," below). Visitors staying at any of these should seriously consider a day trip that takes in the **Padmanabhapuram Palace** (see review below), on the way to **Kanniyakumari,** India's southernmost tip, where you can enjoy one of the most interesting cultural experiences on the subcontinent (see box below).

From the terraced viewing area you will see two rock islands, one of which is the site of the **Swami Vivekananda Rock Memorial** (Tues–Sun 8am–5pm; Rs 10/20¢ daily *darshan:* viewing of a deity), reached by half-hourly ferry (Rs 20/40¢ round-trip). The memorial commemorates a Hindu guru and social reformer's meditative sojourn on the island in 1892. Several bookstores selling spiritual tomes are found on the island, but the best experience is to be had in the **Dhyana Mandapam,** a room where absolute silence is maintained so that pilgrims can meditate before a golden *om* symbol; children may not enter. A set of **Parvati's footprints** is enshrined in a purpose-built temple on the island. On the adjacent rocky island, a massive sculpture of the celebrated ancient Tamil poet-savant **Thiruvalluvar** stands 40m (133 ft.) high, punctuating the horizon like some bizarre homage to New York's Statue of Liberty.

The only attraction in the town itself is the famous **Kumari Amman Temple** ✸ (daily 4:30–11:30am and 5:30–8:30pm), dedicated to Kanniyakumari, a virgin goddess. Devotees enter the temple through the north gate, making their way around various corridors and bridges before viewing the deity, here depicted as a young girl doing penance with a rosary in her right hand. It's said that her sparkling nose jewel—seen glowing from some distance away—was installed by Parasurama himself. Non-Hindus wishing to enter the temple must remove their shoes, and men must remove their shirts and wear a *dhoti* (although a *lunghi* passes; purchase one before you leave Kovalam). A willing temple priest will lead you on a very brisk (queue-jumping) tour of the temple, ending with the obligatory suggestion that a donation would be quite acceptable.

If, for some reason, you get trapped in this ramshackle pilgrim-choked town, head for **Hotel Maadhini** (East Car St.; ✆ **04652/34-6787**), where you will be woken pre-dawn with tea and an urgent suggestion to watch the rising sun from your balcony. Double rooms, with carpets, attached bathrooms, and hot water, cost between Rs 350 ($7.60) and Rs 900 ($20).

En route back toward Kerala, you can buy cheap, delicious palm fruits from children on the side of the road and visit the fantastic palace in the town of **Padmanabhapuram,** capital of Travancore until 1790 (see below).

Padmanabhapuram Palace ✸✸✸   Although technically in Tamil Nadu (but a mere 55km/34 miles south of Trivandrum), this gorgeous palace—one of the finest examples of secular architecture in India—was for several centuries the traditional home of Kerala's Travancore royal family. It's still well-maintained, and a meditation room features two lamps that have burned since its construction, tended by two dutiful ladies. Built over a number of generations during the 17th and 18th centuries, the palace exemplifies the aesthetic and functional

---

Tips **Women: Don't Flaunt It**

Women should take care not to flaunt their bodies on Kovalam's beaches. Stories abound of women being harassed, and it is not uncommon for even teenage boys to boldly grab the breasts of Western bathers. Some argue that it's because some Western women consort with local men, and their "shameless" displays of affection create the impression that all foreign women are brazen hussies, keen to be had by virile Indian men. In short: Unless you're on a resort beach, where you'll be watched over by a "lifeguard," cover up and don't go it alone.

appeal of Kerala's distinctive architectural style: sloping tiled roofs; elaborate slat-
ted balconies; cool, polished floors; and slanting walls and wooden shutters—all
effectively designed to counter the intense sunlight and heat. The private living
quarters of the royal family are a maze of open corridors and pillared verandas;
outside, small garden areas feature open courtyards where the sunlight can
be enjoyed. Note that the king's chamber is furnished with a bed made from 64
different types of medicated wood and has its own beautifully decorated prayer
room.

Padmanabapuram is located 55km (34 miles) south of Trivandrum. Admission Rs 10 (20¢) adults, Rs 5 (10¢)
children; parking Rs 20 (40¢). Tues–Sun 9am–4:30pm. Ticket office closed 1–2pm.

WHERE TO STAY & DINE

Backpackers head for the budget hotels on the fringes of Kovalam's beaches
which, during peak season (Dec and Jan), are overrun by tourists and relentless
hawkers. Most lodging is less pleasant than cheap, and you're likely to be at the
constant mercy of blaring music from the beach and its sprawl of cafes. Note
that these cafes are fine for a snack but each should be judged according to the
number of customers. The rule of thumb is: If it's empty, the food has been
standing around too long. Your safest bet for a proper meal in Kovalam is the
restaurant of **Hotel Rockholm** (Lighthouse Rd.; ✆ **0471/248-0607**), where
you can dine on a terrace with ocean views; fresh seafood is always available, and
it's carefully prepared. Also, even if you haven't opted to stay at the beautiful
Surya Samudra resort (see below), it's worthwhile to dine at **Octopus.** Seafood
is the order of the day: tiger prawns fried in ginger garlic, shark or barracuda
steak grilled with ginger and chili, a wholesome tuna salad made with freshly
caught fish, or perfectly fried mussels—all delivered daily by the local fishermen.
Vegetarians are well catered to—try the green papaya curry or red spinach prepared in a coconut sauce—and there is also a selection of Western dishes, including a rather good spaetzle (the owner is, after all, German).

If you want to overnight close to Kovalam's tourist beach action, head for one
of the establishments at Samudra Beach, like the government-run **KTDC Samudra** (G.V. Raja Rd., Kovalam 695 527; ✆ **0471/248-0089** or 0471/248-1412,
-1413; fax 0471/248-0242; www.ktdc.com; doubles from Rs 3,600/$78). It's
sterile but enjoys a remarkable setting, perched close to the beach with fine views,
a swimming pool, and Ayurvedic masseurs. The best-situated of all the hotels is
the run-down **Kovalam Ashok Beach Resort** (✆ **0471/248-0101;** fax 0471/
248-1522; www.kovalamashok.com), which at press time was being bought by a
private hotel chain, so it may be renamed. The sprawling property—a great big
chunk of concrete designed by well-known Indian architect Charles Correa—
needs considerable attention, but if you're looking for good views over the Lakshadweep Sea and lots of amenities, it may be worthwhile to check how
renovations are getting along.

The resorts reviewed below are situated away from mainstream Kovalam and
offer peace, tranquillity, and charm, as well as some of the world's most pristine
stretches of coastline.

Bethsaida Hermitage   Ten kilometers (6 miles) south of Kovalam, this collection of thatched bamboo and stone beach cottages was conceived by a local
priest who wanted to start an eco-friendly endeavor that could be used to aid a
local orphanage. Set on a semi-private beach, amid 8 hectares (20 acres) of
coconut palms, this is truly a back-to-nature experience, with very simple, clean

accommodations (coconut wood bed, table chair, and overhead fan) in a variety of configurations. Reserve one of the most recently built rooms, which have bamboo-walled open-to-the-sky bathrooms. Hot water is at the mercy of an occasionally moody electrical system, and you need to bring your own toiletries. Don't arrive expecting luxury (for that, go next door to Surya Samudra; see below); this is the place to indulge your inner hippie—red and yellow tie-dyed fabrics are used extensively, and there are even several "cave" rooms. Tranquillity is the order of the day, and you'll feel good knowing that your room cost (slightly overpriced, considering) will contribute to the welfare of some 2,500 children.

Pullinkudi, Mullar, Kovalam Beach, Thiruvananthapuram 695 521. ⓒ and fax **471/248-1554.** 28 units. Doubles: $46 cave room; $70 cottage; $100 traditional *tharavad* with bay view. Rates include breakfast. 15% discount May–July. Credit cards for deposits only. Minimum 7-night stay over the Christmas and New Year period. **Amenities:** Restaurant; indoor games; travel desk; airport transfers; Ayurvedic massage; prayer hall; meditation center.

Lagoona Davina ✸✸   Converted into a charming sanctuary by English owner Davina Taylor Phillips, this charming little resort is popular with visitors who don't like to pack their own suitcases; send Davina your clothing sizes, and she'll have comfortable handmade cotton garments waiting in your room upon your arrival, along with personally chosen eco-friendly Ayurvedic toiletries. Guest rooms are small but lovely, each with a canopied four-poster bed covered in hand-loomed linen and mosquito net, freshly cut flowers, and bright yellow walls. Guests in the main house or in one of the Maharaja rooms also enjoy the services of a personal room attendant, who will pick you up at the airport if necessary. Various Ayurvedic treatments are available. You can relax after a stint on the beach in the small swimming pool near the edge of the lagoon—for solo female travelers, Davina arranges for someone to discreetly keep watch while you're lying on the beach.

Pachalloor 695 527. ⓒ **0471/238-0049** or -4857. Fax 0471/246-2935. www.lagoonadavina.com. 6 units, 1 cottage. Doubles (Nov–May/June–Oct): $126/$50 main guesthouse with sea view; $132/$66 sea-view Maharaja room; $64/$25 Eagles Nest room without sea view. 20% supplement for Christmas and New Year. MC, V. Credit card payments made in India incur 5% service charge. **Amenities:** Restaurant; pool; cultural programs; boating; backwater excursions; library with indoor games; travel assistance; car hires; boutique; Ayurvedic massage, yoga, meditation and reiki; tailoring.

Maharaju Ayurvedic Health Resort ✸ *Finds*   This low-key newcomer has all the spirit of Surya Samudra (a short walk down the road; see below), without the beach views, spacious layout, and price tag. Guest bungalows have been built to mimic traditional Kerala-style architecture, with banana-curved tiled roofs, open-to-the-sky bathrooms (with coconut palm trees), and spacious interiors with natural air-conditioning. Choose between a more traditional wooden Kerala house and a cheaper, more spacious garden house; these are large enough for two double beds (covered with Indian print bedcovers and draped with mosquito nets), and have two separate mini-verandas and their own sizeable gardens. Try to book cottage no. 1, which is private and looks directly into a dense coconut grove. There are hammocks to laze in while enjoying the after-effects of a glowing massage session—the highly respected Ayurvedic doctor practices his art in Switzerland during the off season, and his army of nearly 30 masseurs are frequently on loan to the area's upmarket resorts. Due to strict Ayurvedic principles, alcohol is not available. The beach (which Surya Samudra overlooks) is a 5-minute stroll away.

Pullinkudi, Mullar P.O. Thiruvananthapuram 695 521. ⓒ **0471/246-7288.** Fax 0471/248-2788. www.maharaju resorts.com. maharaju@netddl.com. 10 units. Doubles: $80 Maharaj suite; $80 Kerala wooden houses; $60 garden house; extra bed add 20%. Ayurvedic packages available. No credit cards. **Amenities:** Restaurant; Ayurvedic center; Kalaripayattu training center; travel assistance; car hires; room service; doctor-on-call. *In room:* Minibar (in garden house only).

Nikki's Nest ⭐   This is another resort set away from the tourist crowds and overlooking a secluded beach; it's a good alternative if Davina's is full. Accommodations are in roomy thatched-roofed cottages (reserve an A/C unit here) or three restored traditional wooden Kerala houses. No matter which guest cottage you choose, you'll enjoy first-rate views of the ocean and beach below, thanks to the resort's elevated location on a small hill. A number of Ayurvedic treatments are on offer. Located in the small village of Chowara, within verdant gardens and a collection of orchids, Nikki's Nest is virtually unknown to local taxi drivers but is located 12km (7½ miles) south of Trivandrum and a half-hour from the airport.

Azhimala Shiva Temple Rd., Pulinkudi, Chowara, S. Kovalam, Thiruvananthapuram 695 501. ⓒ 0471/248-1822, -3821, or -3822. Fax 0471/248-1182. www.nikkisnest.com. nikkisnest@hotelskerala.com. 15 units. Doubles: $100 (May–Sept), $170 (Dec 15–Jan 15) big Kerala house; $65 (May–Sept), $125 (Dec 15–Jan 15) Kerala house; $60 (May–Sept), $100 (Dec 15–Jan 15) A/C cottage; $40 (May–Sept), $85 (Dec 15–Jan 15) non-A/C cottage; add 20% per extra person. Rates include breakfast. AE, DC, MC, V. **Amenities:** Restaurant; pool; cultural programs; Ayurvedic spa; airport and railway transfers; currency exchange; shop; room service; laundry; doctor-on-call.

Poovar Island Resort ⭐⭐⭐   Kerala's southernmost resort, at the border between Kerala and Tamil Nadu on a remote stretch of river lagoon, is a tranquil, paradisiacal place of granite rock walkways and rubber-tree footbridges, sloping red-tiled roofs, and chocolate-brown villas. Add to the facts that this resort offers some of the best service, best food, and best Ayurvedic treatments in all of Kerala and is visited only by fishermen (the only way to reach this island retreat is by boat), and you see why this understated boutique resort is providing Samudra with some stiff competition. Catch the hotel water-taxi from the resort's mainland jetty and you land in a hammock-lounging, pool-lazing chill-out zone for weary travelers. Taking advantage of its island setting, Poovar has floating Malaysian teakwood cottages with elephant-grass roofs moored to jetties on the waters of the gorgeous Neyyar River not far from the estuary where it meets the Arabian Sea. Landlubbers can get cozy in quaint, rustic cottages (a little bigger than those moored at the jetty) with flecked-chocolate exteriors covered in a mixture of sandy soil, hay, and coal tar, and capped by Kerala-style tiled roofs. Interiors have blond-hued wood furniture; textured fabrics in cool orange, lime, yellow, and blue; and gorgeous bedside Tiffin lamps; antiques are thrown in for local flavor. Bathrooms are tiny throughout (particularly on the floaters, which only have showers). Idle away your time watching fishermen from your private veranda or from the sunken bar at the large and lovely cross-shaped pool; or consign yourself to the excellent bamboo-walled Ayurvedic center, staffed by two doctors and a handful of top-notch nononsense masseurs. Expect outstanding service in every department.

K.P. 7/911, Poruthiyoor, Kulathoor Panchayat, Pozhiyoor P.O. Trivandrum 695 513, Kerala. ⓒ 0471/221-2068, -2069, or -2073. Fax 0471/221-2092. www.floatelsindia.com. poovarisland@sify.com. 34 units (22 on land, 12 floating). Doubles: $80 superior rooms (Apr 1–Oct 14), $130 (Oct 15–Dec 21 and Jan 5–Mar 31), $200 (Dec 22–Jan 4) includes all meals; $120 floating cottage (Apr 1–Oct 14); $150 (Oct 15–Dec 21 and Jan 5–Mar 31); $150 deluxe floating villas (Apr 1–Oct 14), $225 (Oct 15–Dec 21 and Jan 5–Mar 31) includes airport/station transfers and complimentary soft bar, $325 (Dec 22–Jan 4) includes all meals; $25 extra bed. All rates include boat transfers, breakfast, and backwater cruise. AE, MC, V. **Amenities:** 2 restaurants (1 floating); bar; cake and pastry service; packed meal service; cultural performances; pool; gym; boating (kayaks, paddleboats); fishing trips; bird-watching; backwater cruises; Ayurvedic center; sightseeing and tours; car hires; currency exchange; shop; salon; 24-hr. room service (on land only); babysitting; laundry; doctor-on-call; small library; photographer (with prior notice). *In room:* A/C, TV (on land and in deluxe floating cottages), tea-and coffee-making facility (in floating cottages).

Somatheeram ⭐   Dalí would have loved this shabby-chic "Ayurvedic hospital" carved out of red sandy soil and perched on a terraced cliff overlooking a beach. Somatheeram has been inundated with awards for "Best Ayurvedic Centre" (mostly from Kerala's Tourism Department), and that is the primary reason to book here. European "patients" shuffle around in pastel dressing gowns with serene expressions on their golden-tanned faces; you'll swear everyone is recovering from a particularly blissful enema. Some accommodations are in traditional wooden Kerala houses, which have the standard shaded verandas and hand-carved pillars and are comfortable but not overly luxurious. Opt for an ordinary *nalukettu* room in one of the four-bedroom *tharavadu* houses, and ask for one with a good view of the ocean below. Substantially cheaper, the cottages are very basic round thatched structures built of stone or brick. For travelers on a tight budget, the adjacent sister resort, **Manaltheeram** (*C* **0471/248-1610;** www.manaltheeram. com) has sea-view thatched villas for $90 during the peak season.

Chowara P.O. 695 501. *C* **0471/248-1601.** Fax 0471/248-0600. www.somatheeram.com. somatheeram@ vsnl.com. 55 units. Doubles ($85–$200 deluxe suite; $60–$160 deluxe Kerala house; $50–$120 ordinary Kerala house; $40–$90 special cottages; $25–$70 ordinary cottages; $15–$50 mini cottages; 25% extra per person sharing. AE, DC, MC, V. **Amenities:** Restaurant; Internet cafe; cultural performances; beach games; beach guards; boating; yoga and meditation; indoor games; travel and tour assistance; currency exchange; tailor; gift shop; room service; laundry; doctor-on-call (Ayurvedic hospital). *In room:* Fridge in deluxe units.

Surya Samudra Beach Garden ★★★ Named for the gods of the sun and the sea, this is Kerala's most famous resort (at least for those who subscribe to *Condé Nast Traveler* or who have flipped through the picture-perfect *Hip Hotels*), and deservedly so. The small collection of purely traditional cottages sits on a terraced hillside overlooking the sea, with access to two gorgeous beaches. The original "Octagon cottage suite" was built as a private getaway during the 1970s by Klaus Schleusener, a German professor working in Madras. Alarmed at how centuries-old carved wooden cottages from villages around Kerala were being torn down to make way for modern homes, Schleusener was the first person to come up with the inspired idea of transplanting them into an environment aimed at well-heeled tourists with excellent taste. Spread over 8 hectares (20 acres) amid terraced gardens of hibiscus trees, coconut palms, and various indigenous palms, and interspersed with rustic pathways, Surya is not as slick (or coolly detached) as some five-star hotels, but the atmosphere is so romantic and the setting so glorious that you could easily spend your entire holiday here. Start the day with a yogic salutation to the sun, and end the day being lulled into dreamland by the sound of the ocean, with nothing but squirrels, lizards, insects, and spiders (all nonpoisonous, you're assured) to keep you company. You have a variety of accommodations to choose from, most with antique beds, beamed ceilings, heavy rosewood shutters, planter's chairs, peaceful verandas, and fans whirring lazily overhead. Without a doubt, the best options are the sea-facing rooms and suites, which have private patios and picture-frame windows looking onto the Arabian Sea, where villagers put their catamarans to work. The small beach cottages are good value for budget-conscious travelers who want a view. You can be picky and find incidental faults such as loose toilet seats and inconsistent housekeeping, but the luxury of unfettered tranquillity more than makes up for such slight oversights. The hotel is also relatively accessible: It's 40 minutes from Trivandrum airport, and a 90-minute walk along the beach to Kovalam.

Pulinkudi, Mullar P.O. Thirvanathapuram 695 521. *C* 0471/226-7333. Fax 0471/226-7124. www.suryasamudra. com. 16 units. Doubles: Low season (May–July); high season (Aug–Oct); peak season (Nov–Apr); Christmas/New Year season (Dec 22–Jan 6). $120–$360 garden suites depending on season ($480 Dec 31); $110–$300 sea-front rooms depending on season ($400 Dec 31); $110–$270 A/C garden rooms depending on season ($360 Dec 31); $110–$270 garden house depending on season ($360 Dec 31); $80–$180 small beach cottages depending on season ($240 Dec 31); $100–$180 garden-view cottages depending on season ($240 Dec 31). Children under 6 stay free if no extra bed required; extra bed 20% more. All rates include breakfast and airport or train station

transfers. Dec 31 rate includes complimentary drink, gala buffet dinner, and entertainment programs. MC, V.
Amenities: Restaurant; pool; beach lifeguard; boating; Ayurvedic spa; tour arrangements; foreign exchange; shop; room service; babysitting (by prior booking); doctor-on-call; small library; personal butler and valet ($20 per day). *In room:* Minibar, tea- and coffee-making facility. A/C in garden rooms.

Travancore Heritage ⚡ Massive billboards along the highway south of Trivandrum announce the establishment of this recent addition to the tourism boom along Kerala's southern coast. Set on 3 hectares (7 acres) of land, amid tamarind and jackfruit trees and coconut palms, Travancore Heritage is separated from the beach by 152 steps; all but two guest rooms have views of the ocean. This is the place to come if you prefer your heritage faux. With sloping red-tile roofs, wooden walls and floors, high-pitched ceilings, and covered pillared verandas, structures recall the traditional style of the region; the main building is modeled on the royal palace at Edapally and features some wonderful reproductions and charming views from its upstairs balcony. Guest rooms are furnished with high wood-frame beds, old wicker-backed planter's chairs, and blinds made from gilded white *lungi* material. Views from the premium rooms, two of which have tubs rather than showers, are quite a bit better than their standard counterparts. Staff are helpful and friendly, and there's a fine Ayurvedic center.

Chowara P.O., Trivandrum 695 501. © **0471/226-7828** or -7832. Fax 0471/226-7201. www.thetravancore heritage.com. travancoreheritage@vsnl.net. 45 units. Doubles: $85 heritage home, $95 heritage premium, $155 pool mansion (Apr–Sept 30); $105 heritage home, $130 heritage premium, $225 pool mansion (Oct 1–Mar 31); $30 extra bed. MC, V. **Amenities:** Restaurant; cultural performances; pool and kids' pool; beach volleyball; Jacuzzi; indoor games; travel, car hires, and tour assistance; currency exchange; room service; doctor-on-call; library. *In room:* A/C, TV, coffee-making facility.

5 Lakshadweep

Between 200km (124 miles) and 450km (279 miles) W of Kerala's coast

Ask any globe-trotting island-hopper if the globe still holds any undiscovered gems, and Lakshadweep will be the among the first names to crop up. One of India's best-kept secrets, the 36 atolls and coral reefs making up the remote Union Territory of Lakshadweep (or Laccadives) are an extension of the better-known Maldives island group, where booming tourism has spawned luxury resorts. Only three Lakshadweep islands—Agatti, Kadmat, and Bangaram—are open to foreign tourists, and the Indian government employs a strictly enforced entry permit system. All the islands are "owned" by the indigenous people, and land is unavailable for purchase by non-natives—even a man marrying a local woman may not buy land here.

Only 10 islands in the archipelago are populated, almost exclusively by Malayalam-speaking Sunni Muslims who make their living from fishing and harvesting coconut coir. Only Minicoy Island, which is closest to the nearby Maldives, shares aspects of its neighbor's culture, including a Maldivian dialect known as Mahl.

Being Muslim, the islands are officially dry, and alcohol is only available on Bangaram, which is technically uninhabited; avoid carrying any liquor with you. You are, however, strongly advised to bring insect repellent since the mosquitoes become alarmingly active once the sun descends.

ESSENTIALS

PERMITS No foreigner may visit the islands without prebooked accommodations. Visitors intending to stay at the Bangaram Island Resort can have all permit arrangements made through the **Casino Hotel Group central reservations** (Casino Hotel, Willingdon Island, Cochin 682 003; © **0484/266-8221;**

fax 0484/266-8001; casino@vsnl.com). Foreigners must supply the hotel with your name, address, place and date of birth, passport number, place of issue, date of issue, and date of expiry. The Casino Hotel Group will also happily book your flight to and from Kochi for you.

To make your own permit arrangements (a laborious process), contact the **Society for Nature, Tourism and Sports (SPORTS)** run by Lakshadweep Tourism (© **0484/266-8387**) in Kochi, or contact their Delhi office (© **011/2338-6807**).

VISITOR INFORMATION See "Permits," above. For details about Lakshadweep, contact the Assistant Manager, SPORTS, Lakshadweep Administrative Office, Willingdon Island, Kochi; © **0484/266-8387.**

GETTING THERE Unless you fancy a time-munching trip from Cochin by ship (anything between 14 and 20 hr.), the only way to get to Bangaram is on one of Indian Airways' costly flights ($320 at press time) from Cochin. You arrive at the tiny airfield on Agatti (Agathi) Island, after which you'll be detained by some bothersome paperwork.

After this you'll be met by a resort representative, who'll usher you to a waiting boat anchored near the shore not far from the airport for a memorable 90-minute journey to nearby Bangaram Island. During the monsoon season (May 15–Sept 15), a helicopter is used instead of a boat; transfers cost $100 per person.

DIVING THE REEFS

Experienced divers rank the reefs of Lakshadweep among the best diving destinations in Asia, particularly the coral islands of Bangaram, Tinakara, Pirelli 1, and Pirelli 2. Bangaram Island Resort hosts **Lacadives,** a small dive center that is the first and only CMAS (an international underwater-sports federation) dive organization in India, with its headquarters on the island of Kadmat. Lacadives offers diving courses, rents out equipment, and conducts two dives a day (at 9:30am and 2:30pm). If you're not a qualified diver, you can rent a mask and go on one of the resort's snorkeling trips to a nearby wreck where an assortment of marine fauna will have you begging for more. The resort can organize big-game fishing with local boats, but anglers should bring your own equipment. For details, contact the **Lacadives Diving Centre,** Bangaram Island Resort, Bangaram (www.lacadives.com; lacadives@hotmail.com; in Kochi: Lakshmi Niwas, 43/2051, K. Colony, Kadavanthra P.O., Kochi 682 020, © **98/4703-3395,** fax 0484220-6766; in Mumbai: E-20, Everest Building, Tardeo Rd., Mumbai 400 034, © **022/5662-7381** or -7382, fax 022/2495-1644).

WHERE TO STAY

Bangaram Island Resort ★★★ Lodging options are limited, so thank heavens for the Casino Hotel Group's keen appreciation for this unique environment. Borrowed from the pages of an old-style holiday brochure, this peaceful 51-hectare (128-acre) island is all silver beaches and towering coconut palms—no newspapers, television, minibars, or even air-conditioning get in the way of experiencing the beauty of the island. Eco-consciously designed so as to all but disappear into the surroundings, the modest 14-year-old resort is quite basic, with the emphasis on the captivating setting rather than fussy luxuries. Guest cottages, arranged in a row a short distance back from the beach, are spartan and clean: palm-frond thatch-covered huts with simple cane furniture, mesh screen windows, and private porches from which to admire the ocean. Cottages have electricity and running water (which is not heated but is never cold; it's taken straight from the ground, so although it's safe for showering, it has a detectably high salinity level and a slight sulphuric smell). The atmosphere here is so removed from workaday worries that you'll battle to find excuses for not simply reclining in your hammock and staring into the magnificent cobalt waters. On the other hand, you could discover a new addiction: diving, which is a major drawing card. On foot (take shoes for coral-covered stretches), you can skirt the entire island in about an hour; en route you will discover a host of stunning milky-white beaches to call your own. Wandering around the island, you can also venture inland where, among the trees, you'll find the huts of the Lakshadweep locals who come to the island from time to time to harvest their coconuts. There's an Ayurvedic massage center for those days when the sunbathing gets too stressful, and early risers can salute the rising sun with yoga on the helipad at 6:30am. The buffet meals unfortunately are served indoors, but the best spot to be in the evenings is at the circular bar near the water's edge, where, among other things, barman Joseph mixes a mean Bangaram Binge—a feisty blend of dark Indian rum and coconut milk, completed with one of his signature palm frond swizzle sticks. (At press time, plans for upgrading facilities were being held up by a government dispute.)

Bangaram Island, Lakshadweep. Reservations: Casino Hotel, Willingdon Island, Cochin 682 003. © 0484/266-8221. Fax 0484/266-8001. www.casinogroup.com. casino@vsnl.com. 30 cottages. Doubles: $240 standard room, $270 peak season (Dec 21–Jan 20); $450 2-bedroom deluxe, $530 peak season; $100 extra person. Rates include all meals. Boat transfers $30 per person. AE, DC, MC, V. **Amenities:** Restaurant; bar; Ayurvedic center; boat transfers; dive center; deep-sea fishing; island trips; kayaks, catamarans.

6 The Cardamom Hills & Periyar Wildlife Sanctuary

190km (118 miles) E of Kochi

Each year, around half a million travelers make their way up into the Cardamom Hills, where the crisp, cool air is redolent with the scents of spices, and soaring mountains give way to tea plantations and dense jungle. Most people head straight to Thekaddy to explore the Periyar Wildlife Sanctuary, the stomping grounds for large herds of wild elephants. Periyar is one of India's largest and most popular reserves, and the site of one of the best-organized trek experiences in India. The best time to visit is in late spring and summer (Dec–Apr), when streams and watering holes dry up and herds of wildlife come from the depths of the jungle to drink and bathe in the Periyar lake.

Another worthwhile destination in the Cardamom Hills, particularly if you're overlanding from Madurai in Tamil Nadu, is the region around **Munnar**, a 2- to 4-hour drive north of Thekkady. At a much greater altitude than Periyar, Munnar (pronounced *Moo*-naar) is a collection of vast green tea estates first established by a Scotsman in the late 19th century—it's hardly surprising, then, that the area is sometimes referred to as Kerala's Scottish highlands. In the days of the Raj, it became a popular "hill station"—a place to escape from the summer heat in the plains. Today the landscape—for the most part—retains a classic hill station atmosphere. Watched over by Mount Anamudi, south India's highest peak, Munnar's primary attractions are its gorgeous views of rolling hills covered with tea and cardamom plantations, and the cool climate—great for leisurely walks and cycle-tours (not to mention a close encounter with the rare tahr, a variety of mountain goat or ibex).

ESSENTIALS

VISITOR INFORMATION   All Periyar Wildlife Sanctuary inquiries should be made through the **Wildlife Information Centre** (© 0486/232-2028; daily

---

Finding Serenity on the Way to Periyar

En route from Cochin (110km/68 miles) to Periyar (90km/55 miles), and a mere 30km (19 miles) from Kottayam, **Serenity** ★★ is a lavishly converted 1920s bungalow on Kanam Estate, in the heart of a rubber plantation. It has a choice of six guest rooms, all with high wood-beam ceilings, generous windows, polished floors, cane chairs, and outlandish traditional masks mounted on display stands. Reservations are made through the Malabar House Residency in Cochin (1/268, 1/269 Parade Rd., Fort Cochin 682 001; ✆ **0484/221-6666;** fax 0484/221-7777; www.malabarhouse.com; info@malabarhouse.com).

6:30am–5pm; near the jetty within the reserve); entry to the park (Rs 50/$1.05) is between 6am and 6pm. Easiest by far is to ask your hotel to make arrangements; all the resorts will book and transfer you to the KTDC-arranged excursions (see "Exploring the Periyar Wildlife Sanctuary," below). The **Idukki District Tourism Information Office** (✆ **0486/232-2620**) is located in Kumily, the nearest village to the park, but it has very erratic opening hours.

The best source of information in Munnar is Joseph Iype, a self-proclaimed Munnarphile who runs the **Free Tourist Information Centre** (Main Bazaar; ✆ **0486/253-1136** or -0349; daily 9am–1pm and 3–6pm). Joseph will provide you with maps, articles, and advice, and can help arrange transport and accommodations (yes, he also has his own cottage to rent). Alternatively, the **Tourist Information Centre** (✆ **0486/253-0679**) in Old Munnar is good for arranging wildlife tours and local sightseeing excursions.

GETTING THERE   From Cochin   Periyar is a 6-hour drive east of Cochin, a fairly long but enjoyable drive that traverses mountain roads ascending 900m (3,000 ft.) above sea level; to cut down on travel time, perhaps arrange your itinerary so that you depart from (or to) Kottayam or Alleppey. Munnar is a 2- to 3-hour drive north of Periyar (100km/62 miles), and another beautiful drive; you'll pass tea plantations and spice-growing embankments and drive through lovely sections of forest, quite different from Kerala's coastal region. See "Fast Facts: Cochin," above, for information on car hires.

From Madurai, Tamil Nadu   The drive from Madurai to Munnar (or you can bypass Munnar and go direct to Periyar) is also stunning, traversing many a mountain pass and scenic countryside. The drive from Madurai to Periyar should take about 4 hours. *Note:* Traveling by bus is at best arduous and time-consuming, at worst hair-raising.

GETTING AROUND   You can pick up a ride on a rickshaw or taxi almost anywhere in **Kumily,** where hordes of vehicles wait at the bus stand. Overcharging foreigners is common; try to ascertain from your hotel what the going rate for a particular route is, and bargain upfront. Taxicabs and auto-rickshaws are readily available in and around **Munnar,** or you can arrange a car and driver through your hotel.

EXPLORING THE PERIYAR WILDLIFE SANCTUARY

Originally the hunting grounds of the Maharajah of Travancore, the Periyar Wildlife Sanctuary was declared a wildlife reserve in 1933. In 1979 it became a Project Tiger Reserve—India's homegrown initiative to protect the big cats' dwindling numbers. Today Periyar covers 777 sq. km (191,979 acres), and is divided into core, buffer, and tourist zones. Although tiger sightings are rare, particularly in the tourist zone, the reserve is home to elephants, sloth bears, sambar, Indian bison or gaur, wild dog, leopard, spotted deer, Malabar flying squirrel, barking deer, Nilgiri tahr, some 260 species of birds, and over 2,000 species of flowering plants, including at least 150 different kinds of orchids.

The best way to experience Periyar is with the privately run Periyar Tiger Trail (see below); other than this, all access to the park is arranged through the KTDC. These excursions are cheap, making them popular with exuberant domestic tourists who somewhat inhibit the serenity of the experience. Most opt for the 2-hour **boat cruise** on the Periyar lake (Rs 100/$2.10 on top deck; Rs 50/$1.05 on lower), from where you can view animals coming to drink at the water's edge. Unfortunately, you're more likely to experience nonstop din from children (and their parents) who refuse to obey pleas for silence, preferring to rove around the boat and camcord each other. Boats depart at 7am, 9:30am, 11:30am, 2pm, and 4pm. A better option: Ask about the **private boat launches,** also offered by KTDC; these cost around $30 and take a maximum of 12 passengers. Also recommended are the **daily walks;** these 3-hour treks depart at 7am and 3pm, and provide you with the opportunity to admire some of the stunning flora of the region. And to ensure you have a truly close-up encounter with a pachyderm, you can mount one on a 30-minute **elephant ride** in the park (Rs 30/60¢; departing every 30 min. 11am–12:30pm and 2–4:30pm). More determined naturists can arrange to spend a night in one of the two **observation towers,** but you'll require all your own provisions and a sleeping bag.

Note: Whatever activities you have in mind, you're better off making all your arrangements through your hotel. Avoid any unsolicited offers from "guides" promising to take you on walks or tours into the reserve; this will only waste your time and test your patience.

The Periyar Tiger Trail ★★★ *Moments*   By far the most exciting and tranquil way to experience the park (and one of the best in India) is on an exclusive 2- or 3-day "Periyar Tiger Trail" organized by **TourIndia** (the same company that innovated the backwaters houseboat scene). Armed with anti-leech footwear and a sleeping bag (supplied), and accompanied by a naturist and a game ranger armed with a rifle, you are taken farther into the tourist zone than any other operator is allowed to penetrate. What's more, you are led and looked

---

Tips Alternatives to Spotting Elephants in Periyar

You can pick up a range of spices from a massive number of shops lining the streets of Kumily, the nearest town to Periyar. The best option is to head straight for **Kerala Spices Centre** (Thekkady Rd.), where the chatty owner will offer to take you on a complimentary 4km to 5km (2½-3-mile) tour of the various plantations (transport not included, of course). He also sells nuts and delicious cardamom tea, and he's more than likely to invite you to join him for a cuppa *chai* prepared by his wife in their home around the back. Just down the road from Spice Village and Cardamom County, daily **Kathakali** performances are held at the **Mudra Kathakali Centre** (Thekkady Rd.; ℭ **0481/256-7982,** 0481/252-5230, or 98-4731-0710; Rs 150/$3.15). Shows feature graduates of the Kalamandalam school. Show times (usually at 6 or 6:30pm) change with the seasons, so call ahead.

after by a team of reformed poachers (sandalwood, cinnamon bark, and bison being their loot of choice) who know the terrain and the wildlife better than anyone. They skillfully track and spot animals, carry all the gear, strike camp, cook, clean, and—most important—stand sentinel throughout the night when the danger of being trampled by elephants becomes a serious risk. They also now play an essential role in catching poachers who remain active in the reserve.

You'll almost certainly come across elephants, wild pigs, sambar, black monkeys, wild dogs, and bison, and when you're not trekking to your next campsite, you'll be relaxing under forest cover or alongside a lake tributary. Meals are wholesome, authentic Keralan vegetarian fare: sweet *chai* and pleasant snack lunches served on silver trays with the grass for a tablecloth and an electronic beetle symphony. Ablutions are performed in the great outdoors. If you have any special interests, such as ornithology, TourIndia will make arrangements to have a specialist guide you. *Note:* These exceptional hiking expeditions are limited to five visitors at a time, and only 20 participants are accepted per week, so book early, particularly in peak (winter) season.

IX/1007 Kumily, Thekkady Rd., near Kerala Spices Centre, Kumily 685 509. ℂ 0486/232-3208 or -3209. Reservations: Post Box no. 163, Mahatma Gandhi Rd., Trivandrum 695 001. ℂ 0471/233-0437 or -1507. Fax 0471/233-1407. www.richsoft.com/tourindia. tourindia@vsnl.com. A 3-day, 2-night expedition, which involves around 30km (19 miles) of hiking and includes all gear, food, guides, and a forest officer, costs around $250 per person for 2 people sharing. Up to 5 people can be accommodated, in which case the cost is around $150 per person. Individual interests are catered to and special packages can be devised.

EXPLORING MUNNAR: HOME OF TEA & TAHRS

Munnar township is itself rather unpleasant and increasingly clogged by impulsive development; thankfully, the region's real attractions lie on its outskirts and have so far withstood the onslaught of tourist exploitation.

With plantations spread out as far as the eye can see, watching the mists creep over the valleys and come to rest like a blanket on the jade-colored hills is almost as refreshing as luxuriating in the cool climate—a welcome relief before you descend to the tropical Keralan coast or to sultry Madurai in neighboring Tamil Nadu.

Almost all the plantations are owned by the powerful Tata company, the same mighty conglomerate that produces India's buses, Sumo four-by-fours, and the Taj hotel chain. **Tea factory visits** can be arranged either through your hotel or by contacting Tata's regional office (℗ **0486/253-0561** or -0565); the latter may prove more difficult since visitors are not actively encouraged.

To get up close to some of the world's last Nilgiri tahr (a variety of mountain goat or ibex), visit nearby **Eravikulam National Park.** Existing only in the mountain grasslands of the Western Ghats at altitudes above 1,200m (3,840 ft.), the tahr is as endangered as the tiger, with fewer than 2,000 left. Of course, sighting what is basically a goat, no matter how rare, may not be as exhilarating as spotting a tiger, but your chances are far higher—in fact the tahrs have grown so used to visitors that you can get within a few yards of them. Enter the park at the Rajamala entrance, 15km (9⅓ miles) from Munnar, where you can buy tickets in the forest office (daily 7am–6pm; foreigners Rs 50/$1.05, light vehicles Rs 10/20¢, three-wheelers Rs 5/10¢). Avoid the usual noisy crowds by arriving early.

WHERE TO STAY & DINE
IN & AROUND PERIYAR

With the exception of the atmospheric KTDC Lake Palace, which is inside the park, visitors to Periyar are limited to accommodations options that lie within a few minutes of each other along Thekaddy Road (which links nearby Kumily with

Once in a Blue Bloom

If you're not in too much of a rush to get to India's southern highlands, plan your visit for 2006, when you can glimpse the next blooming of the rare and exotic **Neelakurunji plant.** Its violet blossoms transform the hillsides around Munnar for 1 month every 12 years. A pleasant 34km (21-mile) trip from Munnar, Top Station—the highest point on the Munnar–Kodaikanal road, from where you enjoy panoramic views of the surrounding plains and hills—is *the* place to witness this natural spectacle.

the park gate). Of these, the Shalimar Spice Garden Resort, located just off Thekaddy Road (see below), is by far your best bet. Even if you don't stay at the resort, a table at **Mangiatutto,** the excellent in-house restaurant, is worth booking. The name means "eat it all," and that's exactly what you'll want to do. Keralite cuisine is served the traditional way (on banana leaves), but the Italian dishes are quite fabulous. Try the rich, delicious guinea fowl when it's available, or ask for the ever-so-subtly-spicy roast quail, which isn't always on the menu. Homemade pasta is prepared especially for the Bianca Alpomodora, tossed in Tuscan olive oil that's brought all the way from Italy in owner Maria Fernhof's luggage. The **Periyar Room,** the air-conditioned indoor-outdoor restaurant at the Taj Garden Retreat (see below), is another popular option and ideal for a romantic evening.

Cardamom County   You wouldn't say so from the dull lobby, but Thekkady's newest hotel has some good suites with fine views into the Periyar sanctuary. Small cottages with tiled roofs and average-size rooms are terraced against a hill that slopes sharply up from the very public (and often noisy) kidney-shaped pool; bored waiters from the adjacent restaurant pass the time ogling the guests as they sunbathe. Units have high ceilings, fans, and uninspiring black wooden furniture on red terra-cotta floor tiles. Those located higher up the steep hillside (nos. 305–314) offer superb views; ask for room no. 303 or 304 (or even 317)—these have private balconies.

Thekkady Rd., Thekkady 685 536. (C) **0486/232-2866** or -2806. Fax 0486/232-2807. www.cardamomcounty. com. 45 units. Doubles: Rs 2,800 ($62) non-A/C superior; Rs 3,400 ($74) superior; Rs 3,750 deluxe ($80); Rs 5,000 ($110) suite. AE, DC, MC, V. **Amenities:** Restaurant; pool; health club; Ayurvedic center; fishing pond; indoor game room; tours; currency exchange; small shop; room service (6am–10pm); babysitting on request. *In room:* TV, minibar.

KTDC Lake Palace   The major draw of this old-fashioned stone, wood, and tile-roofed retreat—the former game lodge of the Maharajah of Travancore—is the gorgeous setting, best enjoyed from the wraparound veranda from where you're likely to spot a variety of game. In fact, the sense of wonderful remoteness kicks in when you take the 15-minute boat ride across Periyar Lake to reach the forested peninsula, inhabited only by hotel staff, a handful of fellow guests, and wild animals. The six "deluxe" guest suites are rather simple and forlorn, however: A few pieces of antique teak furniture (including four-poster twin or double beds), faux tiger-skin upholstery, and fake ivory tusks, tastelessly framing the dressing table mirrors, set the tone. Ask for a room on the east side, where the views are best. At press time, management was talking of refurbishments—musty carpets are to be removed to reveal teak flooring—but it's doubtful, given that the place is government-run, that the worn mattresses will be replaced. That aside, it's great not to have to travel to start your exploration—arrange for a predawn wake-up call and guide to take you into the jungle on foot.

Inside Periyar Wildlife Sanctuary. Reservations: Aranya Nivas and Lake Palace, Thekkady 685 536. © **0486/ 232-2023.** Fax 0486/232-2282. www.ktdc.com. aranyanivas@vsnl.com. ktdc@vsnl.com. 6 units. Doubles: Rs 6,500/$140 (Oct 1—Dec 20, Jan 21–May 31, and Aug 1–Sept 30); Rs 7,500/$164 (Dec 21–Jan 20); Rs 4,500/$120 (June and July); Rs 1,500 ($33) extra person. Rates include all meals. AE, DC, MC, V. **Amenities:** Restaurant; beer available; Ayurvedic treatments; travel assistance; boat cruises; car hires; currency exchange; laundry; doctor-on-call. *In room:* TV, minibar.

Shalimar Spice Garden Resort ★★★

In the off-the-map "village" of Murikkady, just 4km (2½ miles) from Thekkady, this pristine resort, situated on a 2.4-hectare (6-acre) plantation of palms, hardwood, fruit, coffee, and fragrant spices, offers the most enchanting accommodations in the region. Italian owner-architect Maria Angela Fernhof has combined her own brand of minimalist Euro-chic design with beautiful antique Keralan furniture and objets d'art from around the subcontinent, working hard to retain the benefit of light in such a dense forest setting. Scattered over a landscaped terraced hillock behind the lobby (situated in a 300-year-old traditional *pathayam,* or granary), granite and pebble pathways lead you to the thatch-roofed guest rooms and cottages. Through their teak and rosewood doorways, cool interiors are filled with antique furniture and carefully chosen ornaments. Cottages are modern and beautiful, with whitewashed walls and pale terra-cotta tile floors, crystal stained glass, and breezy loggias; the en-suite bathrooms all have windows letting in natural light. The "rooms" are simpler and smaller than the cottages but no less elegant; instead of bathtubs, they feature drench showers. Shalimar's small Ayurvedic center draws a regular European clientele; it's built according to ancient traditions with a stone floor, handmade brick walls, and an open fire for heating the medicated oils. Up the terraced hill, along garden pathways decorated with stone bowls once used for grinding spices, the lilac-blue granite-bordered pool sits in a sun-drenched clearing. Outside and in, the scents of cinnamon, tea, pepper, cardamom, jasmine, guava, orange, goose-berry, mulberry, tapioca, passion fruit, and tamarind fill the air. If you're interested in horticulture, ask Vinod, one of the waiters, to show you around the property—he's an accidental botanist with endless patience.

Murikkady P.O. 685 535. © **0486/232-2132.** Fax 0486/232-3022. www.shalimarkerala.com. shalimar_ resort@vsnl.com. 12 units. Doubles: $60 cottage, $50 room Apr 1–Oct 31; $130 cottage, $100 room Nov 1–Dec 19 and Jan 6–Mar 31; $150 cottage, $120 room Dec 20–Jan 6; extra bed is 30% of room rate; children under 6 free without extra bed. Add $10 for breakfast or add $40–$50 for all meals. Payment is required 60 days in advance. MC, V. **Amenities:** Restaurant; pool; Ayurvedic center; yoga; boat rides; bird-watching; sightseeing; trekking; taxi rental; currency exchange; specialty shop; babysitter by prior request; laundry; doctor-on-call; valet/butler by prior request.

Spice Village Nature Habitat ★★ *Kids*

Alive with fragrant spices and lush greenery, this "rustic village" resort has not only hosted its fair share of celebs but serves as a template for unpretentious yet quality holiday accommodations. Spread over a huge area around a network of pathways and intersections (if you're averse to walking, choose a low-numbered room, as these are closer to the public areas), the whitewashed bungalow cottages are all topped with thatch—a swell of thick elephant grass that plunges to the ground in an exaggerated curve, almost swallowing the red-tiled veranda; interiors are spacious but simply furnished. The well-priced and very private deluxe guest units are recommended; each has direct access to a private patio and garden, separate shower cubicle in the bathroom, and even a small kitchenette. From the moment you arrive, when you're welcomed with a mint-lime soda and the delicate smell of incense, staff are eager to please: Guided plantation tours, Periyar excursions, Ayurvedic spa treatments, and various culturally flavored activities make up the to-do list. Nature lovers may be interested in visiting the resort's Wildlife Resource Center.

Thekkady-Kumily Rd., Thekkady 685 536. ℭ **0486/232-2314**. Fax 0486/232-2317. www.casinogroup.com. 52 units. Doubles: $132 standard villa ($149 Dec 21–Jan 20); $165 deluxe villa; $35 extra person. Rates include breakfast. AE, DC, MC, V. **Amenities:** Restaurant; bar; cultural performances; pool; badminton; recreation room; Ayurvedic spa; nature center; wildlife excursions; cooking demonstrations; plantation visits; shop; room service.

Taj Garden Retreat Thekkady 🐾🐾   The delightful guest villas at this lush resort are mounted on 3.3m (11-ft.) stilts affording sweeping vistas of the verdant plantation-filled hills and valleys below. For the best views, try to book room no. 302, 501, or 601. The thatched-roofed guest rooms all feature high, pitched ceilings and private viewing decks; they're spacious and smartly furnished, with plenty of wood and attractive floral prints in natural fabrics. The gardens are also lovely, with indigenous trees as well as a number of exotic plants and flowers; during the season a naturalist is on-site to talk you through the botany. The multi-cuisine restaurant here is the only real fine-dining establishment in the vicinity.

Amalambika Rd., Thekady, Idukki District, Kerala 685 536. ℭ **0486/232-2401**, -2402, -2403, -2404, -2405, -2506, or -2407. Fax 0486/232-2106. www.tajhotels.com. retreat.thekkady@tajhotels.com. 32 units. Doubles: $120 Oct–Apr; $70 May–Sept; $140 Dec 20–Jan 5; $20 extra bed. AE, DC, MC, V. **Amenities:** Restaurant; bar; banquet hall; pool; badminton; Ayurvedic center; forest treks; boat safaris; plantation visits; game viewing; activity room; treehouse for kids; travel assistance; car hires; currency exchange; babysitting; doctor-on-call; nature library. *In room:* TV; minibar; tea- and coffee-making facility.

AROUND MUNNAR

For real Raj nostalgia, head for the **High Range Club** (ℭ **0486/253-0724**), which has tennis courts, a golf course, and a billiards table guarded by looming animal trophies. It's popular with wealthy Indians and has only 10 cottages, so book well in advance; double rooms cost between $40 and $54. Even more affordable is the **Eastend Edassery** (Temple Rd.; ℭ **0486/253-0451;** www.edassery group.com), which has clean, pleasant guest rooms and several garden cottages. Rates range from Rs 1,350 ($30) for a deluxe cottage to Rs 2,200 ($48) for a large duplex suite. For a less personal experience, **Tea County Hill Resort** (Munnar 685 612; ℭ **0486/253-0460;** fax 0486/253-0970; reservations: ℭ **0471/231-8976;** www.ktdc.com; ktdc@vsnl.com) is one of the better government-run hotel-resorts in India. The property occupies a sprawling, lovely estate atop a low-lying hill. Deluxe guest rooms are clean and comfortable, with small dressing rooms, tubs in the bathrooms, tiled floors, and small balconies with picturesque views. Plenty of guest facilities keep you distracted, including a very slick beer parlor with colonial ambience, and an elegant restaurant; order the Malabari fish curry or tandoori chicken.

Club Mahindra Lakeview 🐾 *Kids*   Located smack in the middle of Tata's Tea Estates, 22km (14 miles) from Munnar, Club Mahindra's guest rooms live up to the name, with lovely views of the lake below. An ideal spot to watch the mists swirl over the tea-plant-covered slopes below, Mahindra is a pleasant resort aimed at wealthy Indian families. Choose to stay in either the main building, with its sophisticated, colonial country-club flavor (planters' chairs, four-poster beds, and faux fireplaces), or in the more down-to-earth home-away-from-home apartments, which come with basic cooking facilities. A team of people are at the ready to keep the kids busy while you relax in the Tea Room, sampling local varieties. Or opt for one of the formidable assortment of activities—from meditative yoga to rappelling on a rock-face. In the glass-fronted restaurant, Chef

Sawarkar prepares a mean Nilgiri *korma,* a curry specialty from the Nilgiri hills. Club Mahindra is often booked up with timeshare participants, so advance reservations are recommended. Note that room rates soar over the Christmas/ New Year period.

Chinnakanal Village, Munnar 685 618. ✆ **0486/284-9224,** -9226, -9228, -9290, or -9291. Fax 0486/284-9227. www.clubmahindra.com. reservations@clubmahindra.com. 92 units. Doubles (Oct 1–June 15/Dec 20–Jan 5/June 16–Sept 30): $120/$150/$60 superior; $130/$180/$60 deluxe; $225/$275/$110 suite in main block; $250/$300/$120 1-bedroom deluxe suite; $300/$350/$145 2-bedroom deluxe suite. AE, DC, MC, V. **Amenities:** Restaurant; yoga; boating; camping; adventure activities; children's activity center; travel and tour assistance; plantation tours; provisions shop; salon; 24-hr. room service; laundry; doctor-on-call. *In room:* A/C, TV.

The Siena Village ★★ (Value) It's a striking half-hour drive from scruffy Munnar town to this interesting resort in what feels like genuine hill country. Still relatively new, accommodations are spread around a wide expanse of neatly trimmed lawns and a central open-air pavilion where barbecue dinners are held with a campfire and entertaining cultural performances. Split-level deluxe guest rooms are homey; these have downstairs living rooms with working fireplaces, treated wooden floors, and private balconies with lovely dam views. Ask for one with an upstairs bedroom. Bathrooms are smallish and don't have tubs. The **Peppermill Restaurant,** which only opens for breakfast (included in the price) and lunch, has a small upstairs section from where you can enjoy lovely views. A playground and activity center help keep younger visitors occupied.

Chinnakanal Village, Munnar 685 618. ✆ **0486/284-9261,** -9328, or -9461. www.thesienavillage.com. 26 units. Doubles: Rs 1,600 ($35) standard; Rs 2,700 ($60) deluxe; Rs 3,200 ($70) luxury suite; Rs 400 ($8.75) extra person; children under 5 free in parent's room. Rates include breakfast. Add Rs 1,000 ($22) for all meals. MC, V. **Amenities:** Restaurant; alcohol available; cybercafe; indoor games; travel desk, sightseeing assistance; plantation tours; car hires; conferencing; shop; laundry; doctor-on-call. *In room:* TV. Deluxe guest rooms have fireplaces.

Windermere Estate ★ Just outside Munnar on a 24-hectare (60-acre) estate, this intimate undertaking includes a stone farmhouse and two-unit Coffee Cottages and warm service to make visitors feel like personal guests. Accommodations are bright and clean, with wooden ceilings and floors and dark cane furniture. The surrounding landscape is exceptionally good for scenic walks, and you can try your luck fishing in one of several nearby streams.

P.O. Box 21, Pothamedu, Munnar 685 612. ✆ **0486/253-0512** or -0978. Reservations: c/o Molly Simon, Trikkakara, Kochi 682 021. ✆ **0484/242-5237.** Fax 0484/242-7575. www.windermeremunnar.com. email@windermeremunnar.com. 7 units. Doubles (Apr–Sept/Oct–Mar): $90/$110 farmhouse; $110/$145 cottage. Rates include breakfast and lunch or dinner. Payment in advance at Kochi. No credit cards. **Amenities:** Dining room; fishing; trekking; doctor-on-call; TV in sitting room.

7 Malabar: Northern Kerala

Even though northern Kerala's history as a major spice trade destination is well documented, it remains relatively untouched by tourism. This is largely because of the 8-hour drive to get here from Kerala's better-favored beaches and backwaters. Nevertheless, this can be a wonderful region to explore if you are looking to get far away from the tourist crowds, and have time to spare. Certainly if you're traveling overland, from Goa or Karnataka to Kerala, it makes excellent sense to spend a day or two exploring this undervalued part of the subcontinent, particularly the **Wyanad Hills,** which remains one of India's last true wildernesses and has one of the most interesting accommodations options on the subcontinent.

ESSENTIALS

VISITOR INFORMATION   In Calicut, a **Kerala Tourism information booth** (© 0495/270-2606; Mon–Sat 10am–1pm and 2–5pm) is at the railway station. In Kannur, inquire at the **Kannur District Tourism Promotion Council** (Taluk Office Campus; © 0497/270-6336).

GETTING THERE   By Road   Kannur and Calicut are both on National Highway 17, which gets tricky in places as you head farther north. To get from Calicut to Vythiri in the Wyanad mountain ranges, you need to take the Calicut–Bangalore highway, which makes its way through Ooty, in Tamil Nadu, and Mysore, in Karnataka.

By Air   There are regular flight connections to **Karipur Airport** (© 0495/271-2762)—located 25km (16 miles) south of Calicut—with Mumbai, Chennai, and Coimbatore, and less frequent connections with Goa. Taxicabs are available for transfers into the city and should cost no more than Rs 150 ($3.15).

By Train   Calicut is an important jumping-off point for trains running up and down the coast of Kerala; there are daily trains from Mumbai and Delhi. Daytime journeys are wonderful if you're keen on enjoying fantastic views. Dial © 133 for the **Calicut Railway Station.**

GETTING AROUND   By Taxi & Auto-Rickshaw   Autos are fine for short trips in Calicut and Kannur, but for longer journeys you will have to hire a car and driver.

CALICUT & THE WYANAD RAINFOREST
Calicut is 146km (90 miles) NW of Kochi

Malabar trade, which is focused on spices and textiles, once centered on the teeming coastal town of **Calicut,** unofficial capital of the north, and incidentally from which the term *calico* (white, unbleached cotton) is derived. Vasco da Gama was first welcomed here in 1498; at the nearby village of Kappad, a commemorative plaque memorializes the spot where the Portuguese explorer is said to have landed. Now also known as Kozhikode, the city is of marginal interest to travelers, being more of a go-between point for journeys farther south or north, or inland to Kerala's highest rainfall region, the **Wyanad Hills** ★★★, one of India's last true wildernesses and home to the magical **Green Magic Nature Resort** (see below).

Archaeological evidence suggests that civilizations inhabited the Wyanad around a millennium before Christ. In this fertile rainforest, tribal populations continue to practice ancient rituals as they eke out a simple existence, relying on the barter system and living in harmony with nature. Mild temperatures and extremely high rainfall make the region great for growing coffee, cardamom, pepper, and rubber; plantations stretch over hills in every direction.

Not Quite Kung Fu Fighting

While in Calicut you can watch students perform Kerala's spectacularly acrobatic, high-flying martial art form, Kalaripayattu (see the sidebar "Kathakali & Kalaripayattu: Kerala's Colorful Art Forms," earlier in this chapter) at **C.V.N. Kalari Nadakkavu** (E. Nadakkavu, Nadakkavu P.O., Kozkikode 673 011; © 0495/76-9114 or -8214; cvnkalari-clt@usa.net). The school holds open classes 6 to 8:30am and 4 to 6:30pm—with prior notice, foreigners with some martial arts training are allowed to join classes. Ayurvedic treatments are given during the day.

Placating the Gods with *Theyyams*

Peculiar to the tribal region of northern Malabar, this ritual dance form evolved as a means of placating ancient village gods and ancestors. Combining temple ritual, rustic ballads, and folk art, *theyyams* are essentially representations of the collective consciousness of the village. Heavily made-up men with masks, elaborate costumes, spectacular jewelry, and 2m (6-ft.) -high headgear essentially become oracle-like incarnations or manifestations of the godhead or of a valorous ancestor. The ceremony begins with a song of praise, performed in honor of the presiding deity; this is followed by a dance strongly influenced by Kalaripayattu, the traditional Keralan martial art thought to predate the better-known Far Eastern forms like kung fu. *Theyyams* traditionally last an entire day and include a great deal of music, singing, and lighting of torches—oil lamps are ceremoniously brandished as shields and swords. *Theyyams* are usually held between December and May. To ensure your chances of seeing a performance, visit the **Sri Muthappan Temple** at Parassini Kadavu, 18km (11 miles) from Kannur, which has early morning and evening performances throughout the year.

KANNUR

92km (57 miles) NW of Calicut; 266km (165 miles) N of Kochi

Kannur is a pretty coastal town predominantly inhabited by what is locally known as the Malabar Muslim. Unlike North India, where Islam was more often than not established through violent conquest, here it arrived initially through trade, and grew through love; Arab sailors coming to Malabar in search of precious spices married local women, establishing the Mappila, or Malabar Muslim, community, which in turn developed its own Arabi-Malayalam songs and poems and the "Mappila Pattu." This oral record of their unique history contrasts, for instance, the broadminded Calicut rulers with the intolerant Portuguese tyrants.

Tourism in this northerly region of Kerala is only recently coming into its own, which has distinct advantages if you're looking to get away from the crowds. It also means that infrastructure remains scant. Don't be put off, especially if you are traveling by road between Karnataka and destinations in south Kerala.

If you're looking to find a safe, practically untouched sunbathing and swimming spot, head for **Muzhapilangad Beach,** 15km (9 miles) south of Kannur, where you'll probably have much of the 4km (2½-mile) sandy stretch all to yourself. Closer to the city, which the Europeans called Cannanore, the paranoid Portuguese built the imposing **Fort St. Angelo** (daily 10am–4:30pm; no charge), a monumental laterite edifice from which visitors can view the fishing harbor below. Seventy kilometers (43 miles) north of Kannur lies **Bekal,** Kerala's largest fort, thought to date back to the mid–17th century, though there is no accurate account of its construction. Bekal Fort (© **0499/277-2900**) is open to visitors daily between 9am and 5pm; admission is $5.

WHERE TO STAY
CALICUT

You'll find a number of cheap hotels along Calicut's beachfront. Built as the Malabar English Club in 1890, the **Beach Hotel** (Beach Rd., Calicut 673 032; © **0495/276-2055,** -2056, or -2057; fax 0495/236-5363) retains an air of history (it's where the likes of Somerset Maugham and Jawaharlal Nehru chose to stay). You can get a beach-facing suite for Rs 850 ($19) or a simpler air-conditioned room for Rs 600 ($13). Slightly more expensive, but still relatively good value, the **Fortune Hotel** (© 495/276-8888; www.fortunecalicut.com; doubles: Rs 1,900–Rs 2,500/$42–$55)) is a pleasant low-rise hotel with central air-conditioning and immaculately clean and comfortable rooms with small balconies. If you want a double bed, you need to reserve a Fortune room. The hotel is on a noisy main road, so you should ask for a room on a higher floor. A swimming pool is located on the third floor.

Taj Residency Calicut 🏵🏵   With the opening of its swanky Ayurvedic treatment center in 1999, this luxury business-orientated hotel, the best in Calicut, is steadily drawing more leisure and health travelers. Guest rooms are carpeted and feature dark red wood furniture offset by dark green upholstery and pale curtains and bedcovers; a small sitting area under wooden ceiling beams adds space and character. The lobby is bright and welcoming with wood-paneled pillars, cast-iron chandeliers, and wood-beam pitched ceilings; the sloping red terra-cotta tiled roof echoes the architecture of the region. If you do go for an Ayurvedic rejuvenation program, you can be assured of professional service and the knowledge that any treatments will be made in consultation with the resident astrologer.

P.T. Usha Rd., Kozhikode 673 032. © 0495/276-5354. Fax 0495/276-6448. www.tajhotels.com. residency.calicut@tajhotels.com. 74 units. Doubles: $75 standard; $90 residency room (includes breakfast and happy hour); $95 executive suite (includes breakfast). AE, DC, MC, V. **Amenities:** 2 restaurants; bar; pool; kids' pool; tennis on request; health club; Ayurvedic center; travel assistance; car hire; business center; currency exchange; shopping arcade; 24-hr. room service; laundry, dry cleaning; doctor-on-call. *In room:* A/C, TV.

IN & AROUND WYANAD

It takes around 2 hours to drive the 90km (56 miles) from the coastal city of Calicut to Vythiri, the nearest village to the Wyanad's exciting Green Magic Nature Resort (see below). If you're unsure about Green Magic but want to be close to the rainforest, the more staid **Vythiri Resort** 🏵 (Vythiri, Lakkidi P.O., Wyanad 673 576; © 0493/265-5366; fax 0493/265-5368; primeland@eth.net) is recommended, not least for its excellent Ayurvedic facilities. Doubles cost between $75 (tribal hut) and $90 (cottage), with all meals included.

Green Magic Nature Resort 🏵🏵🏵   If you've always dreamed of sleeping in a treehouse, in the heart of a forest dense with Ceylon oak and giant ficus trees, and with the sights and sounds of the rainforest canopy and its attendant animals below you, look no further. A cluster of treehouses built using age-old tribal techniques, separated with bamboo curtain "walls" and boasting plenty of living space and private wraparound balconies, the apartments (lit with hurricane lanterns) are fitted with rattan furniture, quilted mattresses with mosquito nets, and—best of all—attached bathrooms where you can shower and flush high above the world, watched by only your neighbors the giant Malabar squirrels. It's a heart-stopping experience getting to your room (there are lodges on the ground if you suffer from vertigo); one treehouse requires getting into a pulley-rigged bamboo cage and being hoisted 26m (85 ft.) up in the air—a simple but safe procedure using water-weight technology; another is reached via a swing bridge—quite daunting when you return to your room after dinner in the dead of night. You don't have to be an Indiana Jones to fall in love with Wyanad. You're pampered by the helpful staff, fed three excellent vegetarian meals per day, and supplied with natural Ayurvedic toiletries (red sandalwood and turmeric for your face, waka bark for your body, and rice charcoal for your teeth). And you get to explore the forest on (and later bathe) an elephant. Before you leave, you're asked to plant a tree, leaving not only your personal legacy but something living to come back to. Green Magic is situated 10km (6¼ miles) off the highway on an unpaved motorable road; if you don't have your own vehicle, the resort will arrange to collect you from Calicut. (The squeamish may want to note that leeches appear when it's rainy or whenever you get near water.)

Post Lakkidi, Vythiri. Reservations: Post Box no. 163, M.G. Rd., Trivandrum 695 001. ℂ **0471/233-0437** or -1507. Fax 0471/233-1407. www.richsoft.com/tourindia. tourindia@vsnl.com, tourindia@asianetindia.com. 3 treehouse units and 8 lodges. Doubles: $150 treehouse; $110 cottage. Rates include all meals. No credit cards. **Amenities:** Dining area; elephant rides; hiking; bird-watching; airport transfers; room service within reason.

Tranquil—The Plantation Hideaway ✮
Experience life on a 160-hectare (400-acre) working coffee plantation at the edge of the Wyanad National Park with the welcoming family owners, Hector and Jini Dey. Situated in a 70-year-old planter's bungalow, which has a pool and an Ayurvedic wing, accommodations are aptly named Coffee, Cloves, and Cardamom, and are individually designed. The Deys are very good about arranging tours of the nearby pepper, cardamom, coffee, banana, and coconut plantations. They can also organize a traditional *theyyam* performance (see "Placating the Gods with *Theyyams*," above) in a local temple. The nearby Eddakkal Caves, with wall carvings dating from the Neolithic Age, are also worth a peek. With a few developed sites in the neighborhood, this is not the back-to-nature experience of Green Magic.

Kuppamudi Coffee Estate, Kolagapara P.O., Sultan Battery, Wyanad 673 591. ℂ **0493/262-0244.** Fax 0493/ 262-2358. www.plantationhideaway.com. ivorytower@vsnl.com. Reservations: TravelsKerala, Karimpatta Rd., opposite Medical Trust Hospital, Pallimukku, Kochi 682 016. ℂ **0484/238-1038.** Fax 0484/236-4485. info@travelkerala.com. 6 units. Doubles: Rs 6,500 ($140); Rs 1,500 ($33) children over 12 sharing parent's room. Rates include all meals and taxes. AE, MC, V. **Amenities:** Restaurant; pool; Ayurvedic treatments; plantation tours; sightseeing; laundry. *In room:* TV.

NEAR KANNUR
The best place to overnight in this northernmost part of Kerala is a family-run guesthouse called **Ayisha Manzil** ✮✮ in Thalassery, which has a terrace looking onto the sea from its majestic position atop a cliff. Built by an East India Company tradesman in 1862, this lovely two-story mansion was bought by a family of Muslim spice traders in 1900. Today, it is still run by the Moosas, and combines modern facilities with sumptuous wooden antiques and unique family heirlooms. The guesthouse has a pool and a dining room where traditional Keralite and Malabari dishes are served. The six en-suite guest rooms differ in size and layout; upstairs accommodations are more private. Each room has either one or two double beds. Doubles, including all meals and beach transfers, cost around $150. The only drawbacks are that you may be told that there's a 2-night minimum stay, and that you must bring your own alcohol. If you're after a thoroughly unusual dining experience, ask to have breakfast on "the island." Nearby excursions include outings to Thalassery's fruit markets, or a tour through the property's original cinnamon plantation, apparently the largest in Asia. Ayisha Manzil (Court Rd., Thalassery 670 101; ℂ **0490/234-1590**) is 80km (50 miles) from Calicut's airport, and Thalassery (or Tellicherry) is served by trains from Calicut as well as Bangalore and Chennai. Transfers are easily organized.

6

Tamil Nadu: The Temple Tour

If your idea of India is one of ancient temples thick with incense and chanting masses worshiping dimly lit deities covered with vermilion paste and crushed marigolds, then Tamil Nadu is where your mental images will be replaced by vivid memories. Occupying a long stretch of Indian Ocean coastline known as the Coromandel, India's southernmost state is dominated by religion in nearly every aspect of life. For many, this is the Hindu heartland—home to one of India's oldest civilizations, the Dravidians, who pretty much escaped the Mughal influence that permeated so much of the cultural development in the north. Ruled predominantly by the powerful Chola, Pallava, and Pandyan dynasties, Dravidian culture flourished for more than a thousand years, developing a unique political and social hierarchy, still evident in the strong caste differences prevalent here, the strictly vegetarian fare, and a fervent nationalist sensibility.

Thanks to heavy summer downpours, Tamil Nadu is green and lush—particularly in the Cauvery Delta toward the west, where the great Dravidian kingdoms were established and some of the finest temples built, like the 11th-century **Brihadeshwara Temple,** situated in Thanjavur, the Chola capital for 400 years. By contrast, **Chennai** (formerly Madras), the capital established by the British in the 17th century, is a thoroughly unpleasant metropolis. It's primarily of interest as a gateway to some of the region's best attractions, like nearby **Kanchipuram,** one of the seven sacred cities of India, and the **Sri Venkateshvara Temple** (just over the border in Andhra Pradesh), said to be the wealthiest temple in the world. There, devotees line up for hours—even days—to hand over an annual 1.5 billion rupees to help Vishnu settle his debt with the God of Wealth. Just 2 hours south of Chennai lies the seaside village of **Mamallapuram,** where the Pallavas built the earliest examples of monumental architecture in southern India during the 5th and 9th centuries right near the water's edge. From here it's a relaxing 2½-hour drive further south to charming **Pondicherry,** Tamil's former French coastal colony. Although the French officially left years ago, Pondicherry's Gallic spirit is still very much alive—traditional Indian snack joints feature signs proclaiming MEALS READY; BIEN VENUE, locals clad in *lungis* (traditional Indian clothing) converse in French, and gorgeous antiques-filled Indo-French colonial mansions have been restored as hotels—the kind of "temple" that will appeal to the lazy hedonist in you. Having caught your breath in the wide boulevards of Pondicherry, you can either travel to Tiruchirappalli, exploring the holy temple town of **Srirangam** and nearby **Thanjavur,** or head to the **Sri Meenakshi-Sundareshwar Temple** at Madurai. A place of intense spiritual activity, this temple is where 15,000 pilgrims gather daily to celebrate the divine union

Fun Fact **Rule of the Screen Gods**

It's not just temple gods who are worshipped here—much as in California, screen gods are adored by the local population, enough to elect them to the highest political office. The majority of Tami Nadu's leaders have started off on the big screen. Across the state, you'll see massive billboards featuring the swollen face of **Jayalalitha,** a controversial actress-turned-politician who is currently Tamil Nadu's incorrigible chief minister. Kicked out of office on corruption charges in 2001, she jumped back in to reclaim her position, tossing her successor in jail. Once again declaring herself the voice of the people, she immediately set to work initiating a piece of state legislation to prevent the conversion of Hindus to other religions—a bill that no doubt earned her great favor with the powerful Brahmins who control the temples that so deeply influence the lives of the ordinary people.

of the goddess Meenakshi (Parvati) and her eternal lover, Sundareshwar (Shiva)—it's one of the most evocative experiences in all of India.

Note: **Kanniyakumari,** the venerated southernmost tip of Tamil Nadu, is discussed in chapter 5.

1 Chennai

Chennai is neither ancient nor lovely. Formerly called Madras, the capital of Tamil Nadu is a teeming, sprawling, bustling industrial metro established on the site of a fishing village in 1639 as the first British settlement in India. Today it is often choked by pollution, acrid smells—and people. The city is only marginally fascinating—it's a strange mix of British Raj–era monuments, Portuguese churches, Hindu temples, and one of the longest urban beaches on earth. Most travelers arrive here simply because it's a transport hub and soon leave, discouraged by the intense heat, polluted air, and fever-pitch crowds. Its star attraction—**Kanchipuram,** city of "a thousand temples"—is a day excursion away.

ESSENTIALS
GETTING THERE & AWAY   By Air   Jet Airways has daily flights to Chennai's international **Meenambakkam Airport** (© **044/2232-9971** or -9972; or dial 140) from all major destinations in India; both Madurai and Tiruchirappalli can be reached by flights from here. Aringar Anna International Terminal and Kamarajar Domestic Terminal are situated about 12km (7½ miles) from the center. The 30-minute taxi ride from the airport to downtown Chennai should cost Rs 300 ($6.50).

By Train   Chennai has two major railway stations. **Chennai Central** (Georgetown) connects Chennai with most major destinations around India, while **Egmore** is the point of arrival and departure for trains within Tamil Nadu or Kerala. Some trains from within the state now also pull in at the **Tambaram** station, an hour from Chennai. You can get recorded train information by dialing the computerized © **1361** (remember to have your train number). To plan train

Tamil Nadu

travel, we suggest you go online to **www.srailways.com** or **www.southernrailway. org**. Or book your train at your hotel, a travel agency (see below), or the Rajaji Bhavan Complex (ground floor) in Besant Nagar.

By Road   You may not realize it by glancing at a map, but Tamil Nadu is a fairly massive chunk of India, and it will take over 15 hours to drive from Chennai to Kanniyakumari in the far southwest of the state. Nevertheless, getting around is best done from the relative comfort of a rented car, with a driver who knows the way to the best temples, and knows when and how to avoid peak traffic. The drive between Chennai and Bangalore, in Karnataka, should take around 8 hours along National Highway 4. If you're moving on to Mamallapuram (about 1 hr. from Chennai), take the East Coast Road. Regular buses are available for travel to almost any point in the state, Bangalore, and Tirupati; contact the **State Express Transport Corporation Bus Stand** (© 044/2534-1835; daily 7am–9pm).

VISITOR INFORMATION   For general tourist information, contact **Indiatourism** (© 1913). Staff at the Indiatourism offices (154 Anna Salai; © 044/2846-0285 or -1459; fax 044/2846-0195; indtour@vsnl.com; Mon–Fri 9am–6pm, Sat 9am–1pm), across the road from Spencer's, are busy but attentive. *Hallo! Madras* is a highly recommended monthly booklet with detailed information (Rs 10/20¢). CityInfo's useful *Chennai This Fortnight* is another comprehensive visitors' guide (Rs 30/65¢); it highlights hotels, restaurants, and shopping options, and has listings for just about everything, from suggested walks to entertainment events. *Salaam Chennai* (Rs 52/$1.05) is another similar publication released every 2 months. *Glance* is a tourist information booklet distributed four times a year; it covers both Chennai and Pondicherry.

ORIENTATION & NEIGHBORHOODS   Extending westward from the Bay of Bengal, Chennai is quite unwieldy. Linking the north and south of the city is Anna Salai, which starts out as G.S.T. Road (or Mount Rd.) near the airport in the southwest, and terminates at Fort St. George in George Town in the northeast. Two major rivers snake their way through the city—the Cooum River in the north, and the Adyar River several kilometers south. Between these, the most popular section of Marina Beach stretches between the sea and the city's busiest districts, where you'll find most of its hotels and a number of attractions. George Town lies just north of the Cooum's confluence with the Bay of Bengal. Southwest of George Town (around the Cooum River), Egmore and Triplicane form the heart of the commercial city. Farther south, the neighborhoods of San Thome and Mylapore are where you'll find the most significant religious monuments—**San Thome Cathedral** and the **Kapalishvara Temple.**

GETTING AROUND   **By Taxi & Auto-Rickshaw**   Chennai is a large, sprawling city, and its many sights are spread out and quite impossible to cover on foot. Auto-rickshaw drivers in this city are particularly adept at squeezing impossible fares out of foreign visitors—you would be well-warned to avoid them entirely. If you choose to take a taxi, keep in mind that although the official rate is Rs 7 (15¢) per kilometer, meters are often unreliable. Determine the distance and rate, and negotiate taxi fares before setting out. At night (after 9pm), fares may double. **Call taxis** are a good option: Try **Bharat Call Taxi** (© 044/2814-2233), **Chennai Call Taxi** (© 044/2538-4455), **or Fast Track** (© 044/2473-2020). In "Fast Facts: Chennai," see "Taxis" for more, and "Car Rentals" for longer (1 or more days) excursions.

GUIDED TOURS & TRAVEL AGENTS   You can sign up for an exhaustive range of tours of the city and the entire state at **Tamil Nadu Tourism** (4 E.V.R. Rd., opposite Central Railway Station, Park Town; ✆ **044/2538-2916,** 044/ 2536-0294, or 044/2538-4356; fax 044/2536-1385; www.tamilnadutourism. org). Again, most of these tours are geared toward domestic tourists. We recommend that you approach a private operator instead, such as **Sita World Travel** (✆ **044/2825-2943** or 044/2827-0985; www.sitaindia.com; maa@sitaincoming. com); **Travel House** (✆ **044/2852-0003;** www.travelhouseindia.com); or **Madura Travel Service** (✆ **044/2825-2002** or 044/2825-3858; www.madura travel.com).

FAST FACTS: Chennai

Airlines   Phone numbers you may need are: **Jet Airways** (✆ **044/2841-4141,** 044/2858-7910, -7920; or airport 044/2234-0215, -0217); **Indian Airlines** (✆ **141;** reservations 044/2855-5200, -5201, -5205, -5207); and **Air Sahara** (✆ **044/2827-2027,** -1961, 044/2826-3661, or inquiries 044/2823-1873).

Ambulance   Dial ✆ **102.**

American Express   G-17 Spencer Plaza, Anna Salai; ✆ **044/2852-3638** or -3640. Open Monday to Friday 9:30am to 6:30pm; Saturday 9:30am to 2:30pm.

Area Code   The area code for **Chennai** is **044.**

ATMs   **UTI** and **IDBI** banks have numerous ATMs around the city; ask your hotel concierge about a machine near you. There's an **HSBC** ATM in Spencer's Mall.

Banks/Currency Exchange   **Thomas Cook:** Eldorado Building, 112 Nungambakkam High Rd. (✆ **044/2827-2610**); Ceebros Centre, 45 Monteith Rd. (✆ **044/2855-3276** or -4600); 20 Rajaji Rd., George Town (✆ **044/ 2534-2374** or 044/2533-0105). Open Monday to Saturday 9am to 6pm.

Bookstores   **Higginbothams** (116 Anna Salai; ✆ **044/2821-3519;** daily 9am–7:30pm) has a massive selection of books and Indian music.

Car Rentals   **Europcar** (✆ **044/2495-3239**) and **Welcome Tours and Travels** (✆ **044/2846-0614** or -0908) both have a wide range of vehicles for rent at reasonable rates. Other car-rental companies include **Aviation Express** (✆ **044/2234-6013,** 044/2233-0205, 044/2435-0195, or -4073) and **Bala Service** (✆ **044/2822-4444**).

Drugstore   Located on the second floor of Spencer Plaza (769 Anna Salai) is **Health & Glow** (✆ **044/2851-2285;** Mon–Sat 9am–8pm, Sun 11am–7pm).

Embassies/Consulates   **United Kingdom:** 24 Anderson Rd.; ✆ **044/2827-3136/7;** Monday to Friday 8:30am to 4pm. **United States:** 220 Anna Salai; ✆ **044/2811-2000;** Monday to Friday 8:15am to 5pm. **Canada:** 3rd Floor, Dhun Building, 827 Anna Salai; ✆ **044/2852-9818;** Monday to Thursday 9:30am to 5:30pm, Friday 9am to 1pm. **New Zealand:** "Maithri," 32 Cathedral Rd.; ✆ **044/2811-2472/3;** Monday to Friday 8am to 4:45pm, Saturday 8 to 11:45am.

Emergencies   Call **Apollo Hospital** at ✆ **044/2829-1111** or -0792.

Hospitals **Apollo Hospital** (21 Greams Lane, off Greams Rd.; © **044/2829-3333** or **-0200**) offers the city's top service and also has a good round-the-clock pharmacy.

Police For emergencies, dial © **100**. For traffic police, dial © **103**.

Post Office Although the **General Post Office** (Rajaji Salai; © **044**) is in George Town, you're best off making use of the **Head Post Office** on Anna Salai. Its hours are Monday to Sunday 10am to 8:30pm.

Taxis Among the call-taxi services are **Metro** (© **044/2821-4848**), **Fast Track** (© **044/2473-2020**), and **Rent-a-Benz** (© **044/2822-4444**). Generally, these services charge a minimum of Rs 30 (65¢) for the first 3km, and thereafter Rs 8 (17¢) per kilometer. There's a nighttime surcharge of 25%, and you'll be expected to pay a waiting fee.

WHAT TO SEE & DO

Unfortunately, the city's monuments are very spread out, and getting around can be nightmarish; select a few choice attractions and get an air-conditioned taxi for the day. Presuming you've already spent the night in Chennai, try a predawn start by taking in the early-morning activities along the 12km (7½-mile) **Marina Beach;** you can watch fishing boats being launched (around 6am). If you'd rather sleep in, save the beach for dusk, when it becomes a colorful pageant of boys playing cricket, vendors flogging souvenirs, and food carts offering fast-food snacks. Disappointingly, the world's second-longest city beach is also one of its largest latrines and has a distinctly post-apocalyptic air to it; stick to the area in the vicinity of Triplicane, along Kamarajar Road.

The 8th-century **Parthasarathy Temple** (off Triplicane High Rd., west of South Beach Rd.; daily 7am–noon and 4–8pm) is near the main drag of Marina Beach; dedicated to Krishna, it is believed to be Chennai's oldest temple. South lies Mylapore's **San Thome Cathedral Basilica** (San Thome High Rd., Mylapore; daily 6am–6pm), where the so-called final resting place of Thomas the Apostle has become a neon-lit attraction. Legend has it that St. Thomas, one of Christ's disciples, was martyred at St. Thomas Mount (see below) after spending the final years of his life preaching on a nearby beach. Stained-glass windows recount the saint's tale, and wooden panels depict Christ's final days on earth. The interior is also decked with bits of tinsel and neon-pink polystyrene hearts dangling from the ceiling; other modern kitsch additions include a relief-sculpted crucifix with a neon orange border and a halo of fairy lights.

Near the basilica is the **Kapalishvara Temple** ★★ (off Kutchery Rd. and Chitrukullan N. St., Mylapore; daily 4am–noon and 4–8pm), a classic example of Dravidian architecture, where thronging devotees will give you an idea of what Tamil Nadu's devout worship is all about. The temple is marked by a 36m (120-ft.) *gopuram* (gateway) tower adorned with detailed figures and inscriptions dating back to A.D. 1250. The place really comes alive during the Aru-pathumoovar Festival, 10 days in March.

Built by the Portuguese, nearby **Luz Church** (Luz Church Rd., Mylapore) is the oldest church in Chennai. If it's peace and quiet that appeal to you, visit the 16th-century church of **Senhora da Expectação,** atop **St. Thomas Mount.** Built in 1523 by the Portuguese, the little church provides fine views over the city and is serenely removed from the city's nonstop commotion. Alternatively, spend some time roaming the gardens of the **Theosophical Society,** a sprawling campus of rambling pathways and countless trees. The society's headquarters are the Huddlestone mansion, built in 1776, where relief imagery and quotations representing various faiths are on display (E. Adyar; ✆ **044/2491-3528;** Mon–Sat 8:30–10am and 2–4pm).

Chennai's **Government Museum** ✦ (Pantheon Rd.; ✆ **044/2826-9638;** admission $5; Sat–Thurs 9:30am–5pm) is considered one of the finest receptacles of bronze sculpture in the country; visit if you're keen on museums, or need to escape from the sun. While in Egmore, pop into **St. Andrew's Kirk** (off Periyar E.V.R. High Rd., northeast of Egmore Station, Egmore; ✆ **044/2538-3508;** open daily)—inspired by London's St. Martin-in-the-Field. St. Andrew's steeple rises 50m (160 ft.) into the air; you can climb this to reach a small balcony for a good city view. To experience grand architectural heritage, set aside a few hours to visit **Fort St. George** ✦✦ (Kamarajar Rd.)—the first bastion of British power in India went into construction in 1640. The cluster of gray and white colonial buildings with pillared neoclassical facades now houses the Tamil Nadu State Legislature and the Secretariat. Visit its **Fort Museum** (✆ **044/2536-1127;** Sat–Thurs 10am–5pm; admission Rs 100/$2.10) to see the collection of portraiture, oil paintings, sketches, and etchings that reveal the nature of colonial life in early Madras.

Just north of the fort is the red sandstone **High Court** (Mon–Sat 10am–5pm), built in the mid–19th century in the Indo-Saracenic style, and still in use today. Guided tours of the building take in the various courtrooms, many which are remarkably decorated. Busy **George Town,** bounded by Rajaji Salai and N.S.C Bose Road, was once known as "Black Town," a racist appellation for a settlement occupied by East India Company textile workers who came from Andhra Pradesh in the mid-1600s (the name Chennai, incidentally, is derived from the name given to the area by the dyers and weavers who lived here: Chennapatnam). Today, George Town is a bustling collection of streets that should be explored on foot—not a good idea in the middle of the day.

DAY TRIP TO THE SACRED CITY OF KANCHIPURAM ✦✦✦

All of Kanchipuram's roads lead to *gopurams,* the unmistakable temple gateways that tower over you as you prepare to enter the sacred shrines. This 2,000-year-old city of "a thousand temples"—also called Kanchi—features on many travel itineraries, and is best seen as a day trip out of Chennai. With a rich heritage, it's famous as a seat of both Shaivaite and Vaishnavite devotion and for exquisite silk saris. It was here that the Dravidian style really had its roots, and the sheer profusion of temples makes this an ideal place to get a feel for how South Indian temple architecture has developed over the centuries. The oldest structure in town is the **Kailasantha Temple** (Putleri St.; 1.5km/¾ mile) out of the town center; daily 8:30am–noon and 4–6pm), entered via a small gateway that pre-empts the larger *gopurams* found throughout South India. Built by the same Pallava king responsible for Mamallapuram's Shore Temple, Kailasantha shows signs of evolution from its seaside forebear; it's also less overwhelming than many of the more grandiose Tamil temples.

The 57m (180-ft.) white *gopuram* marking the entrance to the 9th-century Shaivite **Ekambareswara Temple** (Puthupalayam St.; 6am–12:30pm and 4–8pm) was added as late as the 16th century. Through a passageway, visitors enter a courtyard and the "thousand-pillared" hall (though the number of pillars has dwindled significantly over the years). Within the temple, a mango tree believed to be 2,500 years old apparently yields four different varieties of the fruit—legend has it that it was here that Shiva and Parvati were married, and that Parvati fashioned a lingam of earth, one of the five sacred Hindu elements. As a test of her devotion, Shiva sent a flood through the town that destroyed everything in its path except the lingam (phallic symbol), which she protected from the deluge with her body.

Dedicated to the *Shakti* cult, which celebrates creation's female aspect, the 14th-century **Kamakshi Amman Temple** (Amman Koli St.; daily 5am– 12:30pm and 4–8:30pm) was built by the Cholas. Apparently, the tank there is so sacred that demons sent to bathe were cleansed of their malevolent ways. Other worthwhile temples include the **Vaikunta Perumal Temple** and the **Varadaraja Temple,** both of which are dedicated to Vishnu.

Note that Kanchi's temples close from 12:30 until 4pm, which means that you'll need to head out rather early or—better still—arrive in time for evening *puja* (prayer). However, traffic into and out of Chennai can get hellish during peak hours. If you're hot and hungry, head for the air-conditioned room at the vegetarian restaurant in **Hotel Saravana Bhavan** (504 Gandhi Rd.; ✆ **04112/ 22-2505;** 7am–10pm). Feast on reasonably priced South Indian *dosas* (pancakes) or order a *thali* (multicourse) platter.

Kanchipuram is 80km (50 miles) southwest of Chennai. Ask about guided tours of the temple town at the tourist office. Otherwise, guides can be picked up around the Kailasanatha Temple for around Rs 250 to Rs 300 ($5.35– $6.50); ask to see certification.

WHERE TO STAY

Given the generally insalubrious conditions of much of Chennai city, you're best off forking out for a decent hotel. Best of all, head down the coast to **Fisherman's Cove** resort, which is right on the beach, a mere 50 minutes' drive from Chennai airport and near one of Tamil's top temple destinations (see Mamallapuram's lodging reviews, below).

Should you decide to spend the night in town, the **Park** (reviewed below), which blew the lid off Tamil Nadu's hospitality industry when it opened in 2002, is *the* place to be, and at press time offered excellent value for money. If for some reason the Park does not suit you, Chennai has a large inventory of luxury hotels providing reliable comfort and standardized service. These include **Meridien** (www.royalmeridien-chennai.com), two **Taj** hotels (www.tajhotels. com; the **Taj Coromandel** has the best restaurant in town, but you'll find better value for money if you book a "heritage executive" room in the lovely, laidback **Taj Connemara** for $220), a **Radisson** (www.radisson.com), and two **Sheratons** (www.welcomgroup.com). None of these, particularly the fabulously refurbished **Welcomgroup Chola Sheraton** ✪✪ ($90), will disappoint you.

For a good option near the airport, opt for **Le Royal Meridien** (✆ **044/ 2231-4343;** www.royalmeridien-chennai.com; doubles from $160). Even closer

---

A Taxing State of Affairs

Comfortable hotels are considered an ultimate luxury—or sin—in Tamil Nadu, where a hefty 25% "luxury" tax is tacked onto each bill; this is over and above the 10% expenditure tax that must also be added. You'll also find a hefty 80% surcharge on imported liquor.

is the **Trident,** where you can get a courtyard- or pool-facing room (© **044/ 2234-4747;** reservations@tridentch.com; doubles from $160); the hotel runs a courtesy airport shuttle, and has a discounted rate for guests checking out within 12 hours.

For travelers on a really tight budget, prospects are grim. Your best option is the **YWCA International Guest House** (1086 EVR Periyar Salai, behind Egmore Station; © **044/2532-4234;** fax 044/2532-4263; doubles from $16), which has clean accommodations with en-suite bathrooms and Western toilets. It has a restaurant, and the staff are friendly and helpful.

The Park ★★★   Even the most jaded visitor to one of India's dullest cities will be bowled over by Chennai's newest hotel, a dazzling contemporary space that could easily occupy the pages of *Wallpaper.* Guest rooms are a fabulous blend of comfort, style, and functionalism—for a mere $10 more, opt for a luxury room. Guest rooms follow the same contemporary-chic design of the public areas, making up for the lack of views with thoughtful, artistic touches, and the beds are tremendously comfortable. If you don't get a room here, be sure to pop in for a bite or a drink—this is where you'll find the best nightlife option in the city, the **Leather Bar** (see below). The fabulous 24-hour eatery off the lobby, **601,** is recommended as much for its contemporary design as for its unusual, varied menu—order meze platters and seafood tapas to share, or opt for the fabulous seared fish kebab, prepared in the tandoor oven and served with a garlic sauce. Still in its early stages when we visited, the Park has since added a rooftop health club and spa, as well as a Thai restaurant. (***Note:*** If you're not a fan of modern design, you might be more comfortable at the recently overhauled **Welcomgroup Chola Sheraton,** which currently charges a similar rate.)

601 Anna Salai, Chennai 600 006. © **044/2714-4000.** Fax: 044/2714-4100. www.theparkhotels.com. sales. che@theparkhotels.com. 250 units. Doubles: $90 deluxe; $100 luxury. Note that these special introductory rates are subject to change. AE, DC, MC, V. **Amenities:** 2 restaurants; bar; nightclub; health club; gym; spa; travel assistance; car hire; secretarial services; currency exchange; 24-hr. room service; laundry; doctor-on-call. *In room:* A/C, TV, minibar, tea- and coffee-making facilities, electronic safe.

Ramada Raj Park   A turbaned doorman greets you at the entrance to the marble-and-chandelier lobby of this well-priced business hotel. Conveniently located and efficiently managed, this is one of Chennai's best moderately priced options. Executive guest units are done in elegant albeit slightly old-fashioned decor, with comfortable beds, writing desks, and bathtubs. Deluxe guest rooms come with all the modern conveniences but are a little smaller, with an Indian-meets-faux-rococo flavor. Suites are plush, but not overstated, with two of everything and elegant high-backed sofas, armchairs, and a chaise longue in the sitting room. A pool and health club were planned; ask about their progress.

180 T.T.K. Rd., Alwarpet, Chennai 600 018. © **044/2498-7777,** 044/2499-3738, or 044/2467-0002. Fax 044/ 2499-0749. www.rajpark.com. reservation@rajpark.com. 87 units. Doubles: $57 deluxe; $65 executive; $95 suite; $15 extra bed. 25% tax. Rates include breakfast. AE, DC, MC, V. **Amenities:** Restaurant; bar; car hire; shop; 24-hr. room service; laundry; doctor-on-call. *In room:* A/C, TV, dataport, minibar, tea- and coffee-making facilities (suites only), hair dryer (executive rooms only), ironing equipment.

WHERE TO DINE

Chennai is a great place to discover the flavors of South India, particularly the cuisine of the Chettinad, best sampled at **Raintree,** the beautiful alfresco restaurant located at the Taj Connemara (reviewed below). You'll find many of the world's tastes represented in the city. Besides trying the classy **601** at the Park Hotel (see above), head for **Bella Ciao** (4 Sree Krishna Enclave, off Water Land

Dr., Kottivakkam Beach; ℂ **040/2451-1130**), where Ciro Cattaneo serves authentic pizzas and pastas at a venue near the beach.

Annalakshmi ⭐⭐⭐ INDIAN VEGETARIAN   Chennai's most famous vegetarian establishment is jam-packed with Indian artifacts and objets d'art. Unusually enough, it is administered by volunteers. It was founded in 1995 by an Indian guru named Swami Shantanand, and the food is prepared by local mothers, grandmothers, and devotees of the guru, with proceeds going to various charitable projects. Today it has outlets in Singapore, Perth, and Kuala Lumpur. Various set menus provide a good introduction to the different tastes of Indian cuisine; there are separate menus for lunch and dinner, and an entire menu is devoted to juices. From the a la carte selection, try French beans coconut curry or potato Chettinad. In season, try the herbal wine known as ambrosia *aroghya paan,* said to have Ayurvedic healing properties, or the date-and-honey milkshake.

804 Anna Salai. ℂ **044/2852-5109.** Main courses Rs 80–Rs 160 ($1.70–$2.40). Set menus Rs 250–Rs 600 ($5.35–$13). AE, DC, MC, V. Tues–Sun noon–2:45pm and 7:30–9:45pm. A 2nd branch is at Anna Nagar E. (ℂ 044/2628-3366).

Benjarong ⭐⭐⭐ THAI   Popular with Chennai's U.S. consular general, Benjarong (the name refers to the hand-painted gold porcelain used in Royal Thai households) is the city's best Thai restaurant, frequented by the local elite as well as international diplomats. You're welcomed with a fruit-ginger drink—a refreshing concoction to whet the appetite—and with a selection of taste-size treats called *mein kam,* wrapped in leaves. The spicy *tom yam* soup is possibly the best you'll get outside Bangkok, made using *goong* (prawn brains) and tempered with ginger. Signature dishes include chargrilled duck *(ped yang)* done to perfection; also wonderful is spicy *gai pahd bai graprou,* ground chicken tossed with chilies and hot basil. If you're up for something simpler, green curry prawn is a standout favorite, or go for fish delicately flavored with tamarind. Top off the evening with *tub tim siam* (water chestnut in chilled coconut milk) or jackfruit custard and ice cream.

146 T.T.K. Rd., Alwarpet. ℂ **044/2432-2640.** Reservations essential on weekends. Main courses Rs 98–Rs 598 ($2–$13). AE, DC, MC, V. Daily 12:30–2:45pm and 7:30–11:45pm.

Raintree ⭐⭐⭐ CHETTINAD   It was here in 1988 in this fabulous outdoor restaurant—the best restaurant in the state, and one of the best in India—that Chettinad cuisine first came out of the Chettiar family kitchen and into the commercial arena. At the entrance, a pair of Brahmin ladies skillfully prepare savory South Indian vegetable starters. Nearby is a stage for nightly classical dance and music programs, and the best seats are under fairy lights and massive rain trees that give the place its name. After sipping a welcome drink—a wide-brimmed copper goblet of *vasantha neer,* honey-sweetened tender coconut water, delicately flavored with mint leaves—you can't go wrong with *kozhi Chettinad,* boneless chicken in an authentic Chettinad sauce, best had with *appams* (rice flour pancakes); or try the *karaikudi kari* (lamb chops). For the really adventurous, *moolai melagu* is tender lamb brain cooked in a peppery masala. Order rice flavored with tamarind as an accompaniment. End with the delicious coconut dessert, *elaneer payasam.*

Taj Connemara, Binny Rd. ℂ **044/2852-0123.** Reservations essential in winter season. Main courses Rs 135–Rs 475 ($3–$10). Weekend buffet Rs 550 ($12). AE, DC, MC, V. Daily 7:30pm–midnight.

CHENNAI AFTER DARK

If there's one place you need to grab a drink, it's Chennai, and the best place to do so is the **Leather Bar** ⭐⭐⭐, at the Park hotel. Go not just for the beautiful leather floor and suede-covered walls or the gorgeous clientele, but for the super-hip tunes belting from the orbital DJ booth, transporting you far away from Chennai's heat and hectic crowds. For more highbrow entertainment, check the local papers or ask your concierge to assist you. Or make an appointment to visit Kalakshetra (below).

Kalakshetra ⭐   Occupying 40 hectares (99 acres), Kalakshetra ("the Temple of Art") is a school for traditional music and dance. It has produced some of the country's most revered modern-day dancers. It was set up in 1936 by Rukmani Devi Arundale, a follower of Annie Besant (who co-founded the Theosophical Society). Devi studied ballet under Anna Pavlova, Russia's great ballerina; back in Madras, she studied *dasi attam,* traditionally restricted to temple dancers. She later set up the International Centre for the Arts, which was specifically concerned with reviving *dasi attam,* also known as *Bharatnatyam.* Visitors interested in observing day classes are welcome, and performances are staged in the school's auditorium.

Thiruvanmiyur, E. Coast Rd., 29km (18 miles) south of Chennai. ✆ 044/2491-1844.

THE WORLD'S WEALTHIEST TEMPLE: A SIDE TRIP TO ANDHRA PRADESH ⭐⭐⭐

Situated on a peak of the Tirumala Hills, overlooking Tirupati (just across the Tamil Nadu border into Andhra Pradesh), is the most active religious pilgrim-age destination on earth, drawing more than 10 million devoted pilgrims every year—apparently, more than either Jerusalem or Rome. The richest in all India, and potentially the wealthiest single temple or church on earth, the Dravidian-style **Sri Venkateshvara Temple** is said to be the heart of Hindu piety, but in many ways it appears to exist expressly for the collection of wealth connected to a legendary loan: Lord Venkateshwara, the living form of Vishnu, apparently borrowed an enormous amount of money from the God of Wealth in order to secure a dowry for his bride. Devotees donate generously in order to help their god settle his debt—the loan must be repaid in full, with interest, before the end of this epoch. Annual donations of jewelry, cash, and gold total around 1.5 bil-lion rupees. Much of this goes towards the temple kitchens, which prepare meals for pilgrims and also produce the famous *laddu* sweets given to visitors.

The inner shrine is presided over by a diamond-ornamented 2m (6-ft.) black idol that stands at the end of a narrow passage. Pilgrims queue for hours, some-times days, excitedly preparing for *darshan*—the extraordinarily brief moment when you're all but pushed past the god by guards to ensure that the sanctum doesn't become clogged with devotees, many of whom succumb to the moment by falling to the ground. Waiting amid the mass of anxious, highly charged pil-grims, you'll get a good sense of the religious fervor of the Hindu faith. By the time you reach the moment of *darshan,* thousands of excited, expectant wor-shippers will be behind you, chanting Vishnu's name. Once out of the inner shrine (one of the few in South India that non-Hindus can enter), you'll make your way past a massive fish tank–like enclosure, where temple clerks count the day's takings—possibly the most cash you're ever likely to see in one place.

Note: As you're waiting in line, you'll see many shaven heads—it's common practice for believers to have their heads tonsured before going before the deity

> ### *Tips* Jumping the Queue
>
> Wealthier pilgrims can now make use of a computerized virtual queue system that streamlines the *darshan* experience. Pilgrims buy an armband imprinted with their *darshan* time, shaving hours—even days—off their wait in line. Foreign visitors should bring their passports and appeal to the Assistant Executive Officer (A.E.O.) (ask one of the temple police for directions) for a special *darshan* ticket, which costs Rs 100 ($2.10). Paid at a special counter, it cuts waiting time to around 2 hours. Note that men must wear long pants or *lungis*. Prior to entering the queue, you'll be asked to sign allegiance to the god. Avoid taking part if you suffer from claustrophobia, since you'll still have to spend an hour or two within cagelike passages designed to prevent line-jumping. Temple activities commence at 3am with a wake-up call to the idol *(suprabhatham)* and continue until 12:45am the following morning.

as a devotional sacrifice. As a result, a lucrative human hair business contributes significantly to the temple coffers—Far East wig manufacturers are major consumers of world-renowned Tirumala hair, shorn by a fleet of barbers permanently in the service of the temple.

ESSENTIALS The easiest ways to get here are by train from Chennai (or Hyderabad, Bangalore, or Mumbai) or by one of the twice-weekly **Indian Airlines** (© 08574/25349) flights to and from Chennai and Hyderabad (taxis into town should cost around Rs 100/$2.10). To overnight, make sure to prebook a room at **Hotel Guestline** (© 08574/8-0800; guestlinetirupati@rediffmail.com; doubles Rs 1,300–Rs 1,900/$28–$42), which is located 3.2km (2 miles) from the busy city and draws a more upmarket crowd. Don't expect luxury, however—just basic Western comforts (A/C, TV) in the rooms, and two restaurants, a pool, and a health club.

2 Mamallapuram (Mahabalipurum) ✦✦✦

51km (31 miles) S of Chennai

A visit to this once-thriving port city of the Pallavas, a dynasty that ruled much of South India between the 4th and 9th centuries A.D., is an excellent introduction to South Indian temple architecture. Established by Mamalla, "the Great Wrestler," the tourist town of Mamallapuram attracts thousands to view the earliest examples of monumental architecture in southern India—incredible rock-cut shrines that celebrate Hinduism's sacred pantheon and legends. Even today, the sounds of sculptors chipping away at blocks of stone—creating carvings for temples, hotel foyers, and tourists—echo through the streets, a reminder of the sort of devoted craftsmanship that must have possessed the original masons who created the World Heritage monuments of Mamallapuram. It's possible to survey the best monuments in a morning, provided you get an early start (ideally, long before domestic tourists arrive en masse around mid-morning). This leaves you time to unwind on the pleasant beach and dine on succulent seafood at a village cafe (for a song). But if you don't plan on hanging around, you can move on to Pondicherry after lunch and be sipping Gallic cocktails before sundown.

ESSENTIALS

GETTING THERE & AWAY   Mamallapuram is 2 hours south from Chennai, on the East Coast Highway. Buses from Chennai arrive and depart every half-hour, and tourist taxis congregate around the bus stand (E. Raja St.). Pondicherry is 2½ hours away by road.

VISITOR INFORMATION   The **Government of Tamil Nadu Tourist Office** (Kovalam Rd.; ✆ **04114/244-2232;** daily 9:45am–5:45pm) can supply you with limited information and a map of Tamil Nadu or booklets on the town. You can also rent a **camping site** with Western toilet facilities (Rs 100/$2.10 per night), or a simple **cottage** with a sea view (Rs 300/$6.50).

GETTING AROUND   All of the town's attractions can be reached on foot, or you can rent a bicycle or catch an auto-rickshaw.

GUIDES & TOURS   **Hi-Tours** (123 East Raja St.; ✆ **04114/44-3260;** www. hitours.com) runs a smooth operation and will customize a tour of the state for you. They will organize flights, train tickets, taxis, and hotels at decent rates. **Guides** are available at the entrances to the Panch Rathas and Shore Temple; they charge around Rs 250 ($5.35), but for this amount you're probably better off arranging a knowledgeable English guide while you're in Chennai—either through your hotel or one of the tourist offices (see "Visitor Information" for Chennai). You can also make arrangements for a special guide, in advance, through the **Archaeological Survey of India** in Chennai (✆ **044/2536-0397**).

EXPLORING THE SHRINES & TEMPLES

Mamallapuram's monolithic shrines and rock-cut cave temples lie scattered over a landscape heaped with boulders and rocky hillocks. Among these, the excellent **Shore Temple,** built to Lord Shiva, and the **Five Rathas,** a cluster of temples named for the five Pandava brothers of *Mahabharata* fame, are definitely worth seeking out, while the celebrated **Arjuna's Penance** is the largest relief-carving on earth—try to see these as early in the day as possible, before busloads of noisy holiday-makers descend. Also try to view **Mahishamardini Mandapa** (and give the nearby government-run Sculpture Museum a miss). If you feel the need to visit an active temple, head for **Talasayana Perumal Temple,** dedicated to Vishnu. It stands on the site of an original 9th-century Pallava temple but was rebuilt during the 14th century by the Vijayanagar King Parang Kusan, who feared that the sea would eventually erode Shore Temple. Half-hour *puja* (prayer) sessions are conducted daily at 9am, 11:30am, 5:30pm, and 8pm. About 4km (2½ miles) north of Mamallapuram, **Tiger Cave** ⋘ (Covelong Rd.) is the site of an 8th-century shrine to the tiger-loving goddess Durga. It's thought that the shallow cave, with its sculpted *yalis* (mythical beasts) framing the entrance, might have been used for open-air performances. Seventeen kilometers (11 miles) west of Mamallapuram, in the Kanchipuram district, **Tirukkazhukundram,** named for the holy kites (eagle-type birds) that make their home here, are popular with pilgrims who come to witness the Brahmin priests feeding the two birds of prey at midday. *Note:* Herpetologists or beleaguered parents may wish to make a pilgrimage of a very different kind: Set up by the famous herpetologist Romulus Whitaker, **Crocodile Bank** (15km/9 miles north of Mamallapuram; Rs 20/40¢; Wed–Mon 8:30am–5:30pm) is a breeding and research center that sustains around 5,000 crocodiles, including 14 of the world's 26 species.

Arjuna's Penance ⋘⋘⋘   Opposite Talasayana Perumal Temple, the world's largest bas-relief is commonly referred to as "The Descent of the Ganges," depicting the sacred penance performed by one of the Pandava brothers. Standing on one leg, the meditative Arjuna contemplates Shiva—a painful reparation performed while lively representations of the gods, celestial nymphs, elephants, monkeys, and other creatures look on. A naturally occurring cleft down the rock is said to represent the Ganges, a symbol that comes to life during the rainy season when water flows into a tank below. Just a few meters away, to the left of Arjuna's Penance, is **Krishna Mandapam** ⋆, another bas-relief, carved in the mid–7th century; this one depicts Krishna using his divine strength to lift a mountain to protect people from imminent floods. The duality of the god's nature is expressed in carvings of him going about his more mundane activities, including flirting with his milkmaids. Near Arjuna's Penance, to the north, is the huge spherical boulder known as **Krishna's Butter Ball,** balancing on a hillside.

W. Raja St.

Mahishasuramardini Cave ⋆⋆ A lighthouse tops the hill where you'll find a number of superb rock-cut shrines—seek out **Mahishasuramardini Mandapa,** remarkable for the two impressive friezes at each end of its long veranda. In the panel to the right, Durga, the terrifying mother of the universe, is seated astride her lion *vahana* wielding an assortment of weapons. She is in the process of destroying the buffalo-headed demon, Mahisha, who disturbs the delicate balance of life. At the opposite end of the veranda, Vishnu is depicted sleeping peacefully on his serpent bed, the sea of eternity; gathered around him, the gods appeal to him to continue the creation. Also atop the hill, the **Adivaraha Mandap** features various sculpted figures and mythical scenes, including one large panel of Vishnu as a gigantic boar.

W. Raja St.

Panch Pandava Rathas ⋆⋆⋆ The initial sight of these five *(panch)* monolithic stone shrines, set in a sandy fenced-off clearing, is dramatic, even though the structures themselves—named for the five brother-heroes of the *Mahabharata* and resembling temple chariots *(rathas)*—are incomplete. The ancient sculpting techniques are astonishing: Carved out of single pieces of rock from the top down, these shrines reveal perfect, precise planning. The dome-shaped *shikhara* (tower finial) found on some of the temples became the template for later South Indian temples, successful experiments that were further refined and enlarged.

E. Raja St., 1km (a half mile) south of Arjuna's Penance. Tickets available from ASI booth at the entrance. A single ticket for entrance to both the Five Rathas and the Shore Temple costs Rs 250 ($5.35). Daily 6:30am–5:30pm. Approved guides can be hired at the entrance.

Shore Temple ⋆⋆⋆ Perched at the edge of a sandy beach on the Bay of Bengal, where it has been subjected to centuries of battering by salt water and oceanic winds, this early-8th-century stone temple is considered to be one of the oldest temples in South India, and a forerunner of the Dravidian style. Its two carved towers inspired a style that spread throughout the region and to more distant Asian shores. Vishnu is found reclining inside one shrine, while two others are dedicated to Shiva. A low boundary wall topped by rock-cut Nandi bulls surrounds the temple, and a veritable pride of lions rear their heads from the base of the pillars.

Northeast of the Panch Pandava Rathas, at the beach. Tickets available from ASI booth at the entrance. A single ticket for entrance to both the Five Rathas and the Shore Temple costs Rs 250 ($5.35). Daily 6:30am–5:30pm. Approved guides can be hired at the entrance.

WHERE TO STAY

If you want to be closer to Mamallapuram's temples, you have two good seafront options. In the process of being overhauled, **Temple Bay** is a wonderfully situated chalet-style resort with good amenities (pool, travel desk, salon) and a view of the Shore Temple from the restaurant. Its best accommodations are the cottages overlooking the ocean with private patios; these have air-conditioning, TV, and minibars (© **04114/244-2251,** -2252, -2253, or -2254; grttemplebay@ vsnl.net; doubles Rs 2,995/$65). Located just 3km (2 miles) from Mamallapuram (near Tiger Caves), **Ideal Beach Resort** is a little more run-down but fairly well managed, with a range of standard amenities. The best thing about it (besides the price) is its location, right on the beach. Ask for an upstairs unit with an ocean view (© **04114/24-2251;** www.idealresort.com; doubles Rs 1,250–Rs 2,000/$27–$44).

Taj Fisherman's Cove ✹✹✹   Built on the site of a 17th-century Dutch fort, this bright, breezy, beach-front resort is set on 8.8 manicured hectares (22 acres) with a labyrinth of tidy, shrub-lined pathways. Completely overhauled in 2000, it's a great refuge, within easy striking distance of both Chennai and Mamallapuram. Most guest rooms are in the main hotel block (those with sea views have expansive floor-to-ceiling windows). The shell-shaped cottages closer to the beach are delightful, with bamboo-enclosed alfresco showers; private hammocks; bright interiors in shades of orange, yellow, and green; and a breezy patio with a beautiful Chettinad swing. Those cottages facing the sea directly (nos. C4–C14) are the best spots from which to admire the surf. Larger luxury sea-facing cottages are also available; each one has a totally private garden with palm trees supporting your own hammock and cane-strung rockers on a covered porch. Interiors are a little more formal and old-fashioned, but also more spacious, with high-pitched ceilings and an indoor bathroom that has a separate tub and shower. When you're not out exploring ancient temples, you can try out the huge number of activities on offer, laze around a pool with a sunken swim-up bar, stroll along the beach to the nearby village of Kovalam (also known as Covelong), or peruse the menu of the thatched beachside **Bay View Restaurant.**

Covelong Beach, Kanchipuram District, Chennai 603 112. © **04114/27-4304.** Fax 04114/27-4303. www.taj hotels.com. fishcove.Chennai@tajhotels.com. 50 units; 38 cottages. Doubles (Oct 1–Dec 22/Dec 23–Jan 5/Jan 6–Apr 30/May–Sept): $145/$165/$155/$120 standard; $155/$170/$165/$130 standard sea-view; $175/$190/$185/$150 cottage garden-view; $195/$230/$205/$175 cottage sea-view; $215/$260/$225/$190 villa; $30 New Year supplement; $20 extra bed. AE, MC, V. **Amenities:** 2 restaurants; 2 bars; pool; kids' pool; tennis; Jacuzzi; health club; beach volleyball; badminton; jet-skiing; sea kayaking; windsurfing; bicycles; children's activity center; indoor games; concierge; travel desk; catamaran trips; fishing excursions; ecology tours; car hire; currency exchange; shopping arcade; 24-hr. room service; Ayurvedic massage center; babysitting; doctor-on-call; library. *In room:* A/C, TV, minibar, tea- and coffee-making facilities, hair dryer.

WHERE TO DINE

Seafood, not surprisingly, is popular and abundant; it's also amazingly affordable, with the most expensive item being lobster at Rs 1,000 ($22) per kilogram (2.2 lb.). *Note:* None of the following take credit cards. **Sea Shore** (Fisherman Colony, Mamallapuram Beach; © **04114/42780**) is the cleanest of the shack-style restaurants situated directly on the beach, and it opens first thing in the morning. It has a great view of the Shore Temple, and at press time an upstairs section with even better views was being added. Tables are covered with simple Indian throws and the chairs are plastic, but the seafood is fit for a king. Have your choice of fresh lobster, tiger prawns, calamari, tuna, or shark—all washed down with an ice-cold Kingfisher. Another recommended shack-style beach restaurant with a view of the Shore Temple, **Luna Magica** (✆ **04114/244-2521**) is where Chef Rajindran has been pulling in customers since 1992. Also check out **Gazebo** on East Raja Street (✆ **04114/244-2525**), a relaxed fan-cooled all-day restaurant with Indian-print throws over the tables and brown rattan chairs; Bob Marley and classical Indian tunes set the mood. Freshly caught lobster is available grilled, boiled, braised (country-style), or Thermidor-style. If you tire of affordable seafood, the usual Indian suspects are on offer; *palak paneer,* vegetable *dal frezi,* and Madras-style chicken curry are popular.

3 Pondicherry ★★★

189km (117 miles) S of Chennai

Pondicherry's ancient history dates back to the Vedic era; the Romans traded here 2 millennia ago, and the Portuguese arrived in 1521. Dutch and Danish traders followed, but it was the French—who purchased the town in the late 17th century, only relinquishing their hold in 1954—who left the most enduring legacy. Now a Union Territory, with its own local government, this seaside colony retains its French élan, tempered by South Indian warmth, making it one of India's most relaxing destinations. Besides hanging out in your antiques-filled colonial hotel or sauntering around the oceanfront **French Quarter** (where you'll see old men in thick-rimmed spectacles under the apparent illusion that they're in a Parisian *arrondissement*), you can visit **Auroville,** an interesting experiment in alternative living, also optimistically known as the City of Dawn, or join the New Age travelers here to visit the ashram of **Sri Aurobindo.** Ashramic allure and Aurovillian aura aside, Pondy is the type of charming seaside town where you arrive for a quick overnighter and end up staying; like Goa, it has a number of expats to prove it. And, yes, it's far friendlier than Bordeaux.

ESSENTIALS

GETTING THERE & AWAY   Pondicherry is best reached by road from Chennai, a 4-hour drive, mostly along a two-lane highway. To get here by train, you must first travel to Viluppuram (1 hr. away), on the Chennai-Rameswaram line. Inquire at the **railway station** (South Blvd.; ✆ **01413/233-6684**) about outbound trains.

VISITOR INFORMATION   Pondicherry's **Tourism Information Centre** (40 Goubert Ave.; ✆ **0413/233-9497** or -4575; fax 0413/235-8389; www.nic.in/pondicherry.com; www.tourisminpondicherry.com) can help you with maps, brochures, and tour bookings. Available in bookstores, *The Guide—Pondicherry* costs Rs 30 (60¢) and carries extensive local listings.

GETTING AROUND   **By Taxi & Auto-Rickshaw**   Auto-rickshaws prowl the streets in some areas, actively soliciting fares. Overcharging is rife, but if you've got several kilometers to cover, it may be worthwhile to hire one for a couple of extra rupees simply to avoid walking in the sun.

By Bicycle   By Indian standards, the streets and sidewalks of Pondicherry are immaculate, and ideal for exploration by bike. You can rent a bike (Rs 5/10¢ per hour; Rs 40/85¢ per day) from Le Café on Beach Road, or from the Pondicherry Tourism Information Centre (see above). Ask about hiring the services of a guide who can cycle along with you.

By Boat   Offshore cruises are available through the **Tourism Information Counter** (40 Goubert Ave.; ✆ **0413/233-9497**). A 2-hour cruise costs Rs 100 ($2.10) per person, or you can charter a boat for Rs 1,200 ($26) for 2 hours.

GUIDED TOURS   Heritage walks and other guided tours and sightseeing trips can be arranged through Pondicherry Tourism (see above). The **Indian National Trust for Art & Cultural Heritage** (**INTACH,** 14 Labordonnais S.; *©* **0413/222-5991** or -7324) can also help with guided walks.

WHAT TO SEE & DO

Pondicherry's tree-lined French Quarter is one of India's most prepossessing neighborhoods, and a real contrast to the area across the "Grand Canal" aqueduct that the French used to refer to as "black town"—a more typically Tamil neighborhood, with tiny shops lining crowded streets. If you want to unwind, stick to the French Quarter (or "white town"), with its wide boulevards, uncluttered roads, bilingual signs, stately government buildings, and gorgeous residential villas. Besides taking a few strolls, the only other attractions—and really, this is one place you will feel entirely guilt-free simply lazing on your hotel terrace for the duration of your stay—are the **Aurobindo Ashram,** and a trip to **Auroville,** the City of Dawn.

While wandering the Quarter, you may want to take a look at the **Sacred Heart of Jesus (Eglise de Sacre Coeur de Jésus),** an 18th-century neo-Gothic Catholic church on South Boulevard. The facade of the **Immaculate Conception Cathedral** (Mission St.) has an air of pageantry enhanced by colorful banners (note that many Christian devotees remove their shoes before entering). Dedicated to Ganesha, the elephant-headed god, **Sri Manakula Vinayagar Temple** is off a side street so popular that it's cordoned off during the early evening hours; a temple elephant marks the entrance. For a quick glimpse of local historic memorabilia and collectibles, visit the **Pondicherry Museum** (49 Rue St. Louis; *©* **0413/233-6203;** Tues–Sun 9:45am–5:15pm), housed in a 17th-century colonial mansion once occupied by the French administrator. The museum features a collection of carriages and carts, stone sculptures, and a formidable bronze gallery. Along the same road, which runs along the northern end of a square known as **Government Place,** is **Raj Nivas,** the late-18th-century mansion occupied by Pondicherry's lieutenant governor.

Looking for a Higher Level of Consciousness?

Located in the heart of Pondicherry, **Aurobindo Ashram** *⚑* draws a global mix of ardent devotees and ordinary people searching for peace or looking to improve their meditation skills. Aurobindo Ghose, a politically active British-educated Bengali who sought asylum from the British in this small French enclave, took to meditation and yoga while developing theories of enlightenment that integrated his personal spirituality with the tenets of modern science. He also met Mirra Alfassa here, an artist on a similar spiritual quest; she became his soul mate, earning her the appellation "The Mother." Founded as a place to foster evolution to a higher level of spiritual consciousness, the ashram opened in 1926. With a significant following and numerous published titles to his credit, Aurobindo died in 1950. Today, those who share his vision of a better world place flowers and other gestures of remembrance upon the memorial chambers (samadhis) of Sri Aurobindo and The Mother, which lie one above the other in the center of the peaceful main courtyard beneath a frangipani tree. For more information, contact the ashram (Rue de la Marine; *©* **0413/233-4836;** daily 8am–noon and 2–6pm; free admission; no children under 3).

At twilight, head for **Goubert Salai** (Beach Rd.). The most interesting sights along the promenade (aside from the locals enjoying themselves) include the colonial **Hôtel de Ville** (now the Municipal Offices building) and the 4m (12-ft.) statue of Gandhi standing at the pier. Cultural events, art exhibitions, and film screenings are conducted regularly by Pondicherry's **Alliance Française** (*C* **0413/233-8146;** fax 0413/233-4351; afpondy@satyam.net.in; Mon–Fri 8:30am–12:30pm and 2:30–6pm; temporary membership Rs 100/$2.10); contact this active organization for information regarding specific events.

SCIENCE FICTION IN THE CITY OF DAWN ★★

The **Auroville** project began life in 1964, conceived by Sri Aurobindo's French-born disciple, Mirra Alfassa—"The Mother" (see "Looking for a Higher Level of Consciousness?" above). She spoke of a place on earth that could not be claimed or owned by any nation, one where all humanity could live freely and in peace—a city that would ultimately become a living embodiment of human unity. Largely designed by French architect Roger Anger, Auroville drew a motley global group, and was inaugurated in 1968 when soil from around the world was symbolically placed in an urn along with the Auroville Charter.

At its spiritual and physical heart is the futuristic spherical structure known as **Matrimandir,** a place dedicated to the universal mother—a symbolic space devoted to the divine creatrix. An ongoing project, the structure is a flattened dome spanning 36m (115 ft.) in diameter, surrounded by gardens, an amphitheater covered with red Agra stone, and meditation rooms. As development continues, glistening gold discs are fixed to the outer surface of the dome, enhancing the structure's sci-fi image. The white marble chamber of the dome houses the "Inner Room," which contains a crystal that reflects the sun's rays and produces a concentrated light that is used for enhanced meditation. Visitors who obtain passes can have a brief peak at this chamber between 4 and 5pm each day, and it's possible to stay for meditation until 6pm. Radiating from the Mandir and its gardens, the city is architecturally conceived along the lines of a galaxy, evolving organically within certain parameters. The original design planned accommodations for 50,000 residents but there currently are about 1,500, all committed to being "willing servitors of the Divine Consciousness." Auroville is far more than a place for devotional meditation; it's an experiment in self-sufficient living that takes both nature and culture into account. Its architectural innovation and utopian idealism make this a place of interest for anyone with a penchant for the unusual, the ethereal, or the novel.

Auroville is 8km (5 miles) north of Pondicherry. Auto-rickshaws charge around Rs 150 ($3.15) for the round-trip. Pondy's tourist office also organizes tours. Stop at the Tourist Information Centre 1st, where you can pick up brochures, shop, snack, and even watch a video presentation. *C* **0413/262/2239.** Fax 0413/262-2704. www.auroville-india.com. Mon–Sat 9am–1pm and 1:30–5:30pm; Sun 9am–1pm and 2–4pm.

WHERE TO STAY

If you're looking for very affordable lodging in the heart of the French Quarter, **Satsanga Restaurant** (see "Where to Dine," below) has 10 clean, simple air-conditioned rooms costing Rs 600 ($13).

Hotel de l'Orient ★★★ *Value* Tamil and Cajun spices scent the air of this award-winning heritage hotel (Pondicherry's best)—a 1760s manor house located in the heart of the French Quarter. The hotel has been beautifully restored, and captures the period grandeur of a nobleman's mansion. Each of the 10 guest rooms—set around an inner courtyard shaded by citrus and neem trees—is themed and named for a former French colony. Comfortable and airy, with shuttered windows, high ceilings (some original wood ceiling beams), private patios, and tall French doors, its rooms are elegantly attired in pinks, yellows, and cool emerald. Most of the furniture pieces are French colonial antiques. Bathrooms are very chic, though small (only four have tubs, so specify if you want one). Casimbazaar (no. 6) is the best of the standard rooms, but it's worthwhile to pay the extra $20 for an executive suite; these have original four-poster beds and private drawing rooms with Pondicheriennes (local planter's chairs). Avoid staying in Masulipatam on the ground floor—it can get noisy. Accommodations overlook the courtyard restaurant, **Carte Blanche,** where local "Creole" cuisine, a blend of South Indian and French, is served. A second, air-conditioned dining room is inside, where you can avoid mosquitoes. You can enjoy serene views of Pondicherry from the rooftop courtyard.

17 rue Romain Rolland, Pondicherry 605 001. © 0413/34-3067. Fax 0413/22-7829. www.neemranahotels. com. orient1804@satyam.net.in. Delhi reservations: Neemrana Hotels Private Ltd., A-58 Nizamuddin E., New Delhi 110 013. © 011/2461-6145. Fax 011/2462-1112. sales@neemrana.com. 10 units. Doubles: Rs 3,000 ($65) executive suite; Rs 2,500 ($55) luxury suite; Rs 2,000 ($44) standard room; Rs 1,500 ($33) ordinary attic room. AE, MC, V. **Amenities:** Restaurant; gift shop. *In room:* A/C, TV (executive suites only).

Hotel de Pondicherry ★★ You may have trouble deciding which of the individually styled guest rooms—designed by the talented Vasanthi Manet—in this beautifully restored Indo-French colonial mansion is your favorite, though "Mahe de Labourdonnais" is arguably the finest of the double rooms. All the high-ceilinged guest rooms are *trés* chic, blending Indian and colonial accents with wood-frame beds covered with crisp white sheets and satin bedcovers. Bathrooms (with drench showers) are bright and cheerful. The small hotel has a number of handsome public sitting areas with planter's chairs and smart cane sofas covered with bright pink cushions; fans whir overhead. The hotel offers little besides great dining facilities (no room service), but staff try hard, and rates are very reasonable.

38 Dumas St, Pondicherry 605 001. © 0413/22-7409. Fax 0413/33-0057. hotel_de_pondichery@yahoo.com. 9 units. Doubles: Rs 1,500–Rs 2,250 ($33–$50); Rs 350 ($7.60) extra bed. AE, DC, MC, V. **Amenities:** 3 restaurants; tours; travel assistance; currency exchange; laundry; doctor-on-call. *In room:* A/C.

Villa Helena ★★ *Value* Owned by Roselyne Guitry, a perfumer from Burgundy who has lived in Bangkok, Delhi, and now Pondicherry, this guesthouse started out as a place in which Roselyne could keep her gorgeous collection of antiques and traditional furniture. Now she operates this delightful villa as a nonprofit hobby and an opportunity to meet people from around the world. A natural decorator, she claims that the place was thrown together, but furnishings and features show remarkable taste. A communal porch with gracious arches and pillars, where you can relax in planters' chairs, is a plus, while the guest rooms (which have lovely high ceilings that extend into the shower-only bathrooms) feature an eclectic blend of classical and colonial knickknacks picked up by Roselyne from all over Asia. Upstairs is an enormous suite, which is more like an apartment: In addition to a large bedroom and its own terrace, it has two living rooms, one of which features a desk that's large enough to double as a dining table, and a sofa that doubles as a bed. The beds here are the best in town—proper thick-pile mattresses. *Note:* At press time, Roselyne was planning to start another similarly stylish guesthouse, with a more inherently Indian flavor. Contact her for details.

14 Suffren St., Pondicherry 605 001. © 0413/22-6789, -7075, or 98-4306-9443. Fax 0413/22-7087. villahelena @satyam.net.in. 4 units. Doubles: Rs 1,500 ($33) standard; Rs 2,500 ($55) suite. Rates include breakfast. Coffee and soft drinks on demand. No credit cards. **Amenities:** Dining facility; sightseeing and travel assistance. *In room:* A/C, TV.

Good Food to Go

If you miss some of the comforts of home, you'll delight in **Church Gate** (198 Mission St.; © **0413/34-9146;** Mon–Sat 8:30am–noon and 3:30–9pm, Sun 8:30am–1:30pm). A grocery store billing itself "The Complete Shop," this is where you'll find imported food, pastries, fresh local fruit, and toiletries. It's an ideal place to stock up for a day trip or picnic or to get something wholesome for your minibar.

WHERE TO DINE

When it comes to the best fusion food in town, it's a bit of a toss-up between The Bistro/Indochine, reviewed below, and the classy Hotel de l'Orient's **Carte Blanche** ★★ (see above). If you opt for the latter's leafy courtyard (residents get first option), make sure you order a dish involving fish—it's caught locally and is so fresh it almost moves. **Satsanga** (30 Labourdonnais St.; © **0413/222-5867**) is a relaxing all-day eatery operated by an expat from the south of France who has been in Pondy for 33 years and who now resides in Auroville. If you're a carnivore, opt for the green pepper filet *(filet au poivre vert)* or the fish *Provençale*—not always on the menu, but worth asking for anyway.

The Bistro/Indochine ★★ FRENCH/ECLECTIC CAFE   These two restaurants at the atmospheric Hotel de Pondicherry share the same menu and venue; the Bistro transforms into the more exotic-sounding Indochine in the evenings. Set beneath a thatched roof, the venue has roll-down blinds, cane furniture, and green plastic seats for the spillover; fans work to kept customers cool, and potted plants add to the courtyard-cafe atmosphere. The menu is eclectic, with pizzas, hamburgers, savory pancakes, and great salads on offer. Pondicherry beef *paupiettes* and prawn *a la* Normandy are house faves. Also at Hotel de Pondicherry, the upstairs restaurant, **Le Club** ★★, prides itself on serving authentic traditional French cuisine, using only the finest French herbs, cream, and butter. The menu offers chateaubriand *a la béarnaise,* chicken with mustard sauce, crab with saffron sauce, shallow fried prawns with basil and cream, and squid prepared with mustard and egg yolk.

Hotel de Pondicherry, 38 Rue Dumas St. © **0413/222-7409.** Breakfast Rs 85–Rs 195 ($1.80–$4.25); continental brunch Rs 175 ($3.70); main courses Rs 85–Rs 195 ($1.80–$4.25); Le Club main courses Rs 145–Rs 325 ($3–$7). AE, DC, MC, V. Open all day; Le Club 10am–1pm and 5–10:30pm.

Rendezvous Café ★★ FRENCH/ITALIAN/INDIAN/CHINESE   Vincent, the owner of this popular cafe, started out as a sailor cooking meals for ship's crews. One day he visited this century-old Indo-French restaurant and became violently ill. Instead of complaining, he decided to buy the restaurant and tap into its potential. With a shabby colonial-chic atmosphere, the restaurant derives much of its charm from the relaxed setting, with a large thatched-roof area upstairs. It stocks cigars, imported beers, and Scotch, especially for the European expats and diplomats who hang out here. Seafood is a specialty; have the lobster either in a rich garlic-butter sauce, or mildly spiced and grilled in the tandoor. Alternatively, try traditional Pondicherry prawn curry served with steamed white rice. The pork is bred by Jesuit priests in Kodaikanal; try the pork vindaloo or the more conventional roast pork, arguably the best in town.

30 Rue Suffren. © **0413/233-9132.** Main courses Rs 80–Rs 400 ($1.70–$8.75). AE, DC, MC, V. Wed–Mon 8am–3pm and 6–10:30pm.

SHOPPING

Auromirayan (95 Canteen St.; © **0413/233-9351;** Mon–Sat 9:30am–12:30pm and 4:30–8:30pm; cash only) is the factory shop for leather goods (shoes, handbags, belts) produced in Auroville. The tiny **Boutique Auroshree** (18 Jawaharlal Nehru St.; © **0413/22-2117**) sells clothes and handicrafts from all over India; it has a small selection of silver jewelry, Tanjore miniatures, and handcrafted sandalwood items. **Little Shop** (21 Rue de la Compagnie; © **0413/34-3272;** Mon–Sat 9:30am–1pm and 3–7pm) is a tiny diversion in the vicinity of the museum where you can buy local handmade pottery, ceramic table lamps, and frosted glassware. **Splendour** (16 Goubert Ave.; © **0413/33-6398;** Thurs–Tues 9:30am–1pm and 4–8:30pm) sells goods exclusively produced by the Aurobindo Society. Besides toys, belts, bags, and incense, you can pick up a wide range of books on the Society and Sri Aurobindo. **Focus** bookstore (Mission St.; closed Sun), next to Immaculate Conception Cathedral, has hundreds of books on Indian culture and religion.

4 Thanjavur (Tanjore) & Tiruchirappalli

Tiruchirappalli is 325km (200 miles) SW of Chennai; Thanjavur is 55km (34 miles) E of Tiruchirappalli

Tiruchirappalli, or "the City of the Three-Headed Demon," sprawls at the foot of the colossal **Rock Fort,** where the Vijayanagar empire built its once-impregnable citadel when they wrestled power from the Cholas in the 10th century. The Vijayanagars and their successors, the Nayaks of Madurai, started work on one of South India's largest and most impressive temple towns, **Srirangam,** on an island created by the Cauvery and one of its tributaries, just beyond Tiruchirappalli.

During the bitter Carnatic wars, French and British forces battled for control of the city, both keen to establish control of the looming hilltop fortress. Today a number of neo-Gothic Christian monuments remain as evidence of the British influence during the 18th and 19th centuries, when a cantonment was established here and when much of the present-day city was built.

Almost directly east of Tiruchirappalli (or Trichy, as it's thankfully known), **Thanjavur** was the capital of the Chola empire—which included present-day Kerala, Sri Lanka, and parts of Indonesia. Its 11th-century **Brihadeshwara Temple** is a World Heritage monument and, together with Mamallapuram and Madurai, an important stop on Tamil's temple route.

ESSENTIALS

GETTING THERE & AWAY You can fly to Trichy from Chennai (every day except Mon and Fri) or from Fort Cochin in Kerala (Mon, Wed, and Fri). The airport is 8km (5 miles) from the city. Chennai is 7 hours away by road; slightly quicker by train—several daily trains (3 hr.) connect Trichy with Madurai. To get to Thanjavur from Trichy, either hire a car for the 1-hour journey, or spend

---

Tips **A Recommended Guide**

In the tourist information center at the front entrance of Brihadeshwara Temple, you should be able to locate **K. T. Raja** (© **98-4249-9772**), who has been working as a guide for more than a quarter of a century. He'll not only show you local temples, he'll arrange trips to outlying temple towns. Guide fees are about Rs 425 ($9) per day.

2 hours traveling by train. From Pondicherry, the fastest way to get to Trichy is by hired car; alternatively, check the current train schedule.

ORIENTATION   Trichy's hotels are situated in the British-built Cantonment, separated from the busy industrial and bazaar neighborhood where the Rock Fort is situated. Srirangam is a few kilometers north of Rock Fort.

VISITOR INFORMATION   Mr. Janarthanam at Trichy's **Government of Tamil Nadu Tourism Department** (1 Williams Rd., Cantonment; © **04324/ 246-0136;** daily 10am–5:45pm) can supply you with information, maps, and brochures. **Thanjavur's tourist office** (Hotel Tamil Nadu Complex Jawan Bhavan; © **04362/233-0984;** Mon–Fri 10am–5:45pm) provides good information on local sights and can help with transport.

GETTING AROUND   It may be worthwhile to hire a car and driver through your hotel or the tourist information center. You can even manage to see all the major attractions in a single, exhausting day.

WHAT TO SEE & DO
TIRUCHIRAPPALLI

Spend anywhere from a half to a full day here, devoting the majority of your time to the atmospheric temple town of **Srirangam.** In the evening, climb the steps to the summit of **Rock Fort** (Rs 1/2¢, entrance at China Bazaar) in time to witness the sun setting over the city. This is also the time you're likely to encounter the greatest number of devotees coming to worship at the Shiva temple (off-limits to non-Hindus) and paying tribute to the elephant-headed god, Ganesh, at his summit shrine. Little of the old fortification has survived (though some inscriptions date back to the 3rd c. B.C.), but you may be interested to know that at 3,800 million years old, the rock itself is said to be one of the oldest on Earth, predating the Himalayan range by around a million years.

Srirangam 🏵🏵🏵   Just 7km (4 miles) beyond Trichy, the vibrant, ancient holy town of Srirangam—one of India's biggest temple complexes—is the site of the sprawling **Sri Ranganathaswamy Temple,** whose seven concentric boundary walls *(prakara)* enclose 240 hectares (600 acres) devoted to the Hindu faith. Within the temple walls, a web of lanes lined with houses, shops, and businesses is also enclosed, making for fascinating exploration of what feels like a heaving medieval village. Dedicated to Vishnu, worshipped here as Ranganatha, the town sees almost nonstop feverish and colorful activity, with communal gatherings and festivals held throughout the year. The original 10th-century temple was destroyed by a Delhi sultan, but reconstruction began in the late 14th century. Ongoing expansion by Trichy's successive rulers culminated in the late 20th century, with the elaborately carved and brightly painted **Rajagopuram,** not

---

⎛Tips⎞ Need a Break?

In a city where dependable non-hotel restaurants are in short supply, **Rock City** (28 Nandhi Koil St.; © **0431/270-6324**), a relatively slick-looking joint seemingly cut into the base of Rock Fort, is a godsend. The major drawback here is that no one speaks much English, so you're best off sticking to what you know from the wide-ranging menu of popular Indian, tandoori, and Chinese dishes—the Dolmond pepper chicken is recommended. Open for lunch and dinner, the restaurant accepts credit cards.

only the largest of the 21 *gopurams* (tower gateways) that surround the immense complex, but said to be the largest in Asia, soaring to a height of 72m (230 ft.). The most important shrines are within the inner four boundary walls, entered via a high gateway where smaller shrines mark the point beyond which lower-caste Hindus could not venture. Within this enclosure, you'll find a temple to the goddess Ranganayaki, as well as the **thousand-pillared hall,** which dates back to the Chola period. Arguably the most impressive of all is the nearby **Seshagirirayar Mandapa,** where the pillars are decorated with stone carvings of rearing horses mounted by warriors. For a memorable view of the entire complex, make sure to purchase a ticket to climb to the rooftop.

7km (4 miles) north of Trichy. Free admission. No photography allowed inside the sanctum.

THANJAVUR

Brihadeshvara Temple ★★★   This granite temple, a World Heritage Site built by the Chola kings a thousand years ago, was only recently reopened for worship; today the large complex is very much alive with devotees. Standing in a vast courtyard, surrounded by a number of subsidiary shrines, the temple was built—no doubt at great expense—by the Chola Rajaraja I for the worship of Shiva. Pyramidal in shape, the monumental tower or *vimana* over the inner sanctum rises almost 70m (224 ft.) and is visible for miles around. It's capped by an octagonal cupola carved from a single block of granite that was hauled into place along a ramp that is said to have been 6km (4 miles) long. Within the sanctum is a 4m (13-ft.) lingam; facing the sanctum, a colossal 25-ton Nandi monolith, carved from solid granite, dominates the courtyard. Numerous extant inscriptions on the molded plinth describe the enormous wealth of the temple (much of it booty from Rajaraja's successful campaigns), as well as the copious acts of ritual and celebration that took place here. In its heyday, an enormous staff was maintained to attend to the temple's varied activities; these included everything from administration to procuring dancing girls.

West of Thanjavur bus stand. Visitors can make prior arrangements for entry to the sanctum and the upper floors of the temple by contacting the temple administration (✆ 04362/24-3139). Alternatively, contact the local tourist office.

Thanjavur Palace Complex & Art Gallery ★★   Built as the home of the Nayak rulers, the 16th-century **Royal Palace** has fallen into a state of minor ruin but is home to the impressive **Thanjavur Art Gallery** (daily 10am–1pm and 2–5pm; admission Rs 10/20¢), which houses an eclectic collection of stone and bronze idols, mostly from the Chola period. Within the palace, you should also climb the narrow and tricky steps of the **arsenal tower** for fantastic views of the complex and the entire city, including Brihadeshvara Temple. Inside the 17th-century **Durbar Hall,** built by the Marathas, who ruled after the Nayaks, are 11th-century statues of Vishnu and Parvathi, exhibited in Washington, D.C., in 1865. Near the museum is the **Saraswati Mahal Library,** which houses a collection of rare books—including Sanskrit works and 18,623 palm-leaf manuscripts—assembled by the Maratha ruler Serfoji II, who ruled until 1832 and was known as a great patron of the arts. The attached **Museum** (Thurs–Tues 9:30am–1pm and 1:30–5:30pm; free admission) has highlights from the collection, including some detailed drawings of Chinese torture and punishment techniques. Give both the **Sadar Mahal Palace** and its **Royal Museum** a miss.

E. Main Rd. For information about Thanjavur Art Gallery, contact the Art Gallery Society (✆ 04362/ 233-9823). Daily 9am–1pm and 3–6pm.

WHERE TO STAY & DINE

You may end up spending the night in both Trichy and Thanjavur, a pity, because neither has exciting accommodations options. But a stay may be hard to avoid—onward travel in either direction takes 2 hours, so you'd need to move at quite a pace, and Tamil Nadu's heat will inevitably slow you down.

TIRUCHIRAPALLI

Hotel Sangam Tiruchirappalli   Popular with tour groups, this friendly 30-year-old hotel benefits considerably from its location a short distance out of the city center, so it offers less noise and polluted congestion and a greater sense of space, enhanced by decent lawns. Marble and plaid are primary motifs, and linoleum surfaces are popular here, but Sangam's large guest rooms are adequately furnished and immaculately clean. Ask for a room overlooking the swimming pool (these have even numbers). The restaurant, **Chembian,** where Chef Madi prepares some interesting dishes, is also agreeable—try the *kozhi milaau,* fragrant chicken flavored with ginger and tamarind.

Collector's Office Rd., Tiruchirappalli 620 001. ℂ **0431/241-4700** or -4480. Fax 0431/41-5779. www.hotel sangam.com. 60 units. Doubles: $107; $155 including all meals. AE, DC, MC, V. **Amenities:** 2 restaurants; bar; pool; health club; travel counter; shopping arcade; 24-hr. room service; laundry and dry cleaning; doctor-on-call. *In room:* A/C, TV, minibar (in some rooms).

Jenneys Residency   The lobby of this well-equipped five-floor business hotel is decked out in white marble, with large reflective pillars in a sort of fantasy of temple architecture. Recently refurbished, the centrally air-conditioned guest units are comfortable enough, with standard Western comforts that include fair-size bathrooms and tubs. They offer great value but tend to pick up noise from the busy main road outside. Some of the rooms offer excellent views of the Rock Fort. The theme bar here is very popular with locals—especially on weekends.

3/14 McDonald's Rd., Tiruchirappalli 620 001. ℂ 0431/241-4414. Fax 0431/46-1451. www.jenneysresidency. com. 123 units. Doubles: $40 executive; $55 deluxe; $75 luxury suite; $100 presidential suite; $10 extra bed. Rates include breakfast. AE, DC, MC, V. **Amenities:** 2 restaurants; bar; pool; health club; travel agency; currency exchange; florist; shopping arcade; salon; 24-hr. room service; Ayurvedic massage; laundry; doctor-on-call; valet. *In room:* A/C, TV, minibar.

THANJAVUR

The best hotel in town, **Hotel Sangam Thanjavur** (ℂ **04362/233-9451** or -9452; www.hotelsangam.com; doubles: Rs 1,650/$36 walk-in rate, Rs 4,590/$102 published rate) benefits greatly from its quiet location on Trichy Road, away from the town center. Fronted by neat gardens, it has comfortable, relatively new guest rooms (A/C, TV, minibar) and a good range of amenities (room service; pool; health club), and the staff is very helpful. The restaurant, **Thillana,** is one of India's rare small-town restaurants where your server not only manages to make convincing recommendations, but the food (rather spicy) actually meets your expectations—order chicken Chettinad, a Tamil favorite that explodes with tangy flavor, or vegetables sautéed in spicy Chettinad masala (avoid the Chinese and Continental dishes on offer).

For Thanjavur's best bargain, book into the **Ideal River View Resort,** cottage-style apartments clustered on the banks of a branch of the Cauvery River. Situated 3km (2 miles) out of town, the resort enjoys a remote setting amid paddy fields and wild vegetation. Each air-conditioned guest room has a balcony facing the Vennar River. With doubles at Rs 1,100 ($24) and an impressive range of amenities, including a pool, boating, riding, tennis, fortune-tellers, and Ayurvedic massage (© **04362/235-0533** or 044/2823-7583; www.idealresort. com), this is really unbeatable value.

5 Madurai ⋆⋆⋆

498km (308 miles) SW of Chennai; 160km (99 miles) W of Trichy

Located on the banks of the Vaigai River, Madurai—apparently named for the nectar that flowed from Shiva's hair as a blessing for the new city (*madhuram* is the Tamil word for sweetness)—was built by the Pandyan king Kulasekara and was the capital of a kingdom that ruled much of South India during the 4th century B.C., and that conducted trade as far afield as Greece and Rome.

Madurai also became a center for the great festivals of poetry and writing—the **Tamil Sangams**—that were being held more than 2 millennia ago. According to legend, the great literary academics would toss works of literature into the holy water of the Golden Tank around which the temple was built, and only those that floated were deemed to be of any value. Through the millennia, various dynasties have battled over the city. The Vijayanagars built much of the temple during their reign, which lasted until the 16th century, when the Nayaks came to power, who in turn ruled until the arrival of the British in 1736. Modern Madurai embodies the spirit of Tamil Nadu's deeply embedded temple culture, and the labyrinthine **Meenakshi Temple**—celebrating the love of the Meenakshi goddess and her groom, Sundareswarar (the "Handsome God"), an avatar of Lord Shiva—is easily our first choice in Tamil's temple destinations.

ESSENTIALS

GETTING THERE & AWAY Daily flights connect Madurai to Chennai or Mumbai. The **airport** (© **0452/267-1333**) is 12km (7½ miles) south of the city center. Contact **Indian Airlines** (© **0452/274-1234** or -1236, or 0452/267-0133 at the airport; Mon–Sat 10am–5pm). For information about new services offered by **Jet Airways,** call © **0452/252-6970,** -6971, or -6972. Trains from all over southern India pull in at **Madurai Junction Railway Station** (W. Veli St.; © **0452/274-3131**). The journey from Chennai is 10 hours; from Bangalore, it's 12 hours. From Pondicherry it's a long haul either by car or train; best to stay over at Trichy.

VISITOR INFORMATION Staff at the **Government of Tamil Nadu Tourist Office** (W. Veli St., next to the Tamil Nadu Hotel; © **0452/233-4757;** www.maduraicity.com; daily 10am–5:45pm) provides maps, advice on government-sponsored hotels and shops, and recommendations on guides. As elsewhere, beware of fake "official guides" you meet on the streets.

GETTING AROUND Rickshaw drivers tend to have a field day with foreign visitors; establish a flat rate before heading off.

FESTIVAL If you're in town for the **Chittrai Festival** (Apr–May), when Meenakshi's marriage to Sundareswarar is celebrated, you're in for a treat—the town attains a fever-pitch radiance.

WHAT TO SEE & DO

The principal reason to visit Madurai—for you as well as for tens of thousands of Hindu pilgrims—is to experience the ecstatic spiritual life of the **Meenakshi Temple;** what little else there is to see and do in town will pale in comparison.

Legend recalls that Meenakshi began life as a glorious princess, born of fire with three breasts and eyes like a fish. As she grew older, she overpowered all the gods with her impossible beauty until she encountered Shiva, who transformed her heart to ghee (butter) and married her. While sitting inside the temple itself can provide hours of entertainment and an appreciation of Tamil's vivid spirituality (as well as a sense of its religious commerce), the streets immediately around the great temple are full of character, and are best experienced by simply wandering around. Not far from the temple, the **Tirumala Nayak Mahal** (Palace Rd.; ℂ **0452/273-2945;** daily 9am–1pm and 2–5pm; admission Rs 1/2¢) is a 17-century Indo-Saracenic palace built by Tirumala Nayak and later restored to some extent by Madras governor Lord Napier. Not all that much of the palace remains except for the large pillared courtyard known as the "Heavenly Pavil-ion," where a nightly *son et lumière* show (6 or 6:45pm; Rs 100/$2.10) sheds light on Madurai's history.

It was in Madurai in 1921 that Mahatma Gandhi historically exchanged his *kuta* wardrobe for the *dhoti,* or loincloth, typically worn by the poor. Today the bloodstained *dhoti* he wore when he was assassinated is encased in a glass shrine at the **Gandhi Memorial Museum** (Tamukkam, 5km/3 miles east of the city center; www.madurai.com/gandhi.htm; daily 10am–1pm and 2–5:30pm; free admission), which chronicles India's history leading up to independence. Avoid the adjacent **Government Museum,** where visitors experience two million years of history in 30 seconds as they whiz past a 9th-century Vishnu statue, 12th-century Pandyan works, undated Chola statues, and a stuffed polar bear.

If you're still not tired of temples, 8km (5 miles) from Madurai, **Thiruppa-rankundram Temple** makes for a pleasant outing, particularly on Tuesday and Friday, when women with marriage or family troubles sit on the temple floor and create colorful patterns on the ground using flowers and candles as offerings to Durga. Nearby, **Owayat,** the 40-year-old temple elephant, shuffles and waits to bestow blessings on those willing to donate a rupee.

Shri Meenakshi-Sundareshwarar Temple ★★★

One of South India's biggest, busiest pilgrimage sites (around 15,000 pilgrims each day; 10,000 more on Fri), this sprawling temple, always undergoing renovation and repairs, is a place of intense spiritual activity almost unparalleled in India. A high wall surrounds the complex, and 12 looming *gopurams* (pyramidal gateways) mark the various entrances. Garish stucco gods, demons, beasts, and heroes smother these towers in a writhing, fascinating mass of symbolism, vividly painted in a riot of bright colors reminiscent of a Disney cartoon. Traditionally, entrance to the complex is through the eastern **Ashta Shakti Mandapa,** a hall of pillars graced by sculptural representations of the goddess Shakti in her many aspects. Adjacent to this, in the **Meenakshi Nayaka Mandapa,** is where pilgrims purchase all manner of devo-tional paraphernalia and holy souvenirs. Near the inner gate, a temple elephant, daubed with eye shadow and blusher, earns her keep by accepting a few rupees' donation in exchange for a blessing—bestowed with a light tap of her dexterous trunk. From here you can wander at will, finding your way at some stage to the **Temple Art Museum,** housed in the impressive 16th-century Hall of a Thousand Pillars. This hall has 985 elegantly sculpted columns, including a set of "musical pillars" that produce the seven Carnatic musical notes when tapped (a ticket offi-cer will gladly demonstrate in exchange for a tip).

All around the complex of shrines and effigies, various *pujas* (prayers) and rit-uals are conducted, some under the guiding hand of a bare-chested Brahmin priest, others as spontaneous expressions of personal, elated devotion. Against one stone image of buxom Meenakshi, devotees actually throw balls of ghee—a ritual prayer tossed at her to keep her cool, her heart apparently having turned to butter when she met Shiva. On other statues, layer upon layer of ghee and oil have turned surfaces smooth and black, stained with years of turmeric and vermilion powder sprinkled and dabbed by believers seeking blessings and hope.

At the heart of the complex are the **sanctums of the goddess Meenakshi (Parvati)** and **Sundareshvara (Shiva).** What often eludes visitors to the heaving temple at Madurai is the city's deeply imbedded cult of fertility; behind the reverence and severity of worship, the Meenakshi temple is a celebration of the divine union of the eternal lovers, represented symbolically at the end of the day when they are ceremoniously carried (a ritual you can observe until they enter the inner sanctum, which is off-limits to non-Hindus) and brought together for an evening of celestial fornication. This is the time to head for the stairs around the great tank, where devotees gather to chat and relax at the end of the day.

Bounded by N., E., S., and W. Chitrai sts. ✆ 0452/274-4360. www.maduraimeenakshi.org. Daily 5am–12:30pm and 4–9:30pm. Admission free. No entrance to main shrines for non-Hindus. Deposit shoes outside entrance. Thousand Pillar Museum: Adults Rs 2 (4¢), children under 12 Rs 1 (2¢). daily 7am–6pm.

WHERE TO STAY

Taj Garden Retreat Madurai ★★ Situated on a hillock known as Pasumalai, and blessed with sprawling tree-filled grounds, this colonial-style hotel—without a doubt your best option in Madurai—offers panoramic views of the Temple City. Arrived at by a long driveway (a sign en route warns of PEACOCKS CROSSING), this was the original residence of Sir William Harvey. The main building, built in 1891, is decorated with hunting trophies and includes a well-stocked colonial-style bar. Accommodations are spread over five different blocks; opt for the spacious deluxe rooms that are housed in the original colonial buildings and offer fantastic views from wide bay windows (book room nos. 21 and 22) and shared balconies. Superior rooms are no less comfortable, offering either pool or garden views. Among the hotel's offerings is resident palmist Mr. Mani, who has looked into the futures of nearly 25,000 people with "almost accuracy"!

40 T.P.K. Rd., Pasumalai, Madurai 625 004. ✆ 0452/277-1601. Fax 0452/277-1636. www.tajhotels.com. 62 units. Doubles (Oct–Apr/May–Sept/Dec 23–Jan 5): $120/$100/$135 standard; $145/$110/$165 superior/Old World rooms; $160/$135/$175 deluxe; $20 extra bed. 35% tax. AE, DC, MC, V. **Amenities:** Restaurant; bar; pool; tennis court; badminton court; jogging track; Ayurvedic center; nursery; travel desk, car hire; 24-hr. room service; babysitting; laundry, dry cleaning; doctor-on-call; pharmacy service; palmist. *In room:* A/C, TV, minibar, hair dryer. Deluxe rooms have tea- and coffee-making facilities.

WHERE TO DINE

The city has a fair number of scruffy dining halls that are well attended by locals—and with good reason. *Thali* (multicourse) meals served in these dime-a-dozen joints are delicious and extremely economical. But if the idea of eating with your fingers makes you gag, head for the classy all-day restaurant at **Taj Garden Retreat Madurai** (see above). Situated on the fairy-lights-adorned rooftop of the 1970s-style Supreme Hotel, the pleasant **Surya Rooftop Restaurant** ★ (110 W. Permal Maistry St.; ✆ **0452/254-3151;** daily 4pm–midnight; Rs 30–Rs 90/60¢–$1.90) opens in time for an early sun-downer session, making it a popular place from which to admire the setting sun on the Meenakshi Temple. A personal favorite is Hyderabadi vegetable balls, great with *tawa paratha,* a soft tandoori bread. Portions are generous and neatly served.

7

Karnataka & Hyderabad: Kingdoms of the South

Sixteenth-century visitors to the royal courts of present-day Karnataka returned to Europe with stupendous tales of wealth—cities overflowing with jewels, and streets littered with diamonds. Over the centuries, the lush, green state that occupies a vast chunk of India's southwestern seaboard saw numerous kingdoms rise and fall, powerful dynasties that left a legacy of impressive palaces and monumental cities that now lie scattered throughout the interior, some of them well off the beaten track, but worth the effort and time it takes to seek them out.

The post-independence state of Karnataka, unified in 1950 on the basis of common language, is predominantly made up of the once-princely state of Mysore and the Berar territories of the Nizam of Hyderabad's kingdom. Once one of the richest cities in India, Hyderabad is now the vibrant capital of Andhra Pradesh, and a possible excursion from Bangalore, state capital of Karnataka. **Bangalore,** in many ways the country's most "Western" city, is today famous for its energetic nightlife and computer and technology industries. Although it offers little by way of sightseeing attractions, it's a great place to relax; you can shop by day and explore the pubs and clubs at night before you take the overnight train to explore the ghost city of **Hampi.** This great medieval Hindu capital of the South is said to have once rivaled Rome in size and wealth. The ruins of the 14th-century Vijayanagar kingdom are set in a boulder-strewn landscape that proves fascinating in its own right—deservedly Karnataka's most famous attraction.

Karnataka's other primary destination is **Mysore,** the famous "City of Incense," where the vibrant markets are still perfumed with the aromas of jasmine and musk, sandalwood, and frangipani. Ruled by India's most enlightened maharajas, Mysore is home to some 17 palaces, of which **Amba Vilas** is arguably India's most opulent. Just a few hours south of Mysore is **Rajiv Gandhi National Park,** home to herds of wild elephant and the more elusive Bengal tiger, while northward lie the **"Jewel Box" temples** built by the mighty Hoysala warriors in the cities of Belur and Hal, best reached via Sravanabelgola, home to one of the oldest and most important Jain pilgrimage sites in India: a 18m (60-ft.) **statue of the naked Lord Gomateswara,** said to be the tallest monolithic statue on earth and one of the most spiritually satisfying destinations in India.

Karnataka

Tips Planning Your Tour

Most travelers head directly for **Bangalore**, Karnataka's capital, using it as a base to fly to **Hyderabad,** capital of Andhra Pradesh (discussed at the end of the chapter), or as a base from which to catch an overnight train to and from the "lost city" of **Hampi,** which lies 320km (198 miles) north. (Note that many younger, more adventurous travelers, usually backpackers, catch a bus from Goa and head straight here.) Remote and serene, Hampi is good for a few relaxing days—at least 3 if you intend to explore the under-visited **temples of the Chalukyas,** which lie north of Hampi. The second principal destination in Karnataka is **Mysore,** again usually reached from Bangalore. If you're in Tamil Nadu or Kerala, it's also possible to drive directly to Mysore, passing the **Rajiv Gandhi National Park,** or to approach it from the coastal city of **Mangalore,** connected to Goa and Kerala via the Konkan railway. Spend at least a day in Mysore before spending the next day or two visiting the beautifully decorated **11th-century temples** at Belur and Halebid, and the nearby **Jain monolithic statues** at Sravanabeloga. Karnataka also has a few stunning **beaches,** just south of the Goan border, but unless you can make do with the limited facilities, save your sunbathing for Goa and Kerala.

1 Bangalore

If you've been in India a while, the capital of Karnataka will probably feel like a long, soothing break from the endless commotion. The first city in India to get electricity, Bangalore continues, in many ways, to blaze the trail in terms of the country's quest for a modern identity. Once known as the Garden City (and less encouragingly as Pensioner's Paradise), the country's most pristine city evolved significantly when the high-tech revolution hit and it suddenly found itself at the center of the nation's massive computer hardware and software industries. Its cosmopolitan spirit fueled as much by its luminous pub and cafe culture as by the influx of international businesspeople, India's high-tech hub has a high-energy buzz, yet it's tangibly calmer and cleaner than most other places in the country, with far and away the best climate of any Indian city—no doubt the reason the majority of upwardly mobile Indians rank it the number-one city in which to live.

Unless you go in for the cafe society, you won't find very many attractions. The city's real appeal is its zesty contemporary Indian lifestyle and its usefulness as a base for getting to the extraordinary temples and ruins of the Deccan interior and the vibrant cities of Hyderabad and Mysore.

ESSENTIALS

GETTING THERE & MOVING ON   By Air   Bangalore's airport (13km/8 miles north) is the busiest in South India, connected to most of the major cities in India (including Hyderabad). There are even several Air-India flights to London and New York. To get to your hotel from the airport, it's best to use a taxi (about Rs 150/$3.15 to most hotels) from the prepaid counter.

By Train   Bangalore is a major transport hub, reached by a significant number of rail connections. Journeys from North Indian cities, however, are extremely time-consuming; the fastest connection with Delhi takes 35 hours, while Mumbai is 24 hours away. From Chennai (Tamil Nadu), take the 5-hour Shatabdi Express. To get to Mysore, catch the 2-hour Shatabdi Express (departs Wed–Mon at 11am). For Hyderabad, catch the comfortable overnight Rajdhani Express (departs four times a week at 6:35pm).

By Road   For the greatest amount of freedom, you should hire a car and driver, particularly if you plant to get off the beaten track.

VISITOR INFORMATION   Karnataka State Tourism Development Corporation (KSTDC) tourist information counters are found at the railway station (℃ **080/287-0068;** daily 7am–10pm) and at the airport (℃ **080/526-8012;** daily 7:30am–1:30pm and 2–7:30pm). **Karnataka Tourism** (1st Floor, F Block, Cauvery Bhavan, Kempe Gowda Rd.; ℃ **080/221-5489;** www.karnatakatourism.com) is reliable for sightseeing information rather than info on accommodations and dining; ask for a copy of *Bangalore This Fortnight.* The **Government of India Tourist Office** is at the KSFC Building, 48 Church St. (℃ **080/558-5417;** Mon–Fri 9:30am–6pm, Sat 9am–1pm).

GETTING AROUND   By Auto-Rickshaw   Insist that the meter is used. Generally, the first kilometer will cost Rs 9; each kilometer after that will cost Rs 4. After 10pm, drivers will try to skewer you for double; pay 50% the displayed amount.

With Car & Driver   Plan on spending in the region of Rs 150 per hour, or Rs 400 for a 4-day tour, which will include 40km of free mileage. To hire a car and driver, try **Dial-a-Car** (℃ **080/526-1737**), which operates around-the-clock.

GUIDED TOURS & TRAVEL AGENTS   KSTDC (104/1 Kasturba Rd.; ℃ **080/221-2901**) conducts sightseeing tours around the state. **Sita Travels** (1 St. Mark's Rd.; ℃ **080/558-8892**) and **Marco Polo Tours** (Janardhan Towers, 2 Residency Rd.; ℃ **080/227-4484;** fax 080/223-6671) are reliable all-rounders. **Cosmopole Travels** (℃ **080/228-1591**) is useful for event destinations such as the Nrityagram Dance Village.

FAST FACTS: Bangalore

Airlines **Jet Airways:** ℃ 080/227-6617, -6618, -6619, or airport 080/526-6898. **Indian Airlines:** ℃ 080/221-1914 or 080/526-6233.

Area Code The area code for **Bangalore** is **080**.

ATMs Visit the shop-intensive vicinity of M.G. Road.

Bookstores **Strand Book Stall** is at 113 Manipal Centre, Dickenson Road (℃ 080/558-0000). **Higginbothams** is at 68 M.G. Rd. **Sankar's Book Stall** is at 15/2 Madras Bank Rd. (℃ 080/558-6867).

Car Rentals **Gullivers Tours & Travels** is at South Black 201/202 Manipal Centre, 47 Dickenson Rd. (℃ 080/558-8001).

Currency Exchange Exchange cash or get credit card advances from **Wall Street Finances** (3 House of Lords, 13/14 St. Mark's Rd.; ℃ 080/227-1812; Mon–Sat 9:30am–6pm) and **ANZ Grindlays** (Raheja Towers, M.G. Rd.;

Mon–Fri 10:30am–2:30pm, Sat 10:30am–12:30pm). Alternatively, you can go to **Thomas Cook** (55 M.G. Rd.; ✆ 080/558-1337; Mon–Sat 9:30am–6pm).

Drugstores Twenty-four-hour chemists include **Khoday's Pharma** (214 Westminster, Cunningham Rd.; ✆ 080/228-1540); **Mallige Pharmacy** (31/32 Crescent Rd.; ✆ 080/226-7662); and **Mallya Hospital** (Vittal Mallya Rd., south of Cubbon Park; ✆ 080/227-7979).

Emergencies Dial ✆ **100** for police emergencies.

Hospital Both **Manipal Hospital** (98 Rustumbagh Airport Rd.; ✆ **080/526-6646**) and **St. John's Medical College and Hospital** (Sarjapur Rd.; ✆ **080/ 553-0724** or **-0734**) are decent options.

Internet Access See "Cafe Society," below.

Mobile Phones You can rent a phone from **Smart Cell Rentals** (50 Shrungar Complex, M.G. Rd.; ✆ 080/559-4647) or **Global Access** (14 St. Marks Plaza, St. Marks Rd.; ✆ 080/299-6560).

Police Contact **Cubbon Park Station** at ✆ 080/556-6242 or **100**.

Post Office As always, your best bet for sending mail is through your hotel. The **GPO** (✆ 080/286-6772 or -7901; Mon–Sat 10am–6pm, Sun 10:30am–1pm) is architecturally interesting. It's located at the intersection of Raj Bhavan and Ambedkar Road.

Railway For inquiries, dial ✆ **131** or 132.

Taxis Call **Bangalore Radio Taxi** (✆ 080/332-0152 or -7589).

WHAT TO SEE & DO

Although it was ruled by various dynasties, Bangalore's chief historical sights date back to the 18th-century reign of Hyder Ali and his son Tipu Sultan, "the Lion of Mysore," who put up the most spirited resistance to British imperialism. But more than anything, Bangalore is about experiencing an Indian city that's brimming over with pubs, restaurants, and positive energy—a great place for walking, window-shopping and, at night, letting your hair down. The Garden City also has lovely parks, some of which date back over 2 centuries, of which the botanical gardens at **Lal Bagh** are the most impressive.

Set off early for Bugle Hill, site of the **Bull Temple** (daily 7:30am–12:30pm and 5:30–8:30pm). Built by the city's original architect, Kempe Gowda, this 16th-century black-granite statue of Nandi (Shiva's sacred bull "vehicle") literally dwarfs his "master," and is kept glistening by regular applications of coconut oil. Nearby is a Ganesha temple **(Sri Dodda Ganapathi),** which houses an enormous statue of the elephant-headed deity made of rank-smelling butter.

Picnicking with the family and cricketing with the boys are popular pastimes in **Cubbon Park** (Cantonment), laid out in 1864 by the Mysore engineer, Richard Sankey. Today many visitors come to view the lovely buildings that surround the park as well as to visit the **Government Museum and Venkatappa Art Gallery** (✆ 080/286-4483; Tues–Sun 10am–5pm; Rs 4/10¢), which focuses on sculpture. It contains works from Khajuraho, Bihar, and Madhya Pradesh dating back to the 10th century, Buddhist figures from the 4th- and 5th-century Gandhara school, and Hoysala carvings from Belur, Halebid, and Hampi—not that these are really a match for the real thing, seen on location.

While in the vicinity, take a walk or drive past **Vidhana Vidhi** to admire its Greco-colonial-style buildings, including India's largest state headquarters, **Vidhana Soudha,** Karnataka's State Legislature and Secretariat building (no entry allowed), to marvel at what is termed "neo-Dravidian" architecture. Its blend of styles from across India is capped by one of India's most recognizable symbols—the four-headed gold lion of Ashoka, India's celebrated early Buddhist king. Over the entrance, a gleaming gold-lettered sign bears the somewhat ironic slogan GOVERNMENT WORK IS GOD'S WORK. Across the road from the Vidhana Soudha, fringing Cubbon Park, is Karnataka's two-story High Court building, or **Attara Kacheri,** an attractive design with red bricks and monumental Corinthian columns.

If it's a real garden you're after, head straight for the botanical gardens at **Lal Bagh** (daily 9am–6pm; Rs 2/5¢), conceived and laid out by Sultan Hydar Ali in 1760. His son, Tipu, expanded the gardens further, planting exotic plants from Persia, Kabul, Turkey, and Mauritius (tropical and subtropical species) over 96 hectares (240 acres). Highlights include the Lawn Clock and the British-built glasshouse, structurally based on London's Crystal Palace. After visiting the Gardens, be sure to pop in for a meal at *the* Bangalore lunch institution, **Mavalli Tiffin Rooms** (see "Where to Dine," below), a short distance from the entrance.

Tipu Sultan's Summer Palace (daily 9am–5pm; Rs 2/5¢), built toward the end of the 18th century entirely from timber, is a relic in a city committed more to progress than to preservation. It has a somewhat sophomoric exhibition with extensive text about Tipu's life and military conquests as well as those of his father, Hydar Ali Khan. Next door is an enormously active 17th-century temple, built by the Wodeyar kings, and just north are the ruins of the **Bangalore Fort (Kempe Gowda),** largely destroyed during the Anglo-Mysore War.

WHERE TO STAY

Bangalore has a huge range of excellent top-quality hotels, of which our personal favorites are **The Park.hotel** for its contemporary über-slick styling and in-house nightlife, and the **Taj West End Hotel** for its heritage atmosphere (both reviewed below). You may want to compare online rates with the following hotels, which offer the same top-end luxury and amenities. **Hotel Windsor Sheraton & Towers,** popular with Bollywood's elite and high-profile businesspeople and politicians (including Tony Blair), retains the look and character of a neoclassical English country house; ask for a room in the Manor Block (© **080/226-9898;** fax 080/226-4941; www.welcomgroup.com). The **Oberoi** (© **080/558-5858;** www.oberoihotels.com; doubles from $255) is another excellent hotel, set amid gardens with lovely views over the lawns and the swimming pool. Standard units

---

Cafe Society

Caffeine is a popular fix in a city where public socializing is the pastime of choice for a money-wielding cosmopolitan crowd. Get yours at **Java City** (24/1 Lavelle Rd.; daily 10am–11pm), where you can also indulge in a slice of rum-and-chocolate cake (other branches are at 47 Church St. and 13 Cunningham Rd.). Or head for cool **Cinnamon Barista** (11 Walton Rd., off Lavelle Rd.), attached to the highly recommended Cinnamon boutique. You can surf the Internet while getting your caffeine rush at **Café Coffee Day,** Bangalore's first cybercafe (13 Brigade Rd.; © **080/559-1602;** daily 8am–10:30pm; Rs 50/$1 for 1 hr. and two coffees).

are not quite as large or as elegant as those at the Windsor Sheraton, but they're spacious enough and luxuriously decorated with floral fabrics and antique finishes; ask for a room on an upper floor for better views. But for over-the-top opulence, the **Leela Palace**—judged by *Forbes Magazine* one of the world's best new business hotels in 2001—is the hands-down winner. A baroque rendition of contemporary Indo-Saracenic architecture, looming large in pale pink, it offers enormous "conservatory" rooms with private balconies and, along with all the modern conveniences, elegant four-poster beds, rococo gold-gilt lamps, and silk duvet covers. Deluxe rooms are also very spacious and styled in the same manner (✆ **080/521-1234;** www.theleela.com; doubles: $190 deluxe, $210 conservatory). In the moderate price range, opt for the Taj-run **Gateway Hotel on Residency Road;** its best accommodations are the recently refurbished "executive" guest rooms. Ask for an even-numbered, pool-facing room on the fourth floor (✆ **080/558-4545;** www.tajhotels.com; doubles from $105). Even cheaper, **St. Mark's** is a small, neat business hotel (✆ **080/227-9090;** www.stmarkshotel. com) with doubles from Rs 3,200 ($70). Our budget recommendation is **New Victoria Hotel;** this simple, welcoming hotel offers basic en-suite rooms set around a pleasant courtyard (✆ **080/558-4076;** fax 080/558-4945; doubles: Rs 1,360/$30).

The Park.hotel ✰✰✰   Themed around Bangalore's reputation as India's information-technology city and its historic connection with silk production, this compact boutique hotel features top-class interiors by Tina Ellis of London-based Conran and Partners that could be from the pages of *Wallpaper* magazine. In the lobby—dominated by a gigantic silk curtain—rough, smooth, and suede textures are offset with brushed metal and a row of large white orbs of light. The white-marble reception counter is topped by orange Apple laptops—behind the counter, staff wear pale gray jackets over white T-shirts. The four floors are styled around a palette of strong chromatic elements that refer to the Indian landscape; pale lime and iris purple suggest the mountains, while a desert oasis is alluded to with ultramarine and saffron. Guest rooms are on the small side and don't have great views (ask for a pool-facing room), but they are beautifully finished— oak flooring, designer rugs, black-and-white photographs of Bangalore, oak-and-leather director chairs, and minimalist metal-framed four-poster beds. Bathrooms are great, with large rain showers that adjust to give you a water massage. Rooms on the desert-themed Residence Floor come with a host of additional services including airport transfers, late checkout, sparkling wine on arrival, head and shoulder massage, Internet access, in-room fax and laptop on request, DVD player, and access to the elegant private lounge, where breakfast and all-day tea and coffee are served.

14/7 M.G. Rd., Bangalore 560 001. ✆ **080/559-4666.** Fax 080/559-467. www.theparkhotels.com. 109 units. Doubles: $160 deluxe; $170 deluxe balcony; $180 deluxe terrace; $200 luxury; $225 Residence; $250–$300 suite. AE, DC, MC, V. **Amenities:** 2 restaurants; lounge bar; pool; health spa; indoor games; travel services; sightseeing; currency exchange; gift shop; 24-hr. room service; babysitting; laundry; doctor-on-call; valet; library. *In room:* A/C, TV, dataport, minibar.

Taj West End Hotel ✰✰✰   A member of The Leading Hotels of the World, West End dates back to 1887, when it was a 10-room Victorian boardinghouse; today the luxury hotel retains its old-world charm while providing guests with modern conveniences. Stately yet simple, the lobby features a central tree, green marble pillars, a skylight, and chandeliers; it opens onto a bar and a good Italian specialty restaurant. Accommodations are spread over more than 8 hectares (20 acres) of gardens with wonderful old banyan trees—thankfully, a leather-seat

Mercedes whisks you to your room after check-in. Rooms comprise various pitched-roof–veranda blocks and more recent structures modeled on similar colonial architecture; each has a private balcony looking onto the extensive gardens. Try to book in the Heritage Wing, which has four-poster beds and old-Bangalore-theme lithographs. "Superior" rooms are by comparison rather ordinary, but the private balcony with lovely views is a consolation. If you value your space, fork out the extra cash for an executive suite; these are massive, warm-toned, carpeted spaces with long balconies and high arched ceilings. Bathrooms are large, with separate tub and shower, and a walk-in dressing room.

Race Course Rd., Bangalore 560 001. © 080/225-5055. Fax 080/220-0010 or 080/220-4475. www.tajhotels. com. 129 units. Doubles: $220 superior; $250 luxury (includes one-way airport transfer); $290 Taj Club; $350–$500 suites; $30 extra bed. Taj Club rooms and suites include breakfast and airport transfers. AE, DC, MC, V. **Amenities:** 3 restaurants; 3 bars; 2 tennis courts; golf and riding on request; fitness center; travel assistance; car hire; currency exchange; shopping arcade; salon; 24-hr. room service; babysitting; laundry and dry cleaning; doctor-on-call. *In room:* A/C, TV, minibar, hair dryer. Taj Club units have fax machines.

WHERE TO DINE

Most of the best restaurants are located in hotels; besides Karavalli, reviewed below, the following are worth mention: At Taj West End's **Paradise Island,** Thai chef Umpaan is justifiably proud of his creations; have the popular chicken satay starter or the raw papaya salad. For seafood, order the stir-fried garlic-and-pepper prawns. Or try *Kai Hai Boy Toey*—chicken leg cutlets steamed, wrapped in pandanus leaves (grown on-site), and then deep-fried. For North and South Indian cuisine, **Jamavar** at the Leela Palace is one of Bangalore's class acts, with arguably the best tandoor dishes in town. For specialty South Indian cuisine, there's no better place than **Dakshin,** the upmarket restaurant at the Hotel Windsor Sheraton. If you need to give your system a break from spicy cuisine, **i-t.ALIA** is Bangalore's most stylish Italian restaurant, situated in The Park.hotel. If you want to get out of the hotel atmosphere, head for the slightly cramped terrace of **Sunny's** (35/2 Kasturba Cross Rd., off Lavelle Rd.; © **080/ 224-3642**), a three-level restaurant with a cafe-style Mediterranean atmosphere, where you'll develop a sense of Bangalore's growing sophistication. Favorites here include baked brie with toasted almonds; stir-fried calamari with basil and garlic; angel-hair pasta with fresh chunky tomatoes and extra-virgin olive oil; and the flavorful, slightly spiced lamb lasagna, served piping hot.

Art ★★ ECLECTIC/FUSION   Pretentious as the name sounds, this is one of Bangalore's hippest restaurants, done out in bright shades of yellow and orange. Chef Ramdeo Das really does prepare each dish as though it were a work of art. A standout entree is "Birds in Flight," a seafood combo comprising prawns prepared in olive oil and lemon juice, and fresh fish stuffed with smoked salmon, served on a bed of spinach and broccoli and topped with a creamy basil sauce. Cheaper, quick meals are also available.

Cosmo Village, Magrath Rd. © 080/509-3090. Main courses Rs 200–Rs 850 ($4.30–$19). AE, DC, MC, V. Daily 12:30–3:30pm and 7–11:30pm.

Ebony ★ ECLECTIC INDIAN   Here's an unexpected treat on the rooftop of a lurid city-center building. After the unpromising elevator ride up, you can dine alfresco and enjoy the best city views in Bangalore. Try mutton *pulao,* based on a Parsi recipe; it's made with tender meat and potatoes steeped in Persian spices (cinnamon, cardamom, and rose petals), then layered with saffron-flavored rice before being cooked with an onion-based gravy. Another fantastic meat dish is Manan's pepper mutton; this comes from the temple town of Kumbakonam (Tamil Nadu), where Manan is the owner of a small eatery. The mutton is cooked in a paste made from roasted pepper, coriander seeds, and Indian spices. If you'd prefer to avoid meat, try *subz sunheri mausam*—mushrooms, baby corn, and *paneer* in a creamy flour gravy made with *ajwain* (thyme-like spice); have it with garlic *naan* (bread). Thai food is served on Thursday and Friday (reserve ahead).

13th Floor, Ivory Tower Hotel, Barton Centre, 84 M.G. Rd. ✆ 080/558-9333 or -5164. Main courses Rs 90–Rs 275 ($1.90–$6). AE, DC, MC, V. Daily 7:30–11:30pm.

Karavalli ✹✹✹ INDIAN For more than a decade, this indoor-outdoor restaurant has been wowing guests and winning awards. Sit in the garden area under umbrellas, with twinkling lights, bamboo trees and, in keeping with the traditions of the *vaasthu* design concept, water cascading down a rockery. For seafood lovers, Karavalli is a godsend, with Goan baby lobster, Mangalorean black pomfret, and pearlspot caught off the shores of Cochin in Kerala. The west coast also provides fresh bekti, shrimp, tiger prawns, scampi, squid, sear, sole, and ladyfish, while the varying cuisines of India's southern coastal regions provide inspiration for dishes originally found in home kitchens.

Taj Gateway Hotel, 66 Residency Rd. ✆ 080/558-4545. Main courses Rs 155–Rs 545 ($3.20–$12). Lunch thali Rs 265–Rs 295 ($6–$6.50). AE, DC, MC, V. Daily 12:30–3pm and 7:30–11pm.

Mavalli Tiffin Rooms (MTR) ✹✹ *Moments* SOUTH INDIAN VEGETARIAN Possibly *the* essential Bangalore eating experience, this is an excellent spot to sample the chaos of a traditional "tiffin" (lunch or snack) room, where scores of locals rush in for the Indian version of fast food, served since 1924 with attitude and gusto from shiny silver buckets by obnoxious waiters in white *dhotis*. Eat with your fingers from a silver tray onto which various authentic South Indian concoctions are heaped and continuously replenished. You sit in rather indecorous surroundings (the current venue was built in 1949, and hasn't changed at all in over 40 years) on brown plastic chairs at marble-top tables with orange steel legs; unless you want to watch *naan* breads being prepared by men seated on the floor, you should grab a table upstairs. Adjacent, the **MTR Store** sells a wide range of South Indian treats and delicacies, including popular sweets (like *badam malwa* and *ladu*) and ready-to-eat savories.

14 Lal Bagh Rd. ✆ 080/222-0022. Reservations are recommended for Sat–Sun. A typical meal costs Rs 75 ($1.60); individual items Rs 5–Rs 20 (10¢–40¢). No credit cards. Tues–Sun 12:30–2:45pm and 8–9:30pm.

Moksh ✹✹✹ VEGETARIAN/CONTEMPORARY INDIAN When Moksh opened in May 2002, would-be diners were hauling out their business cards to try and wrest tables from those who'd bothered to make a booking. The menu covers the gamut of vegetarian dishes. Vegetarian kebabs include *mutterwali tikki,* spicy green peas made into a patty packed with cumin and *paneer* (cheese), and then griddle-fried. Two of the best dishes are *chhenna paaturi,* which is *paneer* marinated with raisins, mustard, and green chilies, then wrapped in a banana leaf and steamed; and tandoori *phool,* made from florets of broccoli, cottage cheese, black olives, pimento, and ginger, grilled in the tandoor oven in a rice batter. As an aperitif, try the house specialty, *ananas da panna,* a tangy digestive drink made with crushed, roasted pineapple, cumin, and mint. Alternatively, try the *phaalsa* blush, made from a Rajasthani elderberry that grows for only a few weeks a year.

The Chancery, 10/6 Lavelle Rd. ✆ 080/227-6767. Reservations essential. Main courses Rs 95–Rs 175 ($2.05–$3.75). AE, DC, MC, V. Daily 12:30–3pm and 7:30–11pm.

Swinging in the Hip City of Bangalore

Spend at least an hour schmoozing on beanbags at The Park.hotel's **i-BAR** 🌟🌟🌟 (closed Mon)—currently the most happening spot in Bangalore—or dancing to house and trance on the small dance floor, where DJ Sasha mixes up a swinging party. Alternatively, head for **13th Floor–The Cocktail Lounge** 🌟🌟 (Ivory Tower Hotel; M.G. Rd.; 7–11:30pm), a sexy 120-seater rooftop lounge where you get a large dose of the Bangalore skyline. **Liquor Café** 🌟🌟 is a groovy lounge bar on the covered rooftop of a building that houses several smart restaurants (including Art—see "Where to Dine," above); it attracts a hip young crowd who come for the funky, laid-back acid lounge music (Cosmo Village, Magrath Rd.; ✆ 080/509-3090; 7–11:30pm).

Named for the Greek god of sleep, **Hypnos** 🌟 is a cocktail lounge that does anything but, even in the Moroccan Square where you can smoke *Shishas* (hookahs) filled with apple, strawberry, or grape tobacco while tucking into Lebanese and Mediterranean fusion cuisine (Gem Plaza, Infantry Rd.; ✆ 080/532-3901, -3902, -3903, or -3904). Single men are technically unwelcome at **180 Proof** 🌟, and the Mafioso-style management ensures that the industrial-chic atmosphere is enhanced by the highest-profile Bangalorean crowd. Housed in a lovely stone building that looks like a historic monument, this is probably *the* place in Bangalore to strut your stuff on the dance floor: Three locally based DJs run the show with a blend of rock, hip-hop and, from 8:30pm on, trance music, occasionally joined by record-spinners from Mumbai, San Francisco, and the U.K. (40 St. Marks Rd.; ✆ 080/299-7290; daily noon–11:30pm). You pay heavily (Rs 500–Rs 1,000/$11–$22) to get into **Insomnia** 🌟, a pleasant split-level club with a bar upstairs and a cozy DJ-operated dance floor down below (Le Meridien, ✆ 080/226-2233). **NASA** (1/A Church St.; ✆ 080/558-6512; daily 11am–11:30pm) is worth a giggle: Staff are decked out in pilot outfits, and the interior is like the inside of a sci-fi space module; the bar is called the "Fuel Tank" and the loo is known as the "Humanoid Disposal" area. It's good for an afternoon pint, but happy hours draw massive crowds. For a London pub vibe, head for the tartan-and-leatherette watering hole **Underground** (65 Blue Moon Complex, M.G. Rd.; ✆ 080/558-9991; daily 11:30am–11:30pm). The Oberoi Hotel's smart **Polo Club** combines deep leather sofas with ubiquitous TV sports entertainment. Cigar aficionados should head for the **Jockey Club** at the Taj Residency, where expat wives meet every Thursday.

SHOPPING

You'll find the city's major shopping centers along and around **M.G. Road, Commercial Street,** and **Brigade Road.** M.G. Road is where you'll find the fixed-price tourist-orientated (no bargains or bargaining) **Cauvery Arts and Crafts Emporium, Central Cottage Industries Emporium,** and **Karnataka State Silk Industries Emporium.** Fabulous silks and home textiles, as well as contemporary silverware from Neemrana and traditional silver jewelry from

Amrapali and Jaipur, are some of the highlights available in **Shop Ananya,** located next to the Hotel Sarovar on 9/1 Dhondusa Annexe (© **080/299-8922**). With four levels of saris and *salwar kameez* (for women) and *sherwanis* (for men), and a nonstop clientele, you can understand why staff at **Deepam Silk International** insist that there is "nowhere else in the whole world" better to shop for silk garments (67 Blumoon Complex, M.G. Rd.; © **080/558-8760**). **Ashok Silks** (Shrungar Shopping Complex, M.G. Rd.; © **080/558-7623**) also sells a huge range of quality silk garments.

Cinnamon 👁👁   Some of India's top designers are represented in this cool, stylish boutique, which often hosts small exhibitions. Abraham and Thakore, considered the country's top design duo, have a range here, and this is the only place in India outside Jaipur that you'll find clothing by Brigette Singh. Bangalorean designer Jason Cheriyan refuses to sell his work anywhere else. The shop is open daily from 10:30am to 8pm. It accepts American Express, MasterCard, and Visa. 11 Walton Rd., off Lavelle Rd. © **080/221-2426** or 080/222-9794.

BANGALORE AFTER DARK

Check the local dailies for information about cultural events. Besides art exhibitions and traditional performances, Bangalore draws major international artists, including pop and rock stars.

The violin-shaped auditorium known as **Chowdaiah Memorial Hall** (Gayathri Devi Park Extension, Vyalikaval; © **080/344-5810**) hosts regular classical music performances, as well as film, dance, and drama. Plays are regularly staged at **Rabindra Kalakshetra** (Jayachamarachendra Rd.; © **080/222-1271**), where you can also catch occasional art exhibitions.

Fluid Space (S-105&106 Manipal Centre, 47 Dickenson Rd.; © **080/509-2305;** www.fluidspace.org) is a small, chic, contemporary art and design exhibit space. Also check out **Gallerie Zen** (121 Dickenson Rd.; © **080/558-1578;** www.zenmrl.net).

Nrityagram Dance Village (along the Bangalore-Pune Hwy., 35km/22 miles from Bangalore) is a renowned center for Indian dance training. Performances feature students as well as established artists. Organized tours of the facility include lecture-demonstrations designed to introduce you to Indian culture, life philosophy, and both *kathak* and *odissi* dance forms (© **080/846-6313;** Sept–May, Tues–Sun 10am–5pm; tours Rs 20/40¢ per person; advance bookings essential). A through-the-night dance and music festival is held in February; it attracts almost 30,000 spectators, so decent seating is at a premium.

2 Mysore 👁👁👁

140km (87 miles) SW of Bangalore; 473km (293 miles) N of Chennai; 1,177km (730 miles) SE of Mumbai

A city of palatial buildings and tree-lined boulevards, laid-back Mysore is possessed of a quaint charm, a dignified hangover from the days when it was the capital of a rich princely state. It remains a popular destination for travelers, particularly for its **Maharajah's Palace.** Built over a period of 15 years at the turn of the 20th century at a cost of over Rs 4 million, this astonishing Indo-Saracenic palace is testament to the affluence of one of India's notably wealthy ruling families. During the 10-day **Dussehra Festival,** held here during the first half of October, the entire city is dressed up in show-off style; each night **Mysore Palace** is lit up by 80,000 bulbs, and on the final evening of festivities, the maharajah himself leads one of the country's most spectacular processions through the city streets. But Mysore is also an ideal base from which to explore the temples known as the **"Jewel Boxes"** of Hoysala architecture, which lie some 3 hours north, as well as the nearby Jain pilgrimage site at **Sravanabelgola.**

ESSENTIALS

GETTING THERE & AWAY   Trains from Bangalore (3 hr.) and Hassan (for Hoysala heartland; 2–3 hr.) pull in regularly at the **railway station** (© **131** or 0821/42-2103), situated at the intersection of Jhansi Laxmi Bai Road and Irwin Road. For the Rajiv Gandhi National Park, your best option is to hire a car.

VISITOR INFORMATION   For information, visit the **Karnataka Tourist Office** (Old Exhibition Building, Irwin Rd.; © **0821/44-2096; Mon–Sat 10am–5:30pm;** closed the 2nd Sat of each month).

GETTING AROUND   Negotiate **taxi** prices in advance, or hire a vehicle for the day. **Auto-rickshaws** are cheap and plentiful; insist that drivers use their meters.

GUIDED TOURS & TRAVEL AGENTS   Operating since 1976, **Seagull Travels** (8 Best Western Ramanashree Hotel Complex, Bangalore-Niligiri Rd.; © **0821/52-9732** or -0535, or 0821/43-5095; fax 0821/52-0549; www.seagull travels.com; daily 8:30am–8pm) handles a wide range of travel needs, including ticketing, taxi arrangements, and individually packaged tours (although prices can fluctuate arbitrarily). Seagull is Mysore's only agent for the government's popular Jungle Lodges and Resorts, including the popular Kabini River Lodge (see below). Another local travel agent is **Skyway International Travels** (10 Madhu Nivas, Gandhi Sq.; © **0821/42-6823** or -6824; fax 0821/42-2762; www.skywaytour.com). Don't pay for any taxi or vehicle without first checking its condition. You can organize a car through your hotel travel desk, but it's likely to be more expensive.

WHAT TO SEE & DO

Besides Mysore's most famous palace, the Maharajah's Palace, and an excursion to Keshava Temple, you might want to visit the **Jagan Mohan Palace** (west of Mysore Palace, Dewan's Rd.; daily 8:30am–5pm; Rs 10/20¢), which once served as the royal auditorium. The building now exhibits South India's oddest assortment of kitsch memorabilia from the massive private collection of the Wodeyars. Southeast of downtown (3km/2 miles away), **Chamundi Hill** is where you can join throngs of huffing-puffing pilgrims, some of who recite or read Hindu verses along the way. Stop first at the **Shiva Temple,** where devotees meander around the statue in a clockwise direction while a friendly priest dishes out sacred water and dollops of vermilion paste. The summit of the hill is very active with pilgrims come to pay their respects to Durga. You can buy a *darshan* ticket from the computerized ticketing booth and then join the queue for a peek at the deity inside the **Sri Chamundeswari Temple,** or you can wander around the hilltop exploring smaller temples, many of which serve as bases for bright-robed grinning *sadhus* (holy persons) wanting to sell you a private photo opportunity.

Finally, no trip to Mysore is complete without getting lost in the dizzying aromas of jasmine, musk, sandalwood, frangipani, and incense as you wander through the city's vibrant **market.** Mysore is also famous for its silk and sandal-wood oil, and you can witness the production of both by taking a side trip to Vidyaranyapuram, 15 minutes away. For an escorted tour of the **Government Silk Weaving Factory,** call © **0821/48-1803;** the **Government Sandal Oil Factory** is right next door.

Maharajah's Palace (Amba Vilas) ☆☆☆   Generally considered *the* palace in South India, this was designed by Henry Irving at the turn of the 20th century;

15 years of nonstop construction produced a fabulous domed, arched, colon-naded, and turreted structure with lavish interiors—teak ceilings, carved marble handrails, gilded pillared halls, ivory deities, rococo lamp stands, Italian crystal chandeliers, stained-glass windows, miles of white marble floors, and ceilings made from stained glass brought all the way from Glasgow. You'll be hard-pressed to find an undecorated section of wall or ceiling; frescoes, paintings, statues, and delicate relief carvings recall religious as well as secular scenes, including glorious state processions. Within the inner courtyards, growling stone felines guard stair-ways, while elsewhere, elaborately carved rosewood doors mark the entrances of yet more splendid halls and chambers. Paintings by Raja Ravi Varma, golden chariots, gilt-framed mirrors, stately family portraits (including a wax sculpture of the maharajah), and all manner of ornate fantasy objects add to the spectacle of abundant wealth. Overlooking the parade grounds, brought to life during the **Dussehra Festival** (Sept or Oct), a terraced grandstand pavilion is covered by a heavily decorated and frescoed ceiling, while huge, decaying chandeliers dangle precariously over the seating

Don't bother to purchase an additional ticket for the disappointing **Maharajah's Residential Palace,** where a sad display of items gathers dust.

Ramvilas Rd., Mizra Rd., and Purandara Rd. ✆ 0821/42-2620. Admission: Amber Vilas Rs 15 (30¢); Residential Palace Rs 15 (30¢). Daily 10am–5:30pm.

Keshava Temple 🌟🌟🌟 Situated 38km (25 miles) from Mysore in the small village of Somnathpur, this is perhaps the best-preserved and most complete Hoysala monument in existence. Also referred to as the Chennakeshava Temple, this beautiful religious monument is presided over by Vijayanarayana, one of the 24 incarnations of Vishnu. Built as early as 1268, it is constructed entirely of soapstone and rests on a raised plinth; typical of Hoysala temples, it has a star-shaped ground plan and exquisitely sculpted interiors. It's really worth exploring in detail, and you may have to urge or bribe the caretaker to crank up the gen-erator so that you have enough light to properly observe the three shrines in the temple. Somnathpur is serene and remote, and the lawns around the monument are ideal for picnicking—ask your hotel for a packed lunch.

Somnathpur is 38km (24 miles) east of Mysore. Admission $5. Daily 9am–6pm.

WHERE TO STAY

The Green Hotel 🌟🌟 This award-winning hotel began life as Chittaranjan Palace, built in the 1920s by Wodeyar IV as a retreat for his three sisters. Today it looks and feels pretty much how you would imagine the home of a royal fam-ily in decline would look. The palace proper has a motley assortment of antique furniture and colorful memorabilia that rivals some of the other tourist distrac-tions in town. Light filters through stained-glass windows, and the large, open public spaces are swathed in teak and brimming with old-world charm, despite the incessant noise from the main road alongside. This erstwhile princess retreat also offers some charming lodging options. Choose one of the seven guest rooms in the original palace: The Princess's Room is enormous, with antique furniture, blue Indian throws, and sheer curtains over narrow slit windows. For added color, try the Deluxe Bollywood room, where the antique wooden headboards are decorated with brightly colored renditions of old Bollywood starlets on painted glass. Guest rooms in the garden block (built when the palace became a film studio) offer value but are simple and lack the historical flavor of the palace.

Chittaranjan Palace, 2270 Vinoba Rd., Jayalamipuram, Mysore 570 012. ✆ 0821/51-2536 or 0821/41-4635. Fax 0821/51-6139. www.greenhotelindia.com. 31 units. Doubles: Rs 1,830–Rs 3,750 ($40–$80) palace rooms; Rs 4,750 ($105) Maharani's suite; Rs 1,300–Rs 2,000 ($28–$44) garden rooms; Rs 2,250 ($50) garden suites; Rs 575 ($13) extra bed Rates include breakfast. MC, V. **Amenities:** Restaurant; bar; volleyball; croquet; boule; indoor games; travel services; green auto-rickshaw service; room service on request; laundry; doctor-on-call; library.

WHERE TO DINE

Visitors with a sweet tooth will get a kick out of the local specialty, *pak*, which is made from corn flour and liters of ghee (clarified butter). You'll find a number of outlets at Devaraja Market. Try the famous **Guru Sweet Mart** (Sayaji Rao Rd.) for your sugar rush.

Lalitha Mahal Palace Hotel Restaurant ⋆ ECLECTIC   Once the ballroom of the maharajah's sumptuous guesthouse, the glorious baroque hall has an immensely high ceiling with domed skylights made of Belgian glass. Hindustani music, performed live at lunch and dinner, fills this pillared palatial space. Come here for a poke around the royal facilities, but don't expect too much from the food: Even though you're eating off delicate decorative china and silver thali platters, the cheap cutlery gives the game away. Thalis are enjoyable, however, and quite filling. Also worth trying are the Mangalore fish curry and *lassoni malai tikka*, chicken in a garlic-flavored masala prepared in the tandoor oven, and best enjoyed with *naan* or *roti*. If you're more interested in a snack, the menu includes items such as a Maharajah club sandwich or hamburger.

Lalitha Mahal Palace Hotel, T. Narsipur Rd. © 0821/57-1265. Reservations recommended. Main courses Rs 100–Rs 550 ($2.10–$12). AE, DC, MC, V. Daily 12:30–2:45pm and 8–11pm.

Le Olive Garden ⋆ *Finds* NORTH INDIAN/ECLECTIC   At this restaurant, situated in a peaceful neighborhood away from central Mysore, you dine alfresco in a leafy garden with geese, turkeys, rabbits, and wind chimes for company. Arranged on landscaped terracing, the dining area is surrounded by water and reached by tiny bridges. Most of the dishes are Indian, with a good range of kebabs on offer, but you can also order Chinese or choose from a small selection of Continental dishes. Although it's not on the menu, ask for *rogan gosht*, made with slightly fatty mutton and cooked in rich masala gravy made with cashew nuts.

Chamappaji Rd., opposite Horse Park, Nazarbad. © 0821/44-8762. Main courses Rs 60–Rs 150 ($1.25–$3.15). V. Daily 11am–3pm and 6:30pm–midnight.

VISITING RAJIV GANDHI NATIONAL PARK

Originally the private property of the Maharajah of Mysore, Karnataka's most popular elephant hangout became a national park in 1955, 3 years after the princely state of Mysore was absorbed into post-colonial India. Situated 95km (59 miles) southwest of Mysore, and spread over 511 sq. km (195 sq. miles) filled with teak, rosewood, sandal, and silver oak trees, Rajiv Gandhi National Park is also generously populated by *dhole* (wild dogs), *gaur* (Indian bison), antelope, sloth bears, panthers, otter, crocodiles, cobras and pythons, falcons, eagles, and great Indian horned owls. Keep an eye peeled for tiny *muntjac* deer; they stand only .6m (2 ft.) tall and are crowned by finger-length antlers. The big draw, of course, are the tigers (between 60 and 65 tigers reside here), but sightings are subject to a great deal of luck—although when Goldie Hawn came here to shoot a documentary, she apparently spotted several. Ms. Hawn stayed at the popular **Kabini River Lodge,** the most practical place to be if you want to have access to the park without any organizational fuss. A charmingly rustic retreat some 6 hours by car from Bangalore (3 hr. from Mysore), Kabini is spread over 22 hectares (55 acres), incorporating lush forest and largely untamed vegetation, just the way a "jungle resort" should be. Its centerpiece is the maharajah's original 18th-century hunting lodge.

Accommodations are adequate, although those with the best position (the river-facing cottages) lack the comfort of the air-conditioned rooms, which are also significantly smarter; expect small bathrooms, dated green sofas, and lumpy mattresses covered with charming Indian throws. Besides eyeballing the skies for birds like hoopoes and drongos, a program of wildlife safaris, brief coracle (boat) trips, elephant rides, and—of course—dining and drinking tea are laid out for you according to a precise schedule. The lodge was set up by Col. John Felix Wakefield, who at 90 still takes his meals on the terrace overlooking the river. A tiger hunter in his youth, now a celebrated sanctuary-tourism reformer, Wakefield can be a lively source of information about the region. Book a room at Kabini well in advance, and plan to arrive there at least an hour before the afternoon safari, which begins at 4:30pm (© **08228/32181** or 080/559-7021; www.junglelodges.com; standard package 2 days, 1 night per person, $125 A/C room; includes all meals, safaris, park entrance, and elephant and boat rides). For companies that offer the services of a car and driver for the 3-hour drive, see "Guided Tours & Travel Agents" under Mysore "Essentials," above.

3 Exploring the Hoysala Heartland: Belur, Halebid & Sravanabelagola

Halebid is 220km (136 miles) W of Bangalore; Belur is 14km (9 miles) SW of Halebid

The Hoysalas were a race of warriors who found time to allow their art to flourish despite regular military campaigns. What remains of this once-powerful dynasty are beautiful temples, usually commissioned to commemorate their victories or covenants made with their gods. Situated at the edge of the Western Ghats, the existing temples of the once-powerful cities of **Belur** and **Halebid** are often referred to as the "Jewel Boxes" of Hoysala architecture, and are comparable with the religious monuments of Khajuraho (in Madhya Pradesh) and Konark (in Orissa). The artists who created these compact, assiduously sculpted temples demonstrated enormous regard for the rules of proportion, and went to extreme lengths to ensure absolute spatial precision. Exterior temple walls are invariably covered in detailed sculpted decoration, while inside you will discover hand-lathe–turned filigreed pillars and figures with moveable jewelry, also carved from stone. The gods paraded at these temples are over 8 centuries old, yet continue to impress with the vigor with which they carry out their superhuman duties, slaying demons and moving mountains, while celestial maidens admire their reflections in eternally reflective mirrors.

In quite a different vein, the living pilgrimage center at **Sravanabelagola** is where you will find the world's tallest monolithic sculpture. A naked ascetic saint, the statue of Gomateswara is one of the biggest Jain pilgrimages in the country—lacking any decoration whatsoever, yet awesome in its sheer grandeur.

To see these highlights of Karnataka's religious heritage, you have to veer off the main drag a little. Fortunately, if you're pressed for time, it is possible to cover all three destinations with ease in a single day. Most visitors base their exploration of this region out of the dusty, dull town of Hassan, but the coffee-growing town of Chikmagalur offers far more glowing surroundings, highlighted by the pleasant accommodations of a **Taj Garden Retreat.**

ESSENTIALS
GETTING THERE & AROUND

The most convenient way to see the Hoysala sights is to hire a car and driver in Mysore or even Bangalore. A more affordable option is to catch a train from

Mysore to Hassan (3 hr. away), from where you can pick up a taxi for a full day of sightseeing. Hassan can also be reached overland from Mangalore (see "Traveling Via Mangalore," below). If you need to hire a vehicle in Hassan, we recommend you contact **Mr. Altaf** (© **08172/56338;** or ask the manager at Hotel Southern Star to give him a call), who offers excellent rates, and ask for **Abdul Rafiek,** an affable driver with masterful control over his ancient Ambassador. Extraordinarily, Abdul even uses his indicators.

VISITOR INFORMATION

Visit the friendly **Regional Tourist Office** (Vartha Bhavan, B.M. Rd.; © **08172/ 68862**) if you need to stock up on brochures. You can also deepen your knowledge at the **Belur Reception Centre** (© **08177/22218**) at the entrance to the temple courtyard, or at the Hotel Mayura Velapuri's **Belur Tourist Information Centre** (Temple Rd.; © **08177/22209**). In Halebid, there's a **Tourist Help Desk** (Mon–Sat 10am–5:30pm) at the Hoysalesvara Temple. You can pick up ASI-certified **guides** outside each of the two main temples in Belur and Halebid.

BELUR

Now a sleepy hamlet, Belur was the capital of the Hoysala kings at the height of their reign. The magnificent soapstone **Temple of Lord Channakeshava** ★★★ (daily 8am–8:30pm; free admission), built over a period of 103 years, was commissioned to commemorate the victory of Vishnuvardhana over the Cholas from Tamil Nadu; apparently, it was so admired by Belur's iconoclastic Muslim invaders that they decided to leave it intact.

Built on a star-shaped plan, the temple stands on a raised platform within a courtyard surrounded by an outer wall. After you survey the courtyard, approach the temple by climbing the short flight of steps. Despite its compact scale, the profusion of carved decoration is spectacular, the multicornered shape of the temple allowing maximum space for sculptures of Vishnu and a vast retinue of Hindu images. Covering the flat-roofed building are detailed representations of myriad themes—ranging from erotica to religious mythology, everyday events to episodes from the *Ramayana*—arranged in bands that wrap around the entire exterior, forming delightful compositions. The temple itself is borne by almost 650 stone elephants. Don't miss the various bracket figures, which are considered the highlight of Hoysala workmanship. Use a torch to study the temple interior, at the center of which is a pillar adorned with smaller versions of the temple's 10,000 sculpted images. Belur is a living temple, and a silver-plated image of Vishnu within the inner sanctum is still worshipped; *puja* (prayer) is performed at 9am and 7pm each day, and the inner sanctums are closed between 1 and 3pm and 5 and 6pm.

HALEBID

Once known as Dwara Samudra, "the gateway to the sea," Halebid usurped Belur's position as the Hoysalan capital in the 12th century. Unfortunately, when the Muslim invaders arrived, Halebid failed to escape their wrath. Appropriately, its current name means "destroyed city," as it consists of only a dusty road and some well-crafted temples amid a lush landscape with the Western Ghats as a distant backdrop. The exquisitely sculpted **Hoysalashwara Temple** ★★★ (sunrise to sunset; free admission; shoe-check Rs 1/2¢) is the largest of the Hoysalan temples (Hoysalashwara actually consists of two distinct temples resting upon a star-shaped platform, both dedicated to Shiva). It has more complex and detailed carvings than those at Belur. You can discover the 20,000-odd sculptures in and around the temple on your own, or enlist the services of a **guide** (who will approach you as you arrive at the monument; expect to pay around Rs 70/$1.50, but do include a tip). You can visit the on-site **Archaeological Museum** (Sat–Thurs 10am–5pm; Rs 2/4¢) to see more stone statues of Hindu gods, gathered from Halebid and its immediate environs. If you want more of the same, without the touristy vibe, head for the **Kedareshvara Temple,** 300m (960 ft.) away and marked by its serene location.

Also in Halebid are several **Jain Bastis** that allude to the religious tolerance of the Hoysala kings who extended patronage to other faiths. Although lacking the immense carved decoration of the Hindu monuments, the **Parswanathasamy Temple** (daily 10am–5pm; free admission) enjoys a lovely lakeside location.

SRAVANABELAGOLA ✦✦✦
For members of the peace-loving, nonviolent Jain faith, this is one of the oldest and most important pilgrimage centers, famous for its 18m (60-ft.) statue of Lord Gomateswara, said to be the tallest monolithic statue on earth, reached by climbing the 635 steps that lead to the summit of the hill. Naked and imposing, the statue is a symbolic representation of worldly renunciation. Commissioned in A.D. 981, the colossal **Statue of Gomateswara** ✦✦✦ is a representation of Bahubali; son of the first Jain Tirthankara, Bahubali renounced his kingdom and sought enlightenment by standing naked and motionless for an entire year while contemplating the meaning of life. Seen in detail on the legs of the statue, the creepers and plants twisting their way up his body are symbolic of his motionless mission of spiritual discovery. A special celebration is held here every 12 years, when the giant monolith is bathed with bucketfuls of milk and honey and other condiments. The next ceremony takes place in 2005.

WHERE TO STAY & DINE
Accommodations options close to the temples are limited and hardly the stuff of kings. You'll find a number of government-run hotels in both Belur and Halebid; these have restaurants of questionable quality and extremely basic rooms. In Halebid, the tourism department's **Hotel Mayura Shanthala** (Temple Rd.;

Tips Traveling Via Mangalore

Once a seaport of some significance, Mangalore is an important center for the processing and export of Karnataka's spices, coffee, and cashews. It is known as the *bidi* cigarette capital of the world. (The bidi is also known as the "pauper's puff." Apparently 90 people die every hour in India from tobacco-related cancer.) Its greatest significance for travelers is that it makes a convenient pit stop on the section of the Konkan Railway that runs between Goa and Kerala, and provides road access to Belur, Halebid, and Sravanabelgola, as well as Mysore. **Taj Manjuran** (✆ 0824/42-0420; www.tajhotels.com; doubles from $45) is the best hotel in Mangalore. Accommodations are comfortable, if not particularly luxurious; suite no. 401 ($82) has the best views, taking in the river and the ocean. Staff will arrange trips to the beach and local temples, as well as tours of a cashew-nut factory or tours to see how Mangalore's famous tiles are made.

© **08177/3224;** double $3–$4) is within striking distance of a number of temples. Belur's **Hotel Mayura Velapuri** (© **08177/22209;** double $4) is located just outside the temple entrance. Better to opt for **Hotel Southern Star Hassan,** a relatively new and welcome addition to Hassan's otherwise dismal accommodations scene. It offers pleasant service (including sightseeing advice) and safe dining. It's certainly not luxury level, but guest rooms are comfortable and clean; views from odd-numbered rooms are of a less built-up part of the town (© **08172/51816** or -51817; www.ushashriramhotels.com; doubles from Rs 1,350/$30).

Taj Garden Retreat Chikmagalur 🌟🌟   Just outside the small coffee-growing town of Chikmagalur, this hillside retreat—originally built as a government rest house—is comfortable and idyllically remote, with sloping red-tile roofs echoing the style of the local colonial Malnad plantation homes. Reserve one of the cottages (only $5 more); these have high-pitched ceilings, polished floors, two double beds, and large balconies with scenic views. (Reserve no. 119 for an especially large balcony.) The attached bathrooms are spacious but have showers only. Visits to nearby coffee plantations set off daily at 3:30pm; also ask about excursions to the Bhadra Wildlife Sanctuary and surrounding hills.

K.M. Rd., opposite Pavitravana Jyothinagar Post, Chikmagalur. © **08262/20202** or -20404. Fax 08262/20222. www.tajhotels.com. 29 units. Doubles: $70 standard; $75 standard pool-view; $80 cottage; $20 extra bed. AE, DC, MC, V. **Amenities:** Restaurant; bar; pool; pool table; table tennis; cycling; travel assistance; car hire; currency exchange; fax service; laundry; doctor-on-call. *In room:* A/C, TV, minibar, tea- and coffee-making facilities.

4 Hampi & the Ruined City of Vijayanagar 🌟🌟🌟

Hampi is 460km (285 miles) NW of Bangalore; 13km (8 miles) E of Hospet

The surreal, boulder-strewn landscape of Karnataka's hinterland is the backdrop to the largest complex of ruins in India. Hampi, capital of one of India's most formidable empires, the powerful Vijayanagara—whose rule stretched from the Arabian Sea to the Indian Ocean—was home to a population of half a million, and protected by more than a million soldiers. Set in a vast valley sprawling from the banks of the Tungabhadra River, the splendid "City of Victory"—where even the king's horses were adorned in jewels—is now a sprawling ghost city with numerous temples, fortification ramparts, stables, royal apartments, and palaces, popular with determined sightseers and Bollywood location scouts. Hampi's distance from anywhere makes it difficult to get to, but this remoteness is to a large extent its charm, with a serene atmosphere you can easily enjoy for 2 or 3 days, particularly if you've booked at **Hampi's Boulders** (see "Where to Stay & Dine," below), a comfortable new resort within striking distance of the ruins.

ESSENTIALS

GETTING THERE   The overnight **Hospet Express** leaves Bangalore daily at 10pm, arriving in unremarkable Hospet, the nearest town, at 7:50am. From Hyderabad, the Rayalseema Express departs at 5:30pm and arrives early the following morning, at 5:15am. Hampi is 15km (9 miles) away. Taxis charge around Rs 100 ($2.10) for the one-way trip; be sure to negotiate.

VISITOR INFORMATION   If you reserve lodging at **Hampi's Boulders** (see "Where to Stay & Dine," below), you'll have no better source of information than your host, Bobby. In Hampi Bazaar, the government-run **tourist office** (© **0839/41339;** daily 10am–5:30pm) can organize coach bookings (not recommended) and English-speaking guides. At Hotel Malligi in Hospet, you can hire an **audioguide,** featuring Bollywood voices, for around Rs 50 ($1.05). In Hampi, you can pick up information and guides from the **information office** (© **08394/51339**) on Bazaar Street.

GETTING AROUND **By Taxi & Auto-Rickshaw** Hampi's ruins cover 39 sq. km (15 sq. miles), and should be explored on wheels. Bicycles are fine for the energetic, but only in winter (for rent in Hampi Bazaar). Taxis (around Rs 500/$11 for a full day, without A/C) or even auto-rickshaws (count on Rs 250/$5.35 to Rs 300/$6.50) are better if you'd rather not deal with maps, heat, and dirt tracks. Do, however, get out on foot whenever you can.

EXPLORING THE RUINED CITY OF VIJAYANAGARA

For anyone with dreams of Indiana Jones–style adventuring, the Hampi ruins provide the perfect setting—an ancient city with isolated ruins scattered among impossibly balanced wind-smoothed boulders and immense stretches of verdant landscape. Various excavations have uncovered evidence to suggest that Vijayanagara was occupied as long ago as the 3rd-century-B.C. Mauryan era. During early medieval times, armies were regularly dispatched to the Deccan by the Delhi Sultanate as part of its campaign to establish an empire that would encompass the whole of India. During one such campaign in the early 14th century, the invading forces captured Harihara and Bukka, two princes of Warangal, and took them to Delhi, where they fell in with the Sultanate. This allegiance eventually saw Harihara being crowned king of the region that is today known as Hampi. In celebration, Harihara lay the foundations of Vijayanagara, his new capital, on the southern banks of the Tungabhadra. His brother, Bukka, succeeded him 20 years later and ensured widespread support by issuing an edict that granted all religions equal protection. The monarchs who followed extended patronage to all manner of artists, poets, philosophers, and academics, effectively making Vijayanagara a center of learning that, in its grandeur, captivated visitors from as far as Arabia, Portugal, and Italy.

The kingdom reached its zenith during the reign of Krishna Deva Raya (1509–29), when international trade flourished under progressive commercial practices and foreign trade agreements. Early accounts of the city tell of its massive fortifications, broad boulevards, grand gateways, efficient irrigation systems, and splendid civic amenities. The fall of the kingdom of Vijayanagara came in 1565 when five allied Deccan sultans laid siege to the city, which they then apparently ransacked—their soldiers looting, killing, and destroying at will.

While some of the individual ruins can only be visited on purchase of a ticket, most of Hampi is a veritable free-for-all, with tame security in the form of a handful of guards at the major monuments. This means that you can mix and match your itinerary as you see fit, moving between the different locations in a taxi or—if you're up for it—on a bicycle. Pick up information or engage the services of an official guide from the government tourist office in Hampi. You can see Hampi's highlights in a morning if you set out early enough. However, it's spread over a vast area, and exploring can be quite exhausting, particularly in the midday heat—don't overdo it, or even the most impressive monuments begin to look like more of the same.

Hampi Bazaar is a broad, dusty boulevard lined with stalls and restaurants. It leads to the entrance of the **Virupaksha Temple** ★★★, which predates the Vijayanagara kingdom yet remains a center of living Hindu faith (even though Hindu idols have been removed from the surrounding temples). Virupaksha's towering *gopuram* is lavishly sculpted and rises several stories; within its courtyards, monkeys and children careen around ancient pillars, while a sad-faced temple ele-phant takes tips for much-rehearsed blessings granted with her trunk. In the far right corner of the complex, tucked within a chamber, look for the shadow of the main *gopuram,* which falls—miraculously, it would seem—as an inverted image on the temple wall, created by light passing through a small window. South of Virupaksha Temple is a temple housing a massive **Shiva lingam** (phallic symbol) standing in a pool of water. Carved from a single rock, the lingam is adjacent to a fantastic **monolithic statue of Narasimha** ✿✿, the man-lion avatar of Vishnu. Although partially damaged, the one-piece carving dating to the first half of the 16th century is one of the finest sculptures at Hampi.

Some distance from the bazaar, on a high elevation, is the spectacular **Vitthala Temple** ✿✿✿, dedicated to an incarnation of Vishnu, and one of the most fabu-lous and famous of Hampi's monuments. One of Hinduism's most enduring images, an ornate **stone chariot** ✿✿✿, is found here. With solid stone wheels that can turn on their axles, the chariot faces a shaded dance hall where ancient musi-cal dramas were once played out and from where you can now enjoy panoramic views of Vijayanagara. The pillars of the temple are commonly referred to as "musical pillars," each one producing a different note when tapped.

Nearby, the **King's Balance** was once a scale-like instrument used to measure out grain or even gold against the weight of the king. The weighed item was then given to the priests (or to the poor, depending on your guide's story).

The **royal enclosure** ✿ incorporates the ruined palaces where the Vijayana-gara kings would have lived and held court. Not much survives, but you can still visit the **Hazara Rama temple** where the royals went to worship, a small **stepped tank,** and the **Mahanavami Dibba,** a platform where performances and entertainments were held. On the outskirts of the royal complex, you need to buy a ticket to see the Zenana enclosure, where the two-story Indo-Saracenic pavilion known as the **Kamala (Lotus) Mahal** ✿✿ features massive pillars, del-icately punctuated arches, and fine stucco ornamentation; its unusual design blends elements of Muslim and Hindu architecture. Within the same enclosure are quarters believed to have been used by Hampi's Amazonian female guards, described by several Portuguese travelers. Just outside the enclosure are the superb **Elephant Stables** ✿✿✿.

13km (8 miles) east of Hospet, Belary District. Guides can be hired through the government tourist office in Hampi Bazaar for Rs 150 ($3.15) half day and Rs 350 ($7.60) full day. Entrance to Virupaksha Temple Rs 2 (4¢); free 6:30–8am. Entrance to Lotus Mahal and Elephant Stables Rs 225 ($5).

WHERE TO STAY & DINE

Hampi's Boulders ✿✿   The name says it all: This new resort (opened in 2002 by the engaging proprietor, Bobby) is set in and among the enormous natural boulders that define Karnataka's splendid landscape. Private, remote, and immersed in nature, Boulders resides alongside the Tungabhadra River on a 16-hectare (40-acre) spread, amid bamboo trees, coconut groves, mango trees, coffee plantations, and the namesake rocks. It's a mere 6km (4 miles) from Hampi, reached by crossing the river in a coracle (small boat) after a pleasant half-hour walk. Nearby, in the 4,800-hectare (12,000-acre) animal sanctuary, you can spot wolves, wild dogs, panthers, hyenas, foxes, jackals, sloth bears, and crocodiles. Accommodations in the Executive Cottage are top-notch; living rock boulders bulge through the walls, and the entire structure feels like a miniature castle (where, in the huge bathroom, the "throne" allows the occupant to gaze onto the river). There's also a gorgeous veranda and a rooftop viewing-platform. Guest cottages are pleasantly furnished, with attached bathrooms and private patios; the floors are marble and the ambience and furniture simple, but they're still far better than anything else near Hampi, and the setting is unmatched. Meals are served in a semi-exposed circular granite-walled thatched-roof dining area where there's no menu, but five-course meals are whipped up according to your mood.

Narayanpet, Bandi Harlapur-P.O., Munirabad-R-S, Koppal District and TQ. (*C*) 08539/75829 or 08539/75939. Fax 08539/75940. info@hampiboulders.com. 15 units; camping facilities available. Doubles: Rs 2,700 ($60) standard; Rs 6,000 ($130) executive. No credit cards. **Amenities:** Restaurant; bar; children's pool and play area; guided tours and safaris; watersports; fishing; beach volleyball; river rafting; rock climbing; birding; shop; laundry; doctor-on-call.

5 Hyderabad

490km (304 miles) N of Bangalore

One of the largest and wealthiest of India's former princely states, Hyderabad built its fortune on the trade of pearls, gold, steel, fabric and, above all, diamonds, which some believe remain hidden beneath the foundations of **Golconda Fort,** precursor to the city some 10km (6¼ miles) away. Once the most famous diamond kingdom in the world, Golconda was home to the Koh-I-Noor, as well as the Orloff, Regent, and Hope dynasties, famous for their typically bloody histories. It was in fact Golconda's legendary wealth that attracted the attention of the voracious Mughal emperor Aurangzeb, and with the aid of an inside agent he captured the fortress in 1678. Aurangzeb's invasion marked the temporary decline of the city, but when the Mughal empire began to fade, the enterprising local viceroy, Asaf Jah I, promptly proclaimed himself *nizam* (ruler) and established independent rule over the Deccan state. Under the notoriously opulent nizams of the Asaf Jahi dynasty, their power cemented by an alliance forged in 1798 with the British East India Company, Hyderabad again became a major influence, and even contributed to the British military campaigns against the recalcitrant Tipu Sultan of Mysore.

Hyderabad is more than 400 years old but is today as famous for its burgeoning information technology and biotech research industries as it is for its minarets. Like Bangalore, this is one of India's fastest-growing cities (with a projected population of 7.5 million by 2015), but unlike most, Hyderabad is actually getting greener and cleaner. A substantial part of the city is the suburb of Cyberabad, where Microsoft and Oracle are but two major players in the development known as Hi-Tech City, responsible for the city's much-needed economic upswing.

Despite its newfound attractiveness as a business destination, the city remains steeped in history, and you're just as likely to share the road with camels and bullock carts, and haggle alongside Muslim women covered from head to toe in black *burkhas,* as you are to converse with cellphone-wielding yuppies. There may not be much by way of specific sights to see in Hyderabad, but it's a pleasantly manageable city with a vibrant culture, excellent-value luxury hotels, and a heavenly cuisine—perhaps the most enduring legacy of the decadent tastes and patronage of the cultured nizams who first put the city on the map.

ESSENTIALS

GETTING THERE & AWAY Hyderabad is pretty much slap-bang in the middle of very little else, so you're best off flying in, not least because you're unlikely to spend much time in Hyderabad proper (unless you plan to shop endlessly for pearls and eat yourself stupid). There are daily 2-hour flights from Delhi and 1-hour flights from Bangalore, Mumbai, Chennai, Kolkata, and

Tirupati. **Begumpet Airport** (off Sardar Patel Rd.; © **140** for general enquiries, 142 for recorded flight information) is 8km (5 miles) north of the city; a taxi into town should cost Rs 150 ($3.15). **Trains** to and from Bangalore, Tirupati, Chennai, and Mumbai take at least 14 hours; book an overnight journey several days in advance. There are two main stations: Nampally (also known as Hyderabad station) and Secunderabad, with most longer-distance trains arriving at the latter. Call © **1345** for specific information about outbound services.

VISITOR INFORMATION   For the lowdown on sights, tours, and events, visit **Andhra Pradesh Travel & Tourism Development Corporation** (© **040/ 2345-3036;** daily 6:30am–8pm), on the corner where Secretariat Road becomes Tank Bund. Avoid **Andhra Pradesh Tourism** right next door; the stench that hangs in the air from the fish market nearby competes with the incompetence of the staff. There are also information counters at the railway stations. *Channel 6* (Rs 15/30¢) is a monthly booklet listing a wealth of information about the twin cities of Hyderabad and Secunderabad. *Hyderabad CityInfo* (Rs 30/60¢) appears every 2 weeks and provides extensive information about hotels, restaurants, and current events. *Primetime Prism* is filled with useful information about destinations all over the state.

GETTING AROUND   Hyderabad—actually comprising the twin cities of Hyderabad and Secunderabad—is spread over a vast area, and its few sights are scattered, so you're best off renting a car and driver for a half or full day. See **Sita World Travel** (details below) for car hire or call **Cosy Cabs** (Karan Apartments, Begumpet; © **040/2776-2023**). Note that the Old City is best explored on foot.

GUIDED TOURS & TRAVEL AGENTS   The **Andhra Pradesh Travel & Tourism Development Corporation** (see "Visitor information," above) runs full-day guided tours of the city (Rs 130/$2.75) and 3-day trips to Tirupati (Rs 950/$21, including a night's accommodation; see chapter 6). **Sita World Travel** (3-5-874 Hyderguda Rd.; Mon–Fri 9:30am–6pm, Sat 9:30am–1:30pm) can make all your travel, sightseeing, and car-hire arrangements. For alternate quotes, call **Mercury Travels** (© **040/2781-2712**).

WHAT TO SEE & DO

To see Hyderabad in a day, first drive to the **Qutb Shahi Tombs,** where Hyderabad's dynastic rulers are buried. Standing at the center of its own garden, Sultan Muhammed Quli Qutb Shah's tomb is considered the most impressive. Built around the same time as his tomb, the mortuary bath **(Hamaam)**—where the dead were washed before being laid to rest—lies at the center of the enclosure. From here, consider walking to **Golconda Fort;** have your driver show you the route, which is about 2km (1¼ mile) and takes you through lively villages where you may even be invited in for a cup of *chai* and a chat. Allow at least an hour to explore the ruins of the historic citadel, arranging for your driver to pick you up at the entrance. Next, head to **Charminar,** a four-sided archway with soaring minarets. It was laid out by Mohammad Quli Qutb Shahi as the centerpiece of a great new city when Golconda's disease epidemics forced him to move his seat to the banks of the Musi River. Explore the Old City quarter on foot, heading westward into **Laad Bazaar** ✸✸✸, where double-story houses with tiny wooden shutters line narrow lanes. Wandering through these perpetually congested narrow lanes, you'll encounter numerous *burkha*-wearing women scanning the stalls for bargains, and you're likely to score a deal on anything from old saris, pearls, *bidri* (surface ornamentation) work, and silver and gold jewelry, to paper kites, henna, turmeric, and cheap china. *Lac* bangles, made from shellac encrusted with shiny, colorful stones, are a Hyderabadi specialty that you'll find in huge quantities here. It's also where the people of Hyderabad go to buy traditional bridal wear, or *Khopdia Joda,* consisting of a *kurta* pajama, *choli,* and *ghunghat.*

India's second-largest mosque, **Mecca Masjid** (Kishan Prasad Rd., near Charminar), is said to have been built with a few bricks brought from Mecca, and attracts thousands of worshippers during *Namaaz,* Friday prayers. It's off-limits to non-Muslims during prayers, but visitors are welcome at other times. Leave your shoes with an attendant before making your way through a long room that houses the tombs of the nizams of the Asaf Jahi dynasty. Non-Muslims cannot enter the prayer hall but can view proceedings through a screen. In Gulzar Hauz is **Jami Masjid,** Hyderabad's oldest functioning mosque, dating back to 1597.

Round off the day by watching the sun set over Cyberabad from the white-marble **Birla Mandir** ✦ (Kalabahad Hill; daily 7am–noon and 2–9pm; free admission). Commissioned by the Birlas, India's foremost industrial magnates, the main temple is dedicated to Lord Venkateshwara, and is pleasantly free of greedy "guides" and the like.

Golconda Fort ✦✦   Sitting at an elevated height on the outskirts of Hyderabad, Golconda—seat of the Qutb Shahis—was once a magnificent citadel and center of the world diamond trade. The fort took 62 years to build, and when it fell to Aurangzeb in 1678, he tore the place apart looking for diamonds and gold. Left to the birds of prey that circle high above the once-daunting battlements, Golconda would have become a tranquil retreat were it not for its popularity with visitors, who noisily explore the ramparts of Hyderabad's most illustrious attraction. That's why it's best to visit as soon as it opens, or around twilight when it's far cooler and the dimming evening sky sheds a mysterious aura over the stone ruins.

Enclosing the graffiti-smeared remains of bazaars, homes, fields, barracks, armories, mosques, camel stables, Turkish baths, and water reservoirs, the battlements incorporate 87 bastions and extend some 7km (4½ miles) in circumference. Four of the original eight gates are still in use; present-day visitors enter via the **Bala Hissar gate**—large teakwood doors with metal spikes designed to withstand charging elephants. Guides can assist by demonstrating the tremendous acoustics of the structure—a clap here is heard clearly when you are at the fort's highest point, 1km (.62 miles) away; this was once an invaluable security-cum-intercom system. The Royal Palace complex comprises buildings constructed by the Qutb Shahi kings during different periods. Most are decorated with floral designs, glazed tilework on the walls, and cut-plaster decorations indicative of the Qutb Shahi style. Sadly, where royalty once went about their daily lives, rats, bats, garbage, grime, and tourists have taken over. At the top of the fort is the **Baradari,** reached

---

Tips **Getting a Guide**

You'll be confronted by many would-be guides at the entrance to the Golconda Fort—ask around for **M. D. Rathmath** or **Shaik Rajiv.** Both have a good grasp of English. The going rate is Rs 250 ($5.35) for 2 to 3 hours. At the end of the day, the guides gather on the lawn outside the fort entrance, near the ticket booth; join them if you're interested in learning more about Hyderabad culture.

Asthmatics Say "A-aah!"

One of the world's largest alternative medicinal gatherings takes place annually at the **Namally Exhibition Grounds** in Hyderabad, usually on June 7 or 8. Just as the monsoon sets in and brings with it all sorts of seasonal respiratory illnesses, hundreds of thousands of asthmatics from all over India flock to the city to receive an unusual cure administered orally by the Bathini Gowd brothers. A special herbal medicine is stuffed into the mouth of a 2- or 3-inch *murrel* (sardine). The fish is then slipped into the patient's mouth, who swallows the slithering creature alive (the Gowds claim that the wriggling fish increases the efficacy of the medicine because it clears the patient's throat). The result: For more than 162 years, countless people have reported relief from a variety of respiratory-type disorders. Said to have been given to an ancestor of the present-day Gowds by a Hindu holy man back in 1845, the secret formula has been passed down through the generations and administered free of charge in accordance with the saint's wishes. Visit **www.fish-medicine.org** for more information.

by three stone stairways. As you make your way up, look along the walls for the remains of limestone pipes once part of a sophisticated sewerage system that used Persian wheels to carry water up the hill so that it could be piped down for bathing and flushing cistern systems. The climb to the top is worth it for the excellent views alone.

The fort hosts an extremely popular **sound-and-light show** that recounts the history of Golconda using the illuminated ruins as a backdrop. There are performances in English each night; but be warned that power failures can disrupt the performance—and be sure to take insect repellent.

Situated 6km (4 miles) west of the city. 📞 040/2351-2401. Admission Rs 100 ($2.10). Daily 7am–6pm. English sound-and-light show: Daily Mar–Oct, 7–8pm; Nov–Feb, 6:30–7:30pm. Admission Rs 25 (50¢). Tickets available 30 min. before the show; line up early.

Salar Jung Museum ⭐⭐⭐   Marketed as the world's largest private collection of art, artifacts, and antiques, this eclectic assortment of more than 30,000 different exhibits was assembled by three Nawabs Salar Jung, who served as prime ministers *(wazirs)* to the nizams of Hyderabad. It's a truly fascinating collection—particularly the textiles and fine art section, which includes a fine collection of Indian miniature paintings demonstrating the evolution of styles and the differences between Rajput, Deccan, Pahari, and Mughal paintings. One of the most valuable pieces must be a 9th-century edition of the *Koran*, written in beautiful Kufic script. The weaponry collection includes a diamond-encrusted sword used ceremonially by the Salar Jungs, as well as pieces used by Mughal emperors. There's something to be said for the sheer profusion of design objects, ranging from boxes studded with precious gems and vessels blown from Indo-Persian glass to a chair made of solid ivory, a gift from Louis XV to Tipu Sultan. In one room, large crowds are drawn to a famous musical clock with a toy watchman who emerges from behind a door every hour in time to beat a melodious gong. Give yourself at least 90 minutes to explore.

C. L. Badari, Malakpet. 📞 040/2452-3211. Admission Rs 150 ($3.15). Sat–Thurs 10am–4:15 or 5pm.

WHERE TO STAY

At press time, the exquisite **Falaknuma Palace** (Tank Bund Rd.), a work of astonishing architectural opulence that has hosted the likes of King George V, was in the process of being converted into a heritage hotel by the Taj hotel group. This is likely going to be the best place to stay in Hyderabad; visit www.tajhotels.com for ongoing developments.

A good budget option is **Green Park.** Catering primarily to business travelers, Green Park may not rank particularly high in terms of luxury and sophistication, but it's clean, comfortable, and convenient to the nearby airport. Ask for a garden-facing guest room (© **040/2375-7575;** www.hotelgreenpark.com; doubles from Rs 2,650/$58, breakfast included).

ITC Hotel Kakatiya Sheraton & Towers ★★★   Not as opulently over-the-top as Taj Krishna, this is billed as the best business hotel in town. Public spaces are smartly dressed in a vibrant and culturally evocative assortment of objets d'art typical of the region—decorative silver *bidri* pieces, detailed frescoes, and elegant furniture finished in rich fabrics. Guest rooms are wonderfully spacious; even the cheapest corporate rooms are large and attractively finished (twins only). The best views are of Hussain Sagar Lake, the city, and the pool (book a room with a number ending in 01, 03 or 05 for the least obstructed view). The atmosphere here is one of down-to-earth sophistication, and staff are friendly and helpful, if not always on the ball.

Begumpet, Hyderabad 500 016. © 040/2340-0132. Fax 040/2340-1045. www.welcomgroup.com. 188 units. Doubles: $135 corporate; $165 executive club (includes breakfast and happy hour); $215 Sheraton towers; $290–$515 suites. Tower rooms and suites include breakfast, airport transfers, and happy hours. AE, MC, V. **Amenities:** 4 restaurants; 2 bars; tea pavilion; patisserie; pool with Jacuzzi; health club; currency exchange; concierge; travel desk; shopping arcade; florist; salon; room service; laundry; dry cleaning; doctor. *In room:* A/C, TV, minibar.

Taj Krishna ★★★   Situated in the upmarket suburb of Banjara Hills, Hyderabad's most luxurious hotel is fashioned to emulate the opulence and (sometimes high-kitsch) style of an Indian palace; guests have included Lady Diana, Shimon Peres, the Dalai Lama, and Kofi Anan. Between its sumptuous arches, *zardozi* (embroidered) panels, and mother-of-pearl inlaid marble pillars, its lobby is packed full of Belgian chandeliers, ornately engraved mirrors, rococo marble statues, Asian vases, an original French gold-encrusted ornamental grandfather clock, and a fountain spouting water into a dark marble koi pond. The best guest rooms are those on the two Taj Club floors, which have beautiful wooden floors, embroidered sheer curtains, and large bathrooms; Club benefits include breakfast, cocktails, and airport pickup. Book an even-numbered room facing the lake and the acre-long pool area. Note that if you opt for a cheaper room, you'll be more comfortable at the Sheraton. Krishna has some of the city's most exclusive restaurants (see "Where to Dine," below), its best nightlife option, and close proximity to shopping outlets. The Krishna is very popular, which can tax the general efficiency of staff and elevators when occupancy is up.

Rd. No. 1, Banjara Hills, Hyderabad 500 034. © 040/2666-2323 or 040/2339-2323. Fax 040/2666-1313. www.tajhotels.com. 257 units. Doubles: $145 superior; $175 deluxe; $225 Taj Club (includes breakfast and airport transfers); $250 executive suite; $300 deluxe suite; $450 luxury suite; $750 presidential suite; $25 extra bed. AE, MC, V. **Amenities:** 3 restaurants; bar; tea lounge; nightclub; pool; clay tennis court; squash, badminton, golf, and sightseeing by arrangement; health club; concierge; travel desk; car hire; limousine service; currency exchange; salon; florist service; bookshop; pearl shop; 24-hr. room service; laundry; dry cleaning; doctor-on-call. *In room:* A/C, TV, dataport; minibar.

Viceroy ⭐ *Value*   This smart business hotel has a reputation for good value and fine service. It's so popular, in fact, that a new conference-oriented wing has just been completed, almost doubling the room inventory. Offering prime views of the lake from some of its guest rooms, this hotel is marked by unfussy design— as the name implies, decor pays homage to the days of the Raj, with paintings of English lords and ladies throughout. Ask specifically for a lake-facing room; at night, when Hussain Sagar is lit up, the view is quite lovely. Guest rooms are laid out for business convenience, so they're no-nonsense, though strangely enough dressed in shades of lilac, pink, and blue.

Tank Bund Rd., Hyderabad 500 080. ℂ 040/2753-8383. Fax 040/2753-8797. www.viceroyhotels.com. 298 units. Doubles: $72 deluxe; $82 lake-view; $100 corporate club (includes privileges); $135–$160 suites; $15 extra bed. Rates include breakfast. AE, DC, MC, V. **Amenities:** 4 restaurants; bar; pool; health club; concierge; currency exchange; Internet lounge; shops; salon; room service; laundry; doctor. *In room:* A/C, TV, dataport. Corporate Club and suites: Minibar. Corporate Club only: Hair dryer and tea- and coffee-making facilities.

WHERE TO DINE

Hyderabad is known for its *dum*-style cooking, the practice of sealing the pot or dish and slowly simmering its ingredients over a slow fire, thereby increasing the absorption of aromatic spices. Lavishly decorated in vibrant blues and distinctively Hyderabadi objets d'art, **Dum Pukht** ⭐⭐⭐ (Kakatiya Sheraton & Towers; ℂ **040/2340-1045;** Rs 150–Rs 600/$3.15–$13) is the city's most celebrated upmarket restaurant, and known for its *dum*-style dishes. (*Dum Pukht* literally means cooking by locking in the steam.) Try the chef's *kareli ki nahari,* mutton shanks cooked in their own juices and marrow, tinged with cardamom and saffron. Melt-in-the-mouth *kakori* kebabs prepared from finely minced mutton, cloves, and cinnamon are skewered, chargrilled, and drizzled with saffron.

One of the best examples of *dum*-style cooking is biryani, the Hyderabad's most fashionable dish, and best made with marinated mutton which, together with basmati rice and spices, is prepared in a sealed pot for juicy results. Available practically anywhere, it's best enjoyed with a spicy *salan* (chili curry) and yogurt chutney. **Azizia,** adjacent the Nampally railway station, is said to be the home of biryani, and its chefs claim to be descended from the nizams' master chefs.

Another place that serves authentic biryani, among other delights, is **Firdaus** ⭐⭐⭐ (Taj Krishna, Rd. no. 1, Banjara Hills; ℂ **040/2339-2323;** Rs 125–Rs 465/$2.60–$10). At this large, elegant restaurant, waiters serve dishes fit for the nizams against a backdrop of live *ghazal* music. You're in capable hands with the young, enigmatic Chef Sunil, whose kebabs are quite fantastic. Have the *shikampuri kebab,* tender lamb with yogurt and coriander.

To sample all the delights of the region in a value-packed buffet, head for the Viceroy hotel's **Patio** coffee shop (see "Where to Stay," above) on Friday night, when a great-value Hyderabadi *Shahi-Dastarkhan* ("royal dining experience") is laid out. You can sample Chef Vishi's authentic *nahari* soup (a strong, pungent, powerful, and possibly acquired taste), flavorful biryani, and rich *haleem,* made with lamb and wheat powder cooked to a sticky-smooth consistency—in truth, somewhat akin to mashed mince.

8

The Heart of India: Delhi, the Taj, Uttar Pradesh & Madhya Pradesh

The capital of India, Delhi, and its neighboring state, Uttar Pradesh, are the geographical and historical heart of India, with ancient cities and awesome monuments that make for definite inclusion in the itineraries of most first-time visitors to the subcontinent.

With comfortable accommodations options and a host of interesting sights, Delhi is a good place to acclimatize. But the main reason most visitors touch down here is its proximity to some of North India's most impressive sights, like the **Golden Temple** at Amritsar, one of the most spiritual destinations in India (see chapter 10); **Jaipur,** capital of Rajasthan, "land of princes" (see chapter 9); and **Agra,** third point of the Golden Triangle. The Mughal capital of Agra is famed for the timeless beauty of its monuments, of which the **Taj Mahal** is the most famous, but it is in the city of **Varanasi** that time has indeed stopped. Believed to be the oldest living city in the world, Varanasi is the holiest destination in Hindu India, where true believers come to die in order to achieve *moksha*—the final liberation of the soul from the continuous rebirth cycle of Hindu life. Rising like a densely populated crust from the banks of the Ganges, the city is saturated with a sense of the sacred,

though the crowds and filth you may encounter in the city's tiny medieval lanes are not for the faint-hearted. For those travelers who prefer to keep the chaos of India at arm's length, it's better perhaps to head for **Lucknow,** the state capital, where space and serenity prevail, and the decadence and good taste of the ruling *nawabs* (Shiite Muslim ruler or landowner) live on in the rich cuisine and majestic *imambaras* (tombs).

South of Uttar Pradesh sprawls the **Madhya Pradesh,** a vast landlocked state that contains some of the loveliest untouched vistas on the subcontinent. The most famous sights here are the deserted palaces of **Orchha** and the erotic shrines of **Khajuraho**—both easily included as side trips between Delhi or Agra and Varanasi. Deeper south, which sees a great deal less tourist traffic, lie **Sanchi,** one of the finest Buddhist *stupa* (commemorative cairn) complexes in Asia, and **Mandu,** an exotic Mughal stronghold. To the east lies **Bandhavgarh National Park,** with the densest concentration of tigers in India. These excursions will suit those keen to escape the hassle of more tourist-oriented destinations, but they take careful planning to reach; details are provided throughout the chapter.

1 Delhi

200km (124 miles) from Agra; 261km (324 miles) from Jaipur; 604km (375 miles) from Jodhpur

The capital of the world's largest democracy has a truly fascinating history, but with a population of 14 million sprawling over some 1,500 sq. km (585 sq. miles), and plagued by the subcontinent's highest levels of pollution, growth, and poverty, Delhi's delights are not immediately apparent. Even Delhiites, the majority of whom have been born elsewhere, seldom show pride in the city they now call home, bemoaning its drab mixture of civil servants, aspiring politicians, and avaricious businesspeople; the ever-expanding slums and "unauthorized" colonies; the relatively high levels of crime; and the demise of traditional ways. Yet Delhi is in many ways the essence of modern India, with its startling paradox of old and new, foreign and familiar. And it remains the best starting point for exploring North India, not only because of its excellent transport connections and relatively sophisticated infrastructure, but because the history of Delhi, one of the oldest cities in the world, is essentially the history of India (see "A Tale of Seven Cities," below).

The city is littered with crumbling tombs and ruins, most of which are not even on the tourist map. They—like the elephant trundling alongside a traffic-logged road, where handwritten posters for CUSTOM CONFISCATED GOODS SOLD HERE vie with glossy fashion billboards—are just part of the strange fabric of Delhi. It doesn't have the vibrancy of Mumbai or the atmosphere of Kolkata, but in one day you can you go from marveling at the sheer grace of the soaring **Qutb Minar tower,** built in 1199 by the Turkish Slave King Qutb-ud-din Aibak to celebrate his victory over the Hindu Rajputs, to gawking at that 1920s British imperialist masterpiece, the palatial **Rashtrapati Bhavan.** You can wander through the sculptural **Jantar Mantar,** a huge, open-air astrological observatory built in 1725 by Jai Singh, creator and ruler of Jaipur, to the still-sacred atmosphere surrounding the **tomb of the 14th-century Sufi saint,** Sheikh Nizamuddin Aulia, or the **16th-century garden tomb of the Mughal Emperor Humayun,** precursor to the Taj. Or, after the chaos of exploring the crowded streets of 17th-century **Shahjahanabad,** Delhi's oldest living city, you can escape to **Rajghat,** the park where Gandhi was cremated in 1948, or to the **Lodi Gardens,** where lawns and golfing greens are studded with the crumbling 15th-century tombs of once powerful dynasties.

The Plight of the Delhi Beggars

Some 50,000 people live on Delhi's pavements or squalid open lots. These squatters are predominantly from rural areas, many of them forced to move off their ancestral lands to make way for a network of dams that are being constructed across North India despite fierce opposition. Oblivious to the blatant injustice these people have suffered, Delhi's municipal authorities passed a law in September 2002 that makes it an offense to give money to beggars at traffic lights, in part because "it portrays an adverse picture of our country." Begging has in fact been illegal since the 1959 Beggars Act, and those arrested have to bribe the police to avoid spending up to 3 years in jail, but this is the first time the *actual act of giving* has been penalized. As local human-rights lawyers argue, the authorities are effectively criminalizing poverty. And if you deny the desperate the right to beg, they are left with one alternative. Crime.

And still you haven't covered the half of it. . . . But despite its host of attractions, unless you're staying in one of its top hotels (of which the Imperial is almost a destination in its own right), Delhi is not a very relaxing destination, and it is as famous for its pollution (it was rated the 4th most polluted city in the world through the 1990s) as it is for its sights. Unless you're a history buff or here on business, spend as much time as you need to recover from jet lag, choosing to view only a few of its many attractions (the best of which are listed below), and then move on, for the rest of India, with its awesome array of experiences and beauty, awaits.

ESSENTIALS

VISITOR INFORMATION   To pick up a free map of Delhi or to get up-to-date information on sights, city tours, and taxi/rickshaw prices, head for the **Government of India Tourist Office** at 88 Janpath (near Connaught Place; ✆ 011/2332-0005; Mon–Fri 9am–6pm, Sat 9am–2pm). You will also find Government of India Tourist Offices at both airports and at the railway stations. Do not confuse these with so-called "government authorized" tourist offices, which are not authorized by anyone and are very adept at fleecing the unsuspecting. You will find these fakes particularly along Janpath and at the New Delhi railway station; make sure you seek assistance only at 88 Janpath. Note that the Government of India Tourist Office can supply information but will not make bookings. If you intend to travel anywhere during your sojourn in India by train, you are urged to make all your reservations in Delhi. You can make bookings at the helpful India Railways Counter at the airport. Alternatively, for information and bookings, visit the **Delhi Tourism and Transport Development Corporation** (**DTTDC;** Bombay Life Building, Middle Circle; ✆ 011/2331-4229; Mon–Fri 9am–6pm, Sat 9am–1pm), or see "Getting There By Train," below.

GETTING THERE   By Air   Most major international airlines operate in what is one of the best-connected cities in south Asia. Delhi has separate domestic and international airports that lie 8km (5 miles) apart; a free hourly shuttle bus runs between them. Note that the domestic airport has two terminals, 1A and 1B, also connected by free shuttle bus (1A is for Indian Airlines; check which one you need to be at when leaving). The **Indira Ghandi International Airport** ✆ 011/2569-6021) lies 20km (12 miles) southwest of Connaught Place (the city center), 25 to 50 minutes away. The cheapest way to get into town is to catch a State Transport bus (Rs 60/$1.25 plus luggage fee), but if you've just crossed time zones you'll want to opt for a taxi. If you've just arrived in India, don't hire a rickshaw; they may be cheaper than taxis, but they're very slow and bound to be uncomfortable if you're burdened with luggage—plus, you will almost certainly be pressured into handing over more money even if the price has been discussed upfront. Choosing, let alone negotiating with, a taxi driver is likely to make your head spin, so it's best to book a taxi at the official **prepaid taxi kiosk** (just outside the arrivals hall; ask for directions, and don't be sidelined). It offers fixed rates; there are three categories, and luggage determines the final rate, but expect to pay between Rs 150 ($3.15) and Rs 300 ($6.50) into the center of town (25% more after 11pm). Alternatively, find out what the current prepaid rate is and try to bargain it down with one of the taxi touts outside—remember to always agree on the price upfront. Better still, ask your hotel to arrange the transfer, though this will more than double the price. Note that you can change money at the international airport at the State Bank of India (24 hr.), but you can't draw money on your credit card.

The Heart of India: Delhi, Uttar Pradesh & Madhya Pradesh

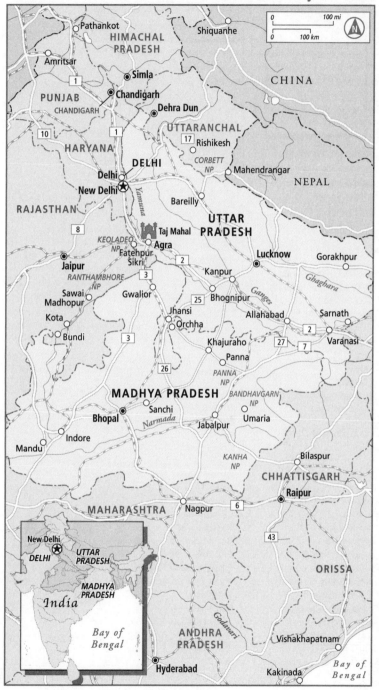

Delhi

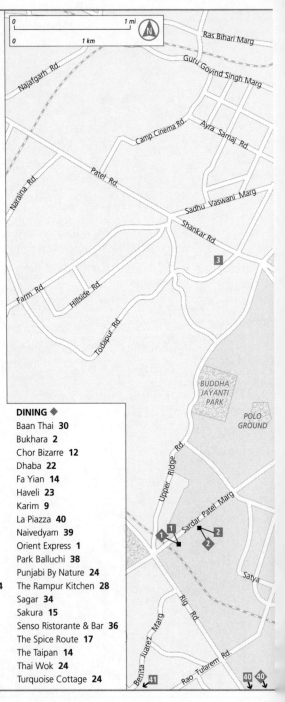

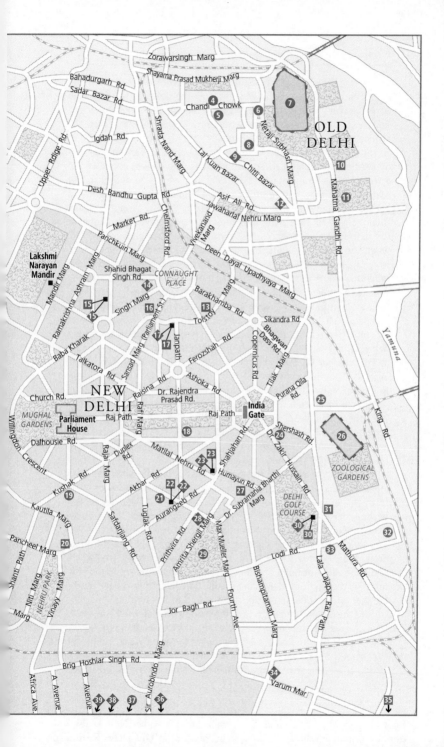

A Tale of Seven Cities

Chosen by the strategically astute invaders who attacked from the north, east, and west, Delhi was not only the gateway to the fertile Gangetic plains and watered by its own Yamuna River, but it enjoyed some protection from the west by the Aravalli Mountains that cross latter-day Rajasthan, and by the Himalayas to the north. Despite this, waves of invaders resulted in the creation—and more often than not destruction—of at least seven distinct cities. The earliest accounts and archaeological finds date back to 1000 B.C., when—according to the *Mahabharata* epic, most revered of Hindu religious texts—the Pandavas and their cousins the Kauravas did battle for the city of **Indraprastha**, thought to be located under the present ruins of Purana Qila, citadel of the sixth capital. But the earliest existing ruins date back to A.D. 736, when the Tomara Rajputs, one of the self-anointed warrior clans to which Rajasthan gave birth, built the fortress **Lal Kot,** around which grew **Qila Rai Pithora,** today known as the first city of Delhi. In 1180 the Tomaras were ousted by the Chauhans Rajputs, who were in turn forced back to Rajasthan by the Slave King Qutb-ud-din Aibak, a Turkish general who built the **Qutb Complex** in 1199, which today remains one of the most interesting sights in the city (see "The Top Attractions," below). Aibak served under the Afghani Muhammad Ghuri until Ghuri's assassination in 1206. Aibak took over the Indian spoils of war, founding the Delhi Sultanate, which was to rule over Delhi and the surrounding region for almost 2 centuries. In 1303, the Delhi Sultan Ala-ud-din Khalji built the second city, **Siri,** near present-day Hauz Khas. Then the Tughluqs built **Tughlaqabad,** 8km (5 miles) east of the Qutb complex, but this was deserted in 1321 and little remains today of what is now referred to as the third city. After a brief sojourn in latter-day Maharashtra, the Tughluqs moved the city again in 1327, this time between Lal Kot and Siri, and named this fourth city **Jahanpanah.** A mere 27 years later it was moved again, this time some distance north to an eminently sensible position next to the Yamuna River. Named **Ferozabad,** this sprawling fifth city was, according to legend, one of the richest in the world. But how the mighty do fall or, according to the Persian prophecy, "Whoever builds a new city in Delhi will lose it." Timur drove the Tughluqs out of Delhi, and while his successors, the Sayyids and Lodis, did not build brand-new cities, their tombs are found scattered in the appropriately named **Lodi Gardens.** Their defeat by the Mughal (of Mongol) Babur signaled the end of Sultanate rule and the start of the Mughal empire, one of the world's greatest medieval dynasties, who were to rule over the region for more than 200 years.

It was Babur who first moved the capital to nearby Agra, but his son **Humayun** chose to return to Delhi in 1534, only to be forced into exile by the advancing army of the Afghan Sher Shah, who took possession

By Train   Of the five stations, most trains arrive at either **New Delhi Station,** a 10-minute walk from Connaught Place, or at **Old Delhi Station** in

of **Purana Qila** (literally "old fort") in 1540, and renamed the citadel **Shergahr,** the sixth city. Fifteen years later, Humayun finally ousted the Afghan, only to die an ignominious death a year later, falling down his library steps—his tomb, which can be seen from the southern gate of Purana Qila, remains one of Delhi's top attractions.

Humayun's son, Akbar—generally revered for his religious tolerance and diplomacy—again chose to move the capital back to Agra. Only after Akbar's grandson, Shah Jahan, built the Taj Mahal for his wife, did Delhi again became the capital in 1638. Shah Jahan, the greatest architect of the Mughal dynasty, rebuilt an entirely new city, using materials from the ruins of Ferozabad (and, it is said, the corpses of criminals in the foundations), and—not known for his humility—named it **Shahjahanabad.** Shahjahanabad is still very much inhabited, and is today usually referred to as "Old Delhi," with many of the city's top attractions. After Shah Jahan was viciously deposed by his son, Aurengzeb (see "The Life & Sordid Times of the Mughals," later in this chapter), Mughal power began to wane, and with it the importance of Delhi. It was only with the advent of British power that Delhi again played a pivotal role in the affairs of India. After the "Indian Mutiny" (or "Great Revolt," depending on who's talking), a direct result of the racist and exploitative policies of the British East India Company, India was annexed by Britain as its colony in 1858, and Delhi was declared the Raj capital in 1911. The last (at least for the time being) of Delhi's cities to be built, **New Delhi** took shape between 1911 and 1933. Designed by the British imperialist architects Lutyens and Baker, the simple, almost brutal classicism of New Delhi's major buildings are considered the finest artifacts of the British empire, their sheer scale symbolizing its fascist ideals. But again Delhi was lost to her rulers, and in 1947 India's first democratically elected prime minister was sworn into power. The bungalows of New Delhi became home to Indian masters. Ever a city of paradoxes, Delhi's jubilation was tinged with tragedy, for this was also for many the demise of ancient Delhi: With the division ("Partition") of the subcontinent into India and Pakistan, bloody street battles between Hindu and Muslim broke out, leading to the wide-scale immigration of Delhi's urbane Muslim population to Pakistan, and an even bigger, reverse influx of Punjabis from what was now Pakistan. Primarily farmers, but with a reputation for hard work and business acumen, the Punjabi immigrants effectively doubled the population of Delhi and forever changed its image of itself as a birthplace of civilization. As William Dalrymple describes it in *City of Djinns,* Delhi—"grandest of grand old aristocratic dowagers"—had become "a nouveau-riche heiress: all show and vulgarity and conspicuous consumption." But if one thing is constant, it is Delhi's ability to reconstitute herself—who knows what she will grow into next?

Shahjahanabad. If you're traveling to Agra, you may need to catch the passenger train that leaves from the Nizamuddin station, south of Connaught Place (rail inquiries: ⓒ **131** or 011/23366177; for reservations from 8am–8pm, dial ⓒ 011/23348686). All stations are well-serviced by taxis and auto-rickshaws. Again, negotiate the fare upfront—expect to pay Rs 30 (60¢) to Connaught Place; Rs 45 (95¢) to Shahjahanabad/Old Delhi. Note that if you plan to travel elsewhere in India by train, it's worth prebooking all your train trips in Delhi. It's easiest to do this with a recommended travel agent like **Cozy Travel** (ⓒ **011/ 2777-4768;** cozy@ndf.vsnl.net.in), near the New Delhi railway station exit gate.

GETTING AROUND   Delhi finally has a subway, but this can get over-crowded and claustrophobic, and women traveling alone will get unwelcome attention. As is the case elsewhere, subways also provide no sense of the city layout or passing sights. The best way to get around is still in Delhi's black-and-yellow taxis or, for short distances, auto-rickshaws (look out for those marked with a green line to indicate their eco-friendly CNG-power status), but be sure to agree on the price upfront. For instance, traveling from Connaught Place to Red Fort shouldn't cost more than Rs 50 ($1.05) by auto-rickshaw, Rs 90 ($1.90) by taxi. If you feel you're being overcharged, accuse the driver of cheating, threaten to report him, and warn him that under Section 420 of the Indian Penal Code he could be imprisoned (not yet in force, but it should put the fear in him!); to complain, dial ⓒ **011/2331-9334.** If the idea of having to haggle like this turns your stomach, **Dial-a-Cab** (ⓒ **1920**) offers a convenient, albeit more expensive, alternative, with a fleet of air-conditioned cars outfitted with working meters. If you'd prefer to hire a car and driver for a half or full day, arrange this through your hotel or, for the best possible rate and reliable drivers, through the tourist office at 88 Janpath. You can also contact the charming **Rinku** (see "Guided Tours," below). If you plan to tour North India by car, set-ting off from Delhi, contact **Journeys** (ⓒ **011/2432-3523;** journeys@giasdl01. vsnl.net.in), a reputable operator with good drivers; or **Shyam Singh** (ⓒ **011/ 6851-7777;** shyam125@hotmail.com), a quiet, sober, and excellent driver who can provide you with a quote if you give him a rough itinerary that includes the number of days, destinations, and vehicle specification (A/C or not, for exam-ple). He will then pick you up from the Delhi airport (or even the Agra or Jaipur airports) and accompany you for the remainder of your trip.

Note: It is inadvisable to travel anywhere during rush hour—you will almost certainly find yourself in a traffic jam in one of the most polluted cities in the world.

GUIDED TOURS   You can book an air-conditioned bus tour of New Delhi (8am–1pm daily) and/or Old Delhi (daily 2:15–5pm) at the tourist office at 88 Janpath (See "Visitor Information," above). Expect to pay about Rs 150 ($3.15) for one tour, Rs 250 ($5.35) for both. Slightly cheaper tours are offered by the DTTDC (see "Visitor Information," above). Both offer long-distance tours that include trips to Agra, Jaipur, and Rishikesh. If you want to create your own half- or full-day tour from the attractions listed below, contact **Rinku** (ⓒ **011/2556-5016** or 98-1119-4983; rinku_dhall@yahoo.co.in or sanjeevjoney@rediffmail. com). Rinku is not, strictly speaking, a guide (he cannot, for instance, give you a detailed history of an attraction), but he knows the city forwards and backwards, knows when you should hire a guide (usually available at every entrance) and how much it should cost, knows when you need to remove your shoes or cover your shoulders, and can tell you whether you can include that last sight before the rush hour takes over. He drives around with a friend in a non-air-conditioned van (Rs 500/$11 for a full day), but if you'd like him to arrange more salubrious trans-portation, give him advance warning (like all taxi drivers/guides in India, Rinku will try to take you to a travel agent or shop from whom he will make a commission, but unlike most, he won't press you further if you decline). For an excellent introduction to Hinduism, as well as visits to some of the lesser-known sights in Old Delhi, book into **Master Paying Guest House** (see "Where To Stay," later in this chapter)—the erudite proprietor gives one of the best tours we had in India. For expensive customized tours of the city and farther afield, contact **American Express** (see "Fast Facts," below) or **Cox & Kings** (see chapter 2). Another company worth highlighting is **Exotic Journeys** (© **011/2617-8685;** exotic@del2.vsnl.net.in)—all you need to do is supply proprietor Raj Singh with your budget (as low as Rs 1,200/$26 a day, including car and driver and accommodations), number of days, and area of interest, and he will customize an excellent trip, kicking off with 2 days of sightseeing in Delhi.

FAST FACTS: Delhi

Airlines Most international airline offices are located on Janpath, Connaught Place, and Barakhamba Road. The best domestic airline, **Jet Airways,** is located at Jetair House, 13 Community Centre Yusuf Sarai (© **011/ 2651-7443;** booking offices © 011/2685-3700). **Indian Airlines** is located at Safdarjung Airport (© **011/2462-2220**) and is open 24 hours; for general inquiries call © **141;** for departures call © **143.**

Ambulance For **Centralised Accident & Trauma Service** call © **1099.** For air ambulance call **East West Rescue** at © 011/2469-9229 or -0429.

American Express The office is located at A-Block Connaught Place (© **011/ 2332-4119**).

Area Code The area code for **Delhi** is **011.**

ATMs There are hundreds of ATMs in the city; ask your hotel which is the closest. Alternatively, head for Connaught Place, where (among others) HSBC, Standard Chartered Grindlays, and Citibank ATMs offer 24-hour cash machines that take Visa and MasterCard.

Banks Hours are Monday to Friday 10am to 2pm, Saturday 10am to noon. It's quickest to use 24-hour ATMs. See "ATMs," above.

Car Hires See "Getting Around," above.

Currency Exchange The international airport has 24-hour currency exchange but no facilities to let you draw money on your credit cards, so bring foreign notes or traveler's checks if you intend to catch a taxi from here. Thomas Cook is located at the airport and at the Hotel Imperial (see "Where to Stay," later in this chapter). See above for American Express. For cash withdrawals or exchange, see "ATMs" and "Banks," above.

Doctors & Dentists Most hotels listed here have doctors on call. The hotels are also your best bet for finding a reputable dentist.

Drugstores There are numerous 24-hour drugstores throughout the city. Best to ask your hotel to arrange a delivery or pickup.

Embassies & Consulates **U.S.:** Shanti Path, Chanakyapuri (© **011/2419-8000**). **U.K:** Shanti Path, Chanakyapuri (© **011/2687-2161**). **Australia:** 1/50-G Shanti Path, Chanakyapuri (© **011/2688-8223**). **Canada:** 7/8 Shanti Path Chanakyapuri (© **011/2687-6500**). **New Zealand:** 50-N Nyaya Marg (© **011/2688-3170**).

Emergencies For police call (*C* **100**; for local stations ask your hotel or call the Government of India Tourist Office. See "Ambulance," above.

Hospitals **All India Institute of Medicinal Sciences** ((*C* **011/2686-4851**), on Ansari Nagar, has a 24-hour trauma unit. Alternatively, head for **East West Medical Centre,** a private clinic located at 38 Golf Links Rd. ((*C* **011/2336-1014**), also with 24-hour emergency service.

Internet Access There are numerous outlets; try **Café Wired World** (34 Bawa Potteries Complex, Aruna Asaf Ali Marg, Vasant Kunj).

Mobile Phones **Airtel** has counters at both airports.

Newspapers/Magazines **The Indian Express** and **The Times of India** are both good national dailies that provide the lowdown on (largely) the political scene. **Outlook** and **India Today** are weekly news magazines that cover a range of issues; of the two, *Outlook* is more populist and interesting to read. **Outlook Traveller** (www.outlooktraveller.com) is a top-quality locally produced travel magazine. **First City** is a monthly magazine recommended for its comprehensive reviews and listings.

Police See "Emergencies," above.

Post Office P.O. Parliament St. ((*C* **011/2371-5605**). Best to ask your hotel to post items.

Restrooms Avoid.

Safety Delhi, like the rest of India, is relatively safe, though the city has seen an increase in crime. It's unwise for women to travel alone at night.

Taxis See "Getting Around," above.

Weather Delhi's summers are notoriously unbearable; October/November to February are the best times to go.

THE TOP ATTRACTIONS

India's capital has more sights than any other city in India, but they are concentrated in three distinct areas—Old Delhi, New Delhi, and South Delhi (known as the **Qutb Minar Complex**)—which can be tackled as separate tours or grouped together. Most organized tours spend a half day covering the top attractions in New Delhi, and another half day exploring the 17th-century capital, Shahjahanabad. Commonly referred to as "Old Delhi," Shahjahanabad lies a mere 5km (3 miles) north of centrally located Connaught Place, the commercial heart of New Delhi, but it feels a hundred years away (400 to be exact). If you do only one sightseeing excursion, make it here, for this is most authentically India, where the imposing **Lal Qila (Red Fort)** and the **Jami Masjid,** India's largest mosque, pay testament to the vision and power of Shah Jahan, and the chaos and pungent smells from the overcrowded and ancient streets are a heady reminder that you are far from home. Surrounding and immediately south of Connaught Place is New Delhi, built by British imperialist architects Baker and Lutyens. Its primary attractions are the architectural gems centered around **Rajpath** and **Rashtrapati Bhavan,** official residence of the president of India. Of Delhi's remaining cities, all of which are today deserted and in ruins, only the 12th-century **Qutb Minar,** a World Heritage Monument built in Delhi's first city and surprisingly intact, is definitely worth inclusion in your itinerary. (*Note:* Most museums in Delhi close Mon.)

SHAHJAHANABAD (OLD DELHI) ✹✹✹

Still surrounded by crumbling city walls and three surviving gates, the vibrant, bustling Shahjahanabad, built over a period of 10 years by Emperor Shah Jahan, is very much a separate city—predominantly a labyrinth of tiny lanes lined with 17th-century *havelis* (Indian mansions), their balustrades broken and once-ornate facades defaced with rusted signs and sprouting satellite dishes. Old Delhi is inhabited by a predominantly Muslim population that seldom ventures beyond the ancient city walls.

The best way to explore the area is to catch a taxi or auto-rickshaw to the Red Fort (see below), then set off in a cycle rickshaw (or on foot if it's too congested) down the principal street, **Chandni Chowk,** which leads from the main entrance to the Red Fort. Along this busy commercial street are mosques, a church, and a number of temples. First up, opposite the fort, is the **Digambar Jain Temple,** the oldest Jain temple in Delhi and surprisingly simple compared with other Jain temples, which are renowned for the intricacy of their carvings. Attached is a **bird hospital,** which smells less charming than it sounds. If you're pressed for time, skip these and proceed to the vibrant **Gauri Shankar Temple** (just look for the mounds of marigolds, sold to worshippers as they enter), which has an 800-year-old lingam. Or stop at the **Sisganj Gurudwara Temple,** an unassuming but superbly atmospheric and welcoming Sikh temple, which marks the spot where Guru Tegh Bahadur, the ninth Sikh guru, was beheaded by the fundamentalist Aurangzeb (Shah Jahan's vicious son). You will be expected to hand over your shoes at a super-efficient kiosk and wash your hands and feet at the cheap taps bizarrely plumbed right at the temple entrance; on the way out you may be offered food—politely decline (rich with ghee, it will have your stomach churning). A little farther along is **Sunehri Masjid,** recognizable by its three gilt domes from where the Persian invader Nadir Shah enjoyed a bird's-eye view as his men massacred some 3,000 of Shahjahanabad's citizens in 1739.

Either turn right into Kinari Bazaar (see below) or head the length of Chandni Chowk to **Fatehpuri Masjid,** designed by one of Shah Jahan's wives, take a detour right into Church Mission Marg and then left into **Khari Baoli**—reputed to be Asia's biggest spice market—the colors, textures, and aromas that literally spill out into the street are worth the side trip. Then double back down Chandni Chowk, turn right into the jam-packed **Kinari Bazaar,** and possibly stop to admire the cheap gold (we're talking mostly tinsel) and silver trinkets and accessories. Or keep going until the right turn into **Dariba Kalan,** "the jewelers' lane," where you can bargain hard for gorgeous baubles. Go south down Dariba Kalan to reach **Jami Masjid,** India's largest mosque, keeping an eye out on the right for the tall spire of the **Shiv Temple.** Having explored Jami Masjid (see below), you can head west down **Chawri Bazaar** for brass and copper icons and other souvenirs, then up Nai Sarak (which specializes in the most magnificent stationery, some bound into diaries). Or head south to **Churiwali Gali,** the "lane of bangle-sellers," and make a final stop at **Karim's** to sample the authentic Mughlai cooking that has kept patrons coming back for over 100 years.

This done, you've pretty much covered Shahjahanabad's top attractions by rickshaw. A few more sights of interest within the old city walls may attract the die-hard tourist. The pretty **Zinat-ul Masjid (Daryaganj),** or "Cloud Mosque," built in 1710 by one of Aurangzeb's daughters, lies south, but doesn't see as much traffic as nearby **Rajghat** (Mahatma Gandhi Rd.; sunrise to sunset), where Mahatma Gandhi, "Father of the Nation," was cremated. There's not much to see besides the black granite plinth inscribed with his last words "He Ram!"

("Oh God!"), but it's worth getting here at 5pm on Friday, when devotees gather to sing melancholic *bhajans*. Nearby, the **Gandhi Memorial Museum** (📞 011/ 2331-1793; Tues–Sun 9:30am–5:30pm) documents his life and last rites, which must have been immensely moving. Also within the old city walls is **Feroze Shah Kotla (Bahadur Shah Zafar Marg)**, the ruins of the palace of the fifth city, Ferozabad. The principal attraction here is the pristine polished sandstone pillar from the 3rd century B.C. that rises from the palace's crumbling remains. One of many pillars left by the Mauryan emperor Ashoka throughout North India, it was moved from the Punjab and erected here in 1356. North of the Red Fort is **St. James Church** (Lothian Rd.; daily 8am–noon and 2–5pm). Consecrated in 1836, Delhi's oldest church was built by Col. James Skinner—the son of a Scotsman and his Rajput wife, who became one of Delhi's most flamboyant 19th-century characters—to repay a promise made during battle.

Lal Qila (Red Fort) ⭐⭐   Built by Shah Jahan, the most prolific architect and builder of the Mughal empire, Lal Qila must have been a very modern departure from the labyrinthine Agra Fort (which is older but a great deal better preserved and atmospheric). It was the seat of Mughal power from 1639 to 1857. Named after the red sandstone used in its construction, the Red Fort covers an area of almost 2km (1 mile). Visitors enter through the three-story **Lahore Gate,** one of six impressive gateways; pass through **Chatta Chowk,** which has some quaint shops selling cheap souvenirs (especially handbags); and arrive at the **Naqqar Khana,** where the emperor's musicians used to play. From here you look up into the **Diwan-I-Am,** the 60-pillared "hall of public audience," from where Emperor Shah Jahan used to listen to his subjects' queries and complaints as he sat cross-legged upon the beautifully carved throne (an age-old custom that his nasty son, Aurangzeb, discontinued). Behind this lie the **Rang Mahal,** the royal quarters of the wives and mistresses, and the **Mumtaz Mahal,** probably used by a favored wife or by Princess Jahanara, who evoked such envy in her sister's heart (see "Agra" introduction, later in this chapter). Next up is the **Khas Mahal,** which housed the emperor's personal quarters (he would greet his subjects across the Yamuna River from the balcony); the gilded **Diwan-I-Khas,** where the emperor would hold court with his inner circle from the famous jewel-encrusted Peacock Throne (taken by the Persian invader Nadir Shah in 1739 and still in Iran); and finally the **Hamams,** or royal baths, whose fountains of rose-scented water would give modern-day spas a run for their money. In front of the Hamams is the **Moti Masjid,** built by Aurangzeb exclusively for his own use— a far cry from the Jami Masjid his father built to celebrate the faith along with thousands of his subjects.

A few examples of beautiful carving, inlay, and gilding remain, particularly in the Diwan-I-Khas, but after so many years of successive plunder it takes some contemplation (and a guide) to imagine just how plush and glorious the palaces and gardens must have been in their heyday; they were ruined when the British ripped up the gardens and built their ugly barracks (the fort is incidentally still a military stronghold, with much of it off-limits). Consider hiring a guide at the entrance, but negotiate the fee upfront and don't expect much by way of dialogue (guides often speak English by rote and don't understand queries); do expect to be hassled for more money. If you're staying in an upmarket hotel, arrange a guide through the concierge.

Chandni Chowk. 📞 011/6327-3703. Rs 100 ($2.10). Rs 100 ($2.10) guide. Free on Fri, so avoid visiting then. Evening light shows in season (call to check times). Daily 6am–7pm.

Jami Masjid ✮✮   Commissioned by Shah Jahan in 1656, this took 5,000 laborers 6 years to complete and is still the largest mosque in Asia, accommodating up to 25,000 worshippers during holy festivals such as Id. Sadly, non-Muslims are not allowed in during prayers, but photographs (sold elsewhere) of the thousands of supplicant worshippers provide some idea of the atmosphere as you wander the huge 28m (90-ft.) square expanse within. The central pool is for washing hands, face, and feet; to the west (facing Mecca) is the main prayer hall with the traditional *mihrab* for the prayer leader. You can ascend to the top of the southern minaret to enjoy fantastic views of Old Delhi and beyond to the distinctly different rooftops and high-rises of New Delhi—the climb is pretty stiff, but worth it. *Note:* If your knees or shoulders are bare, you'll have to rent a scarf or *lungi* (sarong or covering cloth) at the entrance to cover up.

Off Netaji Subhash Marg. Rs 10 (20¢). Closed for prayers and after 5pm.

NEW DELHI

Almost all of New Delhi's attractions lie south of **Connaught Place,** which you will no doubt visit to make onward bookings, get cash, eat, or shop. Built on concentric circles surrounding a central park, the retail heart of New Delhi was designed by Robert Tor Russell in the late 1920s. With its deep colonnaded verandas, gleaming banks, and host of burger joints and pizzerias, it's a far cry from Chandni Chowk but is still quite chaotic, crawling with touts and hucksters whose aim is to part you from your money as quickly and seductively as possible. From here, the closest attraction well worth visiting (unless you're moving on to Jaipur) is the **Jantar Mantar** ✮ (daily 9am–7pm), which lies on Sansad Marg, on the way to Rashtrapati Bhavan. It's one of five open-air observatories built in the 18th century by Maharaja Jai Sing II, the eccentric genius who built Jaipur. The sculptural qualities of the huge instruments he designed are worth a visit alone, but note that the Jantar Mantar in Jaipur is both bigger and better preserved (see chapter 9).

The easiest way to take in central New Delhi's imperial architecture—for many the chief attraction—is to drive to **India Gate,** built to commemorate those who died in World War I, and where an eternal flame burns in memory of those who gave their lives in the 1971 Indo-Pakistan war. Then set off on foot west along the **Rajpath** (the 3.2km/2-mile boulevard once known as King's Way) to the beautifully ornate gates of **Rashtrapati Bhavan,** flanked by the two almost identical **Secretariat buildings.** Having covered the architectural attractions of New Delhi, you can double back to the **National Museum** (see below) or catch a ride to the **National Gallery of Modern Art,** which lies near India Gate (Jaipur House; ✆ **011/2338-2835;** Tues–Sun 10am–5pm). Farther west lies the **Crafts Museum** (see below). Although the National Gallery is one of India's largest museums of modern art, it's pretty staid fare and unlikely to thrill those used to such Western shrines as London's Tate Modern or New York's Museum of Modern Art.

Other museums you may consider in the area include the **Gandhi Smriti** ✮ (Tees January Marg; ✆ **011/2301-1480;** daily 10am–5pm). The colonial bungalow where Gandhi stayed when he was in Delhi, and where he was assassinated, it's more atmospheric than the museum near Raj Ghat in Old Delhi. The **Nehru Memorial Museum and Library** (Teen Murti Marg; ✆ **011/2301-6350;** Tues–Sun 9:30am–5pm; free admission) was the grand home of India's own "Kennedy clan": Nehru was India's first prime minister, a role his daughter and grandson, Indira and Rajiv respectively, were also to play before both were assassinated. Those interested in contemporary Indian history may wish to visit the **Indira Gandhi Memorial Museum** (1 Safdarjung Rd.; Tues–Sun 9:30am–5pm; free admission). A huge force in post-independence India (see "India Past to Present," in the appendix), Gandhi was murdered here by her Sikh body-guards. Among the displays (which provide a real sense of the woman) is her blood-soaked sari, as well as the clothes worn by her son Rajiv when he was killed in 1991.

The best temples to visit in central New Delhi are the **Lakshmi Narayan Mandir** ⟨ (west of Connaught Place, on Mandir Marg), an ornate yet contemporary Hindu temple built by the wealthy industrialist B. D. Birla in 1938; and **Bangla Sahib Gurudwara** ⟨⟨ (off Ashoka Rd.), Delhi's principal Sikh temple. If you aren't heading north to the Golden Temple at Amritsar (see chapter 10 for more on Sikhism), a visit to the *gurudwara* is highly recommended, if only to experience the warm and welcoming atmosphere that seems to pervade all Sikh places of worship—evident in details like the efficient shoe deposit (which is free), genuinely devoted guides (available at the entrance), devotional hymns (sung constantly sunrise till 9pm), free food (served three times daily), and *prasad* (communion) offered as you leave—be warned that it's very oily and you won't give offense if you decline. The *gurudwara* is certainly an interesting contrast to Lakshmi Narayan Mandir; a visit to one of the first Hindu temples to open its doors to all castes (including "outcasts" like the foreign Britishers) makes you feel very much like a tourist, whereas the more embracing atmosphere of the *gurudwaras* have you feeling rather humbled.

If all this sightseeing has you beat, you can retreat to the **Lodi Gardens** (5km/3 miles south of Connaught Place), where green lawns surround the crumbling tombs of the 15th-century Sayyid and Lodi dynasties—the tombs are not well-preserved, but the green, shaded oasis may suffice as a break from the hectic traffic or shopping at nearby Khan Market (though I'd opt for a hotel pool). The 18th-century **Safdarjang's Tomb** lies just south of the Lodi Gardens, but more impressive by far is **Humayun's Tomb** (a short rickshaw ride west) and the nearby **Hazrat Nizamuddin Aulia** (both discussed below).

Finally, the special-interest traveler may be keen to know that you can view India's largest collection of rare stamps free of charge at the **National Philatelic Museum,** located at the post office at Dak Bhavan (Sansad Marg, enter at back of post office; Mon–Fri 9:30am–4:30pm, closed 12:30–2:30pm).

New Delhi's Imperial Architecture ⟨⟨⟨ Nehru wrote that "New Delhi is the visible symbol of British power, with all its ostentation and wasteful extravagance," but no one with any design interest fails to be impressed by the sheer scale and beauty of these buildings and the subtle blending of Indian influence on an otherwise stripped-down Western classicism—a far cry from the ornate Indo-Saracenic style chief architect Sir Edwin Lutyens so deplored. Lutyens, known for his racist views, in fact despised all Indian architecture (he was convinced that the Taj was the work of an Italian designer), but he was forced to include some "native" elements in his designs. Clearly, at first glance the buildings are a symbol of imperial power intended to utterly dwarf and humble the individual, yet these Indian influences, such as the neo-Buddhist dome, tiny helmet-like *chattris* (cenotaphs), and filigree stonework, only add to the stately beauty. Once the home of the viceroy of India, this is today the official residence of the president of India and is closed to the public (though the Mughal Gardens, which are among the best in India, are open to the public in Feb). The slender column near the entrance gates was donated by the Maharaja of Jaipur. The two Secretariat buildings, designed by Sir Herbert Baker, show a similar subtle blend of colonial and Mughal influences and today house the Ministry of Home Affairs and the Home and Finance ministries. Northeast, at the end of Sansad Marg, is Sansad Bhavan (once the Parliament House), also designed by Baker, from where the country is managed (or not, as Booker Prize–winner Arundhati Roy argues so succinctly in *The Algebra of Injustice*—a recommended but somewhat depressing read). Take a drive around the roads that lie just south of here (Krishna Menon Marg, for instance) to view the lovely bungalows, also designed by Lutyens, that line the tree-lined avenues.

The National Museum ✿✿   Okay, so this museum boasts 150,000 pieces covering some 5 millennia, but it is frustratingly hard for the layperson to traverse these hallowed corridors, some of which lie boarded up and empty, and all of which have displays with little or no information. That said, you can still find gems, like the **12th-century statue** of the cosmic dance of Lord Shiva (South Indian bronzes), which is almost an Indian archetype; and the truly wonderful collection of **miniature paintings**—this is one area (2nd floor) where you will easily spend a few hours. And if you have any interest in history, the sheer antiquity of many of the pieces will amaze—it has the country's finest collection of Indus Valley relics (ca. 2700 B.C.), as well as those garnered from central Asia's "Silk Route," but again very little is displayed in an accessible manner. This means that it takes time and effort (and preferably a guide, whom you will have to hire before you arrive) to appreciate the wealth of history that lies throughout the 30-odd galleries spread over three floors.

Corner of Janpath and Rajpath. ℭ 011/2301-5938. Tues–Sun 10am–5pm.

The Crafts Museum ✿   If you plan to shop for crafts in India, this serves as an excellent introduction to what's out there, though when it comes to the antiques, like the 200-year-old life-size Bhuta figures from Karnataka or the Charrake bowls from Kerala, you'll be lucky to pick up anything nearly as beautiful. Some 20,000 artifacts—some more art than craft—are housed in five separate galleries, showcasing the creativity that has thrived here for centuries, not to mention the numerous ways in which it's expressed, depending on where you travel. The **Crafts Museum Shop** is also worth your time, at the very least to familiarize yourself with the best crafts and textiles.

Bhairon Marg. ℭ 011/2337-1887. Free admission. Tues–Sun 10am–5pm. Closed July–Sept.

Humayun's Tomb ✿✿✿   This tomb, built for the second Mughal emperor, launched a great Mughal architectural legacy—even the Taj, which was built by Humayun's great-grandson, was inspired by it. Though the Taj's beauty (and the money spent) eclipsed this magnificent example of a garden tomb, it's well worth a visit, even if your intention is to visit its progeny. Paid for by Humayun's "senior" wife, Haji Begum, and designed by the Persian (Iranian) architect Mirak Mirza Ghiyas, it's another grand testimony to love. Set in peaceful surrounds, the tomb features an artful combination of red sandstone and white marble, which plays with the wonderful symmetry and scale used by the makers of the Mughal empire. Though it doesn't have the fine detailing of the Taj, aspects such as the intricately carved stone trellis windows are lovely. If you're traveling on to Agra, it is interesting to see how the Mughals' prolonged stay started to influence design elements (the Persian finial that mounts the central marble dome was, for instance, later supplanted by the lotus). There are a number of outlying tombs, and if you want to do more than simply wander through the garden and marvel at the sheer generosity of scale, this is one place where the services of a guide are worthwhile. Hire one through your hotel or the central tourism office.

Lodi and Mathura Rd. © 011/2462-5275. Rs 50 ($1.05). Daily sunrise–sunset.

Hazrat Nizamuddin Aulia ✦   Originally built in 1325, but added to during the following 2 centuries, the tomb of the saint Sheikh Nizamuddin Aulia (along with a few prominent others, including the favorite daughter of Shah Jahan) is one of the holiest Muslim pilgrimages in India. It is certainly one of Delhi's most fascinating attractions, not least because the only way to get here is to traverse the narrow medieval lanes of old Nizamuddin on foot. The entire experience will transport you back even further than a foray into Shahjahanabad. This is not for the faint-hearted (or perhaps the recently arrived), however—the lanes are claustrophobic, you will be hassled by hawkers (perhaps best to purchase some flowers as sign of your good intentions upfront), and the smells are almost as assaulting as the hawkers who bar your way. Once there, you will almost certainly be pressured by a sheikh into making a heftier donation (some Rs 100/ $2.10) than is strictly necessary—a far cry from the sacred Dargah in Ajmer (see chapter 9). This would in fact be a three-star attraction if it weren't for the sense that outsiders are not really welcome (though many have reported otherwise)—note that the main structure is a mosque, Jam-at Khana Masjid, and is closed to women. Best to dress decorously (women should even consider covering their heads), pick up some flowers along the way, get here on a Thursday evening when *qawwals* gather to sing the most spiritually evocative devotional songs, and just sit and soak up the medieval atmosphere.

Nizamuddin (6km/4 miles) south of Connaught Place. Donation expected.

SOUTH DELHI

Delhi's sprawling suburbs keep expanding southward, impervious of the remnants of the ancient cities they surround. Die-hard historians may feel impelled to visit the ruins of **Siri** (the 2nd city), **Tughlaqabad** (the 3rd) and **Jahanpanah** (the 4th), but the principal attraction here is the **Qutb Complex** (see below), built in the area that comprised the first city of Delhi. Located in Mehrauli Archaeological Park, it has a number of historic sites centered around the Dargah of Qutb Sahib, as well as a number of cafes and boutiques frequented by Delhi's well-heeled.

Nearby is **Hauz Kas** (on the Delhi–Mehrauli road; © 011/2644-4029; Tues–Sun 9 or 9:30am to between 5:30 and 7pm, depending on season; free admission). The upmarket suburb is known for its glossy boutiques and restaurants that—so typical of Delhi—have sprung up around the 14th-century reservoir and ruins (including the tomb of Feroze Shah Tughlaq). Rail enthusiasts should not miss **The National Railway Museum** (© 011/2688-1816; Tues–Sun 9:30am–1:30pm and 2:30–5pm), said to be one of the world's most impressive—hardly surprising given India's huge network. It is situated southwest of the Lodi Gardens, on Chanakyapuri.

Qutb Complex ✦✦✦   Originally built by Qutbuddin Aiback, first of the Delhi Sultanates who were to rule for some 4 centuries, the complex surrounds the Qutb Minar, the sandstone Victory Tower that he started in 1193. The Minar was added to by his successor, Iltutmish (whose tomb lies in one corner); and the topmost stories, reaching 70m (234 ft.), were built in 1368 by Feroze Shah Tughlag. It is remarkably well-preserved, and photographs don't really do the tower justice—not in scale, nor in the detail of its carving. The surrounding buildings show some of the earliest Islamic construction techniques used in India, as well as the first mingling of Islamic and Hindu decorative styles— Koranic texts are inscribed in the Minar and Alai Darwaza (old gateway to the complex), while Hindu motifs embellish the pillars of the Quwwat-ul-Islam ("Might of Islam") mosque. The iron pillar in the courtyard dates back to the 4th century.

WHERE TO STAY

The capital draws countless diplomats and businesspeople, which in turn has led to a thriving (and relatively pricey) five-star accommodations sector, with little innovation in the guesthouse or B&B areas (the exception being the **Master Paying Guest House,** reviewed later in this chapter, which is the best place by far to stay if you're watching your rupees). As a result, you'll probably need to fork out if you want a certain level of luxury—not a bad idea if this is your first stop in India. Although a five-star hotel may serve as a gentle introduction to India, most are a bland reproduction of what you can expect anywhere in the world, and some are downright hideous despite the hefty price tag. This is why we've come up with a special sidebar of all five-star properties we didn't include in our top picks: "Five-star Hotels That Didn't Make the Grade," below (useful if they're part of a package you're buying). With so much parity in the top-end market, our hands-down recommendation is **The Imperial,** a hotel with a classy and colonial old-world atmosphere, friendly staff, superb restaurants, and the most central location (it's walking distance to Connaught Place). More of a brand, but still the ultimate in luxury, the **Oberoi** has the most lavishly cozy rooms of all the top-end hotels in Delhi, but you'll shell out for the privilege. It's worth checking the going rate at **Hyatt Regency,** which is not as conveniently located as either of these but operates specials throughout the year—you can stay here for as little as $100 a night. Alternatively, check out **Oberoi Maidens,** Delhi's oldest hotel and one of the best-value options in Delhi. To decide among these, check out the full reviews below, and their websites. If you favor the trend toward intimate boutique-style hotels, **The Manor** (© **011/2692-5151;** www. themanordelhi.com; from $170) is a small luxury hotel that has been featured in a number of design books and magazines like *Tatler* and *Condé Nast Traveler*. Located in Friends Colony, a smart residential quarter in the southwestern part of New Delhi, it has a fabulous chef, gracious lawns with a pool, and an intimate atmosphere (18 rooms total). It is really one of the most elegant (all muted colors) and contemporary (a great mix of materials like silk, terrazzo, onyx, and granite) options in Delhi, but a few details (like stained carpets) need attention. Check it out yourself.

Note that if you're literally in transit, the **Radisson** ✪ (NH 8, New Delhi 110 037; © **011/2677-9191;** fax 011/2612-9090; www.radisson.com/newdelhi.in) is your best bet near the airport. It's perched on the edge of a major highway, but guest rooms (from $225) are large and sumptuous, with contemporary furnishing and king-size beds. Ask for a pool- or garden-facing unit.

Note: The prices below are sometimes given in rupees, with U.S. dollar conversions; others are stated in U.S. dollars only, which is how many hotels targeting foreign markets quote their rates.

NEW DELHI
Very Expensive
The Imperial ★★★ *Value*   This gracious establishment (built in 1931) is the best hotel in Delhi—certainly for anyone wanting something a little more

Five-Star Hotels That Didn't Make the Grade

A stone's throw from Rajpath, but looming like a large glass-faced office block, **Le Meridien** (Windsor Place, New Delhi 110 001; ℂ **011/ 2371-0101;** www.lemeridien-newdelhi.com; doubles from $260) has twinkling lights over its entrance. Endless holiday promotions and photo booths create a mall-like ambience during the day; at night the soaring accommodations atrium (Delhi's tallest) is dark and feels a bit like a casino. Accommodations are comfortable enough, but as a place to relax and feel pampered, the hotel is a bit of a letdown. With its large room inventory and numerous food outlets, the **Grand Inter- Continental** (Barakhamba Ave., Connaught Place, New Delhi 110 001; ℂ 011/2341-1001; www.interconti.com; from $225 double) feels a bit like a small indoor city, offering practically everything you need so you never have to step outside, but the ambience is staid and the accom- modations tasteless. **The Metropolitan Hotel Nikko CEN** (Bangla Sahib Rd., New Delhi 110 001; ℂ **011/2334-2000**), a member of the Japanese hotel chain, has a refined atmosphere, with a wildly eclectic mix of baroque furnishings and decorative elements. Unfortunately, the only real highlights here are the very chi-chi spa and authentic Japanese restaurant; guest rooms are small and cluttered, with pastel pink walls and ornate two-poster beds. And rooms are expensive—from $300. The Taj Group has two five-star options in the city—and of the two, the **Taj Mahal Hotel** (see below) is far preferable. Slightly cheaper, the **Taj Palace Hotel** 🏵 (2 Sadar Patel Marg, Diplomatic Enclave, New Delhi 110 021; ℂ 011/2611-0202; www.tajhotels.com; doubles from $270) pulsates with the energy of Delhi's bourgeoisie; at night it becomes a haven for see-and-be-seen weddings and gigantic corporate functions. The Western-style deluxe guest rooms are large and overlook the pool. Unfortunately, all the high-end social functions seem to have had a negative impact on service (this hotel has the longest check-out line in Delhi). Better value, and right next door, is the **Welcomgroup Maurya Sheraton Hotel and Towers** 🏵🏵 (Diplomatic Enclave, New Delhi 110 021; ℂ 011/2611-2233; www.welcomgroup.com; from $220 double). Its location in the diplomatic sector is its major drawback; on the pos- itive side, it has two excellent Indian specialty restaurants. The other so-called five-star option in this neighborhood is the government-run **Ashok,** but it's tired and poorly managed, so definitely avoid this one.

Even farther south, both relatively new, are the **Parkroyal Inter- Continental** 🏵 (Nehru Place, New Delhi 110 019; ℂ 011/2622-4288; www.newdelhi.intercontinental.com; from $270), which is a little more intimate than many of its competitors, with comfortable rooms and top-notch fittings and amenities (the best rooms have views of the Bahai Lotus Temple); and the **Marriott WelcomHotel** 🏵 (District Cen- tre, Saket, New Delhi 110 017; ℂ 011/2652-1122; newdelhi.marriott@ welcomgroup.com), which offers the best value in the five-star category—deluxe doubles for only $170. Guest rooms are rather small, however, and the double-glazed bedroom windows fail to completely block out noise, so ask for a room on an upper floor.

atmospheric than any chain, no matter how luxurious, can hope to offer. Only at the Imperial can you recover from your jet lag in luxury while experiencing something of the elegance of colonial-era Delhi—without even setting foot out of the lobby. It's also incredibly convenient (only a short stroll to Connaught Place) yet tranquil (it has one of the deepest, largest pools in Delhi). It's comfortable as well, having undergone a major renovation that has left the Raj-era atmosphere untouched but has provided every amenity you'd expect from a five-star hotel. Spacious guest rooms with wonderfully high ceilings are furnished in colonial-era elegance (opt for an Imperial or Heritage Room). However, it is the public areas, like the double-volume colonnaded veranda and grand 1911 bar, that are a sheer delight—huge, elegant (it's a word that tends to crop up whenever you try to describe the Imperial), and everywhere a showcase of Delhi's imperial past. A huge collection of original art adorns every corridor (a veritable museum of 18th- and 19th-century art, which you can explore with the resident curator). Silver-service breakfasts are among the best in the world. This quiet, dignified hotel is not only the perfect place to acclimatize, but a place we believe ranks among the top city destinations in the world.

1 Janpath, New Delhi 110 001. © 011/2334-1234. Fax 011/2334-2255. www.theimperialindia.com. 230 units. $250–$290 double; $400–$1,100 suite. AE, DC, MC, V. **Amenities:** 5 restaurants; bar; pool, fitness center; concierge; travel desk; car hire; Thomas Cook currency exchange; bookshop; salon; 24-hr. room service; babysitting; laundry, dry cleaning; doctor-on-call; valet; art gallery. *In room:* A/C, TV, dataport, fax machine (except 1st floor), minibar, tea- and coffee-making facilities or butler service, hair dryer, electronic safe, scale. Deluxe rooms and suites have DVD player.

The Oberoi ★★★   If you like being treated with the reverence of a celebrity, this is the place to stay—just ask Harrison Ford, Mick Jagger, Nelson Mandela, and Salman Rushdie. Even if you're not a star, staff are trained to genuflect—a typical characteristic of all the Oberoi hotels. Service aside, the hotel's location— east of the Lodi Gardens (near Humayun's Tomb) and surrounded by the green oasis of Delhi's golf course—makes for tranquillity. Its sophisticated elegance is also very relaxing—after a morning's sightseeing somewhere like Shahjahanabad, it's a great retreat. Recently renovated, the carpeted guest rooms are richly textured, with upholstered carved wood furniture and bright pink scatter cushions offset with pale floral and paisley fabrics; walls feature artworks illustrating the rich variety of Indian culture. Bathrooms aren't huge but are impeccably decked out with top-notch fittings. The higher up your room, the better the view; odd-numbered rooms have views of Humayun's Tomb. The massive deluxe suites have private balconies, timber floors with rugs, large bathrooms with Jacuzzi tubs and bidets, cabinets with decorative inlay, and two-poster beds; executive suites are similarly lovely but more compact and not quite as lavish. Guest rooms on the top four floors not only have the benefit of excellent views, but include DVD players, complimentary breakfast, and free airport transfers. (**Note:** If jet lag has weakened your immune system, ask the manager of the Chinese restaurant to whip up a hot concoction of ginger, black pepper, mint, and honey for you.)

Dr. Zakir Hussain Marg, New Delhi 110 003. © 011/2436-3030. Fax 011/2436-0484. www.oberoihotels. com. reservations@oberoidel.com. 287 units. Doubles: $320—$375 standard; $575 executive suite; $825 deluxe suite; $1,300–$1,500 Presidential-Curzon. AE, DC, MC, V. **Amenities:** 4 restaurants; bar; patisserie; pool; health club; concierge; travel desk; car hire; limousine service; shopping arcade; bookshop; salon; 24-hr. room service; babysitting; laundry; dry cleaning; doctor-on-call; valet. *In room:* A/C, TV, dataport, fax machines (except 1st floor), minibar, tea- and coffee-making facilities or butler service, hair dryer, electronic safe, scale. Deluxe rooms and suites have DVD player.

The Park ★   The Park is small and has a pretty exterior, but its aspirations are high. A member of Small Luxury Hotels of the World, it fancies itself a boutique hotel, but with 224 rooms, it's a tad big for the category. That said, accommodations, while not particularly spacious, do a good job of differentiating themselves from the look-alike luxury hotel rooms found elsewhere. Hushed shades of teal, gray, and beige create a soothing ambience in what is generally a luxurious space for a guest room; bathrooms are small, with tubs and elegant chrome fittings. Because of the curved shape of the hotel, guest rooms vary in size: The largest are near the elevators and at the corners of each floor. Try to reserve no. 209, 211, 309, 311, 409, or 411—these have double beds. More expensive deluxe rooms occupy two separate floors of the "Residence" and are even more aesthetically pleasing, with smart furniture, in-room VCD (Video Compact Disc) players and Internet access, remote-controlled curtains, a bedside electronic console, and wonderful spring mattresses. Bathrooms have separate walk-in showers and Jacuzzi jets in the tub. There's a full spa, and salsa fans will enjoy the lobby-level **Latino Bar,** with its funky Spanish decor and music. The Park is in the same price category as The Imperial, however, and you know our preference!

15 Parliament St., New Delhi 110 001. ℂ 011/2374-3000. Fax 011/2373-4400. resv.del@theparkhotels. com. 224 units. Doubles: $250 superior; $275 deluxe; $300–$375 suites; $25 extra bed. Deluxe rooms and suites include airport transfers, breakfast, and happy hour. AE, DC, MC, V. **Amenities:** Restaurant; restaurant-pub; bar; pool; health club; gym; sauna; steam; travel desk; confectionery shop; gift shop; salon; 24-hr. room service; massage; babysitting; laundry; doctor-on-call. *In room:* A/C, TV, dataport, hair dryer; electronic safe. Residence rooms and suites include butler service, minibar, VCD player, personal hi-fi, computer on request. Suites have a fax machine.

Taj Mahal Hotel 🌟🌟   This opulent, slightly brash hotel is not quite so massively over-the-top or overwhelming as its older sister, the Taj Palace Hotel, but it does have an exciting atmosphere and a range of superefficient amenities. Its major drawing card, however, is the high esteem in which it is held locally—this is one of the best places to watch the Delhi glitterati at play and work. Capped by *zardozi* domes, the carefully decorated lobby sees a variety of beautiful models and high-powered execs swishing in and out the front door. Despite wonderful service and every amenity you could wish for, guest rooms are unexceptional. You can splurge on a luxurious room on the Taj Club floor, where you'll enjoy a dedicated check-in after being fetched from the airport in a limousine, but at this price you may as well consider the Oberoi. A good-value alternative is to book at the Ambassador (see below) and hang out here (it has a great pool and restaurants) during the day.

Number One Mansingh Rd., New Delhi 110 011. ℂ 011/2302-6162. Fax 011/2302-6070. www.tajhotels. com. mahal.delhi@tajhotels.com. 300 units. Doubles: $300 superior; $320 deluxe; $355 Taj Club (includes breakfast, limousine airport transfers, valet, and cocktail hour); $650 executive suite; $800 luxury suite. AE, DC, MC, V. **Amenities:** 3 restaurants; bar; pool; health center; concierge; travel desk; car hire; shopping arcade; bookshop; salon; 24-hr. room service; babysitting; doctor-on-call. *In room:* A/C, TV, dataport, minibar, tea- and coffee-making facilities, electronic safe.

Expensive

The Ambassador Hotel 🌟   Not far from the Lodi Gardens and Humayan's Tomb, this hotel—operating since 1945—has an old-fashioned edge, with plenty of wood paneling and understated luxury. But it's not particularly elegant, and not as good value as Claridges (see below). Standard guest rooms are small and cluttered. For the best value, book a superior guest room ($10 more), where French doors open onto private balconies. The bathrooms are large and enjoy natural light. Also pretty good value ($175) is the suite-size executive room, where a sliding door divides the bedroom from the comfortably furnished sitting room; sadly, the original Victorian fireplaces are now used for potted plants. Guests are entitled to make use of the extensive facilities offered by the flagship Taj Mahal hotel. The **Yellow Brick Road** coffee shop is bright and laid-back, with an open-kitchen concept and an ode-to-early-20th-century Americana decor. Less opulent and grandiose than some of the other upmarket hotels in town, this is a comfortable alternative with less formal but pleasant service.

Sujan Singh Park, Cornwallis Rd., New Delhi 110 003. ℂ **011/2463-2600.** Fax 011/2463-2252. www.tajhotels. com. ambassador.delhi@tajhotels.com. 88 units. Doubles: $150 standard; $160 superior; $175 executive room; $180 deluxe suite. **Amenities:** 2 restaurants; restaurant-bar; travel desk; currency exchange; bookshop; shopping arcade; salon; 24-hr. room service; babysitting; doctor-on-call; access to Taj Mahal hotel facilities. *In room:* A/C, TV, dataport, minibar, tea- and coffee-making facilities, hair dryer, scale.

Claridges 👁👁 With nearly half a century behind it, this smart hotel retains more authentic old-fashioned charm and period elegance than the Ambassador. It began as a small guesthouse in a smart residential neighborhood., and is convenient to many central Delhi sights. The cheapest accommodations are smart but slightly cramped. By contrast, the slightly more expensive "Regal" rooms are enormous; nos. 128, 228, 132, and 232 face the centrally located pool. Decor varies in style and color, but most rooms are carpeted and have some antique furniture and large bathrooms with tubs; those adjacent to the pool have marble floors and rugs (sacrificing a historical ambience for a more contemporary look). It may not offer quite the same sophisticated luxury as the city's over-represented Western chains, but the Victorian aesthetic lingers, and you'll find friendly service and more than adequate amenities here.

12 Aurangzeb Rd., New Delhi 110 011. ℂ **011/2301-0211.** Fax 011/2301-0625. claridges.hotel@gems.vsnl. net.in. 162 units. Doubles: $120 viceregal room; $140 regal room; $200 viceregal suite; $250 regal suite; $275 luxury suite; $20 extra bed; children under 12 stay free in parent's room. AE, DC, MC, V. **Amenities:** 4 restaurants; bar; patisserie; pool; tennis court; health club; gym; sauna; steam; travel agency, car hire; business center; currency exchange; shopping arcade; salon; 24-hr. room service; babysitting; laundry, dry cleaning; doctor-on-call. *In room:* A/C, TV, minibar, hair dryer.

The Hans Plaza 👁 Staff at this small hotel, conveniently located near Connaught Place, are wonderfully friendly and enthusiastic, which is a major draw. Filled with the piped-in sounds of Simon and Garfunkel, the lobby is very 1980s, which is when the hotel was built. The deluxe guest rooms vary quite a bit: Ask for one on the 16th floor and you'll enjoy double beds with firm, comfortable mattresses and comfortable sofas, all in bronze-toned fabrics—very, neat, clean, and unexceptional. Ask for one on the 18th floor, and you'll have a recently renovated room with wooden flooring and larger windows, but then don't expect the same good bed or furniture. The rooftop restaurant and bar afford grand views of the city.

15 Barakhamba Rd., Connaught Place, New Delhi. ℂ **011/2331-6861** through -6870. Fax 011/2331-4830. www.hansgroup.com. 67 units. Doubles: $160 superior; $190 executive; $240 executive suite; $260 deluxe suite. AE, DC, MC, V. **Amenities:** 2 restaurants; bar; travel desk; currency exchange; 24-hr. room service; babysitting; laundry, dry cleaning; doctor-on-call. *In room:* A/C, TV, dataport , minibar, hair dryer, electronic safe.

Moderate

There is nothing exceptional in this price category; the recommended options are all located in the pleasant Sunder Nagar neighborhood, not far from Humayun's Tomb. Of these, the 50-room **Jukaso Inn** (49–50 Sunder Nagar; ℂ **011/2435-0308,** -0309, or -2137; fax 011/2435-4402; http://indiamart. com/jukasoinn) is the best option, not least because it has the most amenities (restaurant, room service, travel assistance). Ignore the tiny standard guest rooms (Rs 2,700/$60) and pay a meager Rs 200 ($4.30) more for a superior room; although cramped and rather dark, they demonstrate better taste than the cheaper units. Ask for room no. 107 for marble flooring, a set of double beds, and a tub in the bathroom. Public areas have gleaming white marble floors, but the best place to be is on the yellow painted terrace with its potted plants, tiny fountain, and wooden seats. Also in Sunder Nagar, located across the way from an open park, **La Sagrita Tourist Home** (14 Sunder Nagar; ℂ **011/2435-8572; www.lasagrita.com**) is the most peaceful of the lodgings in the area. Its major advantage is the generous amount of natural light that filters into some of the guest rooms; specifically request room no. 203, which is large, with two double beds and plenty of window space. There's no restaurant, but the private garden makes a decent escape.

Inexpensive

Master Paying Guest House ✸✸ (Value)   Staying here is quite simply your best opportunity to discover what "real" Delhiites are all about: sophisticated, charming, and extremely knowledgeable. Filled with warmth and good taste, the guesthouse is owned and run by Avnish and Urvashi Puri. It's their energy and creative panache that make this a satisfying experience, as amenities are pretty basic. The five guest rooms occupy the two floors above their home; two of the rooms are located on the rooftop terrace. All rooms share two sets of immaculately clean bathroom facilities (showers only). You'll find comfortable beds, writing tables, and a carefully sourced objet d'art in each room, while the entire house is decorated with sculpted gods, handicrafts, and artworks. There's an aqua purification system, so you'll shower in cleaner water than the bottled stuff you drink, and an emergency generator deals with Delhi's unpredictable electricity supply. Hot water bottles and heaters are provided in winter, and there's air-conditioning when it gets warm. Home-cooked meals are prepared from fresh market ingredients and served in a small dining room—simply order by ringing a bell and jotting down your request. On the rooftop terrace, you'll find a scented garden nook as well as a meditation room cluttered with images of gurus and gods, and enthusiasts can enjoy an early morning yoga session. The guesthouse is 4km (2½ miles) from Connaught Place. Avnish offers a wonderful "Hidden Delhi" experiential tour through the city, showing you a world never seen by most visitors to Delhi, and he'll unravel Hinduism's spiritual origins in a profoundly logical way. Reserve in advance, and arrange for a pickup if you want to avoid haggling with taxi drivers at the airport. The only drawback for some is that you feel more like a guest in someone's house than in a hotel, but again, this is the whole idea, and a very gentle introduction to India.

R-500 New Rajinder Nagar, New Delhi 110 060. ℂ **011/2574-1089** or 011/2585-0914. www.master-guest house.com. 5 units. Doubles: Rs 400–Rs 750 ($8.75–$16). No credit cards. **Amenities:** Dining room; yoga; meditation; Reiki; transport assistance; airport transfers; sightseeing; excursions; laundry; hospital nearby; Internet access. *In room:* A/C, heater. The Mughal room has a safe.

SOUTH DELHI

Hyatt Regency ✸✸✸   Interesting design, unusual layout, and wonderful contemporary guest rooms mark this as one of the city's best hotels, and—depending on the day—certainly a winner when it comes to value. The lobby bears a faint resemblance to a Hindu temple, with mirrored panels and vaulted ceilings over rug-covered marble floors; accommodations have parquet wood floors and queen-size beds with lovely white duvets and thick mattresses. Pool-facing rooms are only $20 more and are a much better size, while the "bay rooms" are even larger and not only have sleek designer furniture, but also gorgeous bathrooms with glass basins, large walk-in showers, and tubs. Hyatt Regency features the city's most authentic Italian restaurant (don't miss the pizzas here) and the famous **Djinns** pub (see "Delhi After Dark," below). Expect fabulous service in all departments.

Bhikaji Cama Place, Ring Rd., New Delhi 110 066. © **011/2679-1234.** Fax 011/2679-1212. www.delhi.hyatt. com. 518 units. Doubles from $215, but check website for current specials. AE, DC, MC, V. **Amenities:** 4 restaurants; bar; nightclub; patisserie; pool; 2 tennis courts; fitness club; travel desk; currency exchange; shop; 24-hr. room service; babysitting; laundry; dry cleaning; doctor-on-call. *In room:* A/C, TV, dataport, minibar.

NORTH DELHI

Oberoi Maidens ✿✿ *Value*   This Georgian gem is a little out of the center of Delhi, but it has more character and charm than competitors charging twice its tariff. Delhi's oldest hotel, it retains much of its grand ambience, hinting at what it might have been like when Luytens stayed here while supervising the development of the Raj Bhavan. Stained-glass windows, thick columns, stately arches, and deep corridors open to huge rooms on one side and small sunlit balconies on the other, all recalling a bygone style. Accommodations are carpeted, have high ceilings, and are done in elegant textiles. Room no. 105 is a particularly good option, with a second, smaller bedroom, and a large bathroom. It also receives plenty of natural light, whereas some units have small windows. Lovely grounds, inundated with lovely trees and bushes, and a period kidney-shaped pool, add further serenity, only disrupted when parties and weddings are hosted here (it's an understandably popular venue for wealthy families). *Note:* This hotel has been earmarked for extensive upgrading in the not-too-distant future.

7 Sham Nath Marg, Delhi 110 054. © **011/2397-5464.** Fax 011/2398-0771 or -0595. www.oberoihotels. com. 56 units. Doubles: $150 standard; $250 suite. **Amenities:** 2 restaurants; bar; pool; 2 tennis courts; gym equipment; travel assistance; car hire; currency exchange; 24-hr. room service; babysitting; laundry; doctor-on-call. *In room:* A/C, TV, minibar.

WHERE TO DINE

Delhi doesn't enjoy the same reputation for its dining scene as Mumbai, but it's becoming increasingly lively as Delhi's smart, design-conscious elite step out to see and be seen. That said, an irritating trend (at least for voyeurs) among the moneyed crowd is to eat at "members only" restaurants. The most popular of these very hip joints is **Oriental Octopus** (Habitat World, India Habitat Centre, Lodhi Rd.), where you dine at curved, meandering tables shared by gorgeous designer-clad Delhiites—a million miles from the streets of Shahjahanabad. See if your concierge can arrange a reservation, or find a member and tag along. The food isn't bad either—start with Singaporean steamed spring rolls, and move on to Malaysian black pepper prawns tossed in garlic and crushed pepper. The best food in Delhi is Asian (make every effort to dine at The Spice Route at The Imperial), but if you're too nervous to dive into the heavily spiced cuisine, you'll find the best pizzas in town served at the Hyatt Regency's **La Piazza** ✿✿ (Bhikaji Cama Place, Ring Rd.; © **011/2679-1234**). Besides surprisingly authentic Italian cuisine, there's an extensive wine list. The list includes some superb vintages from around the world, though the prices may have you gagging into your glass.

VERY EXPENSIVE

Baan Thai ✿✿✿ THAI   Authenticity is also a focus at this stylish, rather romantic restaurant at the Oberoi; many of the exotic ingredients are, like resident chef Tseng Te Chang, flown in from Thailand, while seafood comes from the Keralite port of Cochin. Start with *tom yam koong,* spicy prawn soup flavored with lemon grass, kafir leaves, galangal, and lime, to prepare your palate. Tseng Te Chang makes a mean green curry from garden-fresh chilies and imported Thai spices, with your choice of duck, lamb, catfish, tenderloin, chicken, or vegetables. Other popular items include deep-fried pomfret topped with raw mango salad, stir-fried crab, and grilled duck in Thai wine sauce. Save space for a light dessert: The homemade ice creams include coconut and pandanus flavors.

The Oberoi, Dr. Zakir Hussain Marg. © **011/2436-3030**. Main courses Rs 300–Rs 875 ($6.50–$19). AE, DC, MC, V. Daily 12:30–2:45pm and 7:30–11:30pm.

Bukhara ★★★ NORTH-WEST FRONTIER   Staff at this international culinary flagship are immensely proud of the fact that Bill Clinton apparently chose to stay at the Maurya Sheraton "because of our restaurant," and report that when Putin was in town, he wanted to dine here three times a day. It's a cozy venue, with stone walls and cushioned-covered stools at mock log-top tables. In a busy display kitchen where meat and vegetables hang from sword-like kebab spears, chefs slave to produce delicacies from a menu that hasn't changed in over 25 years. The best way to experience Bhukara's internationally celebrated cuisine is to order an assorted kebab platter (there's even one named in Clinton's honor). Finish off with a traditional rice-based *phirni* pudding.

Welcomgroup Maurya Sheraton Hotel, Diplomatic Enclave. © **011/2611-2233**. Reservations before 8:30pm only. Main courses Rs 350–Rs 950 ($7.60–$20). AE, DC, MC, V. Open for lunch and dinner; call for hours.

Haveli ★★★ NORTH INDIAN   Besides the fact that Haveli's food is exceptional, it's almost worth a visit just to admire the sumptuous decor. One wall showcases fine floral frescoes and decorative reliefs, while the ceiling is adorned with carved wooden haveli eaves, gilt tiles, and Belgian chandeliers. In the evenings, music and cultural performances are staged on a raised marble platform under a beautiful canopy. A great way to get a taste for North Indian cuisine is to order a Maharaja *thali*, a silver platter filled with tandoori prawns, masala chicken, spicy lamb, mixed vegetable curry, and heavenly black *dal*, a lentil specialty that's cooked for up to 20 hours over hot charcoal. Try the signature *murgh tikka lababdar*, chicken cooked in the tandoor oven with a tangy coriander gravy; or try *murgh haveli*, a mild chicken curry flavored with mace and cardamom.

Taj Mahal Hotel, Number One Mansingh Rd. © **011/2302-6162**. Main courses Rs 260–Rs 800 ($5.40–$18). Thalis Rs 800–Rs 900 ($18–$20). AE, DC, MC, V. Daily 12:30–2:45pm and 7:30–11:45pm.

Masala Art ★★ CONTEMPORARY INDIAN   Artistic rendering of classic Indian cuisine is all the rage in the country's upscale city restaurants, and Masala Art makes a very conscious attempt to dazzle. The chefs turn cooking into performance art, putting on engaging food demonstrations at mealtimes; spectators eat whatever delicacies are produced. There are daily a la carte specials; look for prawns flavored with raw mango, and *galouti* kebabs prepared with finely minced lamb and 126 different herbs. If you're up for sharing a small feast, order *khushk raan*, a whole leg of lamb pot-roasted in a secret, heavenly marinade. Order homemade puffy *phulka* bread, made from ground wheat, on the side, and be sure to have a glass of fresh sugar-cane juice.

Taj Palace Hotel, 2 Sadar Patel Marg, Diplomatic Enclave. © **011/2611-0202**. Main courses Rs 325–Rs 750 ($7–$16). Food shows Rs 900 ($20) seafood, Rs 750 ($16) vegetarian or meat; lunches slightly less. AE, DC, MC, V. Daily 12:30–2:45pm and 7:30–11:45pm.

Orient Express ★★ FRENCH   You're best off dressing up for a meal in this posh replica of a Pullman Orient Express train carriage; look anything less than debonair and you're likely to be ignored. Enjoy pre-boarding drinks on the "platform," as the bar area is called, and scan the humidor for an expensive cigar. Your four-course journey is inspired by the countries through which the Orient Express passes on its Paris-to-Istanbul run, and is likely to include items such as kirsch-flavored quail, Camembert soufflé with paprika sauce, pan-seared reef cod with raw papaya salad, and the extremely popular oven-roasted New Zealand rack of lamb, encrusted with herbs and almonds and served with lamb jus. Fish is flown in fresh daily—from France. Although the menu changes three or four times a year, one item will never be replaced: the sinful but wonderful warm chocolate pudding with a liquid chocolate center.

Taj Palace Hotel, 2 Sadar Patel Marg, Diplomatic Enclave. ✆ 011/2611-0202. Reservations essential. Children under 17 not allowed for dinner. 4-course meal Rs 1,895 ($42) non-vegetarian, Rs 1,595 ($35) vegetarian. AE, DC, MC, V. Daily 12:30–2:30pm and 7–11:30pm.

Sakura ✿✿ JAPANESE   Located in the Japanese-owned and -run Hotel Nikko, this is one of the best Japanese restaurants in Delhi. Both master chefs hail from Japan, and most ingredients, including all fish, are flown in fresh on a daily basis. Though you may feel a little guilty about coming to India to eat Japanese, the chefs are known to also combine Japanese and Indian flavors to create unique fusion items. Ask about any special platters that may be available, or try the red snapper or barbecued eel in a sweet soy sauce.

The Metropolitan Hotel Nikko, Bangla Sahib Rd. ✆ 011/2334-2000. Main courses Rs 290–Rs 1,250 ($6.40–$28). Set menus: Rs 600–Rs 880 ($13–$19) vegetarian; Rs 1,350–Rs 2,200 ($30–$48) non-vegetarian. AE, DC, MC, V. Daily 7–9:30am, noon–2:30pm, and 6–10:30pm.

Senso Ristorante & Bar ✿ ITALIAN   Think of the milk bar in *A Clockwork Orange,* and you'll have some idea of the 1970s-meets-futuristic decor in this favored haunt of Delhi's ultra-sophisticated 20-something crowd. All-white faux-leather armchairs are offset by shades of gray and cracked stone underfoot; silver mirror-ball effects and sheer curtains with metallic baubles add drama to a venue that has a fresh but unadventurous selection of dishes from a constantly changing menu. There's pomfret from Mumbai, salmon from Norway, and lamb from Australia. Chicken lasagna, *penne arrabiata,* and various pizzas are available. It may be a good idea to settle for a light buffalo mozzarella caprese salad followed by deep-fried calamari, and then settle into a night of schmoozing and grooving in the fabulous lounge bar downstairs.

33 Basant Lok Community Centre, Vasant Vihar. ✆ 011/2615-5533 or -5534. Main courses Rs 250–Rs 921 ($5.35–$20). AE, DC, MC, V. Restaurant: 12:30–3pm and 7:30–midnight. Bar: 11:30am–11:30pm.

The Spice Route ✿✿✿ ASIAN   It was voted one of the top 10 restaurants in the world by *Condé Nast Traveler,* and it certainly lives up to its promise with a vast menu that makes the mouth water at the variety of flavors and ingredients. The decor alone is worth a visit—every nook and cranny is hand-painted by temple artists flown in from Kerala, and antique beams, pillars, and ceilings are all imbued with meaning. The restaurant took 9 years to complete, and is divided into nine sections, each representing an aspect of the "journey of life"—for instance, the Wealth section is embellished with 24-karat gold leaf, whereas the Ancestral section has replicas of panels from Thai temples. If the evening is balmy, sit in the tranquil courtyard and be prepared to be blown away by the food—the best *tom kha kai* ever (the classic Thai soup, made with spicy chicken and coconut milk, flavored with lemon grass and kafir leaves) and mouthwatering *chemeen thoren*—Kerala-style prawns, stir-fried with coconut, curry leaves, and black tamarind, and flavored with mustard seeds. *Kung nang phad khing* is stir-fried lobster with ginger and Thai black mushrooms, and *malu miris* is composed of vegetables, coral mushrooms, and water chestnuts cooked in a Sri Lankan curry. As indicated by the name, the menu takes you on a complex culinary journey, from the Malabar Coast to Sri Lanka, Malaysia to Indonesia, Thailand to Vietnam. And although the lobster and the like are pretty pricey, you won't regret ordering them. There are plenty of other dishes in the Rs 300 ($6.50) range. Service is superb—smart, discreet, and helpful.

The Imperial, 1 Janpath. ✆ **011/2334-1234.** Main courses Rs 215–Rs 850 ($4.60–$19). AE, DC, MC, V. Daily 12.30–3pm and 7:30–11:30pm.

The Taipan ⭐⭐⭐ CHINESE   Singaporean chef Sam Wong is a determined perfectionist, and his contribution to New Delhi's culinary scene has earned him the nickname "the Dim Sum Lord." Steamed and served in special bamboo baskets, Chinese *dim sum* are tiny dumplings filled with an assortment of tasty morsels; they draw a dedicated following, and it's quite possible to fill up on these starters without even moving on to the main courses. And, at lunchtime, when you can enjoy the fantastic view over Delhi Golf Course, an assorted platter of dim sum is ideal for a tasty midday meal that won't leave you feeling stuffed for the rest of the day. If you're up for a complete meal, bear in mind that Sam is a master of Peking duck, a dish not to be missed.

The Oberoi, Dr. Zakir Hussain Marg. ✆ **011/2436-3030.** Reservations recommended, essential on the weekend. Main courses Rs 300–Rs 1,450 ($6.50–$32); average dish Rs 780 ($17). AE, DC, MC, V. Daily 12:30–2:45pm and 7:30–11:45pm.

EXPENSIVE

Thai Wok ⭐⭐⭐ THAI   This is one of the best ways to enjoy Delhi, which is probably why Delhi's smart crowd loves this designer-chic rooftop restaurant, with views of the Qutb Minar. Reached via an ancient elevator and a short set of stairs, the artful alfresco setting includes a bright-orange walled area with cushioned seating, wind-blown canopies, and wall torches; you should reserve well ahead to sit here. The energetic hostess will make plenty of recommendations; find out if the wonderful pork spareribs, marinated in Thai herbs and topped with a honey and garlic sauce, are on offer. Seafood dishes are exceptional; try red snapper in chili-sour sauce, prawns stir-fried with fresh green chilies and sweet basil, or deep-fried filet of sole tossed in chopped garlic and freshly crushed black pepper. On Sunday, a value-packed buffet draws a big crowd. Try one of the delightfully decadent cocktails. The wine list has vintages from France, Italy, Spain, Australia, Chile, New Zealand, and California.

1091/1 Ambavata Complex, Mehrauli. ✆ **011/2664-4289.** Reservations highly recommended. Main courses Rs 155–Rs 395 ($3.20–$8.70). AE, MC, V. Noon–11pm.

Turquoise Cottage ⭐ THAI/CHINESE   Another option (like Thai Wok) if you're in the Qutb Minar area, this smart Asian restaurant has turquoise walls, dark stone floors with turquoise tiles, wrought-iron furniture, contemporary chandeliers, and a fish tank or two. Start with an assortment of *dim sum* dumplings (mouthful-size portions of minced seafood, chicken, meat, or vegetables wrapped in handmade wontons and steamed). Then move on to a barbecue platter; it comes with spareribs, grilled chicken, filet of sole, and prawns. Other interesting dishes include black pepper crab, spicy basil prawns, crispy shredded lamb, stuffed squid, and pork chops prepared with fragrant lemon grass. After you've eaten, join the young, hip crowd in the bar downstairs.

81/3 Adhchini, Sri Aurobindo Marg. ✆ **011/2685-396** or 011/2696-3234. Main courses Rs 175–Rs 650 ($3.70–$14). AE, DC, MC, V. Daily noon–3pm and 7:30–11:30pm.

MODERATE

Sagar (18 Defense Colony Market; © 011/2461-7832) is one of Delhi's favorite restaurant chains, serving reliable South Indian food at reasonable prices. Have one of the South Indian thali platters, and eat with your hands. End your meal with a filtered Madrasi coffee, or you can start your day the same way—the restaurant opens at 8am, which is the best time for a traditional *masala dosa,* South India's favorite breakfast pancake, stuffed with spicy potato filling.

Chor Bizarre ✿✿ NORTH INDIAN/KASHMIRI   A fantasy of kitsch twisted into a unique and wonderful space that is more irreverent museum than diner, this is one restaurant that truly lives up to its name. Chor Bizarre literally means "thieves' market," and in it you'll discover fascinating odds and ends, mis-matched settings, out-of-place furnishings, and reassembled bits and pieces, innovatively displayed to create one of India's most visually dynamic restaurants. One table was previously a maharaja's bed, while a 1927 vintage Fiat has become the buffet-carrying "*Chaat* mobile." You'll find matchboxes, coins, chessboards, antique combs, ivory sandals, jewelry, a jukebox, gorgeous chandeliers, and some carefully chosen works of art. Start with deep-fried lotus roots, prepared Kashmiri-style, and move on to marinated lamb brain, seared with spices. Car-damom-flavored lamb meatballs are another delicious Kashmiri specialty, slow-cooked over an open flame. Alternatively, if you're up for a feast, try the Maharaja Thali, filled with treats and served from a traditional royal platter. Ask about walking tours that combine lunch with sights in Old Delhi.

Hotel Broadway, 4/15 A Asaf Ali Rd. (central New Delhi). © 011/2327-3821. Main courses Rs 100–Rs 295 ($2.10–6.40); thalis Rs 225–Rs 295 ($4.80–$6.40). AE, DC, MC, V. Daily noon–3:30pm and 7:30–11:30pm.

Fa Yian ✿ *Finds* CHINESE   Judging by the exterior and the neighborhood, this might at first seem the type of place you don't want to be at night. But grit your teeth and venture inside—the brainchild of Gregory Kuok, this is the most authentic Chinese restaurant in Delhi, and the well-established menu has been tried and tested by some of the city's fussiest diners for well over a decade. Steamed wheat dumplings, filled with prawns, chicken, or vegetables and served with a garlic soya dip, are what gave Fa Yian its excellent reputation. The dumplings are prepared, along with the homemade noodles, fresh each day. Try these as a starter, followed by honey chicken, pepper-salt jumbo prawns, or the Fa Yian hot pot, which is prepared at the table according to your taste. Fish, brought in from Mumbai and steamed with a delicate hint of ginger, is lovely. Set over two levels, the ambience is relaxed and simple; ask for a table upstairs, where the red walls add a dash of warmth. Service is friendly and casual.

A Block, 25/2 Middle Circle, Connaught Place. © 011/2332-4603. Main courses Rs 80–Rs 395 ($1.70–$8.70). AE, DC, MC, V. Daily noon–3pm and 7–11pm.

Park Balluchi ✿✿✿ MUGHLAI/AFHGHANI   A regular winner of India's Tourism Award for the country's best restaurant, Park Balluchi enjoys a magical setting on the grounds of Delhi's leafy Deer Park, in Hauz Khas. Turbaned wait-ers in waistcoats and long shirts serve an extensive range of kebabs and spicy tan-door items. For some light drama, order Afghani-style *murgh-potli* (tandoori chicken): chicken breast stuffed with minced mutton and served over a flaming sword. The specialty at Balluchi is the *dohra kebab,* a unique combination of two meats. Vegetarians should order *mewa paneer tukra,* Indian cottage cheese stuffed with raisins, sultanas, walnuts, and other nuts; preparation of this dish takes at least 12 hours. Be sure to get a side order of *peshawri naan,* bread cooked in the tandoor oven with poppy seeds and coriander leaves. The garden views make this an ideal lunch venue.

Deer Park, Hauz Khas Village. © 011/2685-9369. Reservations for dinner and weekends essential. Main courses Rs 120–Rs 430 ($2.50–$9.40), average price Rs 220 ($4.70). AE, DC, MC, V. Daily noon–11pm and 3:30–7pm.

Punjabi By Nature ✸✸ PUNJABI   You'll know from the many Sikh families that eat here that this is one of Delhi's best-regarded Punjabi restaurants, with two floors for diners and a pub upstairs. On the first floor is a display kitchen where you can watch tandoori items and desserts being made; ask for a table here, where it's more atmospheric. Try tandoori trout, flown in from the icy streams of Himachal Pradesh, or masala quail *(bataear masaledar)*. Lobster is brought fresh from Mumbai, and cooked to perfection in the tandoor oven. Vegetarians can look forward to tandoori broccoli, prepared in a mustard marinade, or *sarson ka saag,* fresh spinach served with homemade cornbread. Look for this infant franchise in Mumbai and, eventually, London.

Note: **Dhaba** (The Claridges, 12 Aurangzeb Rd.; © 011/2301-0211) is another pleasant Punjabi restaurant. Done up like a roadside truck stop, it's where you can sample a refined, hygienic version of the simple, tasty food served along North India's busy highways.

11 Basant Lok, Vasant Vihar. © 011/2851-6665, -6666, -6667, -6668, or -6669. Main courses Rs 150– Rs 395 ($3.15–$8.70); prawns Rs 435 ($9.50); lobster Rs 750 ($16). AE, DC, MC, V. Daily 12:30–11:30pm.

The Rampur Kitchen ✸✸ NORTH INDIAN   Named for a former princely capital in Uttar Pradesh, this bright, yellow-walled restaurant is a fantastic place for meat-eaters, and ideal if you've been browsing the Khan Market. It's intimate and extremely clean, with modern artworks depicting scenes from Delhi life. The Muslim food here is rich—the chefs don't exactly hold back on the ghee. Try *seekh kebab Rampuri,* tasty mutton kebabs that are generously spiced, mixed with boiled egg whites, and grilled over charcoal. *Gosht nahari* is a delicious mutton dish prepared in thick, spicy onion gravy and cooked overnight on a slow fire. Another delicacy is *haleem,* made from a thick mutton paste mixed with spices and pulses and garnished with chilies and ginger; order tasty *sheermal* bread as an accompaniment. Alcohol is not available.

8A Khan Market. © 011/2463-1222 or 011/2460-3366. Reservations not accepted on weekends. Main courses Rs 80–Rs 220 ($1.70–$4.70). DC, MC, V. Daily 12:30–3:30pm and 7–11:30pm.

INEXPENSIVE

Karim Restaurant ✸ MUGHLAI   In the heart of Old Delhi, not far from the Jami Masjid, this legendary eatery dates back to 1913, when it was opened by a chef who hailed from a family of royal cooks who served, among others, the great Mughal emperor, Akbar. Come here for the food, and don't be put off by the informal setting; this is the genuine thing. It's primarily a meat-eaters' hangout, and the real princely treats are mutton *burra* kebabs. The butter-cooked chicken *(makhani murgh-e-jahangiri)* is also wonderful, prepared according to a little-known recipe. You can also sample exotic fare such as spiced goat trotters, or the advance-order *bakra* feast—lamb stuffed with chicken, rice, eggs, and dried fruit.

16 Jami Masjid, Matiya Mahal, opposite Hotel Bombay Orient. © 011/2326-9800. www.karimhoteldelhi.com. Main courses Rs 80–Rs 300 ($1.70–$6.50); bakra Rs 3,000 ($65). No credit cards. Tues–Sun 7am–midnight.

Naivedyam ✸✸ SOUTH INDIAN VEGETARIAN   Delhi has three branches of this fantastic little South Indian restaurant; the one in Hauz Khas is the original, atmospherically decorated with mirror-framed Tanjore paintings and pillars that have been beautifully carved and embossed. Soothing temple music fills the subtly lit interior. You start your meal with a spicy lentil soup, called *rasam,* which is drunk as a curative and is something of an acquired taste. *Thalis,* or multicourse platters, are served at meal times, and are a good way to sample a variety of tastes from the South. Alternatively, you can choose from a whole range of *dosas* (akin to a pancake). Try *tangam paper masala dosai;* it's made from rice and lentil flour, and topped with spicy boiled potatoes. The ingredients may sound ridiculously simple, but *dosas* easily become addictive. On the side you'll be served a *chatni,* made from ground coconut and green chilies, and *sambar,* a souplike concoction of lentils, tamarind, and vegetables. Tea and coffee are served in the style typical of the South, but there's no alcohol. You'll recognize the restaurant by the stone Nandi bull statue that faces the front entrance.

1 Hauz Khas Village. © 011/2696-0426. Main courses Rs 45–Rs 75 (95¢–$1.60); thali Rs 90 ($1.90). AE, DC, MC, V. Daily 11am–11pm.

SHOPPING

The Delhi shopping experience is to some extent less exciting than in, say, Mumbai or Jaipur, but this has as much to do with the sprawling size of the city as anything—best to concentrate on one area at a time. If this is your first port of call, try not to load your luggage too early with stuff to take home. Note that most shops and markets close on Sunday. Besides the areas described below, you can spend an entire day covering the old city of Shahjahanabad (see "Top Attractions," above). Finally, the recommended shops below are only a fraction of what's out there; if you know what you're looking for, it's best to inquire at both your hotel and the Janpath tourist office for more alternatives.

CONNAUGHT PLACE   If you want to get an idea of what lies ahead on your travels, you should definitely visit **Cottage Industries Emporium** on Janpath (walking distance from the Imperial Hotel and Connaught Place), a huge multistory complex brimming with quality goods from all over India (© **011/ 2335-8863**). Alternatively, visit a few of the 22 **State Government Emporiums** that line Baba Kharak Singh Marg; some recommended options are Himachal for blankets and shawls in particular (© **011/2336-3087**); Tamil Nadu ("Poompuhar") for sandalwood objects (© **011/2336-3913**); Uttar Pradesh ("Gangotri") for the stone-inlay work made famous by the Taj, as well as copper/brasswork and leather goods (© **011/2334-3559**); the **Kashmir Emporium** for superb carpets; and Orissa (Utkalika) for fabrics and traditional paintings (the latter off the beaten tourist track). If you're not moving on to Rajasthan, don't miss visiting both this and the **Gujari Emporium.** Both Cottage Industries Emporium (CIE) and the State Government Emporiums have fixed prices, so you won't pick up any bargains, but you are spared the incessant bartering you will have to master elsewhere.

⌐Finds The Shawl-*Wallah* & the Rug Princess

For beautiful quality shawls, call **Ikram** (© 011/2684-8848). Tell him your price range and color choices, and he'll bring samples to your hotel room. One of the best places to buy fine rugs, the quality of which is notoriously difficult to determine, is not in a shop but at the home of **Meenakshi Devi;** her prices are good, and she'll take orders for special sizes and colors (© 011/2462-6394 or -6461).

Diagonally opposite CIE, also on Janpath, is the **Tibetan Market,** where it is said you will pick up a better selection of items (from antique locks to silver jewelry) at better prices than you will anywhere in Tibet.

Having walked its length, you will find yourself in Connaught Place, the retail heart of imperial Delhi, where hundreds of outlets vie for your rupees. Visit **Benaras Silk House** for saris and the most beautiful fabrics on earth (N-13 Connaught Place, opposite Shindia House; ℂ 011/2331-4751). Then go to **Handloom House** to compare selection and prices (9A Connaught Place; ℂ 011/2332-3057). Head to **Jain Super Store** (172 Palika Bazaar, Gate 6) for perfumes, incense, and teas; **M Zee Handicrafts** (48 Palika Bazaar, Gate 3) for silver jewelry; or **Shaw Brothers** (Shop 8, Palika Bazaar; ℂ 011/2332-7327) for pure high-quality Kashmiri shawls and elegant Pashminas—the latter is pretty much a must-see. For jewelry, try **Bholanath** (L23 Connaught Circus) or nearby **Kapur di Hatti** (L 16).

Khan Market & Sundar Nagar Market   Khan Market is good for books, music, and DVDs. Sundar Nagar is considered the best market to trawl for authentic antiques, interesting secondhand goods, and unique artworks. A number of its reputable outlets include **Natesans** (13 Sundar Nagar Market), renowned for the quality of its artifacts and antiquities; and **Poonam Backliwat** (Shop 5, Sundar Nagar Market), where you can pick up items of jewelry worn during Mughal times, as well as sculptures and miniature and glass paintings.

South Delhi   Seek out **Ravissant** (ℂ 011/2683-7278; www.cest-ravissant. com) in New Friends Colony for beautiful contemporary pewter and silver houseware items (or visit the outlet conveniently located in the Oberoi hotel lobby). **Santushti Shopping Complex** is an upscale collection of shops (predominantly boutiques) housed in landscaped gardens 15 minutes from the center. Patronized by embassy wives, it's worth visiting for its lovely atmosphere and to browse **Anokhi** (ℂ 011/2688-3078; also in Khan Market, which is closer to the center) for its highly fashionable blend of Western- and Eastern-style clothing (see "Jaipur: Shopping" in chapter 9 for full review of the Anokhi headquarters); or visit **Lotus Eaters** to pick up a pretty jewelry item.

Even farther south (convenient to visit after viewing the Qutb Minar) are trendy **Hauz Khas Village,** set against a 12th-century backdrop; and, slightly southeast (40 min. from the center), **Greater Kailash**—the latter shopping area (divided into M and N blocks) is the least atmospheric but has a large variety of shops in an upmarket atmosphere. Hauz Khas is where you should seek out designer boutique outlets, like **Ritu Kumar** (E-4; ℂ 011/2656-8986). Or simply head straight for **Ogaan** (H-2 Hauz Khas; ℂ 011/2696-7595)—the formalwear version of Anokhi, it's perfect for unusual Indo-West and contemporary Indian designer clothing (it stocks a number of well-known labels). **Tandon's** (4 Aurobindo Place; ℂ 011/2696-6552) has high-quality Lucknow "Chikan" embroidered linen and clothing. If you're returning to Delhi and have bought fabric, head to **Kavita & Vanita Swahney** for wonderful tailor-made garments at unbelievably good prices (B-78 Greater Kailash; ℂ 011/2646-4633). The most famous shop in N Block is **FabIndia** (N14; ℂ 011/2621-2183), specializing in stylish ethnic Indian homewear and clothing for all ages—highly recommended.

DELHI AFTER DARK

For current events and entertainment, pick up a copy of the weekly *Delhi Diary* or the monthly *First City.* A worthwhile daily event is **Dances of India,** held at the Parsi Anjuman Hall, Bahadur, Shah Zafar Marg (© **011/2331-7831**). One of the most interesting (though touristy) evening shows in Delhi is the sound-and-light show held at the **Red Fort;** most hotels will arrange tickets (Rs 20/40¢). Cultural attractions aside, Delhi is in many ways most interesting at nighttime, when the "conspicuous consumers" to whom William Dalrymple refers in his *City of Djinns* head out and shmooze—to this end, **Djinns** ✹✹✹ (Bhikaiji Cama Place, Ring Rd.; © **011/2679-1234**), named after Dalrymple's book, is worth a look. Located in the Hyatt Regency, the legendary pub attracts a mixed, hard-partying crowd, in some ways as incongruous as the kitsch collectibles—anything and everything, from a red London telephone booth to a 1988 Iron Maiden concert poster (with Kiss, David Lee Roth, and Guns 'n' Roses supporting!), is on display. Alternatively, head for the Basant Lok Community Centre, where you can cruise a variety of options. **Senso Ristorante & Bar** ✹✹✹ (33 Basant Lok Community Centre, Vasant Vihar; © **011/2615-5533** or -5534) has a style-conscious, ultra-chic bar-lounge with a vinyl bar counter, modern white chairs, green antique-style sofas, and mirrored tables. Choice, funky music is always playing, and there are some worthwhile parties on Saturday nights.

The Other Side ✹✹, downstairs at Turquoise Cottage (81/3 Adhchini, Sri Aurobindo Marg; © **011/2685-396**), has a popular bar that draws a vibrant crowd. It has exposed brick walls decorated with an assortment of Western-inspired obsessions; one nook is dedicated to vintage cars, another is filled with Rolling Stones album covers, and still another is decorated with saddles.

2 Agra

200km (124 miles) from Delhi; 60km (37 miles) from Bharatpur, Rajasthan; 120km (75 miles) from Gwalior

Agra is invariably included on every first-time visitor's itinerary, for who visits India without visiting the Taj? Home to three generations of one of the most dynamic dynasties in the medieval world, their talent and wealth immortalized in stone and marble, Agra is home to the finest examples of Mughal architecture in India, of which the Taj is simply the most famous. The beauty of these buildings will bowl you over, but knowing something of the history that played itself out on these stages (akin to reading a Shakespearean drama) makes the entire Agra experience come alive.

To soak up this fascinating history in the walls and rooms that resonated to Mughal voices, you should ideally set aside 2 full days here and hire the services of a good guide. And, if your budget can stretch that far, there's only one place to stay: the palatial **Amarvilas,** where every room has a view of the Taj.

ESSENTIALS

VISITOR INFORMATION   The **Government of India Tourist Office** is at 191 The Mall (© **0562/222-6378;** goito@nda.vsnl.net.in; Mon–Sat 9am–5:30pm). A **Tourism Reception Centre** is at Agra Cantonment Railway Station (© **0562/236-8598**). Not as much on the ball, the state **U.P. Tourism Bureau** is at 64 Taj Rd (© **0562/236-0517**); it has the same hours as the Government of India Tourist Office.

GETTING THERE & AWAY   By Road   Agra lies less than 4 hours away, on a good double-carriage highway from Delhi. Should you need to stop for refreshments, the **Country Inn** at Kosi, 99km (61 miles) from Delhi, is a good bet. Many operators in Delhi offer bus tours to Agra; see "Visitor Information" in the Delhi section, earlier in this chapter. Easy connections between Jaipur and Agra are strangely absent; best to hire a car and driver.

By Air   You can fly from Delhi (35 min.); the same flight continues onward to Khajuraho and Varanasi. Agra is also connected to Mumbai and Kolkata. Kheria airport is a 20-minute ride from downtown; a taxi should cost you Rs 100 to Rs 150 ($2.10–$3.15), an auto-rickshaw Rs 50 ($1.05). Jet Airways and Indian Airlines both have offices at the Hotel Clarks Shiraz (see later in this chapter).

By Train   The **Shatabdi Express** leaves New Delhi at 6am daily, arriving at Agra Cantonment Railway Station (2km/1 mile from downtown) at 8am; it returns to Delhi at 8:18pm and 10:50pm. Alternatively, you can catch the **Taj Express,** which leaves Delhi's Nizamuddin Station at 7:15am and 9:45am, returning to Delhi at 6:35pm and 9:45pm. **Agra Cantonment Railway Station** (inquiries ✆ **131** or 133; reservations 0562/2364131) has prepaid taxi/auto-rickshaw hire (Rs 50–Rs 90/$1.05–$1.90) at Platform 1; this is also where you can book a city sightseeing tour. Trains from Rajasthan pull in at the Agra Fort Station. (Avoid the inconveniently located Agra City Station.)

GETTING AROUND   By Taxi & Auto-Rickshaw   As is the case everywhere in India, make sure you negotiate your taxi or auto-rickshaw rate upfront (or use the prepaid facility). Hiring an air-conditioned car for 4 hours should run you Rs 600 ($13), a full day Rs 1,150 ($25). Unless you're traveling to Fatehpur Sikri, an auto-rickshaw should suffice. **Islam** is a reliable auto-rickshaw-*wallah* originally from Nepal; if you'd like to hire his services for a day, or for the duration of your stay in Agra, he can be contacted at ✆ **0562/223-4061** during the day, or at ✆ **0562/248-1137** (his neighbor) after 9pm. In an attempt to cut down on the air pollution that threatens the Taj, motorized transport is not allowed in the Taj Sanctuary area (2km/1-mile radius); walk or hire a cycle-rickshaw.

GUIDED TOURS   U.P. State Tourism Development Corporation (Tourist Bungalow, Raja-ki-Mandi; ✆ **0562/2351720**) operates city tours that cover all the major sights and conveniently coincide with the arrival times of the Taj Express. Traveling around with a tour group is, however, far from the ideal way to experience the mystery and magical allure of the Taj or Fatehpur Sikri. To book one of the best guides in Agra (if not India!), contact the intelligent and knowledgeable **Rajiv Rajawat** before you even get to India, to ensure he is available on the days you'd like to use his services. Rajiv's mobile number is ✆ **98-3702-3601;** or contact him at rajivrajawat@yahoo.com.

WHAT TO SEE & DO

Agra is today a large industrial city with a woeful infrastructure, but sightseeing here is quite manageable given that there are five major attractions and very little else to keep you here. Ideally, you will see the **Taj** at dawn, then visit **Itmad-ud-Daulah's tomb** and **Agra Fort,** and move on to **Fatehpur Sikri** the following dawn. Besides those sights listed below, you may also want to make time to visit the beautiful **Jami Masjid,** built in 1648 by Jahanara Begum, Shah Jahan's favorite daughter, who clearly inherited some of his aesthetic sensitivities. It is in the heart of the medieval part of Agra, best approached by cycle- or auto-rickshaw; you can stop along the way to bargain for jewelry, fabrics, or carpets. The other sight worth swinging by is the **Dayal Bagh Temple**—begun 95 years ago, it is still under construction and is being built by the progeny of the laborers who built the Taj; the families guard their traditional craft techniques like gold, passing them on only to the sons in the family. Other minor attractions

Agra

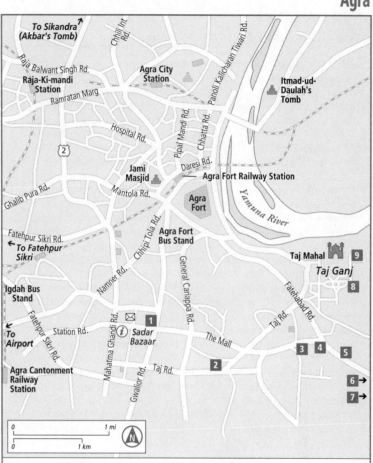

To Sikandra (Akbar's Tomb)

Chhili Int. Rd.

Raja Balwant Singh Rd.

Raja-Ki-mandi Station

Agra City Station

Panioli Kalicharan Tiwari Rd.

Itmad-ud-Daulah's Tomb

Ramratan Marg

Hospital Rd.

Pipal Mandi Rd.

Chhatta Rd.

Daresi Rd.

Jami Masjid

Agra Fort Railway Station

Mantola Rd.

Agra Fort

Yamuna River

Ghalib Pura Rd.

Fatehpur Sikri Rd.

← To Fatehpur Sikri

Agra Fort Bus Stand

Chhipi Tola Rd.

Namner Rd.

General Cariappa Rd.

Taj Mahal

Taj Ganj

9

8

Fatehabad Rd.

Igdah Bus Stand

Fatehpur Sikri Rd.

Station Rd.

Mahatma Ghandi Rd.

Sadar Bazaar

1

The Mall

Taj Rd.

3 4

5

← To Airport

Gwalior Rd.

Taj Rd.

2

6 →

7 →

Agra Cantonment Railway Station

0 ——— 1 mi
0 ——— 1 km

N

New Delhi

Agra

UTTAR PRADESH

ACCOMMODATIONS

Amarvilas Hotel **8**

Hotel Agra Ashok **1**

Hotel Clarks Shiraz **2**

Hotel Sheela **9**

Jaypee Palace Hotel **7**

Mansingh Palace **3**

Welcomgroup Mughul Sheraton **5**

Taj View Hotel **4**

The Trident **6**

ⓘ Information
✉ Post Office

The Life & Sordid Times of the Mughals

Babur, the first Mughal emperor—inspired by the Persians' belief that a cultured leader should re-create the Islamic ideal of a "garden of paradise" here on earth—built three gardens on the banks of the Yamuna. But Agra only took shape as a city under the third Mughal emperor, Babur's grandson, Akbar. Son of the poet-astronomer-philosopher Humayun (whose tomb is in Delhi, described earlier in this chapter), Akbar moved the capital here in 1566. Akbar was as versatile as his father but a better statesman, revered for his religious tolerance and relatively understated lifestyle. He took the throne at age 13 and ruled for almost 50 years, during which time he consolidated the Mughal empire and wooed the Hindu "underlings" by abolishing taxes, banning the slaughter of cows, promoting Hindu warriors within his army, and taking a Rajput princess as his bride, who bore him a son, Jahangir. In gratitude, Akbar built a brand-new city, **Fatehpur Sikri,** which lies 40km (25 miles) southwest and is today one of Agra's top attractions.

The grandeur of this statement of gratitude indicates that Akbar must have, at least at first, been a very indulgent father, though his joy must later have been tinged with disappointment, for at an age when he himself was ruling India, his only surviving son, Jahangir, was relishing his reputation as a womanizer and acquiring a deep affection for alcohol, opium, painting, and poetry. When Jahangir fell in love with **Nur Jahan,** his "light of the world," who was at the time married, Akbar opposed the alliance. But after her husband died, under mysterious circumstances, it must be said, and Jahangir promised to give up "the pleasures of the world," Akbar gave his consent. Jahangir had a coin minted in her honor, and when he was crowned emperor in Agra Fort in 1628, it was the strong-willed and ambitious Nur Jahan who ruled the

---

are ill-kept and a disappointment after viewing those reviewed below. Note that Bharatpur, where the Keoladeo Ghana National Park lies (see chapter 9), is only 54km (34 miles) from Agra.

Taj Mahal ✶✶✶   You expect to be disappointed when coming face to face with an icon that is almost an archetype, but nothing can really prepare you for the beauty of the Taj Mahal. Built by Shah Jahan as an eternal symbol of his love for his favorite wife, whom he called Mumtaz Mahal ("Elect of the Palace"), it has immortalized him forever as one of the great architectural patrons of the world. It's not just the perfect symmetry, the ethereal luminescence, the wonderful proportions, or the sheer scale (which is virtually impossible to imagine from staring at its oft-reproduced image), but the exquisite detailing covering every inch of marble that justifies it as a wonder of the world. What appears from afar to be perfectly proportioned white marble magnificence is in fact a massive bejeweled box, with *pietra dura* adorning the interior and exterior—said by some to be an Italian technique imported to Agra by Jahangir, and said by others to be a craft originating in Persia. These intricately carved floral bouquets are inlaid with precious stones: agate, jasper, malachite, turquoise, tiger's eye, lapis lazuli, coral, carnelian—every stone known to man, as well as different shades of marble, slate,

empire from behind the *jali* screens for 16 years. She built a magnificent garden tomb, known today as the "mini-Taj." for her father. By the time Jahangir died in 1644, reputedly a drunkard, Akbar must have been turning in his tomb (yet another of Agra's top tombs).

It was Jahangir's third son, **Shah Jahan** (not born of Nur Jahan), who came to power—apparently after murdering his two elder brothers, their two children, and two male cousins. Known as the architect of the dynasty, the fifth Mughal emperor began renovating the Agra Fort at age 16, but achieved the apotheosis of Mughal design when he built the Taj Mahal for his beloved **Mumtaz** (incidentally, the niece of Nur Jahan). Bored, he moved the capital to Delhi when he was 47, building an entirely new city from scratch, designing modern geometric palaces (including a separate royal apartment for his favored daughter, Jahanara Begum) and beautiful gardens within the new Red Fort. But he was to pay a bitter price for the favoritism he showed Jahanara and his son, **Dara Shukoh.** His pious third son, **Aurangzeb,** aided by **Roshanara Begum** (Jahanara's embittered younger sister), seized the throne by betraying and/or murdering most of their siblings. Aurangzeb, the last of the great Mughal emperors, became the most repressive ruler North India had yet seen, destroying Hindu temples and images throughout the region and banning the playing of music or any other form of indulgent pleasure, even poisoning Roshanara when he caught her in an illicit liaison with 9 men in her quarters at the Red Fort. Known as much for his cruelty as his ambition, Aurangzeb imprisoned his father in Agra Fort, and sent him a platter upon which he garnished the head of his favorite son, Dara. He instructed his servant to present it with the words, "Your son sends you this to let you see that he does not forget you."

and sandstone. Beautiful calligraphy, inlaid with black marble, is carefully increased in size as the eye moves higher, creating an optical illusion of perfectly balanced typography, with the letters the same size from whichever angle you look. Carved relief work, again usually of flowers, which symbolized paradise on earth for the Mughals, decorates much of the interior, while the delicacy of the filigree screens that surround the cenotaph, carved out of a single piece of marble, is simply astounding. The tomb is flanked by two mosques—one is a prerequisite, but the other is a "dummy" built only in the interests of symmetry; both buildings are worthy of examination in their own right. At the center of it all lies Mumtaz Mahal's cenotaph with the words HELP US OH LORD TO BEAR WHAT WE CANNOT BEAR; Shah Jahan's cenotaph was added later.

Work started in 1641, and the structure took 20,000 laborers 22 years to complete—legend has it that Shah Jahan cut off the hands of the architect (Persian-born Ustad Ahmad Lahori) and laborers to ensure that they would never build another, but there is little to substantiate this sensational story. You rather suspect that if alive today, he would order just such a punitive measure for the developers of a massive retail complex on the river Yamuna: It was undertaken without adequate research into how it will affect the river, and there is a very real

---

Tips **Be the First to Arrive**

Get to the Taj entrance at dawn, before it opens, then rush—run if you must—straight to the cenotaph chamber (remember to remove your shoes before ascending the marble steps). If you manage to get there first, you will hear what might aptly be described as "the sound of infinity"— the vibration created by air moving through the huge ventilated dome. As soon as the first visitor walks in, jabbering away, it reverberates throughout the room, and the sacred moment is lost until closing time again.

---

threat that the Taj, situated on the banks of the Yamuna, will be flooded during the next monsoons.

The Taj changes color depending on the time of day, and many recommend that you witness this by visiting in the morning and evening; your ticket is valid for one entry only, however—either pack a picnic and stay the day, or come in the morning.

Note: The Taj is closed on Monday. It is free for Indian visitors on Friday, which increases the crowds significantly, so avoid this day. Your Taj ticket also entitles you to a small discount at the other four major attractions, so keep it on hand and show it when paying to enter the others.

Finally, to understand the symbolism of the Taj, as well as what has been lost since Shah Jahan's day (such as the plunder of the pearl-encrusted silks that covered Mumtaz's cenotaph), it's definitely worth hiring the services of a good (read: official) guide, arranged through your hotel.

Tajganj. *C* **0562/233-0496.** Rs 500 ($11). Tues–Sun dawn (about 6am) to dusk (about 7:30pm). Ask whether moonlight viewing has resumed.

Agra Fort 👁👁👁   Built by Akbar (or by his 4,000 workmen) on the west bank of the Yamuna, the Agra Fort first took shape between 1565 and 1573, but each successive emperor was to add his imprint, and today the towering red-sandstone ramparts house a variety of palace apartments, representing the different building styles of Akbar and Shah Jahan. Jahangir's **"chain of justice"** (1605), by which any of his subjects could call on him, provides some insight into the ruling qualities of the man many dismiss as a drunkard. Entrance is through the impressive **Amar Singh Gate,** and you pass on your right-hand side the **Jahangiri Mahal,** the palace that housed the women of the court, dating to Akbar's reign (ca. 1570). In front is a stone pool with steps both inside and outside—legend has it that was filled with rose petals during Nur Jahan's time, so that she could bathe in their scent. Much of the exterior (the jutting *jarokhas,* for example, and the domed *chattris*) and almost the entire interior were clearly built by Hindu workmen, who used Hindu building styles and decorative motifs—indicative of Akbar's all-embracing religious tolerance. Adjacent, facing the **Anguri Bagh** (the **Grape Garden,** where flowing water, flower beds, hidden lamps, and hanging jewels would have transformed it into a fantasy garden), is **Khas Mahal** (1636), built overlooking the cooling breezes of the Yamuna. You are now entering Shah Jahan's palaces, immediately recognizable by the extensive use of white marble. Historians also point out that here—unlike in Akbar's buildings, which feature straightforward Hindu elements next to Islamic—a subtle blend of Hindu and Persian elements resulted in a totally new style, the "Mughal style," with its classical purity. The Khas Mahal is flanked by two

Golden Pavilions (a reference to the fact that they were once gilded), the bedrooms of the princesses Jahanara and Roshanara, before the latter plotted the downfall of her father and sister. On the left is the **Mussaman Burj,** an octagonal tower open to the cooling breezes, which may have been the emperor's bedroom. Romantic accounts would have us believe that Shah Jahan, imprisoned by his son, would gaze at the Taj Mahal until his death of a broken heart in 1666. However, evidence points to death by a massive dose of opium, complicated by the prolonged use of aphrodisiacs. Near the tower are the mirrored **Sheesh Mahal** and the **Mina Masjid (Gem Mosque)**; adjacent is the **Diwan-i-Khas (Hall of Private Audience;** 1637), its marble columns inlaid with semi-precious stones in *pietra dura* floral patterns. In front of the Diwan-i-Khas are two **thrones** (from where the emperor watched elephant fights below); facing these is **Machchhi Bhavan (Fish House)**, once filled with the sounds of trickling water. Beyond lies the **Diwan-i-Am (Hall of Public Audience)**, the arcaded hall where the emperor would listen to the complaints of his subject, seated on the Peacock Throne (see "Lal Qila (Red Fort)," in Delhi). Note the insensitive placement of the tomb of John Russell Colvin, who died here during the Mutiny and was laid to rest in front of the Diwan-I-Am. The ugly barracks to the north are also 19th-century British additions. From here on, most of the buildings (except for the **Nagina Masjid,** the private mosque of the ladies of the court) are closed to the public, being at press time structurally unsound.

Note: As is the case at the Taj, avoid Friday when entry is free for Indian visitors, making the place unpleasantly crowded.

Yamuna Kinara Rd. Rs 300 ($6.50). Keep ticket until visit is over. Daily 7am–6pm.

Itimad-ud-Daulah's Tomb ★★★   Described as a mini-Taj, this "bejeweled marble box" is the tomb of Mirza Ghiyath Beg, who served under Akbar and fathered Nur Jahan, the powerful wife of Jahangir who helped promote her father to his position as Lord of the Treasury and enshrined him here—proof of her power. Also built of translucent white marble, it was the most innovative building of 17th-century India, and marked the transition from the heavy red sandstone so favored by previous Mughal emperors. It no doubt inspired Shah Jahan with its beautiful symmetry and detailing; the *pietra duras* are as delicate as embroidery, and the dense gilding and paintwork feature typical Persian motifs, such as the wine-vase and the dish and cup, much favored by Jahangir at the time. The scale may be far less grand than that of the Taj, but the polychrome geometric ornamentation is more obviously decorative, and given the beauty of the proportions and the intricacy of its inlays and mosaics, it's amazing how little traffic this tomb sees relative to the Taj. It definitely warrants a short visit, if only to get a sense of how almost generic opulence was to the Mughal court.

Eastern Bank of Yamuna (30 min. from Taj). Rs 110 ($2.40). Admission for Indians is free on Fri, so avoid that crowded day. Daily 6am–6:30pm.

Sikandra (Akbar's Tomb) ★★   Someone once described the rise and fall of the Mughal empire as rulers who started "as titans and finished as jewelers." To this end, Akbar's tomb is a less elegant version of the bejeweled tombs of his great-granddaughter (or his daughter-in-law's father), yet more ornate than that of his father Humayun (see "Delhi: The Top Attractions"). That said, the perfect symmetry is typical of Persian architecture, and the scale is huge; the gateway alone, featuring more than 20 panels inlaid with intricate geometric patterning, will stop you in your tracks. Geometric patterning in fact dominates, with relatively few floral designs, as befits the last "titan" ruler. It's not surprising to hear that the tomb is believed to have been designed by Akbar; the detailing reflects the altogether more restrained lifestyle and masculine personality of this great ruler.

8km (5 miles) from Agra on NH 2. ✆ **0562/237-1230.** Rs 235 ($5). Free on Fri for Indians, so may be crowded. Daily 7am–5:15pm.

Fatehpur Sikri ⭐⭐⭐   Built from scratch in 1571 by Akbar in honor of the Sufi saint Salim Chisti, who had predicted the birth of a son (see "The Dargah Sharif & Other Ajmer Gems" in chapter 9), this grand ghost city is carved entirely from red sandstone. It was only inhabited for 14 years, after which— some say because of water shortages—it had to be abandoned. It's a bizarre experience wandering through these magnificent, architecturally fascinating sandstone arches, courtyards, and buildings (try to get here right when it opens, the only time it's peaceful), which combine a fine sense of proportion—indicative of Akbar's Persian ancestry—with strong Hindu and Jain design elements, indicative again of his embracing attitude to the conquered. Upon entering, you will see the **Diwan-i-Khas,** thought to be a debating chamber, on the right. Facing it is the **Ankh Michali,** thought to be the treasury, which has mythical Hindu creatures carved on its stone struts. To the left is the large **Pachisi Court,** where Parcheesi was played with live pieces: the ladies of the harem. It is said that Akbar learned much about the personalities of his court and enemies by watching how they played, won, and lost. Surrounding the court are, from the left, the **Diwan-i-Am,** a large pavilion where public hearings were held; the **Turkish Sultana's House,** an ornate sandstone pavilion; and the **Abdar Khana,** where drinking water and fruit were apparently stored. Walk between the two latter buildings to enter **Akbar's private quarters.** Facing the **Anoop Talao**— the four-quartered pool—are the rooms in which he slept (note the ventilating shaft near his built-in bed) and his personal library (note the built-in shelves). Also overlooking the Pachisi Court is the **Panch Mahal,** the tallest pavilion, where Akbar's wives could watch the games and enjoy the breeze without being seen. Behind the Panch Mahal are the female quarters, including **Maryam's House** and the **Haram Sara Complex.** The harem leads to **Jodha Bai's Palace,** a large courtyard surrounded by pavilions—note the green glazed roof tiles. To the east is **Birbal's House,** a two-story pavilion noted for its carvings; beyond lie the **servants' cells.** From here you exit to visit the **Jami Masjid,** a mosque even more spectacular than the larger one his grandson built in Delhi. Set like a glittering pearl amid the towering red sandstone bastions, punctuated by a grand gateway, is the white marble *dargah* (tomb) of Salim Chisti, which has some of the most beautiful carved screens in India. It attracts pilgrims from all over India, particularly (given his prediction for Akbar) the childless, who make their wish while tying a cotton thread onto the screens that surround the tomb.

Again, the services of a good guide are indispensable to a visit here (don't bother hiring one of the "official" guides at the entrance, however).

37km (23 miles) west of Agra. No phone. Rs 485 ($10.50). Daily 7am–7pm. Avoid crowds on Fri when admission is free for Indian visitors.

WHERE TO STAY

Given that it is one of the most-visited tourist destinations in the world, Agra's accommodations options are a real disappointment, no doubt a case of resting on the Taj's laurels. The big exception is **Amarvilas,** which—even if it means scrimping elsewhere—is worth every cent, not least for its proximity to the Taj and the views. Within the moderate price category, all located south and south-west (known as the Cantonment) of the Taj, there is incredible price parity (about $60); of these only the **Trident** and **Jaypee Palace Hotel** offer good value. The best budget option, conveniently located within Tajganj (where the Taj is located), is the **Hotel Sheela,** also reviewed below.

EXPENSIVE

Amarvilas 🏵🏵🏵 *Value*   Given the rather dire alternatives, it is really worth splurging on this extraordinary hotel, which—despite the fact that it's not cheap—offers value, because it is located just 600m (1,900 ft.) from the Taj, of which every room has a beautiful view. Here you can literally sip a cappuccino in your king-size bed at dawn, watching the subtle color variations the monument undergoes as the sun rises; or you can order a cocktail on your private balcony at sunset, admiring the ethereal marble silhouette as staff light the burners that line the hotel's grand stepped terraces that lead down to the central pool. The lobby, bar, and lounge all offer the same surreal views of the Taj, but even those public spaces that don't offer a feast for the eye are lovely, with large reflecting pools, colonnaded courts, terraced lawns, and pillowed pavilions. By day some of the exteriors look a little bland and in need of the detailing featured in the interior, but at night it's a pure *Arabian Nights* fantasy, when burning braziers provide a wonderful contrast to the fountains and trickling streams. The rooms, which are compact but extremely luxurious, are pure Vilas (see the Rajvilas review under "Jaipur" in chapter 9), showcasing the best-quality Indian craftsmanship available but with every modern amenity, including a walk-in cupboard and marble bathroom with separate tub and shower. The only difference between the deluxe (standard) and superior is that the latter has a small balcony (recommended!). The in-house spa also has views of the Taj—lying there, gazing at the dream-like monument, you might just have to ask the masseuse to pinch you. Without a doubt it's the best hotel in town, yet service isn't always smooth; this may irritate the well-traveled, though staff will go out of their way to make up for any problems. Note also that blaring temple music from town is ever-present when the windows are open, but with an open mind this can add to the charm.

Taj East Gate End, Taj Nagari Scheme, Agra 282 001. ✆ **0562/223-1515.** Fax 0562/223-1516. www.oberoi hotels.com. 106 units. Doubles: $350 deluxe; $370 superior; $450–$850 suites. AE, DC, MC, V. **Amenities:** 2 restaurants; lounge; bar; cultural performances/entertainers; pool; fitness center; Banyan spa; travel services; salon; 24-hr. room service; laundry; doctor-on-call. *In room:* A/C, TV/DVD, minibar; personal butler; hair dryer.

Taj-View Hotel 🏵   Within 1km (a half mile) of the Taj, this is a comfortable albeit unexceptional option. Although little can be done to change the exterior, which looks like a 1970s apartment block, extensive renovations at press time may spruce up the guest rooms, which are showing their age (at least those in the least expensive category). You pay at least $20 extra for a Taj-facing room, which has a view so distant that it's probably better value to book a city-facing room (request one on an upper floor). With extensive landscaped lawns and a quiet, relaxing marble pool with its own swim-up bar, this is a fair place to come home to after the rush of sightseeing. It's more competitively priced than the brash Sheraton, but not as good value as the Trident or Jaypee.

Fatehabad Rd., Taj Ganj, Agra 282 001. ✆ **0562/223-2400** through -2418. Fax 0562/223-2420. www.tajhotels. com. 100 units. Doubles (Oct–Apr/May–Sept): $95/$70 standard; $115/$75 superior Taj-view; $135/$80 deluxe Taj-view; $155/$85 executive suite Taj-view. AE, DC, MC, V. **Amenities:** 2 restaurants; seasonal poolside barbecue; bar; cultural performances by arrangement; pool; tennis court; putting green; fitness center; currency exchange; shops; massage; travel services; car rental; airport transfers; sightseeing; babysitting; 24-hr. room service; laundry; doctor-on-call; astrologer. *In room:* A/C, TV, minibar.

Welcomgroup Mughal Sheraton ★ *Kids*   Before Amarvilas, this was billed the best lodging in town, but despite its awards for design (it's supposed to emulate the palatial residence of a Mughal king but looks tawdry in comparison to Amarvilas), this hotel had a rather frenetic ambience: The classical music that is constantly piped through the vast marble lobby is drowned out by the ever-present buzz of people who gather to drink, chat, and wait for sightseeing buses to depart, and your room may end up being the only place to relax. Given the high traffic, personal service can also be elusive at times. Guest rooms are large, but those in the lowest price category—the so-called Chamber of Kings—are slightly cluttered, with an unfortunate choice of lurid green and yellow carpets. You'll have to fork out a good deal more ($45) for the better-designed Chamber of Emperors rooms; given the distance of the view, the Taj-facing guest rooms are overpriced. On the plus side, it offers sprawling gardens, relative proximity to the Taj, and an endless list of facilities. And, with a children's amusement park and an army of nannies, it's aimed at the top end of the domestic family market.

194 Fatehabad Rd., Taj Ganj, Agra 282 001. ✆ **0562/233-1701.** Fax 0562/233-1730. www.welcomgroup.com. 288 units. Doubles: $140 Chamber of Kings; $185 Chamber of Emperors; $195 Taj-facing Mughal chambers exclusive; $600 suite. AE, DC, MC, V. **Amenities:** 5 restaurants; bar; nightclub; cultural performances; entertainers; pool; 2 tennis courts; croquet; badminton; boating; miniature golf; billiards; jogging track; health club; sauna; children's amusement park; travel services; currency exchange; bank; shopping arcade; salon; 24-hr. room service; doctor-on-call; astrologer. *In room:* A/C, TV, minibar. Chamber of Emperors rooms have hair dryers, tea- and coffee-making facilities.

MODERATE

If for some reason the hotels recommended below are full, three more options are clean and relatively comfortable, though all show their age. The previously government-run **Hotel Agra Ashok,** which has recently changed hands (it may even have changed name by 2004), has neat and fairly spacious guest rooms and a number of amenities such as an in-house restaurant, 24-hour room service, a pool, a travel desk, and laundry (✆ **0562/236-1231** or -1232; moonagra@yahoo.com; doubles from Rs 2,995/$64). Styled as a faux fortress-palace, **Mansigh Palace** has similar amenities (✆ **0562/233-1771;** www.mansinghhotels.com; doubles from Rs 2,995/$64). Despite the unpromising lobby, guest rooms are unexpectedly pleasant, with comfortable beds, far roomier and attractive than those at **Hotel Clarks Shiraz,** which has similar amenities and is less than 3km (2 miles) away from the Taj. Other than this, the large lawns are the most attractive feature of this white concrete edifice. Guest rooms are small, relatively comfortable, but extremely dull and dated with cheap touches like the TV remote that is chained to the bedside table. A few of the rooms (top floor) have Taj views; those with odd numbers on the top floor of the main wing are best (✆ **0562/222-6121** or -6132; www.hotelclarkshiraz.com; doubles from Rs 3,000/$65).

Jaypee Palace Hotel ★★ *Value*   This huge hotel and convention center sits practically undiscovered at the edge of town; priced way below its competition, it is Agra's best-kept secret. The red-sandstone buildings have a formal look, more reminiscent of a modern library or museum than a palace, but it's wonderfully quiet (at least at press time; a huge tour group could change this). The hotel is set on 10-hectare (25-acre) grounds with well-tended gardens, lovely walkways, fountains, and pergolas—you can even take a camel ride through the grounds. Fresh flowers breathe life into the large, carpeted guest rooms, which have comfortable beds with firm mattresses (specify that you want a double bed when you book—only a few are available), upholstered sofas, and well-considered work areas designed for businesspeople. Rooms are relatively tasteful, dressed in shades of blue and mushroom; deluxe rooms have balconies, while executive rooms are much bigger but lack the balcony. Agra's largest health club is situated here, where you can enjoy a yoga session or aromatherapy treatment. Golf lovers note: Guests receive coupons to play golf at a private course when you return to Delhi.

Fatehabad Rd., Agra 282 003. © **0562/233-0800.** Fax 0562/233-0850. www.jaypeehotels.com. 350 units. Doubles: $60 deluxe; $65 executive. AE, DC, MC, V. **Amenities:** 4 restaurants; tea lounge; bar; disco; pool; putting greens; tennis; squash; jogging track; bowling alley; billiards; table tennis; health club; aerobics; spa; children's play areas; virtual reality games; travel and transport counter; airport transfers; helipad; helicopter; currency exchange; in-house banking facility; shopping plaza; florist; salon; 24-hr. room service; babysitting; laundry; doctor-on-call. *In room:* A/C, TV, minibar, tea- and coffee-making facilities, hair dryer. Executive rooms have electronic safe.

The Trident 🌟🌟   Another desperate attempt to emulate Agra's architectural heritage, this hotel uses the same red sandstone favored by the Mughal kings, but that is where the similarity ends. It is a tranquil option, though, with cool, neat, public spaces and service that is generally a great deal slicker than elsewhere in Agra—not surprising given that this it's an Oberoi-managed hotel. Guest rooms, which are decently proportioned, have clay tile floors with rugs and are coordinated in shades of tan, maroon, and green—hardly the height of elegance, but soothing enough. Attached bathrooms feature tubs and green marble floors. Accommodations are arranged around a lovely central garden, with manicured lawns, trimmed hedges, and a swimming pool. As is the case elsewhere, a variety of cultural performances are held at night, including dancing, singing, and pottery demonstrations.

Taj Nagri Scheme, Fatehbad Rd., Agra 282 001. © **0562/233-1818.** Fax 0562/233-1827. www.oberoihotels. com. 140 units. Doubles: $60 superior room; $20 extra bed; children under 12 free in parent's room. AE, DC, MC, V. **Amenities:** Restaurant; bar; pool; table tennis; travel agent; airport transfers; bookstore; jewelry store; salon; 24-hr. room service; babysitting; laundry; doctor-on-call. *In room:* A/C, TV, minibar, tea- and coffee-making facilities, electronic safe.

INEXPENSIVE

Hotel Sheela (Value   As far as budget lodging goes in the immediate vicinity of the Taj Mahal, you won't do better than this peaceful complex of neat, cream-walled buildings with a pleasant garden courtyard filled with bougainvillea, parrots, peacocks, and squirrels. Aimed at the budget traveler, accommodations are very spartan, with patterned vinyl flooring and wallpaper designed like faux miniature brickwork, and beds with firm but thin mattresses. The en-suite tiled bathrooms are clean and have towels; hot water is available in winter. Bedrooms have fans, mosquito screens over the windows, and air coolers for summer. Ravi Sharma is an affable, helpful host who'll help with sightseeing endeavors, guides, and organizing a taxi. During the winter season, you are advised to reserve in advance or risk ending up in one of the nearby hovels.

East Gate, Taj Ganj, Agra 282 001. © **0562/233-1194** or -3074. 22 units. Doubles: Rs 200–Rs 350 ($4.30–$7.60). No credit cards. **Amenities:** Restaurant; taxi hire; sightseeing assistance; telephone. *In room:* Air cooler.

WHERE TO DINE

As is the case with accommodations, dining (and nightlife) options are limited in Agra, and you may as well dine in your hotel. But if you're "slumming" elsewhere and have cash to burn, **Esphahan** is definitely worth a splurge.

Chiman Lal Puri Wallah (Moments NORTH INDIAN   Raja Babu is the proprietor of this fifth-generation family eatery, where mountains of cheap, satisfying *puri* (deep-fried bread) and vegetable curry are served in a grubby two-level corner shop not far from Agra's Jami Masjid. Using the fingers of your right hand, mop up the curry with the wafer-thin *puris,* adding the mint chutney and curd to taste. You'll be offered more *puris* and *subji* (the curry, or stew) until you flatly refuse to eat anything more; then comes saffron-flavored *kheer,* a traditional rice pudding. The "menu" does not change. Ever. Simple, yet exceptionally tasty, this is real Indian dining.

Chimman Chauraha. ✆ 0562/236-7430. Meals around Rs 30 (60¢). No credit cards. Daily 7am–11pm.

Esphahan ✦✦✦ INDIAN Even if you aren't staying at Amarvilas, you should dine at this Indian specialty restaurant—not only are the cuisine, service, and live Indian music superb, but arriving at the flame-lit latter-day palace is one of Agra's most memorable moments. (When you reserve, ask to have your pre-dinner cocktail on the veranda so you can watch the sunset hues color the Taj and the magnificent pool area below.) Start with *tandoori phool,* stuffed cauliflower in a Kashmiri cumin marinade; or Sunhera *jheenga,* tiger prawns marinated in citrus yogurt; or succulent *murgh makhmali* kebab—cubed chicken breast in a cream and mace marinade—you'll wish you'd ordered this melt-in-the-mouth starter as a main. But you have so much more to choose from. The Bharwaan *gucchi* (stuffed Kashmiri morels in saffron gravy) is recommended. However, Jahangirabadi *murgh* biryani (sandalwood-flavored chicken layered in saffron basmati rice) is a tad dry and dull. All dishes are served with *dal,* seasonal vegetables, and a choice of Indian bread. It makes for a memorable evening out, and the perfect place to celebrate seeing the Taj.

Amarvilas, Taj East Gate End. ✆ 0562/223-1515. Reservations essential. Rs 300–Rs 1,100 ($6.50–$24). AE, MC, V. Daily 7–10pm.

Only ✦ *Value* NORTH INDIAN/INTERNATIONAL Although it's touristy (recommended by every guidebook on the planet), the aptly named Only caters as much to the domestic family as to the foreign market, and is never empty—*always* a good sign. You'll be welcomed as you enter by exuberant Rajasthani dancers, the service is super-slick and fast, the atmosphere (air-conditioned!) is convivial, and the simple food delicious, though nothing approximating gourmet. Start with *bagam bahar,* seasonal vegetables and fruits cooked in sour cream and mild spices and topped with a spinach paste, and make sure you sample the vast array of breads (try the *aloo paratha:* flour bread, softened with butter and studded with potato and coriander, cooked in a clay oven). The *murgh tukole* (chicken slices simmered in a thick spicy gravy) and chicken *tikka* (boneless, tenderized spicy chicken served with onion, lemon, and chutney) are both delicious.

45 Taj Rd. ✆ 0562/322-6834. Rs 55–Rs 365 ($1.10–$8). AE, MC, V. Daily 7–10pm.

SHOPPING

Agra is famous for its marble and softstone inlay, as well as *zardori*-embroidered fabrics, leather goods, brassware, carpets, and jewelry. However, it's hard work dealing with the touts and hawkers who have been making their money from tourists for generations (300 years, to be exact). Given the sights you need to cover, you may feel too exhausted to deal with this, but the energetic should explore the following shopping areas around the Taj Complex: **Sadar Bazaar** and **Fatehabad Road** (visit **Cottage Industries Exposition,** just to get an idea of quality; prices are very high). **Sanjay Place** is also worth exploring.

3 Varanasi (Benares)

320km (198 miles) SE of Lucknow; 765km (474 miles) SE of Delhi

A crumbling maze of a city that rises from the *ghats* (steps) on the western banks of the Ganges, Varanasi is in many senses the quintessential India. With an ancient history—Mark Twain famously described it as "older than history, older than tradition, older even than legend, and looks twice as old as all of them put together"—it is also one of the most sacred cities in the world today. Kashi, or "City of Light, where the eternal light of Shiva intersects the earth," as Varanasi is seen by devotees, is the holiest of Indian pilgrimages, home of Shiva, where the devout come to wash away their sins. It is also one of the holiest *tirthas* (literally a "crossing" where mortals can cross over to the divine, or the gods and goddesses come to bathe on earth), where many return to die in the hope that they may achieve *moksha,* the salvation of the soul from the cycle of birth, death, and rebirth.

Named after the confluence of two rivers, Varuna and Asi, the city is centered on the ghats that line the waterfront, each honoring Shiva in the form of a *linga*—the rounded phallic-like shaft of stone found on every ghat. Cruise the waterfront at dawn and you will witness the most surreal scenes, when devotees come to bathe, meditate, and perform ancient rituals to greet the sun. Or even come at sunset, when *pundits* (priests) at Dashswamedh Ghat perform *arti* with complicated fire rituals, and pilgrims light candles to float along the sacred waters.

Earliest accounts of the city go back 8,000 years, and "the city of learning and burning," as it is affectionately referred to, has attracted pilgrims from time immemorial, not all of them Hindu—even Buddha visited here in 500 B.C. after he achieved enlightenment, sharing his wisdom at nearby Sarnath. Successive raids by Muslim invaders (the last of whom was the Mughal emperor Aurangzeb) led to the destruction of many of the original Hindu temples, which means that most of the buildings here date back no further than the 18th century. Yet the sense of ancient history is almost palpable. Getting lost in the impossibly cramped labyrinth, you are crowded by pilgrims purchasing flowers for *puja* (offering, or prayer), grieving relatives bearing corpses, chanting priests sounding gongs, and sacred cows rooting in the rubbish—an experience you will never forget.

ESSENTIALS

VISITOR INFORMATION   The **Government of India Tourist Office** is located at 15B The Mall, Cantonment (© **0542/234-3744;** daily 9am–5:30pm). A satellite information counter is open during flight arrivals. The **U.P. Tourist Office** is on Parade Kothi (© **0542/234-1162;** daily 10am–5pm); a satellite counter is at the railway station (© **0542/234-6370;** Mon–Fri 6am–8pm).

GETTING THERE   By Road   Unless you have a lot of time on your hands, driving to Varanasi means spending too much time on the road.

By Air   The airport is 23km (14 miles) from the Cantonment (Cantt.) area, where the most comfortable hotels are located, and 30km (18 miles) from the riverfront. Best to fly in with **Jet Airways** (© **0542/251-1444**) from Delhi via Khajuraho; the flight lasts 75 minutes. **Indian Airlines** (© **0542/234-3746**) flies in from Agra, Delhi, Lucknow, and Mumbai. **Sahara Airlines** (© **0542/234-3094**) connects the city with Kolkata and Bangalore. A taxi should run you Rs 280 ($6) to the Cantonment; the airport shuttle charges Rs 35 (75¢), but you may be in for a lengthy wait while it fills up.

By Train Varanasi is conveniently reached by overnight train from Delhi; the Kashi Vishwanath Express takes 18 hours. It is also connected with a host of other cities and towns. For inquiries, call 🕐 **1331;** for reservations, call 🕐 **0542/ 234-8031** or -8231. Prepaid taxis are available from the station. (Note that Mughal Sarai is 17km/11 miles out of town, so try to arrange to get off at Varanasi Cantonment.)

GETTING AROUND **By Auto-Rickshaw & Cycle-Rickshaw** The narrow lanes and extremely crowded streets of the "old city" and the lanes in and around Godaulia are penetrable only by two-wheelers and extremely determined cycle-rickshaws. These are also useful—if sometimes bone-jarring—ways of getting from your hotel to the area near the ghats and other attractions. Once at (or near) the ghats, set off on foot. Bear in mind that Varanasi is a city of transport tricksters, and there is little chance of escaping at least one rickshaw-related con job. Ask your hotel what the current going rate is for any trip in either an auto- or cycle-rickshaw, and bargain for the correct fare. Be further warned that rickshaw-*wallahs* will readily agree to take you somewhere without the faintest idea where it is. Once you've been onboard for several minutes, you will suddenly be asked where it is you want to go; to avoid falling into this annoying and time-wasting trap, ensure that the driver can repeat the name of your destination to you in recognizable English. To hire a car and driver, expect to pay at least Rs 375 ($8) half day or Rs 750 ($16) full day.

GUIDED TOURS At press time, the city offered no organized tours. We certainly recommend that you explore the area with a personal guide, if only to know which temples you can enter or which street food to sample, and to help avoid getting lost or conned. **Dhananjay (Deejay) Singh** is a government-approved guide who is a font of knowledge and an absolutely charming host; contact him at 🕐 **0542/222-475.** (Explore the old city on foot or by boat, then arrange a car.) Alternatively, you can arrange both guide and car through your hotel, or contact the **Tourist Office** (see "Visitor Information," above) to arrange for an approved guide and vehicle (🕐 **0542/234-3744**). To hire a boat (with oarsman), head for Dahsaswamedh; the price should be Rs 50 ($1.05) per hour.

FESTIVALS Varanasi is in many ways like a huge trippy trance party that started centuries ago and has just kept going, its revelers refusing to discard their costumes and come down to earth. So there's no real reason to time your visit with a festival—on the contrary, any increase in numbers is worth avoiding. That said, the huge **Dev Deepavali** is by all accounts a spectacle, held during the full moon in November, when almost every ghat and building is covered in glowing earthen lamps, and the river is aglitter with floating candles (but with about 100,000 pilgrims about, you may never even get to the river). Other auspicious occasions are **Mahashivatri** (Jan/Feb), **Holi** (Mar/Apr), **Ganga Dasha-hara** (May/June), and **Sri Krishna Janmashtami** (Sept/Nov).

WHAT TO SEE & DO

If you do only one thing in Varanasi, take a **boat cruise** past the ghats at dawn (see below); you can repeat this at sunset or, better still, head for **Dashaswamedh Ghat** to watch the **Ganga Fire Arti.** For 45 minutes, priests perform age-old prayer rituals with conch shells and burning braziers accompanied by drummers, while children hawk candles for you to light and set adrift. Aside from these two must-sees, you should set aside some time to wander the ancient lanes of the **old city,** particularly those centered around the **Kashi Vishwanath Temple** (see below)—but a few hours of picking your way past cow pats

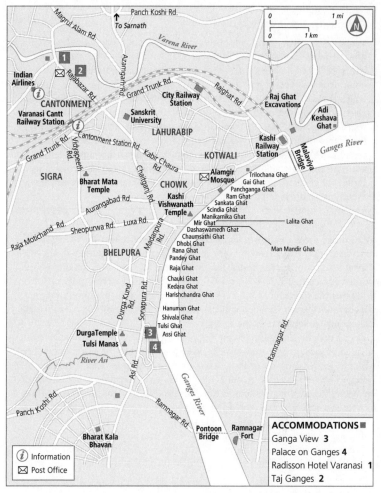

amid the incessant din of clanging temple gongs, not to mention striking out to view the 24-hour cremations at **Manikarnika Ghat,** is likely to have you craving some peace and solitude. Hire a car and visit **Sarnath,** where Buddha first revealed his Eightfold Path to Nirvana, or explore the fascinating collection in the **Bharat Kala Bhavan Museum** at the Hindu University. Both experiences are enriched by having a good guide with you.

Ramnagar Fort (Rs 7/15¢), the palace of the former Maharaja of Varanasi, is billed as another worthwhile attraction. Although the actual palace is beautiful in a run-down sort of way, and the location (the only Varanasi site on the east bank of the river) is lovely, the museum is filled with dusty, moth-eaten and decaying exhibits, such as the once ornate *howdas* (elephant seats) that transported the royal family—fascinating in a way to see such beauty so discarded. Do stop for a glance at the palace's grand Durbar Hall, though it's hard to see through the filthy windows. The lack of care says much about the dedication of the current young maharaja. Although he is said to involve himself in local

---

Moments Up in Flames

You need a pretty strong constitution to hang around Varanasi's burning ghats (**Harish Chandar** or **Manikarnika** ghats) and watch a human corpse, wrapped in little more than a sheet, being cremated in public view. Bodies are burned around the clock at these famous open-air cremation sites, which draw a constant crowd of grievers, curious pilgrims, gawking travelers, and confused cows. Only Varanasi's "Untouchables" are allowed to touch the bodies, placing them on wood piles, where they are covered with more logs (for a fee you are told the kinds of wood used and their significance) before being doused in a flammable paste and lightly coated with incense powder—the latter used to disguise the smell of burning flesh. No photography is allowed, and you are expected to treat the mourners with the respect their grief deserves.

---

tourism, his name certainly does not enjoy the reverence that the maharajas of Rajasthan still evoke. Last but not least of Varanasi's fascinating sights, the **Bharat Mata,** or **Mother India Temple** (located just north of the old city) is worth highlighting, if only because it is the incarnation of the spoken Hindu belief that the very land of India is sacred (ironic, given the pollution). Pilgrims walk around a large relief map of the subcontinent before Partition, featuring all its holy *tirthas,* mountains, and rivers.

If you have the energy, note that Varanasi has produced some of India's most talented musicians (the great Ravi Shankar was born here; if you're unfamiliar with his genius, purchase without delay the CD *Chants of India,* produced by George Harrison—highly recommended). Ask your hotel what performances are being hosted while you are in town, or head for the **International Music Centre** in Ganesh Mahal on Wednesday and Saturday for live Indian classical music performances by up-and-coming artists.

If you'd like to learn to play the **tabla** (set of two small drums) in Varanasi, which is renowned for its tabla merchants, head for the **Triveni Music Centre** (D24/38 Pandey Ghat) and ask for Nandlal. Nandlal and his father also stage regular concerts at Triveni.

CRUISING THE GHATS ✸✸✸

Drifting along the Ganges, admiring the densely textured backdrop of 18th- and 19th-century temples and palaces that line the 90-odd bathing ghats, you will be confronted with one of the most spiritually uplifting or downright weird tableaus on the entire crazy subcontinent: Down below, waist-deep pilgrims raise their arms in supplication, priests meditate by staring directly into the rising sun or are frozen in complicated yoga positions, wrestlers limber up, and disinterested onlookers toss live rats from the towering walls of the old city, among other assorted goings-on. Note that you'll need to get here between 4:30am and 6am (check sunrise times with your hotel, as well as the time it takes to get to the ghats), so plan an early wake-up call. You should be able to hire a boat anywhere along the ghats, but most people either catch one from **Assi Ghat,** the southernmost ghat, or—particularly if you're staying in the Cantonment area— from **Dashaswamedh** (meaning "10-horse-sacrifice," referring to an ancient sacrifice performed by Brahma). Situated roughly halfway, this is the most accessible and popular ghat and is always crawling with pilgrims, hawkers, and priests surveying the scene from under bamboo umbrellas. Boats here operate at a fixed rate (at press time) of Rs 50 ($1.05) per hour. The following descriptions of the 100-odd ghats assume that you will leave from here; note that it's worth traveling both north and south. You can do another trip in the evening as the sun is setting, but don't travel too far—no boating is allowed after sunset.

Heading North from Dashaswamedh Ghat   From here you pass **Man Mandir Ghat** which, along with the beautiful palace that overlooks it, was built by the Maharaja Man Singh of Amber in 1600 (Jai Singh, who built the Jantar Mantars, converted the palace into an observatory in 1710; it's open daily 9:30am–5pm). Next is **Mir Ghat,** where the New Vishwanath Temple, Vishalakshi shrine, and Dharma Kupa (where the Lord of Death relinquished his hold over those who die in Varanasi), are found. North lies **Lalita Ghat,** with its distinctive Nepalese Temple, and then the "burning" **Manikarnika Ghat,** the principal and favored cremation grounds of Varanasi, where you can see funeral-pyre flames burning 24 hours, tended by the *doms,* or "Untouchables"—touching the dead is considered polluting to all but these low castes. Boats are requested to keep their distance as a sign of respect. On this ghat is the venerated **Manikarnika Kund,** the world's first *tirtha* (sacred place), said to have been dug out by Vishnu, whose sweat filled it as he created the world as ordered by Shiva. Some say that Shiva shivered in delight when he saw what Vishnu had created, dropping an earring into the pool; others say that it was the earring of Sati, Shiva's dead wife, hence the name Manikarnika: "jeweled earring." Between the Kund and the ghat is what is supposed to be Vishnu's footprint. Adjacent is **Scindia Ghat,** with its distinctive half-submerged Shiva temple, toppled by weight, then **Ram Ghat** and **Panchganga Ghat** (said to be empowered by the five mythical streams that flow here into the Ganges), and one of the five *tirthas* that pilgrims need to perform rituals at. Behind the ghat glowers the **Alamgir Mosque,** built by Aurangzeb on a Hindu temple he destroyed; note also the almost submerged cells where the Kashi pundits (priests) are freeze-framed in meditation poses. Proceed from here to **Gai, Trilochana,** and **Raj** ghats, but it's best (if you still want to proceed south) to turn back at Panchganga (or explore the north banks further on foot).

Heading South   Passing the **Chaumsathi Ghat,** where the temple houses images of Kali and Durga, and **Dhobi Ghat,** alive with the sound of laundrymen rhythmically beating clothing that have been "purified" by the Ganges, you come to **Kedara Ghat,** notable for its red-and-white-striped South Indian–style temple. Farther south lie **Harishchandra Ghat,** Varanasi's second cremation ghat (though

---

(Fun Fact The Polluted Elixir of Life

According to religious belief, the Ganges is *amrita,* elixir of life, "cleanser of sin," "eternal womb," and "purifier of souls." Even from a scientific point of view, the river once had an almost miraculous ability to purify itself—up to 100 years ago, microbes such as cholera could not survive in these sacred waters. Sadly, the Ganges is today one of the most polluted rivers in the world. This is mostly due to the chemical toxins dumped by industrial factories that line the river, but Varanasi's ancient sewers and a population with equally ancient attitudes toward waste disposal (including the dumping of an annual estimated 45,000 uncremated corpses) are problems the Uttar Pradesh Water Board struggles to overcome.

less popular because it also houses an electric crematorium), and **Tulsi Ghat,** named in honor of Goswami Tulsidas, a revered Hindu poet. Nearby is **Lolark Kund,** where childless women come to bathe and pray for progeny. The final stop (or the first, if your accommodations options make a south-north journey more convenient) is the **Assi Ghat,** a simple clay bank situated at the confluence of the Ganga and Assi rivers. From here you can walk to **Durga Temple,** which lies farther west from the ghat. *Note:* If you want to walk from Assi Ghat to Dashaswamedh, the trip will take a leisurely 60 to 90 minutes.

Kashi Vishwanath Temple ★★   Of the more than 2,000 temples in Varanasi, the most important is Kashi Vishwanath Temple, or "Golden Temple," dedicated to Lord Shiva, the presiding deity of the city. Because of repeated destruction by the invading sultans and later by Aurangzeb, the current Vishwanath is a relatively modern building: It was built in 1777 by the Maharani of Indore, and the *shikhara* (spire) and ceilings were plated with 820kg (1,808 lb.) of gold, a gift from the Maharaja Ranjit Singh, in 1839. Five major *aartis* are held daily, but the temple is always abuzz with worshippers. Sadly, non-Hindus may not enter, but by taking a stroll through the Vishwanath Gali (lane) that runs the length of it, you can get a glimpse of the interior, which exudes pungent smells and constant noise. For a small donation, you can also climb to one of the second floors or rooftops of the shops that line the lane and get a good view. Note that adjacent is the **Gyanvapi Mosque,** built by Aurangzeb on a Hindu temple site and heavily guarded to ensure that no trouble erupts. Ironically, this is also the starting point for many pilgrims on their quest to visit all the *tirthas* in a ritual journey, accompanied by a priest who keeps reciting the *sankalpa,* or "declaration of intent." Nearby is the **Annapurna Temple,** dedicated to Shakti.

Vishwanath Gali. Closed to non-Hindus.

Bharat Kala Bhavan Museum ★★   As is usually the case in India, this museum suffers from poor curatorship, with exhibits—which are marvelous—haphazardly displayed and poorly labeled. You may even have trouble persuading the guards to turn all the lights on—hence the need for a good guide. The miniature-painting collection is superb, as are many of the Hindu and Buddhist sculptures and Mughal artifacts, though again, without a guide there is no way to know, for instance, that the otherwise nondescript coin behind the glass was minted by the Mughal emperor Akbar—and in keeping with his legendary religious tolerance, it has a Hindu symbol printed on the one side and an Islamic on the other. Set aside 2 hours to explore.

Varanasi Hindu University. July–Apr, Mon–Sat 11am–4pm. May and June, closes at 12:30pm. Admission Rs 40 (85¢).

Sarnath ★   After gaining enlightenment, this is where Buddha gave his first sermon some 2,500 years ago, and he continued to return here with his followers. For many centuries this was a Buddhist center of learning, housing some 3,000 monks, but successive Muslim invasions and later lootings destroyed the monasteries and much of the art. Today it still attracts many pilgrims, but—unless you're very familiar with Buddha's personal history or are an archaeologist—the site itself is nowhere near as inspiring as his teachings. The most impressive sight is the **Dhamekh Stupa,** if only for its sheer age. Built around A.D. 500, with a massive girth, it still towers 31m (102 ft.) into the air and is said to mark the very spot where Buddha revealed his Eightfold Path leading to nirvana. The ruins of the **Dharmarajika Stupa** lie immediately north of the entrance. Beyond is the **Ashokan Pillar**—the *stupa* is said to have been one of 28 built by Ashoka, the 3rd-century-B.C. Mauryan king and bloodthirsty warrior who was to become one of the most passionate converts to Buddhism. Beyond these are the ruins of monasteries. Across the road from the entrance to the main site is the **Sarnath Archaeological Museum,** where you can view the four-headed lion that once topped the Ashoka Pillar. The lion, with the wheel beneath representing Buddha's "wheel of dharma," is today the national emblem for India. East of the Dhamek Stupa is the **Mulagandha Kuti,** which houses an image of Buddha (against his wishes, images of Buddha abounded after his death). The walls contain frescoes pertaining to his life history—a good crash course for the novice if accompanied by a guide.

Sarnath is 10km (6¼ miles) north of Varanasi. Admission Rs 100 ($2.10). Daily 9am–5pm. Museum Sat–Thurs 10am–5pm.

WHERE TO STAY

In a general sense, you have two options: You can stay in one of the waterfront lodgings, most of which (with the exception of the two reviewed below) are very basic; or you can spend the night in the relative peace and comfort of the Cantonment area, where the most "luxurious" options are. Still, other than those reviewed below, the Cantonment hotels are all looking very frayed if not downright decaying. The downside of staying in the Cantonment is that you feel very cut off from the real Varanasi, and require an earlier morning wake-up call to get to the ghats; for the sunset *arti,* when the streets are often jammed, it may take 30 minutes to get there, and you'll walk the last part. Staying on the Ganges means you have no chance of unwinding at a pool, but if you manage to bag a river-facing room you will have the serenity of a waterfront view, with the surreal experience of Varanasi on your doorstep. *Note:* Staying in one of the budget hotels away from the ghats is not advisable unless you're used to budget traveling; many have no windows, and the noise is incessant.

CANTONMENT

Radisson Hotel Varanasi ★★ *(Value)*   Varanasi's newest top-end hotel is giving Taj Ganges (see below) a real run for its money with its fresh, relatively stylish accommodations for (at press time) a great deal less money. Guest rooms are large and comfortable (the thick mattresses are the best in town), with thick drapes and chocolate-brown furniture offset by brushed orange walls. The green marble bathrooms—also the best in town—are moderately proportioned, with green marble floors and gleaming fittings. There's also a full spa and a smallish pool with wooden deck chairs and its own bar; complimentary breakfasts are served in the bright sunflower-themed coffee shop. The free railway station transfer is very convenient if you're arriving by overnight train from Delhi.

The Mall, Cantonment, Varanasi 221 002. © 0542/250-1515. Fax 0542/250-1516. www.radisson.com. radvar@ sify.com. 117 units. Doubles, including breakfast and railway transfers: High season (Oct–Apr): $65 superior room; $125 suite. Low season: $55–$100; $10 extra bed. **Amenities:** 2 restaurants; bar; pool; travel desk; foreign exchange; 24-hr. room service; babysitting; doctor-on-call. *In room:* A/C, TV, dataport, minibar, tea- and coffee-making facilities, hair dryer, iron and ironing board.

Taj Ganges ★★   Before the Radisson opened, Taj Ganges was undisputedly the best hotel in town, but this had more to do with the pathetic competition than any superior features. Within an ugly 1970s monolith, rooms are small and look a little tired; the exceptions are the top-end suites (book no. 527, which occupies a top corner and is very spacious and gracious, albeit old-fashioned). What distinguishes this old five-star stalwart are service and the vast array of amenities, as well as a real passion for the region; the hotel hires the best guides in the city, shopping tips are excellent, and the travel desk will arrange tours as far afield as Bodgaya. It also has sprawling grounds (5 hectares/12 acres) and the best restaurant in town (this does not mean that the meal will be the best you have in India). Note that the Taj Ganges offers the most romantic Ganges boat tour in town: A beautiful old horse-drawn carriage, once belonging to the maharajas, clip-clops through the old city to the ghats in style, after which you board the most luxurious boat on the Ganges, with a mattressed rooftop on which you can recline in comfort while watching the surreal scenes drift by. There are plans to turn the **Nadesar Palace** (on the grounds) into luxurious suites, which will give it the edge it needs over the modern Radissons of the world.

Nadesar Palace, Varanasi 221 002. ☎ **0542/234-5100**, -5117, or -8067. Fax 0542/220-4898. www.tajhotels. com. 130 units. Doubles: $130 "superior" (standard); $140 large; $165–$190 suites; $20 extra person. AE, MC, V. **Amenities:** 2 restaurants; bar; pool; tennis; badminton; table tennis; yoga; travel desk; 24-hr. room service; massage; laundry; doctor-on-call; astrologer. *In room:* A/C, TV, minibar.

WATERFRONT

Ganga View Guesthouse 🔎🔎 *(Value)* You're required to remove your shoes upon entering this lovely colonial lodge at the edge of the Ganges, and it's an appropriate gesture of respect given the effort that has turned this budget guest-house—the best on the Ganges—into such a comfortable haven. In fact, it's so popular with certain repeat guests (many of them artists and musicians) that you'd do well to book your room up to a year in advance. The gorgeous, simple guest rooms feature marble floors and French doors that open onto enclosed cor-ridors filled with ornamental columns, charming bric-a-brac, antique furniture, and animal trophies. Straw mats and colorful Indian throws add character to the tiny bedrooms. There is no formal dining area, but room service is available. A delightful covered courtyard is stuffed full of portraits, religious artifacts, memo-rabilia, objets d'art, and books. Upstairs, an open-air terrace packed with potted plants and stylish cane furniture has excellent views of activity at the ghats.

Asi Ghat, Varanasi 221 006. ☎ **0542/231-3218**. Fax 0542/236-9695. 12 units. Doubles: Rs 1,500 ($33) A/C; Rs 1,000 ($22) non-A/C. No credit cards. **Amenities:** Musical performances; taxi and sightseeing arrange-ments; room service; laundry. *In room:* A/C (half).

Palace on Ganges 🔎 It's no palace, but for the waterfront this is an elegant and smart (it only opened in Oct 2002) option. Guest rooms are small but lovely, with marble floors and rugs, king-size beds with hard foam mattresses, and the best amenities on the Ganges. Walls are decorated with artworks reflect-ing aspects of different Indian heritage sites, and each room is a tribute to a dif-ferent regional style. Bathrooms, which only have showers, are done in colorful tiles. The heritage theme is carried throughout, with polished brown marble stairways, dark wood paneling, and intricately carved period furniture featuring inlaid decorative tiles. Although its location overlooking the Ganges is one of the selling points of the hotel, views from the rooftop terrace include an unpleasant garbage dump at the water's edge—this is scheduled to be converted into a gar-den by 2004, but don't hold your breath (or do).

B-1/158 Assighat, Varanasi 221 001. ☎ **0542/231-5050**, -4304, or -4305. Fax 0542/231-4306 or 0542/ 220-4898. www.palaceonganges.com. 22 units. Doubles: Rs 2,990 ($66). AE, MC, V. **Amenities:** Restaurant; travel desk; car hire; 24-hr. room service; laundry; doctor-on-call. *In room:* A/C, TV, minibar.

WHERE TO DINE

Varanasi's best and smartest restaurant is **Varuna** (☎ **0542/234-5100**), in the Taj Ganges, which features a vast menu of Indian specialties (illustrated with

Moments **Street Dentistry**

Opposite the elaborately carved facade of the peaceful **Phulwari Restaurant** (opposite Jaipuria Dharamshala, D 37/33 Baradeo, Godowlia; © **0542/ 240-0286**), be on the lookout for one of Varanasi's street dentists. Barechested and dreadlocked, this old man pulls teeth and does makeshift fillings at the side of the busy road. With the help of his young trainee assistant, he also applies dentures using "Rapid Repair" acrylic paste. If you're not too squeamish, hang around to watch him deftly pull a tooth using a pair of pliers.

chilies to indicate those that are super-strength), a comfortable air-conditioned interior, and helpful service. For the works, served on a traditional Varanasi silver platter, order the Satvik Thali (Rs 425/$9.25). That said, this is very much a hotel restaurant, and you may not be in the Cantonment area at lunchtime. For an authentic yet hygienic Varanasi meal while exploring the old city, head for one of the restaurants below.

Bread of Life Bakery & Restaurant ☆ BAKERY/INTERNATIONAL CAFE This restaurant was established by James and Monika Hetherington, an American interior designer and a German flight attendant. The decor is a tad sterile (fake African violets on white-vinyl-top tables), but the windows and small roadside terrace overlook an interesting street. You can enjoy wholesome Western dishes and freshly baked breads and muffins knowing that you are making a positive contribution—all profits go to local charities, including the Mother Teresa Hospice. Daily specials include steaming-hot vegetable moussaka, chickpea goulash, ratatouille, and warm Portuguese salad. Satisfy your sweet-tooth craving with a generous helping of authentic German Black Forest cake. Hot dishes take a while to arrive, so you can be certain that everything is freshly prepared and, in a city known for food-related mishaps, that hygiene is a priority. Thick and fruity, the banana *lassi* is particularly good.

B3/322 Shivala, Varanasi 221 001. © 0542/227-5012. www.bolbar.com. Main courses Rs 50–Rs 110 ($1.05–$2.30). Daily specials around Rs 80 ($1.70). No credit cards. Daily 9am–9pm.

The Keshari Restaurant *Value* INDIAN A stern-looking, bespectacled clerk sits counting cash at the entrance of this busy, cramped restaurant (ideal if you're exploring the old city) hidden away down a near-impossible-to-find back street. Inside, fans hover overhead and an ancient cooling system blasts away while waiters dash between tables packed with locals, pilgrims, and bewildered foreigners. There's a huge selection of Indian, Chinese, and Continental dishes on offer, but stick to Indian fare, which includes biryanis, *pulao,* and a selection of breads. Try a *thali* (multicourse platter); have the huge Keshari thali if you're particularly ravenous. The Keshari special *dosa* (pancake) is filled with creamy *paneer* (cheese) and cashew nuts. *Lassis* are fantastic, with chunks of real fruit. To get here, head down the alleyway opposite the La-Ra Hotel.

Off Dasashwamedh Rd., near Godaulia crossing. © 0542/40-1472. Main courses Rs 30–Rs 65 (60¢–$1.35); thali Rs 100 ($2.10). No credit cards. Daily 9am–10:30pm.

SHOPPING

Varanasi is famous above all for its silk—every Indian bride wants to marry wearing a Benares sari, and around 3,000kg (6,614 lb.) of silk is consumed by the weaving units daily. Wander through the old city, or ask at your hotel or the tourist office for recommended wholesalers. **Silk Ways** (© 0542/221-0791), near Chhave Mahal Cinema, has the most gossamer-like scarves, among other things. Or head for the following recommended sari shops in Chowk: **Narayan Das Jagdish Das** (© 0542/240-0561 or -0593); **Ushnak Mal Mool Chand** (© 0542/227-6253); or **Quddus & Sons** (cellphone: © 98-3905-5001). You can also try **Kabir Sarees** in Madanpura (© 0542/240-1971) or **Banarsi Saree. com** in Rathyatra (Varanasi © 0542/236-1464 or -1465).

4 Lucknow

497km (308 miles) SE of Delhi

Situated on the banks of the Gomti River, Lucknow, capital of Uttar Pradesh, has a relatively calm disposition, its urbane gentility and relative absence of beggars and touts a welcome change from the heady assault that so marks the experience in more popular North Indian cities. Lucknowites are in fact given to a peculiar strain of pomposity that seems entirely out of place in the 21st century—locals call out to you in *pukka* high-falutin' English "Good evening" at three in the afternoon, and a firm "How are you, gentleman?" is popular among locals keen to demonstrate their eloquent English, no matter how limited it really is.

Lucknow owes its sense of pride and heritage to the cultured Avadh Nawabs: A minor dynasty founded by the Persian aristocrat Nawab Saadat Khan Burhan-ul-Mulk, the *nawabs* ruled the independent state of Avadh (or Oudh, as the British called it), which grew in splendor—so much so that by the middle of the 18th century (coinciding with the decline of Delhi), Lucknow was India's largest and most prosperous city, filled with grandiose palaces, gilded cupolas, and pleasure gardens. It was to retain this reputation for almost a century—in 1850 a correspondent for *The Times* of London favorably compared Lucknow with Rome, Athens, and Constantinople. While the nawabs were known as men of refinement and taste, fond of poetry and courtly dance, they had some decadent predilections, highlighted by the last nawab's weakness for *muta*, temporary marriages that often lasted a single night.

When the British summarily unseated the last nawab and annexed Avadh in 1856, it helped spark the notorious Mutiny, known in India as the First War of Independence, during which 2,000 people were killed on the grounds of Lucknow's Residency. Much of Lucknow's former glory was further dissipated when, after Partition in 1947, the city's cultured elite emigrated en masse to Pakistan. Now the capital of a state plagued with corruption, Lucknow continues to draw the spotlight for the various political intrigues played out here by the state government.

ESSENTIALS

VISITOR INFORMATION　There's a **U.P. Tourism Reception Counter** (© 0522/225-2533) at Charbagh Station. The **U.P. Tourism Regional Office** (© 0522/263-8105) is at 10 Station Rd.; best to browse www.lucknowonline. com before your visit.

GETTING THERE　By car, the trip from Delhi takes roughly 10 hours, by bus 12 hours; far better to fly. Lucknow's **Amausi Airport** is 14km (9 miles) from the town center (Rs 150–Rs 250/$3.15–$5.35 for a prepaid taxi into town). Lucknow is served by all the main domestic airlines. Flights from Delhi take an hour. Other connected cities include Mumbai, Kolkata, Chennai, Bangalore, Hyderabad, Ahmedabad, and Varanasi. The **Lucknow Mail** leaves Delhi at 10pm and arrives in Lucknow at 7:05am the following day. Alternatively, enjoy the scenery by catching the **Lucknow Shatabdi Express** at 6:20am; the train pulls in at Lucknow's **Charbagh Station** at 12:10pm.

GETTING AROUND   By Taxi & Auto-Rickshaw   You can see just about everything Lucknow has to offer in half a day. Hire an auto-rickshaw or a taxi with a driver for the duration; be sure to settle the price in advance.

GUIDED TOURS & TRAVEL AGENTS   One of the most reputable travel agents in Lucknow is **Tornos House** (© 0522/238-0610; tornos@satyam. net.in), which supplies transport and keen guides who can take you to little-known places of interest. If you're lucky, Earl Figg, one of the directors of Tornos, will be available to show you around; ask for him by name. For around Rs 75 ($1.60), you can join the **U.P. Tourism** bus tour of Lucknow, taking in the city's most popular sights, including the Residency, the three Imambaras, the Clock Tower, the Picture Gallery, and the Martyr's Memorial. The tour begins at Hotel Gomti. **Sita World Travel** (Rana Pratap Marg; © 0522/220-9611) is a consistently reliable national travel agent.

FESTIVALS   Rooted in Shia Muslim traditions, Lucknow enjoys some unique customs, the most significant of which is **Muharram,** a festival that commemorates the martyrdom of Imam Hussein, the Prophet's grandson. Whereas in other parts of the world, Muharram lasts between 10 and 12 days, in Lucknow it extends over 2 months and 8 days. During this time, people gather in the Shia *imambaras* in the presence of *taazias* (replicas of the tombs of the martyrs), and it's not uncommon to see men flagellating themselves with knives and chains and even tearing open their skulls as symbolic acts of their need to be forgiven for being unable to help defend the martyr.

THINGS TO SEE & DO

You can easily see Lucknow's significant sights in a morning. At the top of the list is the **Bara (Great) Imambara** (see below). Your ticket also provides access to the nearby **Chhota (Little) Imambara** ✿, which contains the tombs of its creator, Mohammed Ali Shah and his mother. Built in 1837, it features opulent and ornate interiors with colorful stucco walls, gilt-edged mirrors, a golden domed silver pulpit *(mimbar),* and chandeliers that are lit during Muharram.

La Martinière College ✿✿, a lovely stone mansion off Kalidas Marg, is one of the architectural highlights of Lucknow, and although it's not really open to visitors, you can admire the facade and wander around the grounds (permission to visit can be arranged in advance; call the principal at © 0522/222-3863). Huge, rampant stone lions with gaping jaws stand upon the mansion gables, and it's said that fires were lit to illuminate the glaring eyes of these beasts to scare off the wild animals of the surrounding swamps.

Although **The Residency** (M.G. Rd.; Rs 100/$2.10; daily 7am–5:30pm) is billed as one of the city's top attractions, the ruins here hold little appeal unless you're intimate with their history. The home of the British Resident appointed to look into the affairs of the Oudh, where more than 2,000 British residents and Indians loyal to the Raj died during the Mutiny, it bears the scars of fierce bombardment, and the sprawling complex of burnt-out, skeletal buildings is in pretty much the same state as the day the siege ended. Feel free to skip this, and head for the bazaars where you can experience Lucknow's colorful daily life. In the predominantly Shiite Muslim area of the Chowk, women in black *burkas* go about their daily shopping, while merchants in white prayer caps operate their businesses in premises downstairs from their family homes, protected from the sun by wooden shutters and *jali* screens.

Lucknow is famous for *attar,* the scented oils used to make perfumes. Used by Muslim women, the oils are made from a magnificent variety of flowers and fruits; some fragrances are created to smell like the earth during monsoon rains. Chowk Bazaar is filled with attar shops; to purchase a sample, visit **Izhar Ahmad & Sons,** or the granddaddy of them all, **Azam Ali-Alam Ali Industry,** which has been producing attars for centuries.

Try to take lunch at either branch of the famous **Tunday Kababi** (see "Where to Dine," below), which serves cheap, delicious bazaar food.

Bara Imambara ★★ Built in 1784, Lucknow's most significant monument is a large edifice of grandiose proportions, built of *lakhauri* bricks plastered with lime and decorated with molding. The Great Imambara houses what is said to be the largest vaulted hall in the world. The hall's interior is kept cool by massive hollow walls that also help lighten the load of the structure, completely unsupported by pillars or beams. Dripping with Belgian chandeliers and other ornate embellishments, the hall is where the *taziyas* (paper shrines representing the graves of Imam Hussain and the martyrs of Karbala) are kept when not being carried through the streets of the city each year during the solemn month of Muharram. Visitors to the Bara Imambara enter through the **Rumi Darwaza,** an 18m (60-ft.) tower that stands like a sentinel overlooking the city's grand monuments. For a truly atmospheric experience with fabulous views of the complex and of the surrounding neighborhood, head upstairs to the attic's labyrinthine maze called the *bulbulya;* just above this is a flat roof where you can relax and observe the city. Adjacent the Bara Imambara, the **Asafi Mosque** is off-limits to non-Muslims. Across from it is an atmospheric step well, or *bauli.*

Hussainabad. Admission Rs 10 (20¢). Open 7am–7pm; closed during Muharram.

WHERE TO STAY

La Place Park Inn ★ (*Value* Conveniently situated near the city center, this smart business hotel with a neoclassical facade may not have fantastic views or any real sense of history, but it offers comfortable, quiet, and spacious accommodations. Elegant and uncluttered, the deluxe guest rooms have green marble floors, smart sofas, and good, firm mattresses. Bathrooms are also a decent size, and have tubs. If you don't mind a few extra dollars, the executive rooms are fabulously large, with plenty of cupboard space, separate sitting areas, and wonderful king-size beds. Stylish, but hardly ostentatious, La Place features a reliable restaurant and public areas punctuated with watercolors and color lithographs illustrating Lucknow's past. The inn has no pool.

6 Shahnajaf Rd., Lucknow 226 001. ✆ 0522/222-0220, 0522/228-2201, -2202, -2203, or -2204. Fax 0522/222-0522. www.parkinnlucknow.com. 50 units. Doubles: Rs 2,600 ($57) deluxe; Rs 3,200 ($72) executive; Rs 4,200 ($92) executive suite. AE, DC, MC, V. **Amenities:** Restaurant; bar; airport transfers; currency exchange; 24-hr. room service; laundry; doctor-on-call. *In room:* A/C, TV, minibar.

Taj Residency Lucknow ★★ Grandiose yet charming, this white neo-colonial-style building, set in vast landscaped gardens, is by far Lucknow's loveliest option. With its palatial white marble lobby and elegant architectural flourishes, it was originally conceived as a leisure hotel and is now aimed at business travelers and politicians. Accommodations are excellent; standard rooms are carpeted with high ceilings and plush furniture, and bathrooms have tubs and are scented with potpourri and hibiscus flowers. Ask for a room with a good view of Martinière College, or choose a ground-floor deluxe room for heaps of space, a king-size four-poster bed, and a private balcony. There's a great swimming pool, from where you can admire the hotel's arched and colonnaded rear facade.

Gomti Nagar, Lucknow 226 010. © **0522/239-3939**, -1201, -1202, or 1203. Fax 0522/239-2282 or -2465. www.tajhotels.com. 110 units. Doubles: $155 standard; $175 executive (includes breakfast); $215 deluxe; $300 suite; $20 extra bed. **Amenities:** 2 restaurants; bar; pool; fitness center (gymnasium, steam bath, Jacuzzi, massage); travel desk; sightseeing; guide service; car hire; currency exchange; shopping arcade; florist; salon; 24-hr. room service; babysitting; laundry; dry cleaning; doctor-on-call; photographer. *In room:* A/C, TV, minibar, tea- and coffee-making facilities, hair dryer.

WHERE TO DINE

Gastronomically inclined, the nawabs of Lucknow considered the skillful preparation of food an art form. Their kitchens (or *bawarchi khana*) took pride of place in the royal courts, and it's a matter of legend that Nawab Salar Jung paid his cook an exorbitant (at the time) Rs 1,200 ($26) per month. Today Lucknow is known for its rich, spicy meat dishes. Melt-in-the-mouth kebabs, biryanis, and tandoori chicken items are particularly favored, and cream, saffron, raisins, cashews, and almonds are all commonly used. A popular dessert is the royal bread-and-butter pudding, *shahi tukra*. The influence of the nawabs lives on not only in the city's two top hotel restaurants, but also in the bazaars at Chowk and Aminabad, where the busier stalls are excellent for traditional no-frills food.

Falaknuma ★★ LUCKNOWI On the ninth floor of the Clarks Hotel, Falaknuma—a popular choice with local diners—offers excellent views of the city, so be sure to grab a table near a window. Live Indian music is performed every night except Tuesday. It offers a good variety of mouthwatering Lucknowi specialties; if you've never had *kakori kebab,* made with minced lamb and mixed Indian spices, try it here with *roomali roti.* Also excellent is Avadhi *murgh korma,* spring chicken cooked in golden gravy that's rich and spicy. The host, Mr. Srivastava, has been keeping guests satisfied for over a decade.

Clarks Avadh, 8 Mahatma Gandhi Marg. © **0522/261-6500** through -6509. Main courses Rs 135–Rs 325 ($3–$7). AE, DC, MC, V. Daily 1–3:15pm and 8–11:15pm.

Oudhyana ★★★ LUCKNOWI/INDIAN Local chef Gulam Rasool has been preparing fabulous food for the Taj group for 2 decades. Ever since he returned to his hometown to work in the city's best fine-dining establishment, people have been coming from as far as Kanpur to enjoy his kebabs. Start with a soothing *thandai* (a chilled blend of chopped almonds, cashew nuts, and pistachios blended with milk and a dash of pepper), and then move on to a kebab platter while sampling rich saffron-flavored bread *(sheermal),* fresh from the tandoor. Favorites include *galawat ke kebab* (pan-fried medallions of minced lamb), *kakori kebab* (minced lamb blended with saffron, rose petals, and cardamom), and *murgh tikka "mirza hasnoo"* (chicken marinated in yogurt, flavored with saffron, and chargrilled with exotic spices). Alternative meat dishes include *murgh ambari,* chicken tikka prepared with a marinade of royal cumin and tomato gravy; and *nargisi kofta,* an Avadhi dish with lamb and egg. Leave room for a traditional Lucknowi dessert—deep-fried bread soaked in sweetened milk and saffron-flavored *rabri,* and finished with pistachios and almonds.

Taj Residency, Gomti Nagar. © **0522/239-3939**. Reservations recommended for dining between 8 and 9pm. Main courses Rs 140–Rs 425 ($3–$9.25). AE, DC, MC, V. Daily 12:30–3pm and 7:30–11:30pm.

Tunday Kababi ★★ *Moments* LUCKNOWI KEBABS Hectically popular, you'll recognize this bazaar-based hot spot by the scene out front; Tunday's chefs sweat over huge metallic ovens and grills, where they prepare delicious chicken for scores of expectant customers. Over a century old, this Muslim family-run establishment is named for an ancestor with a physical disability *(tunday)*. The place may look grubby and unkempt, but the mutton kebabs and tandoori chicken have represented the city at international food festivals.

Naaz Cinema Rd., Aminabad. (*0522/221-6535. Kebabs Rs 8–Rs 16 (15¢–35¢). Half tandoori chicken Rs 50 ($1.05). No credit cards. Daily 11am–11pm.

5 Khajuraho ★★★

600km (372 miles) SE of Delhi; 415km (257 miles) SW of Varanasi; 395km (245 miles) SE of Agra

Legend has it that when the Moon God saw the young maiden Hemavati bathing in a river, her beauty was such that he descended to earth to engage in a passionate affair. Before his return to the celestial realm, he swore she would bear a son who would one day erect a great temple to celebrate the beauty of their divine love. Thus the founder of the mighty Chandela dynasty, a robust clan of the warrior Rajputs, was born, and between A.D. 900 and 1100, the Chandela kings—who settled in remote Khajuraho, where they were clearly unhindered by the usual distractions of fighting off invading forces—built not one but 85 temples, almost all of them featuring exquisite sculptures of men and women joyfully engaging in the most intimate and erotic acts. The Chandelas held sway here until the start of the 13th century, when the Sultans of Delhi increased their hold over vast swaths of central North India. By the end of the 15th century, the temples were abandoned, hidden deep within thick jungle, until their accidental discovery by a British military adventurer in 1838. By this time, 7 centuries after the political decline of their Chandela creators, only 22 of the original 85 temples remained. Today these UNESCO World Heritage monuments are famous for their transgressive, taboo-breaking erotic sculptures, images that are almost as intimately associated with India as the Taj. But the temples also represent an outstanding synthesis of advanced architecture and refined sculpture, and their beauty means that a trip here should definitely be included in your North India itinerary, particularly if you plan to fly from Agra or Delhi to Varanasi.

ESSENTIALS

GETTING THERE & AWAY   By Air   It's most convenient to fly in from Delhi or Agra and fly on to Varanasi the following day. During the high season (winter), daily Indian Airlines and Jet Airways flights do exactly this. Khajuraho's

---

Fun Fact India's Ancient Sex Manual

Khajuraho's shops are filled with an endless variety of versions of the *Kama Sutra,* an ancient avatar of modern-day do-it-yourself sex manuals. With information about everything from "increasing the size of the male organ" to the benefits of "slaps and screams" and "bites and scratches," the ancient treatise on sensory pleasures—recorded by the scribe Vatsyayana from oral accounts sometime between the 1st and 6th century A.D.—remains the most famous Indian text in the world. The first English translation was published in 1883 by the Victorian adventurer Richard Burton, who adapted the text in order to dodge charges of obscenity; among other confusing details, he used the Sanskrit words *lingam* and *yoni* to denote the sexual organs.

airport is 3km (2 miles) from the town center; a taxi should cost Rs 100 ($2.10), an auto-rickshaw Rs 50 ($1.05).

By Train & Road We cannot sufficiently emphasize the appalling state of the roads in Madhya Pradesh. Avoid lengthy road travel at all costs and don't travel at night; rent the services of a sturdy 4WD and driver, and check that your vehicle has at least one spare wheel. If you're traveling from Delhi, Mumbai, or Chennai, you will disembark at Jhansi (175km/108 miles from Khajuraho). From New Delhi, catch the Bhopal Shatabdi Express, which leaves the capital at 6am and pulls in at Jhansi at 10:25am. From here, MPSRTC runs a bus service from Jhansi to Khajuraho, scheduled to meet the train from Delhi (Rs 150/ $3.15), or you can catch a taxi (Rs 1,500/$33) to Khajuraho (4 hr.). You can also rent a car and driver for a few days if you have plans to see more of the region—note that Orchha (20km/12 miles from Jhansi) is definitely worth a stop en route to Khajuraho (Orchha is discussed later in the chapter). If you're traveling from Mumbai, Kolkata, or Varanasi, you will arrive at Satna, which is 117km (72 miles) or 3 hours from town.

VISITOR INFORMATION MP Tourism (© 07686/274-051; mptkhaj@ sancharnet.in) is in the Chandela Cultural Centre, Khajuraho. Note that the state tourism website, **www.mptourism.com**, and **www.khajuraho-temples. com** are both excellent sources. A **Government of India tourism office** is located opposite the Western Group of Temples.

GETTING AROUND **By Taxi, Auto-Rickshaw, & Cycle-Rickshaw** You will be flooded with offers to take you from Khajuraho's airport to your accommodations; in return, touts and drivers expect you to use their services for the duration of your stay, and will even continue to lurk outside your hotel. Make it clear that yours is a one-time fare, and stick to cycle-rickshaws and walking for the duration of your stay. To visit the Panna temples, expect to pay Rs 700 ($15) for a taxi.

GUIDES Guides charge Rs 280 ($6) per half day and Rs 450 ($9.80) for a full day. You can hire the services of a reliable guide at **Raja Café** (opposite the Western Group of temples; see below). Alternatively, the MPSTDC offers a "Walkman Tour"—an audiocassette-assisted tour purchased at the MP Tourism counter at the entrance to the Western Group; this costs Rs 50 ($1.05), as well as a refundable deposit of Rs 500 ($11).

FESTIVALS The **Khajuraho Dance Festival** ★★ is held between February 25 and March 2, when the temples are transformed into a magical backdrop for India's top classical dancers, who perform traditional Odissi, Kuchipudi, and Bharatnatyam dance forms, as well as contemporary Indian dance styles. For up-to-date information, visit **www.khajuraho-temples.com**.

EXPLORING KHAJURAHO'S TEMPLES

Known for the profusion of sculptural embellishments on both exterior and interior walls, Khajuraho's temples are also recognizable for the exaggerated vertical sweep in the majority of the temples, with a series of *shikharas* (spires) that grow successively higher. Serving as both metaphoric and literal "stairways to heaven," these shikharas are believed to be a visual echo of the soaring Himalayan mountains, abode of Lord Shiva. Most of the sculpted temples are elevated on large plinths (often also shared by four smaller corner shrines), and follow the same five-part design. After admiring the raised entrance area, you will enter a

---

Tips **Services Unlimited**

As you wend your way around town, older teenage boys will try to "adopt" you by starting up polite conversations—a pattern you will quickly recognize—before getting down to the business of offering their services for a range of possible needs: tour guides, transport, bicycle hire, shopping assistance, advice, or a tour of the local village school. All are money-making enterprises of which you should be wary. On the other hand, there is little harm in enjoying the company and charm of a local host; best to simply make it clear that you have no intention of parting with your money and leave it to your new friend to decide whether or not to stick around.

---

colonnaded hall which leads to a smaller vestibule and then an inner courtyard, around which is an enclosed sanctum. You can circumnavigate (move around the temple in a clockwise direction, in the manner of the ritual *pradakshina*, with your right shoulder nearest the temple building) the sanctum to view the beautifully rendered friezes of gods, nymphs, animals, and energetically twisting bodies locked together in acts of hot-blooded passion.

Originally spread across a large open area, unprotected by walls, the temples— most of them built from sandstone lugged on bullock carts from the banks of the River Ken 30km (19 miles) away—are today roughly divided into three sections according to geographic location: the Western, Eastern, and Southern groups. The most spectacular—and those most obviously dripping with erotic sculpture—are within the Western Group. The Eastern Group is located near the old village, and the Southern Group, which is the most missable, lies south of this. As none of the temples outside the Western Group are likely to evoke quite the same delighted reaction, see these first if you're pushed for time or tired; they're also conveniently located near the majority of hotels. Try to enter as soon as they open (sunrise), not only for the quality of light but also to avoid the busloads of tourists who will almost certainly detract from the experience.

You can cover the Western Group in 2 hours. Amitabh Bachchan, arguably India's most popular screen icon, narrates the fascinating history of Khajuraho for the 50-minute **sound-and-light show** held here each night at 6:30pm. Try to time your visit to the Eastern Group for about 3 or 4pm, so you can enjoy the sunset while you return either to the Western Group or to the imminently more peaceful Chaturbhuj temple in the South Group. To save time and get the most out of the experience, an official guide—hired through the Raja Café, tourist office, or your hotel—is highly recommended; avoid all unofficial touts and guides. Note that you can rent an audiocassette-assisted tour, which is useful if you don't want to be accompanied by a guide.

WESTERN GROUP ★★★

As you make your way around the complex in a clockwise direction, the first important structure you'll encounter is the **Lakshmana Temple** ★★★, one of the three largest in Khajuraho. Built in commemoration of military victory and temporal power, it is thought to be one of the earliest Chandela temples, completed around A.D. 954, yet relatively intact. The structure is as high as it is long, and its raised platform is, like the entire temple, heavily decorated with a variety of sculptures that allude to the pleasures, pastimes, lifestyle, desires, and conquests of the Chandela dynasty. Here you will witness an astonishing diversity of scenes: horse-mounted hunters pursuing their prey, musicians providing lively entertainment for the court, couples drunk on love and liquor, female attendants fanning their king, elephants engaged in playful battle, soldiers on the march and, of course, amorous couples keeping themselves occupied in the most literal of pleasures. Higher up, above bands of images of Shiva and Vishnu, are the voluptuous depictions of women engaged in worldly activity while draped in little more than jewelry and gossamer-like garments.

Inside the temple, covered with more depictions of gorgeous women and deities in their various avatars and incarnations, light pours in through high balconies on each side of the structure, and shadows are cast seductively over the imaginatively carved walls. The main shrine was built to house the three-headed image of Vishnu-Vaikuntha, which features one human head and the head of two of Vishnu's avatars (incarnations), a lion and a boar.

Opposite the temple are two smaller structures, the **Devi Mandap** and the **Varaha Mandap** ☆. The latter is an open sandstone pavilion on a high platform with 14 pillars supporting a high pyramidal roof with a flat ceiling carved with lovely lotus designs. A large stone sculpture of Varaha, the incarnation of Vishnu as the Boar, dominates the space. Varaha's polished monolithic body is carved with hundreds of tiny Brahmanical gods and goddesses.

At the northeastern end of the Western Group complex, a number of magnificent temples are found in close proximity to one another. Thought to have been built between A.D. 1017 and 1029, the elegantly proportioned **Kandariya Mahadev Temple** ☆☆☆ is considered the finest temple in Khajuraho, with 872 statues adorning the interior and exterior. Within niches around the temple are images of Ganesh and the seven mother goddesses or *Sapta Matrikas*. Again, among the sculptures of Shiva and the other deities is a profusion of female figures engaged in daily activities made lovely by the sheer exuberance of the sculptural technique: A woman stretches, another plays with a ball, another admires her reflection in a mirror. You won't have to search too hard to find fascinating erotic panels; kissing, caressing couples are depicted with their bodies entwined in blissful union.

To enter the temple building, you pass through the beautiful entrance *toran;* sculpted from a single piece of stone, this is a floral garland that stems from the mouths of *makaras,* ever-watchful mythical crocodiles, and is carried across the doorway by flying nymphs. Within the temple chambers, the walls are covered with exquisite carvings and sculptures: Don't forget to look upward to appreciate the sculpted flower and leaf motifs of the ceilings. There's a Shiva lingam deep within the *garbha griha,* or "womb chamber"; devotees today place flowers on and around the lingam.

Next to the Kandariya Mahadev Temple is the small **Mahadev Shrine,** which features a sculpted figure of what is thought to be the emblem of the Chandela dynasty, a raging lion fighting with a kneeling figure. Alongside it is the **Devi Jagadambi Temple** ☆☆—note the graceful woman who stands half-naked as she interrupts her bath, possibly to catch a glimpse of Shiva's wedding procession. The southern wall includes a panel with a woman climbing up her lover's stout, standing body so that she can kiss him passionately. Although originally dedicated to Vishnu, the temple now houses a large image of Devi Jagadambi, the goddess of the universe, also known as Kali, one of the avatars of Shiva's divine consort. In both this and the nearby **Chitragupta Temple** ☆, images of Parvati and Shiva in the throes of amorous passion are symbolic of the "cosmic union that makes the world go round." Chitragupta, which was poorly renovated by the Maharaja of Chattarpur, is dedicated to Surya, the sun god; the relief carving around the entrance is the temple's highlight. Within the temple is the figure of Surya riding his sun chariot across the eternal sky.

Back near the entrance of the complex stands the **Temple of Vishvanatha** *⍟*, built in A.D. 1002 by King Dhanga, and notable for three female figures that decorate the building. One maiden plays the flute, her back sensuously exposed to the viewer, another cradles a baby, and the third has a parrot seated on her wrist. Opposite the main entrance of the temple is the **Nandi Pavilion** (or *mandap*), in which one of the largest figures of Shiva's companion, Nandi the bull, can be found, sculpted from a single piece of stone.

Outside the walls of the Western Group complex, but right alongside the Lakshman Temple, is the still-functioning **Matangeshvar Temple.** It is here that the annual Maha-Shivratri Festival culminates when the Shiva-Parvati marriage ceremony is accompanied by latter-day wedding rituals, lasting through the entire night in a fantastic collaboration of myth and reality.

Across the road from the entrance to the Western Group is the **Archaeological Museum,** with its modest selection of sculptures collected from various Khajuraho sites. The advantage of spending a few minutes here is that you get to see close-up details of types of carved figures that usually occur high up on the temple *shikharas.*

Main Rd., opposite the State Bank of India. Admission Rs 250 ($5.35). Daily 6:30am–sunset. English-language sound-and-light show Mar–Aug 7:30pm, Sept–Feb 7pm; Rs 200 ($4.30). Archaeological Museum open Sat–Thurs 10am–5pm; Rs 5 (10¢). No photography in the museum.

EASTERN GROUP

The Eastern Group comprises both Hindu and Jain temples. The entrance to the Jain **Shantinath Temple** is guarded by a pair of mythical lions; inside, you are confronted by esoteric charts detailing some of the finer points of Jain philosophy. Photographs of important sculptures and Jain architecture line some of the walls, while the individual shrine entrances are carved with amorous, nonerotic couples and other figures. The main shrine contains a large sculpted image of a naked saint. Throughout the temple, devotees place grains of rice and nuts as tributes at the feet of the various saints.

The **Parsvanatha Temple** *⍟* dates to the middle of the 10th century A.D. and is the finest and best preserved of Khajuraho's old Jain temples. Since Jainism promotes an ascetic doctrine, there are no erotic images here, but the sculptural decoration is rich nonetheless. In a large panel at the right side of the entrance are images of meditating and naked Jain saints *(tirthankaras),* while the temple exterior is covered in decorative sculptures of voluptuous maidens, embracing couples, and solo male figures representing various Hindu deities. This is a strong indication that the temple—which recalls the temples of the Western Group—was perhaps originally Hindu. In the same complex, the **Adinath Temple** has been modified and reconstructed with plastered masonry and even concrete.

Moving north to the Hindu temples, you will pass the **Ghantai Temple;** built in A.D. 1148, it is named for the pretty sculpted bells that adorn its pillars. Passing between the Javari Temple and the granite and sandstone "Brahma" Temple (more likely to be dedicated to Shiva given the presence of a linga), you come to the northernmost of the Eastern Group temples, the Hindu **Vamana Temple,** built between A.D. 1050 and 1075. Vamana is the short, plump, dwarf incarnation of Vishnu. The entrance to the inner sanctum of this temple is decorated with small erotic relief panels; within the sanctum you will see Vishnu in many forms, including the Buddha, believed to be one of his incarnations.

SOUTHERN GROUP

One of the last temples to be built, **Duladeo Temple** dates back to the 12th century A.D. but has been subjected to later restoration. Standing on the banks of the Khuddar stream, facing east, the temple is dedicated to Shiva. Elaborately crowned and ornamented *apsaras,* flying *vidyadharas,* crocodile-mounted *ashtavasu* figures, and sculptures of over-ornamented and stereotypically endowed characters in relatively shallow relief decorate the interior. Like the Parshvanath Temple, the walls of Duladeo feature a narrow band of sculptures that depict the celestial garland carriers and musicians in attendance at the wedding of Shiva and Parvati.

The unexceptional **Chaturbhuj Temple,** 3km (2 miles) south of Duladeo, sees very little traffic but has a remarkable sculpture of Vishnu and is a peaceful place at the best of times, not least at sunset. Nearby excavations continue to unearth new temple complexes, as Khajuraho keeps revealing more hidden gems.

EXCURSIONS

Panna National Park 🦌   A mere 27km (17 miles) from Khajuraho, Panna covers 542 sq. km (211 sq. miles) of dry deciduous forests, fed by the Ken River—jungles of teak, Indian ebony, and flame-of-the-forest trees alternate with wide-open grassy plains in what were once the hunting grounds of several royal families. Although Panna has as few as 25 tigers, sightings have begun to escalate in recent years, so this is a good place to visit if you're unlikely to make it to any other tiger reserve. You're certainly likely to encounter *nilgai,* Indian gazelle, *sambar,* and four-horned antelope; sightings are dramatically improved if you undertake a rather relaxing elephant safari. Adjacent the park is the ancient town of Panna, home to the largest diamond mines in Asia.

27km (17 miles) from Khajuraho. © 07732/252-134. Bookings through Forest Department, located at the park entrance. Park fees: Rs 200 ($4.30) admission; Rs 50 ($1.05) vehicle entry; Rs 75 ($1.60) guide; Rs 25 (50¢) still camera; Rs 200 ($4.30) video camera; Rs 300 ($6.50) elephant rides. Daily 6:30–10:30am and 3–5pm.

WHERE TO STAY

If you're simply overnighting, it's best to stay in the village, from where you can walk to the majority of temples—the Trident is your best bet here. For those who want a more romantic, earthy experience and a visit to Panna National Park, Ken River Lodge is the place to be. Be warned that at present there is no fabulous lodging option to be found here, though currently in the pipeline is the establishment of Khajuraho's first heritage accommodations, at the hitherto deserted 19th-century **Rajgarh Palace.** Situated some 25km (15 miles) from the village, at the foot of the Manijagarh Hills, this beautiful palace has exceptional views, and the end result is likely to be spectacular. You can get updated information about developments from the local tourism bureau.

IN KHAJURAHO

There are a few so-called luxury options situated along Khajuraho's main road; if they're not included below, it's because they really aren't worth it. A large strip of hotels and guesthouses is dedicated to backpackers; rooms vary considerably. Budget hunters should head for **Hotel Surya** (Jain Temple Rd.; © 07686/27-4145), where Rs 600 ($13) buys you a clean, spartan room with an air-conditioner and attached drench shower (ask for a room with a balcony from where you can watch early risers practice yoga in the garden).

Jass Trident ★★ *Value*   The service and atmosphere make this hotel—which has a bizarrely futuristic appearance from the outside—the best Khajuraho has to offer. Bright white marble-floored public spaces are decorated with attractive Indian artworks, and you can spend some time wandering through the passages studying the collection of large Mughal paintings. The beige-carpeted guest bedrooms are fairly spacious and modestly dressed in pale fabrics and dark wood. The three suites include enormous sitting rooms with sofas and tiny kitchenettes. All guest rooms have balconies and either garden, pool, or mountain views; those overlooking the pool on the first floor (reached via a twisting marble staircase with an impressive chandelier hanging from a domed ceiling) are best. In the new wing, rooms are decorated in pale blue hues and have minibars and balconies with mountain views. The low-key atmosphere is enhanced by friendly, helpful staff (this is part of the Oberoi group, after all) and the ambient Indian music that constantly drifts through the hotel.

By-Pass Rd., Khajuraho 471 606. © 07686/27-2344. Fax 07686/27-2345. www.oberoihotels.com. 93 units. Doubles: $60 standard; $100 suite. AE, DC, MC, V. **Amenities:** Restaurant; bar; pool; tennis court; health club; travel assistance; sightseeing; guides; car hire; airport transfers; currency exchange; shopping arcade; 24-hr. room service; babysitting; laundry; doctor-on-call. *In room:* A/C, TV. Some units have minibar; suites have kitchenette with fridge.

OUTSIDE KHAJURAHO

Ken River Lodge ★★ *Kids Value*   A short distance from the entrance to Panna National Park (about 30 min. from Khajuraho), this small resort (eight solid huttents and three larger villas) is located right on the river and has a great deal more charm than its pricier counterparts in town. Three kilometers (2 miles) off the main road, it's an ideal hideaway in a gorgeous forest setting, where fishing enthusiasts can cast a line and hope for one of India's famous fighting *mahseer*. Accommodations are novel: army-style tents with an attached two-level structure made of wood, stone, mud, and brick, with a children's bedroom upstairs and a large bathroom (shower only) downstairs. The main bedroom, which is tented (only some of which have water coolers), has grass mats, small rugs, and two large single beds (no doubles) with thin mattresses covered with Indian-style throws. Each tent also has a small private "porch." Tent no. 6 is the most secluded, while no. 1 is nearest the restaurant and bar. Meals are taken on a large wood-and-mud platform built into a series of trees alongside the river. A thatched roof, tribal-design moldings, and a treetop observation deck contribute to the resort's immense appeal. If this isn't good enough, private romantic dinners can be arranged on a tiny private island in the middle of the river.

Village Madla, District Panna 488 001. © 07732/27-5235. In Delhi contact Mr. Manav Khandiya (© 98-1002-4711). shyamindrasingh@yahoo.co.uk. 11 units. Rs 1,500 ($33) per person, all meals included; Rs 3,500 ($76) per person includes all meals and two all-inclusive safaris to Panna National Park; elephant rides extra. No credit cards. **Amenities:** Restaurant; bar; boating; fishing; tours and safaris; room service; laundry; doctor-on-call. *In room:* Water coolers (some units).

WHERE TO DINE

If you're down with a case of culinary homesickness, Khajuraho is awash with eateries proclaiming to serve "authentic" Italian dishes. Of these, **Mediterraneo** (Jain Temple Rd., opposite Surya Hotel; daily 7:30am–10:30pm; no credit cards), an alfresco rooftop restaurant, is your best bet. Gigantic letters along the side of the building exclaim MEDITERRANEO CHEF TRAINED IN ROME, and although this is certainly not true, the owner is from Rome, and the menu does offer a range of Italian favorites, including pizza (when available), pasta, and chicken dishes prepared with "Italian herbs."

Head Case?

Not sure who you are or where you're headed? **Shastri Di** is an aura and forehead analyst who will help you "know thyself better." He can be contacted through the Mediterraneo Restaurant (see above).

Apsara ECLECTIC/NORTH INDIAN   This smart and reliable restaurant at the Jass Trident hotel is the best place in town, particularly for North Indian cuisine (a range of other dishes is also available). With lovely views of the gardens and pool, and comfortable cane furniture, the atmosphere is relaxed and bright, enhanced by the charming maitre d'. Some of the recommended Indian options are a mulligatawny soup flavored with curry leaves; fish marinated in mustard-flavored yogurt and cooked in the clay oven; potatoes stuffed with cottage cheese and nuts in a saffron-flavored curry; skewered minced lamb flavored with mint and carefully cooked over a charcoal flame; and spinach-and-cottage-cheese dumplings. If you only want a light bite, the sandwiches are outstanding. Don't miss out on the coffee mousse flavored with Tia Maria.

Jass Trident, Khajuraho. ℂ **07686/27-2344.** Main courses Rs 140–Rs 490 ($3–$11). AE, DC, MC, V. Daily 12:30–2pm and 7:30–9.30pm.

SHOPPING

Khajuraho can be a nightmare for tourists. In contrast with the tranquil village atmosphere, hawkers and touts ooze from every corner and have record-setting persistence. You'll no doubt develop a gut-wrenching dislike for the overstretched shopping areas in and around the main square, where everyone seems to demand that you step into yet another handicrafts shop to "just look, no buy." Do not enter any shop in Khajuraho with anyone other than fellow travelers. If you make a purchase on your own, you'll save yourself around 20%, which is the standard commission, borne by you, demanded by "agents" (taxi drivers, guides, or someone who has "befriended" you) for their "service" of bringing foreign business to local stores.

Amid all the hard-sell look-alike shops is one shining light. **Artist** (Surya Hotel Complex, Jain Temple Rd.; ℂ **07686/27-4496;** dilipartist@yahoo.com; daily 9:30am–1:30pm and 3–10pm) is an appropriately named outlet for Pichhwai and Mughal paintings rendered by Dilip Singh and his two brothers, whose late father was a recipient of a National Award for Art many years back. The Singh brothers' paintings vary in subject, size, and quality, but the selection includes something to suit everyone's pocket. Miniatures start at a mere Rs 10 (20¢), and the most expensive paintings sell for up to Rs 13,000 ($280). Besides exquisite paintings on silk, fabric, and paper, you can also buy clever foldaway chairs, tables, and ornamental pieces at prices so low they'll make your head spin. If you want quality original art that reflects Mughal culture and history (and eroticism), be sure to spend some time in either of the two Artist outlets in Khajuraho. You can also commission a work if there's something in particular that you want to take home with you.

6 Orchha

440km (273 miles) SE of Delhi; 238km (148 miles) S of Agra; 120km (75 miles) SE of Gwalior

Located on a rocky island on the Betwa River, the deserted royal citadel of Raja Rudra Pratap is one of India's most fabulous Mughal heritage sites, yet Orchha (literally "hidden place") is mercifully free of development, making this a wonderfully relaxing stop. Founded in 1531, it was the capital of the Bundela kings until 1738. Today the weathered temples, palaces, and cenotaphs are the royal quarters of emerald parakeets and black-faced langurs, while traditional whitewashed, flat-roofed structures house the laid-back villagers. Besides the palace complex, three beautiful temples are worth seeking out, as well as 14 graceful *chhatris* (cenotaphs) commemorating the Orchha rulers, built upstream along the riverbank. Most of these sights can be covered in a day excursion on the way to Khajuraho, but to get the most out of this surreally tranquil haven, spend at least 1 night here.

ESSENTIALS

VISITOR INFORMATION   There is no official tourism bureau. Two-hour audio tours (Rs 50/$1.05 plus Rs 500/$11 refundable deposit) are available from **MPTDC Sheesh Mahal,** which acts as an informal tourism office (see "Where to Stay & Dine," below). They will arrange day trips and transfers.

GETTING THERE   The best way to get to Orchha is to catch a train to Jhansi, where trains from Delhi, Mumbai, or Chennai pull in, dropping visitors on their way to Khajuraho (see "Khajuraho: Getting There," earlier in this chapter). You can catch an auto-rickshaw from Jhansi to Orchha (20km/12 miles) for about Rs 150 ($3.15). Alternatively, with time on your hands, you can hire a car and driver and travel by road from Agra, overnighting at Gwalior (see "The Gems of Gwalior," below).

EXPLORING ORCHHA'S FORGOTTEN MONUMENTS

The monuments of Orchha are fairly spread out, but close enough to be explored entirely on foot. You can spend a quick-paced morning poking through the ruins in which you're most interested, or take your time and spread your explorations over an entire day. A few of the sights require a ticket, which you can purchase from a booth at the front of the Raj Mahal (daily 9am–5pm); the Rs 30 (60¢) ticket provides access to all the main monuments.

Visible as you enter the village, Orchha's fortified palace complex is approached by a multi-arched medieval bridge. Once over the bridge, you'll first encounter the earliest of the palaces, **Raj Mahal** ✦, built during the 16th century by the deeply religious Madhukar Shah, who befriended the Mughal Emperor Akbar, an alliance that was to serve the rulers of Orchha well. Look for the bold, colorful murals on walls and ceilings, and climb to the uppermost levels of the palace for a more complete view of the entire complex. A pathway leads to the two-story **Rai Praveen Mahal;** according to legend, it was built in the mid–17th century for a concubine who the then-ruling Raja loved to watch dance. Surrounded by lovely lawns, the palace includes a ground-level hall where performances were once held, and naturally cooled subterranean apartments. Deemed Orchha's finest palace, with delicate *chhatris* (dome-shaped cenotaphs) and ornate stone *jali* screens along its outer walls, the **Jahangir Mahal** ✦✦ is distinguished by its domed pavilions, fortified bastions, and ornamental gateway flanked by stone elephants holding bells in their trunk, perhaps to announce the entry of the man in whose honor the palace was built: Emperor Jahangir, Akbar's son (see "The Life & Sordid Times of the Mughals," earlier in the chapter). He is said to have promised to visit, but accounts vary as to whether he actually arrived. The sandstone exterior bears the remains of beautiful turquoise- and lapis lazuli–tiled embellishments, while interior walls are decorated with lovely carvings. For a long-winded audio guide to the palace complex, make inquiries at the **Sheesh Mahal Hotel,** a section of the palace complex built by a local king as a country getaway some time after Orchha's decline. If you wander along the paths heading away from the palace complex (to your left after you cross the bridge), you'll encounter the ruins of a number of small, atmospheric temples amid fields belonging to local farmers.

With both Persian and Rajput architectural influences, the seven-story **Chaturbhuj Mandir** ✫ looms hauntingly over Orchha village. Reached by a steep flight of steps, the 16th-century temple consists of an expansive vaulted assembly hall with impressive spires; make your way up the narrow spiral staircases for lovely views from the temple roof. Never used, the temple was supposed to have housed an image of Lord Rama brought from Ayodhya by the wife of Orchha's king. Upon arriving, she found the temple incomplete, so she temporarily installed the deity in her palace. When Chaturbhuj was finally completed, the god refused to be moved, so the queen's palace became the **Ram Raja Mandir** (daily 8am–12:30pm and 7–9:30pm), today one of Orchha's main attractions for Hindus, despite its secular architecture.

Behind Ram Raja Mandir is a paved path that leads to the **Lakshminarayan Mandir** ✫✫, atop a low hill less than 1km (a half mile) from the village. The walk takes you past lovely flat-roofed houses that line part of the pathway. The 17th-century temple features interesting murals depicting military battles and religious myths. Although it's usually open to ticket-holders between 9am and 5pm, the temple is sometimes locked up, with no trace of the attendant.

After you explore the village and its trinket-filled stores, don't miss the 14 sandstone *chhatris,* or cenotaphs, alongside the Betwa River. Built as memorials to expired rulers of the Bundelkhand, they celebrate old alliances, combining elements of Mughal architecture, such as the arches, and Hindu temple design, such as the *sikharas* (spires).

WHERE TO STAY

Orchha is small but popular, with few decent lodging options, so be sure to book well in advance, particularly in winter when the tour groups arrive en masse. The best room in Orchha is the atmospherically shabby **Royal Suite** ✫✫ in the otherwise overrated **Sheesh Mahal Hotel** (✆ **07680/25-2624** or 011/ 2336-6528; www.mptourism.com; Rs 2,995/$64). An enormous room, with a domed ceiling over an assortment of paintings, cabinets, and fascinating Raj-era relics, the suite has its own dining area and a wonderful terrace with magical views. Even the bathroom is huge, with a marble tub and polished stone flooring. Note that the hotel's ordinary guest rooms are dungeons, with bleak furnishings. Like most government-run establishments, the place is poorly managed. Despite its obvious shortcomings, the Sheesh Mahal, no doubt due to its heritage status, is usually booked up days in advance.

The Orchha Resort ✫   Orchha's smartest hotel enjoys a good location on the banks of the Betwa River near the cenotaphs. Popular with European tour groups, the resort is attractive and includes 11 deluxe tents arranged around the tennis court; these really are the best value. They're comfortably furnished and include all the regular amenities as well as en-suite toilets and showers and a small porch from where you have an incredible, close-up view of several impressive cenotaphs. Guest rooms in the main building are more expensive; they have marble floors, smallish bathrooms with tubs, and good-quality fabrics in shades

The Gems of Gwalior

If you've chosen to travel by rail or road from Agra, which lies 118km (73 miles) north, to Khajuraho via Orchha, which is 120km (75 miles) south, set aside a day to explore Gwalior's fine sights. To see them all necessitates an overnight stay in the palace that is part of the attraction and one of the best heritage properties in central India.

Looming over the three cities of modern Gwalior—Lashkar, Morar, and Gwalior—its 3km (2-mile) long thick walls built atop steep cliff surfaces, the **Gwalior Fort** ✹ (daily 8am–6pm) is believed to date back to the 3rd century A.D. The oldest surviving Hindu fort in the Bundelkund, it changed hands repeatedly and was admired by all who invaded it— even the first Mughal emperor, Babur, who admired very little else of India, famously described it as "the pearl among the fortresses of the Hindi" (though he still allowed his army to desecrate the Jain rock-cut sculptures, viewed as you approach the Urwahi Gate). Within the ancient walls are a number of palaces, temples, step wells, and underground pools (best to hire a taxi, available at the entrance), but its most significant structure is the monumental **Man Mandir Palace** (Rs 100/ $2.10), built by Raja Man Singh of the Tomara dynasty in the 15th century. Ornamented with a variety of glazed tile patterns, this is considered one of the finest examples of pre-Mughal Hindu palace architecture in India. Now housing a rather good **Archaeological Museum** (Sat–Thurs 10am–5pm; Rs 5/10¢), the **Gujari Mahal** was also built by Man Singh, this time for his favorite wife, a queen of the Gujjar tribe; he famously fell in love with her after he witnessed her courageously separate two warring buffaloes.

The oldest temple in the fort is the **Teli-ka Mandir** (Rs 100/$2.10), or **Temple of the Caste of Oil Sellers,** dating back to the 9th century. Built in the South Indian, or Dravidian, style, it was originally dedicated to Vishnu and apparently used as a soda factory by the British when they occupied the fort in the 1800s. Just north of here is a large pool of water known as the **Suraj Kund.** It was here that a divine hermit named Gwalipa, for whom the fort is named, is believed to have cured the fort's founder, King Suraj Sen, of leprosy. Other notable temples are the late-11th-century **Sas Mandir (Temple of the Mother-in-law)** and the **Bahu Mandir (Temple of the Daughter-in-law)**, which form an elegant pair (Rs 100/$2.10).

of green or red. Do beware of the slippery area around the pool when you go for a post-sightseeing dip. Owned by Jains, the restaurant is strictly vegetarian.

Kanchanaghat, Orchha, Tikamgarh District 472 246. ☎ **07680/25-2677** or -2678. Fax 07680/25-2677. Reservations: Oswal Motels and Resorts, A-17 Shopping Arcade, Sadar Bazaar, Agra 282 001. ☎ 0562/236-3240 or -3411. Fax 0562/236-3407. 45 units. Doubles: Rs 1,600 ($35) tent; Rs 2,950 ($64) room. AE, MC, V. **Amenities:** Restaurant; pool; tennis court; health club; sauna; table tennis; gift shop; 24-hr. room service; laundry; doctor-on-call. *In room:* A/C, TV, minibar.

The last rulers of Gwalior were the Scindia clan, and during the British era the Scindia maharaja, Jiyaji Rao, was known to be one of the most decadent of the Rajput rulers. In 1875 he built the over-the-top 19th-century **Jai Vilas Palace** for the express purpose of impressing the Prince of Wales. He filled it with treasures imported from Europe; in the Durbar Hall are the world's heaviest chandeliers, each weighing 3½ tons, which hang over the largest handmade carpet in Asia. In the dining room you can see the electric silver-and-crystal toy train the maharaja used to dispense drinks and cigars around the massive dinner table—apparently refusing to stop the train in front of those he disliked. Jai Vilas Palace (© **0751/232-1101**; Thurs–Tues 10am–5pm; Rs 175/ $3.70) is, incidentally, still occupied by his descendants.

Gwalior's has a long-standing tradition of musical excellence and innovation, and to this end the **Sarod Ghar** traces and showcases this legacy in the beautiful sandstone home of the Bagnash family. You might inquire about the **musical recitals** occasionally held in the museum's marble courtyard (© **0751/242-5607**; www.sarod.com; Rs 10/ 20¢; Tues–Sun 10am–1pm and 2–5pm). Or find out whether musicians are performing at the simple white memorial **Tomb of Miyan Tansen.** One of India's greatest musicians, Miyan Tansen was considered one of the *navratna* (nine gems) of Mughal Emperor Akbar's court. For recital information contact **MP State Tourism DC** (© **0751/234-0370**; mptgwalior@ sify.com).

The best place to overnight is the **Taj Usha Kiran Palace Hotel** (© **0751/232-3993** or -3994, **0751/232-3213** or -3214; www.tajhotels. com). Scindia royalty once resided here, and this small, handsome hotel retains an evocative old-world atmosphere. Most accommodations (A/C, TV, minibar) are arranged around a courtyard with a decorative fountain. Carpeted, with high ceilings, pleasant sitting areas, and furniture that once belonged to the maharaja, the deluxe accommodations represent good value ($60). Around the hotel building, you'll discover broad passages, 51 differently designed sandstone trellises, ornate chandeliers, and an upstairs terrace affording views of Jai Vilas Palace and Gwalior Fort, ideal as a sundowner venue. If you do spend the night, you might want to watch the 45-minute. sound-and-light show held at the fortress each night at 7:30pm October through March (8:30pm in summer).

7 Bandhavgarh National Park

237km (147 miles) S of Khajuraho

Known as "Kipling Country," despite the fact that the writer never set foot here, the nature reserves of Madhya Pradesh are archetypal India, with vast tracts of jungle, open grassy plains and, of course, tigers. Bandhavgarh National Park occupies 437 sq. km (168 sq. miles), making it a great deal smaller than its more famous cousin, Kahna National Park. But despite its relatively diminutive size,

---

Fun Fact **The White Tiger of Rewa**

The last elusive white tiger ever to roam free was a Bandhavgarh cub that was snared by Martand Singh, who bred the animal in captivity in order to exploit his deviant genes and so produce a new "genus"—the "White Tiger of Rewa." Today, the only places you'll see white tigers are zoos.

---

the park is home to some 50 to 70 tigers, the highest density of tigers of any park on earth, and your chances of sighting one are as high as at Ranthambhore, in Rajasthan. Once the personal hunting grounds of local maharajas, who almost wiped out the tiger population, Bandhavgarh continues to experience problems with wayward poachers, usually suppliers for China's lucrative traditional medicine industry. But, as locals will assure you, your chances of seeing a wild tiger (those at Ranthambhore are almost tame) are still unmatched anywhere else in India. Best of all, you will approach your predator on elephant-back, giving the entire experience a totally unreal air.

Besides the sought-after tiger, the sanctuary is home to spotted deer, *sambar, nilgai* antelope, barking deer, shy *chinkara* (Indian gazelle), and wild boar; leopards and sloth bears are far more elusive. The varied topography includes dramatic cliffs that proved a natural location for the 14th-century **Bandhavgarh Fort.** If you give enough notice, you can arrange to visit the reserve's rock-cut caves, with inscriptions dating as far back as the 2nd century B.C.

ESSENTIALS

VISITOR INFORMATION   Entry to Bandhavgarh is via the tiny village of Tala, where a number of lodges and resorts, a handful of *dhabas* (snack shacks), and several souvenir stalls are the only distractions from park activities. Try to get any information you require in advance. Contact **M.P. Tourism** at the White Tiger Forest Lodge at Bandhavgarh (✆ **07627/65-308**) or the **Project Tiger Field Director** in Umaria (✆ **07653/22-214;** fdbtr@bom6.vsnl.net.in). You can also contact **M.P. Tourism** in Delhi (204–205, 2nd Floor, Kanishka Shopping Plaza, 19 Ashoka Rd.; ✆ **011/2334-1187** or 011/2336-6528; fax 011/2334-7264; www.mptourism.com) or in Mumbai (74 World Trade Centre, Cuffe Parade, Colaba).

GETTING THERE   By Road   Set aside an entire day for road journeys from destinations within Madhya Pradesh; surfaces are terrible at best, consisting of little more than endless potholes linked by clusters of asphalt and islands of sand. The nearest town of tourist interest is Khajuraho—what should be about a 5-hour journey takes around 10 hours.

By Air   If you can afford it, take advantage of the helicopter trips from Delhi offered by several of the upmarket resorts in Bandhavgarh. If you decide to catch a commercial flight, Jabalpur is the nearest airport. It is situated 165km (102 miles) away; the 4-hour onward taxi trip will cost upward of Rs 3,000 ($65).

By Train   Umaria, 45 minutes from Tala, is the nearest railhead. The best train from Delhi is the **Utkal Express,** which leaves Nizamuddin station at 12:50pm and arrives in Umaria the following day at 6:30am, a little too late for early entry to the park. Taxi rides to Tala cost around Rs 500 ($11). Other nearby railheads include Katni and Jabalpur.

WHEN TO GO   Sightings are best February through June, when the heat forces more animals to search for water, although the park opens as early as October (depending on the monsoon situation). Although the park attracts smaller crowds than Corbett and Ranthambhore, avoid Bandhavgarh for the week before and after the Diwali, Holi, and New Year holidays, when the park may be filled with queue-jumping VIPs and noisy families.

ORGANIZING YOUR BANDHAVGARH SAFARI

Regarding entry fees and permits, the best plan is to book accommodations that include *everything;* the resorts and lodges we've reviewed below will take care of all your safari arrangements. Get to the park first thing in the morning, when you will join the line of open-top jeeps and other 4WDs waiting at the entrance for the daily rush, which starts promptly at dawn. If you've hired a vehicle and driver privately, you will have to pay a small fee for the services of a park guide who will accompany you; this and other charges for entry permits, cameras, and such are all paid at the park entrance. jeep safaris can cover a relatively large area within the park, but most sightings occur as a result of information shared among the various drivers and guides. Elephant-mounted *mahouts* head out early to search for tigers; once they locate them, the mahouts wait at the nearest road until safari jeeps begin to congregate and word spreads, ensuring the arrival of other vehicle-driven visitors. Rs 300 ($6.50) buys you an elephant-back ride for an unnervingly close-up view of the tigers, usually encountered minding their own business deep within the sal forest. You then have around 5 minutes to capture the elusive cat on film before your elephant returns to the road to pick up new passengers.

With any luck, your guide will be as interested in showing you the terrain, which is rugged and beautiful, as he is in finding your tiger. He may point out other species such as the *chital,* blue bull antelope, and *sambar;* and the many bird species such as spotted black kites, crested serpent eagles, storks, ibises, hornbills, white-eyed buzzards, black vultures, golden-backed woodpeckers, kingfishers, and dove parakeets. If all else fails, there are plenty of black-faced langur monkeys and rhesus macaques to keep you amused.

Tip: During the afternoon, the park offers more-substantial elephant safaris that are as much relaxing as they are a good opportunity to see more tigers in the wild, this time without feeling like you're part of a tourist conveyor belt.

Park entrance is at Tala. Park fees: Rs 200 ($4.30) admission; Rs 100 ($2.10) vehicle entry; Rs 90 ($1.90) compulsory guide fee; Rs 25 (50¢) camera charge; Rs 200 ($4.30) video camera charge; Rs 300 ($6.50) elephant ride per person. Daily 6:15–10am and 3–6pm.

WHERE TO STAY

Note that rates quoted are "Jungle Plan" packages, which include all meals and two safaris into the park as well as all entrance, guide, and vehicle fees. Besides Bandhavgarh Jungle Lodge, two upmarket tented options are worth considering, though neither offers the same good value. Consisting of 15 smart but simply furnished twin-bedded tents, each with attached bathroom (shower only) and private porch, **Jungle Camp** is the most expensive ($280 double) and has the stylistic edge. Due to a conflict with the son of the local maharaja on whose grounds the camp previously stood, it has recently shifted to a new location, unfortunately some distance from the park entrance, though the area offers scenic walks. Meals are buffet-style, and a raging fire provides the entertainment at night. Book through B/21 Kailash Enclave II, New Delhi 110 048 (© **011/ 2685-4626**).

Bandhavgarh Jungle Lodge ⭐ (Value)   A stone's throw from the park entrance, in a garden of medicinal plants, fruit trees, and colorful flowers, this is the loveliest and best-value place to stay in Tala. Opt for one of the charming village-style mud-and-dung walled huts (wall-to-wall rugs; firm, comfortable beds; screened windows; and basic but clean attached bathrooms with showers) rather than the concrete cottages, which are less atmospheric but have tiled bathrooms with tubs. At night, all you have for company are the sounds of the jungle and a hot-water bottle tucked under white linen and a thick quilt. Service is pleasant and personal, and the emphasis on the environment means that solar power is used for cooking and for hot water. Meals and safaris are included in the fee. Conversation in the lovely *boma*-style restaurant, serving adequate Anglo-Indian cuisine, usually revolves around tiger sightings and poaching.

Reservations: WelcomHeritage, C-7, 2nd Floor, J-Block Market, Saket, New Delhi 110 017. ℂ **011/686-8992** or -8993, 011/685-0438, 011/656-1869 or -1875. Fax 011/686-8994. www.welcomheritage.com. 18 units. Doubles: Rs 5,600 ($123); Rs 2,100 ($46) extra bed. Rates include all meals, taxes, and jungle excursions. MC, V. **Amenities:** Restaurant; laundry; resident naturalist; video library.

8 Bhopal & Sanchi

Bhopal is 744km (461 miles) S of Delhi. Sanchi is 46km (28 miles) NE of Bhopal.

Despite its exciting marketplaces, grand old mosques, and lovely palaces, the capital of Madhya Pradesh is perhaps best known as the site of the world's worst urban industrial disaster. But most foreign visitors find themselves in Bhopal in order to visit nearby Sanchi, a UNESCO World Heritage Site, and one of the most impressive Buddhist monuments in Asia. Architecturally unique and far from the beaten tourist track, the monuments and surrounding ruins are tranquil, free of hawkers and touts, and a worthwhile diversion from the more frequented destinations of Varanasi, Agra, Khajuraho, and Delhi.

If Bhopal's few monuments, its market, and the glorious Buddhist monuments at Sanchi leave you with time on your hands, head for the caves of **Bhimbetka,** where red-and-black prehistoric drawings recall the antics of ancient dancers and hunters, sticklike in the company of tigers and charging bulls.

ESSENTIALS

VISITOR INFORMATION   For extensive information about any destination in Madhya Pradesh, as well as transport options, contact the extremely helpful Yogesh Argal at the **Madhya Pradesh State Tourism Development Corporation (MPSTDC;** 4th Floor, Gangorti Complex, TT Nagar; ℂ **0755/277-8383;** mail@mptourism.com). The website, **www.mptourism.com,** is also excellent. Sanchi is 46km (28 miles) from Bhopal, less than 2 hours by road. Regular train services from Bhopal pass through Sanchi.

GETTING THERE & AWAY   As the state capital, Bhopal is well connected by air with numerous cities (including Delhi, Mumbai, Gwalior, and Indore). Bhopal is also on a main railway line, and frequent **trains** connect the city with Delhi, Agra, Gwalior, Jhansi (for Orchha), Mumbai, and Hyderabad.

GETTING AROUND   Taxis and auto-rickshaws are common and easy to flag down.

GUIDED TOURS   Mrs. Chopra, of **Radiant Travels** (24 Ahmedabad Rd.; ℂ **0755/273-8540** or -8541), is not only an experienced tour guide, but introduces visitors to basic Indian cuisine with vegetarian meals at her home.

The Bhopal Gas Tragedy

On the night of December 2, 1984, a tank at the Union Carbide pesticide manufacturing plant near Bhopal ruptured, leaking highly poisonous methyl isocyanate gas into the atmosphere. By the time it had dissipated, 1,600 people were dead—but final estimates are as high as 20,000. A claim of $6 billion in compensation was initially demanded by the government, but it settled out of court for $470 million. Adding insult to injury, the money, paid to the government, took 7 years and many more deaths before even a fraction of it reached the victims. Almost 2 decades later, survivors continue to protest the haphazard and inadequate manner in which the families of the victims were compensated. Evidence suggests that the continuing effects of the gas disaster may have affected as many as 300,000 people afflicted with various cancers and birth defects. Effigies of the Union Carbide bosses are regularly burned at memorial protests (failing to reach more than the evening news), and many victims continue to go without aid or recourse from the law. Meanwhile, Union Carbide, having abandoned the factory, has started up elsewhere as Eveready Industries India Ltd.

WHAT TO SEE & DO IN BHOPAL

No one spends much time in Bhopal itself, but the "City of Lakes" is not without its charms, and a handful of sights are worth setting time aside for. Note that most places are closed on Monday, and on Friday mosques are off-limits, unless you're Muslim.

A visit to the **Chowk (Bazaar),** in the heart of the old city, can be a wonderful way to gain insight into the daily lives of Bhopal's warm, friendly citizens. Its ramshackle streets are lined with old havelis and atmospheric stalls; it's impossible not to get involved in the village vibe, where shopping, hard-core haggling, and gossiping occupy one's time. Shop around for embroidered velvet cushions, *tussar* silk, silver jewelry, and intricate beadwork. While you're in the Chowk, visit the lovely **Jami Masjid** (built in 1837, it features gold-spiked minarets, distinguishing it from the "Pearl Mosque") or the **Moti Masjid,** farther south. Sporting three large white Mughal domes and two soaring minarets, **Taj-ul-Masajid** ⚘, one of India's largest mosques, was started at the end of the last century by Bhopal's eighth ruler, the great queen Shah Jahan Begum, but was only completed in the 1970s.

Designed by the preeminent Indian architect, Charles Correa, the breezy, modern **Bharat Bhavan** ⚘⚘ (Shamla Hills; © **0755/266-0353;** Tues–Sun: Feb–Oct, 2–8pm and Nov–Jan, 1–7pm; Rs 10/20¢, Fri free), overlooking Upper Lake, is one of the best cultural centers in the country, showcasing some wonderful contemporary and tribal art exhibitions.

If you're set on seeing a white tiger, **Van Vihar National Park** is the place to do it. Zoo conditions here are better than elsewhere in India, but it's still a depressing place to see a wild animal (Zoo Rd.; Wed–Mon 7–11am and 3–5:30pm; Rs 100/$2.10, vehicle entry Rs 30/60¢; carnivores are fed around 4pm).

EXPLORING THE BUDDHIST COMPLEX AT SANCHI ⚘⚘⚘

Now a deserted site resembling an *X-Files* set, the monuments of Sanchi have not only survived despite nearly 2,000 years of neglect, but the *stupa* at Sanchi is considered India's finest and most evocative example of ancient Buddhist architecture. The Mauryan emperor Ashoka, famous for converting to Buddhism after massacring thousands during his military campaigns in Orissa, was responsible for laying the foundations in the 3rd century B.C. Set upon a squat hill affording lovely views of the surrounding countryside, the complex of *stupas* (fat, domelike monuments housing Buddhist relics), monasteries, and temples probably owes its location as much to the serenity of the site as it does to its proximity to the once-prosperous city of Vidisha, where Ashoka's devoted Buddhist wife, Mahadevi, lived. Located at the confluence of the Bes and the Betwa rivers and two important trade routes, the Buddhist complex elicited the patronage of Vidisha's wealthy merchant communities. Even during the invasions of the Hun, life at Sanchi appears to have gone undisturbed, and is believed to have continued until the 13th century A.D., when a resurgence of Hinduism and an increasingly militant Islamic movement led to a decline of Buddhism in India. The site was deserted for more than 500 years before its rediscovery—again by a British military adventurer-type—in 1818. Today, aside from the attractive complex of ruins, Sanchi is little more than a railway station, a few guesthouses, snack stands, a museum, a restaurant, and a shop.

During the excavation that has taken place over the last century, the ruins of around 55 temples, pillars, monasteries, stupas, and other structures have been unearthed. It appears that Sanchi is unique in that its monuments cover the gamut of Buddhist architectural structures—dating from the 3rd century B.C. to the 12th century A.D.

The star attraction is Ashoka's large hemispherical stupa, which rises from the ground like a massive stone-carved alien craft. Around the middle of the 2nd century B.C., a balustrade was erected around the stupa, and the mound was covered in stone by the rulers of the Sunga dynasty. Facing the cardinal directions and contributing to the mystical appearance of the main stupa are the four intricately carved gateways, erected around 25 B.C. under the later Satvahana rulers. These striking entranceways feature finely detailed panels depicting incidents from the life of the Buddha and tales from the *Jakatas*. At that time, the current understanding of the Buddha in human form had not yet emerged, and instead he is symbolically depicted as a bodhi tree, lotus, wheel, pair of feet, or stupa.

The Sanchi monasteries consist of a central courtyard surrounded by cells that served as the sleeping quarters for the nuns or monks. Of these, the best is **Monastery 51,** which was first excavated in the 19th century.

WHERE TO STAY & DINE

Jehan Numa Palace ★★ *Value*   Built in 1890 as a royal guesthouse, this handsome low-rise white colonial-era building is fronted by attractive lawns with fountains, hedges, and colorful bougainvilleas. Costing the same as a standard room, the two original heritage suites (ask specifically for either "Bourbon" or "Goddard") are very swish, with huge bedrooms, poster-beds, Regency furniture, spacious bathrooms with separate tubs and showers, and private patios. Executive guest rooms are off verandas around a fountain courtyard; these are large, with French doors and high ceilings. Standard rooms, in a new wing, are best avoided, as are the "cottage rooms." Colored with natural vegetable dyes, the eco-friendly linens are handmade by a local cottage industry, and walls are decorated with local handicrafts. Service is excellent. Facilities include Bhopal's largest pool and a fitness center offering Ayurvedic massage.

15/ Shamla Hill, Bhopal 462 013. (*C*) **0755/266-1100.** Fax 0755/266-1720. www.hoteljehanumapalace.com. 60 units. Doubles: Rs 2,300 ($50) cottage; Rs 3,290 ($71) standard room; Rs 3,290 ($71) executive room; Rs 3,290 ($71) heritage suite. Rates include breakfast. AE, DC, MC, V. **Amenities:** 2 restaurants; bar; club-cum-pub; garden barbecue; patisserie; pool; tennis court; jogging track; horseback-riding; health club; gym; Jacuzzi; sauna; steam; mini-golf; table tennis; pool table; concierge; barber shop; 24-hr. room service; massage; laundry; doctor-on-call. *In room:* A/C, TV, minibar. Suites have tea- and coffee-making facilities, hair dryer.

9 The Fortress City of Mandu *★★★*

90km (56 miles) from Indore

Built at a cool height of over 600m (2,000 ft.) on the southwestern edge of the Malwa Plateau, with sweeping views of the Nimar Plains below, Mandu was once the largest fortified city on earth, and playpen to some of central India's most powerful rulers. Initially christened by the Malwa sultans as the "City of Joy," the medieval capital inspired its rulers to celebrate the most pleasurable of pastimes—one of Mandu's most famous palaces was built solely to house some 15,000 concubines, and it is said that the Mughal emperor Humayun was so mesmerized by Mandu's sanguine beauty that he developed an opium habit during his stay here. Today the exotic ghost city—still one of the most atmospheric destinations in India—draws but a handful of tourists, which makes the excursion here all the more rewarding. It's a mere hour away from the industrial hub of Indore, yet Mandu, even more so than Orchha, is rural India at its best: a place of enduring beauty, both natural and man-made, with panoramic views. It's the perfect antidote to the well-traveled North India circuits. You can visit Mandu as a rather long day trip out of Indore, but for those willing to sacrifice luxury for serenity, it's worth spending a night or two here to revel in silence, fresh air, and wide-open space.

ESSENTIALS

GETTING THERE & AWAY   To visit Mandu, you have to travel via Indore, which is connected to important regional centers by daily flights and regular train services. The airport ((*C*) **0731/241-0452** or -3747) is 8km (5 miles) out of the center. The train trip from Bhopal lasts 6 hours; from Delhi 13 hours; from Mumbai 15 hours. Unless you plan to get to Mandu by bus (a long, tiring, but very cheap journey), hire a taxi; a recommended operator is **President Travels** (Hotel President, 163 R.N.T. Rd., Indore; (*C*) **0731/253-3472**).

VISITOR INFORMATION   **Madhya Pradesh Tourism** has an office at the Tourist Bungalow in Indore ((*C*) **0731/252-8653** or -1818; mptourismind@ sancharnet.in). In Mandu, ask the manager at the **MPSTDC Tourist Cottages** ((*C*) **07292/26-3235**) for assistance.

GETTING AROUND   Indore has plenty of **taxis** and **auto-rickshaws;** ask the driver to use his meter. In Mandu, you can hire a **bicycle,** or ride on the back of a **motorcycle** with a local guide as your driver.

EXPLORING MANDU

After passing through the narrow gates of the fortress and continuing for some distance, you'll arrive in "downtown" Mandu (a collection of shops and stalls in the vicinity of the **Central Group** of monuments). As soon as you emerge from your car or bus, you'll be approached by a local guide, who will offer his services with a nervous but easygoing disposition. Even if your guide—and there are only a couple in Mandu—is not a certified expert, this is one place where it can be fun to have someone show you around and enrich your experience with a version of history that overplays the myth, romance, and fantasy of the place (but do agree on a price upfront and establish that he speaks passable English).

If you don't plan to spend the night in Mandu, start your tour immediately with the 15th-century **Jami Masjid** ✪; said to have been inspired by the mosque in Damascus, this colossal colonnaded structure bears some Hindu influences, such as the carvings of lotus flowers and decorative bells. Adjacent the mosque is the **mausoleum of Hoshang Shah,** the first white marble tomb in India, said to have inspired those in Agra; it's ultimately missable. The **Royal Enclave** ✪✪ (Rs 100/$2.10; daily 9am–5pm) is dominated by the enormous **Jahaz Mahal,** commonly known as the "ship palace." Built between two artificial lakes, it certainly was intended to be the ultimate stone pleasure cruiser, where the sultan Ghiyas Shah kept his 15,000 courtesans and an additional thousand Amazonians from Turkey and Abyssinia to guard them. Behind the ship palace is the **Hindola Mahal;** its oddly sloping buttress walls have given it the nickname "Swinging Palace," which may have been a more appropriate moniker for the Jahaz Mahal.

Mandu's main road stretches southward, through open fields dotted with ruins and a few village houses, and continues into the **Rewa Kund** group of monuments (Rs 100/$2.10; daily sunrise to sunset), where the passionate romance between Maharaja Baz Bahadur, the last independent sultan of Malwa, and the beautiful Hindu shepherdess, Rupmati, is preserved in striking stone constructions. Apparently smitten by Rupmati's glorious singing voice, Baz built the **Rupmati Pavilion** ✪✪ so that she could see her village in the Narmada Valley below, but things went awry when the Mughal emperor Akbar came to hear of her legendary beauty and voice and wanted to take her home as a souvenir. After a fierce battle in which Baz was defeated, his beloved committed suicide. The view from the pavilion, which stands on the edge of a sheer precipice rising 365m (1,168 ft.) from the valley floor, is still sublime. On the way back from the pavilion, stop at **Baz Bahadur's Palace,** where the acoustics enjoyed by the musically inclined king remain quite astonishing, even if some of the restoration work is a bit ham-fisted.

WHERE TO STAY & DINE

If the budget lodgings at Mandu are too basic, Indore has a number of fine business-orientated hotels where you'll find comfort and extensive facilities. The best of which is the **Taj Residency** (✆ **0731/25-5770;** www.tajhotels.com; doubles from $75). The amenities and comforts here match those of any smart city hotel, and the surrounding lawns and gardens are lovely.

Hotel Rupmati   Close to the village bazaar on the edge of a cliff with fantastic views, this is the most impressive of Mandu's small selection of spartan hotels. Guest rooms are in a long stone building. Each large, pink-walled unit has a thin rock-hard mattress with white linen and a blanket; there's a small balcony. Attention has been paid to the lawns, and the cleanliness and tranquillity of the place make up for the budget facilities.

If you can't get in here, you'll have to try the **MPSTDC Tourist Cottages,** situated on the bank of Mandu's largest lake, the Sagar Talaab (✆ **07292/26-3235;** www.mptourism.com; from Rs 450/$9.80).

Mandu 454 010. (✆ **07292/63-270/9.** Reservations in Indore: (✆ 0731/270-2055. 10 units. Doubles: Rs 750 ($17) A/C; Rs 400 ($8.75) non-A/C. No credit cards. **Amenities:** Restaurant; children's play area; limited room service. *In room:* 6 units have A/C, TV.

Rajasthan: Land of Princes

For many, Rajasthan is the very essence of India, with crenelated forts and impregnable palaces that rise like giant fairy-tale sets above dusty sun-scorched plains and shimmering lakes. It's a place peopled by proud turbaned men and delicately boned women in saris of dazzling colors. Much of India's second-largest state (similar in size to France) is covered by the ever-encroaching Thar Desert, but despite its aridity, Rajasthan was once remarkably prosperous: Traders from as far afield as Persia and China had to cross its dry plains to reach the southern ports of Gujarat, something the warrior princes of Rajasthan were quick to capitalize on. Today the principal attraction of Rajasthan—the post-independence name for Rajputana, literally "land of princes"—is the large variety of forts and palaces its aristocrats built throughout the centuries, making it the most popular destination in India outside of the Taj. But Rajasthan offers so much more than desert castles and culture—from tracking tigers in the Ranthambhore jungle (incidentally, the best place to spot wild tigers in Asia) to gaping at the world's most intricately carved marble temples high above sea level on historic Mount Abu. The land of princes is rich with possibilities and offers easy road access to the less-traveled state of Gujarat, discussed at the end of this chapter.

You could plan to spend your entire trip to India in Rajasthan, which is within easy striking distance of Delhi (and the Taj) by train, plane, or road.

Certainly you'll need at least a week to take in the major destinations, of which the lake city of Udaipur and the desert fort of Jaisalmer—the only fort in the world still inhabited by villagers—are top highlights. Also vying for your time: the "blue city" of Jodhpur, which has the state's most impressive and best-preserved fort as well as the largest palace in India; the tiny town of Pushkar, built around the sacred Brahmin lake and host to the biggest *mela* (cattle fair) in Asia; the painted *havelis* (historic homes or mansions) of the Shekawati region, referred to as India's open-air gallery; the tiny Keoladeo "Ghana" National Park, which boasts the largest concentration and variety of bird life in Asia; the untainted, almost medieval atmosphere of little towns like Bundi; and the bumper-to-bumper shops and bazaars in Jaipur, the state and retail capital of Rajasthan. Shopping, in fact, is another of the state's chief attractions: Because of the liberal patronage of the wealthy Rajput princes, skilled artisans from all over the East settled here to adorn the aristocrats and their palaces. Today these same skills are on sale to the world's designers and travelers, and no one—from die-hard bargain-hunters to chi-chi fashionistas—leaves Rajasthan empty-handed. The question is simply how to choose from an unbelievable array of textiles, jewelry, paintings, handbags, rugs, pottery, diaries—even kitchen utensils—and then how to fit them into your bulging suitcase.

Land of Thirst: Rajasthan Today

Still very much a traditional, feudal society, the country's second-largest state is also one of its poorest, with the highest population growth rate in the country. Although official estimates indicate that poverty is on the decrease, sheer numbers rather than percentages paint a more depressing picture—more than one million city-dwellers live in slums. Some 400,000 have no regular access to pure drinking water, and 330,000 have no access to proper toilet facilities. The plight of Rajasthan's people has in recent years been exacerbated by the worst drought in living memory—4 years of little rain has resulted in the widespread deaths of livestock and the decimation of crops. During the 2000 heat wave, when temperatures often averaged 122°F (50°C), many wells ran dry; 2 years later, reports of malnutrition and hunger continue to make headlines. Many blame the government for undermining traditional ways of coping with drought: Widespread irrigation schemes have made farmers rely on taps and tanks rather than take a frugal approach to water. Regardless, the fact remains that—even with the prayed-for return of rain next year—it will be difficult for the rural sector to fully recover.

But perhaps the best reason to visit Rajasthan is to experience its unusual hotels: The state has almost 80 heritage properties—castles, palaces, forts, and ornate havelis—many of which are still home to India's oldest monarchies. This must be the only place in the world where, armed with a credit card, you can find yourself sleeping in a king's bed, having earlier dined with the aristocrat whose forebears built and quite often died for the castle walls that surround it. Known for their valor and honor, and later for their decadence (see "Once Were Warriors: The History of the Rajput," below), the Rajputs are superb hosts, and it is almost possible to believe that you, too, are of aristocratic blood, as a turbaned aide awaits your every wish while you marvel at the starry night from the bastion of your castle. Long live the king (and queen), for you are it.

1 Planning Your Trip to Rajasthan

Rajasthan has so much to see, with long travel distances between top sites, that a trip here requires some careful planning (particularly if you're going to hire a car and driver, which in some ways is the best way to tour the state). The following serves as an overview.

The three biggest cities in Rajasthan, all with airports, are **Jaipur,** the "Pink City"; **Jodhpur,** the "Blue City"; and **Udaipur,** the "White City." All are worthwhile destinations, not least because they offer easy access to great excursions. The tiny **Jaisalmer,** or "Gold City," is the most awkward to reach, and although some find it the highlight of their Rajasthan trip, others feel it isn't worth the schlep it takes to get there.

For most, the entry point is the state capital of Jaipur, near the eastern border, and the third point (the others being nearby Delhi and Agra/Taj) of the

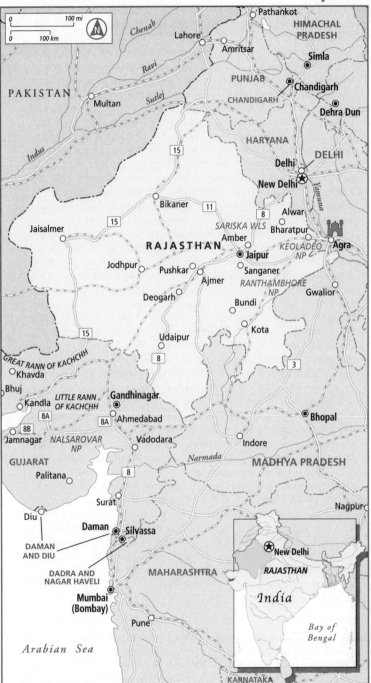

Rajasthan

0 100 mi
0 100 km

Chenab

Pathankot

HIMACHAL
PRADESH

Lahore
Amritsar

Simla

Ravi

PUNJAB

Chandigarh

PAKISTAN

Multan

Sutlej

CHANDIGARH

Dehra Dun

Indus

HARYANA

DELHI

Delhi

15

New Delhi

Bikaner

11

Alwar

8

Jaisalmer

15

SARISKA WLS

Bharatpur

R A J A S T H A N

Amber

Yamuna

Jaipur

KEOLADEO
NP

Agra

Jodhpur

Pushkar

Sanganer

Ajmer

RANTHAMBHORE
NP

Gwalior

Deogarh

Bundi

15

Udaipur

Kota

8

3

GREAT RANN OF KACHCHH

Khavda

Bhuj

LITTLE RANN
OF KACHCHH

Gandhinagar

Bhopal

Kandla

8A

Ahmedabad

8A

Jamnagar

8B

NALSAROVAR
NP

Vadodara

Indore

GUJARAT

Palitana

Narmada

MADHYA PRADESH

8

Surat

Nagpur

Diu

Daman

Silvassa

New Delhi

DAMAN
AND DIU

RAJASTHAN

DADRA AND
NAGAR HAVELI

India

MAHARASHTRA

Mumbai
(Bombay)

Pune

Bay of
Bengal

Arabian Sea

KARNATAKA

Once Were Warriors: The History of the Rajput

Rajasthan's history is inextricably entwined with that of its self-proclaimed aristocracy: a warrior clan, calling themselves the *Rajput,* that emerged sometime during the 6th and 7th centuries. Given that no one too low in the social hierarchy could take the profession (like bearing arms) of a higher caste, this new clan, comprising both indigenous people and foreign invaders such as the Huns, held a special "rebirth" ceremony—purifying themselves with fire—at Mount Abu, where they assigned themselves a mythical descent from the sun and the moon. In calling themselves Rajputs (a corruption of the word *Raj Putra,* "sons of princes"), they officially segregated themselves from the rest of society. Proud and bloodthirsty, yet with a strict code of honor, they were to dominate the history of the region right up until independence, and are still treated with deference by their mostly loyal subjects.

The Rajputs offered their subjects protection in return for revenue, and together formed a kind of loose kinship in which each leader was entitled to unequal shares within the territory of his clan. The term they used for this collective sharing of power was "brotherhood," but predictably the clan did not remain a homogenous unit, and bitter internecine wars were fought. Besides these ongoing internal battles, the Hindu Rajputs had to defend their territory from repeated invasions by the Mughals and Maharashtras, but given the Rajputs' ferocity and unconquerable spirit, the most skillful invasion came in the form of diplomacy, when the great Mughal emperor Akbar married the daughter of Raja Bihar Mal, ruler of the Kachchwaha Rajputs (Jaipur region), who then bore him his first son, Jahangir.

Jahangir was to become the next Mughal emperor, and the bond between Mughal and Rajput was cemented when he in turn married another Kachchwaha princess (his mother's niece). A period of tremendous prosperity for the Kachchwaha clan followed, as their military prowess helped the Mughals conquer large swaths of India in return for booty. But many of the Rajput clans—particularly the Mewar (in the Udaipur region)—were dismayed by what they saw as a capitulation to Mughal imperialism. In the end it was English diplomacy that truly tamed the maharajas. Rather than waste money and men going to war with the Rajput kings, the English offered them a treaty. This gave "the Britishers" control of Rajputana, but in return the empire recognized the royal status of the Rajputs and allowed them to keep the majority of the taxes extorted from their subjects and the many travelers who still plied the trade routes in the Thar Desert.

much-traveled **Golden Triangle.** Should you choose to start your trip here, you are in fact well-positioned to visit some of Rajasthan's top sites: Only a few hours from the city is the **Ranthambhore National Park**—where, given 2 days, you are virtually assured of spotting a wild tiger—and Bharatpur's **Keoladeo National Park,** a must-see for birders, and virtually on the way from Agra. Jaipur is also within easy striking distance of **Bundi,** an untouched, off-the-beaten-track rural

This resulted in a period of unprecedented decadence for the Rajputs, who now spent their days hunting for tigers, playing polo, and flying to Europe to stock up on the latest Cartier jewels and Belgian crystal. Legends abound of their spectacular hedonism, but perhaps the most famous surround the Maharaja Jay Singh of Alwar (north of Jaipur), who wore black silk gloves when he shook hands with the English king and reputedly used elderly women and children as tiger bait. When Singh visited the showrooms of Rolls-Royce in London, he was affronted when the salesman implied that he couldn't afford to purchase one of the sleek new models—he promptly purchased 10, shipped them home, tore their roofs off, and used them to collect garbage. The English tolerated his bizarre behavior until, after being thrown from his horse during a polo match, he doused the animal with fuel and set it alight. Having ignored previous reports of child molestation, the horse-loving British finally acted with outrage and exiled him from the state.

Above all, the Rajput maharajas expressed their newfound wealth and decadence by embarking on a frenzied building spree, spending vast fortunes on gilding and furnishing new palaces and forts, which reached its peak in Jodhpur, with the completion of the Umaid Bhawan Palace in the 1930s, at the time the largest private residence in the world.

When the imperialists were finally forced to withdraw, the "special relationship" that existed between the Rajputs and the British was honored for another 3 decades—they were allowed to keep their titles and enjoyed a large government-funded "pension," but their loyalty to the British, even during the bloody 1857 uprisings, was to cost them in the long run.

In 1972 Prime Minister Indira Gandhi—sensibly, but no doubt in a bid to win popular votes—stripped the Rajputs of both stipends and titles. This left the former aristocracy almost destitute, unable to maintain either their lifestyles or their sprawling properties.

While many sold their properties and retired to live in middle-class comfort in Delhi or Mumbai, still others started opening their doors to paying guests like Jackie Kennedy and members of the English aristocracy, who came to recapture the romance of Raj-era India. By the dawn of a new millennium, these once-proud warriors had become first-rate hoteliers, offering people from all walks of life the opportunity to experience the princely lifestyle of Rajasthan.

town that lies some hours away by train or car, as well as nearby **Ajmer,** gateway to the sacred lake of Pushkar and site of the state's most famous camel fair.

Other than its proximity to these sites, however, as well as the excellent rail and flight connections to the rest of India, the only good reason to dally in Jaipur itself is to indulge in some retail therapy (or stay at Rajvilas, one of India's best hotels). Most visitors planning to travel farther by car circle Rajasthan in a

counterclockwise direction, starting off in Jaipur and traveling the rather circuitous route west to Jodhpur (with a sojourn in Pushkar—a highly recommended option, particularly for younger travelers); then, from Jodhpur, you
make the 5½- to 6-hour drive west to Jaisalmer for a few nights before you
return to Jodhpur. An alternative route to Jaisalmer, which means you don't have
to travel both to and from Jodhpur, is to travel from Jaipur through the
Shekhawati region to Bikaner, and from there on to Jaisalmer, before you travel
east again to Jodhpur. (The other alternative is to skip Jaisalmer altogether, and
if you're short on time this is what you may have to do, but we think it's a must-
see city.) From Jodhpur you then travel south to Udaipur, the most relaxing
place to end the journey, however you choose to plan it.

For someone with limited time (say, only enough to visit one of Rajasthan's
cities), it's far better to fly direct to Udaipur—the prettiest of Rajasthan's cities
and with great lodging options in all price brackets. From Udaipur you can
take a wonderful (but long) day trip to the **Kumbalgarh Reserve** to take in
Ranakpur's exquisitely carved **Jain temples** and the impressive **Kumbalgarh
Fort** before overnighting at **Devi Garh,** one of India's top hotels. Alternatively,
you can head east from Udaipur to Bundi, via the historic fort of **Chittaurgarh,**
and then move on to **Ranthambhore National Park.** Or take the short trip
directly south to the relatively undiscovered **palaces of Dungarpur,** or head out
west to **Mount Abu,** the state's only hill station and sacred pilgrimage of the
Jains, who come to visit the famous **Dilwara Temples.** Jodhpur and its majestic
Mehrangarh Fort lie only 5 hours north of Udaipur by road, and you can break
up the trip by overnighting at one of the recommended heritage properties along
the way.

The state's other must-see city is Jaisalmer, which is rather inconveniently situated on the far-flung western outreaches of Rajasthan's Thar Desert. To get there,
you either have to set off from Jodhpur or travel via the less-than-spectacular
desert town of Bikaner—both routes involve a lot of driving (Jodhpur is a 5½-
to 6-hr. drive away; Bikaner a 4½- to 5-hr. drive). You can also opt to travel from
Jodhpur to Jaisalmer by overnight train, but this means keeping a close watch
on your baggage and carrying a warm blanket—the desert nights are bitterly
cold. Ideally, to cover all or some of these connections, the long-term hire of
a car and driver is highly recommended—this is really the best way to tour
Rajasthan because it means you can travel at your own pace, avoid public transport (or the daily grind of haggling with taxis), and get right off the beaten track.
That said, Rajasthan's potholed roads make for slow going, drivers have unknown
rules (but clearly the big trucks and cows rule, no matter what the circumstances), and traveling by night is only for the suicidal—even day trips will have
you at times closing your eyes in supplication to some higher being.

Most operators are not keen to provide a breakdown of pricing, leaving you
with the distinct feeling that you are being ripped off. To avoid this, hire through
the **RTDC Transport Unit** (or at least get a quote from them). The RTDC own
a number of vehicles or will contract out specific requests for vehicles; call them
at (℃ **0141/237-5466** or 0141/231-5714 (or write to rtdcpr@sancharnet.in). At
press time, an air-conditioned car and driver cost about Rs 2,400 ($50) for
250km (155 miles) per day, every kilometer thereafter costing Rs 9 (20¢). A very
romantic way to go—but certainly not the fastest—is in an air-conditioned
Ambassador, India's quaint homegrown brand of sedans, which provides you
with a real sense of being in another world, not to mention another era.

2 Jaipur

259km (160 miles) SW of Delhi; 232km (144 miles) W of Agra

After independence, Jaipur became the administrative and commercial capital of what was known as Rajputana, a suitable conclusion to the dreams of its founder Maharaja Sawai Jai Singh II, a man famed for his talents as a politician, mathematician, and astronomer. At age 13 he ascended the throne of the Kachchwaha Rajputs, a clan that had enjoyed tremendous prosperity and power as a result of their canny alliance, dating back to Humayun's reign, with the Mughal emperors. It was in fact the emperor Aurangzeb, a fanatically pious Muslim, who—despite the fact that Jai Singh was a Hindu prince—named him Sawai, meaning "one and a quarter," for his larger-than-life intellect and wit. Having proved his prowess as a military tactician for Aurangzeb, growing the emperor's royal coffers substantially, Jai Singh felt it safe to move his capital from the claustrophobic hills surrounding Amber to a dry lake in the valley below.

Begun in 1727 and completed in just 8 years, Jaipur was the first city in India to enjoy rigorous town planning according to the principles laid down in "Shilpa Shastra," an ancient Indian treatise on architecture. The city is protected by high walls, with wide, straight avenues that divide it into nine sectors (apparently reflecting the nine divisions of the universe, resembling the Indian horoscope), each named after the commodity and caste who lived and practiced their specific skills here—the order and space was at the time a total revolution in Indian cities. Although these market names still provide some clue as to what can be found in the otherwise rather uniform rows of shops that line the streets, the overall significance of these historic divisions is today lost to the traveler on foot trying to negotiate the chaos of the filth-strewn streets and pushy traders.

Despite the romantic nickname the "Pink City," Jaipur is not one of Rajasthan's most attractive cities, which is why, after taking in the centrally located City Palace (where the principal sights are located), it's probably wise to concentrate on sites farther afield: Amber Fort, first royal residence of the maharajas of Kachchwaha, lies 11km (7 miles) north; and popular **Samode Palace** is an hour's drive away. But if the heat has you beat and the very thought of traipsing through another fort or durbar hall leaves you feeling exhausted, check out some of the shopping recommendations. A central repository for the region's wonderful crafts, Jaipur is famous for its gems and jewelry, enamel- and brassware, blue pottery, embroidered leather footwear, rugs, tie-and-dye cotton fabrics, fine *Kota doria* saris, and ready-made linen and homewear.

ESSENTIALS

VISITOR INFO   The **Rajasthan Tourist Development Corporation (RTDC)** information bureau is located on Platform 1 at the Jaipur Railway Station (© **0141/220-3531** or -2586; Mon–Sat 10am–5pm; closed 2nd Sat of every month). The main office is located at the **RTDC Tourist Hotel** (© **0141/511-0591** or -0596; same hours as station office) on M.I. Road, the main thoroughfare in Jaipur. For predeparture planning, check out the RTDC's website at www.rajasthantourismindia.com, or contact them at rtdcpr@sancharnet.in. You'll find the less helpful **Government of India tourist office** at the Khasa Kothi hotel (© **0141/236-8461;** Mon–Fri 9am–6pm, Sat 9am–1:30pm).

To find out about any events or festivals or current arts and entertainment listings, pick up a copy of the daily *Hindustan Times* or the *Jaipur Vision.*

Fun Fact Why Pink?

Jaipur is known as the Pink City, a rather idealized description of the terra-cotta-colored lime plaster that coats the old part of the city's walls, buildings, and temples. The reasons for painting the town pink are unknown, but various theories have been tossed about, from using pink to cut down glare, to Jai Singh II's apparent devotion to Lord Shiva (whose favorite color is reputedly terra-cotta). Others believe Singh wanted to imitate the color of the sandstone used in the forts and palaces of his Mughal emperor-friends. The most popular reason (spread no doubt by "Britishers" during the Raj era) is that pink is the traditional color of hospitality, and the city was freshly painted and paved with pink gravel to warmly welcome Edward VII for his visit here in 1876. In 2000 the city was again painted for a state visit, this time by former U.S. president Bill Clinton, and a few streets became off-limits to cars—thankfully, this is still the case at Bapu Bazaar, which as a consequence is the best place to browse.

GETTING THERE

BY AIR   Both **Jet Airways** (© **0141/236-0763,** 0141/241-2222, or airport 0141/254-9215) and **Indian Airlines** (© **0141/274-3500** or airport 0141/2721519) connect the city with Delhi (40 min.), Jodhpur (45 min.), Udaipur (1hr., 40 min.), Mumbai (directly 1 hr., 30 min.; hopper 4 hr., 20 min.), and Kolkata (1 hr., 55 min). Sanganer Airport lies 15 minutes south of the center of town; most hotels are 30 minutes away. A taxi ride should cost Rs 250 to Rs 300 ($5.35–$6.50); the airport bus is Rs 30 (60¢).

BY TRAIN   The Jaipur Railway Station, located west of the old city, is open Monday to Saturday 8am to 2pm and 2:15 to 8pm, Sunday 8am to 2pm. You can reach Jaipur by train from just about anywhere. The Shatabdi Express connects Jaipur with Delhi in 4½ hours; from Agra the train takes about 7 hours. Dial © **131** for railway inquiries and © **135** for reservations. Reservations for foreign tourists are made at counter 769. Note that you will be inundated with rickshaw-*wallas* on arrival—to avoid this you may want to utilize the prepaid auto-rickshaw counter at the railway station.

BY BUS   Buses arrive at the Inter-state Bus Terminal on Station Road. For information call © **0141/220-5790,** -5621, or -6143.

BY CAR   As is the case everywhere, you will need to hire a driver with your car. The Jaipur–Delhi National Highway no. 8 has been improved and transformed into a dual carriage road that should get you between the two cities in 4 hours. The single-road highway between Agra and Jaipur through Fatehpur Sikri and Baratphur is in good condition—all you have to worry about are the other drivers.

GETTING AROUND   The best way to get around the crowded city center is on foot or by rickshaw. A rickshaw should set you back Rs 50/$1.05 per hour—always discuss the fare upfront. You can hire a car and driver for approximately 1 hour (16km/10 miles) for Rs 160 ($3.35); 2 hours (32km/20 miles) Rs 310 ($6.70); 4 hours (40km/25 miles) Rs 390 ($8.70); 5 hours (50km/31 miles) Rs 485 ($10). Arya Niwas (see "Where to Stay," below) offers a 3-hour round-trip to Amber for Rs 350 ($7.60). If your intention is to hire a car and driver to tour Rajasthan at your own pace, contact **RTDC Transport Unit** (✆ **0141/ 237-5466** or 0141/231-5714) or **Rajasthan Tours** at the Rambagh Palace in Jaipur (✆ **0141/238-1668** or -1041). For more information on hiring a car and driver, see chapter 2.

GUIDED TOURS   You may be in for a frustrating time if you hire guides, registered or not, who hang around outside attractions—many have their English commentary down pat but more often than not can't engage in dialogue. Better to organize a guide through your hotel; or contact **Rajasthan Travel** (✆ **0141/236-5408**) or **Sita World Travel** (✆ **0141/237-3996,** 0141/240-3434, or -2020). Expect to pay about Rs 250 ($5.35) for 4 hours. If you don't mind groups (and the guide may, once again, have limited knowledge of English), RTDC offers several tours. A packed half-day (5-hr.) tour, departing 8am, 11:30am, and 1:30pm, covers Hawa Mahal, Amer Palace and Fort, Jal Mahal, Gaitor Maharaja Cenotaphs, City Palace and Museum, Jantar Mantar, Central Museum, and Jawahar Kala Kendra. The cost is Rs 90 ($1.90). The 8am tour is advisable. The full-day tour (9am–6pm) includes all of the above as well as the Nahargarh and Jaigarh forts and Birla Planetarium; it costs Rs 135 ($2.85). Tours depart from the information bureau on platform 1, Jaipur station. The **Indian Tourism Development Corporation (ITDC)** offers a similar full-day tour (Rs 105/$2.15; Rs 160/$3.35 A/C), departing at 9:30am from Ashok Travels & Tours, Khasa Kothi; to book, call ✆ **0141/236-8461** (www.theashok group.com). A **Jaipur by Night tour** (✆ **0141/220-2586** or -3531) comprises dinner at Nahagarh Fort. A far classier option is dinner booked at Rambagh Palace or Rajvilas.

CITY LAYOUT   The major attractions and best bazaars lie within the walls of the old city. Just south of the wall lies the Mirza Ismail (M.I.) Road—running west to east, this major thoroughfare is where most of the primary retail outlets and a few good restaurants are located. Farther south (but still within walking distance) lie the Albert Hall and Museum of Indology.

FESTIVALS   As is the case everywhere in India, Jaipur seems to celebrate something new every month, but the following are worth noting: In March, when Holi celebrants throughout the country splash color on anything that moves, Jaipur also celebrates an **Elephant Festival.** The massive pachyderms—dressed to the nines and decorated with paint—march through the city's streets to the City Palace, accompanied by loud drumbeats and chanting. The event also sees a tug-of-war between the elephants and their *mahoots* (elephant trainers/ caretakers), as well as men playing polo—on elephant-back, of course. Make sure you book accommodations in advance during this period.

(**Moments   Sunset over Jaipur**

See the pink city at its rosiest from Nahargarh Fort (or "Tiger Fort") when the sun sinks behind the Aravalli Hills. Then—as night falls—watch the city skyline turn into the twinkling jewels for which it is famed. The view is always a winner, but during the festival of Diwali in November, when firecrackers explode above the city, it's one you will never forget. The fort (Rs 5/10¢ entry) itself is largely in ruins, but the great vantage point alone is worth the trip. An RTDC-run cafe serves drinks and snacks.

The following month (Apr) is **Gangaur,** when the women of Rajasthan pray for the longevity of their husbands or for husbands fair and kind to the goddess Parvati (also known as Gangaur). This culminates with a procession to Gangaur Temple by the symbolic Siva, accompanied by elephants, to take his bride home. **Teej** (July–Aug) sees Rajasthan's always colorfully clad women dressed in full regalia to celebrate the onset of the monsoon, while **Diwali**—the "festival of lights"—is celebrated throughout India in November.

FAST FACTS: Jaipur

American Express Located on M.I. Road (near Ganpati Plaza), the office is open from Monday to Saturday 9:30am to 6pm.

Area Code For Jaipur, the area code is **0141**.

Banks You'll find several banks and ATMS on M.I. Road.

Climate Summers have a mean maximum temperature of 104°F (40°C) (and a minimum of 75°F/26°C), while winters range between mean maximum of 70°F (22°C) and 48°F (8°C). Best months are October through February.

Directory For assistance call ⓒ **197**.

Emergencies Ambulance ⓒ **102**; Fire ⓒ **101**; Police ⓒ **100**.

Hospitals The **Santokba Durlabji Memorial Hospital** (ⓒ **0141/256-6251** to -57) is located on Bhawani Singh Marg.

Newspapers/Books You can pick up an amazing selection of newspapers, magazines, and books (considering its inconspicuous location and minute size) from Books Corner on M.I. Road, including the *Jaipur Vision* and *Trains at a Glance.*

Police The HQ is on Station Road (ⓒ **0141/231-1677**).

Post Office The GPO is on M.I. Road (Mon–Sat 9am–6pm).

WHAT TO SEE & DO

The principal attraction of the old city of Jaipur is its **City Palace** (see below), the nearby **Jantar Mantar** (also described below), and the much-photographed **Hawa Mahal (Palace of Wind).** Built by Sawai Pratap Singh in 1799, Hawa Mahal is principally a five-story facade of 593 latticed-stone screened windows, behind which the ladies of the palace could view the city without being seen. You can walk along the corridors that line the windows, which are mostly one room thick, but the building's principal attraction is the facade, which can be viewed from street level (entrance from Sireh Deorhi Bazaar; 9am–4:30pm; Rs 5/ 10¢). Also within the city complex, opposite the Chandra Mahal, is **Govindji Temple** (daily 5–11am and 6–8pm), the most famous in the city and dedicated to Lord Krishna, Jai Singh II's favorite deity. The Krishna image was brought here from Brindavan in the late 17th century; devotees are only allowed a brief glimpse of it seven times a day.

In the new part of the city lies **Ram Niwas Bagh,** the city garden, which houses a depressing zoo and aviary. At the heart of the garden lies Albert Hall, which houses the **Central Museum** (ⓒ **0141/257-0099;** Sat–Thurs 10am– 4:30pm; Rs 30/60¢). Designed by the prolific architect and past master of the hybrid Indo-Saracenic style of architecture, Swinton Jacob, this is of principal interest from an architectural point of view, and a slow turn around the building in a car will suffice for many. That's not to say that the exhibits are devoid of interest—the eclectic collection covers a wide range of objects, from musical instruments to bottled organs, and the tiny terra-cotta figures demonstrating myriad yoga positions are worth a look. A short drive due south lies the even stranger **Museum of Indology** (© 0141/2607455; daily 8am–6pm; Rs 40/ 85¢), where an incredible selection of objects—all collected in one lifetime by the writer Acharya Vyakul—has been crammed into countless dusty display cases in every nook and cranny of his house. The collection is as eclectic as they come, including such items as a map of India painted on a grain of rice, misprinted rupees, a 180-million-year-old fossil, a letter written by Jai Singh, and the Gayatri Mantra written on a single strand of hair. It's a great shame more money is not available to edit and present this collection more professionally.

On M.I. Road you'll find **Raj Mandir**—one of the most over-the-top cinemas in the country. This is the place to watch a Bollywood blockbuster, though you may have to wait in line for hours to do so. Look out for the **statue of Sawai Jai Singh II** nearby, at the Panch Batti intersection. The most disappointing attraction in the city is the **Jawahar Kala Kendra**—designed by the Indian architect Charles Correa in 1993, it has enjoyed exposure as a great example of contemporary Indian design and is celebrated as a center for the arts, with large exhibition spaces and studios for artists. Although the architecture may impress some, it is now all but empty of artists, and the exhibition spaces contain little more than a few broken chairs and the mattress of a homeless student. It may pass for art in the minds of the Turner Prize judges, but it looks very much like an indulgent waste of money.

CITY ESCAPES   If the populous nature of Jaipur gets to be too much, take a trip to **Amber Fort** (see below), which can be covered in a few hours. Do bear in mind, however, that even here the crush of people can be exhausting, particularly over weekends; try to get here as soon as it opens. Time allowing, you may want to include a visit to **Jaigarh Fort** (daily 9am–4:30pm; Rs 20/40¢), whose walls snake high above Amber, creating a crenelated horizon. Built for defense purposes by Sawai Jai Singh II, it has a number of buildings, gardens, and reservoirs as well as the world's largest cannon on wheels and the only surviving medieval cannon foundry, but its principal attraction is the panoramic view across Amber.

On the way to Amber you'll see the turnoff for the imposing hilltop fort of **Nahargarh** (see "Sunset over Jaipur," above). Just below it is **Gaitor,** a walled garden that houses the marble *chhatris*—erected over cremation platforms—of the Kachchwaha rulers. Needless to say, the most impressive one belongs to Jai Singh II. Farther along the Amber road you will see the **Jal Mahal,** a lake palace originally built by Sawai Pratap Singh in 1799, who spent much of his childhood at Udaipur's Lake Palace. Sadly, Man Sagar Lake is dry from the protracted drought, stripping it of much of its romance. If it's romance you're after, take a leisurely drive to **Samode Palace** (see "Where to Stay," below; lunch Rs 425/ $9.25) or—even better—book a table at **Rajvilas** for dinner (see "Where to Dine," below).

East of Jaipur (8km/5 miles), on the road to Agra, you will find relative peace and fresh air at **Sisodia Rani Gardens** (© 0141/268-0494; daily 8am–6pm; Rs 1/2¢). Constructed by the Kachchwaha kings during the 18th and 19th centuries, it comprises terraced gardens with painted pavilions, the largest being **Sisodia Rani Ka Bagh,** built by the ever-prolific Jai Singh II for his Sisodia queen in yet another clever alliance—this time with the Rajputs from the Udaipur region. Her small palace—the perfect retreat from royal intrigue—has featured in a number of Bollywood movies. Behind the gardens a flight of stairs leads to a temple dedicated to Hanuman, the monkey god—hundreds of monkeys descend here at 4pm when the priests feed them. A little farther along the Agra road is pretty **Galta,** a gorge filled with sacred *kunds* (natural pools or reservoirs), all fed by pure spring water that falls from a rock resembling a carved cow's mouth, and surrounded by temples.

TOP ATTRACTIONS

City Palace (and Maharaja Sawai Man Singh II Museum) ★★★   The former ruling family still lives in the seven-story Chandra Mahal ("Moon Palace") built by Sawai Jai Singh II, but the outer and inner courtyards have been converted into a museum. The first courtyard is where you'll find the **Mubarak Mahal (Welcome Palace),** a "reception center" constructed by Maharaja Sawai Madho Singh II, grandfather of the present maharaja. Mubarak houses the textile and costume section, where regal costumes provide some insight into the tremendous wealth and status that the family enjoyed, as well as the extraordinarily high level of craftsmanship available to them over the centuries. These include embroidery so fine it looks like printwork, some of the best *bandhini odhnis* (tie-dye veils) to come out of Sanganer, Kashmiri shawls, gossamer muslin from Bangladesh, and silk saris from Varanasi. The **Armoury,** with a selection of exquisitely crafted yet truly vicious-looking daggers and swords, is housed in the adjacent palace—if Mughal history, with all its valor and intrigue, has caught your imagination, ask one of the attendants to point out the items belonging to the emperors Akbar, Jahangir, and Shah Jahan. The next courtyard reveals the raised **Diwan-i-Khas (Hall of Private Audience),** built in sandstone and marble. Look for the sun emblems decorating the walls—like most Rajput princes the Kachchwaha clan belonged to the warrior caste, who traced their origins back to the sun (see "Once Were Warriors: The History of the Rajput," earlier in this chapter). To the west is the **Pritam Niwas Chowk,** or **"Peacock Courtyard,"** with its four beautifully painted doorways—from here you can search for signs of life from the royal residence that towers above. Finally, the **Diwan-i-Am (Hall of Public Audience)** houses a simply fantastic collection of miniature paintings, carpets, manuscripts, and photographs—look for the self-portraits of eccentric Ram Singh II, who found expression for his vanity in a passion for photography. Trying to see everything here is time-consuming, but for many this is the real highlight of the visit.

Fun Fact I'll Take My Ganges Water to Go, Thanks

Inside the Diwan-i-Khas are two huge silver urns, each weighing 345kg (760 lb.)—according to the *Guinness Book of Records,* these are the largest silver objects in the world. The Maharaja Sawai Madho Singh II, a devout Hindu, had these made before attending the coronation of King Edward VII in England to ensure that he had a constant supply of Ganges water to drink and purify himself with from extended contact with the "outcastes."

Chokri Shahad, Old City. Entrance through Atish Gate or Nakkar Gate. Get here as soon as it opens. ⓒ 0141/ 260-8055. Rs 150 ($3.15); still camera free. Daily 9:30am–4:45pm.

Jantar Mantar ★★★ Living proof of the genius of Sawai Jai Singh, this medieval observatory (built 1728–34) is the largest of its kind in the world, and the best preserved of Jai Singh's five observatories. Whether or not you understand how the instruments are read, the sheer sculptural shapes of the stone and marble objects and the monumental size of many (like the 23m/74-ft.-high Samrat Yantra, which forecasts crop prospects based on "the declination and hour of the heavenly bodies") are worth the trip and make for great photographs. It looks more like a modern art exhibition or sci-fi set—hard to believe these instruments were constructed in the 18th century and remain functional—some are still used to forecast how hot the summer will be, when the monsoon will arrive, and how long it will last. There are 18 instruments in all, erected between 1728 and 1734 by Sawai Jai Singh—many of his own invention. Try to get here before the sun gets too hot. You can hire a guide at the gate for Rs 150 ($3.15) but will probably do better arranging one through your hotel.

Follow signs from city palace. Rs 10 (22¢). 9am–4:30pm.

Amber (or Amer) Fort ★★ Amber was the capital of the Kachchwahas from 1037 to 1727, when Sawai Jai Singh II moved the capital to Jaipur. The approach is through a narrow pass, and the fort, an imposing edifice that grew over a period of 2 centuries, is naturally fortified by the Aravalli Hills, making it an ideal stronghold. It's a stiff 20-minute climb to **Suraj Pol (Sun Gate),** beyond which lies a beautiful complex of palaces, halls, pavilions, gardens, and temples—either travel by car or pretend you are of royal blood and ascend on elephant-back (Rs 400/$8.75 for one to four riders). Having entered through Suraj Pol into Jaleb Chowk, where more elephants take riders for a turn around the courtyard, take the flight of stairs up through **Singh Pol (Lion Gate)** to the **Diwan-i-Am (Hall of Public Audience),** a raised platform with 27 colonnades. Opposite you'll see the ornately carved silver doors leading to the **Shila Devi Temple,** which contains an image of the vicious goddess Kali, the appropriate family deity for the warring Rajput Kachchwaha. The massive three-story, intricately decorated **Ganesh Pol (Elephant Gate)** leads to the private apartments of the royal family, built around a Mughal-style garden courtyard. The **Sheesh Mahal (Mirror Palace)**—covered in mirror mosaics and colored glass—would have been the private quarters of the maharaja and his maharani, literally transformed into a glittering jewel box in flickering candlelight. Above is **Jas Mandir,** a hall of private audience, with floral glass inlays and alabaster relief work. Opposite, across the garden, is the **Sukh Mahal (Pleasure Palace)**—note the perforations in the marble walls and channels where water was piped to cool the rooms. South lies the oldest part, the **Palace of Man Singh I.** If you want to explore the old town and its many temples, exit again through the Chand Pol, opposite Suraj Pol. *Note:* As is the case elsewhere, the press of bodies and noise levels can seriously detract from the experience—try to get here at 9am to avoid the heat and crowds, particularly on weekends.

Amber, 11km (7 miles) N of Jaipur. ⓒ 0141/253-0293. Rs 50 ($1.05). Daily 9am–4:30pm.

WHERE TO STAY

Jaipur has a plethora of places to stay, from standard Holiday Inns to backpacker hostels. But no one in his right mind comes to Rajasthan to overnight in a bland room in some nondescript hotel chain when he could be sleeping in the very room where a maharaja seduced his maharani, or in the royal apartments of the family guests—hence our focus on heritage hotels. The following reviews represent the best in the city, in a variety of price categories. The exception to this is Rajvilas, which not only imitates the heritage property concept, but improves upon it.

You may come across a few heritage properties that did not make the selection, such as the **Jai Mahal Palace** (© **0141/222-3636;** www.tajhotels.com; Rs 5,000–Rs 5,600/$110–$123 double). The hotel is architecturally splendid, with buildings dating back to 1745, but it's neither as grand as Taj Rambagh nor as romantic and authentic as Samode or Alsisar Havelis (which also offer much better value for your money). The **Raj Mahal Palace** (© **0141/238-3260** or -3262) is a 14-room mansion that in its heyday (when Man Singh II and his beautiful wife, Gayatri Devi, moved here from Rambagh) hosted the likes of Jackie Kennedy, Prince Philip, and Princess Diana. It still has a gracious feel (not to mention the biggest hotel rooms in India), but is badly in need of refurbishment. If you're into nostalgia, check it out on www.royalfamilyjaipur.com, then book room no. 107, where the maharaja hosted Mrs. Kennedy. This is also the best place to bring kids, with huge family suites, large grounds, and a pool; rates are from Rs 2,200 ($48) double. Sadly, a similar air of decay hangs over **Bissau Palace** (© **0141/230-4371** or -4391; www.bissaupalace.com; from Rs 750/ $16, Rs 990–Rs 1,800/$20–$40 for A/C room). Built by the Rawal (Duke) of Bissau, with original buildings dating back to 1787, it offers much the same facilities as the cheaper Diggi Palace, with the advantage of a small pool. **Raj Palace** (© **0141/263-4077;** www.rajpalace.com; $90–$350) is the most recent heritage conversion, but frankly, it's overpriced and just too kitsch for our taste.

Budget travelers looking for a lively atmosphere may want to check out **Arya Niwas** (© **0141/237-2456;** www.aryaniwas.com; from Rs 450/$9.80). This is not a heritage hotel but it is incredibly popular with a wide array of international travelers, many of whom appear to spend a great deal of time sitting in the wicker chairs that line the deep veranda overlooking a small patch of lawn. It's efficiently run, with good-value tours and car hires, and the canteen-style dining hall has a great reputation. The building and rooms have a very institutional feel, however—unlike the similarly priced, more laid-back Diggi Palace (see below).

Note: The prices below are sometimes given in rupees, with U.S. dollar conversions; others are in U.S. dollars only, which is how many hotels targeting foreign markets quote their rates.

Alsisar Haveli 👁👁 *(Value* This is the most elegant heritage property in its price category in Jaipur, offering excellent value for money, and in slightly better condition than Narain Niwas. Built in 1892 and still owned by the Kachchwaha clan of Rajputs, it has all the traditional elements of Rajput architecture—scalloped arches and pretty cupolas, painted ceilings and colored glass windows, and a maze of corridors and stairs threaded around and through inner courtyards. Rooms vary in size, but all are furnished with antiques and the block-printed fabrics typical of the region, and most have a padded alcove area for lounging. The only drawback is that some of the mattresses are a tad soft, and the bathroom fittings—plastic taps and pink shower curtains (all showers are in tubs)—are perfectly serviceable, but ugly. You can take tea around the pool, or retreat to the tables on the lawn for total peace. The lounge is beautifully furnished, but it is the dining hall that sets the place apart: Unlike the oppressive rooms so typical of heritage properties (like Samode Haveli), Alsisar's is filled with light thanks to the floor-to-ceiling glass walls and spotless white tablecloths. Food is good, albeit not memorable; breakfast will run you Rs 135 to Rs 150 ($1.80–$3.15), while lunch and dinner (both buffets) cost Rs 300 ($6.50).

Sansar Chandra Rd., Jaipur, 302 001. © 0141/236-8290 or -4685. Fax 0141/236-4652. www.alsisar.com. 36 units. Rs 2,000 ($44) double; Rs 2,400 ($53) suite. AE, DC, MC, V. **Amenities:** Restaurant; bar; pool; laundry. *In room:* A/C, TV, minibar, hair dryer.

Diggi Palace ⭐ *Value*   This to our mind is the best budget option in Jaipur, where you get the opportunity to overnight in a 200-year-old heritage property for a fraction of the rate charged by Alsisar Haveli and Narain Niwas (though service and facilities are correspondingly not in the same class). Architecturally, the building reflects traditional Rajput style. Rooms, which vary in size, all feature cool, clean white tiles and whitewashed walls; some have antique furniture offset with bright block-printed fabrics. Book an air-conditioned room to beat the heat—they're also larger and still a steal at Rs 750 ($16)—or, if you want your own veranda, ask for one of the larger Rs 950 ($21) rooms, particularly those overlooking the garden. The "palace"—it would be more honest to describe it as a haveli—is within walking distance of the Ram Niwas Gardens and central museum. The only drawback is that it has no pool, but the leafy, well-established gardens are a wonderful respite, filled with birdsong. The open-air, first-floor veranda is where meals are served; dinner costs Rs 40 to Rs 95 (85¢–$2).

Shivaji Marg, C-scheme, Sawai Ram Singh Hwy., Jaipur 302 004. © 0141/237-3091, 0141/236-6120, 0141/236-6196. Fax 0141/230-359. diggihtl@datainfosys.net. 40 units. Double: Rs 300–Rs 450 ($6.50–$9.80), Rs 750 ($16) A/C; Rs 950 ($21) suite. No credit cards. **Amenities:** Dining hall; laundry. *In room:* TV in some, A/C in some.

Narain Niwas Palace ⭐   Like Alsisar, Narain Niwas provides you with an opportunity to live in a heritage property for relatively little money (though Alsisar currently has the edge in terms of atmosphere and service). Built in 1928 by Gen. Amar Singh, Thakur of Kanota and then commander of the Jaipur State forces, Narain Niwas was originally a country residence to which the thakur would retreat from the walled city. The 3-hectare (7-acre) property remains an oasis, but the city now surrounds it. Since opening as a heritage hotel in 1978, it has been featured in glossy design publications like Taschen's *Indian Interiors*. Not surprisingly, staying in a room like the much-photographed suite no. 36, with its high ceilings, four-poster antique bed, fresco-painted walls and ceilings, and Raj-era chandelier, is like overnighting in a museum. (Sadly, the off-camera bathroom is very disappointing—with no tub and in serious need of a face-lift.) Standard room nos. 51 to 57 are worth booking; individually furnished with antique beds and chairs, these feature pretty frescoes and block-print fabrics and are close to the pool, opening onto a particularly lush part of the garden—an essential balm after tackling Jaipur's streets. Buffet-style meals are taken on the lawns or in the dining hall which, like the antiques-filled lounge, features scalloped arches decorated with frescoes, and colored glass windows and baubles.

Kanota Bagh, Narain Sing Rd., Jaipur 302 004. © 0141/256-1291 or -3448. Fax 0141/256-1045. 31 units. Rs 2,000 ($44) double; Rs 2,500 ($55) suite. AE, DC, MC, V. **Amenities:** Dining hall; bar; pool; travel desk; car hires; laundry. *In room:* A/C, TV in some, minibar, hair dryer.

Rajvilas ⭐⭐⭐   Rajvilas is one of those luxury hotels that is a destination in its own right. It has won awards every year since it opened in December 1997 (including *Tatler*'s "Hotel of the Year" and *Gourmet*'s "Most Exotic Resort in the

World") and is arguably the best of the Oberio's flagship Vilas properties—this is, after all, where Bill Clinton stayed during his state visit to India and where Mr. Oberoi himself chose to celebrate his daughter's recent marriage. With a budget of $20 million, no expense was spared in showcasing the fine craftsman-ship typical of the region to create and decorate what is ostensibly a traditional fortified Rajasthani palace—and though it may not have the history of an orig-inal heritage hotel, it more than makes up for this with a level of comfort and luxury that true heritage properties simply cannot match. Set amid 13 hectares (32 acres) of orchards, formal gardens, and decorative pools, accommodations are separate from the main fort (which houses the public spaces) in clusters of rooms—between four and six around each central courtyard—and a few luxury tents, all comfortably decorated with a tasteful blend of colonial and Rajasthani influences. The discreet yet attentive staff (115 culled from 7,200 interviews) will not let you lift a finger, enabling even the most demanding guest to relish "living in the princely style of Rajasthan." The restaurant serves excellent food, with a wide range of Eastern and Western options, and even the spa, offering every conceivable treatment, is an award-winner. The only drawback (aside from the top-scale prices) is that you feel totally disconnected from Jaipur; then again, for many this in itself is an excellent reason to book here.

Goner Rd., Jaipur 303 012. ℂ 800/5-OBEROI toll-free in the U.S. and Canada, or 0141/268-0101. Fax 0141/268-0202. www.oberoihotels.com. 71 units. $370 double; $450 tents. AE, DC, MC, V. **Amenities:** Restaurant; library/bar; pool (the 3 villas have private pools); mini golf; tennis courts; croquet; gymnasium; health and beauty spa; elephant, horse, and camel riding; concierge; complimentary airport transfers; helipad; room serv-ice; laundry. *In room:* A/C, TV, CD/DVD player (complimentary access to music and films), minibar, hair dryer.

Samode Haveli ★★ Ever since Samode Haveli made it into that glossy tome to style, *Hip Hotels: Budget,* and was selected by the author, Herbert Ypma, as one of his top 10 hotels in the world, it has enjoyed unprecedented popularity. One of the few accommodations options within the old walled city (the nearby Raj Palace is not in the same class), this 200-year-old city mansion oozes authen-ticity, with higgledy-piggledy rooms of various sizes furnished in typical Rajasthani antiques and featuring pillars and cusped arches painted in traditional motifs, tiny colored glass windows, marble floors, and deep alcoves for loung-ing. Bathrooms have enjoyed recent upgrades, and most now have separate showers (or showers only). Best rooms are those housed in the *zenana* (tradi-tionally the part of the house where women were secluded), particularly the Sheesh Mahal suite, in which every inch of wall and ceiling is covered in tiny glass mirrors or delicately executed miniature paintings—the effect in candle-light is not dissimilar to the celebrated Sheesh Mahal at Amber Fort (though it's worth mentioning that some find the extra-low ceilings and numerous pillars claustrophobic). For all its romance and gracious atmosphere, this is no honey-mooners' delight—only two rooms (nos. 114 and 115) have double beds. The main drawbacks here are the dining hall, which, despite being beautifully deco-rated, feels gloomy and oppressive, particularly during the day; the mediocre food; and the service, which is extremely patchy. The recently constructed pool area, with adjoining spa, is a very welcome addition.

Samode Haveli, Gangapole, Jaipur 302 992. ℂ 0141/263-2407, -2370, or -1942. Fax 0141/263-1397. www.samode.com. 22 units. Rs 3,100 ($66) double; Rs 3,950 ($85) suite. AE, DC, MC, V. **Amenities:** Dining hall; bar; pool; fitness center; steam room; airport transfers; massage; laundry. *In room:* A/C, TV, minibar, hair dryer.

Taj Rambagh Palace ★★★ If you're hell-bent on experiencing the blue blood of heritage properties, Rambagh Palace is both the largest (19 hectares/

47 acres) and most elegant option in Jaipur; its origins date back to 1835. Converted into a hotel in 1957, it is today a favorite of Bollywood stars and worth visiting for a drink or dinner even if you're not staying here. Of the three room categories, the standards (which the Taj calls "superior") are disappointing—particularly those located in the new wing—and feature underlit carpeted corridors off which run endless rooms with low ceilings and tacky hotel furniture. Then again, you probably won't spend a great deal of time in your room; you'll be too busy luxuriating in the gracious, beautiful palace buildings (which, incidentally, house one of Rajasthan's classiest bars, the **Polo**) or strolling the sweeping lawns. To feel as if you're actually living in a palace apartment, however, opt for a luxury room (no. 317 is just fabulous)—old-fashioned in a colonial rather than Rajasthani sense, elegant and spacious, they really are worth the extra $70 (but bear in mind that for a few dollars more you could be staying at Rajvilas, with its infinitely superior service). Dining at the swish **Suvarna Mahal** is a grand affair (see review below), and certainly the hotel has every amenity you could wish for (except an outdoor pool), but you sense that a certain complacency has crept in—even the best heritage hotel in Jaipur can't rest on its laurels forever.

Sawani Sing Rd., Jaipur 302 005. ℂ **0141/238-1919**; 212/515-5889 in the U.S. Fax 0141/238-1098. www.tajhotels.com. rambagh.jaipur@tajhotels.com. 90 units. Rs 8,000–Rs 11,000 ($175–$240) double; Rs 13,000–Rs 30,000 ($284–$654) suite. AE, DC, MC, V. **Amenities:** 2 restaurants; bar; indoor pool; tennis; badminton and squash courts; health club; croquet; travel desk and car hires; concierge; business center; room service; laundry; camel rides; astrologer; henna. *In room:* A/C, TV, minibar, hair dryer.

AROUND JAIPUR

Samode Palace ⭐⭐   An hour's drive (45km/28 miles) from Jaipur, the 400-year-old Samode Palace is popular, pretty, and very commercialized. Once an exclusive retreat for those in the know, its starring role in the 1984 mini-series *The Far Pavilions* put it on the map, resulting in some touristy additions like the new wing with its charmless low-ceilinged rooms, most of which overlook a parking lot. The original palace suites are beautiful, however: huge, with loads of natural light and furnished with a mix of antiques and contemporary pieces. Bathrooms need renovating but are adequate. Best value-for-money option is one of the rooms overlooking the lovely pool area (nos. 207, 216, 308, and 405 are a few)—ask for one with a balcony. Many use this as a relaxing retreat from Jaipur, whose major attractions can be covered in a day trip, and it's also a good steppingstone into the Shekawati. However, the palace is far more commercial than, say, Deogarh Mahal (a 280km/174-mile drive from Jaipur), and there's not much to see or do here besides wander around the town to meet the tourist-savvy locals or shop for block-print fabrics and bangles. An interesting and good-value alternative lies 10 minutes away, at Samode Bagh, a large garden established by the royal family. Featuring delightful en-suite tents (situated a little too close to each other, frankly), Samode Bagh has enjoyed increased attention ever since it was included in *Hip Hotels: Budget*. The tent walls feature beautiful Mughal-inspired patterns and are attractively furnished with carpets, standing lamps, and pretty wooden beds and chairs. The Bagh has its own pool and tennis courts. All in all, it's an extremely peaceful getaway, as long as you have your own car. Sadly, as at all Samode properties, service is at best unpredictable.

Reservations through Samode Haveli, Gangapole, Jaipur 302 992. ℂ **0141/263-2407**, -2370, or -1942. Fax 0141/263-1397. www.samode.com. 35 units (Palace); 50 units (Bagh). Rs 4,000 ($87) double; Rs 6,000–Rs 10,000 ($130–$218) suite. Bagh Rs 3,060 ($66) double. AE, DC, MC, V. **Amenities:** Restaurant; bar; pool; tennis; gym; badminton; table tennis; massage; laundry; camel safari. *In room:* A/C, TV, minibar, hair dryer.

WHERE TO DINE

All the hotels reviewed above have dining halls or restaurants that usually serve buffets featuring mediocre to good North Indian food and mediocre to inedible "Continental" options. If you're spending more than 1 night or looking for somewhere to lunch, check out the following options. Note that you'll find the largest concentration of restaurants along M.I. Road, which is also the main shopping drag outside the old city. If you're feeling peckish or thirsty during a visit to the City Palace, take a table on the courtyard at the **Palace Cafe,** inside the palace walls near the Jaleb Chowk entrance (✆ **0141/262-6449;** Mon–Fri 9am–6pm, Sat–Sun 9–11am). It's a serene place with outdoor seating and an air-conditioned interior where historic photographs line the walls. Order a cold beer or a refreshing pot of tea and some cucumber sandwiches.

For a more authentic experience, head to Johair Bazaar to shop, stopping at **Laxmi Misthan Bhandar (LMB)** ∉∉ (✆ **0141/256-5844;** daily 1:30–3:30pm and 7–11pm; Rs 50–Rs 120/$1.05–$2.60). Anyone with even half a sweet tooth shouldn't miss stepping out of the madness of the bazaar into this cool oasis—even if it's just to salivate over the huge selection of sweets beautifully (and hygienically) displayed behind glass counters. Sample the *paneer ghewar* (honeycomb soaked in treacle)—claimed to be the best in India. Beyond the takeout area lies the large air-conditioned restaurant. Recently renovated by what appears to be a set designer with a love for the flamboyant 1980s, it remains strictly Brahman (no onion or garlic are used in preparation—they are believed to inflame the senses), and no meat or alcohol are allowed on the premises. Try the freshly prepared *samosas* (Rs 13/25¢), and wash them down with the most delicious banana *lassi* (yogurt drink) in Jaipur.

Chanakya ∉ Ⓥⓐⓛⓤⓔ NORTH INDIAN/VEGETARIAN   Like Niros (which is located a little farther down M.I. Rd.), Chanakya is crammed with Jaipur businesspeople and Indian families relishing *koftas* (dumplings) and thalis from the extensive vegetarian-only menu. The *koftas* are particularly recommended: choose between the standard *malai kofta* (potato dumplings in a creamy, spicy sauce) or the *hariyala kofta* (vegetable dumplings served in a spinach sauce). To sample a bit of almost everything on the menu, order the Chanakya Special Thali—at Rs 170 ($3.60), it's the most expensive item on the menu but it's big enough to share. The bread menu is extensive (25 options), and the restaurant enjoys a deservedly high reputation for the stuffed *paratha*—ideal as a starter or an addition to *kofta*. Be warned, however, that this (like just about everything on offer) is rich—cooked and coated with pure ghee (butter). Continental choices ("baked macroni [sic]"; "vegetable cutlet with boiled vegetable") are best avoided. Waiters speak English, and service is excellent. No alcohol is served.

M.I. Rd. ✆ **0141/237-6161** or 0141/237-8461. Main courses Rs 55–Rs 170 ($1.05–$3.60). AC, DC, MC, V. Daily noon–11pm.

Niros ∉∉ NORTH INDIAN/CHINESE   The name is the only inauthentic aspect of this very professionally run restaurant, where the constant traffic includes large, extended Indian families, Bollywood celebs, and foreign travelers drawn by its reputation. Well-situated on the shopping route, Niros does good Chinese as well as typical Rajasthani meat and vegetarian dishes. Plus, if your stomach is starting to curdle from the traditional (and liberal) use of ghee as a cooking medium, you'll be happy to know that Niros's chefs use only refined soybean oil. House specialties include *laal maas* (mutton cooked in a spicy red gravy) and *reshmi* kebab (mutton marinated in traditional spices and chargrilled).

The *korma* dishes are all prepared in a deliciously creamy cashew-nut-based sauce. *Note:* You may find the ever-popular chicken *tikka masala* a tad spicier than usual. Waiters speak English, and service is excellent.

M.I. Rd. ⓒ 0141/237-4493. www.nirosindia.com. Rs 70–Rs 175 ($1.50–$3.70). AE, DC, MC, V. Daily noon–4pm and 7–11pm.

Surya Mahal ✦✦✦ INDIAN FUSION/CONTINENTAL The courtyard adjoining the Surya Mahal restaurant is the most romantic place to have dinner in Jaipur. Lit by huge burning braziers, the courtyard features a raised platform where beautiful Rajasthani women give a short performance of their traditional dance. Service is superb, as is the food—this is one place where the "Continental" cuisine is as good as the Indian; hardly surprising, considering that executive chef Daniel Patterson has worked in a number of Relais & Châteaux properties and Michelin-starred restaurants (including Aureole in New York City). Specialty Indian dishes include the kebab platter (any of the tandoor dishes are highly recommended) and traditional *thali* (multicourse platters). The *bhuney murgh ke pasandey*—chunks of chicken breast steeped in a sandalwood-saffron marinade and cooked in the tandoor—is delicious (ask for it as a main), as is the seafood Malai curry—fresh Calcutta *bekti* (a freshwater fish) and prawns simmered in a mild coconut and curry sauce. A traditional Rajasthani lamb preparation, *laal maas,* was disappointing—chewy and not complex enough. All Indian dishes are served with dal, curried vegetables, steamed rice, Indian bread (choose from a variety), and chutneys. If you don't feel like eating Indian, try the sweet potato and honey soup, followed by spinach-and-tomato ravioli with succulent tandoori *paneer* (cottage cheese)—comparatively bland but a balm for a sensitive stomach.

Rajvilas (see "Where to Stay," above). Reservations essential. Rs 475–Rs 995 ($10–$22). AE, DC, MC, V. Daily 12:30–3pm and 7:30–10:30pm.

Suvarna Mahal ✦ NORTH INDIAN/CHINESE/CONTINENTAL The main reason to dine here is not the food—which is ultimately forgettable—but the grand colonial atmosphere of the room. Having had a drink at the elegant Polo bar, or grabbed a seat on the deep veranda that overlooks the lawns where a puppet show and/or Rajasthani dancers offer predinner entertainment, you are shown through enormous doors to a well-dressed table in a soaring double-volume space, where a wonderfully opulent, old-fashioned atmosphere is only enhanced by chandeliers, huge gilded mirrors, and walls covered in rich gold fabric. Not all the waiters have a good grasp of the menu (or English), so insist on speaking to the maitre d'—he recommended the *hariya murg tikka* (chicken marinated in spicy coriander-flavored marinade and cooked over charcoal), but this was after we'd ordered a very bland *palak paneer.* He also recommended the extensive Chinese menu (cooked by a resident Chinese chef), which he claimed

---

(Tips *Lassi* Heaven

Across the road from Niros is Lassiwallah, favored by the locals as *the* place to experience a *lassi* (cold yogurt drink). Not only is the *lassi* (salty or sweet; sadly, no banana) exquisitely creamy, but the price includes the large terra-cotta mug it's served in—to be kept as a memento or (as the locals do) thrown away after use.

the locals prefer over any other in Jaipur, if not Rajasthan. Continental food is also offered.

Taj Rambagh Palace (see "Where to Stay," above). ℂ **0141/238-1919.** Rs 295–Rs 375 ($6.50–$8). Prawns Rs 675 ($15). AE, DC, V. Daily 7–11pm.

SHOPPING
Only Mumbai comes close to offering the array of goods found here, and foreign buyers for wholesale and retail outlets descend in droves to stock up on textiles, rugs, pottery, jewelry, shoes, miniature paintings, and ready-made clothing and housewares. It's a cornucopia here, and the pressure to buy is immense—not least because everyone seems to be a tout for someone (see "Understanding the Commission System," below). Finding your way around the old city is relatively easy—the divisions based on what is produced still hold true, though you'll find much more besides. Following are a few rough guidelines.

For jewelry and gems, head for **Johari Bazaar** in the old city—the gem center of Jaipur (look for Bhuramal Rajmal Surana; ℂ **0141/256-0628**). Alternatively, wander through **Chameliwala Market,** beyond the Zarawar Singh Gate, on Amber Road. If you're in search of silver jewelry, **Silver Mountain** (ℂ **0141/ 237-5913**), located in the market, is recommended. In fact, numerous factories and showrooms run the length of Amber Road, including those specializing in hand-blocked prints, blue pottery, and antiques. If you're looking to take home some of Jaipur's famous blue pottery, you'll find the largest concentration on Amber Road.

The cutting, polishing, and selling of gems and the making of silver jewelry take place in the predominantly Muslim area of Pahar Ganj in the Surajpol Bazaar. Jewelry designers from all over the world continue to nurture the superlative gem-cutting and -setting skills of these craftsmen, but here as in Johari Bazaar, be aware that bargains are hard to come by—more often than not, you really do get what you pay for. If you're knowledgeable enough, shop for gems and jewelry in the bazaars, but for most, a trip to the shops listed below is recommended.

Fabric is another must-buy, as the finest quality silk, chiffon, and cotton is transformed through traditional block printing and tie-and-dye techniques, creating intricate patterns with vibrant contrasts and colors. The finest tie-dye process is known as *bandhni* (literally "to tie"): Tiny circles are made by tying the cloth with thread in a detailed design; the cloth is often sold with the thread still tied on and is traditionally worn unironed, showing off the crinkly circles. **Bapu Bazaar** (around the corner from the Johari bazaar) is where you can bargain for a wide range of textiles and ready-made garments, as well as traditional leather shoes and bangles of glass and lacquer; it's also by far the most pleasant shopping street because it's pedestrianized.

If you're looking for great inexpensive gifts, take a look at the tiny workshops producing beautiful bangles in **Maniharon Ka Rasta,** an alley off Tripolia Bazaar. Other old-city shops worth highlighting are **Saurashtra Oriental Arts** (5–6 Jorawar Singh Gate, Amber Rd.; ℂ **0141/255-2026**), for embroidered textiles; and **Bharat Boot House** (off Johari Bazaar; ℂ **0141/256-4914**).

If you're interested in block-printed fabrics, a trip to Sanganer, a village 16km (10 miles) south of Jaipur, is a must—here printing takes place in the courtyard of almost every house. Famous as the birthplace of blockwork (and home to the largest handmade-paper industry in India), this is where you'll find the most refined block-printed work in the world. Visit **Shilpi Handicrafts** (© 0141/273-1106) for fabrics, and **Salim's** (© 0141/273-0076) for a range of handmade paper you'll be loathe to write on!

BLUE POTTERY

Kripal Singh Shekhawat ★★★   If you want to make sure you're purchasing top-quality blue glazed pottery, make an appointment to view the work of Jaipur's most famous ceramist, Kripal Singh. Made from ground, blue quartz stone and utilizing traditional designs, his work is nothing short of exquisite. B-18A Shiv Marg (near Jaipur Inn), Bani Park. © 0141/220-1127.

BOOKS

Books Corner ★ BOOKS   You could easily miss this corner shop, but even though it's tiny, it's chockablock with magazines and books. If you're looking for more information on India, coffee-table books on Rajasthan, or just a good paperback read, this has the best selection around, at the fairest prices. M.I. Rd. © 0141/236-6323.

CLOTHING & HOUSEWARES

Anokhi ★★★   This company was created by a British designer who has the items made here for import to the U.K. and elsewhere. The combination of Eastern and Western influence on design has resulted in elegant and flattering shapes (particularly the knee-length *kurta* styles, worn with wide, floppy pants) with a modern twist. The designer also produces a wide range of feminine houseware items (anything from duvet covers to napkins) and a gorgeous (but small) range of dresses for little girls. Prices are higher than in the bazaars, but the quality of design and workmanship is in another league. 2 Tilak Marg. © 0141/275-0860.

JEWELRY

Amrapali ★★   In 1980, two young entrepreneurs, Rajesh Ajmera and Rajiv Arora, saw a gap in the market and started adapting traditional jewelry styles to appeal to a broader international market. Conveniently situated near Panch Batti and the city gate that leads into Jauhri Bazaar, Amrapali is famous for its tribal silver jewelry, but the gold showroom also contains some rare examples of kundan jewelry, a technique in which each gem is set by pressing fine strips of highly purified gold around it. M.I. Rd. © **0141/237-7940** or 0141/236-2768.

Durlabhji Jewellers (Emerald House) ⭑ When a new emerald mine was discovered in Rhodesia (now Zimbabwe) in the 1920s, Mr. M. S. Durlabhji got on the very next boat and traveled south. Once there, he took one look at the deep-green quality of the emeralds and purchased the entire consignment, then continued to purchase every stone until the mine ran dry. Today his son Yogendra has a collection of emerald jewelry that makes jewelers across the world green with envy. Subhash Marg, C-Scheme. © **0141/236-3061** or 0141/237-4175.

Gem Palace ⭑⭑⭑ When the maharajas of Rajasthan were suddenly deprived of their privy purses in 1972, many were forced to sell off the family jewels. Gem Palace, whose owners had been serving their needs for four generations, was a discreet place to do so. Today you can admire these priceless items in the museum created by owner Sudhir Kasliwal, after which you can take a look at his craftsmen at work creating new pieces, destined for the necks, wrists, and fingers of the privileged all over the world. This is arguably the best jewelry shop in Jaipur, but not the place to pick up a bargain. M.I. Rd. © **0141/236-3061** or 0141/237-4175.

PASHMINAS

New Gandhi Handloom Coop ⭑⭑ *(Value* This tiny store is stuffed with a selection of Pashminas of varying quality—the cheapest cost Rs 100 ($2.10) and are available in just about every color under the sun. The extremely helpful Kashmiri gentleman will of course tempt you to spend a great deal more on one of his pure Pashminas—prices aren't going to be any lower, even in Kashmir. Johari Bazaar, Old City.

3 The National Parks

The two most famous parks in Rajasthan, both within easy striking distance of Jaipur, are **Bharatpur-Keoladeo Ghana National Park,** a 2,600-hectare (6,400-acre) tract of land that attracts the largest concentration and variety of birdlife in Asia, and **Ranthambhore National Park,** which enjoys an enviable reputation as the one area where you are virtually guaranteed to see a tiger. Also relatively close to Jaipur (110km/68 miles; 2 hr.) is **Sariska National Park,** a tiger reserve, but we have yet to meet anyone who actually saw a tiger here. The Sariska Palace Hotel, an aspiring luxury hotel built by the Machiavellian Maharaja Jay Singh of Alwar (see "Once Were Warriors: The History of the Rajput," earlier in this chapter), is a rather lovely French-Indo concoction (if you like your buildings looking like over-the-top confections) furnished with many original pieces (rotting trophies included). Reports of service have been less than satisfactory, and it's really only worthwhile to pop in for tea if you're in the area. By contrast, the Ranthambhore is far more beautiful and has two excellent accommodations options as well as a fascinating conservation history.

BHARATPUR/KEOLADEO GHANA NATIONAL PARK

Referred to as the Eastern Gateway to Rajasthan, Bharatpur lies almost exactly halfway between Delhi (152km/94 miles) and Jaipur (176km/109 miles), and is a mere 55km (34 miles) from the Taj Mahal. The town itself holds no fascination, but a few kilometers south on National Highway 11 is the Keoladeo "Ghana" National Park. Recognized by UNESCO as a World Heritage Site, the park is definitely worth visiting if you're a keen birder, but—particularly given the recent drought—it's not a must-see for people who don't know the difference between a lark and a peacock.

A natural depression of land that was initially flooded by Maharaja Suraj Mal in 1726, the park abounds in large tracts of wetlands (covering more than a 3rd of the terrain) as well as wood, scrub, and grasslands, a combination that attracts a large number of migratory birds that fly thousands of miles to find sanctuary here. It was not always so—for centuries, the area was the Maharaja of Bharatpur's private hunting reserve, and in 1902 it was inaugurated by Lord Curzon as an official duck-shoot reserve (some 20 species of duck are found here). In the most shameful incident in the park's history, Lord Linlithgow, then Viceroy of India, shot 4,273 birds in one day—the inscription of his record can still be read on a pillar near the Keoladeo temple. Thankfully, the park became a sanctuary in 1956 and was ultimately upgraded to national park status in 1982.

Today the park supports more than 375 bird species, including a large variety of herons, kingfishers, pelicans, storks, and duck. It is the only known wintering region of the rare and endangered Siberian crane, which flies 8,050km (5,000 miles) to get here. The numbers are indeed staggering, and birds will fill your vision throughout the visit—particularly during the winter months (Oct–Feb), when the resident bird population swells to over half a million. The park is also home to 13 snake species (including the oft-spotted python), six species of large herbivores, and mongoose, civet, and otter. A tiger was spotted many years ago, but you sense that the signs urging caution are really there to inject a sense of romance and wildness into what is otherwise a very tame experience. In fact, it is hard to understand how a World Heritage Site that attracts more than a million visitors a year can be so undervalued by those administering it—at dawn scores of people (as well as a few illegal vehicles) take the main road through the park as a shortcut into Bharatpur, feral cattle blithely grazing the grasslands transform the scene into one of ordinary farmland, the loud *khudu-khudu* of generators pumping water disturb the peace in many areas, and a general lack of facilities and tawdry appearance leave a lot to be desired, though the drought has no doubt exacerbated the situation over the past few years.

Tip: If you are staying in the area for a couple of days, an excursion well worth considering is to the architecturally beautiful **Deeg Palaces** (daily 8am–noon and 1–7pm; free), 30km (18 miles) northwest of Bharatpur, particularly in August during the Monsoon Festival, when the 500-odd fountains are turned on.

ESSENTIALS

VISITOR ESSENTIALS   The **wildlife office** is located at the main gate on National Highway 11 (© **05644/22777**). Entry is Rs 200 ($4.30) per person. To really get into the excitement of birding, you should purchase a copy of Salim Ali's *The Book of Indian Birds* (OUP India) or the *Collins Handguide to Birds of the Sub-Continent* and start ticking off those sightings!

GETTING THERE   Bharatpur is a 4½-hour drive from Delhi; it's 55km (34 miles) west of Agra and 175km (108 miles) east of Jaipur. If you travel by train from Delhi, it will take 3½ hours—take the *Paschim Express* or *Golden Temple*. Trains from Agra take 2 hours to get here and 2½ hours to get to Sawai Madhopur (Ranthambhore National Park).

GETTING AROUND   You can set off on foot or rent your own bicycle (passport, Rs 2,000/$44 deposit), but roads are badly maintained and you will often find yourself on foot, only burdened with a bike. You can explore certain areas by boat (Rs 25/50¢), though at press time the drought had put this out of operation. The best way to find your way around the park is with a rickshaw-*wallah* (Rs 150/$3.15 for 2 hr.), many of whom have spent years trundling visitors around and now have a good knowledge of the birdlife as well as keen eyesight (though a less than satisfactory command of English). Official guides (Rs 75/ $1.60) carrying binoculars are also available at the entrance to the park; in a rather unwieldy arrangement, they travel alongside on their bicycles.

WHERE TO STAY & DINE

The government-run **Bharatpur Forest Lodge** (© 05644/22722; Rs 2,795/ $60 double) is the only option inside the park. The 18 rooms are clean but charmless, there is no pool, and you have to pay an entry fee every time you enter the park. On the plus side, it does have a lovely bougainvillea-lined terrace (though you'll have to contend with the monkeys should you choose to eat here), and you don't have to travel far to find the very reason you're here in the first place! It's overpriced, however, which is why our money is on the far more charming **Laxmi Vilas Palace** (see below), a 15- to 20-minute drive away. If you're on a tighter budget, **Hotel Sunbird** (www.hotelsunbird.com; Rs 660– Rs 878/$15–$19 double, including breakfast) and the **Birder's Inn** (© 05644/ 27346; brdinn@yahoo.com; Rs 950/$21 double including breakfast) are both located on National Highway 11 (which can be noisy) and within walking distance of the gates. Both offer pretty basic, but scrupulously clean, en-suite accommodations, with the Birder's Inn set farther back from the road and owned by avid birder Tirath Singh.

Laxmi Vilas Palace ☆   This is not a palace in any sense of the word but an extremely pretty and ornately decorated double-story heritage hotel, originally built in 1899 for the Maharaja of Bharatpur's younger brother and still owned by members of the royal family, who live in a separate wing. Laxmi Vilas Palace is not luxurious, but the rooms—ringed around a central courtyard—are charming, some decorated in original Rajasthani antiques, with the best featuring small double doors leading onto the narrow balcony that circumambulates the exterior. Room no. 203 is a good bargain, a deluxe (the standard category) with a great pastoral view of the mustard fields. Suites are, as always, more spacious. My personal favorite is room no. 301, the "penthouse suite," which is hardly ever rented out because it has no air-conditioning. It's the only room on the rooftop, affording you wonderful privacy, with five double doors, three of which open onto a small private balcony overlooking the fields behind the house. Areas of the hotel look a tad run-down, but the original frescoes are in the process of being repainted by an artisan, and the owners have recently installed a lovely pool. Service is slow but friendly; food is of the tasty home-cooked variety—the dinner buffet offers the usual mix of North Indian and bland Continental (dinner Rs 275/$5.90). Grab a table in the inner courtyard rather than the more claustrophobic dining hall. Lunch prices vary between Rs 50 and Rs 210 ($1.05 and $4.50). Masala cheese toast (Rs 70/$1.50) and vegetable *pakora* (Rs 50/ $1.05) ordered at the pool took a long time to arrive but were well worth it. The hotel jeep can take you to the park or on any other excursions.

Kakaji Ki Kothi, Bharatpur (2.5km/1½ miles from town; 55km/34 miles from Agra) 321 001. © 05644/22-3523 or 05644/23-1199. Fax 05644/22-5259. www.laxmivilas.com. 25 units. Rs 2,450 ($53) double; Rs 2,995

($66) suite. Meals Rs 300 ($6.50); breakfast Rs 175 ($3.70). AE, MC, V. **Amenities:** Dining hall; pool; car rental/transfers; laundry. *In room:* A/C, TV, limited room service.

RANTHAMBHORE NATIONAL PARK

Ranthambhore—for many decades the hunting preserve of the princes of Jaipur—covers a mere 40,000 hectares (98,800 acres) but offers a fascinating combination of crumbling monuments, living temples, wild beauty, and your best chance to spot a wild tiger. Set within a high, jagged escarpment, the Ranthambhore Fort has towered over the park's forests for nearly a thousand years and has witnessed many a bloody combat—even the Mughal emperor Akbar fought a battle for supremacy here in the 16th century. Inside the fort (which is open to visitors from dawn to dusk at no cost) lie a number of ruined palaces, step wells, and a celebrated Ganesha temple visited every year in September by two million pilgrims who take their lives in their hands to worship the Lord Ganesha's birthday (a few years back, a 7-year-old was eaten by a tigress). But it is the forests that lie shimmering in the gorges below, scattered with more ancient crumbling monuments, that attract the foreign pilgrims, who come during the winter months to catch a glimpse of the mighty Bengal tiger. Sightings are recorded almost daily—it is said that between 75% and 95% of all the photographs ever taken of a tiger in the wild have been taken in Ranthambhore. This has meant that the 30-odd tigers living here have become totally habituated to human observation and are almost entirely indifferent to the sight and sound of vehicles and flashing light bulbs.

The success of the park is due in no small measure to the efforts of Fateh Singh Rathore. A member of the princely family of Jodhpur, Rathore was made Field Director of Ranthambhore in 1972, the year tiger hunting was banned in India. Almost singlehandedly Rathore mapped and built the park's roads and persuaded 12 entire villages to move voluntarily, having arranged financial compensation and constructed new villages with modern facilities that included schools, wells, and electricity. He also used a powerful spiritual argument: It is the tiger that always accompanies the goddess and demon-slayer Durga (who embodies the power of good over evil) so it therefore deserves protection; however, its survival would forever be compromised in a habitat shared with man.

Under Rathore's protection, the Ranthambhore tiger population increased from 13 to 40, and his dedicated study and photography of the subjects brought much of the tiger's beauty and plight into the international spotlight. But at no small cost—Rathore was awarded the WWF International Valour Award after a mob of villagers, angry at no longer having access to their ancestral lands for grazing and hunting, attacked him, shattering his kneecaps and fracturing his skull. On his release from the hospital, Rathore simply returned to the village and challenged them to do it again. Today you can have the privilege of meeting one of India's most famous tiger-*wallahs,* Rathore himself, at specially arranged talks at Vanyavilas; or you can meet his godson and daughter-in-law at Sher Bagh, the best accommodations abutting the park.

After a brief scare in the early 1990s, when poaching (apparently by the park's own wardens) almost halved the resident tiger population, numbers stabilized by the year 2000 and currently stand at about 30. With an estimated 90,000 humans and almost a million livestock living within a 5km (3-mile) radius of the park, the pressure on this island of wilderness remains immense, but clearly its popularity will stand it in good stead, as was evidenced when 10,000 cattle recently breached the park's borders and were promptly evicted by police.

Date Rape & Other Tiger Tidbits

Much like the human fingerprint, every tiger's markings are totally unique. Unlike most cats, they have round pupils and are also adept swimmers. Tigers are immensely powerful, strong enough to kill and drag an animal heavier than itself, and can eat over 30kg (66 lb.) of meat in a single night. Females make better hunters, while the males are notoriously lazy—even when it comes to sex. When a female is in heat and makes a mating call, the male will often hide until the female finds him and forces herself on him. By the time hunting was banned in the 1970s, only 2,000 tigers were left out of an estimated population of 50,000 in the 19th century. Today some 60,000 survive throughout the world, of which between 2,000 and 3,000 are found in India.

While tiger sightings are relatively common, don't expect the experience necessarily to be a romantic one. It can be ruined by the presence of other vehicles, particularly the open-topped 20-seater Canters buses that may have screaming kids on board. Only two vehicles are allowed at any sighting but this is not always respected, hence the designation of different routes (see "Getting Around," below), designed to keep number densities spread throughout the park. Even if you don't spot a tiger (and do be prepared for this eventuality), the sheer physical beauty of the park is worth experiencing—from lotus-filled lakes and dense jungle to craggy, boulder-strewn cliffs and golden grasslands. Other species worth looking for include caracal (a wildcat), crocodile, *nilgai* (large antelope resembling cattle), *chital* (spotted deer), black buck (delicate buck with spiraling horns), *chinkara* (a dainty gazelle), and *sambar* (their distinctive barking call often warns of the presence of a tiger nearby). The park also has a leopard population (though they are notoriously shy), wild boar, slothbear, and a rich birdlife—over 400 resident and migrant species.

ESSENTIALS

VISITOR INFORMATION   Unlike at Bharatpur, traffic and numbers are closely regulated. For general information, call the **Sawai Madhopur Tourist Centre** (© 07462/20808). For game-drive bookings in a jeep (avoid the Canter buses), call the **Project Tiger office** (© 07462/20223; Mon–Sat 10am–noon and 3–5pm). If you book with any of the accommodations recommended below, they will arrange all this for you (they also enjoy priority access to the park). Please note, however, that you must let your host know when and how often you would like to go on a game drive as soon as possible—these usually need to be booked 60 days in advance. The price of a seat in a jeep varies depending on where you stay (see below), but the entry fee per jeep is Rs 125 to Rs 200 ($2.60–$4.30) per person; camera fees are extra.

Tip: When asking your host to make a booking, request at least one game drive on Routes 6 or 7 (these cover most of the bodies of water in the park) and another on Route 4 (this is one of the longest drives and encompasses the acacia-dotted golden grass plains). The best time to visit the park is between November and April (Jan–Apr is best for tiger sightings). The park closes during the monsoon season (July–Sept).

GETTING THERE   The nearest airport is Jaipur, which lies 180km (112 miles) away; it is just under a 4-hour drive from here. Alternatively, the sprawling village of Sawai Madhopur (10km/6¼ miles from the park gates) is also well connected by rail to Jaipur (just over 2 hr.), as well as Agra (5 hr.) or Jodhpur (8½ hr.), and is on the main line between Delhi (2½ hr.) and Mumbai. All accommodations options listed will arrange pickup from the station.

GETTING AROUND   A limited number of visitors are allowed entry into the park, hence the need to book your place in a jeep well in advance. There are two game drives: The early morning (Oct–Feb 7–10am; Mar–June 6:30–9:30am) is often preferable to the afternoon drive (Oct–Feb 2:30–5:30pm; Mar–June 3:30–6:30pm), given that temperatures can make for muggy afternoons, but you should pack a warm cover because it can get cold once darkness approaches.

In a strange bureaucratic twist, all jeeps provided by accommodations options in the area are pooled and randomly sent out to pick up guests; guides and routes (which drivers are pretty much forced to stick to) are also randomly allotted. This means you may be on a tight budget yet find yourself in a top-of-the-range jeep with an excellent guide, watching a tiger bathe in the lotus lake that fronts the beautiful 250-year-old Jogi Mahal, while a hapless guest paying top dollar at Vanyavilas trundles around in a noisy, uncomfortable jeep flanked by a monosyllabic guide with halitosis. It's one of the typical ironies of India, and one that will hopefully change in due course.

WHERE TO STAY & DINE

Almost all the best options are on Ranthambhore Road, which flanks the park. If you're on a real budget you may want to consider the government-run **Castle Jhoomar Baori** (© **07462/20495**), a former hunting lodge with a great location (the only choice inside the park) but—as is the case with all RTDC hotels—service is complacent, fittings ancient, and facilities almost nonexistent.

Amanresorts, still in many ways the last word in soulful luxury, is setting up camp at Ranthambhore. **Aman-i-Khas**, the first Aman experience in India, will offer six "suite" tents, each one fully air-conditioned and arranged as rooms divided by cotton curtain "walls." The rooms include a small sitting and dining area, sleeping quarters (complete with king-size bed), and bathroom with tub and shower. The camp will also have a sitting room and library tent, a dining tent, a spa tent, and an outdoor fireplace. Because the camp was due to open in November 2003, we were unable to personally inspect it, but no doubt this will be the best tented camp in India, let alone Ranthambhore. For more information visit www.amanresorts.com.

Sawai Madhopur Lodge ⊛   Built as a hunting lodge by Maharaja Sawai Man Singh II in the 1930s, the original two-story main house is still very attractive, with a deep veranda (furnished with comfortable Deco cane suites) that swoops in a semi-circle overlooking the lawns and outbuildings where many of the standard and superior rooms are located. Given that you could be at Sher Bagh for less money (their rate includes meals), only the seriously unadventurous who prefer to sleep surrounded by mortar (and A/C) should consider staying here—even though it is just a 20-minute drive to the park gates. Standard rooms look like a million other hotel rooms; superiors are simply slightly bigger. The few tired-looking tents are no competition for those at Sher Bagh. Best rooms are the large old-fashioned suites that are located in the original lodge and have lovely views of the property. Alternatively, ask for a room that leads onto the garden close to the pool. The lodge certainly has an old-world charm, but aspects like the pitiful stuffed tiger that guards the pool room, his seams split and claws rotting, and the green-algae tint of the pool, point to poor vision and management. Lunch and dinner buffets will run you Rs 295 and Rs 385 ($6.50 and $8.30) respectively.

Ranthambhore National Park Rd., Sawai Madhophur. © **07462/205-41** or 0746/202-47. Fax 07462/207-18. www.tajhotels.com. 38 units. $160 tents; $170–$190 rooms; $235 suites (all double). Game drives cost a minimum of Rs 1,500 ($33) for 2 people (less if you share your jeep). AE, MC, DC, V. **Amenities:** Dining hall; pool; tennis; croquet; pool table; bicycles; camel cart safaris; horseback riding; laundry. *In room:* A/C, TV, minibar, tea- and coffee-making facilities, hair dryer, room service.

Sher Bagh ★★ *(Value)*   If you're looking for a safari experience in India, this intimate camp is by far your best bet (though unlike its African counterpart, it's not situated in a reserve). The irrepressible and charming owner Jaisal Singh is a superb host and a member of what could be described as Ranthambhore royalty (he is Fateh Singh Rathore's godchild and practically grew up in the park in between bouts of polo playing and hobnobbing with the rich and famous). Accommodations are comprised of a semi-circle of comfortable tents (originally designed for the Maharaja of Jodhpur's hunting expeditions), each with a luxurious en-suite bathroom (no bathtubs, but one of the most satisfying showers in Rajasthan). Tents are a little too close together and hot during the day, but there are a number of places to relax (the coolest place is the 1st-floor bar/lounge area, which enjoys a breeze and has a great selection of books). Sadly, Sher Bagh has no pool—this is the only reason it doesn't have a three-star rating. Tents are not air-conditioned but have fans. Meals are a welcome relief from standard North Indian fare; a full breakfast is served after the morning game drive followed by a light lunch (pesto pasta and salad, perhaps; almost all ingredients are grown on the farm). Cucumber sandwiches and delicious *chai* (tea) are served immediately after the afternoon game drive, followed by a lavish buffet dinner. At night, when the lanterns and torches are lit, the camp really comes into its own. With any luck, Jaisal will cook his special spicy chicken dish on an open fire as he entertains his guests—often a fascinating mix of the wealthy, fashionable, or just plain exhausted Delhiites on a weekend break. Imbibing in G&Ts and idle chatter, feet in the sand and stars above, makes this one of the most relaxing experiences in North India.

Bookings through 59 Regal Building, Parliament St., New Delhi 110 001. © **011/331-6534** or -6445. Fax 011/331-2118. www.sherbagh.com. 12 units. $180 double including all meals. $55 per person per game drive includes everything but the video camera fee. No credit cards. **Amenities:** Dining tent; bar; complimentary station transfer; excursions; laundry. *In room:* Limited room service.

Vanyavilas ★★★   Set on 8 hectares (20 acres) of landscaped gardens, this is by far the most luxurious option in Ranthambhore; in fact, this is the most luxury you can have and be close to any of India's 27 tiger reserves. It opened in 2002 to much fanfare, and the tentlike rooms (replicas of those found at Rajvilas) are indeed out of this world. Rooms feature huge canvas roofs shot through with gold sparkles, teak floors, solid walls hung with artworks, opulent Indo-colonial furnishings, and all the modern conveniences you could possibly need. Bathrooms are the sizes of most hotel rooms and have free-standing claw-foot tubs, fabulous showers, and doors leading out to a private terrace with comfortable day beds on which to rest after plundering the well-stocked minibar. With each generous tent surrounded by a small walled garden, the property does sprawl somewhat, forcing a rather long walk to the pool or restaurant (or call for a golf cart) and, unlike Sher Bagh, the well-manicured surroundings give you little sense of being on the edge of a wilderness. But the superb service, great dining (either in the restaurant or adjacent courtyard), excellent spa, and sheer opulence of the public spaces more than make up for this. Best of all, perhaps, is the opportunity to sit in on one of the regular lectures given by Fateh Singh Rathore, the man who put Ranthambhore on the map.

Ranthambhore Rd., Sawai Madhopur 322 001. ⓒ **800/6-OBEROI** in the U.S., or 07462/239-99. Fax 07462/239-88. www.oberoihotels.com. 25 units. $450 double. Game drives cost a minimum of Rs 1,425 for 2 (less if you share your jeep). AE, MC, V. **Amenities:** Restaurant; pool; gym; spa; billiards room; observation tower; elephant safaris; chauffeur-driven cars; complimentary station transfer; laundry. *In room:* A/C, TV, DVD, CD music system (including selection of CDs and DVDs), minibar, tea- and coffee-making facilities.

SHOPPING

Try and find the time to visit **Dastkar Craft Centre** (clearly marked off Ranthambhore Rd.), which has a selection of pottery, textiles, and ready-made garments produced by the women in the area. Much of it is mediocre, but a few gems can be found at ridiculously low prices. Spending a few rupees here also helps alleviate the overwhelming poverty in the area.

4 Bundi

368km (228 miles) S of Jaipur; 438km (272 miles) SW of Agra

If you see only one off-the-beaten-track town in Rajasthan, the small town of Bundi, established in 1241, should be your first choice. It's worth a visit not just for the architectural magnificence of the palace that clings to the cliff above; the town's lack of modernization and abundance of temples, cenotaphs, and step wells; or even its renowned school of miniature paintings (arguably the best-value paintings in Rajasthan); it's the lack of hustling, which comes as a truly welcome relief. Approached through a gorge, the town is protected by the embracing hills of the Vindhya Range, topped by Taragarh Fort, and life here goes on pretty much as it has for centuries. Because the population is in no way dependent on tourism, you are either greeted with real affection or indifference. There's absolutely no sales pressure—a refreshing change after the constant barrage of "Please come," "Special price for you," and "Just look no buy" that follows you everywhere in the cities and more popular towns.

Exploring Bundi's narrow streets, with tiny cupboardlike shops raised a meter or more above street level to avoid the monsoon floods, feels like seeing the real India. Followed by giggling children who want nothing more than to touch your hand, you will pass old men beating copper pots into perfect shape; tailors working with beautiful fabrics on ancient Singers; huge mounds of orange, red, and yellow spices offset by purple aubergines, red tomatoes, and green peppers; rickshaws carting women adorned in saris of saturated colors; and temples blaring live music—fresh and natural images that will have you grabbing your camera. Besides wandering the streets, a number of attractions are within walking distance, of which the **Garh Palace** ★★★, described by Rudyard Kipling as "the work of goblins" and one of the few examples of pure Rajput style, and **Raniji-ki-Baori** ★★★, called the state's most impressive step well, are not to be missed. Raniji-ki-Baori, which lies in a small park in the center of town, dates back to the 17th century and features ornately carved gates, pillars, and friezes. Garh Palace's exterior is astounding, but sadly, much of the interior is falling apart; entry is now restricted to the **Chitra Shala,** which is decorated with many of the fine murals in the miniature style the town is famous for (free entry; open dawn–dusk; given prior warning, the owner of Haveli Braj Bhushanjee can arrange for you to view palace sections currently closed to the public). The Chitra Shala alone is worth the steep walk up to the imposing gates, as are the views of the town—much of it painted with the same blue seen in the more famous "blue city" of Jodhpur. For an even better vantage point, keep ascending the rough path that leads up to Taragarh (not necessarily to the top), for a great sense of peace (you're unlikely to encounter anyone, bar the Hanuman monkeys and a lone goat herder) and superb photo ops of the town.

Sights farther afield, like the **Sukh Mahal,** a summer palace where Kipling wrote *Kim,* are best explored with Haveli Braj Bhushanjee's picnic and sightseeing tour.

ESSENTIALS

VISITOR INFORMATION The **Tourist Information Bureau** (© 0747/ 22-697) is located at Circuit House, but the owner of the Haveli Braj Bhushanjee heritage hotel (see below) is a mine of information, supplying you with maps, arranging transport, and ready with advice on anything from how much to pay for a rickshaw to opening hours.

GETTING THERE Kota is 130km (80 miles) by road from Sawai Madhopur and 155km (96 miles) from Chittaurgarh, so you can either visit it after you see Ranthambhore and/or Jaipur, or combine it with a trip from Udaipur via Chittaurgarh. To get to Bundi, you have to travel through the industrialized town of Kota. If you have arrived by train (Kota is well connected to the rest of the state, including the main Delhi-to-Mumbai line, Jaipur, Sawai Madhophur, and Chittaurgarh), you will then have to catch a bus, jeep, or taxi to Bundi. A taxi to Bundi will run you Rs 500 ($11); a jeep costs Rs 300 ($6.50). Kota, which dates back to the 12th century, has a number of impressive monuments (particularly the Palace Fort), but it is only worth stopping at if you have arrived too late to catch a taxi to Bundi. If this is the case, recommended overnight options are **Brijraj Bhawan Palace** (© 0744/245-0529) or Welcomegroup's **Umed Bhawan Palace** (© 0744/232-5262).

GETTING AROUND You can get around the town on foot with ease. Should you tire, auto-rickshaws traverse the narrow lanes. If you book into Haveli Braj Bhushanjee, the proprietor will arrange all your transport at very reasonable prices—yet another reason the hotel is so highly recommended.

WHERE TO STAY & DINE

Haveli Braj Bhushanjee ★★ This is without a doubt the best place to stay in Bundi, and—despite the small size of the rooms and basic facilities—one of the most authentic heritage properties in India. Situated on a narrow lane inside the walled city, just below the palace, it also happens to be one of the most professionally run guesthouses in India, managed by the discreetly proud Braj Bhushanjees brothers (four of whose ancestors were prime ministers to Bundi State in the 19th century). Many of the walls are covered with exceptional-quality murals, again typical of the Bundi school of miniature painting, and though each room (like those in so many other guesthouses) is traditionally decorated, the choice of objects, fabrics, and carpets (all sourced from Bundi and surroundings) shows a great deal of thought and innate flair. All the rooms are beautiful (though those overlooking the lane are a tad noisy at times) and feature en-suite "shower rooms"—small, but freshly whitewashed and gleamingly clean. The family is strict Brahmin, so alcohol, meat, garlic, and onion are not allowed on the premises, but dining is of exceptional quality. Rather than a menu,

For the Pleasures of the Raj

Traveling to and from Kota and Bund, you will see fields of wheat, castor beans (from which castor oil is made)—and opium poppies. An ancient crop grown for the pleasures of Rajput kings and queens and Mughal emperors, the poppy is today ostensibly grown for the pharmaceutical industry, but much of it makes its way into the hands of the Mumbai Mafia, and addiction in the area is reported to be rife.

you are served a selection of simple, flavorful home-cooked dishes (Rs 250/ $5.35), either in the Darikhana, where images of ancestors glower and large colored glass baubles hang from the ceiling, or on the terrace, from where you have a picture-perfect view of the illuminated palace at night. The brothers are a wealth of information about the area and can arrange wonderful sightseeing tours on request (they will, for instance, pack a picnic and carry it up to the fort for you). They also have an excellent (and extensive) collection of miniature paintings and other tribal and traditional crafts for sale—you may pay a little more than you would if you purchased direct from the artist (see "Shopping," above), but be assured that the brothers know the difference between a pretty souvenir and a real investment.

Below Fort, opposite Ayurvedic Hospital, Bundi 323 001. © **0747/244-2322** or 0747/244-2509. Fax 0747/ 244-2142. www.kiplingsbundi.com. 17 units. Rs 1,850 ($41) double. AE, DC, MC, V. **Amenities:** Dining hall; laundry. *In room:* TV, hair dryer on request.

SHOPPING

If you want to take home a few miniature paintings (and you do—the style is exquisite and the prices laughably cheap), Bundi is one of the best places to do so. If the vast selection at Haveli Braj Bhushanjee doesn't suffice, the charming Gopal Soni has a **little shop** near the haveli where he paints beautiful miniatures (mostly copies of those in the Chitra Shala) on anything from paper and silk to fingernails! They make a delightful souvenir or gift; prices start from Rs 100 ($2.10). Call © **0747/244-7297** (shop) or 0747/244-3634 (residence).

5 Shekhawati

200km (125 miles) SW of Delhi; 160km (100 miles) NW of Jaipur

The Shekhawati, known as the open-air art gallery of Rajasthan, lies in the roughly triangular area between Delhi, Jaipur, and Bikaner, and encompasses the districts of Jhunjhunun, Sikar, and Churu. Its largely semi-desert, wide-open (uninhabited) spaces offer a peaceful respite from the cities. But the primary drawing card is its remarkable art collection—unusual for the unique painting styles and for the fact that the exhibition space consists of the exterior and interior walls of literally hundreds of havelis, temples, cenotaphs, wells, and forts in the region. The trend for decorating walls in this way would have been imported from the courts of Amber and Jaipur, where the Rajput princes in turn were inspired by the Mughal emperors' patronage of the miniature-mural artform. The Shekhawati's patronage would have been funded by duties imposed on merchandise carried across that section of the Spice Route that traversed their region (cleverly, the local barons here ensured that their duties were lower than those of the house of Jaipur, thereby diverting trade), or by raids across the borders, but patronage truly flourished during the British Raj, a period when the Shekhawati merchants, renowned for their business acumen, moved to the ports of Calcutta, Madras, and Bombay to capitalize on the growing trade in these new centers. There they made small fortunes and celebrated their wealth by adorning their mansions—an age-old urge, but the result here is a great deal more interesting than anything Martha Stewart might have suggested.

The demand was such that skilled artists could not paint fast enough. Even local masons tried their hand, injecting a wonderful naiveté into many of the paintings. Subject matters vary tremendously, from religious stories to local legends of battles and hunts; but perhaps the most amusing are copies of British photographs featuring hot-air balloons, trains, and cars—objects most of the painters had never set their eyes on but faithfully rendered according to the descriptions and prints supplied by their employers, most of whom continued to send money back to their family homes until the 1930s.

Today there are some 30 "painted towns" in the region, but the most essential to include in a first-time itinerary are **Ramgarh** (the town with the most painted buildings), **Nawalgarh** (2nd in number, but with a superior selection, some better preserved than Ramgarh, particularly the restored Anandi Lal Poddar Haveli), **Fatehpur** (together with Juhunjhunu, this is Shekhawati's oldest town, featuring murals that predate any others in the region), and **Mandawa.** Mandawa, a quaint town with a number of beautiful painted buildings, is centrally located with the best accommodations options in the area.

Cantering through the Indian Outback

A great way to experience the real Rajasthan is with **Royal Riding Holidays,** an outfit based at Roop Niwas Palace in Nawalgarh, Shekhawati. You can choose between a variety of 2- to 4-day camel safaris or 3- to 8-day horse safaris on predominantly Marwari horses, the traditional battle horses of Rajputana. Routes cover semi-desert terrain, forests, salt lake, marshes, and flat grasslands, and include visits to local villages and passing nomads. Evening and lunch breaks feature folk music and, on request, anything from a resident masseuse and turban-tying lessons to a lecture on the caste system or local wildlife. Although the purebred Indian horses are well schooled, they are spirited, and you should try to spend a few days before the safari choosing and getting to know your steed (there is no cost for these pre-safari rides). Riders need to be competent and fit as well—the routes cover 25km to 40km (16–25 miles) per day in 4 to 5 hours. Tented camps consist of colorful Asian-style tents with chairs, beds with white sheets and linen, blankets, mosquito nets, hot-water bottles, and a full floor covering. Lighting in tents is by kerosene lamps. Toilet and bath tents are one-piece units. Each bath tent has a wooden floor, towels, looking mirrors, a wash basin, and hangers for clothes. Each toilet tent contains a wooden/metal commode with a pit. Hot water for baths is provided in buckets in both the morning and evening. Cost is between $145 and $175 per person per day, including full board. Contact Royal Riding Holidays (© **0140/262-2949;** www. royalridingholidays.com; horsessafarirajasthan@yahooo.com).

Armed with a good map (see "Visitor Information," below) and a car, it is relatively easy to explore the surrounds on your own—not least because of the usual army of small kids eager to accompany you and point out the relevant sights. But to know more about the history of the buildings, the artisans, and the area, you may wish to hire the services of a guide through the hotels listed below. Most of the buildings are still inhabited and are accessible for a small fee—navigating payment (and whether you should offer to pay at all) is where a guide comes in handy. (Remember that, as is the case in all temples, you will need to *remove your shoes* to enter the inhabited havelis.)

Although the region evokes real passion in some and has resulted in a number of excellent books, it must be said that many of the murals are mere shadows of their former selves, either defaced by human indifference—posters and graffiti mar many of the walls—or faded by the increased water supply to the region, the rise in the water table creating damper conditions. Including this in your itinerary can be tricky as well, unless you are intent on traveling the long haul through Bikaner to Jaisalmer, which means many hours spent on the road.

ESSENTIALS

VISITOR INFORMATION   Jhunjhunu has a tourist office, but you'll have more success finding information and arranging a guide through your hotel. Ilay Cooper's illustrated *The Painted Towns of Shekhawati* (Mapin Guides) is still the original bible, with a concise history of the region as well as a break-down of towns, easy-to-follow maps, and listings of all the sites worth visiting. You can purchase one at Books Corner, in Jaipur, Mandawa Castle, or Desert Resort. Another book worth considering is *Shekhawati: Rajasthan's Painted Homes* by Pankaj Rakesh and Karoki Lewis (Lustre Press Roli books).

GETTING THERE   Public transport is relatively limited, so the easiest way to explore the area is to hire a car and driver in Jaipur (unless you have already done so from Delhi), stop at a few towns along the way, and overnight at Mandawa or Nawalgarh.

GETTING AROUND   Again, you will need a car and driver to go from town to town with ease. Once there, it is relatively easy to explore each area on foot with a guide or by following Ilay Cooper's maps in *The Painted Towns of Shekhawati*.

A suggested driving tour: Travel from Jaipur (or Samode Palace) to Sikar, stopping to look at the *havelis* (historic homes or mansions) in Nawalgarh. Have lunch at Roop Niwas, then set off for Mandawa and overnight. The following day, you can visit Fatehpur and Lachhmangarh before heading south to Sikar and back down to Jaipur.

WHERE TO STAY & DINE

The three heritage properties selected below are your best bets in the region, providing you with central location and comfort (it's worth mentioning that Dundlod Castle, another well-known heritage property in the area, has fallen into disrepute, with very few rooms operating, none of them in a savory condition). If you're traveling here direct from Delhi, a highly recommended overnight stop is the **Neemrana Fort Palace** (www.neemranahotels.com). Situated a few hours from Delhi and on the eastern outskirts of the Shekawati, it is considered one of the best fort conversions in the country. If you're looking to save money and live in one of the original Shekhawati havelis, **Mandawa Haveli** has some nice rooms (ask for the Nilesh room on the 1st floor), though the bathrooms are a tad damp and some are windowless (hotelmandawahaveli@yahoo.com; from Rs 1,100/$24). Alternatively, **Hotel Heritage Mandawa** (www.hotelheritage mandawa.com; from Rs 1,000/$22) offers similar facilities and has wonderfully hospitable owners.

Desert Resort ★★   Situated in the semi-arid Shekhawati Desert and built in the style of a Rajasthani village, this is arguably Rajasthan's most peaceful option, which is no doubt why—together with its unusual architecture—it's featured in the glossy coffee-table tome *Hip Hotels: Escape*. Accommodations consist primarily of circular mud-thatch huts, their organic shapes charmingly decorated with tribal motifs—stark white on dark brown—making features of even the air-conditioning units. Beds are covered in pretty embroidered linen traditional in the area—in fact, almost everything in each hut has been sourced from the Shekhawati. The rustic charm is endearing—but living within circular walls can be a bit of a challenge, particularly when it comes to creating a comfortable headboard. My personal recommendation is to book the suite right next to the pool—it makes no overtures to the tribal theme, being squared off and comfortably furnished with a mix of colonial-era antiques, and it's huge, with some great desert views, even from the bathroom. And you'll be hard-pressed to leave the pool, which is filled daily with fresh spring water, wonderfully soft and a fabulous temperature (no pool loungers, though). Meals are similar to those served at Castle Mandawa, also under the stars, but this time on the manicured lawns; or request a seat at the pool.

Mandawa, Jhunjhunu District, Shekhawati 333 704, Rajasthan. © **0141/237-1194** or -4112. Fax 0141/ 372-084 or 015972/23171. www.mandawahotels.com. 60 units. Rs 2,350–Rs 3,500 ($52–$76) double; Rs 5,995 ($130) suite. AE, MC, V. **Amenities:** Restaurant; bar; pool; badminton; table tennis; croquet; card room; camel/horse/jeep safaris; Ayurvedic massage; laundry. *In room:* A/C, minibar (suites only), hair dryer (on request).

Mandawa Castle ★★   The Castle, well situated to explore the region, is one of the most authentic heritage properties in Rajasthan, not least because of the presence of urbane host Kesri Singh, who was one of the first to start converting the rooms of his 16th-century castle into a hotel in the late 1970s. A thoroughly gregarious and charming host, he usually (assuming he's in residence) invites guests to share a drink with him on one of the turreted battlements that tower above the town roofs before he ushers you to a table on a large roof terrace under the stars. If the hotel is hosting a group, a special fire dance is given by one of the castle's oldest retainers, during which guests help themselves to a tasty buffet. Given the age of the property, the conversion to modern hotel has been remarkably sensitive, maintaining much of the original feel of the castle (no doubt to the approval of the Mandawa ancestors, whose portraits decorate many of the walls) without sacrificing comfort. (Bear in mind that this cannot be said of the new wing, which features boring uniformly sized rooms with none of the authentic charm of the original castle.) If you have a poor sense of direction, the journey from the veranda bar to your room can be challenging, but really, isn't clambering up and down the narrow staircases half the fun? Rooms vary hugely in size, and some have special features like built-in swings and alcoves furnished with bolster cushions. Nos. 304 and 313 are particularly lovely rooms; no. 215 is smaller (standard) but also a good choice. The hotel has a few small drawbacks: Situated in the middle of town, it makes for a strangely urban experience—the town's blaring temple music ceases to charm when it's turned on at the crack of dawn—and it has no gardens or pool to relax in after a day's heavy sightseeing.

Mandawa, Jhunjhunu District, Shekhawati 333 704, Rajasthan. ℂ **0141/237-1194** or -4112. Fax 0141/372-084. www.castlemandawa.com. 70 units. Rs 2,400–Rs 3,500 ($53–$76) double; Rs 3,995 ($86) suite. AE, MC, V. **Amenities:** Dining; veranda bar; badminton; table tennis; camel/horse/jeep safaris; Ayurvedic massage; laundry. *In room:* A/C, minibar (suites only), hair dryer (on request).

Roop Niwas Palace ⭐ An unlikely choice if you're looking for a bit of action, the Roop Niwas "palace" is situated on the outskirts of Nawalgarh, the town that boasts the largest number of painted havelis in Shekawati. The hotel doesn't see even half as much traffic as the Mandawa properties, and as a result has a slightly desolate air. The rural atmosphere and gracious Indo-colonial architecture are still rather charming, however, and even though the surrounding gardens have gone to seed, they still attract strutting peacocks—all very evocative of a decadent era that no longer exists, certainly not in this town. Rooms are clean and furnished with colonial and Rajput pieces, all with en-suite bathrooms (none with tubs). Only the larger (deluxe) rooms have double beds, some with a built-in "couch" that can double as a third bed for a child. Although the pool is currently empty, horse lovers will find the stables a wonderful drawing card, and this is a good option if you're after some real peace and quiet (though if your budget can stretch that far, Desert Resort is a better bet). Guides can be arranged.

Nawalgarh, Distt. Jhunjhunu, Rajasthan. ℂ **0141/262-2949**, -3413, or 0159/742-2008. Fax 0159/7423388. 36 units. Rs 1,700–Rs 1,900 ($37–$42) double. AE. **Amenities:** Dining hall; billiards; horse and camel safaris; laundry. *In room:* A/C (in some deluxe rooms).

6 Pushkar

288km (180 miles) W of Jaipur

On the eastern edge of the vast Thar Desert, with a beautiful backdrop in the embracing arms of the Aravalli Hills, Pushkar is one of the most sacred—and atmospheric—towns in India. Legend has it that the holy lake at its center was created when Brahma dropped the petals of a lotus flower *(pushpa)* from his hand *(kar)*. The tiny temple town that sprung up on the lake shores remains an important pilgrimage site for Hindus, its population swollen in recent years by the hippies who came for a few days and never left—a sore point for visitors who remember its untouched charm, but happily a matter of indifference to the first-time visitor. Their presence has transformed the sleepy desert town into a semi-permanent trance party, however, with *bhang* (marijuana) *lassis* imbibed at the myriad tiny eateries, falafels on every menu, long-bearded rabbis on bicycles, and world music pumping from speakers that line the street bazaar that runs along the northern edge of the lake. This street bazaar is the center of all activity in Pushkar and incidentally one of the best shopping experiences in Rajasthan, where you can pick up the most gorgeous throwaway gear, great secondhand books, and a huge selection of CDs at bargain prices.

Pushkar is somewhat of a mini-Varanasi, only more charming—it really is possible to explore the town entirely on foot, and outside the annual *mela* (cattle fair) it doesn't have the same claustrophobic crowds you find at Varanasi. It takes about 45 minutes to walk around the holy lake and its 52 ghats: Built to represent each of the Rajput maharajas who constructed their "holiday homes" on its banks, ghats are broad sets of stairs from where Hindus pilgrims take ritual baths to cleanse their souls. Note that you will need a "Pushkar Passport" to perambulate without harassment (see "Passport to Pushkar: Saying Your Prayers," below), that shoes need to be removed 9m (30 ft.) from the holy lake (bring cheap flip-flops if you're worried about losing them), and that photography of bathers is prohibited.

Finds   The Dargah Sharif & Other Ajmer Gems

Ajmer is not an attractive town, and most foreigners experience it only as a jumping-off point to the pilgrim town of Pushkar. However, it is worthwhile to plan your journey so that you can spend a few hours exploring Ajmer's fascinating sights (particularly the Dargah, one of the most spiritually resonant destinations in India) before you head the short 11km (7 miles) over a mountain pass to the laid-back atmosphere of Pushkar and its superior selection of accommodations options.

Founded in the 7th century and strategically located within striking distance of the Mewar (Udaipur) and Marwar (Jodhpur) dynasties, as well as encompassing most of the major trade routes, Ajmer has played a pivotal role in the affairs of Rajasthan over the years. The Mughal emperors realized that only by holding this city could they increase their power base in Rajasthan. This is principally why the great Mughal emperor Akbar courted the loyalty of the nearby Amber/Jaipur court, marrying one of its daughters. But Ajmer was important on an emotional and spiritual level too, for only by gaining a foothold in Ajmer could Akbar ensure a safe passage for Muslim pilgrims to the **Dargah Sharif** (or Khwaja Muin-ud-Dir Chisti's Dargah), where the great Sufi saint Khwaja Muin-ud-Dir Chisti, "protector of the poor," was buried in 1235.

Said to possess the ability to grant the wishes and desires of all those who visit it, the **Dargah Sharif** is the most sacred Islamic shrine in India, and a pilgrimage here is considered second in importance only to a visit to Mecca. After a living member of the Sufi sect, Sheikh Salim Chisti, blessed Akbar with the prophecy of a much-longed-for son (Emperor Jahangir, father of Shah Jahan, builder of the Taj), Emperor Akbar himself made the pilgrimage many times, traveling on foot from distant Fatehpur Sikri and presenting the shrine with cauldrons (near the entrance) large enough to cook food for 5,000 people. It was not only Akbar and his offspring who made the pilgrimage—even the Hindu Rajputs came to pay homage to "the divine soul" that lies within.

Today the shrine still attracts hundreds of pilgrims every day, swelling to thousands during special occasions such as Urs Mela (Oct/Nov), the anniversary of Akbar's death. Leaving your shoes at the entrance (Rs 10/20¢ donation to pick up shoes on exit), you pass through the imposing **Nizam Gate** and smaller **Shahjahani Gate;** to the right is **Akbar's mosque,** and opposite is the equally imposing **Buland Darwaza.** Climb the steps to take a peek into the **two huge cauldrons** (3m/10 ft. round) that flank the gates—they come into their own at Urs when they are filled to the brim with a rice dish that is then distributed to the poor. To the right is the Mehfil Khana, built in 1888 by the Nizam of Hyderabad. From here you enter another gateway into the courtyard, where you will find another mosque on the right, this one built by Shah Jahan in his characteristic white marble. You'll also see the great **Chishti's tomb**—the small building topped by a marble dome and enclosed by marble lattice screens. In front of the tomb, the *qawwali* singers are seated, every day repeating the same beautiful haunting melodies (praising the saint) that have been sung for centuries. Everywhere people are abasing themselves and singing, their eyes closed, hands spread wide on the floor or clutching the chest, while others feverishly pray and knot bits of fabrics to the latticework of the tomb or shower it with flowers. It is moving, the sense of faith palpable and, unlike the Dargah in Delhi, the atmosphere is welcoming (though it's best to be discreet: no insensitive clicking of cameras or loud talking). Entry is free, but donations, paid to the office in the main courtyard, are welcome and are directly distributed to the poor. Entered off Dargah Bazaar, the Dargah is open daily, from 4 or 5am to 9 or 10pm depending on the season.

Having laid claim to Ajmer through a diplomatic marriage, Akbar built a red-sandstone fort he called **Daulat Khana** ("abode of riches") in 1572. This was later renamed the Magazine by the British, who maintained a large garrison here, having also realized Ajmer's strategic importance. In 1908 it was again transformed, this time into the largely missable **Rajputana Museum** (Sat–Thurs 10am–4.30pm; Rs 10/ 20¢). The fort is significant mostly from a historical perspective, for it is here in 1660 that the British got a toehold in India when Sir Thomas Roe, representative of the British East India Company, met the emperor Jahangir and gained his permission to establish the first British factory at Surat.

The British also established a number of first-rate educational institutions, particularly **Mayo College** ⟨★, known as the Eton of the East. Originally designed to educate only the sons of the aristocracy, it opened its doors in 1875 to princes arriving on elephant-back, followed by a retinue of 1,000 servants. The school is worth visiting even just to view the building from the road; it's a superb example of Indo-Saracenic architecture, with much symbolic detailing. The sun and the moon, for instance (featured on the college hall roof and on the school coat of arms), signify the mythical descent of the maharajas (see "Once Were Warriors: The History of the Rajput," earlier in this chapter). To enter the school, you will need to get the principal's permission (with a bit of patience, this can be arranged through the gate attendant).

Another Ajmer attraction definitely worth seeing (it will only take about 10 min., and the entry fee is a negligible Rs 4/10¢) is the **Svarna Nagari Hall** ⟨★★ behind the Jain Nasiyan Temple in Anok Chowk. It's a totally unassuming building from the outside, but ascend the stairs to the second floor and you gaze down upon a fantasy world; a breathtaking display that fills the double-volume hall with tiny gilded figures celebrating scenes from Jain mythology. Sadly, no guide is available to explain what it all means, but the workmanship and sheer scale of the display are spellbinding.

Surrounding the lake and encroaching on the hills that enhance the town's wonderful sense of remoteness are some 500 temples, of which the one dedicated to Brahma, said to be 2,000 years old, is the most famous, not least because it's one of only a handful in India dedicated to the Hindu Lord of Creation. The other two worth noting (but a stiff 50-min. climb to reach) are dedicated to his consorts: It is said that Brahma was cursed by his first wife, Savitri, when he briefly took up with another woman, Gayatri—to this day, the temple of Savitri sits sulking on a hill overlooking the temple town, while across the lake, on another hill, no doubt nervous of retribution, the Gayatri Temple keeps a lookout. Ideally, Savitri should be visited at sunset, while a visit to Gayatri should coincide with the beautiful sunrise. *Note:* The Vishnu temple, encountered as you enter town, is the only temple off-limits to non-Hindus.

Unless you're expecting authentic untouched India, Pushkar is a delight to visit any time of the year, with its laid-back, almost European atmosphere offset by the unique aromas of India and tons of tiny shops, temples, Brahmin eateries, and operators offering camel- and horseback safaris into the surrounding desert (about Rs 80/$1.70 per hour; Rs 350/$7.60 full day). But the town is most famous for its annual *mela*—the largest camel, horse, and cattle fair in Asia.

Attracting an estimated 200,000 rural traders, pilgrims, and tourists, the mela sees tiny Pushkar stretched out into sprawling villages of temporary campsites—interspersed with food stalls and open-air theaters—created solely to house, feed, and entertain the swollen population that flocks to the specially built amphitheater on the outskirts of the town to watch the races and attend the auctions. Like most desert destinations, however, it is at night that the atmosphere takes on an unreal intimacy, as pilgrims and tourists get to know each other around the many campfires, Rajasthani dancers and traditional folk singers creating a timeless backdrop. The fair takes place in the Hindu month of Kartik, over the waxing and waning of the full moon that occurs in late October or November.

Tips Passport to Pushkar: Saying Your Prayers

Proof of Pushkar's charm lies in the passport control as you enter the town—many foreigners (mostly Israeli hippies, hence the inclusion of falafels and pitas on the menu of even the most traditional Brahmin eatery) have come to experience its idyllic location and quaint laid-back vibe and never left, marrying locals and starting small businesses. As a result, there is now a moratorium on the length of time you can stay—a maximum of 3 months—so have your passport on hand as you enter. For those who wish to walk onto the ghats lining the lake, you'll need an entirely different kind of passport: Brahmin priests will bully you into making *puja*—prayers that involve a scattering of flowers into the lake—after which you will be expected to make a hefty donation (inquire at your hotel for the going rate or you will almost certainly be ripped off). The priest will then tie a thin red thread around your wrist, which you can then brandish at the next Brahmin priest who will almost certainly approach you, but who will quickly retreat upon seeing your "passport."

On the evening of the full "mela" moon, as the desert sun sets behind the low-slung hills (a spectacular sight at the best of times), temple bells and drums call the devout to *puja,* and hundreds of pilgrims wade into the lake—believed to miraculously cleanse the soul—before lighting clay lamps and setting them afloat on its holy waters, the twinkling lights a surreal reflection of the desert night sky. If you're lucky enough to have booked a room at Pushkar Palace, you can watch this ancient ritual from a deck chair on the terrace (it can be quite a scramble to get a view from the ghats themselves)—a wonderful sight and one of those mystic moments that make a trip to India among the most memorable of your life.

ESSENTIALS

VISITOR INFORMATION   Pushkar doesn't have its own tourist office. The rather useless **RTDC office** is located at the awful RTDC Hotel Sarovar (© 0145/277-2040), and is open daily from 9am to 8pm.

GETTING THERE   Pushkar lies about 3 hours west of Jaipur; a deluxe bus here costs about Rs 75 ($1.60).

GETTING AROUND   Pushkar is easily explored on foot.

WHERE TO STAY & DINE

You really want to get a room overlooking the sacred lake—despite the early morning and evening chanting calls to puja and blaring temple music, it's by far the most atmospheric location in Pushkar. Of the surprisingly limited options that offer direct views onto the lake, Pushkar Palace is the only luxurious option; for the rest you'll have to rough it (we're talking basic furnishings—a plastic chair and bed and the possibility of sharing a bathroom). That said, the following two are well-situated in heritage properties (once belonging to Rajput maharajas) that overlook the lake and are scrupulously clean. **Bharatpur Palace** (© 0145/277-2320) bears no obvious resemblance to a palace but overlooks the ghats and has some rooms with attached bathrooms; none of these have a view, though, so state your preference. Best views are had from the maharaja's room, which is literally just a room with a bed (no attached bathroom), but every wall has double doors opening to views of the lake. Other rooms worth booking are nos. 5 and 6. Rooms range from Rs 200 to Rs 1,000 ($4.30–$22), going up to Rs 3,000 ($65) during the fair. **Lake View** (© 0145/277-2106) has a great rooftop terrace where meals are served, as well as a number of rooms, some with tiny attached bathrooms and lovely views. Rates for these vary between Rs 250 ($5.35) and Rs 300 ($6.50).

The best place to eat is one of the many Brahmin eateries (you won't find meat in Pushkar) that line the bazaar. The usual rule applies: If it's full of customers, food will be freshly prepared and wonderful. At press time, **Prems Venkatesh,** overseen by a Brahmin who cooks his delicious *chapatis* with vegetables of the day and dal over a wood-burning fire, was widely considered the best in town; ask anyone to direct you there. When the sun starts to set, you'll want to be seated at a table at the aptly named **Sunset Café** (on the same road as Pushkar Palace, just a little farther along, and overlooking the lake) with a cold Kingfisher beer; average meals are also served here.

Note that if you haven't prebooked well in advance for the Pushkar mela, which takes place when the full moon appears in late October or early November, finding a decent bed anywhere in town can be hell. During the fair, the

RTDC sets up additional accommodations in the **"Tourist Village Camp,"** which offers huts (Rs 3,450–Rs 6,950/$75–$150), Swiss tents (Rs 3,200– Rs 6,350/$70–$138), and standard tents (Rs 4,150–Rs 5,200/$90–$115). Rates vary depending on dates and include all (vegetarian) meals. (Note that these options, particularly the Swiss tents, are infinitely preferable to the "caravan dormitories" also on offer.) If you want a truly peaceful option, far from the madding crowd (and ideal if you're traveling with children), **Pushkar Resorts** ⋆ has 40 very pleasant cottages set on 6 hectares (15 acres) of palm-dotted lawns (room nos. 1, 2, and 14–16 are the most privately situated). Rooms have TVs and minibars with spruce bathrooms, but it is the verdant garden—a tranquil retreat from the town noise—that is the main attraction. Besides the large pool, a number of activities are on offer (from playing pool to taking a caravan safari into the desert), designed to entertain the upmarket Indian families that frequent the resort. But its location is also the primary drawback: It's 5km (3 miles) from town, so you're likely to feel very cut off from the place you've traveled so far to see. Contact the resort (𝄞 **0145/272-017,** -944, or -945; www.pushkar resorts.com; pushkar@pushkarresorts.com). Another, slightly less upmarket but comfortable option, also on the town's outskirts but within walking distance of the center, is the 32-room **Hotel New Park** (𝄞 0145/277-2464; fax 0145/277- 2199). Each room has TV and attached bathroom, and there's a large pool. If you're on a tight budget, **Chandra,** on Panchkund Road (𝄞 **0145/277-2366**), is a real find: For Rs 150 ($3.15) per person you get to choose one of five very basic but sunny en-suite rooms, with windows overlooking a rose-and-vegetable garden, which in turn services the hippie-style restaurant (reggae music, tables in shack and garden, food "cooked with love by Sukha") that the entrepreneurial Sukha runs just up the road. The center of town is an easy walk away. (Note that Chandra's full name is actually the rather delusional "Hotel Chandra Palace," no doubt bestowed by Sukha after imbibing one of his own *bhang lassis*).

Pushkar Palace ⋆⋆   The pretty 400-year-old palace—its thick white walls reflected in the holy waters of the lake—is by far the best place to stay in Pushkar, not least due to the extensive renovations undertaken by new owners, the Welcome Heritage group, and completed in 2002. The best rooms are the suites below the terrace (nos. 101–105)—these are the closest to the lake, with windows that provide serene (or surreal, depending on the time of day) views directly onto it. Room no. 102 is a particularly good option—it's a corner suite with additional windows. Alternatively, ask for a suite with a balcony. In the deluxe category, the corner rooms (nos. 209, 309, and 409), despite being significantly smaller but comfortably furnished, have the best views—you can literally lie in bed and watch the sunsets, which are stupendous. This is, in fact, one of the best reasons to stay here: the views of the lake, temples, and hills, behind which the sunsets are both thrilling and exclusive to guests. Even if you don't have a room with the best of views (most are set behind the open-air corridors that link the rooms), you can enjoy it all from the terrace (effectively, the roof of the suites), where waiters are on hand to provide the necessary liquid refreshments. Pushkar Palace also arranges a **Royal Desert Camp** during the mela ($250 double, including meals), which is the most luxurious temporary accommodation in town.

The Palace has a sister establishment, **Jagat Palace,** a relatively luxurious property built on the outskirts of town 4 years ago; the same rates apply. The design pays homage to Hindu elements, but it does not appear to have had an

The Ultimate Pit Stop on the Road to Udaipur or Jodhpur

A 4-hour journey southwest of Jaipur (and 3 hr. from Pushkar) and a useful stopover on the road to Udaipur, which lies 135km (84 miles) farther south, or even on the road to Jodhpur, **Deogarh Mahal** 🏨🏨 (© 02904/252-777; fax 02904/252555; www.deogarh.com) is one of the best and most authentic heritage hotels in Rajasthan. An ornate 17th-century fort-palace with domed turrets and balconies that tower over the little village below, and with immaculately restored suites and deluxe rooms featuring original frescoes and antiques, it combines beauty with wonderful service, delicious Rajasthani cuisine, and excellent value. The palace is personally managed by the charming Thakur of Deogarh, who (like Kesri Singh in the Shekawati) makes you feel like a long-lost aristocrat. He is supported by a small, discreet professional staff (tipping, for instance, is only done via a central tipping box, reducing the irritating pressure that is part and parcel of traveling in India). Rooms vary considerably (you are welcome to look around when you arrive and choose), but all are beautifully furnished, with little done to change the authenticity of the architecture (right down to the slightly erratic plumbing). Book one of the six gorgeous suites (no. 235 is a particularly beautiful deluxe suite, available for Rs 3,200/$50; no. 211, the aptly named Royal Suite, goes for Rs 3,995/$86) and pretend that all you survey is yours from your private balcony. There's also a gorgeous pool, and the village is worth exploring. Note that from Deogarh you can take a long but satisfying detour to visit the Ranakpur Temples and Kumbalgarh Fort (see "Top Excursions," below), possibly on your way to Udaipur or Jodhpur; or you can visit them as a round-trip from the Mahal—contact the Mahal regarding planning or transfers from Udaipur, Jodhpur, or Jaipur.

architect on board—the rooms really are lovely, but many of the interior spaces are gloomy, the atmosphere is soulless, and you have to exit the lobby and walk past the parking area to the back of the building to reach the pool (which, by the way, is fabulous). That said, it's probably the most luxurious option if Pushkar Palace is full, though you'll need a car or taxi to get to town.

Pushkar 305 022, Rajasthan. © 0145/277-2001; -2401, -2402; -2953, -2954, or -2957. Fax 0145/277-2226 or -2952. www.hotelpushkarpalace.com. 53 units. Rs 2,200 ($48) deluxe; Rs 5,000 ($110) suite. Extra bed Rs 300–Rs 500 ($6.50–$11). During mela (cattle fair): $200–$300 including breakfast and dinner. AE, DC, MC, V. **Amenities:** Restaurant; bar; pool (2003); laundry. In room: A/C, TV, minibar.

SHOPPING

The main thoroughfare, **Sadar Bazaar,** is just over 1km (a half mile) long, and is lined with tiny shops selling ridiculously cheap (though often low-quality) clothing, excellent music (anything from Hindu temple to Hindi pop to global trance), and the best selection of books west of Delhi. This is definitely the place to come with empty bags—its almost cheaper to stock up on a new wardrobe here than pay hotel laundry fees.

7 Udaipur

405km (250 miles) SW of Jaipur; 260km (160 miles) S of Jodhpur

You'd have to be a real cynic not to love the "City of Sunrise," often described as the most romantic city in India. Built around four lakes, the placid blue waters reflecting ethereal white palaces and temples beyond which the distant Aravalli Hills shimmer, Udaipur has a real sense of space and peace, and the city is mercifully free of the kind of intense capitalist hucksterism that so marks the Indian street experience. This may have something to do with its proud Hindu history, for the city is not only known for its gracious palaces, temperate climate, and beautiful views, but for maintaining a fierce independence from even the most powerful outside influences. It fought bloody wars to repel Turkish, Afghan, Tartar, and Mongol invaders and rejected allegiances with the Mughals, only to acquiesce in 1818, when the state grudgingly came under British political control.

Capital of the legendary Sisodias of Mewar, believed to be direct descendants of the Sun (an insignia you'll see everywhere), Udaipur was built on the shores of Lake Pichola by Udai Singh II in 1559, who returned here after the third and final sacking of the previous Mewar stronghold, Chittaurgarh (see "Top Excursions," below). Udai Singh's son, Pratap, kept the Mughal invaders at bay for a further 25 years and is said to have been so disgusted by Man Singh and the Jaipur raja's obsequious relations with the Mughals that, after one historic meeting, he had the ground where Man Singh had walked washed with Ganges water in order to purify it. In keeping with this family tradition of unyielding Mewar pride, Maharana Fateh Singh was also the only Rajput prince who refused to attend the Delhi Durbar held for King George V in 1911, despite the fact that the British had acknowledged the maharana as the head of the princely states of Rajputana.

Today, much of Udaipur, particularly the old part on the shores of Lake Pichola, where the city's most striking landmarks—the towering **City Palace** and floating **Lake Palace**—are situated, still feels remarkably like a 16th-century Rajput stronghold, and the benevolent maharana is still treated like a reigning king by his devoted and loyal subjects. You can witness this firsthand by attending the temple at nearby Eklingji on a Monday evening, when the maharana—the 76th ruler of one of the world's oldest surviving dynasties—joins his subjects to pay his respects to Shiva.

Try to spend at least 3 to 4 days in Udaipur, whether you spend them aimlessly wandering through its mazelike lanes, taking a slow cruise on Pichola Lake, exploring the giant medieval fortress and palaces that rise from its shores, or setting off to see the intricately carved Jain temples of Ranakpur and the ancient fort of Kumbhalgarh—or whether you do nothing but loll around on a comfortable divan overlooking the lake. You'll find the City of Sunrise the most relaxing part of your sojourn in Rajasthan.

ESSENTIALS

VISITOR INFORMATION   Rajasthan Tourist Development Corporation (RTDC) is inconveniently located in the Tourist Office at Fath Memorial in Surajpole (© **0294/241-1535;** Mon–Sat 10am–5pm). Satellite tourist offices can be found at the railway station (© **0294/241-2984;** Mon–Sat 7:30–11:30am and 4–7pm) and the airport (© **0294/265-5433;** open at flight times). Note that the best places to draw money against your credit card are **Andhra Bank** (Shakti Nagar) and **Bank of Baroda** (opposite Town Hall, Bapu

Udaipur

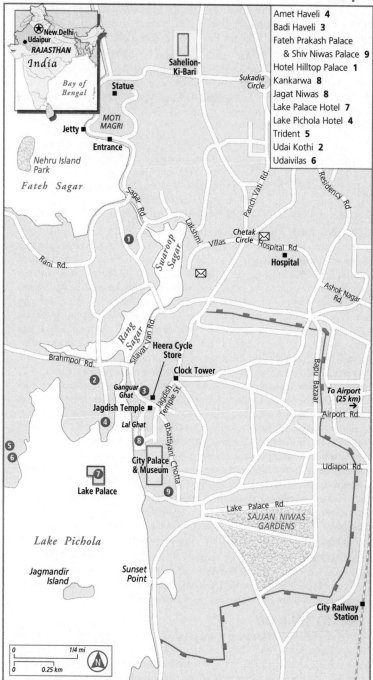

Amet Haveli **4**
Badi Haveli **3**
Fateh Prakash Palace
 & Shiv Niwas Palace **9**
Hotel Hilltop Palace **1**
Kankarwa **8**
Jagat Niwas **8**
Lake Palace Hotel **7**
Lake Pichola Hotel **4**
Trident **5**
Udai Kothi **2**
Udaivilas **6**

New Delhi
Udaipur
RAJASTHAN
India
Bay of Bengal

Sahelion-Ki-Bari

Statue

Sukadia Circle

Jetty

MOTI MAGRI

Entrance

Nehru Island Park

Fateh Sagar

Sagar Rd.

Panch Vati Rd.

Residency Rd.

Rani Rd.

Swaroop Sagar

Lakshmi Villas

Chetak Circle

Hospital Rd.

Hospital

Ashok Nagar Rd.

Rang Sagar

Sllavat Van Rd.

Brahmpol Rd.

Heera Cycle Store

Clock Tower

Bapu Bazaar

To Airport (25 km)

Ganguar Ghat

Jagdish Temple St.

Airport Rd.

Jagdish Temple

Lal Ghat

Bhattiyani Chotta

City Palace & Museum

Udaipol Rd.

Lake Palace

Lake Palace Rd.

SAJJAN NIWAS GARDENS

Lake Pichola

Jagmandir Island

Sunset Point

City Railway Station

0   1/4 mi
0   0.25 km

N

347

Bazaar). A **Thomas Cook office** is conveniently located inside the City Palace, but rates aren't always great. The best private hospital, with 24-hour emergency rooms and pharmacy, is **Udaipur Hospital** (© **0294/242-0223** or -0322).

GETTING THERE   By Air   Dabok Airport (© **0294/265-5453**) is 25km (15 miles) from Udaipur. As always, **Jet Airways** is the preferable option (© **0294/256-1105-60**), connecting the city with Delhi, Mumbai (both 1 hr., 15 min.), and Jaipur (45 min.). **Indian Airlines** (© **0294/241-0999**) covers the same routes as well as Jodhpur. A taxi into town should cost about Rs 250 ($5.35).

By Train/Bus   Udaipur is not well connected to the rest of India by train, with your options limited to Delhi (a 20-hr. overnight journey, stopping along the way at Jaipur; $25) and Ahmedabad ($13), from where you can catch another train to Mumbai. The Udaipur City Station (this is more centrally located than the Udaipur Station) is where to alight. In the unlikely event that you've opted for a bus, you will most likely be dropped off just north of the City Station.

GETTING AROUND   The best way to get around the main tourist sights (the area surrounding the City Palace) is on foot, but if you want to spend a rather satisfying day taking in all the sights in the city, consider renting a **moped** or **bicycle** from Heera Cycle Store (86 Gangaur Ghat Rd., easy walking distance from Jagdish Temple). Given the chaos on Indian roads, hiring a car with driver is probably the way to go; you will certainly need one for the recommended trips farther afield. To hire one for the day, or for a self-planned tour in Rajasthan, head for the RTDC at Surajpole (see "Visitor Information," above). This is also where to check out the range of half- or full-day government tours on offer, though note that organized tours can be too rushed or too slow, and can place you in close contact with odious fellow travelers; the quality of guides often leaves a lot to be desired as well. Should you wish to hire a car and driver from one of the many travel and tour agents that are more conveniently located in the old city (see recommendations below), you might want to call the RTDC just to discern their going rate—at press time, between Rs 900 and Rs 1,200 ($20 and $26) for a full day. Recommended travel and tour agents, all conveniently located within walking distance of the old city sights, are the helpful **Comfort Travels and Tours,** located inside the City Palace (© **0294/241-9746**); **Aravalli Safari,** on Lake Palace Road (© **0294/242-1697**); and the very efficient **Ramesh Dashora,** proprietor of Parul, in the Jagat Niwas Hotel (© **0294/241-5547;** www.rajasthan-travel-bycab.com)—the latter offers guide plus car for Rs 650 ($14) half-day city and Rs 1,200 ($26) full day.

For boat trips on Lake Pichola, see "Top Attractions," below.

FESTIVALS   Udaipur's biggest festivals are the **Mewar Festival,** held every March or April, and the **Holi Festival,** held every March. October's Ashwa Poojan is another celebration worth inquiring about (your hotel should be able to advise on exact dates and where best to experience the festivities).

WHAT TO SEE & DO
If your idea of a holiday is lying at the pool with a good book, only visits to the City and Lake palaces (see "Top Attractions," below) need top your list of things to do in Udaipur proper. The city is the ideal base for a number of day trips, however; the most highly recommended is a round-trip through Kumbhalgarh Wildlife Sanctuary to the Fort, taking in the temples of Ranakpur along the way, and possibly stopping at Eklingji on the way back (see "Top Excursions," below).

For those who are interested in seeing more of the city, the following day tour—to be tailored to your needs—provides an overview of the top sights in and around Udaipur. Start your day by exploring the City Palace, which towers over the city's raison d'etre, the tranquil waters of Lake Pichola, upon which two more palaces can be seen on the islands of Jag Niwas and Jag Mandir (see "Top Attractions," below). Exit through the Tripolia Gate to explore the old city of Udaipur, which sprawls north of the palace, of which the **Jagdish Temple** ✦, the largest in Udaipur, is its chief attraction. Despite some lovely exterior carvings, the temple itself is rather ordinary (if you've seen a number of them elsewhere, that is), but its attraction lies in its massive popularity: the temple has seen a constant stream of people who come to worship Lord Jagannath, an aspect of Vishnu (the black stone image enshrined within), since it first opened its doors in 1652. *Aarti* takes place at around 10am, 7:30pm, and 10pm—try to time your visit for when the prayer-songs make for a most atmospheric experience (remember to remove your shoes before entering). The bronze half-man half-bird statue outside is the vehicle of Vishnu. From the Jagdish Temple you can wander the mazelike streets of old Udaipur, admiring the whitewashed havelis and popping into tiny shops before reaching the clock tower that marks the northern edge. If you haven't picked up a bicycle from **Heera Cycle Store** (86 Gangaur Ghat Rd., near the Jagdish Temple), catch a taxi from here (or have your driver waiting) to the **Bharatiya Lok Kala Museum** (Panch Vati Rd.; daily 9am–6pm; Rs 20/40¢). This is unofficially known as Udaipur's puppet museum (Rajasthan being the birthplace of this favored Indian storytelling medium), where you can watch a good show, staged almost hourly throughout the day (though note that most hotels have a puppet show as part of their evening's entertainment). The folk museum also contains models, instruments, and photographs documenting other local traditions and crafts, but for this you're better off visiting **Shilpgram,** a rather faux rural arts-and-crafts "village" located 5km (3 miles) out of town (reached by following the road that runs along the north of Fateh Sagar Lake; daily 9:30am–6pm; Rs 10/20¢, camel ride Rs 20/40¢; 11am and 7pm folk dance). Created to "promote and preserve the traditional architecture, music, and crafts of the tribal village of western India," Shilpgram has a distinctly artificial feel but may interest cultural anthropologists or those looking to ride a camel and browse for tribal knickknacks that the "traditionally" attired craftspeople will be only too delighted to finally off-load. Along the way, you can stop for a brief wander through **Saheliyon-ki-Bari,** or "Garden of the Maids of Honour" (north of Bharatiya Lok Kala Museum—turn left at the Sukadia Circle; daily 9am–7:30pm; Rs 10/20¢). Created by Sangram Singh in the 18th century for the ladies of his household (some say to re-create the monsoon climate for his sickly daughter), this is billed as Udaipur's finest garden but it suffers from neglect, with none of the fountains operating. Still, it's a peaceful place, and the array of established indigenous trees may interest keen botanists. From Saheliyon-ki-Bari you make your way to nearby **Fateh Sagar Lake,** passing **Moti Magri** on your left, atop which is the statue of Maharana Pratap and his beloved horse, Chetak (largely missable, but the views from here are lovely). Fateh Sagar, the large lake that lies north of Lake Pichola, has a small island garden of its own: The rather neglected **Nehru Park** is usually reached by ferry (daily 8am–6pm), but at press time the severe drought had not only decimated much of the garden, the park was only reachable on foot.

An excellent place to view the sunset is from **Sajjan Garh,** the "Monsoon Palace," built by the Maharan Sajjan Singh as an observatory in the late 19th century. You cannot enter the palace building (it's a restricted security area) but the views of the surrounding lakes, rivers, and mountains are breathtaking. If this sounds like one stop too many after a rather exhausting day, head straight for **Lake Pichola,** where you can either board a boat for the sunset cruise (see below), grab a table on the aptly named **Sunset Terrace** (near the Dovecoat lobby), or sit on the "deck" of the Lake Palace. As the sun sinks behind the distant jagged outline of the Aravalli Hills, bathing the waters in an orange-red hue, you can be forgiven for deciding to extend your stay for just one more day

TOP ATTRACTIONS

City Palace and Museum ✦✦✦   Its cream-colored stone walls towering some 30m (100 ft.) above the mirrorlike waters of the lake, and stretching almost 250m (800 ft.) across its northwestern shore, Udaipur's 300-year-old City Palace actually is comprised of 11 palaces (or *mahals*) built by its successive maharanas, making it by far the largest palace complex in Rajasthan. You should purchase the rather useful guidebook at the entrance (or hire the services of a guide through your hotel) to help you maneuver the sprawling museum, much of it connected by a maze of rather claustrophobic tunnel-like stairways designed to confuse and slow down potential invaders (this is why it's essential to try and get here as soon as the palace doors open—finding yourself trapped between busloads of jeering families who mysteriously come to regular standstills in these airless passages is sheer purgatory). The entire palace is a delight, but highlights include the large peacock mosaics in the 17th-century Mor (Peacock) Chowk; the mirror-encrusted Moti Mahal; the glass and porcelain figures of the Manak (Ruby) Mahal, which has a central garden; the collection of miniatures featuring Krishna legends in Krishna Vilas (dedicated to a 16-year-old princess who committed suicide here); the exquisite Zenana Mahal (Palace of the Queens); and the Chinese and Dutch ceramics of the Chini Mahal. Through cusped windows are superb views of the serene waters of Pichola Lake, on which the white-marble Lake Palace appears to float. The last two palaces built, both now open to visitors wishing to overnight or dine, are the grand but rather staid **Shiv Niwas** and the gorgeous **Fateh Prakash.** The latter is worth visiting for high tea to view the Durbar Hall's royal portrait gallery, with its massive chandeliers and Venetian mirrors, and to see the Crystal Gallery, which has a huge collection of rare cut-crystal furniture and ornaments imported by Maharana Sajjan Singh from England in 1877. (For more on these palaces, see "Where to Stay & Dine," later in this chapter.) Vintage-car lovers should ask about the tour of the Mewar family's Classic Car Collection. Set aside 3 hours to do the palace justice.

Lake Pichola. Rs 100 ($2.10); free for guests staying in the Palace. Daily 9:30am–4:30pm.

Lake Pichola and Lake Palace ✦✦✦   Most beautiful at sunrise and sunset, Lake Pichola reflects what seems to be a picture-perfect inversion of the many whitewashed and cream buildings that rise majestically from its shores and islands, known locally as Jag Niwas and Jag Mandir. Jag Niwas island is entirely covered by the Lake Palace, built by the maharana in 1740 as a summer idyll and today perhaps the most romantic—certainly the most photographed—hotel in India (see "Where to Stay & Dine," later in this chapter). A little farther south is the slightly larger Jag Mandir, upon which the domed Gul Mahal stands. Famous as the star location in the movie *Octopussy,* it has also been a place of refuge: first for the young prince Shah Jahan who—in a typical Mughal ascension—was plotting to overthrow his father, Jahangir (incidentally, it is

> **Fun Fact Indian Solutions to a Global Problem**
>
> The current maharana Shriji Arvind Singhji, 76th custodian of the house of Mewar, combines philanthropic interests with a keen capitalist eye—he owns some 12 heritage hotels throughout Rajasthan, from which a sizable part of the profits are funneled back into his **Maharana of Mewar Charitable Foundation.** Long concerned about the effects of global warming, particularly in Udaipur, which has seen a significant rise in average temperatures, the maharana helped pioneer the world's first solar-powered water taxi, and the world's first solar rickshaw is currently undergoing trials in Udaipur. Because 86% of all the vehicles in India are two-stroke two-wheelers (motorcycles, mopeds, gas-powered scooters), which are responsible for a major percentage of the country's carbon dioxide emissions, this could go a long way toward solving India's pollution problems.

believed, by Udaipurs of course, that the Gul Mahal is what later inspired Jahan to build the Taj Mahal); and later for European women and children, whom Maharana Sarap protected during the Mutiny. You can catch a boat to Jag Mandir from the City Palace (Bansi Ghat) jetty, but once you have alighted there's not much to do but purchase an overpriced refreshment; the trip around the lake including a visit to Sunset Terrace (near Dovecoat Wing) or the Lake Palace Hotel. If you haven't booked a room at the hotel, make sure you come for dinner—the views alone are worth it, but the opulent and elegant setting is sublime (see "Where to Stay & Dine," later in this chapter).

Boats depart from Bansi Ghat at base of City Palace on the hour and operate Apr–Sept, 8–11am and 3—6pm; Oct–Mar, 10am–noon and 2–5pm. Rs 200 ($4.30). To make a table reservation at Lake Palace, call © 0294/ 252-7961.

TOP EXCURSIONS

A number of recommended excursions from Udaipur can either be tackled as round-trips or as stopovers on your way elsewhere in the state. The first option is the easiest, a half-day excursion (at most) that takes in some of the most important temples in Udaipur. The second option—which you can combine with the first for a rather grueling but very satisfying round-trip—takes you to the awesome Jain temples at Ranakpur through the Kumbhulgarh Wildlife Sanctuary, past wonderful pastoral scenes that haven't changed since medieval times, to view the magnificent Kumbhulgarh Fort. From here you can either head northwest for Jodhpur or double back to Udaipur, possibly taking in the temples at Nathdwara, Nagda, and Eklingji. (If you're pressed for time, leave out Nathdwara—beyond the superb examples of *pichwai* paintings, there's not much to see, as non-Hindus may not enter the temple.) To plan this as a round-trip, you will need to hire a driver familiar with the distances and terrain, and overnight along the way (see the listing for Kumbhalgarh Fort, below).

The third outing is another long full-day trip, this time with the sole purpose of viewing Chittaurgarh, site of the most legendary Mewar battles. From here you can return to Udaipur or push on east to the little town of Bundi (see earlier in this chapter), and from there to Jaipur or Ranthambhore National Park.

For those interested in an off-the-beaten-track tourist experience, this time traveling south to the relatively undiscovered Dungarpur Palace, option four is well worth the time, not least for Deco fans who will relish overnighting in the family manse—Udai Bilas Palace, a living Deco museum—before returning or pushing on to Gujarat. If Ranakpur's temples have whet your appetite for more, the fifth option, an excursion to the west ascending the Aravallis to Mount Abu, the only hill station in Rajasthan, and home to the most famous Jain temples in India, can also be tackled from Udaipur, though the distances covered here will necessitate an overnight stay. For details on distances and all excursions, see a full description of the five day trips, below.

An excursion to an attraction that is not described in detail below, but which may interest birders or those in search of more peace, is **Jaisamand Lake,** the second-largest man-made lake in Asia, created in 1691 by Maharana Jai Singh. Located about an hour away from Udaipur, it has a number of marble pavilions but is more famous for the many aquatic birds that have found a home in what is now the **Jaisamand Wildlife Sanctuary.**

DAY TRIP 1: A HALF-DAY TEMPLE EXCURSION

Eklingji & Nagda Temples ⊛⊛   Housing a manifestation of Shiva, the god who guards the fortunes of the rulers of Mewar, Eklingji is a lovely marble temple complex made up of 108 temples, the first of which was built in A.D. 734 by Bappa Rawal, legendary founder of the Sisodia clan, who ruled the Mewar kingdom for hundreds of years. The entire complex, most of it rebuilt in the 15th century, has a wonderfully uplifting atmosphere, particularly during prayer times (see below), and never more so than on Monday evenings when the Maharana of Udaipur comes to pay his respects, walking among his subjects as a mere mortal despite the attendant bowing and scraping. The four-faced black lingam (phallic symbol) apparently marks the spot where Bappa Rawal (that's him riding the peacock) was given the title Darwan (or "servant") of Eklingji by his guru; outside, facing Shiva, is Nandi, Shiva's vehicle. Wander around the temple complex and you'll find a number of carvings from the Kama Sutra; your explorations won't exceed 30 minutes. Deserted **Nagda,** which lies 2km (1¼ miles) north, is a far cry from this vibrant place of worship. All that survives of the site of the ancient capital of Mewar, which dates back to A.D. 626, are the ruins of the "Sas Bahu," a 10th-century Vaishnavite twin temple (*Sas* meaning "mother-in-law" and *Bahu* "daughter-in-law") and the remains of the Adbhutji temple. Regrettably, the temples have been vandalized over the years and look much the worse for wear—unless you're of the archaeological bent, skip it if you're pushed for time.

22km (14 miles) north of Udaipur (30–40-min. drive one-way). Eklingji prayer times: 11:30am, 12:15pm, 12:45pm, 1pm, 6:30pm, 7:15pm, 7:45pm, and 8pm.

Nathdwara ⊛   Said to be the second-richest temple in India, Nathdwara's Shri Nathji temple, home to a 600-year-old black-marble statue of Lord Krishna, is one of the most important pilgrimage sites in India, attracting thousands, particularly during the festivals of Diwali, Holi, and Janmasthami. According to legend, in 1669 as the statue was being carried from Mathura to protect it from the destructive blows of the pious Mughal emperor Aurangzeb, it fell off the wagon at this site; the carriers (no doubt pretty exhausted) took this as a sign and built the temple around the statue. That said, the interior is closed to non-Hindus, so many of you won't even get a glimpse of the statue. The main reason to visit is to view what many believe are the finest examples of *pichwai* paintings that adorn the interior and exterior of the temple. Hand-spun cloth painted with vibrant scenes depicting Krishna's life, these were originally created to teach illiterate low castes (who in the past were also barred from entering the sacred inner sanctum). You can purchase your very own pichhwai paintings in the local bazaar, or look for more examples in Udaipur. Note that this is also a center for traditional *meenakari* (enamel) work.

48km (30 miles) from Udaipur (1-hr. drive one-way).

DAY TRIP 2: A TEMPLE, A FORT & A WONDERFUL DRIVE

Ranakpur Temples ✶✶✶   If you visit only one temple complex in Rajasthan, it should be Jain. Those at Ranakpur offer the finest examples of the complex and sustained levels of craftsmanship the Jains are renowned for, comparable in every way to the more famous Delwara temples at Mount Abu. If anything, a visit here is preferable— despite being a great deal more accessible, it is infinitely more peaceful, with less traffic. Known for their aestheticism and religious fervor (Jains are not only strict vegetarians, but walk with care to ensure no hapless insect should die due to their carelessness; the most orthodox wear permanent masks to protect even the tiniest bug from the possibility of being ingested), the Jain put all their passion (and not inconsiderable wealth) into the creation of ornately carved temples. The Ranakpur temples are jaw-droppingly beautiful, with exquisitely detailed relief carvings (and strangely, a few pieces of tinfoil) covering every inch of pillar, wall, and ceiling. The main triple-volume Chaumukha Temple, built from 1446 and dedicated to Adinatha Rishabdeva, the first Jain *tirthankara*, or "Enlightened One," is surrounded by 66 subsidiary shrines; inside are 1,444 intricately carved pillars—not one of them the same. (Incidentally, the land was donated to the Jains by Rana Kumbha, the warrior who built 32 forts, of which Kumbhalgarh is the most famous.) Note that no leather (not even a belt!) is allowed on the premises, no photography is allowed, and you are requested to dress conservatively (no showing of legs). Menstruating women are also strictly forbidden to enter. *Note:* There are no great accommodations options in the immediate vicinity; best to push on to the **Aodhi,** near Kumbhalgarh Fort (see below) or, if you're on your way to Jodhpur, **Rawla Narlai** (see "Traveling between Udaipur & Jodhpur," later in this chapter).

Tip: Two kilometers (1¼ mile) north (on the way to Jodhpur or Kumbhalgarh), you will pass a traditional **dhurrie carpet "shop"** (✆ **0294/241-7833**), where you can pick up a beautifully crafted 4m by 6m (13-ft. by 20-ft.) carpet for Rs 3,000 ($65)—a great deal cheaper than what you'll pay in the cities.

65km (40 miles) from Udaipur (2½-hr. drive one-way). Open noon–5pm.

Kumbhalgarh Fort ✶✶✶   Built in the 15th century by Rana Kumbha, this mountain fortress is, together with Jodhpur's Meharangir Fort, one of the most impressive sights Rajasthan has to offer. Take one look at the impenetrable walls that snake for 36km (22 miles) along 13 mountain peaks, and you know that this is one of the most inaccessible fortifications ever built by man. It was in fact only captured once, when the Mughal emperor Akbar had its water supply poisoned. This is also where the infant Udai Singh, who was spirited here by his nanny while Chittaurgarh (see below) was being sacked, spent his formative years. The wall, the second longest in the world, culminates in a fairy-tale fort within which lie the **Palace of Rana Kumbha** and the **Bada Mahal** (or **Palace of Clouds,** so named because it literally is in the clouds during the monsoon months). The fort is situated deep within the Kumbhalgarh Wildlife Sanctuary, and the drive there—through tiny villages and pastoral countryside—is one of the great highlights of a trip to Rajasthan and a great contrast to the crowded cities. Kumbhulgarh is considered the most important fort after Chittaurgarh, but its relative accessibility and the charm of the drive make this is the preferable option.

To have adequate time to explore the fort, or to take in Eklingji on the return journey, it's worth overnighting near the fort. The closest and best choice is the lovely **Aodhi Hotel,** owned by the HRH Group of Hotels (www.hrhindia.com; Rs 2,900–Rs 3,000/$60–$65 double; see Fateh Prakash Palace for reservations details). It has spacious, comfortable rooms (each with TV and minibar, and bathroom fittings in a reasonable state) that cling to the hillside and overlook a large pool and a pretty alfresco dining area. Room nos. 4, 5, 10, 11, and 23 enjoy good views.

90km (56 miles) from Udaipur (2-hr. drive one-way; 1 hr. from Ranakpur temples).

DAY TRIP 3: A HISTORY OF VALOR

Chittaurgarh (or Chittor) 👫👫   Chittaurgarh is 3 hours from Udaipur and covers 280 hectares (700 acres), making it a rather long day trip, but it's well worth it if you're armed with information and a good imagination (both of which can be supplied by a good guide; ask your hotel for recommendations). Thrusting 180m (575 ft.) into the sky, the fort houses a number of monuments and memorials, but with much of it in ruins, its primary importance lies in its evocative history. The fort has witnessed some of the bloodiest battles in history, and songs recording the valor and sacrifice of its inhabitants are still sung today.

Built in the 7th century, it remained the capital of Mewar until 1568, when the capital was shifted to Udaipur. During this time Chittaurgarh was ravaged three times, but the story behind the first sacking that took place in 1303 during the reign of Rana Ratan Singh is perhaps the most romantic (see "Battling for a Glimpse of Beauty," below).

Chittaurgarh returned to Rajput rule in 1326 and the Mewar enjoyed 2 centuries of prosperity before it was again laid siege to, this time by Sultan Bahadur Shah of Gujarat. To save the life of the Rajput heir Udai Singh, his nursemaid Panna Dai sacrificed her own infant son, leaving him as a decoy for the murderous sultan and spiriting the tiny heir away to the safety of Kumbhalgarh Fort. The women and children of Chittaurgarh committed *johaur* (suicide) while their men died on the battlefields.

When, at the age of 13, Udai was reinstated at Chittaurgarh, he searched in earnest for a new site for the capital, building Udaipur on the shores of Lake Pichola. Eight years later, the Mughal emperor Akbar, trying to contain the arrogance of Udai Singh—who poured such contempt on Jai (of Jaipur) Singh's collaboration with the emperor—attacked Chittaurgarh. This time 30,000 Rajput lives were lost, and the women and children again flung themselves on the flames rather than be captured by the Muslims. Chittaurgarh was given back to the Rajputs in 1616, much of it in ruins, but by this time the royal family was comfortably ensconced in Udaipur, and the fort was never lived in again.

The fort is approached through seven massive *pols,* or gates—look for the *chhatri* (cenotaph) of the chivalrous Jaimal and his cousin Kala near Bhairon Pol. Jaimal was seriously wounded defending Chittaur against Emperor Akbar but he refused to give up and was carried back into battle on the shoulders of Kala, where both were slain. At Ram Pol is a **memorial to Phatta** who, at 16, having lost his father in battle and witnessed the deaths of his sword-wielding mother and young wife on the battlefield, led his saffron-robed men to certain death while the women of the fort yet again ended their lives by committing *johar.*

Battling for a Glimpse of Beauty

It is said that the rapacious sultan Allauddin Khilji laid siege to the fort because he had become obsessed with tales of the legendary beauty of the Maharana (or Rana) Ratan Singh's queen, Rani Padmini. He promised to withdraw, provided Singh allow him an opportunity to lay eyes on her—an outrageous demand considering that a strange man's gaze was tantamount to the defilement of a Rajput royal woman. But in the spirit of compromise, Singh reluctantly agreed to present him with her reflection in the lotus pond that lay below the palace's women's quarters. The sultan used this opportunity to betray the king, ambushing and capturing him on his departure. The next day a bereft Padmini sent word to the sultan that she would give herself to him in return for her husband and the withdrawal of his troops. She then descended through the seven *pols* (gates), surrounded by what appeared to be her maids-of-honor—Singh's troops, disguised as women. Singh was rescued from the sultan's camp, but the ensuing battle cost the lives of some 7,000 of Singh's men—a crippling loss. When it was clear that the Rajputs would be defeated, the funeral pyres were lit, and Padmini and 13,000 women and children committed *johaur,* flinging themselves onto the flames, after which the last of Singh's men went to meet certain death below the ramparts.

As you enter the final pol, you will see the **Shingara Chauri Mandir,** a typically adorned Jain temple, and the crumbling **15th-century palace** built by Rana Kumbha up ahead. Under the palace lies a series of cellars where Padmini reputedly committed *johar.* Rana Kumbha was one of the Mewar's most powerful rulers: In addition to the palace, he built the **nearby Khumba Shyam Temple,** dedicated to Varah (an incarnation of Lord Vishnu) as well as **Meera Temple,** dedicated to the poet and princess Meera, whose devotion to Krishna reputedly saved her from being poisoned (incidentally, Krishna is depicted as blue as a result of the poison he consumed, thereby saving the world). Note that inside the cenotaph in front of the temple is a **carved figure** of five human bodies with one head—in a rare moment of tolerance, this is supposed to demonstrate that all castes are ultimately equal. Farther south lies Kumbha's **Vijay Stambh,** or **"Tower of Victory"**—a lavishly ornamented tower built by Kumbha to commemorate his victory over the combined forces of Malwa and Gujarat.

Other sites of interest are **Padmini's Palace,** where the sultan Allauddin Khilji gazed upon Padmini's reflection in the lotus pond; the **Kirti Stambh,** a 12th-century tower ornamented with figures from the Jain pantheon; the **Fateh Prakash Palace,** built for the maharana during the 1920s and housing a dry archaeological museum (daily 10am–4:30pm; Rs 5/10¢); and the **Kalika Mata Temple,** originally built as a Sun Temple by Bappa Rawal in the 8th century but rebuilt during the 14th century and dedicated to Kali, goddess of power and valor. Some of the best views are from **Gaumukh ("cow's mouth") Reservoir,** so-called because the spring water trickles through a stone carving of a cow's mouth.

Accommodations in Chittor are limited, with no luxury options. If you *have* to overnight, the best options are **Meera** (© **01472/240-266**) and **Pratap Palace** (© **01472/240-099**).

115km (70 miles) northeast of Udaipur. A tour takes approximately 2 hr. **Note:** You can get here by train, but it's a relatively long trip (3 hr., 30 min. or 4hr., 15 min.), and trains travel at odd times, forcing an overnight stay. The railway station lies 4km (2½ miles) from the base of the fort; from here, you can catch a rickshaw to tour the fort—expect to pay at least Rs 100 ($2.10).

DAY TRIP 4: AN UNDISCOVERED PALACE & DECO DELIGHT

Dungarpur's Palaces ★★★ *(Finds)*   It's hard for anyone flipping through Angelika Taschen's book *Indian Style* to refrain from gasping when they come to the pages recording the magnificent apartments of the 13th-century **Juna Mahal.** A seven-story fortresslike structure that appears to spring forth from its rocky surrounds, the palace doesn't look like much from the outside, but inside, it houses one of the world's most interesting "art galleries": Every wall and column is covered in beautiful, intricate frescoes—tiny paintings; or mosaics with glass, mirror, and tiles; or artfully used porcelain plates embedded into the wall. In one of the large downstairs reception rooms the entire floor is covered in huge (decaying) Persian carpets. Yet even though it houses a treasure trove of art and design, the palace is far from being a tourist attraction: There's no ticket office, no touts, no guides, no visitors—not even a single hawker in sight, only the toothless old retainer whose trembling hands hold the keys while he waits for you to drink it all in before he opens another, even more stunning room. Perhaps it is precisely this— viewing such beauty in absolute solitude—that makes the experience so special, but the artworks are considered to be of the very best in Rajasthan. Don't miss (you're unlikely to, as long as the old man is around to leer at your reaction) the collection of miniature paintings depicting scenes from the Kama Sutra, modestly hidden behind cupboard doors in the maharaja's suite on the top floor.

To view the Juna Mahal, you will likely have to overnight at the nearby **Udai Bilas Palace**—no hardship, as this, too, is a wonderful experience, particularly if you have any interest in the Deco period or relish a sense of nostalgia. Built on the shores of the Gaibsagar Lake (great for birders, with 122 species recorded), it is both scenic and secluded and combines Rajput architecture and murals with original Art Deco furnishings and fittings—the work of the Maharawal Laxman Singhji, who had three new wings built around the lovely Ek Thambia Mahal ("one-pillared palace") in 1940. Still the royal residence of the maharawal and his family (meals are prepared by the beautiful princess Priya), the palace offers 20 old-fashioned rooms (old plumbing, beautiful Deco furniture in need of new springs, no in-room amenities—but simply charming nonetheless) as well as a wonderful pool on the water's edge. If you can afford it, book a suite (our personal preference is for no. 20, but really, it all depends on whether you fall in love with a particular lounge suite or carpet pattern or view). Best to ask whether you can wander around and take your pick; no. 7 is the best standard room.

120km (75 miles) south of Udaipur (2-hr. drive one-way); 175km (108 miles) from Ahmedabad, Gujarat. Udai Bilas rates: Rs 2,000–Rs 3,800 ($44–$82); extra bed Rs 700 ($15). Discounts May–Sept. MC, V. For reservations, contact Udai Bilas Palace, Dungarpur, Rajasthan 314 001 (© **02964/230-808;** fax 02964/231-008; www.udaibilaspalace.com).

DAY TRIP 5: ASCENDING MOUNT ABU

The Rajputs are said to have held the fire ceremony in which they were "reborn" as warriors on these lofty heights, but Mount Abu, so-called "Abode of the

Gods," only became a destination for mere mortals a millennium later, when the British persuaded the Sirohi State to allow them to use it as a retreat from the searing heat of the plateaus that shimmer below. They were later joined by the Rajput princes, who built mini-palaces to show off and entertain the Britishers. At a cool 1,220m (390 ft.) above sea level, this is the only hill station in Rajasthan, and it's within easy striking distance of many of Gujarat's big cities, providing welcome relief for thousands of domestic visitors who come to paddle the central **Nakki Lake** in giant swan boats and view the exquisite sunsets, all accompanied by the inevitable high-spirited carousing of friends and families.

Indeed, unless you're prepared to put on your walking shoes and head for the hills, this is not the most peaceful of places; it's filled with a year-round festive spirit as families and honeymooners throng the streets, clutching ice creams or the manes of the ponies that clatter along, shaking their bells and feathered heads at passersby. Every evening at sunset literally hundreds of people set off for **Sunset Point,** riding in large pramlike vehicles pushed by stringy men or mounting the ponies that congregate here in the hopes of making their masters a few more rupees before the onset of night. The sun sinking into the plains that lie thousands of miles below is a truly wonderful sight, not least because you are sharing it with so many people, the smell of roasting peanuts permeating the air, and there is a rare sense of camaraderie as the crowd gives a final roar of approval when the sun finally slips behind the horizon. If you have no anthropological bent, however, the real reason to venture so far off the beaten track (and unless you approach it from Gujarat, Mount Abu is a long and not altogether satisfactory detour) is to view the Dilwara temples (see below), widely considered the best examples of Jain architecture in India, though to us the temples at Ranakpur (see above) are comparable.

There is a plethora of hotels in town, most awful, but the following two are recommended. **The Jaipur House,** which the latest Jaipur maharaja renovated and turned into an intimate hotel in 2002, is by far the best situated. Because of close family ties, the Jaipur maharaja was given first choice of land by the then-ruler of Sirohi State, and in 1897 he built his Rajput-style mansion on the highest hilltop overlooking Naggi Lake. Guests have a choice of nine rooms—all suites have views of the lake (for truly stupendous views, no. 201, "the Royal Suite," is one of the best in Rajasthan); room no. 107 has no lake views but with two small balconies is the best standard room (avoid no. 106, a horrid "junior suite"). For bookings contact © 02974/235-176 or ctpalace@datainfosys.net. Doubles range from Rs 2,800 to Rs 3,995 ($61–$86). If you prefer a more old-fashioned, laid-back atmosphere and more personable service, **Bikaner House** (also known as Palace Hotel), once the summer residence of the royal Bikaner family, was designed by that master of Indo-Saracenic style, Sir Swinton Jacob, in 1893. Enjoying a tranquil location near the Dilwara temples, it is surrounded by sprawling grounds and forests (including a slightly weedy tennis court). A million miles from the jovial madness that reigns in town, it will suit those who enjoy the timeless elegance of good design (and who don't mind rickety plumbing). Make sure you have a room in the main house; though very little from furnishing to fittings has changed since the maharaja opened it as a hotel in 1962, the staff (under the kind, professional Rajvirsinh) are faultless, and the genteel atmosphere very much captures the graciousness of a bygone era. For bookings, contact © 02974/235-121 or 0297/238-673; bikhouse@datainfosys.net. Rates are Rs 2,200 to Rs 3,150 ($48–$68). The hotels will happily arrange guides or transfers.

Dilwara Temples ☆☆☆ Built between the 11th and 13th centuries, these "hymns in marble"—every interior wall and pillar is covered with the most intricate carvings, none of which are repeated—are worthy of inspiring great devotion, and are said to be unparalleled anywhere else in India (though Ranakpur comes pretty close). Of the five temples, **Vimala Vasahi** (1031), which took 1,500 artists and 1,200 laborers 14 years to complete, and **Luna Vashai** (1231) are the most impressive. The full-color guidebook at the entrance is definitely worth purchasing (not least because photography is not allowed); it gives a pretty detailed breakdown of what you are looking at in each temple. Alternatively, hire the services of a guide through your hotel.

190km (118 miles) from Udaipur (a 5-hr. drive one-way). No entry fee. Dilwara Temples open noon–6pm. Note that no leather, cameras, bare legs, food, recorders, or menstruating women are allowed on the premises, and no one is allowed to enter the cells or touch the sculptures.

WHERE TO STAY & DINE

You will want to book into a hotel or haveli with a view of the lake, particularly on the eastern shore of Lake Pichola. The best are reviewed below, but the following also deserve a mention. The over-the-top Bhagwat Suite (room no. 209, Rs 2,995/$64 double), a large corner room in the **Lake Pichola Hotel** (western shore; ℂ **0294/243-1197;** www.lakepicholahotel.com), has the most wonderful views of the lake and its palaces—you can literally see Lake Palace from your large brass four-poster bed or the glass alcove that juts over the lake. This is by far the best room; others range from livable (2nd floor) to awful (1st floor). If you're literally counting your rupees, **Badi Haveli** (Rs 350/$7.60) is the clean, well-run, well-located (near City Palace), 350-year-old home of a Brahmin family, with monastic but scrupulously clean rooms. Some top-floor rooms have lovely views of the lake (ℂ **0294/241-2588;** hbhaveli@datainfosys.net). Also see the review of Kankarwa, below. At the other end of the scale is the **Trident.** A large, slick, purpose-built hotel—and part of the Oberoi group, with all the professionalism that this entails—it has plenty of amenities and facilities but is set some way from the lake among the tranquil Aravalli Hills, about a 25-minute drive from town. At $165 double, this comfortable option offers relatively good value (pool-facing rooms are best) and will suit the less adventurous traveler, but it's a bit soulless for our taste. Despite the irritating service, we'd opt for the Dovecoat rooms in the **City Palace** (ℂ **0294/432-200;** reservations@tridentudp. com). Note that, as in our Jaipur listings, if a heritage property hasn't been included, it's because it hasn't made the grade.

When it comes to Udaipur's finest dining experiences, you will certainly have to spend an evening at the **Lake Palace Hotel** (see below for details). Catch the boat over before the evening's cultural show starts, then order a cocktail and settle on the "deck" to watch beautiful young Rajasthani women twirl to a hypnotic drumbeat, followed by an amusing puppet show (if your attention starts to wander, take in the sublime views of the City Palace turning pink). Then retire to the dining room where a sumptuous buffet awaits, with more dishes than you can possibly have space for. There have been reports that the quality of the food doesn't match that of the location, but personal experience belies this—we guarantee you'll find something that will delight you, and the entire experience is worth every rupee. At press time the cost was Rs 550 ($12) per person (plus 22% tax and drinks). First preference is given to in-house guests, so book early.

A more casual dining experience is the Fateh Prakash Palace's **Sunset Terrace** (see below). This is indeed the perfect place to watch the sunset, and when the sun finally disappears behind the Aravalli Hills, the ambience just gets more romantic as candles are lit and the Lake Palace, which floats in the foreground, glows like a liner on the lake. That said, the food—which ranges from toasted sandwiches (adequate) to tandoori (overcooked)—is a bit of a letdown. Better fare, and more comfortable seating, is to be had at the **Jagat Niwas terrace, nearby**(see below). Unlike almost everywhere else in town, this restaurant terrace is open to the cooling breezes but totally under cover, which provides some escape from the midday heat. It also has comfortable mattressed alcoves with bolsters where you can curl up with a book or appreciate the sublime views of the lake. This is the kind of place where you could spend an entire afternoon relaxing; in fact, one guest, who wasn't even staying in the hotel, did exactly that every day for the duration of his stay in Udaipur. Service is slow but friendly (some of the waiters have been here 10 years or more), and food is average to good. Stick to the Indian dishes, either the vegetarian (*paneer matar masala,* Indian cheese simmered in a thick gravy with peas and tomatoes; and *paneer do piyaja,* cheese cooked with onion, tomato, and chilies) or the local dishes like fish a la Jagat (slices of the local freshwater fish, caught daily, cooked in a creamy white sauce, and served with chips). Expect to pay Rs 60 to Rs 180 ($1.25–$3.75).

Finally, if you're in the mood for Chinese, the **Hotel Hilltop Palace** (it's clearly a custom-built hotel, and in no way palatial) not only occupies the highest point in Udaipur, it's well-known for its Chinese chef—though it's worth noting that even these dishes have become hybridized, featuring more chili than you'd expect from a Chinese meal. Do ask to dine on the roof terrace (usually only open at night), which has delightful views of the city (the ground-floor hotel restaurant, like the hotel rooms, is nothing special). The hotel is at 5 Ambavgarh (© **0294/432-245,** -246, or -247).

A final note when it comes to dining experiences in Udaipur: Many guidebooks consider "high tea" at the Fateh Prakash Palace a highlight, but personally we find it overrated. Yes, it has lovely views and a grand atmosphere, but the heavy curtains and carpets and general fuddy-duddy atmosphere make it the last place to experience the views and quality of light that is so particular to Udaipur. Do let us know if you differ.

Note: The prices for the accommodations below are sometimes given in rupees, with U.S. dollar conversions; others are stated in U.S. dollars only, which is how many hotels targeting foreign markets quote their rates.

LAKE PICHOLA

Lake Palace Hotel ⭑⭑⭑   Just looking at a photograph of this 18th-century island palace is enough to make you want to start planning a trip to India. It doesn't disappoint, particularly since the standard rooms enjoyed a much-needed upgrade in 2002 (thank heavens for competition, in the shape of Udaivilas, which you can see glowering on the other side of the lake). Everywhere you look—be it from the mango-shaded pool, your room, or the restaurant—you'll have picture-perfect views: the statuesque City Palace walls and crenelated rooftops to the east, the whitewashed havelis and temples of the old city lining the shores of the lake to the north, the Aravalli Hills to the west, or Jag Mandir to the east. The best rooms (besides the suites) are the deluxe rooms facing east—the City Palace is lit up at night, giving you a 24-hour view. The renovations have improved many of the public spaces, and the standard and deluxe rooms now feature opulent fabrics, walls with wood paneling and murals, lovely marble bathrooms, and well-crafted furniture. The huge and opulent suites have thankfully been left as is, and have a timeless grandeur that the City Palace hotels could only wish for—stained-glass windows, marble floors, crystal chandeliers, antique Rajasthani furniture, and old-fashioned pieces that wouldn't be out of place at Balmoral (Queen Elizabeth's favorite residence)—making them the epitome of 20th-century royal splendor, and the most romantic places to celebrate a special occasion. Service and dining are uniformly excellent. Access to the hotel is provided by water taxi, which is on call 24 hours a day. So there's no reason to feel isolated, only wonderfully privileged, as you're helped aboard and whizzed across the waters to your private palace.

P.O. Box 5, Udaipur 313 001. © 0294/252-8800. Fax 0294/252-7975. www.tajhotels.com. 85 units. $370 deluxe lake-view double; $400–$1,000 suite. Extra person $50. AE, DC, MC, V. **Amenities:** 2 restaurants; bar; pool; mini-gym; travel desk (car hires, boat trips); 24-hr. water taxi; currency exchange; shopping; 24-hr. room service; babysitting; doctor-on-call; reading room. In room: TV, A/C, minibar, hair dryer.

EASTERN SHORES OF LAKE PICHOLA

Fateh Prakash & Shiv Niwas Palaces   The last two palaces built within the City Palace walls are now both hotels, but unless you want to overnight in what feels like a wealthy old aunt's large but stuffy apartment, there's only one section worth considering: the relatively new **Dovecoat Wing** (★★ in Fateh Prakash. If you can't afford a room at the Lake Palace, this is the next best location in Udaipur: All the rooms in this wing, which stretches along the shoreline, have the most wonderful views of the Lake Palace and distant Aravalli Hills (perfect at both sunset and dawn); room nos. 511 and 617 even have little sitting rooms that jut over the water. Furnishings are elegant (predominantly salmon and white), bathrooms adequate (obviously done before bathrooms became a real focus in hotel design), and rates offer by far the best value in the palaces. By contrast, Fateh Prakash's much pricier "regal suites," while a great deal larger, are overdressed, overcarpeted, and old-fashioned—not always a bad thing, but these definitely need sprucing up; certainly those that don't even face the lake are a definite no-no. Management may try to persuade you to "upgrade" to these older apartments, but if you don't like the musty, almost claustrophobic atmosphere, insist that they honor your booked room in the lighter, breezier Dovecoat Wing. The crescent-shaped Shiv Niwas Palace, built around the pool courtyard, is positioned farther south, and without the lovely Lake Palace floating before you, its views are a great deal less magical. And that's *if* you get a lake view—again, don't bother staying here if you don't have one (rooms with lake views are listed with rates below). Service in both hotels is well-meaning but will almost certainly try your patience; the aptly named Sunset View Terrace (see above) is the best place to dine—the views are great, but don't expect much from the cuisine.

City Palace Complex, Udaipur 313 001. © **0294/252-8016** or -8019. Fax 0294/252-8006. www.hrhindia. com. Fateh Prakash 28 units. Shiv Niwas 31 units. **Fateh Prakash:** Dovecoat $150; Regal lake-facing suite $250; Regal suite $200. **Shiv Niwas:** Deluxe $100 (no views); Terrace suite $300 (nos. 15 and 16 lake-facing); Historic suite $375 (nos. 6 and 7 lake-facing); Royal suite $475 (nos. 5 and 18 lake-facing); Imperial suite $600 (no. 17 lake-facing). AE, MC, V. **Amenities** (shared by hotels): 3 restaurants; pool; squash; billiards; travel desk; doctor-on-call. In room: A/C, TV, minibar, hair dryer.

Jagat Niwas (★   Like its neighbor the Kankarwa, this 17th-century haveli literally rises from the waters of Lake Pichola. The difference is that Jag Niwas is more hotel than guesthouse, with a laid-back staff, a good travel desk/agent, and in-room amenities like air-conditioning, TVs, and telephones. Approached through a narrow street that runs into the entrance, it is a cluster of buildings around a central courtyard. Rooms vary considerably, with only suites and deluxe rooms providing lake views—of these, nos. 110 and 116 (suites), and no. 102 (deluxe) are particularly pleasing options. Ceilings often feature colored glass baubles typical of Rajasthani havelis; walls have painted murals; fabrics are traditional Rajasthani block prints; and many rooms have alcoves with mattresses. In an irritating oversight, not a single room has a bedside reading lamp. Not all rooms have split air-conditioning—units with this are a great deal quieter than window units, so you might want to request it. The best part of the hotel is the wonderful covered terrace that overlooks the lake (see above) and hosts evening shows. Unless you prefer more hotel-like amenities, choose the more stylish Kankarwa (see below), and come and relax on the terrace here as a visitor. If you want a pool, Udai Kothi (see below) is a better option.

23–25 Lal Ghat, Udaipur 313 001. © 0294/242-0133. Fax 0294/241-8512. www.indianheritagehotels.com. 29 units. Rs 1,250 ($27) standard A/C; Rs 1,400 ($31) deluxe A/C; Rs 1,895 ($42) suite A/C. Extra bed Rs 250 ($5.35). AE, MC, V. **Amenities:** Lakeside terrace restaurant; travel desk/car hires; horseback riding and safaris arranged; laundry; doctor-on-call. *In room:* A/C (specify), TV (some rooms), hair dryer.

Kankarwa ★★ (Value) A short stroll from the City Palace, this is by far the best budget option in town, if not the entire Rajasthan. It's an elegant and professional family-run guesthouse in an ancient haveli right on the shores of Lake Pichola. We loved room no. 204; a simple whitewashed space with white bedding and traditional Rajasthani antiques, it has only two touches of color: the blue waters of the lake reflected outside the *jarokha* window, and a single blood-red lamp that perfectly offsets the cool white—this family has innate style. The compact bathrooms (most with shower only) are also whitewashed or tiled, only adding to the refreshing, clean atmosphere. Room no. 206 is a good twin-bed option with white-pillowed alcove (colored by the stained-glass windows) and a great bathroom with a window (though the tub was stained on our visit). Other good options are nos. 217, 216, and 203—all with the same sense of cool fresh white offset with a touch of color. The Jag Niwas restaurant terrace is right next door, but if you want to enjoy what the family (who have, incidentally, been living here for 200 years) is having for dinner, they will put a lovely wrought-iron table (no plastic here!) on the rooftop terrace, where pink bougainvillea plants grow in pots, framing great lake views. A meal will set you back a mere Rs 100 to Rs 180 ($2.10–$3.75). The only possible drawback is the lack of amenities, but the family works hard at providing assistance. *Note:* Budget travelers may be interested to know that Kankarwa also has two very small but comfortable rooms (no views) for Rs 400 ($8.75) that they don't usually advertise, having such high standards elsewhere.

26 Lal Ghat, Udaipur 313 001. © 0294/241-1457. Fax 0294/252-1403. www.indianheritagehotels.com. Rs 650–Rs 1,200 ($14–$26). MC, V. **Amenities:** Rooftop terrace; laundry.

WESTERN SHORES OF LAKE PICHOLA

Amet Haveli ★ Located directly across the lake from Kankarwa and Jag Niwas, this pretty 350-year-old haveli has enough charm to have found its way into glossy books on Indian style, but it's rather basic for anyone who wants a lot of amenities. Located directly on the shores of Lake Pichola, with views of Kankarwa directly opposite, Amet Haveli was renovated 2 years ago, and rooms remain in good shape. Definitely book one of the suites—the hands-down winner is suite no. 7, which has a large mattressed *jarokha* that juts over the water, providing lovely views of the City Palace and Lake Palace; you can even see the City Palace from your king-size bed. Freshly whitewashed, with simple furnishings (no cupboards to speak of), the room is airy and light, and very good value.

Suite no. 8 is slightly larger, but the views are not nearly as spectacular. The adjacent restaurant, **Ambrai,** is also right on the lake, and has a good reputation for its food (particularly tandoori dishes), but the smell from the lake can at times be a problem.

Outside Chandpole, Udaipur 313 001. ✆ **0294/243-1085.** amethaveli@usa.net or regiudr@datainfosys.net. 7 units. Rs 1,050 ($23) double; Rs 1,450 ($32) suite. No credit cards. **Amenities:** Restaurant; laundry.

Udai Kothi ✦ *Value* Not as well located (with regards to top attractions) as Jagat Niwas or Kankarwa, but still within walking distance of the old city, this small hotel is a relatively authentic replica of a traditional haveli, albeit one with modern amenities (like Udaipur's only rooftop pool), standardized room features and, at press time, top-value rates. There are two room categories—deluxe rooms and suites—all with comfortable *jarokhas* (window seats) from which to enjoy the lake (obviously preferable) or garden view—ask for a room on the third floor for best views. The rooftop terrace is where meals are served—the views at night, when the pool is lit up, are breathtaking, and service overall is generally efficient.

Udai Kothi, Udaipur 313 001. ✆ **294/243-2810** or -2812. Fax 0294/243-0412. www.udaikothi.com. 24 units. Rs 1,250 ($27) deluxe; Rs 1,450 ($32) suite. MC, V. **Amenities:** 2 restaurants; roof terrace; pool; evening cultural shows; health club; Jacuzzi; garden; travel desk; boating; room service; laundry.

Udaivilas ✦✦✦ After the deserved success of the Vilas properties in Jaipur, Agra, and Ranthambhore, Oberoi's latest superdeluxe property, opened in 2002, is a bit of a letdown. Not that it's any less glamorous: The palatial property features huge, beautifully crafted frescoes, a massive central dome that wouldn't look out of place on St. Peter's, hidden alcoves embellished with mosaics, and cool decorative pools everywhere. Intricately crafted pieces and fabrics are artfully combined with Western decor to create the most elegantly dressed rooms and luxurious bathrooms in town. The hotel also has 12 hectares (30 acres) of landscaped gardens, two swimming pools, and an award-winning spa to unwind in. That said, there are a few conceptual flaws, not least of which is the lack of access you have to the lake, despite the fact that the property is built on its shores. Only the superior deluxe (recommended) rooms and suites have lake views, and almost none of the public spaces have views—you can see the lake from the spa pool, but the deck has been designed in such a way that all the loungers face away from the lake waters. Management has promised to look into the problem, so perhaps this will be resolved in some way, but it seems a pity to travel all this way only to find yourself in a resort and room that could be anywhere—no matter how luxurious. Another seemingly good idea that ends up being impractical is the infinity pool that stretches the length of the superior deluxe wing—you plunge straight in, only to find your neighbors swimming past you, kind of ruining the exclusivity of an otherwise absolutely gorgeous room. It also appears that Udaivilas is being used as some sort of training ground: Staff are all very young and very enthusiastic, but their naiveté may irritate the more sophisticated traveler. Udaivilas had only been open for some months when reviewed, so perhaps these are just teething problems; elsewhere, the Oberoi group always runs the best hotels in India. The resort is a 20-minute drive to City Palace.

Haridasji Ki Magri, Udaipur 313 001. ✆ **0294/243-3300.** Fax 0294/243-3200. www.oberoihotels.com. 90 units. $370 deluxe double (no views); $450 superior deluxe; $1,250–$2,000 suite. AE, DC, MC, V. **Amenities:** 2 restaurants; lounge/bar; 9 pools (5 private); Banyan Spa (including Ayurvedic treatments); boating; adjacent wildlife conservatory; travel desk; complimentary limousine transfer from airport; boutique; salon; 24-hr. room service; babysitting; laundry; doctor-on-call; butler service; CD/DVD library. *In room:* A/C, DVD/CD, TV, Internet connections, minibar, tea- and coffee-making facilities, fresh fruit and newspaper daily, hair dryer.

AROUND UDAIPUR

Devi Garh 🐾🐾🐾   "Went to see the City Palace this morning and couldn't wait to return to our very own," one guest remarked, and really, it *is* hard to tear yourself away from what is arguably the best hotel on the subcontinent. Devi Garh is more than beautiful, it is *inspiring,* particularly if you're a modern-design enthusiast. And with a staff-to-guest ratio of 4 to 1, all looking as if they've stepped out of an Armani ad for India, the service levels are unbeatable: extensive, personal, discreet, and intelligent. But what makes this an unparalleled masterpiece is the marriage of the towering exterior of an original 18th-century Rajput palace (which remains totally unchanged) with a totally reinvented minimalist interior. Utilizing the best young designers in India (which put a lie to the perception that design here reached its apotheosis with the Mughals), and financed by the latter-day patron Lekha Poddar, it took 15 years to transform the higgledy-piggledy rooms spread over 14 floors into 23 huge suites. Within the almost stark, soothing space of each suite, there's none of the familiar Rajasthani accents, yet it remains uniquely Indian: Almost everything, from the bed and sofa bases to ashtrays and vases, is carved out of white marble, offset with flashes of color—flower motifs in semi-precious stones, bold swaths of gold inlay, or asymmetrical relief sculpture—designs that reinterpret India's centuries-old craftsmanship in dazzlingly modern ways. If that's not enough, the views of the majestic Aravalli Hills and tiny Delwara village, where life continues as it has for centuries, are perfectly framed by large sheets of squared-off glass—a modern element that is successfully hidden when viewing the pretty *jarokha* windows from the exterior. Below lies a heated green marble pool, tennis court, and spa (with great Ayurvedic treatments on offer), as well as the dining areas where more superb views (and wonderful cuisine) await. The hotel will also arrange camel or horse safaris, jeep treks, or chauffeured tours: Udaipur, Eklingji, Nagda, Nathdwara, Kumbhalgarh Fort, and Ranakpur are all easily explored from here. Make every effort to include a night at this acclaimed *(Condé Nast Traveler, Vogue, Wallpaper)* hotel, though it will no doubt have you wishing you'd planned nothing other than to stay here for the duration of your trip.

26km (16 miles) or 45 min. from Udaipur. Devi Garh, Delwara Village, near Udaipur 313 001. ℂ **02953/289-211,** Delhi 011/335-4554, or 011/372-2200. www.deviresorts.com. 23 units. Rs 8,500–Rs 18,500 ($186–$404); 7 tents at Rs 5,000 ($110). AE, DC, MC, V. **Amenities:** Restaurant; bar; pool; tennis court; health club/gym; spa; horse/camel riding; cycling; kite flying; pool table; table tennis; croquet; travel desk; salon; 24-hr. room service; babysitting; doctor-on-call; astrologer; library. *In room:* TV, AC, DVD/CD, dataport, minibar.

TRAVELING BETWEEN UDAIPUR & JODHPUR

Fort Chanwa 🐾   Somehow it feels more remotely situated than Rohet Garh, but logistically it's a great deal closer to Jodhpur. This red-sandstone fortress is an oasis of relative luxury at the end of a potholed road to Luni. Belonging to the present Jodhpur maharaja's uncle, the 200-year-old property was renovated only 4 years ago, and not always that sensitively. However, interiors (done by the maharani) are very tasteful, and there's a pool, an Ayurvedic massage center, and a very sharp staff to oversee all your needs. The Maharaja suite (no. 9)—a deluxe twin room, with a deep double bed–size alcove, is particularly lovely; a family or group should book nos. 12 and 14. Just a 40-minute drive from Jodhpur, this rural retreat will suit travelers who want to see Jodhpur's top attractions but who prefer to spend the night away from the city's chaos and pollution (or who can't afford the urban oases of Umaid Bhawan or Bal Samand). Transfers from Jodhpur are easily arranged.

Luni village, 35km (22 miles) from Jodhpur. Bookings: 1 PWD Rd., Jodhpur, 342 001. ℂ **0291/432-460** or direct 02931/284-216. www.fortchanwa.com. 31 units. Rs 1,800–Rs 2,400 ($40–$53) double. AE, DC, MC, V. **Amenities:** Restaurant; evening entertainment; pool; sauna; croquet; horse rides; travel desk; village safaris; excursions to Jodhpur; room service; massage; babysitting; laundry. *In room:* A/C, hair dryer on request.

Rawla Narlai 🎯 A 17th-century hunting retreat of the Maharajah of Jodhpur, located in the heart of the arid Aravalli Hills halfway between Udaipur and Jodhpur, the lovely Rawla Narlai was only opened to paying guests in 1995 (and soon after was featured in various glossy magazines). The hotel was sensitively renovated to ensure its authenticity wasn't lost in the process of attaching bathrooms and enlarging the spaces. Rooms all differ but on the whole are really charming (we loved nos. 18 and 19), featuring touches like sepia photographs of the maharaja's ancestors, cusped window frames, frescoed walls, stained-glass windows, pretty alcoves, colored ceiling baubles, *jarokhas*, and views of the Shiva temple that rises from the rock "mountain" that can be seen for miles from the surrounding countryside. If you're on your way to Jodhpur, this is the ideal overnight stop after visiting the Jain temples of Ranakpur (less than an hour away) and/or Kumbhalgarh Fort, but unlike Deogarh Mahal (halfway between Udaipur and Jaipur), it's not really a destination in its own right—at least not until the pool is built.

140km (86 miles) from Udaipur (via Ranakpur 125km/77 miles); 160km (100 miles) from Jodhpur. Reservations through Ajit Bhawan (see "Where to Stay & Dine in Jodhpur," for central Delhi details): Near Circuit House, Jodhpur, 342 006. ℂ **0291/251-0410**, 0291/251-1410, or 0291/251-0610. Fax 0291/251-0674. ajitbhawan@vsnl.com. 19 units. Rs 2,295–Rs 2,900 ($50–$64). AE, MC, V. **Amenities:** Restaurant; horse/camel safaris; rock climbing; excursions; laundry; doctor-on-call.

Rohet Garh 🎯 *(Value)* It's not as pretty as Rawla Narlai, but the 300-year-old Rohet Garh is very professionally run, thanks to the fact that the aristocratic owner Sidharth Singh is still in residence, not only making guests comfortable but also struggling to help remedy local problems like the drought currently blighting the entire region. More important (for hedonists at least), it has a lovely pool in the central courtyard, from which you can access the dining room, smartly attired with white linen tablecloths and napkins and serving good-quality Rajasthani food. The rural peace is very intoxicating—the adjacent village is also not as poor as that at Rawla Narlai, inviting exploration without guilt. Rooms, as is always the case with heritage properties, vary (ask to see what's on offer when

---

(*Fun Fact* **Eighteenth-Century Tree Huggers**

Traveling on the road to or from Jodhpur, you will no doubt come across black buck, a delicate antelope with spiralling horns, and Khedaji, the tough, desert-surviving trees that provide shelter and sustenance for the desert tribes and the black buck. Both animal and tree are sacred to the Bishnoi tribes, so much so that when an 18th-century Jodhpur ruler sent his army out to clear Khedaji trees to make way for a new road, the Bishnoi women clung to the trees in protest— 363 women died with their arms wrapped around their beloved Khedajis before the Jodhpur king intervened. You can still visit the Bishnoi on "village safaris" offered by just about every hotel and guesthouse in town.

you arrive), but all are relatively spacious, featuring the usual frescoes and Rajasthani antiques. Book one of the most recently renovated rooms for the best bathrooms—however, these currently surround the pool, so they are not that private. A couple of the rooms have direct views into the stables for those kids who haven't outgrown the *Black Beauty* phase. Outings include visits to traditional Bishnoi villages and shepherds, with the possibility of witnessing a traditional ceremony.

Rohet Garh, Vill PO Rohet, Distt Pali, Rajasthan. ℂ **02936/268-231** or 0291/243-1161. Fax 0291/264-9368. www.rohetgarh.com. 30 units. Rs 2,000–Rs 3,000 ($44–$65). Extra bed Rs 450 ($9.80). AE, DC, MC, V. **Amenities:** Restaurant; jeep; horse and camel safaris; picnic lunch; laundry; doctor-on-call; cooking classes.

SHOPPING

Udaipur has a number of attractive handicrafts. You're probably best off purchasing them directly from small factories whose touts will beg you to visit, but do beware that the commission system can add significantly to the price, so don't buy the first beautiful thing you see. The main shopping streets run from the City Palace along Jagdish Temple Street to the clock tower and beyond to Hathipol. Good areas are the Surajpol, Bapu Bazaar, Chetak, and Ashwini markets. Udaipur is considered a good place to purchase miniature paintings (it has its own unique style, but if you're looking for a bargain, you're better off purchasing in off-the-beaten-track towns, like Bundi) and *pichwai* paintings—wall hangings painted on cloth or silk, often featuring scenes from Krishna's life, that originated in Nathdwara; see "Top Excursions," earlier in this chapter. Other goods worth keeping an eye out for are puppets and other wooden folk toys, enamel or Meenakari work, dhurrie rugs, tie-dye and block-printed fabrics, embroidered bags and clothing, and silver jewelry. As is always the case, consider carefully before you buy (cheaper is not always better and often means the object is a poor imitation), and always try to bargain. Plenty of places will try to sell you paintings, but if you're looking for top quality (or at least want to understand the difference), you'll need to visit the artist **Kamal Sharma** (ℂ **0294/ 242-3451** or cell 98290/40851, 15A, New Colony, Kala JI-Goora JI). A fourtime national award winner; Sharma works on paper, marble, and silk. To view traditional Udaipur (and Gujarati) embroidery, visit **Jagdish Emporium** on City Palace Road. For beautiful beaded bags, head for Chandpole Road to visit the tiny **Pearl Point** (ℂ **0294/242-1974**) or **Indian Peral Gallery** (ℂ **0294/241- 2160**).

8 Jodhpur

336km (208 miles) E of Jaipur; 260km (160 miles) NW of Udaipur

Founded in 1459 by Rao Jodhaji, chief of the Rathore Rajputs, who ruled over Marwar, "land of death," Jodhpur was to become one of Rajputana's wealthiest cities, capitalizing on its central position on the Delhi–Gujarat trade route and protected by one of the most impenetrable forts in history. Today it is the state's second-largest city, much of it a sprawling, polluted metropolis, but within the old walls—where every building is painted the same bright blue hue, earning Jodhpur the nickname "blue city"—you'll find a teeming maze of narrow medieval streets and bazaars, where life appears much like it has for centuries. Towering above is the **Meherangarh** (literally "majestic'") **Fort,** its impenetrable walls rising like sheer cliffs from the rocky outcrop on which it is built. From its crenelated ramparts you enjoy postcard views of the ancient blue city below and, in the distance, the grand silhouette of the **Umaid Bhawan Palace,** residence of the current maharaja and a tiptop heritage hotel. Within the fort is a typical Rajput palace that today houses one of the state's best-presented museums, artfully displaying the accumulated accouterments of the royal house of Rathore in the beautifully preserved royal apartments.

The labyrinthine old city is a more visually exciting experience than Jaipur, but besides exploring these medieval streets and visiting Mehrangarh Fort and Umaid Bhawan Palace, there's not much to hold you here for more than a day or two—most people use Jodhpur only as a jumping-off point to Jaisalmer or as an overnight stop before traveling on to Jaipur or Udaipur—though a stay at Bal Samand Lake Palace or Umaid Bhawan Palace may have you wishing you'd extended your time here.

ESSENTIALS

VISITOR INFORMATION   The tourist office is located in the **RTDC Goomar Tourist Bungalow,** on High Court Road (© **244/010;** Mon–Sat 8am–noon and 3–6pm). Convenient places to withdraw cash against your ATM card are **UTI Bank** (near Kwality Inn, Chandra Hotel) and **Bank of Baroda** (Sojati Gate).

GETTING THERE   Traveling by car from Udaipur takes approximately 5½ hours with no stops; the journey from Jaipur takes about 6½ to 7 hours. However, Jodhpur is very well connected by rail and air. As always, try to book flights with the more professional **Jet Airways** (© **0291/251-0758**), though you'll have to use Indian Airlines if you want to fly to Udaipur. Jodhpur's **airport** (© **0291/251-2934**) lies 4km (2½ miles) south of the city. Expect to pay about Rs 150 to Rs 200 ($3.15–$4.30) for a taxi into town, a mere Rs 20 to Rs 30 (40¢–60¢) for a rickshaw. Jodhpur's main **train station** is on Station Road, just south of the old city walls. An express train links the city to Delhi in 12½ hours; the Jaipur Intercity Express gets you here from Jaipur in 5 hours. It takes 12 hours by train from Udaipur. *Tip:* If you plan to leave by train, it's advisable to book at least a day in advance—there's a counter at the tourist office (see above), or head for the reservations hall near the station and behind the post office (Mon–Sat 8am–8pm; Sun 8am–2pm).

GETTING AROUND   Rickshaws are the most useful way to get around the old city, but you'll need to hire a taxi if you plan to visit the outlying attractions. To hire a car and driver for the day (or longer—for instance, for a round-trip to Jaisalmer or to Udaipur), contact **Rajasthan Tours** © **0291/251-2428** or 0291/251-2932; bhim@jp1.dot.net.in). The hotel Umaid Bhawan offers guided tours of the fort and market for Rs 350 ($7.60), or will provide a car and driver for a half day for Rs 600 ($13).

FESTIVALS   **Divali** in November is the spectacular festival of lights that happens all over India, but it's particularly exciting when viewed from the gracious lawns of Umaid Bhawan Palace at the grand bash held by Maharaja Gajsinghji II, where you can experience first-hand the deep reverence the former ruler of Jodhpur and Marwar is still treated with—everyone wants to kiss the hem and touch the hand of their beloved father figure. The **Marwar Festival,** held during the full moon in October, is also worth attending, particularly to see the fire dance held on the Osian dunes.

WHAT TO SEE & DO

Having visited the fort and Umaid Bhawan Palace, there's no reason to overextend yourself, but some may opt to include a trip to **Mandore,** which lies 9km

(6 miles) north of the old city. The previous capital of Marwar (not to be confused with Mewar, the princely state of Udaipur), Mandore has as its principal attractions today gardens (in dire need of attention) in which lie the templelike cenotaphs built to honor the Rathore rulers before the final rites were moved to Jaswant Thada (see "Mehrangarh Fort & Museum," below). The largest and grandest of the red-sandstone structures was also the last to be built here; it commemorates the life of Maharaja Dhiraj Ajit Singh, who died in 1763. Beyond, in a totally separate section (pious to the end), is a group of smaller cenotaphs, built to commemorate the female counterparts. Opposite the weird but ultimately missable museum is the **Hall of Heroes,** a collection of 18th-century deities and Rajput heroes carved out of a rock wall. If you haven't tired of temples by now, you can move on to visit the Hindu and Jain temples at **Osian,** 65km (40 miles) north of Jodhpur. You first come across the **Vishnu** and **Harihara temples,** which were built between the 8th and 9th centuries, but more impressive (or at least still alive with worship) are the **Sacchiya Mata** (12th c.) and **Mahavira Jain temples** (8th and 10th c.). See "Ranakpur Temples," earlier in this chapter, for rules on entering a Jain temple. **Village safaris,** in which you are taken into the arid surrounds to get a taste of rural life, sample the food, and learn about traditional remedies and crafts, are also offered by a number of agents in Jodhpur—best to arrange this through the RTDC at the tourist office (see "Visitor Information," above) or Cosy Guest House (see "Where to Stay & Dine," below).

Mehrangarh Fort & Museum ⭐⭐⭐   "The work of angels, fairies and giants . . . he who walks through it loses sense of being among buildings; it as though he walked through mountain gorges . . ." wrote Rudyard Kipling in 1899. For many, this looming 15th-century edifice to Rajput valor is still Rajasthan's most impressive fort, with walls that soar like sheer cliffs 120m (400 ft.) high, literally dwarfing the city at its base, and a proud history of never having fallen to its many invaders. There is an elevator, but choose to walk past the cannon-pockmarked and *sati*-daubed **Loha Gate** (the maharajas' wives would traditionally immortalize their lives by leaving handprints on the fort walls before tossing themselves on the flames to join their deceased husbands). Once at the top, you enjoy not only the most spectacular view, but you enter one of India's finest museums: a rich collection of palanquins, royal cradles, miniature paintings, musical instruments, costumes, furniture, and armor. Every room is worth exploring (allow at least 2 hr., and hire a guide), but among the highlights are the gorgeous **royal chamber** where the maharaja entertained his 30-plus wives (we're not counting concubines); the **Moti Mahal,** featuring the throne on which every Marwar maharaja has been crowned; and the **Phool Mahal,** the "dancing hall" with its pure gold ceiling. A massive **silk and velvet tent,** taken from the emperor Shah Jahan in Delhi, is a vivid illustration of the superlative wealth and decadent pomp with which the Rathore rulers lived. After visiting the courtyard of the **Chamunda (Sun Goddess) temple** (remember to take your shoes off), take the lane that leads to the left to view what is apparently among the rarest collections of cannons in India—again, the view alone is worth it. There is a very good museum shop (look out for the exquisite silk and chiffon fabrics made by Tyeb Khan, awarded the Master Craftsman award in 2001 by the president of India for his outstanding contribution to the nation) and restaurant where you can catch your breath.

On the road that leads to and from the fort, you will notice the **Jaswant Thada,** a white-marble cenotaph built to commemorate the life of Maharaja Jaswant Singh II, who died in 1899, and where the last rites of the Jodhpur rulers have been held since then. It's pretty enough, but after the magnificence of the fort's museum and forts it can be a bit of a letdown, so keep descending into **Sadar Market,** where the sights and aromas of India's ancient and narrow streets—packed with cows, people, goats, carts, and chickens, and remarkably untouristed—may leave you wondering whether you've wandered onto the set of a movie about medieval times. If it all gets too claustrophobic, hire a rickshaw in which to sit in relative comfort and watch the passing parade. All in all, this will be one of the most satisfying mornings you will spend in Rajasthan.

Admission Rs 100. Lift Rs 15 (30¢). Jaswant Thada Rs 10 (20¢). Guide Rs 100 ($2.10). Fort daily 9am–5pm winter, 8.30am–5.30pm summer. Museum closed 1–2.30pm.

Umaid Bhawan Palace ✦✦✦ Situated on another raised outcrop, with sprawling grounds creating an almost rural ambience, this splendid palace was built by Maharaja Umaid Singh (the current maharaja's father) as a poverty-relief exercise to aid his drought-stricken subjects. With 347 rooms, including a cinema, it was at the time the largest private residence in the world—a vivid reminder of the decadence the Rajput rulers enjoyed during the British Raj. Designed by Henry Lanchester, a great admirer of Lutyens (the man who designed New Delhi), it was commenced in 1929, took 3,000 laborers 13 years to complete, and remains one of the best examples of the Indo-Saracenic Art Deco style, topped with a massive dome which rises 56m (184 ft.) high, beyond which the buildings are perfectly symmetrical. If you don't choose to overnight here, you should still visit—if only to have a meal at The Pillars, from where you enjoy a spellbinding view of the fort in the distance. There is also a museum which features photographs of the construction and a model of the building (where you can see that the maharaja quite rightly has kept the best part, with outdoor pool, to himself), as well as items collected by his ancestors.

Note: Amanresorts, the last word in soulful luxury, recently took over management of this hotel palace, and no doubt it will become even better under their watch.

Entrance to the hotel and restaurants (unless you're overnighting) is Rs 300 ($6.50), payable at reception, and you can use this against whatever you eat or drink at either of the restaurants. Museum Rs 50 ($1.05). Daily 9am–5pm.

WHERE TO STAY & DINE

Within the old city are a number of good budget options, including many family "paying guest" accommodations that are listed with the tourist office. If you don't want to take your chances, the following are worth noting. **Haveli Guest**

Tips **The Future in the Palm of Your Hand**

Jodhpur is the home of a well-known astrologer and palmist, **Mr. Sharma,** who is in residence at the Mehrangarh Fort's Moti Mahal Chowk from 9am to 1pm and 2 to 5pm daily; and at the hotel Umaid Bhawan Palace from 7 to 9pm daily. To make an appointment (Rs 150–Rs 300/$3.15– $6.50), call the fort (✆ **0291/254-8790,** ext. 39), the palace (✆ **0291/251-0101,** ext. 6), or the cellphone (✆ **98280-32261**). Remember to remove your nail polish.

House (☏ 0291/261-4615; www.haveliguesthouse.net; Rs 200–Rs 800/$4.30–$18) is a very hospitable and well-run establishment (more of an inn than a haveli) with simple en-suite rooms—make sure you book one that has a view of the fort (Rs 800/$18); you also get good fort views from the rooftop restaurant. For a more homey atmosphere, head for **Cosy Guest House** (☏ 0291/261-2066; cosyguesthouse@yahoo.com; Rs 50–Rs 350/$1.05–$7.60). A Brahmin family-run 15th-century house with an array of basic, monastic rooms (ask for one with an attached bathroom) is aimed at the younger, more adventurous traveler; it's in the oldest, most beautiful part of the blue city, and the views from the rooftop terrace are spectacular (mum cooks pretty good food, too). Because rickshaw drivers are not paid commission, you may struggle to find it: Ask to be dropped off at Novechokiya Road, then follow the signs. The walk is stiff but short—if you're arriving with heavy luggage, ask the owner, Mr. Joshi, to arrange a transfer. If this all sounds a little rough, on the outskirts of town (20 min. from the fort) is the new **Taj Hari Mahal** (☏ 0291/243-9700; www.tajhotels.com; from $110), a very smart five-star hotel built in the style of a Marwari palace. Aimed predominantly at the wealthy business market, this will suit those who have simply had enough of the chaos of India and want to be cocooned from it all in a modern hotel with professional service. Rooms are huge and elegantly dressed, with state-of-the-art conveniences and tiptop bathrooms, and public spaces are also luxurious and cool. Yet the hotel's very modernity and mass-produced furnishings mean it has none of the charm of the Umaid Bhawan or Bal Samand palaces.

Jodhpur is not renowned for its restaurants; you're pretty much limited to dining in hotels. Even if you're not overnighting at Umaid Bhawan, make sure you dine one evening at **Pillars** (see below), the hotel's informal cafe-restaurant where you sit at the base of a cavernous colonnaded veranda that steps down to the palace lawns—get there before the sun goes down to watch the almost surreal changing hues of the sky over the fort, but don't expect miracles from the kitchen (though the *murgh firdosi,* boneless chicken simmered in a rich, spicy gravy, is recommended). Widely regarded as the best restaurant in town, with a great nighttime atmosphere (but do make sure they're serving in the garden), Ajit Bhawan's **On the Rocks** is famous for its tandoori dishes—skewers of spicy vegetables, *paneer* (cheese), or meat, tenderized in a yogurt marinade and cooked over an open fire.

Ajit Bhawan 🌟 *Kids*   Built at the turn of the 20th century for Maharaj Ajit Singh (younger brother of the Maharaja Umaid Singh), this hotel incorporates crenelated castle-like walls and traditional Hindustani elements, resulting in a weird, rather kitsch mishmash. But it's a hugely popular place, and some prefer its more laid-back, down-home atmosphere to Umaid's plush palace. It's also significantly cheaper, and has a wonderful outdoor pool and a good restaurant. The kitsch theme is continued inside as you wander through what appears to be a faux Rajasthani "village," with stone cottages leading off the central dining area and pool. Decor is generally very irreverent, which some may find amusing, but a few rooms have taken the kitsch theme a step too far (like no. 26, which has an indoor waterfall cascading over a rock, buck horns sprouting from its light fixtures, and a tiger skin behind the bed). That said, rooms are in mint condition (many were being renovated at press time), and if you can bag nos. 101 to 104, deluxe rooms each with a little balcony overlooking the pool (the best reason to book here), you'll be quite amused yourself. Car enthusiasts may also dig the fleet of 10 vintage cars on offer—the oldest Buicks and Fords date back to 1928. (Note that the palace was in fact split down the middle after a family feud; the adjacent **Ranbanka Hotel** is a more elegant version of Ajit Bhawan, but it is somehow soulless and a great deal less popular. Rates run between Rs 2,400 and Rs 3,600/$53 and $78 (© **0291/251-2800,** -2801, -2802, or -2803.)

Ajit Bhawan, Jodhpur 342 006. © **0291/251-0410** or -0610. Fax 0291/251-0674. www.ajitbhawan.com. 54 units. Rs 2,400–Rs 3,200 ($53–$71) double; Rs 3,500 ($76) suite; Rs 2,295 ($64) tent. Extra bed Rs 500 ($11). AE, DC, MC, V. **Amenities:** Restaurant; pool; health spa; travel desk; village safaris; folk dancing; fleet of vintage cars for hire. *In room:* TV, A/C, minibar, hair dryer.

Bal Samand Lake Palace ★★
From the outset you need to know that what is being reviewed here are the Royal Suites in the actual palace, and not the new wing with the standard "garden rooms" that lie somewhere behind the palace in the huge gardens—if the Royal Suites aren't available, you may as well book into the Ajit Bhawan. A relatively tiny palace carved out of red sandstone, the Bal Samand appears to grow out of the dam-wall terrace that overlooks the Bal Samand Lake. Surrounded by water, scrubland, and what once must have been the most beautifully landscaped gardens, it's a grand rural oasis second to none, not least because you only share it with a maximum of 16 other guests. Book room no. 1 for the lake views, or the more private room no. 6, which is simply beautiful—a massive double-volume space with fabulous sandstone detailing, lots of lamps for atmospheric lighting, a gorgeous mix of Rajasthani and colonial furniture, a Jacuzzi-size bath, and an atmosphere fit for a king. Room nos. 2 and 3 are quite small by comparison, and room nos. 7, 8, and 9 are on the ground floor—which means they're a little closer to the large, not easily accessible outdoor pool. The biggest drawback is the thin service, which is well-meaning but certainly not up to scratch—most of the hotel staff are situated at the "garden room" wing, where the kitchen is, so room-service food (other than breakfast, which is cooked at the palace) will inevitably be cold. Not that it really matters, considering that the food is the last reason to book here (avoid the European dishes)—this is such a romantic retreat that food may be the last thing on your mind.

7km (412 miles) from Jodhpur. Mandore Rd., Jodhpur 342 026. © **0291/257-1991.** Fax 0291/257-240. bal-samand_1@sify.com. 26 units, 9 suites. Rs 2,900 ($66) garden room (double); Rs 5,000 ($110) suite. AE, MC, V. **Amenities:** Restaurant; pool; room service; laundry.

Devi Bhawan *Value*
This low-slung sandstone residence is a great surprise—a bungalow with free-standing cottages set within a lush, tranquil garden, and personally managed by a wonderful husband-and-wife team. This is by far the best option in this price category (and a great deal better than places like Karni Bhawan, which charges twice this). The en-suite rooms (ask for an air-conditioned garden room) are clean and neat with simple furnishings, and there's not a hint of plastic anywhere (bathroom fittings could be upgraded, however). The dining area spills onto a deep colonnaded veranda with garden views and tables prettily laid out with fabric tablecloths around which black wrought-iron chairs are arranged. Service is very personal, and a number of amenities are offered. All in all, this is a very comfortable and relaxing option, but not one to encourage you to extend your stay in Jodhpur.

Defence Lab. Rd., Ratanada Circle, Jodhpur 342 001. © **0291/251-1067.** Fax 0291/251-2215. devibhawan@ satyamonline.net. 10 units. Rs 800 ($18) deluxe A/C double; Rs 875 ($18) suite/cottage. MC, V. **Amenities:** Restaurant; travel desk; jeep/horse-safaris; Internet access; laundry; doctor-on-call. *In room:* A/C (most rooms), TV.

Umaid Bhawan Palace ★★★   Built on a rocky outcrop in the southeastern part of the city, with lovely views of the fort, this is not only one of Jodhpur's top attractions, but it is regularly cited as one of the top heritage hotels in India. Opened in 1972 to paying guests, it has a range of room categories, of which the standard "palace rooms" were meant to house the administrative staff of the royal household. Some, like no. 211, are the sizes of mini-suites, with doors opening onto the verandas that run the length of the palace. Of the Palace Chambers, nos. 504 and 505 have private balconies with incredible views. Suite no. 510 will delight the Art Deco enthusiast, from the beautiful carpets to the lounge suite, but if this is your bent, nothing less than the Maharaja suite will do, with its superb Art Deco furnishings, fittings, and murals (although the Maharani bagged the best views, her quarters are somehow not as impressive). Regardless of category, some of the rooms have less-satisfactory layouts, so if you're not happy, simply ask to see a few more. And don't expect the latest bathroom fittings and the like—torn between their desire to kept the authenticity of the period, and guests' need for modernity, the maharaja and his team tread a very fine line, and if you have little interest in historical authenticity, you're probably better off at the Taj Hari Mahal. Dining takes place in the grand **Marwar Hall** (often only open for breakfast), the elegant **Risala,** or **Pillars**—the latter is by far your best bet; it shares a menu with Risala but has much more spectacular views. After dinner you can catch the latest Bollywood blockbuster at the in-house cinema. With the exception of one or two surly waiters, staff—headed by the charming Jehangir—go out of their way to ensure that you really are treated like royalty, and the longer you stay, the more the palace feels like home. The biggest drawback, for sun lovers at least, is that the pool, while huge and boasting more wonderful Art Deco murals, is indoors.

Umaid Bhawan, Jodhpur. ✆ 0291/251-0101. Fax 0291/251-0100. 98 units. $185 Palace rooms double; $225 Palace chambers; $325–$329 Vice Regal and Regal suites; $650 Maharaja suite; $750 Maharani suite. $15 extra bed. AE, DC, MC, V. **Amenities:** 3 restaurants; lounge/reading room; indoor pool; tennis; squash; gym/sauna/health spa; billiards room; cinema; travel desk; palmist/astrologer. *In room:* TV, A/C, minibar.

SHOPPING

Jodhpur is famous for its antiques dealers, most lining the road that runs between Ajit Bhawan and Umaid Bhawan. These can be prohibitively pricey, however, particularly when factoring in freight prices. Jodhpur is also good for tie-dye fabrics. The best bazaars are around Sojati Gate, Tripolia, Khanda Falsa, and Lakhara—the latter specializes in colorful lac bangles, which make great gifts. If you're looking for more serious jewelry, head for Station Road. Traditional Jodhpur coats and riding breeches are now only made to order; ask your hotel to recommend a tailor.

9 Jaisalmer

285km (177 miles) W of Jodhpur; 333km (206 miles) SW of Bikaner

Jaisalmer was founded by Rao Jaisal in 1156, making it the oldest "living" city in Rajasthan. A visit here is for many the start of an enduring romance. Located in the heart of the Thar Desert on the far western border of India (it's 55km/ 34 miles from Pakistan), it was strategically positioned on one of the central Asian trade routes, and tremendous fortunes were made by the Rajputs and Jain merchants who levied enormous taxes on caravans laden with silks and spices, particularly during the 14th and 16th centuries. In the 18th century, some merchants, wanting to expand their homes, moved out of the fort to settle on the plateau below. Much as in the Shekawati region, the wealth generated by their taxes was used to decorate the havelis of these wealthy Jain businessmen. Where frescoes satisfied the Shekawats, here power was expressed by the construction of mansions whose soft sandstone facades were then embellished with intricate, almost lacelike carvings. These oft-photographed sandstone mansions are indeed breathtakingly beautiful, but it is Sonar Killa, literally "Golden Fort," that makes it worth traveling this far west. It's not as impressive as Jodhpur's Mehrangarh Fort, but its charm lies in the fact that this is the world's only inhabited medieval fort, its families living in homes they have colonized for more than 800 years. Built entirely from yellow sandstone, the fort rises like a giant sandcastle from its desert surrounds, with great views from the tiny guesthouses that lie within its ramparts. Visitors discover a place with no traffic, minimal pollution (watch out for the cow dung), and a wonderful sense of timelessness. It takes no more than a few hours to tour the fort, including stops to visit the Jain and Hindu temples. And if you want to ride a camel into the sunset, Jaisalmer is probably the place to do it. So plan to spend 2 or more nights, not least because it takes so long to get here.

Jaisalmer's relative inaccessibility keeps tourist numbers down, as does its proximity to Pakistan, with which India has such an uneasy relationship (and felt the need to flex its nuclear muscle at nearby Pokharan in 1998). But ironically, there is less to fear here than on the streets of faraway Delhi and Lahore, where politicians beat their breasts at one another in standoff rituals that predate the evolution of man.

ESSENTIALS

VISITOR INFORMATION You'll find the **RTDC tourist office** near Gadi Sagar Pol (© 02922/252-406; Mon–Sat 8am–6pm).

GETTING THERE At press time, there were no flights to Jaisalmer, and the nearest airport is at Jodhpur (a 5½-hr. drive away, about 2 hr. longer in a bus—not recommended). *Tip:* The best place to stop for lunch or a snack on this route is **Manvar Desert Resort** (© 02928/266-137), which serves a mean chicken *pakora.* It takes 4½ to 5 hours to get from Bikaner to Jaisalmer. The train journey takes just over 6 hours (the overnight Jaisalmer Express) or almost 9 hours (the Jaisalmer Passenger, which travels by day); both trains arrive at the station just 2km (1¼ miles) east of town. Avoid the touts soliciting riders by asking for your hotel to arrange a transfer.

GETTING AROUND Both inside and outside the fort, the town is small enough to explore on foot; for journeys farther afield you will need to hire an auto-rickshaw (at the station or Gadisar Tank) or taxi (Sam's Dunes). For the latter, you'll probably take an all-inclusive trip with your hotel, almost all of which offer safaris of various duration; or contact Harish Bai at **K.K. Travels** (© 02992/253-087; kktravels_2000@yahoo.com).

FESTIVALS The **Desert Festival** held at the end of January or in February (incidentally, the best time of the year to visit Jaisalmer) is the highlight of the year, when dance shows, turban-tying competitions, and camel races are held below the fort, cheered on by colorful crowds who are as much a part of the spectacle as the entertainment.

WHAT TO SEE & DO

Jaisalmer's main attraction is its yellow sandstone **fort,** whose 9m (29-ft.) walls grow in a roughly triangular shape, springing from the three peaks on which it is built and buttressed by 99 bastions. Within you will find a number of elaborately carved havelis overlooking the narrow streets, but the best examples of Jaisalmer's unique **havelis** are situated in the town below. End the evening by taking a trip out to Sam's Dunes to watch the **setting desert sun** from the back of a camel. If you're more sedentary, head for **Mirage,** the rooftop terrace at the Narayan Niwas Palace, for the best view of the Golden Fort; as the sky darkens, the fort starts to glow.

Other attractions are the **Gadisar Tank,** built by the Maharaja Gadi Singh in 1367, which has a few temples and a *chattri* (cenotaph; also spelled *chhatri*) overlooking it but is principally worth visiting to access the nearby **Folklore Museum,** a private museum with some interesting exhibits, particularly the handcrafted items (look for the mobile temple, and the depiction of the tragic love story of Princess Moomal and King Mahendra). Exhibits are not well labeled, however; if the proprietor, Mr. Sharma, is not on hand, a guide could prove useful here. Entrance is Rs 10 (20¢) or donations are welcome; hours are daily 8am to noon and 3 to 6pm.

The best way to visit Jaisalmer's desert surrounds is on a **camel safari** (see below). Many include the following places of interest. **Amar Sagar** is a small settlement with a palace and a restored Jain temple built around the shores of a lake that lies 5km (3 miles) northwest of Jaisalmer. **Barra Bagh,** which lies 6km north of town, is a mini-oasis where you can view a collection of cenotaphs to Jaisalmer's Rajput rulers. Another 10km (6¼ miles) north lies **Lodurva,** once the capital of the Bhatti Rajputs before Jaisalmer was built. The main attractions here are more restored Jain temples, with the usual fine carvings. The entrance to **Thar Desert National Park** lies about an hour (45km/28 miles) from Jaisalmer, near Khuri. Wildlife you are likely to encounter include deer, desert fox, black buck, and the rare long-necked bird known as the Great Indian Bustard.

EXPLORING THE GOLDEN FORT

Some one thousand people still live in the tiny village inside the **Sonar Qila,** or Golden Fort, which has twisting lanes so narrow they can be blocked by a single cow (be warned that these animals *know* that they have the right of way, so step aside). Exploring the fort is easily done in a morning—you access the fort through Gopa Chowk, ascending the battle-scarred ramparts to enter the main courtyard, overlooked by the seven-story **Raj Mahal,** or Maharaja's Palace. Take a look around the Raj Mahal (it's not one of the state's most impressive palaces). The Juna Mahal is the oldest part, dating back to the early 16th century, with various additions and embellishments taking place over the next 200 years. The palace is open from 8am to 1pm and 3 to 5pm, and entry is Rs 30 (60¢). Stop for a cup of *chai* on the Paradise rooftop for the sublime views, or head straight for the beautiful **Jain temples,** which lie west and are only open to non-Jains between 7am and noon. Entrance is free, but you will have to pay to take a camera in; no leather is allowed within the temple, and menstruating women are restricted from entering. Constructed between the 14th and 16th centuries, these temples are typical of Jain craftsmanship, with every wall and pillar as well as the ceiling crawling with the most intricate relief carvings, and large statues representing the Jain *tirthankaras,* or "Enlightened Ones"—note that you cannot enter the caged sanctuaries in which these sculptures sit, or touch or photograph them. A small library has a collection of rare manuscripts, books, and miniature paintings. Take a breather at **Dop Khana ("place of cannon")** for the views, then head north, turning right at some stage to find the **Laxminath Temple** (if you're lost, just ask for directions). Although the Jain temples are worth a visit to see the intricacy of the carvings, this Hindu temple pulsates with energy, particularly if you get there when worshippers chant their devotion (about 10:30am). From here it's a short walk back to the main courtyard.

THE JAISALMER HAVELIS

Haveli is the word that refers to what in India is considered a mansion—a usually rather narrow home with more than one story. Steps lead up to an ornate door through which you enter a central courtyard, around which the family apartments are arranged. The facades of the Jaisalmer havelis, built as elsewhere by the town's wealthy merchants, are unsurpassed for the delicacy of their relief carvings, filigreed windows, and lacelike screens and *jarokhas* (window seats). A testament to the softness of the sandstone but even more to the skill of the *silavats,* Jaisalmer's community of stonemasons, these beautiful facades, some of which date back more than 300 years, have been perfectly preserved, thanks as well to the hot, dry climate. You will find them dotted all over town, but the most impressive are Patwon ki Haveli, Salim Singh ki Haveli, and Nathmalji ki Haveli. **Patwon ki Haveli** actually comprises five ornate houses built by the wealthy Patwon for his five sons between 1800 and 1860. The houses are connected from within (though some are privately owned and not open to the public) and have flat-topped roofs. Inside one of the homes is the Basant Art Emporium, where you can pick up some truly exquisite handicrafts—but certainly not at bargain prices—that the owner has collected from the desert tribes. The Patwon ki Haveli is open daily between 10am and 5pm; admission is Rs 10 (20¢). South of this, near the fort entrance, is the **Salim Singh ki Haveli,** built by a particularly mean-spirited and greedy prime minister who extorted the hell out of the Rajput's kings' subjects, and even squeezed the royal family by providing huge loans and then charging exorbitant interest rates. It was apparently once two stories higher, but legend has it that the Rajput king blew away the top floors in a fit of pique, and Salim Singh was later stabbed to death. It's not necessary to enter it, and it's not always open (though times advertised are 8am–6pm, with admission of Rs 10/20¢). You can't enter **Nathmalji ki Haveli,** but it's still worth swinging by to play "spot the difference" with the beautiful facade. The right and left wings look identical at first glance, but they were separately carved by two brothers—the numerous tiny differences can take hours to discover (this is where a guide comes in handy!). It's on the road to Malka Pole (just ask for directions).

CAMEL TREKKING

Spending some time in the desert on camelback is touted as one of Jaisalmer's must-do activities, and although you can spend a night or even two "camping" out in the desert (some outfitters have semi-permanent camps, with en-suite tents), trekking to sites of interest during the day, most people choose to spend only a few hours in the desert, usually watching the sun set from **Sam's Dunes.** Keep in mind that the popularity of these short trips means you will more than likely be surrounded by noisy travelers in areas that are looking increasingly degraded—with discarded bottles and cigarette packets, and kids cajoling you to buy warm colas and make "donations." If you can cope with staying "on board" a camel train for 2 to 3 hours every morning and afternoon, the best experience is to go on a trek that stops at various desert villages and temples, and lets you enjoy meals around bonfires under the stars and sleep in a temporary but comfortable camp—you will need to pack warm sleepwear for this, and you're pretty much at the mercy of fate when it comes to the group you land up with. It's not always a guarantee, but the pricier the safari, the better your chances. If this sounds like too much of a commitment, and the idea of a communally enjoyed sunset doesn't ruin the romance for you, you can either take a camel ride at sunset from Sam Dunes, about an hour from town by car, or from Khuhri, which lies almost 2 hours away by car. The latter is obviously less popular so it's not as busy, but it is no longer the unspoiled experience it was a decade ago. Almost every hotel and innumerable agents offer camel trips in various locations (you can opt for one just outside of town, where there are no dunes, but lovely fort views), or you can drive out yourself and negotiate directly with one of the camel drivers who line the road with camels—the state of the saddle is a good indication of which one to choose. Personally, we found the entire experience overrated, but then we like our luxuries, of which solitude is highly rated, and never more so than in India.

WHERE TO STAY

Jaisalmer offers two general choices: Stay inside the fort, or stay in the town that sprawls at its base. The ecologically sensitive make a strong argument for the latter: The increase in water usage, mostly due to tourist traffic, which relies on medieval drainage systems, has started to literally pulp the ancient sandstone fort, and clearly the best way to preserve it is to stay in town, which is also where the most luxurious accommodations are. But this means you'll miss out on the daily rituals of the people who live inside the fort's ramparts, and even if tourism is for most now the major source of income, it's still in many ways a very different and authentic experience. Note, however, that if you choose to stay inside the fort, no vehicles are allowed, so you may have to lug your luggage some way, lodgings can be quite claustrophobic, noise can be a problem, and in the midday heat you'll probably long for a pool. A surprising number of options are found within the fort, but none comes near the standard of **Killa Bhawan** (reviewed below). If you're watching your rupees, others worth mentioning are the artfully renovated **Simla** (© 02992/253-061)—the sandstone surfaces of every room and bathroom have been polished to reveal its gleaming, almost marble-like quality to good effect—and the popular **Hotel Paradise** (© 02992/252-674; hotelparadisejsm@yahoo.com). Aimed at budget travelers, Paradise offers very basic, cell-like rooms, but because it's situated right on the fort ramparts it has some awesome desert views (make sure you book a room with one); it also has a great rooftop terrace that draws a convivial crowd. Other well-known options, like **Suraj** (in a beautiful haveli close to the Jain temples; ask for the front room; © 02992/251-623; hotelsurajjaisalmer@hotmail.com) and **Hotel Jaisal Castle** (the first haveli-turned-hotel in the fort; © 02992/252-362; no. 10 is the best room; jaisalcastle@yahoo.com), have an atmospheric charm, but Suraj has no views and Jaisal has a very tired grandeur. From here on, the options only get more basic.

Choices in town are a great deal blander but more comfortable; the well-known but disappointing **Narayan Niwas Palace** has some lovely public spaces but a gloomy indoor pool and very second-rate rooms. The **Mandir Palace** was closed and staff indifferent as to when it was opening. Just out of town on the Sam Road, the **Rang Mahal, Gorbandh,** and **Heritage Inn** neighbor one another like three ugly sisters waiting for some miracle to revive their fortunes. They are relatively modern, incredibly bland and, at press time, very empty. The only real alternative to Fort Rajwada (the most luxurious option in town; reviewed below) is **Jawahar Niwas Palace.** Dating back to the 19th century, this small but lovely Rajput palace was built by the Maharwal Shalivahansinghji of Jaisalmer as a guesthouse, and four generations later the current head of the royal house of Jaisalmer opened it to paying guests. The original palace has large, elegant rooms (the Maharwal suite is the one to book), as well as some good-value rooms in a new wing; it also has a great pool. Renovations were underway at press time, so maintenance and service standards are not reviewed here. Rates are Rs 2,750 to Rs 3,500 ($60–$76) (© **02992/252-208** or 02992/253-540; www. jawaharniwaspalace.com).

Fort Rajwada ★★ (Value) The dapper and stylish entrepreneur Jitendra Rathore, who built Gorbandh, is the energy behind this latest and most luxurious option in Jaisalmer, and he's a mine of information about the town that he loves. Set on the outskirts on 2.4 hectares (6 acres) of land, the hotel has been built in the style of a palace but has all the comforts of the 21st century (barring the constant power failures that, thanks to generators, affect only the TV). Interiors were designed by the opera stage designer Stephanie Engeln, and the public spaces, particularly the double-volume bar, which could have been designed by Philippe Starck, feel like a grand set. Guest rooms are more standard but very comfortable and have great modern bathrooms; ask for one with a fort view. Cuisine is superb (especially the tandoori dishes, which are fragrant and tender), and though service can be on the slow side, it is exceptionally friendly. It's definitely the best choice in town if Killa Bhawan sounds like roughing it. Fort Rajwada also runs a Desert Camp, where you can either dine or overnight after a camel ride at Sam's Dune, though you'll probably be lumped with a package tour that may or may not be the key to a memorable evening—a case of "if you can't beat them, join them."

Outside the fort. No 1 Hotel Complex, Jodhpur–Barmer Link Rd., Jaisalmer. © **02992/253-233** or –533; 02992/253-608 or -609. Fax 02992/253-733. www.fortrajwada.com. 65 units. $70 double; $128 suite. Extra bed $18. AE, DC, MC, V. **Amenities:** 2 restaurants; bar; pool; tennis; health club; billiards room; travel desk; salon; room service; Ayurvedic massage; laundry; doctor-on-call. *In room:* A/C, TV.

Killa Bhawan ★ This intimate and well-run little guesthouse is the most luxurious and stylish option in the fort, and really is a delightful choice given that it's been hewn out of a dwelling that's been around for 700-odd years. Only the lack of amenities, and the fact that most rooms share a communal shower and toilet, stop this place from getting two stars. And bear in mind that the shared shower room is large and luxurious (and cleaned between showers), unlike the usual communal cupboard standard elsewhere. All rooms are beautifully furnished with lovely fabrics (and such thoughtful touches as gowns for guests to don before showering), and the rooftop, which has stunning views, is comfortably furnished with mattresses. Manager Manu and his brother Bharat are always on hand to arrange complimentary tea or coffee or to assist with anything from travel arrangements to dining choices.

Inside the fort. No. 445. © **02992/251-204** or 0299/250-232. Fax 02992/254-518. Kbhawan@yahoo.com. 6 units. Rs 1,650 ($36) double (shared shower); Rs 2,500 ($55) attached bathroom, A/C. MC, V. **Amenities:** Tea and coffee served all day long; laundry.

WHERE TO DINE

If you prefer to eat within the Fort, **Little Tibet** and **Refreshing Point** were recommended at press time. It's best to ask around (though make sure the person you ask doesn't have a vested interest in the answer). Alternatively, walk down into town to **Trio,** hands-down the best restaurant there (see below). Trio also caters for the Royal Desert camp, a permanent tented camp with en-suite tents near Sam's Dunes and run by Fort Rajwada.

Trio ★★★ RAJASTHANI   This unassuming eatery, with its open walls and thin cotton flaps providing a welcome through-breeze (not to mention views of the town and the maharaja's palace), is Jaisalmer's top restaurant and one of the best in Rajasthan. It's not just that the food is delicious, but the chef brings a few interesting variations to signature Rajasthani dishes—a welcome relief to one who has exhausted the almost standardized North Indian menu. The *murgh-e-subz*—succulent, boneless strips of chicken stir-fried with shredded vegetables—is one not to miss. Alternatively, try the *ker sangri* (desert beans and capers), which is unique to a region that traditionally saw little meat. If you have a hearty appetite, the tandoor thali is tops: two chicken preparations (including the ubiquitous but delicious *tikka*), vegetable kebab, mint sauce, and *naan*. Sensitive stomachs can opt for the *kadi pakorao*, flour dumplings cooked in yogurt sauce, or *bhanon aloo*, potatoes stuffed with mint paste and simmered in gravy. All of it washed down with the coldest beers and Cokes in the state.

Near the Amar Sagar Gate, Gandhi Chowk. Rs 50–Rs 250 ($1.05–$5.35). MC, V. Daily noon–3pm and 6.30–9.30pm.

SHOPPING

Whatever you do, don't miss **Barmer Embroidery House** (near Patwon ki Haveli); it's owned by Abhimanyu Rathi, legendary for his fine eye for antique textiles. Designers have been know to cross the Thar just to plunder his exquisite selection. Jaisalmer is also famous for its wool products, particularly rugs, as well as its fine hand embroidery, which turns average skirts and tops into real conversation pieces. Because the town is so easily explored, the best shopping experience is to set aside a morning and wander around, comparing prices before making your selection. Start by exploring the main **Bhatia Market** (begins at the entrance to the fort) and just follow your nose. Note that **Rangoli** has a large collection of embroidered garments, particularly for children, and is a fixed-rate shop (you don't have to bargain), which can be quite a relief. You'll find it opposite the Bank of Baroda, in Gandhi Chowk (✆ 02992/250-215).

10 Gujarat

Home to a predominantly Muslim community, but augmented by Hindus and Jains as well as the semi-nomadic tribes who inhabit the immense salt flats of Kutch, the state of Gujarat has seen its image tarnished by recent spates of politically fueled communal violence, and as a consequence its popularity as a travel destination has dropped off somewhat. But unlike the more volatile Kashmir, Gujarat's atmosphere remains essentially peaceful, and traveling through the state will expose you to a vast, varied, and dramatic Indian landscape, with some of the country's top architectural highlights. The experience is all the more pleasurable because it is so wonderfully free of the hucksters and beggars who plague the more popular tourist trails. Scattered around the state are modest palaces that have been converted into heritage hotels, and off the southern coast is the former Portuguese enclave of **Diu,** where you can laze on the beach and grab a beer far from the teeming crowds of Goa. Gujarat also has a number of excellent wildlife sanctuaries, including **Gir National Park,** last refuge of the Asiatic lion. You can cover the state's top attractions in 5 days, but given the distances, we recommend you set aside at least a week, either catching a train or plane to Ahmedabad from Mumbai, or combining it with a driving tour of Rajasthan.

A DRIVING TOUR OF GUJARAT

You can drive to **Ahmedabad,** Gujarat's major city hub, from popular destinations in Rajasthan, including Mount Abu (215km/133 miles; 7 hr.) and Udaipur (251km/155 miles; 8 hr.). Should you choose to travel by road, two fine Solanki monuments await you in the remote region north of Ahmedabad; the millennium-old **Sun Temple** ✫✫✫ at Modhera is 100km (62 miles) short of Ahmedabad and close to the beautiful **Rani-ka-Vav** ✫✫✫, a *baoli* (well) at Patan. Representing the pinnacle of Solanki architecture, the magnificent Sun Temple predates the great Orissan Sun Temple in Konark. It is positioned in such a way that at dawn and during the equinoxes, the sun would have cast its rays on the deity within the inner sanctum. Built in 1026, it has survived Muslim iconoclasm and numerous natural disasters, but it lost many of its statues to the devastating earthquake of 2001. Considered the most impressive baoli in Gujarat, Rani-ka-Vav was built by a queen in the 11th century and is adorned with 800-odd sculptures that can be admired as you traverse the monumental carved steps leading down to the water's edge. You can make both of these stops en route from Rajasthan to Ahmedabad, after first overnighting at **Balaram Palace** (© **027 42/84278;** www.semaphore.software.com/balaram; Rs 2,200–Rs 3,200/$48–$70 double), a pleasant heritage hotel close to the Rajasthani border. Completed in 1935, the palace overlooks a vast wildlife reserve and features Mughal domes, deep balconies, columned porticoes, and a vast rooftop where moonlit dinners can be arranged.

Established by the Muslim leader Ahmad Shah in 1411 on the banks of the Sabarmati River, the capital, Ahmedabad, has long been the center of a flourishing textile industry, earning it the nickname "Manchester of the East." An important commercial and industrial center, with trading houses and huge textile mills owned by some of India's wealthiest families, the city offers medieval mosques, colorful bazaars, and great modernist buildings designed by Le Corbusier. Full of combustible energy, the city is a fantastic jumble of old and new, where you'll regularly witness camel-drawn carts queuing up at traffic intersections alongside spluttering auto-rickshaws and Tata four-wheel-drives. While you're here, make time to visit the **Calico Museum** ✫✫✫ (© **079/286-8172**); housed in a beautiful 200-year-old haveli made from carved Burmese wood, this is possibly India's best-managed museum. Certainly it's the only one in which a knowledgeable and eloquent guide takes you through sumptuous textile galleries explaining each of the exhibits in detail. Gandhi's **Sabarmati Ashram** ✫✫✫ (© **079/748-3073**) is another supremely peaceful diversion. Time allowing, the Jain **Hatheesing Temple** ✫✫, a beautiful edifice in gleaming marble with 52 cloistered shrines, each with its own marble *tirthankara* idol, is also worth exploring. Built in the 1420s by Ahmed Shah, the **Jama Masjid** ✫✫ is the city's biggest mosque and in close proximity to many beautiful Muslim architectural highlights. Outside the east entrance is the **Tomb of Ahmed Shah,** always adorned with flowers and *chadars* (sacred cloths).

While you're in the city center, visit the 16th-century **Siddi Saiyad Mosque** ✫✫. Note the two wonderful yellow stone latticework (*jali*) screens high on the western wall; the twirling Tree of Life designs have been carved with such intricate detail that you'll have trouble believing they're made from stone at all. Across the road from the mosque is a beautiful 1928 Art Deco haveli, **The**

House of Mangaldas Girdhardas (© 079/550-6946; www.houseofmg.com), which offers Ahmedabad's only heritage accommodations. Try to have lunch at the lovely rooftop restaurant, **Agashiye** ★★, where superb Gujarati *thalis* (multicourse meals) are served. Last but not least (particularly if you're a fan of modern architecture), set aside time to visit Le Corbusier's award-winning **Sanskar Kendra** complex, with its number of galleries and museums.

Offering peace, quiet, great luxury, and a pool, the city's smartest (and most expensive) hotel is **Taj Residency Ummed** (© 079/286-4444; www.tajhotels. com; $135 double), some distance from the city center.

Arguably the best restaurant in Gujarat, **Rajwadu** ★★★ (© 079/664-3845; www.rajwadu.com) is an excellent place for dinner. Reserve a table overlooking the water and arrive around 6:30pm, when the ingredients for the night are offered to the presiding deity, Ram. Then order the delicious vegetarian thali (a mere Rs 168/$3.55). **Vishalla** ★★ (© 079/643-0357) is another great spot to experience Gujarati dining, set in a re-created Gujarati village complete with old carts, buggies, clay pots, and objets d'art. At night, traditional puppet shows and folk-dance performances under lantern light accompany the meal, where 32 different food items are piled onto your leaf platter.

Gujarat Tourism (© 079/658-9683) and **Heritage Walking Tours** (© 079/ 539-1811) are your best bets for excursions around the city.

If you want to escape Ahmedabad's heady vibe, a number of lovely, remote destinations are just hours away. **Utelia** ★★ (70km/43 miles away) is a charming village with natural hot sulphuric springs populated by traditional shepherds known as *Bharwads;* consider spending a night here before continuing on to see the magnificent Jain temple city at Palitana, arguably Gujarat's top attraction. A gorgeous place to overnight is **Palace Utelia** ★★ (© 02714/62222; utelia@ ad1.vsnl.net.in; Rs 2,000–Rs 2,400/$44–$53 European Plan/EP), an Indo-Saracenic mansion built in 1895 by the Thakur of Utelia. Featuring lovely galleries and domes, it's beautifully restored and appealingly furnished—the en-suite guest rooms are enormous and overlook a pleasant courtyard, and even the bathrooms are massive. Book a room with air-conditioning and a private balcony. Outings to the excavated ruins of **Lothal** ★, an ancient city of the Indus Valley civilization (20 min. away), are arranged in *charkas,* vehicles that are part-rickshaw, part-buggy, as are trips to the two nearby wildlife sanctuaries. February through March is foaling season at **Velavadar National Park** ★ (40 km/ 25 miles from Utelia; open mid-Mar to mid-July), a haven for the once extensively hunted black buck, as well as endangered wolves. Birders should visit **Nal Sarovar Bird Sanctuary** (© 07932/54133) between November and February, when around 250 species from as far away as Siberia arrive for the winter; it's a good opportunity to witness the intricate courtship dance of the Sarus crane.

A couple of hours south of Utelia is the fantastic hilltop Jain temple city at **Palitana** ★★★, an essential holy pilgrimage destination for this nonviolent community. A city of gleaming marble monuments housing representations of the few human souls that have managed to be liberated from the cycle of life, Palitana has over 850 temples atop sacred **Mount Satrunjaya** (the "hill that conquers enemies"). The top is reached by climbing (or by being carried up) 3,572 steps—a stiff 2-hour ascent. Amid the massive warren of white marble shrines and temples, you'll encounter many devotees dressed in white, some wearing gauze masks to filter innocent microbes from the air that they breathe. Some of the devotees attain ecstatic heights, practicing their faith with devotional singing, clapping, and humming. Others create devotional patterns on the ground using rice and nuts, or are seen gently waving fly-whisks over the idols as a gesture of respect. Stay at the stately **Nilambagh Palace Hotel** ✦ (© **0278/ 42-4241;** Rs 1,800–Rs 3,500/$40–$76 double) in Bhavnagar (50km/30 miles away), and have staff make all arrangements for your Palitana excursion. Built in 1859, Nilambagh is run by the Maharani of Bhavnagar, who still has servants quaking in her presence. Spacious palace rooms (no. 210 is the classiest) have high ceilings, antique writing desks and dressing tables, oversize canopied beds, traditional lacquered Gujarati armchairs *(sungeda),* and lovely rugs set against stone tile floors.

After the climb to Palitana's holy city, you'll have earned a break on the tiny island of **Diu** off the Gujarat mainland, officially the only place in Gujarat allowed to sell liquor. Here, it's quite common to overhear local sari-clad matriarchs gossiping in exuberant Portuguese—the colonial enclave only became part of India in 1961, when bombs were finally dropped to chase the Portuguese out. Diu remains lost in time, a mellow island appealing to exhausted travelers and Gujarati daytrippers; the latter are here because alcohol is cheap and plentiful. A sprawling fort, elegant Catholic churches, and old Portuguese mansions are on offer, but Diu is best appreciated for its unfettered beaches and languid atmosphere—perfect for a day or two of rejuvenation. Here, you arise from slumber to find the streets all but deserted, the bulk of the male population out at sea. Stay in a villa-style guest room at **Radhika Beach Resort** (© **02875/52553,** -52554, or -52555; www.radhika resort.com; doubles from Rs 1,750/$38) at Nagoa, a popular horseshoe-shaped beach that's safe for swimming.

From Diu, several hours by road takes you through pleasant rural environs to **Gir Sanctuary** (400km/248 miles southwest of Ahmedabad), the only place outside Africa where you can spot lions in the wild. Although Asiatic lions were once found as far away as Bihar, only 300 remain today, and all live in this verdant region of Gujarat, also good for spotting king vultures, paradise flycatchers, pygmy woodpeckers, and crested serpent eagles. Along with around 200 panthers, you may also sight leopard, jungle cat, *cheetal,* rusty spotted cat, *nilgai,* hyena, *chinkara,* and *chowsingha.* Members of the Maldhari community, who rear cattle and live within the sanctuary, frequently lose livestock to the lions. The sanctuary is part of the 260-sq.-km (101-sq.-ft.) Gir National Park, which visitors can enter upon purchase of a permit; Sasan Gir, a one-street village, is the entry point. **Taj Gir Lodge** offers various accommodations, even catering to lion-spotters on a budget (© **02877/85821;** www.tajhotels.com; doubles $110, budget unit $20); the staff here will make all necessary safari arrangements. To see more temples, head to the coast to view the beachfront **Somnath Temple** (45km/30 miles away), considered one of the 12 holiest Shaivite sites.

North of Gir, the **Great Rann of Kutch** ✦✦✦ is one of the most photogenic areas in India, its strange, stark terrain conjuring up a wonderfully haunting atmosphere, proving that deserts are not always a wasteland of sand. Kutch, which was at the heart of the 2001 earthquake that shook Gujarat, is an 18,000-sq.-km (7,020-sq.-ft.) salt flat that was once a navigable lake. For part of the year, the Great Rann becomes submerged in water; but when the floods recede and the clouds disappear, the sky turns a perfect blue and the earth is baked by the relentless sun, converting the vast expanse to a shimmering, hard crust of snow-white salt. This harsh, arid landscape is where the semi-nomadic Rabaris herd their sheep, goats, and camels, wending their way through Rajasthan and

Gujarat on seasonal crossings. Kutch's pastoral communities live in mud-packed toadstool-shaped huts called *bhoongas*—featuring thick walls embellished with molded designs, whitewashed patterns, and brass appliqué (more settled communities will also use pieces of reflective metal or mirrors, making the surfaces sparkle like jewels). Excursions to view these strikingly decorated mud-hut villages inhabited by equally beautifully adorned people, known for their wonderful arts and crafts, are highly recommended. **Bhuj,** Kutch's principal town, is an ideal base from which to explore the region. When villages, handicrafts, and the urge to buy no longer excite you, visit the remote and serene Shivaite monastery at **Than,** where *bidi*-smoking *sadhus* (men who have renounced their worldly possessions) gather to drink *chai* and relax. During the winter the Rann also hosts the largest colony of migratory flamingoes in the world as they arrive near **Khavda;** this is also one of the last habitats of the Asiatic wild ass. Near Bhuj is the ancient seaport of **Mandvi,** where you can visit the fascinating **Vijay Vilas Palace** and watch *dhows* being built. In **Bhuj** you can stay at **Hotel Prince** (© **02832/20370** or -20371; princad1@sancharnet.in; book a deluxe guest room at about Rs 2,000/$44 double). However, better accommodations can be found 30 minutes from Bhuj at **Garha Safari Lodge** ⚑ (Rs 1,600/$35 double), a far more personable place overlooking the Rudrani Dam. En-suite guest rooms are in thatched circular huts styled on Kutch village dwellings, and the lodge organizes full-day outings to Banni villages as well as camel safaris. There's also a good trip to the 5,000-year-old Indus Valley city excavation site at Dholavira, which takes in extraordinary landscapes and shimmering salt-pan flats along the way. Kutchi meals are served in the garden restaurant, accompanied by traditional folk dancing. Book through www.garhatours.com or call © **079/657-9672.**

Returning to Ahmedabad from the Great Rann, it's possible to stop in the Little Rann where—coupled with experiencing the natural drama of a stark landscape powdered with salt crystals—you may encounter herds of Asiatic wild ass, or *onager,* India's last wild horses. Only around 1,000 survive, most in herds in the **Little Rann of Kutch Wildlife Sanctuary.** You can also spot wolves, caracal, and *nilgai,* as well as migratory birds during the winter. You can arrange a jeep safari through **Desert Safaris & Wildlife Tours** (© **02757/82238**).

A LUXURY TRAIN EXCURSION THROUGH GUJARAT

Given the state of Gujarat's roads, not to mention its extreme heat, a good way to explore the westernmost state is by train. Although pricey, **The Royal Orient** (© **011/2578-3960;** www.indianrail.gov.in/royal_orient.html or www.gujarat tourism.com) lives up to its romantic image and does away with the need to organize taxis, sightseeing, meals, and accommodations. The 8-day trip also covers Rajasthan highlights. Departing Delhi every Wednesday afternoon, the 13-coach train offers two- and three-berth cabins with air-conditioning and attached bathrooms; amenities include restaurants, a library, and a bar. Doubles are $400 per day October through March, $300 April through September.

10

Himachal Pradesh: On Top of the World

Proclaimed by ancient Indian texts as *Devbhumi*—"Land of the Gods"—and believed to be the earthly home of the mighty Lord Shiva, this beautiful, far-flung region has an almost palpable presence of divinity. Bordered by Tibet to the east, Jammu and Kashmir to the north, and the Punjab to the west, the landlocked state is one of great topographic diversity, from vast bleak tracts of rust-colored high-altitude Trans-Himalayan desert to dense green deodar forests, apple orchards, cultivated terraces and, everywhere you look, sublime snowcapped mountains. This is also where you'll find the largest concentration of Buddhists, their atmospheric *gompas* (monasteries) a total contrast to the pageantry of Hindu temples.

Shimla, the state capital, is easily accessed from Delhi by train, preferably via the Punjabi town of Amritsar, where the shimmering **Golden Temple** of the Sikhs takes the honors as India's best cultural attraction. Shimla shouldn't hold you longer than it takes to get ready to tackle one of the greatest road adventures in Asia—negotiating the ledges, landslides, and hairpin bends of the **Hindustan-Tibet Road** through the remote valleys of Kinnaur, Lahaul, and Spiti. Hidden from the world for most of the year by a cloak of thick, impenetrable snow, these easternmost districts emerge from their wintry slumber to reveal white-capped Himalayan mountains, lush green meadow-valleys dappled

with flowers, and Tibetan Buddhist *gompas,* of which **Tabo,** a World Heritage Site, is one of the most spiritual destinations in India. Due to limited accessibility (the region only opened to visitors in recent years and requires a special permit) and the impassability of the roads, the region remains the least visited and most exhilarating part of Himachal Pradesh. You should set aside at least 3 to 4 days to explore the area after arriving in Manali, a town somewhat enlivened (some say ruined) by its designated role as Himachal Pradesh's "hippie hot spot" and local honeymoon destination. You can either set off on a trek from this popular adventure center, or head west (via Mandi) to the tea-carpeted hills of the westernmost Kangra Valley and the hill station of **Dharamsala**—seat of the Tibetan government-in-exile and home to the Dalai Lama. Another option is to head north to the lunar landscapes of **Ladakh.**

Although Jammu and Kashmir, India's northernmost state, is a no-go area for rational travelers, Ladakh, the western J&K province on the border of Tibet, is the fortunate exception. It sits astride the Ladakh and Zanskar mountains, surrounded by two of the world's highest ranges—the Greater Himalayas and the mighty Karakoram—and nothing will quite prepare you for the breathtaking stark beauty of the landscape. Jagged peaks, rocky uplands, and vast barren plateaus are the dominant features of this harsh, dry land swept by

Himachal Pradesh

Leh
Shey
LADAKH
ZANSKAR
Gya

H
I
Tso Moriri
M
Kishtwar
Kilar
A
RUPSHU
Sutak
Pang
L
Langera
Sarchu
A
Triloknath
Serai
Y
AMMU
Baralacha La (5100m)
Chamba
Keylong
A
Delhousie
PIR PANJAL RANGE
S
LAHAUL
Batal
Hense
McLeod Ganj
Dhaula Dhar Range
Rohtang
Vashisht
Kunzum La
Kibber
Pass
(4551 m)
Ki Gompa
Dharamsala
(3978 m)
Manali
Kaza
Dhankar
TIBET
Kangra
Katrain
Malana
SPITI
Tabo
Baijnath
Nagar
Manikaran
1A
Kullu
Pin-Parvati
Beas River
20
Pass
Puh
Rewalsar
Mandi
(5400 m)
KINNAUR
HIMACHAL PRADESH
Kalpa
Una
Rekong Peo
To
Narkanda
Sangla
Kinner Kailash
Amritsar
Chitkul
(6050 m)
Shimla
Tons River
Chail
Gangotri
Ludhiana
Yamunotri
1
Chandigarh
UTTARANCHAL
22
PUNJAB
Paonta Sahib
Markanda
UTTAR
PRADESH
Yamuna River
Narwana
1
HARYANA
Panipat

HIMACHAL
PRADESH
New Delhi
India
Bay of
Bengal

383

dust devils and dotted with Buddhist *gompas*, large whitewashed *stupas* (commemorative cairns), and chest-high *mani* walls made from stacks of engraved stones. Aptly nicknamed "Little Tibet," this is India at her remote best. Only visited for the few months of summer when the roads are passable, the world here has been frozen in time; the small Buddhist population continues to live as they have for centuries, totally untouched by outside influences. Spend at least 4 days here (adjusting to the high altitude takes time), then fly out to Delhi and rejoin the 21st century.

1 Staying Active

Himachal Pradesh and Ladakh are exceptional destinations for adventurous travelers. The area has a phenomenal array of trekking routes, and numerous tour operators offer anything from gentle strolls to walks lasting several days—even trips to serious rock faces for hardened climbers. Besides the scenery, a visit here is an ideal opportunity to meet people totally untouched by the modern world—outside of a handful of towns, much of the population in this region is rural and dependent on agriculture. It is also home to some of the world's last nomadic people. **Manali** is a popular starting point for treks into the lush Kullu and Parvati valleys, while **Dharamsala** is a good base from which to explore the Dhauladhar Mountain range. In Ladakh, expeditions out of **Leh** visit the many fascinating Buddhist monasteries, and the **Indus** and **Zanskar rivers** are excellent for white-water rafting. Note that most of the companies listed below are happy to arrange a variety of adventure activities almost anywhere in the Himalayas, including Sikkim (discussed in chapter 12).

IN MANALI   If you arrive in Manali with no prearranged outdoor activities, contact either the **Himalayan Outdoor Centre** (The Mall; ✆ **01902/25-2489, -2581, or 98-1600-3035**)—they offer a wide range of adventure activities, including rafting on the Beas River, skiing (Apr through mid-May), snowboarding, treks, jeep safaris, and tandem paragliding—or **Himalayan Quest Adventures** (above Chopsticks Restaurant, The Mall, Manali; ✆ **01902/25-3139;** fax 01902/25-2404; himquest@yahoo.com), a professional eco-friendly operation offering trekking, jeep safaris, paragliding, and rafting trips throughout the region. Keeping up with the times, the company also offers snowboarding courses; a 5-day package will cost around $45 per day, including all equipment, lodging, and other fees. Besides organizing trekking in Himachal and Ladakh, **Himalayan Journeys The Adventure Company** (The Mall, Manali; ✆ **01902/25-2365;** www.himalayanjourneysindia.com) arranges ski courses, jeep safaris, river-rafting expeditions, mountain-biking tours and, for well-heeled adventurers, luxury heli-skiing packages. This company is associated with Abercrombie & Kent and Equator Expeditions in the United Kingdom, as well as the Australian outfit, Himachal Helicopter Skiing (see below).

IN LEH   San Francisco–based **Geographic Expeditions** ★★★ (www.geoex. com; ✆ **800/777-8183** in the U.S.) offers a 22-day Trans-Himalayan trek that passes through the old kingdom of Zanskar through Ladakh, hitting an altitude of 5,064m (16,880 ft.); although not for the fainthearted, it's an exhilarating way to experience one of India's most untouched regions. For more leisure-oriented travelers, the same company conducts jeep safaris of Ladakh. One of the best treks offered is the arduous **Chadar Trek** ★★★ along the frozen Zanskar

---

Moments   **Chasing the World's Most Expensive White Powder**

Surrounded by soaring snowcapped peaks against a cerulean sky, you climb onto a pair of fat skis and tackle dry, calf-deep powder for heart-stopping, high-powered skiing. If you fancy the idea of being whisked onto pristine Himalayan slopes by helicopter to ski slopes with names like Nasty Nick and Powderbox, where good conditions mean runs of up to a kilometer or more, Manali, in central Himachal Pradesh, is where you should head. You'll need to fork out big bucks for this ultimate adrenaline rush adventure, but the helicopter ride saves you valuable time. From Manali, the snow-covered slopes are a mere 4 minutes away by chopper, a trip that otherwise would involve a grueling 4-day climb. Roddy McKenzie's **Himachal Helicopter Skiing** (© 00 61 3/9593-9853; www.himachal.com) is an Australian outfit with over a decade's experience. Be warned, however: Avalanches are an ever-present risk, and general bad weather, or even low cloud cover, can undo any plans for a chopper's takeoff—and, sorry, no refunds for ski time lost because of poor conditions. McKenzie's operation includes experienced guides who spend considerable time each morning testing the snow for safety prior to drops. Himachal Helicopter Skiing offers weeklong heli-skiing trips for upwards of $6,000 per person, based on two people sharing.

River, starting in Leh and terminating in the village of Padum. At night, temperatures plummet to a bone-chilling –31°F (–35°C), while all day long you defy the slippery ice that is thick enough to support your weight only 2 months a year. In Leh itself, **Indus Himalayan Explorers** (Shamshu Complex, Fort Rd., Leh; © **01982/25-3154,** Delhi 011/2651-0550) is another outfit that undertakes this grueling expedition. The company also arranges less hectic trekking expeditions, as well as yak safaris, skiing, mountain biking, and challenging mountaineering packages for serious climbers. English-speaking mountain guides are provided, as well as all equipment, porters, cooks, and other staff. Also operating along the Chadar route is **Aquaterra Adventures** ★★★ (© **011/ 2921-2641** or -2760; www.treknraft.com), one of the best Indian adventure operators, which runs a wide range of tours and treks customized to suit your personal interests and abilities. Working with highly experienced and knowledgeable guides, Aquaterra is possibly the best choice for discerning travelers looking to raft the Indus or Zanskar rivers in Ladakh or the Beas in Himachal Pradesh. You can also combine trekking and rafting trips, or opt for a unique bicycle camping expedition.

JEEP SAFARI SPECIALISTS   **Banjara Camps & Retreats** ★★ (www.banjara camps.com) operates a number of Trans-Himalayan jeep safaris, which generally start in Delhi and explore different parts of Himachal and Ladakh. Comfortable accommodations (some in beautifully situated deluxe campsites) and good meals accompany you along the way, and you can even design your own customized safari. Another outfitter that allows you to traverse the top of the world in comfort, **Wilderness Trekkers** (www.wilderness-trekkers.org) runs a weeklong adventure that takes in Himachal's Rohtang Pass as well as some of Ladakh's most mesmerizing Buddhist *gompas.*

2 The Golden Temple in Amritsar

410km (254 miles) NW of Delhi

Amritsar (pronounced *Am-ri-sa*) has been the capital of the Sikh religion since the 16th century. Located in the northwestern state of Punjab, a wealthy and prosperous region and home to the majority of India's Sikhs, Amritsar is also home to India's most dazzling temple. A shimmering monument in marble, bronze, and gold leaf, and a vivid architectural celebration of Sikhism's devotion (a faith that actively preaches unity and equality among all religions), the **Golden Temple** is both fascinating and spiritually invigorating, combining sheer physical beauty with a truly sacred atmosphere. The way in which its devotees worship is enough to hold your attention—if not your heart—permanently captive.

ESSENTIALS

VISITOR INFORMATION The best place to get information about the Golden Temple and the Sikh faith is at the temple's own **Information Office** (© **0183/255-3954;** daily 7am–8pm in summer, 7am–7pm in winter). The **Punjab Government Tourist Office** (© **0183/240-2452;** Mon–Fri 9am–5pm) is at the Palace Hotel, opposite the railway station.

GETTING THERE & AWAY The best way to get here is on the Shatabdi Express from Delhi (or you can travel from Mumbai on Frontier Mail); or you can fly from Delhi or Chandigarh with **Indian Airlines** (39A Court Rd.; © **0183/221-3392** or -3393, or 141; Mon–Sat 10am–5pm). Taxis, auto-rickshaws, and bicycle-rickshaws are always available at the station to take you to your hotel. You'll want to avoid spending time tracking down tickets, so either book your return or onward journey in advance, or have your hotel handle your reservation. A computerized reservation facility is located at the Golden Temple complex.

GETTING AROUND Note that Mrs. Bhandari's Guesthouse will make all your transport and sightseeing arrangements for you on a noncommission basis. Besides reasonably priced air-conditioned and non-air-conditioned cars, you can get a guide for Rs 650/$14 (half day) or Rs 1,100/$24 (full day). Cycle-rickshaws are popular, but if you're in a hurry, don't want to do battle with the glaring sun, or need to cover more than a few kilometers, opt for a car or auto-rickshaw instead.

The Five "K's": How to Spot a Sikh

Most orthodox Sikh men wear turbans wrapped around their heads, making them highly visible in all parts of the world. However, there are five other symbols—known as the five *kakkars*—worn by Sikh men to indicate that they are part of Guru Gobind Singh's sacred Khalsa brotherhood, which unites all Sikhs. Traditionally, a Sikh man does not cut his hair or shave his beard. This hair is known as the *kesh,* and is kept neat with a comb known as the *kangha.* As a symbol of dignity and power, he carries a saber or sword, known as the *kirpan,* at all times. You won't see it, but a Sikh man wears loose underpants known as the *kaccha,* said to symbolize modesty. Finally, look on his right wrist: The *karra* is a traditional bangle of steel that indicates fearlessness and strength; pick one up as a reminder of your visit.

Bloody History of the Holy Temple

In 1984, the Sikh fundamentalist Sant Bhindrawale and his followers armed themselves and occupied the Golden Temple as part of a campaign for a separate Sikh state, which they wanted to call Khalistan. Acting on Prime Minister Indira Gandhi's orders, the Indian Army attacked, killing Bhindrawale and others and causing serious damage to the temple. Indira Gandhi was later assassinated by two of her Sikh bodyguards, leading to a massacre in which thousands of Sikhs lost their lives. The Sikh community refused to allow the central government to repair the damage to the temple, instead undertaking the work themselves. Although most of the cracks and crevices have been repaired, the incident has not been forgotten, and you will find many people in Amritsar keen to explain the Sikh side of the story.

The Golden Temple ★★★ *(Moments)*   Prepare to be humbled by what is quite simply the most tangibly spiritual place in the country, one that, in its status as a living monument, even has the edge on the Taj Mahal. Arrive with a few good hours set aside and get lost in its magical beauty. Leave your shoes at the free facility near the entrance, cover your head (bandanas are provided, or you can purchase a "Golden Temple" souvenir bandana from a vendor), and wash your feet by wading through the shallow pool before entering. The most sacred part of the complex is the **Hari Mandir (Divine Temple)** or **Darbar Sahib (Court of the Lord),** which you'll instantly recognize as the marble-and-gold sanctuary at the center of a large body of water within the temple complex. The name "Golden Temple" comes from this gold-plated building, which features copper cupolas and white marble walls encrusted with precious stones arranged in decorative floral patterns that show strong Islamic influence. Four *chattris* flank the structure, which is decorated inside and out with verses from the *Granth Sahib* (the Sikh holy book). Construction of the temple began in 1574, with ongoing restoration and embellishment over the years, including the addition in the 19th century of 100 kilograms of gold to cover the inverted lotus-shaped dome.

To reach the temple, follow the *Parikrama,* which circumscribes the sacred water tank—known as the **Amrit Sarovar,** or the Pool of Nectar—in a clockwise direction. You'll need to cross a marble causeway, the **Guru's Bridge,** which symbolizes the journey of the soul after death, in order to reach the *bangaldar* pavilion on which the temple stands. Access to the bridge is through the marvelous **Darshani Deorhi,** a gateway marked by magnificent silver doors. Here, you will join the many devotees who, especially early and late in the day, pass through the temple to pay their respects (and give a donation) to their Holy Book. Within the Hari Mandir, the scene—which is almost constantly being televised for Sikh viewers around India—is fascinating. Beneath a canopy studded with jewels, scriptures from the Holy Book are sung, while a crowd of fervent yet solemn devotees immerse themselves in the moment. A *chauri,* or whisk, is repeatedly waved dramatically in the air above the Book, while new musicians and singers continually join the ensemble after another participant has paid his respects. Like an organic human machine, lines of Sikhs pay their respects by touching their foreheads to the temple floor and walls, continuing in a clockwise direction at a moderate pace. Simply being among such gracious devotion will fill you with a sense of inner calm. Once you've passed through the Hari Mandir, taking your time to drink in the atmosphere, head back along the Guru's Bridge. It is along this bridge that the *Granth Sahib* is carried between the Hari Mandir and the **Akal Takht** (see "Spiritual Weightlifting," below), the seat of the Sikh parliament, built in 1609 and located directly across from the Hari Mandir.

Don't miss the **Guru-ka-Langar,** a dining hall where each day around 35,000 people are fed by temple volunteers. In an act that symbolizes the Sikh belief in equality of all people, irrespective of caste or creed, anyone and everyone is welcomed and invited to join the communal breaking of bread. Guest quarters are also available for international Sikh visitors (for a nominal fee), and at least 400 simple rooms are provided free of charge to pilgrims. In the **Central Sikh Museum** at the main entrance, galleries display images and remembrances of Sikh gurus, warriors, and saints; note that it includes some graphic portraits of gurus being tortured and executed in terrifying ways.

Unlike in many other temples in India, here you feel genuinely welcome and not at all pressured to take out your wallet. In fact, so proud of their religion, culture, history, and temple are the local Sikhs that you will almost certainly be offered enthusiastic conversation and valuable information by one of the regular devotees—in return for nothing more than your attention. The welcoming information office to the left of the main gate gives helpful advice and information, as well as booklets on Sikhism (see the appendix for a brief précis).

For further information, contact the **Temple Manager** (✆ **0183/255-3953**, -3957, or -3958; fax 0183/255-3919), or call the **Information Office** (✆ 0183/255-3954). Daily 7am–8pm in summer and 7am–7pm in winter. Activity at the temple goes on till late, and even when the last ceremonies of the evening have been concluded, volunteers get to work by cleaning or preparing for the next day. The main gate never closes, and the Hari Mandir is open according to hours determined by the lunar cycle—some 20 hr. in summer and 18 hr. in winter. In summer, the closing ceremony takes place at 11pm and the sanctum is reopened at 2am. In winter, the times are 9:30pm and 4am, respectively.

AN UNUSUAL OUTING

Flag Ceremony at Wagah Border *(Moments*   One of the world's oddest spectator activities, this pompous display of military bravado is a major drawing card for Indian tourists who travel long distances to watch the "Retreat," a high-kicking, toe-stepping, quick-marching ceremony wherein the Indian and Pakistani flags are lowered on either side of the only border that remains open between the two hostile countries. A number of officers from each team puts on a raised-eyebrow performance to the satisfaction of the cheering, chanting crowds, seated

---

Moments **Spiritual Weightlifting**

The best time to visit is for the *Palki Sahib,* or **night ceremony,** during which the *Granth Sahib* is carried from the main shrine in the Hari Mandir to the sanctum where it rests for a few hours until the opening ceremony the following morning. Men can take part in this ceremony by joining one of the vibrant lines that form behind and ahead of the heavy palanquin on which the Holy Book is moved. Several devotees simultaneously help support each arm of the palanquin, but each person has only a few seconds to take part in the auspicious event. As though it were being transported along a human conveyor belt, one person from each side moves away from the palanquin and is replaced by a new shoulder from each of the lines; in this way, everyone gets at least one chance to participate, and you can join the end of the line again and again until your shoulder no longer wishes to cooperate.

---

on specially constructed concrete grandstands on either side. The pointless exercise ends with the furious slamming of the border gates, at which time each side's flag is urgently carried to a room for overnight safekeeping. For anyone interested in unbridled nationalist pride, the Flag Ceremony is a memorable outing (only half an hour from Amritsar). Arrive well ahead of the crowds in order to get a closeup seat—the grimaces of the mighty military men in their rooster caps add to the fun, and you'll get a better look at the Pakistani delegation. Alternatively, find a way of organizing a VIP spot across the road from the crowd; a friendly call to a local politician might do the trick.

Wagah is at the border between India and Pakistan, 32km (20 miles) from Amritsar. A taxi for the round-trip should cost around Rs 650 ($14).

WHERE TO STAY & DINE

Amritsar has several fairly decent hotels, including the **Ritz Plaza Hotel** (45 Mall Rd.; © **0183/222-6606;** fax 0183/256-6027; ritz@del3.vsnl.net.in), which has comfortable rooms, a pool, and all the basic facilities for $42 double. For personal service and a homey stay, however, nothing comes close to the quintessentially Punjabi experience of Mrs. Bhandari's Guesthouse (reviewed below).

Amritsar has scores of *dhabas,* Punjabi-style "fast-food" joints serving tasty and filling *thalis* (multicourse platters) that showcase various traditional dishes. Rs 50 ($1.05) buys you a sizeable spread that you eat with your fingers, dipping piping-hot chapati into tangy concoctions arranged in little heaps on your platter. Check if **New Kundan Dhaba** is still operating (ask at your hotel); it serves the yummiest *dhal* in town. If you want a clean, glitzy restaurant that serves a wide range of dishes, head for **Crystal**. It may not drip with atmosphere, but it's the cleanest and most strikingly popular upmarket restaurant in town, and the food—an eclectic array of dishes (including Chinese and Continental) but with the emphasis on North Indian specialties—is excellent (© **0183/222-5555** or -9999; daily noon–11:30pm; Rs 50–Rs 120/$1.05–$2.50).

Mrs. Bhandari's Guesthouse 🅰🅰🅰 🆅alue   Mrs. Bhandari's is almost as much a reason to visit this corner of North India as the Golden Temple. Situated along a wide avenue in the peaceful, leafy Cantonment neighborhood, this is a very pleasant, comfortable and, above all, homey place in which to enjoy genuine Punjabi hospitality. The fabulously preserved late-Raj family estate packs in beautiful gardens, a welcoming pool, and its own team of curious water buffalo; these provide the essential ingredient (fresh dung) for homemade fire "briquettes." Accommodations vary in size and location, arranged in and around Mrs. Bhandari's charming home. Most rooms resemble "chummeries," the bachelor quarters assigned to Raj officials of junior rank with an attached room for their Indian servant. Interiors are modest but atmospheric, featuring high ceilings, Art Deco tiles, fine Indian throws over firm mattresses, and bathrooms with drench showers or old-fashioned tubs and original piping. The best option is the large "Bambi" suite, just off the dining courtyard (room no. BB3 is also a good option). Mrs. Bhandari has been living here since 1930, but the guesthouse is now run by her warm-spirited daughter, who will help you plan an enjoyable itinerary and organize all transport and temple visits. A one-way transfer from the railway station to the guesthouse is included in the room rate.

No. 10, Cantonment, Amritsar 143 001. © **0183/222-8509** or -2390. Fax 0183/222-2390. http://bhandari_guesthouse@tripod.com. bgha@glide.net.in. 14 units. Doubles: Rs 1,200 ($26); Rs 1,500 ($33) with A/C and heater; Rs 250 ($5.35) extra bed. Camping: Rs 165 ($3.50) per person with own equipment. No credit cards. **Amenities:** Restaurant; pool; tour guide, transport, and taxi arrangements; camping facilities; room service. *In room:* A/C and heater on request.

Visiting Le Corbusier's Chandigarh

Fans of the father of modernism, Le Corbusier, will appreciate the form and functionality of **Chandigarh.** When the Punjab was divided after Partition, Lahore went to Pakistan, leaving the state without a capital; Chandigarh was envisioned as the new headquarters. When Punjab was once again divided into smaller states, the city became a Union Territory serving as the administrative capital for both Punjab and Haryana. Le Corbusier is largely responsible for designing the mesh of rectangular units, or "Sectors," into which the city is divided. Characterized by exposed brickwork, boulder stone masonry, broad boulevards, large landscaped parks with abundant trees, and quadrants of tidy, self-sufficient neighborhoods made up of buildings with louvered screens (brise-soleil) and unfinished concrete surfaces, Le Corbusier's city doesn't quite function as the living organism it's intended to be. Urban decay and waste have crept in, but architecture buffs will find Le Corbusier's structural contributions intriguing. Architectural attractions in Chandigarh include the **Capitol Complex** 𝒜𝒜 (Sector 1), where the geometrical concrete buildings of the **Legislative Assembly,** the **High Court,** and the **Secretariat** represent structural innovation. At the southern end of the complex piazza, the **Vidhan Sabha (Legislative Assembly)** building is capped by a startling cupola, a pyramidal tower, and a cuboid tower, while within the portico is a bright **Cubist mural** by Le Corbusier himself. Also within the complex is the **Open Hand Monument,** a giant metal hand standing 26m (83 ft.) high that is able to rotate in the wind. Symbolizing the give-and-take of ideas, the hand has become the city's official emblem. Technically, tours of the complex start from the reception, but these half-hourly episodes don't always materialize; check with someone from the **Chandigarh Industrial & Tourism Development Corporation (CITCO)** (② 0172/270-4761, -4356, or -4031) in advance, and make arrangements for a permit to gain entry. Locals go to walk, jog, and relax in the 8km (5-mile) long linear park

3 Shimla

107km (66 miles) NE of Chandigarh

In the days when Shimla inspired scenes from Rudyard Kipling's *Kim,* it was a popular pick-up center for lusty British officers and flirtatious maidens keen to create a stir among the scandal-mongers who gathered along The Mall during the summers. Shimla enjoys a proud history as the preferred mountain escape retreat from the unbearable summer heat of the plains (or "downstairs," as many Himachalis refer to their low-altitude neighbors)—a cool spot in which to sink into a life of idle gossip, romantic conquests, and military brown-nosing. Today, this romantic image has been shattered by reckless overconstruction that has torn into the atmosphere of gentility and natural beauty that prevailed not so long ago. Development has now been curbed, but the clogged roads and ugly concrete tenements that cling to the mountainsides beneath historic Shimla detract significantly from the town's former glory.

known as **Leisure Valley**. In Sector 16, the **Rose Garden** is the largest of its kind in Asia. In Sector 10, the **Sculpture Park** adjoining the Cultural Complex is worth exploring. Within the Complex, the **Art and Picture Gallery** (Tues–Sun 11am–4:30pm) includes Modernist works. If you'd like to deepen your knowledge of Chandigarh's planning and construction, visit the **City Museum** (Sector 10), where exhibits document the realization of the city.

Chandigarh's highlight is the **Rock Garden of Nek Chand** 🕉🕉🕉, a surreal fantasyland created by "outsider artist" Nek Chand—a road inspector—from rocks, concrete, and urban rubbish. Set on 8 hectares (20 acres) of wooded landscape, the "garden" comprises a series of maze-like archways, tunnels, pavilions, waterfalls, and bridges, with passages leading from one open-air gallery to another. Each gallery is occupied by unusual characters, figures, and creatures fashioned from an unbelievable array of materials Chand started collecting in 1958; almost half a century later, the garden continues to grow. If the artist is in residence when you visit, he'll be happy to chat with you about his project.

Chandigarh can be visited en route between Amritsar and Shimla, or directly from Delhi by train. The best connections between Delhi and Chandigarh are the daily Shatabdi Express and the Himalayan Queen. From Amritsar, choose the Amritsar Express, which also links Chandigarh with Kalka, starting point for the "toy train" to Shimla. The **railway station** (✆ 0172/265-3131 or 0172/264-1651, -1131, or -1132) is in Sector 17, around 8km (5 miles) from the city center. For railway inquiries, call the **city reservation center** (✆ 0172/270-8573; Mon–Sat 8am–8pm, Sun 8am–2pm). **Chandigarh Tourism** (✆ 0172/270-3839 or -4614) has offices at the airport and at the railway station (✆ 0172/265-8005). If you decide to spend the night, book at **Hotel Mount View** 🕉 (✆ 0172/274-0544, -3268, -2269, -1862, or -1882); insist on a guest room in the renovated section.

Shimla is a useful starting point from which to explore more untouched parts of Himachal, and the town's timbered cottages and wood-gabled buildings retain a degree of charm, but if you're expecting a quiet hill station, you may be disappointed. Shimla sprawls over seven hills fringed by dense forest and magnificent mountains, but the concrete and unchecked urbanization have had a significant impact. The Mall, a promenade on the southern slopes of the ridge, remains a pedestrian preserve, thronged by tourists and local Anglophiles who tend to echo the social mannerisms of the Raj at its most British. Below the ridge, however, an overwhelmingly Indian conglomeration of buildings constitutes the bazaar, and a sweep of modern dwellings has the distinctly untidy appearance of unplanned urban sprawl. Shimla is also in close proximity to a number of lesser-known hill resort getaways: Naldera, Narkanda, Kufri, and Chadwick Falls are all destinations offering relative peace and quiet and scenic splendor guaranteed to capture your imagination. For those seeking adventure and remote beauty, Shimla is a useful confluence of roads leading west to the

---

⌐Tips Plastic in your Wallet

Obtaining cash against credit cards can be highly problematic in Himachal Pradesh and Ladakh. Only a select number of very upmarket hotels and several branches of the Bank of Baroda will advance cash against Visa and MasterCard, and you won't find any ATMs capable of handling international credit card cash advances.

Kangra Valley; north to Kullu, Lahaul, and Ladakh; and east into the valleys of Kinnaur and Spiti.

ESSENTIALS

GETTING THERE & AWAY   By Road   All of the more reputable hotels (see "Where to Stay," below) will arrange transfers from practically any starting point in India, should you wish to arrive in chauffeured style. From Delhi, you'll take National Highway 1 (Grand Trunk Rd.) north to Ambala (in Haryana) and then continue on a fierce and beautiful journey along a hillside road that snakes all the way up to Shimla. You can also drive directly from Chandigarh, following National Highway 21 south until you join the main Delhi–Shimla road.

By Air   Weather can interfere with flights in and out of Shimla's **Jabbarhatti Airport,** 23km (14 miles) from the city. Daily flights connect Shimla with Delhi (1 hr.); these also stop at Kullu's **Bhuntar Airport,** which serves northern Himachal Pradesh.

By Train   The most romantic way to get to Shimla, the **Himalayan Queen** runs from New Delhi to Kalka (640m/2,050 ft. above sea level), where the train switches to narrow-gauge track and continues on to Shimla (at 2,060m/6,500 ft.). Traveling at an average speed of 25kmph to 30kmph (15 mph–48 mph), the journey will consume nearly a full day of your itinerary. Its 96km (60 miles) travels numerous bridges, tunnels, and sharp curves, taking in picturesque views of green forests and meadows, capsicum fields, and red-roofed chalets. The train back to Kalka departs Shimla at 10:35am, arriving in time for you to make the onward connection to Delhi, where you'll arrive before midnight. *Note:* During the high season, it's difficult to secure tickets without at least several days' advance booking.

VISITOR INFORMATION   For friendly, helpful, and enthusiastic assistance on the entire Himachal region, pop into the **Himachal Pradesh Tourism Information Centre (HPTDC)** (© 0177/285-4589; www.himachaltourism.org), where Geeta Ram Ranote will provide you with everything from trekking tips to details of his favorite itineraries; beware, however, of taking on his advice on accommodations—he, like many other government officials, is committed to sending you to HPTDC-run establishments, of which 99.9% are undesirable.

GETTING AROUND   On Foot   Central Shimla is free of traffic, which means that you'll spend much of your time exploring on foot. You'll need some degree of stamina to deal with the numerous steep inclines. A two-stage elevator, **the Lift,** operating between 8am and 10pm, connects the Mall with Cart Road; ticket prices are nominal.

By Car   Shimla has a number of restricted and sealed roads, and farther routes are no-go zones for heavier vehicles. Should you arrive in town by train, you'll find a taxi (and even the odd auto-rickshaw), which will drop you at your hotel—although you may be surprised at the route necessary to get around various "no traffic" zones. Day trips (see "Shimla Excursions," below) will generally require a taxi or jeep—but the prices can fluctuate wildly. Get advice from your hotel on hiring a car and driver at reasonable rates. For prepaid taxi trips, contact © 0177/285-8892, or the **Vishal Himachal Taxi Operator Union** at © 0177/280-5164.

GUIDED TOURS & TRAVEL AGENTS   For intelligent, entertaining, and exclusive **tours of Shimla** itself, your best bet is to make contact with noted local writer Raajah Bhasin, author of *Simla—The Summer Capital of British India*. If he's not too busy rehearsing at the historic Gaiety Theatre, Raajah will provide you with fond memories of the city and an acute understanding of its juicy history. You can make contact with Raajah by inquiring at any of the Oberoi hotels (the Cecil, Clarke's, or Wildflower Hall), for whom he conducts specialized tours.

Government-operated tours are annoying, claustrophobic excursions, best avoided unless you're on a tight budget. The office of the **Himachal Pradesh Tourism Development Corporation** (HPTDC; © 0177/225-2561; www.hptdc.nic.in; Apr 15–June 30 and Sept 1–Oct 31 daily 9am–8pm, rest of year daily 9am–6pm) is along The Mall, near Scandal Point. The Mall has an abundance of travel agencies; use them to arrange transport, tours, and trekking around the state. For jeep safaris out of Shimla into Kinnaur and Spiti, see "Staying Active," earlier in this chapter.

FAST FACTS: Shimla

Ambulance Dial © **0177/280-4648** or 0177/285-2102.

Banks/Currency Exchange You can change cash and traveler's checks, and organize cash advances on certain credit cards, at **ANZ Grindlays** (The Mall; Mon–Fri 9:30am–2:30pm, Sat 9:30am–12:30pm). Guests at the Cecil and Wildflower Hall can also draw money against their credit cards for a small percentage.

Hospital For around-the-clock service, call **Tara Hospital** (© **0177/280-3275**).

Police There's a police office (© **0177/281-2344**) adjacent the Town Hall, on The Mall. It's closed on Sunday.

Post Office The **General Post Office** (Mon–Sat 10am–6pm) is located just above Scandal Corner.

WHAT TO SEE & DO

Shimla's main promenade is **The Mall,** a pedestrian avenue stretching across the length of the city from Gopal Mandir in the west to the suburb of Chhota Shimla, roughly south of the town center. Along this stretch, crumbling remnants of the British Raj abound. Above The Mall is **The Ridge,** a wide-open esplanade watched over by a statue of Gandhi to the east, where the nearby Gothic **Christchurch** is one of Shimla's most imposing structures, situated adjacent the faux-Tudor half-timbered **library.** Note the fresco around the chancel window, designed by Lockwood Kipling, Rudyard's father.

Also on the Mall are the **Telegraph Office,** an interesting example of stone ashlar work completed in 1922 and, to its right, the old **Railway Booking**

Office, a sadly decaying building frequently overrun by obnoxious monkeys. Marking the area where The Ridge joins up with The Mall, **Scandal Point** continues to be a popular social hangout, supposedly taking its name from an unconfirmed scandal involving the elopement of a handsome Patiala prince with the daughter of a British commander-in-chief. Beyond the fire station, after the dressed stone building housing the Municipal Offices, is the **Gaiety Theatre,** originally the Town Hall. Renowned for its excellent acoustics, the Gaiety continues to showcase local dramas on a stage where notable personalities, including Lord Robert Baden-Powell and novelist M. M. Kaye, once graced the planks—not all with great success; a fashionable piece of gossip tells how Rudyard Kipling was booed off the stage.

A short walk east of The Ridge will take you to the start of a rather strenuous but worthwhile hike to the summit of **Jakhu Hill** ✦ which, at an altitude of 2,445m (7,800 ft.), is Shimla's highest point and affords excellent views of the city and surrounding valleys. You need to trudge up a steep 1.5km (1-mile) path, commencing at The Ridge and culminating at Shimla's highest point, to get to the Hanuman temple on Jakhu's summit. Try to make it to the top in time for sunrise or sunset, either of which is glorious. The little temple is dedicated to Hinduism's popular monkey god (who is said to have rested on Jakhu Hill on his return from a mission in the Himalayas). Today his brazen descendants continue to patrol the path and the summit like little monkey Mafioso, so beware of carrying food or doing *anything* likely to provoke them. After you bang the bell at the temple entrance, enter to discover a curious concoction of serious Hindu faith and jovial Christmas pomp suggested by the tinsel and streamer decorations; the priest will happily give you a blessing.

To the west of the city, beyond the Cecil Hotel, is the vast six-story Scottish baronial mansion formerly known as the **Viceregal Lodge** ✦ (Observatory Hill; daily 9am–1pm and 2–5pm; Rs 10/20¢). Built in 1888 at the behest of the British viceroy in an approximation of the Elizabethan style, the lodge is Shimla's single greatest architectural testament to the influence of the British Raj, and its luxuriant woodwork, handsome lawns, and lovely views attract numerous visitors. Even in 1888 it had electric light and an indoor tennis court, both rare for the times. The building was the summer residence of all viceroys until 1947, when India was granted independence and the building renamed Rashtrapati Niwas. The lodge was until recently home to the Indian Institute of Advanced Studies, but it will likely be preserved as a national monument.

SHIMLA EXCURSIONS

A mere 12km (7½ miles) from Shimla, the forested village of **Mashobra** is great for scenic walks but is best visited as an excuse to step into one of India's loveliest hotels, **Wildflower Hall** (see "Where to Stay," below), for high tea or lunch. From the village, you can attempt a trek to the area's highest peak—Shali—which reaches 3,200m (10,000 ft.), or take the 2km (1¼-mile) pedestrian track to the "sacred grove" of Sipur, which is where you'll find the charming indigenous-styled temple dedicated to the local deity, Seep. Because they are considered the personal property of Seep, no trees may be cut here; so superstitious are the locals that they pat themselves down before leaving to ensure no fallen cedar needles have accidentally dropped on them. Beyond Mashobra is the popular picnicking resort of **Naldehra** (23km/14 miles from Shimla), which has an extraordinary 9-hole golf course designed by Lord Curzon (British viceroy of India, 1899–1905). Golfing on the world's highest course is best arranged through your hotel in Shimla.

CHAIL

Chail (2,150m/7,000 ft.), 2 hours from Shimla, can be visited as a day trip out of the capital (or a relaxing, peaceful accommodations alternative; see below). Chail grew out of a romantic scandal, when Bhupinder Singh, the dashing Maharajah of Patiala, eloped with (or abducted, depending on who's telling the story) the daughter of Lord Kitchener. Predictably, the maharajah was forced to return the daughter and was banned from ever again entering the Raj's summer capital. Enraged, the raja combed the neighboring hills in search of a location from where he could literally look down on the town that had snubbed him. Chail was the answer to his ego-driven quest, and there he set about establishing his own "summer capital," building a lavish Georgian palace, as well as the highest cricket pitch in the world (2,444m/7,800 ft.). Sadly, the once-elegant palace has been converted into a poorly managed government-owned hotel.

For those looking for a place to stay nearby, **Banjara Camp** ⚔ (Reservations: 1A Hauz Khas Village, New Delhi 110 016; ⓒ **011/2686-1397;** fax 011/2685-5152; www.banjaracamps.com; Rs 2,600/$57 double) is the best lodging option for adventurous travelers in the vicinity of Shimla, sitting pretty in a clearing overlooking a wide, deep valley just outside Chail. A cluster of smart heavy-duty tents with attached bathrooms encircle a clearing from which, on a clear night, you can see Shimla's lights twinkling across the valley as well as Choor Chandini, the highest peak in this part of the Himalayas. Evenings are spent around a huge bonfire; *paneer*-on-a-toothpick and spicy chicken snacks are served before an Indian buffet is laid out. Days can be spent wandering deep into the forest, where you may even chance upon some rare Himalayan fauna or take an introductory rappelling (abseiling) and rock-climbing lesson.

WHERE TO STAY & DINE

A destination in its own right, the Oberoi's **Wildflower Hall** is by far your best option, but if the rates exceed your budget, nothing can beat the homey Raj-era experience of **Chapslee,** run by the aristocratic Kapurthalas. If for some reason none of the recommendations below suit you, you could try **Clarke's,** a small, modest, Oberoi-owned hotel with dull but perfectly comfortable accommodations. The blue-and-white Tudor exterior is its best asset, though the dining room also has a good reputation (ⓒ **0177/285-1010;** clarkes@sancharnet.in). Alternatively, **Springfields,** a popular Bollywood film location, is a peaceful but slightly tattered alternative to Shimla's main center, with unobstructed mountain views; the better rooms (nos. 1, 5, and 6) have great charm—high ceilings, wooden floorboards, fireplace, large double beds, and generous bathrooms with huge shower areas (ⓒ **0177/282-1297** or -1298; www.ushashriramhotels.com; doubles Rs 3,000–Rs 4,600/$65–$100).

Finally, **high tea** at Wildflower Hall is legendary—sample the local infusions along with traditional Irish tea brack bread—a baked reminder of the Raj, speckled with raisins and sultanas, steeped in Darjeeling tea, and served with unsalted butter and lemon curd.

The Cecil ⭐⭐⭐   Originally built as a private residence back in 1884, the Cecil has hosted the likes of Mahatma Gandhi and continues to draw political figures and noted celebrities. It was rebuilt in the Gothic style of Shimla's most elegant Raj monuments, and the interiors are luxuriously turned out, with plenty of wood paneling, leather, and opulent furniture. Guest rooms are sumptuous and tasteful, with wooden flooring, rich fabrics, and considerable attention to detail; each has a dressing room and a large bathroom with separate tub and shower.

Opt for one of the south-facing rooms (nos. 411–415 are best) with spectacular views of the Shimla Valley foothills; avoid the rooms in the older "Tudor Block," which feels a little claustrophobic and removed from the atmosphere of the main hotel. Facilities include a wonderful spa with a heated pool and a complete range of treatments to add a bit of decadence to your Himalayan sojourn. This is a less intimate, personal experience than Chapslee, but it will suit those who prefer the anonymity of luxury hotels.

Chaura Maidan, Shimla 171 004. ℂ **0177/280-4848.** Fax 0177/281-1024. www.oberoihotels.com. Reservations in New Delhi: ℂ 011/2436-3030. 79 units. $133–$142 double; $24 extra bed. AE, DC, MC, V. **Amenities:** Restaurant; lounge bar; garden lounge; indoor pool; health center (with spa and Thai massage); activity center with billiards; children's activity center; 24-hr. room service; laundry; library. *In room:* A/C, TV, DVD player.

Chapslee ★★ *(Value* On the northeastern spur of the Shimla range, this charming home is the most authentically old-world lodging in town. Owned and lovingly managed by Ratanjit "Reggie" Singh, the regal grandson of Rajah Charanjit Singh of Kapurthala, who bought the estate in 1938, Chapslee remains the quintessential creaky-floorboards Shimla homestead, its Raj-era aura hardly dented by modern conveniences or the slightly fraying Art Deco wallpaper. Originally built in 1835 as the summer residence of a British family, the house received an Edwardian face-lift in 1896 with teak paneling (part of the same consignment used for the Viceregal Lodge), wood parquet floors, and a dramatic staircase; its current incarnation was undertaken when it became the summer residence of the Kapurthala royals. Be sure to request either of the two upstairs suites; the original master bedroom affords lovely valley views, a massive brass four-poster bed, and delicate ornamentation, as well as a vast bathroom with a raised tub, an enormous shower, a bidet, and its own fireplace. Chapslee's obvious aesthetic pleasures are a good match for the fairy-tale view of Shimla at twilight; with whiskey in hand, you can watch the city's lights come on from the garden terrace. Chapslee's excellent kitchen prepares dishes influenced by the British, as well as delectable tandoori chicken and mouthwatering *shami* kebabs.

Chapslee, Shimla 171 001. ℂ **0177/280-2542.** Fax 0177/265-8663. www.chapslee.com. 6 units. Doubles: Rs 5,500–Rs 7,500 ($121–$164); inclusive of all meals, taxes, and service charges in lieu of tips; Rs 500 ($11) winter surcharge. MC, V. **Amenities:** Dining room; bed tea and packed lunches; tennis court; croquet lawn; various drawing rooms.

Wildflower Hall ★★★ *(Kids* Smack-dab in the middle of magnificent deodar cedar forests, atop its own hill a thousand feet above Shimla, surrounded by swirling mist and snowy peaks, this inspired remake of the fire-gutted mountain retreat of Lord Kitchener is the ideal setting for a beautifully eerie alpine fantasy. Affording showstopper views of some of the most spectacularly scenic mountains and valleys in India, this opulent yet surprisingly unpretentious Himalayan resort has all the seductive charms of a luxury boutique hotel, with top-notch facilities and fine service. It's also dressed to perfection: stately architecture, tasteful reproduction furniture, and carefully selected artworks and objets d'art. Guest rooms are well-appointed and spacious, with wood paneling, teak floors, walk-in closets, and exquisite bathrooms—valley-view premium rooms are excellent (nos. 101, 201, and 301 are most prized). Deluxe rooms have the added benefit of private balconies. Besides two outstanding restaurants, there's a gorgeous children's diner fitted with unbreakable everything (including a pizza oven, fairground-style popcorn machine, and oodles of soft toys) and its own movie screen. But the hotel's *pièce de résistance* is the magnificent spa, which offers an impressive range of services (including practically any massage you can imagine: Balinese, Thai, Swedish, Ayurvedic, or even a spot of aromatherapy). For absolute hedonists, there are even private spa suites for couples looking to have a proper pampering.

Mashobra, Chharabara, Shimla 171 012. © 0177/248-0808 or 0177/264-8585. Fax 0177/264-8686. www. oberoihotels.com. reservations@wildflowerhall.com. 85 units. Doubles: $275–$300; $520 suite; $750 Lord Kitchener suite. AE, MC, V. **Amenities:** 2 restaurants; children's restaurant; bar; tennis court; heated indoor pool; spa with gym, sauna, steam, Jacuzzi, and massage facilities, separate spa pavilion, and 2 private spa suites; outdoor Jacuzzi; horses and horse trail; trekking; bird-watching; butterfly-watching; river-rafting; foreign exchange; travel arrangements; car hire; helicopter transfers. *In room:* A/C, TV, dataport, DVD player, minibar, tea- and coffee-making facilities, electronic safe, butler.

SHOPPING

The cool nip in the evening air may well have you stocking up on colorful Kinnauri shawls, mufflers, and caps; Pangwali blankets from Chamba; and multi-colored hand-knitted woolen socks from Lahaul. The best place to shop for these items and more is **Himachal Emporium** (3, The Mall; © **0177/280-1234;** Mon–Sun 10am–7:30pm summer, 10am–7pm winter; closed 1–2:30pm). Try to speak to Mr. Thakur, who has worked here for over a quarter of a century and who is likely to devote some serious time to discussing the quality of rabbit-wool Kullu shawls, Pashminas, Kangra-school miniature paintings, or Buddhist *thangkas* (banners) from Kinnaur and Lahaul-Spiti.

4 Exploring Kinnaur & Spiti ✺✺✺

The arid, dust-covered, snowcapped slopes in the Indo-Tibetan regions of Kinnaur, Spiti, and Lahaul are the stuff adventurers' dreams are made of, offering sublime mountainscapes, twisting roads, and fascinating Tibetan Buddhist communities with atmospheric *gompas* (monasteries). Negotiating the rough, sandy, drop-off ledges of the **Hindustan-Tibet Road** (bizarrely enough, known as National Highway 22) is an action-packed art in itself. The impossible road is made all the more unnerving when buses, trucks, and jeeps headed in the opposite direction seem to appear out of nowhere, and landslides frequently disrupt routes entirely. Although the spectacular scenery is undoubtedly the highlight of any trip through Kinnaur and Spiti, there are also some marvelous monuments, including some of the world's most intriguing Buddhist complexes (such as the World Heritage Site of **Tabo Monastery** in Spiti), as well as high-altitude villages that seem to cling to the sides of mountains or balance on the edges of sharp cliffs.

ESSENTIALS

VISITOR INFORMATION   Pick up information from the **tourism office in Shimla** (or Manali if you're doing the trip in reverse), and make detailed inquiries regarding accessibility and weather developments. Ajay Sud, an ex-army captain and adventurer who runs the **Banjara Camp** near Sangla (among others, including one near Chail; see above) is one of the best sources of information, tips, and assistance in Kinnaur. He's also a very experienced trekker and can give great advice and suggestions for treks throughout the Himalayas (© **011/2686-1397;** www.banjaracamps.com).

GETTING AROUND   Ultra-budget-conscious travelers undertake the journey in state buses that rely on luck as much as faith to reach their destination, while born-to-be-wild adventurers do it on the back of a motorbike. We highly recommend you rent a jeep and driver—the heftier the jeep (a sturdy TATA is your best bet), the better your chances of actually enjoying the adventure. Most of the villages can be explored on foot, and the region lends itself to trekking (see "Staying Active," earlier in this chapter). For one-stop shopping, we highly recommend you utilize the services of Banjara Camp (see "Staying Active," earlier in this chapter), which offers most of the best lodging options and can arrange your entire jeep safari.

INNER LINE PERMITS Foreigners may not travel through the zone closest to the Tibetan border without first obtaining an **Inner Line Permit** from one of several government offices in Himachal. It's a fairly easy, if laborious and frustrating, process (it can take up to a day); you will need your passport, three passport-size photographs, and two copies of both the main page of your passport and your visa, before heading for the SDM (sub-divisional magistrate) office where you complete an application form. The best place to apply is Recong Peo—the SDM's office is located in the Deputy Commissioner's Building near the town's bus stand, next door to the Hotel Snowview. One way of dealing with the slow pace is to apply and then collect your papers the following day after overnighting in beautiful Kalpa nearby. It's a good idea to phone ahead to ensure that the **SDM office** (② **01786/22253**) is open on the day you plan to apply.

THE JOURNEY

Heading east out of Shimla, National Highway 22 takes you to **Narkanda** (2,708m/8,600 ft.), a ski resort where you can take in excellent views, and through the commercial town of **Rampur,** a former princely capital. The road then descends towards the raging Sutlej River, following its contours until you come upon the dusty village of **Jeori.** From here, a twisting, hairpin-heavy climb leads up to the charming village of **Sarahan** (2,165m/7,000 ft., 6 hr. from Shimla), which enjoys spectacular views of the snowcapped peaks across the river. Trapped in time, Sarahan is the site of the famous pagoda-style **Bhimakali Temple** 🏛🏛🏛. You'll have to overnight in Sarahan at the government-run **Hotel Shrikhand** (② **01782/74234;** www.hptdc.nic.in); although it's poorly maintained, it's the only hotel in town, the setting is out-of-this-world, rates are low (from Rs 600/$13), and you'll enjoy incredible views from your room. For the best room deal, book "half the cottage" (Rs 1,000/$22), which gets you a spacious, high-ceilinged room in a separate block with a fireplace, television, and an enclosed porch/sitting room. The hotel has a small bar and a restaurant.

The next morning, follow the same road back down to Jeori. At Karchham (Baspa Junction), you'll take a sharp U-turn and follow the steep dirt tracks of the **Sangla Valley** 🏛🏛🏛, through which the raging Baspa River flows. You won't find any flashy accommodations, but the comfortable **Banjara Camp,** 8km (5 miles) beyond, is an excellent place to spend a night or two, and serves as the perfect base from which to explore the remote hamlet of **Chitkul** 🏛🏛 (3,450m/ 11,000 ft.). Banjara Camp (see "Staying Active," earlier in this chapter; Rs 3,300/$72 double, includes all meals and taxes) comprises 17 comfortable tents with attached toilets and bucket-wash facilities in an open meadow alongside the Baspa River, beneath towering Khargala Peak. Make use of the opportunity to pick Banjara-founder Ajay Sud's brain for details of the best treks in the area. A selection of tasty Indian and Tibetan-inspired dishes is prepared at mealtimes, but there's nothing stopping you from picking up some fresh fish from a local farm and asking the kitchen team to cook it for you.

From Sangla you will have to double back to National Highway 22 to continue east towards Kinnaur's main town of **Recong Peo** (2,670m/8500 ft.), where you must complete the paperwork for your Inner Line Permit, which will permit you to enter the zone closest to the Tibetan border. While waiting for the bureaucratic wheels to turn, you should spend the night in the village of **Kalpa** ⚘⚘ (2,960m/ 9,400 ft.), well worth a visit for its crisp, clear air and view across the valley of the majestic Kinner-Kailash massif; it's a 30-minute drive into the mountain above Recong. **Hotel Kinner Villa** (✆ **01786/26002;** from Rs 1,300/$28 double) is the best place to stay, with simple, clean, and comfortable accommodations. Room no. 201 has the most exquisite view; nos. 101, 104, 202, and 207 aren't bad either. When the hotel's quiet, you'll have to book meals in advance. Note, too, that Kalpa suffers from interminable power failures, so make sure the manager supplies you with candles.

Set out early the following day; once you pass the first Inner Line checkpoint at Jangi, you will notice dramatic changes in the landscape, as fir trees give way to rock and stone sloping up toward distant summits and down into the raging River Sutlej. The journey through Inner Line territory takes you past the off-limits turnoff for the 5,500m (17,600-ft.) high Shipki-La Pass, which heads into China. **Nako Lake** ⚘ and its village lie farther along; beyond the turnoff for Nako, the road attains its most sinister aspect as you enter the notorious section known as the Maling Slide, heavily punctuated with precipitous drops—it's an ideal place to strengthen your faith in the divine. Upon reaching the final Inner Line checkpost at Sumdo—some 115km (71 miles) from Recong Peo and 363km (225 miles) from Shimla—the road heads northwest into the alien landscapes of Spiti.

The Buddhist town of **Tabo** ⚘⚘⚘ (some 6 hr. from Recong) is the most frequented stop in Spiti, and for good reason (see "Top Attractions," below). We recommend you stay at Banjara Retreat (see "Banjara Camps & Retreats" under "Staying Active" above; doubles from Rs 2,600/$57). Architecturally, the building echoes Ladakhi style; simple, clean, comfortable en-suite guest rooms have small, private balconies. Ask for an upper-level room facing the monastery. Omperkash Thakur is not only an efficient manager, but something of a culinary wizard, so there's plenty of carefully prepared food available. Many visitors traveling on a tight budget stay right near the monastery in the **Millennium Monastic Guesthouse & Sarain** (✆ **01906/33333** or 01906/33315), run by the monks. It has simple guest rooms with attached bathrooms, all arranged around a peaceful central courtyard.

Not far from Tabo is the village of **Dhankar** ⚘⚘⚘, which hugs the side of a hill and offers breathtaking glimpses of the surrounding mountains and valley below—a visit to the precariously perched monastery makes for an excellent diversion. Visit Dhankar on your way from Tabo, and then continue on to the town of **Kaza.** As the administrative headquarters of Spiti, Kaza offers little by way of excitement, but unless you really want to spend an entire day on the road, it's a useful base from which to visit the beautiful fortress-like *gompa* of **Kee** ⚘⚘⚘ and the high-altitude village of **Kibber** ⚘⚘. Plan on spending the night here at **Kaza Retreat,** the new inn operated by the Banjara group (see "Visitor Information," above; doubles from Rs 2,600/$57). Guest rooms are simple but have attached Western bathrooms. If you're on a tighter budget, get a room at **Sakya's Abode** (✆ **01906/22256** or -22254; reservations: Solang Hotel, School Rd., Manali; ✆ 01902/25-1824; doubles start from around Rs 600/$13).

From Kaza, either head for Manali to catch your breath, or travel directly to Leh. North of Spiti is **Lahaul** ✦✦✦. Linked to the rest of Himachal by the Rohtang Pass, dotted with villages of flat-roofed houses, fluttering prayer flags, and whitewashed *chortens,* Lahaul is cut off from the world by heavy snow for 8 months of the year. This mountainous region attracts adventurers to its Buddhist monasteries, mountain passes, spectacular glaciers, and high-altitude lakes. Visitors traveling by road to Leh in Ladakh, farther north, pass through Lahaul.

TOP ATTRACTIONS

Bhimakali Temple ✦✦   Chanting and music blast from the temple loudspeakers very early each morning and again in the evenings, transforming Sarahan village into a place that literally resonates with spirituality. Combining Hindu and Buddhist architectural elements, the main section of the temple comprises two pagoda-style pitched slate-roof towers. Built from layers of interlaced stone and timber, the towers rise from a courtyard around which are living quarters and a small museum with a collection of weapons and other unusual ritual objects and relics. Had you visited the temple 200 years ago, you might have witnessed one of the annual human sacrifices that kept the gods satisfied; today, animals suffice. The tower on the right was damaged in an earthquake a century ago, and the presiding deity was relocated to the tower on the left. Climb the stairs to get to the main shrine with its family of idols. Bhimakali is the main deity, while Durga, Ganesha, and even Buddha are all in attendance. The priests don't speak English, but it's worth taking part in the small *puja* (prayer) ceremony, so bring your rupees. Morning and evening prayers are scheduled but don't always take place.

Sarahan village center. No shoes, cameras, leather, or weapons. Daily 7am–8pm.

Tabo ✦✦✦   With a population of only 715, this Buddhist settlement situated at 3,050m (9,760 ft.) elevation in lower Spiti is centered around its celebrated 2,000-year-old monastic complex, said to be the place where the present Dalai Lama will "retire." A serene village of flat-roofed houses topped by thatch packed with branches, mud, and grass, Tabo has as its focus its monastery—or "doctrinal enclave"—consisting of nine temple buildings, chambers for monks and nuns, 23 snow-white *chortens,* and piles of stones, each carved with scriptural inscriptions. The sanctity of this World Heritage Site is topped only by Tholing monastery in Tibet. Don't arrive expecting some cathedral-like masterpiece; Tabo Gompa is a rustic center that is more spiritually than architecturally engaging. A high mud wall surrounds the compound, and the pale mud-covered low-rise monastery buildings suggest nothing of the exquisite wall paintings and stucco statues within. You'll need a torch to properly appreciate many of the frescoes and other artworks that adorn the various dark, ancient spaces; only narrow shafts of natural light from small skylights illuminate the frescoed walls, saturated with rich colors and an incongruous variety of scenes. There's a distinctly surreal, often nightmarish quality to the work—gruesome torture scenes compete with images of meditative contemplation and spiritual discovery.

At the core of the complex is the **Temple of Enlightened Gods (gTsug Lha-khang),** which includes the **Assembly Hall** (or *du-khang*) where there's a 2m (6-ft.) high white stucco image of Vairocana, one of the five spiritual sons of the primordial, self-creative Buddha, or Adibuddha. Below this are two images of the great translator and teacher Rin-Chan-Sang-Po, who is believed to have founded Tabo in A.D. 996. Thirty-three other life-size stucco deities surrounded by stylized flaming circles are bracketed along the walls. Directly behind the assembly hall is the **sanctum,** with five bodhisattvas of the Good Age and beautifully rendered

Indian-style frescoes depicting the life of the Buddha. Monks are initiated in the smaller **Mystic Mandala Temple (dKyil-hKhor-khang),** situated behind the main temples. At the northern edge of the complex is the **Temple of Drompton (Brom-ston Lha-khang),** entered via a small portico and long passage. Only enter the **Mahakala Vajra-bhairava Temple (Gon-Khang)** once you've performed a protective meditation—it's filled with fierce deities that inspire its nickname, "the temple of horrors." Just outside the complex are several contemporary monastic buildings, including an atmospheric guesthouse run by the monks. Above Tabo, across the highway, a group of caves on a sheer cliff-face was once used as monastic dwellings.

365km (226 miles) from Shimla, 295km (183 miles) from Kullu, 47km (29 miles) from Kaza.

Dhankar Monastery ★★★   *Dhankar* means "fort," and a glimpse of this monastery precariously perched on a hill jutting against a sharp mountainside certainly suggests its usefulness as a protective stronghold. Once the castle of the Nono, the ruler of Spiti, the building typifies the traditional architecture of the town. As if wedged between massive craggy outcrops, the rather dirty white-washed flat-topped structures create a dramatic effect against stark fingers of hard rock. Entry to the temple is rather nerve-wracking; access steps and upper-most rooftops drop away to perilously steep rocky slopes. Today, Dhankar is a repository of Bhoti-scripted Buddhist scriptures. You can visit this hilltop monastery as an excursion from Tabo, or en route to your next destination. It makes a sublime detour because it attracts considerably fewer visitors than relatively busy Tabo, and although the monastery interiors are rather small, the astonishing location and wonderful views more than make up for this.

Dhankhar Tashi Choling Monastery, Spiti. Rs 25 (50¢) entry.

Kibber & Ki Gompa ★★★   Just north of Kaza, a road veers off the main highway and zigzags its way up a steep mountainside. At the end of this stretch is Kibber, one of the world's highest inhabited villages, perched on a rocky spur at an altitude of 4,205m (13,450 ft.). Kibber enjoys a reputation as the highest permanent settlement with electricity and accessibility by motor road. Surrounded by limestone rocks and cliffs, the remote and isolated village offers stunning views of the barren valley below. There's even a handful of guesthouses should you require accommodations. Between Kibber and Kaza is Spiti's largest monastery, Ki Gompa, which is almost a thousand years old. Home to a large community of lamas, Ki Gompa is well accustomed to receiving visitors; the monk on duty will brew you a welcoming cup of tea and show you around the different prayer rooms and assembly halls filled with holy relics. The most exciting time to visit is late June or early July, when a festival involving *chaam* dancing and the ceremonial burning of butter sculptures draws large numbers of pilgrims.

Ki Gompa is 12km (7½ miles) northwest of Kaza. Kibber is 4km (2½ miles) farther.

5 The Valley of the Gods: Central Himachal

Central Himachal's fertile valleys—centered around the towns of Mandi, Kullu, and Manali—are watered by the Beas River, and are famous for a variety of fruits, excellent treks, and what is considered—by the stoned hippies of Manali, at least—the finest marijuana in the world.

The drive from Shimla to Manali—starting point for the spectacular road journey to Leh and a number of adventure activities—is around 280km (174 miles) and can be done in a day. The route is scenic, especially in July and August, when the heavy monsoon rains cause the river to swell and waterfalls to cascade spectacularly. Time allowing, it's a good idea to spend the night en route in the scruffy town of Mandi, where you can use the atmospheric Raj Mahal palace hotel as a base for a visit to the nearby hill hamlet of **Rewalsar** 𝕣, a fascinating confluence of Buddhist, Sikh, and Hindu spirituality, centered around a small black lake teeming with fish (supposedly holy) and beautifully reflecting the soaring mountain ranges above. Sacred to all three religions, the lake's banks sport lively Buddhist *gompas,* an important Sikh *gurudwara* (place of worship), and a Hindu temple.

Farther north (about 70km/43 miles), in the heart of the Valley of the Gods, is the unattractive town of **Kullu,** famous for its sheer volume of Hindu temples and the Dussehra Festival (Sept–Oct), which attracts substantial crowds and hundreds of valley gods who arrive to take part in the annual festivities: 9 days of jubilant processions, music, dancing, and markets. Unless you stop specifically to catch any festival action or want to visit the "first and biggest angora farm in Asia," there's no real reason to linger in Kullu.

Bhuntar, not too far south of Kullu, is the turnoff point for drives to Jari, Kasol, and the therapeutic hot springs of **Manikaran,** which is the main jumping-off point for a variety of treks to less-visited villages. **Khirganga,** farther east, is the site of even more thermal water springs, while isolated **Malana,** to the north, is an anthropologist's dream and home of the world's top-rated *ganja,* the famous Malana Gold, according to a recent competition held in Amsterdam. Adventures to any of these remote areas should not be undertaken without the help of a recognized guide—not only is getting lost a strong possibility, but there have been reports of what are believed to be drug-related crimes, including the assault and "disappearance'" of travelers.

ESSENTIALS

GETTING THERE & AROUND   It's possible to avoid Shimla entirely by flying directly to **Bhuntar Airport** 10km (6¼ miles) south of Kullu. In Manali, taxis and auto-rickshaws charge ridiculously inflated rates that fluctuate seasonally and according to the whim of the near-militant local taxi union. If you've used a car and driver to get to Manali, you might consider retaining the service for any further travel, bearing in mind that a sturdy vehicle with off-road capabilities will be essential if you plan on touring Ladakh or the regions east of the Beas River.

VISITOR INFORMATION & TRAVEL AGENTS   For information about the Kullu and Parvati valleys, visit **Himachal Pradesh Tourism** (✆ 01902/22349) in Kullu, near the Maidan. In Manali, the **Tourist Information Centre** (The Mall, Manali; ✆ 01902/25-2175; Mon–Sat 10am–1pm and 1:30–5pm) can give you a pile of booklets on destinations throughout the state (most of these are available from the far friendlier office in Shimla). An ad-saturated tourist map of Manali is available for Rs 15 (30¢), and more detailed books and booklets are available for purchase. **Matkon Travels** (✆ 01902/25-3738, 98-1600-3738, or 98-1604-3738) can also help you with domestic flights and deluxe-bus bookings. Matkon works in conjunction with the **Himalayan Institute of Adventure Sports,** and offers sightseeing, trekking, rafting, paragliding, and skiing opportunities with reliable guides.

MANALI

Yes, it's set amid dense pine forests and shadowed by snowy peaks, but Manali's reputation as a spectacular Himalayan resort is much exaggerated. The primary

> (*Tips* **Avoid the Rush**
>
> The threat of war in the Kashmir has meant that Manali's popularity has soared in recent years. Visitors who once would have gone to Kashmir for the snow and possibility of skiing now swamp Manali during the Indian high season, which stretches from April until the rains hit in early July, and then again from September to November. Manali's charms have been all but eroded by this perverse tourist explosion, which sets off a soulless cash-rally that seems to involve every proprietor, merchant, and taxi-tour operator in town; hotel tariffs also soar during this period. *Bottom line:* Try to avoid this usually peaceful town during these months.

reason to be here is to set off for Leh in Ladakh, a 2-day drive away, or to participate in the many treks or adventure sports, including heli-skiing.

Manali comprises several neighborhoods, each with a distinct personality. North of the Manalsu Nala River is **Old Manali,** with its historic stone buildings; to the west is the pleasant village of **Dhungri;** while messy **Model Town** is a motley collection of concrete buildings tucked behind the main bazaar area, concentrated around The Mall. East of the Beas River, a few kilometers north of Manali is **Vashisht,** a village known for its hot springs and laid-back atmosphere. Unfortunately, Vashisht has lost much of its charm thanks to an influx of long-stay budget tourists; a dunk in the communal hot-water bath of the local temple is hardly reason enough to visit.

The most peaceful area is **Dhungri Village** (around 2km/1¼ miles from the bazaar), where you can stroll through deodar forests or visit a 450-year-old temple where animal sacrifice is still practiced. On the outskirts of the neighborhood, the multi-tiered wooden pagoda-style **Hadimba Devi Temple** ⚘, built in 1553, is Manali's oldest and most interesting shrine, dedicated to the demon goddess Hadimba (an incarnation of Kali). Look around for the sheltered sacrificial stone used for blood rituals during important ceremonies; the central hollow is where the blood from a slain buffalo or goat drains into Hadimba's mouth.

Another good walk takes you through Old Manali (center of cheap backpackers' accommodations), the temple dedicated to Manu, and beyond to silent hillside paths where you'll encounter village women passing the day over idle gossip while their men unhurriedly herd goats and cows toward greener pastures at higher altitudes. Most visitors pay a visit to Manali's two rather modern Buddhist *gompas* in the town's Tibetan quarter south of the bazaar. **Gadhan Thekchhokling gompa** was built in 1969, and is recognizable by its yellow, pagoda-style roof; memorial notices outside draw attention to the extermination of Tibetans in China.

WHERE TO STAY
MANDI & KULLU

If you're traveling by road from Shimla to either Manali or Dharamsala, it's good idea to take a break en route. In Mandi, 70km (43 miles) south of Kullu, the **Raj Mahal** (© **01905/22401** or 01905/23434; fax 01905/23511), a creaky-floorboards "palace," is recommended for its serious time-warp character. Book one of the four enormous Royal Suites (Rs 1,500/$33 double), which showcase an assortment of kitsch furnishings and objets d'art (in one room a stuffed leopard grimaces on a table with rifles for legs!). Generally, the service at Raj Mahal is quite awful, and the ancient plumbing acts up at times, but as a place to lay your head for a night and as a base for visiting nearby Rewalsar, it's adequate. If you're after a more typical (and expensive) hotel experience, carry on to **Apple Valley Resort,** just short of Kullu town. Set on the banks of the Beas River, the luridly decorated country-style cabins with ivy-covered walls and stone chimneys will run you Rs 1,500 to Rs 2,200 ($33–$48) double; book nos. 204, 205, or 206 for the best views. Rates increase by around $10 during the high season (mid-Apr through June and mid-Sept through mid-Jan).

MANALI

For the most atmospheric room in town, you're best off in an original lodge apartment at Johnson's Lodge or the privacy of Leela's Huts; alternatively, stay at **Span Resorts** for its riverside location (see below for reviews of all). Manali's **Private Hoteliers' Information Centre** (The Mall, near the taxi stand) is well established and can assist you in finding suitably priced accommodations if you haven't pre-booked. During the busy season (mid-Apr to early July) you will have difficulty finding any upmarket guest room in Manali at all.

Johnson's Lodge ✦ This recently expanded "lodge," set among lovely lawns, was the first inhabited property in New Manali, and it offers a choice of vintage or brand-new accommodations not too far from the thick of things. Now run by Piya, the cosmopolitan granddaughter of the man who built the original stone lodge apartments, Johnson's may be relatively close to the bazaar, but it remains a tranquil spot with lovely views. If you opt for one of the newly constructed slate, stone, and wood guest rooms in the upper complex, ask for a corner unit—these are larger and have extra windows from which to enjoy the mountain scenes. If you'd prefer an old-fashioned experience, the huge ivy-covered stone-walled balconied apartments in the original building are an atmospheric curiosity, with aging furnishings, original fittings, and loads of space. Wood-beam ceilings, screened windows, and small, homey kitchens add to the ambience. Ask for cottage no. 2, which is the neatest and quietest (and even has a TV). A pleasant, cafe-style restaurant offers all-day dining.

Circuit House Rd., Manali 175 131. ✆ **01902/25-3023** or 01902/25-3764. Fax 01902/24-5123. 18 units. Original apts (4 persons) Rs 3,000–Rs 3,500 ($65–$76) in season (May 15–July 15); 50% discount off season. No credit cards. **Amenities:** Restaurant; laundry; doctor-on-call. *In room:* Some with TV.

Leela Huts ✦ *Kids* Popular with diplomats in need of a real break, this collection of five stone cottages is ideal if you're traveling with children or a group of friends. Set in a large garden of potted plants, fruit trees, and neatly hedged pathways, these rustic, comfortable, and rather large holiday cabins offer a pleasant respite from Manali's bustle, even during the height of the domestic tourist season. Because it's owned and run by a friendly local family, you are assured of friendly, helpful assistance throughout your stay. When the lights go down, as they tend to throughout Himachal, someone soon arrives to tend to your gas lanterns. Although the cottages are self-catering, you have the option of investing in a "cook-on-request" to tend to your culinary desires.

Sunshine Orchards, Club House Rd., Manali 175 131. ✆ **01902/25-2464.** Fax 01902/25-5035. leelahuts@ rediffmail.com. 5 units. 3 2-bedroom cottages at Rs 4,500 ($98) in season, Rs 3,500 ($76) July 1–Sept 15; 2 2-bedroom cottages at Rs 3,500 ($76) in season; Rs 2,500 ($55) July–Sept 15. Non credit cards. **Amenities:** Meals, food, or cook on request; badminton; children's play area; tour and taxi arrangements; in-house doctor. *In room:* TV, kitchenette, fridge, gas cooker, fireplace.

Snowcrest Manor This modest hotel has the best views in town. Perched at the end of a very steep climb, some distance above the sprawling bazaar, Snowcrest is a small hotel built on a slope and offering unimpeded views. Guest rooms are simply furnished and showing their age somewhat, but they're clean and all you'll need for a night or two in this small town. Besides, the panoramic mountain views and small-town hospitality more than make up for any discomfort, and the staff will happily assist with any travel or sightseeing arrangements. Ask for an upper-level deluxe room (the higher you go, the better the views), keep the floral-patterned curtains wide open, and enjoy the modest comforts of this unassuming but well-run inn.

Beyond Log Huts, Manali 175 131. ✆ **01902/25-3351.** Fax 01902/25-3188. Reservations in Delhi ✆ 011/2552-0914 or -0915. www.ushashriramhotels.com/snowcrest.htm. 32 units. Doubles: Rs 1,900 ($42) standard; Rs 2,950 ($64) deluxe; Rs 3,600 ($78) 3-person suite; Rs 500 ($11) extra bed. AE, DC, MC, V. **Amenities:** Restaurant; bar-cum-discotheque; fitness center; travel, tours, sightseeing; adventure activities; business facilities; room service (6am–midnight); laundry; doctor-on-call. In room: A/C, TV.

Span Resorts ⭐ A riverside location, 15km (9 miles) from the center of Manali, makes this resort a peaceful respite from the crowds, enhanced by the generous range of amenities and outdoor activities on offer. Accommodations are in stone-and-wood cottages shaped like stars and spread around well-maintained grounds; they're comfortable and offer a fair degree of privacy. Furnishings are a little disappointing (linoleum seems de rigueur) and there isn't a heck of a lot of space, but each cottage has a fireplace and a covered porch from which to appreciate the relaxed setting and mountain views. There is plenty to keep you occupied during the snowy season, including the best-stocked bar in the state.

Kullu-Manali Hwy., P.O. Katrain 175 129. ✆ **01902/40138** or 01902/40538. Fax 01902/40140. www.span resorts.com. spanres@del3.vsnl.net.in. Reservations: Vijaya (1st Floor), 17 Barakhamba Rd., New Delhi 110 001. ✆ 011/2331-1434. Fax 011/2335-3148. 25 units. Doubles: Rs 5,000 ($110); Rs 625 ($14) children ages 6–12; Rs 1,500 ($33) extra bed. 10% tax. Rates include all meals. DC, MC, V. **Amenities:** Restaurant; bar; tennis; basketball; gym; darts; croquet; card room; table tennis; mini golf; children's park; billiards; badminton; travel assistance, taxis, tours, sightseeing; fishing, river rafting, skiing, horseback riding, trekking, and paragliding by arrangement; 24-hr. room service; laundry; doctor-on-call. In room: A/C, TV, minibar.

WHERE TO DINE

With Manali's tourism boom has come a flood of eating establishments, many of which indulge in unchecked fly-by-night copycat techniques; be sure to check details beyond the name of whichever establishment you choose. Bear in mind that none take credit cards, and most stay open from 9am to 11pm; call to confirm hours.

The best Indian restaurant, with typical Himachali cuisine, is **Mayur** (✆ **01902/52316;** Rs 30–Rs 170/60¢–$1.50). Kangra Valley–born Rajesh Sud has been in the restaurant business since 1970 and opened this Manali institution back in 1978. Fresh, locally caught wild trout, prepared in the tandoor oven with a subtle blend of yogurt and aromatic spices, is the highlight—ask for tandoori trout *machhali*. A good alternative is **Khyber** (✆ **01902/53272;** Rs 55–Rs 250/$1.10–$5.35), where longtime restaurateur Kawaljeet (who's been running the popular nearby **Sher-e-Punjab** *dhaba* since 1972) serves up excellent Punjabi-style chicken, doused with exotic spices and cooked to perfection. With its first-story views over The Mall, Khyber's window tables are great for midafternoon people-watching—particularly when wet weather forces you indoors. For the best Tibetan cuisine, head for **Mount View** (✆ **01902/53617;** Rs 30–Rs 230/60¢–$5), a laid-back diner where you can enjoy the best *momos* (dumplings) in town (try the ones with potato spinach filling). Any of the piping-hot Tibetan broths will pick you up when the cold gets too much, and there's an excellent range of vegetarian Chinese dishes. For Italian (including good coffee), **Il Forno,** housed in a century-old house in Dunghri, is your most authentic option. Verona-born Paolo still speaks passionately about the days before Manali became a bustling tourist center, and the excellent, freshly made pastas (ask if the ravioli is available) and authentic pizzas are prepared by Paolo himself (no phone; Rs 75–Rs 175/$1.50–$3.70). **Johnson's Café** (Johnson's Lodge, The Mall; ✆ **01902/45292;** Rs 30–Rs 230/60¢–$5) is a cozy, informal venue that enjoys a lively atmosphere and has garden seating. It also has fresh trout—locally caught—on the menu, and it's a fine place to have coffee and breakfast while you plan the day's trek.

6 Exploring Dharamsala & the Kangra Valley

Tenzin Gyatso, the 14th Dalai Lama, chose Dharamsala as the capital-in-exile of the Tibetan people after fleeing Chinese oppression in 1959, and whether it's the endless spinning of Buddhist prayer wheels or simply the divine presence of the Dalai Lama, the Tibetan enclave at Dharamsala draws seekers of spiritual enlightenment from all over the world.

Admittedly, a visit to Everyman's spiritual center of the universe seems like the ultimate New Age cliché, but the town and its environs have much more to recommend them than the fervent chanting of *Om mani padme hum* ("Hail to jewel in the lotus"). The natural beauty of the surrounding mountains and mist-soaked valleys compares favorably with that of any of Himachal's best-loved resort towns, and for those not single-mindedly wrapped up in a quest for spiritual fine-tuning with Buddhist lectures and meditation courses, this is an ideal base for walks and treks into the Dhauladhar range. It's also a good place to simply experience a toned-down India at a more leisurely pace.

The hillside town stretches along a spur of the Dhauladhar Mountain range and is divided into two very distinct parts—**Lower Dharamsala** and **McLeod Ganj.** Only the latter is worth considering as a place to stay and explore; here you will encounter brightly robed Buddhist monks with umbrellas and Doc Marten boots, traditionally attired Tibetan women reciting holy mantras, and spiritual tourists somewhat desperately in search of enlightenment. A former British hill station rocked by an earthquake in the early 1900s, McLeod Ganj today harbors several institutes and organizations dedicated to raising funds for the Tibetan people and promoting and preserving Buddhist culture. Among

Enlightenment or Exploitation?

McLeod Ganj is probably the last place you'd expect to encounter any social tension, but if you want to get involved in the local politics, chat up the locals about the refugee situation. Thanks largely to the global popularity of the Dalai Lama and his ability to raise international interest—and massive funding—for the Tibetan cause, the refugees in Dharamsala have managed to maintain their culture, and Tibetans argue that their people work harder and deserve the success they've achieved in the tourist-friendly enclave. On the other hand, Indians bemoan the internationally sponsored wealth that has accumulated around the disenfranchised Tibetans, and some take issue with Tibetan endeavors to rigorously preserve and promote their distinctive culture. It's a fascinating debate, one well worth discussing with the locals.

these is the Government-in-Exile's administration complex, or *Gangchen Kyishong,* where you'll find the fascinating **Library of Tibetan Works and Archives.**

North of Dharamsala are spectacular mountain-hugging drives to the remote towns of Dalhousie and Chamba, while farther south you can visit the charming heritage village of **Pragpur** ★★★ and explore the tea-covered valleys around the historical **Taragarh Palace Hotel** ★★, not far from the town of Palampur.

ESSENTIALS

VISITOR INFORMATION There's a **Tourist Information Office** (daily 10am–1:30pm and 2–5pm) in McLeod Ganj, but you'll be hard-pressed to squeeze anything worthwhile out of the lackluster staff; you'd do better to make enquiries at your hotel. ***CONTACT*** is a free monthly newsletter distributed in and around McLeod Ganj. Although its primary aim is to promote Buddhist issues, it also carries up-to-date information and advertisements regarding cultural events and activities likely to be of interest to foreign visitors. If you are here for massage, meditation, alternative healing, yoga, or Tibetan cooking classes, this publication will point you in the right direction. Also visit **www.contactmag.org** or **www.dharamsalanet.com**.

GETTING THERE & AROUND It's possible to drive from Shimla or Chandigarh to Dharamsala, but there are two great overnight options along the way—choose between **Taragarh Palace,** outside Palampur, or the **Judge's Court,** in Pragpur (see below). The most pleasant way to get to the Kangra Valley directly from Delhi is by train (the drive is almost 12 hr. long). The overnight Panthankot Express from Delhi allows you to rest up before hiring a car for the scenic 3-hour road trip from Panthankot to Dharamsala (80km/50 miles). At press time, flights to Kangra's Gaggal Airport, 15km (9 miles) from Dharamsala, had been suspended until further notice. In Dharamsala, you will find it easy to get either a taxi or auto-rickshaw. (Auto-rickshaws are incredibly impractical, however, because of the engine-killing gradient of the town.) The taxi union is very strong, so if you'd like to avoid the bureaucracy, contact **Bikay,** a private operator who is reliable and can offer a good deal. He's also a useful contact if you are interested in longer day trips. Contact him through his brother Sanjey (✆ **01892/23772** or 01892/25262), or after hours at home (✆ 01892/24976). **Ways Tours & Travels** (Temple Rd., McLeod Ganj; ✆ **01892/21910,** 01892/21355, or 01892/21988; waystour@vsnl.net) can help with all your travel arrangements and can organize individually packaged tours throughout the region. You can also contact them in New Delhi, at House no. 18, New Tibetan Camp, Majnu-Ka-Tilla; call ✆ **011/2381-3254** or 98-1128-9552.

THE TOP ATTRACTIONS

Thekchen Chöling Temple Complex ★★ Life in McLeod Ganj revolves around this Buddhist temple complex, linked to the off-limits private residence of the Dalai Lama. A good example of Buddhism's spiritual and artistic traditions, the complex comprises the **Namgyal Monastery** and the **Tsuglagkhang Temple,** both worth a visit if you're keen to get a sense of active lamastic practice. You'll often encounter monks debating in the courtyard or meditatively preparing colorful sand *mandalas,* ritual diagrams that symbolize the universe and are used in the ritual of spiritual empowerment known as the *kalachakra* ceremony, after which the meticulous designs are destroyed. The *gompa* houses various cultural relics brought from Lhasa during the Cultural Revolution, including a 1,500-year-old idol of Guru Padmasambhav, and a life-size image of

Avalokiteshvara, of whom the Dalai Lama is believed to be an incarnation. Public appearances by the Dalai Lama occur from time to time; consult the local authorities for information. The complex courtyard is the venue for an all-day festival of traditional dance held in honor of His Holiness's birthday on July 6, although the Dalai Lama is not always in attendance on this auspicious day. It's worthwhile to take a break from the prayer wheels and settle in at the tiny, laid-back cafe in the temple complex (which serves primarily as a vocational training opportunity for young Tibetans) to try out the international vegetarian dishes ranging from Indonesian *gado-gado* to Cuban *arro a la cubana.* This is a great place for a cup of pure South Indian coffee or Tibetan herbal tea. Snag the window-side table for beautiful views over the valley below.

Temple Rd. To obtain clearance for a public audience with the Dalai Lama, it's necessary to apply, with your passport, at the Security Office on Bhagsu Rd.

The Tibet Museum 🏛 If you wish to learn more about the plight of the Tibetan people, then step into this sophisticated but rather depressing installation that provides a historical overview of the situation in Tibet. *A Long Look Homeward,* the main exhibition, consists of two parts. The downstairs display highlights the atrocities that have been carried out against millions of Tibetans during the Chinese occupation. Although events are detailed primarily through textual displays, the collection of data is emotionally challenging. Upstairs, the exhibition focuses more on Tibetan history. Particularly moving is the "testimony corner," where visitors can record the names of loved ones whose deaths are a result of the occupation. Lectures, presentations, and video screenings are presented in the small lecture hall; visit **www.thetibetmuseum.com** if you're interested in upcoming events.

Near the main temple and Namgyal Monastery Gate. Admission Rs 5 (1¢).Tues–Sun 10am–6pm.

Norbulingka Institute 🏛🏛🏛 If you're interested in getting a firsthand understanding of the techniques (and unbelievable patience) required to produce authentic Tibetan arts and crafts, the institute is a good starting point. Set in well-tended grounds some 40 minutes from Dharamsala, it comprises workshops, training centers, a temple, a guesthouse, a cafe, and a doll museum. You can contact the management in advance to organize a tour through the facilities, where you can witness the creation of colorful tantric *thangkas* (embroidered wall hangings), paintings, metalware, furniture, and traditional garments. Tibetan language lessons are also available for interested foreigners. The beautiful **Seat of Happiness Temple** 🏛🏛 features astounding murals, including impressions of all 14 Dalai Lamas, and 1,173 images of the Buddha, which decorate the 13m (44-ft.) high temple hall. The gilded copper Buddha Shakyamuni was crafted by Norbulingka's master statue-maker, Pemba Dorje, and is one of the largest of its kind outside Tibet; the arch behind the statue is decorated with sculpted clay images. Head for the richly ornamented temple rooftop for magnificent views of the surrounding landscape. The Institute's **Losel Doll Museum** 🏛🏛 features diorama-style displays of miniature figures (Tibetan dolls) in traditional costumes and historical regalia.

P.O. Sidhpur. ✆ **01892/46402** or 01892/46405. Fax 01892/46404. www.norbulingka.org.

WHERE TO STAY & DINE

The best place to stay is the Tibetan-run **Chonor House,** not least for its dining; if you have a yearning to live in a forest surrounded by nature's bounty, check out **Glenmoor Cottages** (both reviewed below). If you're looking for a real budget

---

The Dalai Lama Speaks Here & Richard Gere Slept There

Tenzin, from Nick's Italian Kitchen (above), is one of the best people to speak to if you're eager to organize an audience with His Holiness. A proud and committed follower of the Dalai Lama, he also organizes occasional talks on Tibet and Buddhism at the restaurant, and is overflowing with personal theories about the local community and the diplomatic situation with the Chinese government. Staunch Richard Gere fans traveling on a limited budget can try to get the Gere Suite of the **Kunga Guesthouse** upstairs from the restaurant; Richard was the first guest when it opened on January 24, 1996.

---

option, consider peaceful **Cheryton Cottage** (Jogibara Rd.; © **01892/21237** or 01892/21993; tcheryl_89@yahoo.com), where Alan and Cheryl Templeton rent out four rooms (Rs 350/$7.60 double) and an entire house (a steal at Rs 1,200/ $26). The rooms are spartan 1970s throwbacks dressed in outrageous colors (of the four units, the aptly named "Blue" and "Pink" have views).

As with many of the towns popular with tourists, McLeod Ganj is disproportionately restaurant-heavy, but the best by far is Chonor House, which specializes in Tibetan cuisine (see below). While Tibetan fare would appear to be the way to go, you'll pretty much find something for everyone—from falafels to focaccia, *momos* (dumplings) to tempura. There's even a nifty grub-'n'-pub style restaurant called **Mc'Llo** (at the top of Temple Rd.; © **01892/21280;** open 9am–late), which is not only an extremely popular hangout for travelers, but prides itself on having once entertained Pierce Brosnan. If you have a yen for Japanese, **Lung Ta,** an intimate diner with meat-free dishes from the land of the rising sun, includes a small floor-seating area with traditional low tables (Jogibara Rd.; © **01892/ 21379;** www.guchusum.org; Mon–Sat noon–8:30pm). Daily set meals feature a curious mix of Japanese vegetarian dishes; on a typical day, you may be offered *kisetsu yasai no agebitashi,* which includes stir-fried fresh seasonal vegetables, cabbage and boiled egg salad, miso salad, and rice.

For Italian, head for **Nick's Italian Kitchen** (in the Kungra Guesthouse, Bhagsu Rd., McLeodganj; © **0189/221-180;** Tues–Sun 11am–9pm), which is something of a local institution. Tenzin, whose father worked as security officer for the Dalai Lama from the age of 18, is—like His Holiness—a proponent of vegetarianism, and his kitchen therefore is strictly non-meat. Gnocchi, cannelloni, and ravioli are prepared fresh every morning, and the eggplant, spinach, and cheese lasagnas are star attractions, as is the aptly named "Pizza Everything."

At the immaculate Norbulingka Institute, **Norling Café** ★★ (© **01892/ 22664;** www.norbulingka.org; call for hours), is great for healthy, wholesome dishes that can be taken on the patio, where you're likely to spot paradise flycatchers darting among the lush vegetation—you can also pre-order meals through the guesthouse.

Chonor House ★★★ *(Value)*   One of the best reasons to spend any amount of time in Dharamsala is to sample each of the exquisitely decorated rooms that make up this charming Tibetan guesthouse at the toe-end of Mcleod Ganj, a stone's throw away from the main *gompa.* Each room is uniquely themed according to different aspects of Tibetan culture; the museum-standard murals created by different experts in conjunction with artists from the Norbulingka Institute (see above) neatly balance the beautifully crafted teak-and-rosewood furniture and hand-knotted carpets rendered by other Norbulingka teams. There are three categories of rooms, each offering different amenities: Some have balconies, some have tubs, and some (like the magnificent "Voyage at Sea" rooms) are simply enormous. "Nomad" features strikingly painted yaks, goats, and traveling tribespeople and also has a lovely balcony from which you have a direct view of the main *gompa*. The terrifically colorful Songsten Suite not only has a separate lounge and private balcony, but also its own shrinelike cabinet showcasing statues of the three great kings of Tibet. There's a neat, homey sitting room furnished with plush sofas and a combination of parquet wood flooring and thick rugs. Indeed, you need hardly step outside the front door to get a good taste of what Tibetan art and culture are all about—this is a treasure chest of style and meticulous attention to the details Westerners probably don't usually think about. Dharamsala's best guesthouse also offers its most impressive dining opportunity. The menu is a veritable encyclopedia of Tibetan dishes—which have a way of becoming quite addictive. Share a plate of *momos* to start—these butter dumplings are steamed to perfection and filled with tasty fresh white cheese. Or experiment with the excellent *bobi*, which allows you to build your own Tibetan spring rolls, a fun alternative to the greasy version popular in Chinese takeout joints. You can build all night, using thinly grilled bread wraps, seasoned glass noodles, mixed vegetables, tofu, and Basmati rice, or have the *bobi* as a starter, after which you can try the delicious fried *pishi* (wontons), deliciously seasoned *shabri* (vegetable balls), or steaming mutton-filled *shabalak* (bread pie). There's even a selection of scrumptious salads (try the cheese, carrot, apple, walnut, and spinach concoction).

Note: Tibetan hospitality at its very best can, of course, do nothing to stop the chorus of barking hounds that seems to be the typical prelude—or interruption—to a good night's sleep.

Thekchen Choling Rd., P.O. McLeod Ganj, Dharamsala 176 219. ✆ **01892/21077**, 01892/21468, or 01892/21006. Fax 01892/21468. www.norbulingka.org. 11 units. Doubles: Rs 1,900–Rs 2,200 ($42–$48); Rs 2,800 ($62) suite; Rs 550 ($12) extra bed. MC, V. **Amenities:** Restaurant; boutique; room service; laundry; TV room. *In room:* Heater, tea-making facility.

Glenmoor Cottages ☆☆ Located on a magnificent property in the midst of a hillside forest, 1km (.62 mile) beyond McLeod Ganj, Glenmoor comprises five private cottages situated around an original colonial manor house, Om Bhawan,

---

A Taste of Tibet

Confused by what's on offer in the Tibetan restaurants of the Indian Himalayan region? Here's a guide: *Gyathuk* is a traditional egg noodle soup, typically prepared with tofu and black-and-white mushrooms. *Thenthuk* is a broth made with handmade pasta. *Pishi* is another name for wontons, often served in a vegetable broth with Tibetan tofu. You'll find Tibetan tofu and dumplings swimming in your *mothuk*, another traditional Tibetan broth. *Gutse rethuk* is a broth made with fresh radish, and it usually also comes with dumplings. *Tseybaklab* is the Tibetan version of a pie, typically accompanied by broth. *Momos* are Tibetan butter dumplings, filled with cheese, vegetables, or meat. *Shabri* are seasoned vegetable balls. *Bobi* are Tibetan spring rolls, filled with glass noodles, tofu, and mixed vegetables. Most Tibetan dishes can be served with vegetables, chicken, mutton, or even pork. *Shabalak* are mutton bread pies, served with broth.

built by a Scotsman in the early 20th century. Dharamsala's most remote and peaceful lodging (you feel as if you're a thousand miles from anything), Glenmoor is owned and run by Ajai Singh, whose family bought the lovely, tree-covered property 6 decades back. The cottages are simple stone structures with pleasant pine interiors and private verandas from which to appreciate the infinite peace and quiet (save for the ceaseless chorus of cicadas) or to watch for exotic birds. The upper cottages are roomier and include both a dressing area and a larger split-level living room; there are only two of these, so book ahead. Guests can enjoy wholesome home-cooked Indian meals and simple continental breakfasts in the small restaurant at the manor house.

Mall Rd., Upper Dharamsala 176 219. ⓒ **01892/21010.** Fax 01892/21021. www.glenmoorcottages.com. glenmoor@vsnl.com. 5 units. Rs 2,800 ($62) upper cottages; Rs 1,800 ($40) lower cottages. Rates exclude meals and taxes. No credit cards. **Amenities:** Restaurant. *In room:* TV in upper cottages or on request.

NEAR DHARAMSALA

If you have the time and want to veer slightly off the beaten track, you should definitely head southeast of Dharamsala toward the gently undulating tea-covered hills of the Kangra Valley. Although it lacks any particular charms of its own, **Palampur** is a popular starting point for Kangra Valley—but you'll be better off passing straight through and continuing for 14km (9 miles) to the romantic **Taragarh Palace,** now run as a heritage hotel (reviewed below). Nearby is **Tashijong Monastery,** a colorful *gompa* established in the years after the Dalai Lama made his home in Dharamsala. The neighboring town of Baijnath is the site of the beautiful Saivite **Vaidyanath Temple complex** ⚜⚜ (Baijnath Main Rd.; daily 5am–9pm in summer and 6am–8pm in winter), one of the more interesting and best-preserved Hindu shrines in Himachal Pradesh, dating back to the early 13th century. Surrounded by a wall decorated by fine carvings, the main temple enshrines a squat Shiva lingam protected by a five-headed metallic cobra; devotees usually cover the lingam with flowers and other offerings.

　　Pragpur ⚜⚜⚜ is a time-trapped village with mud-plastered, slate-roofed houses, elegant *havelis* (mansions), Italianate buildings, and narrow cobblestone roads. Designated as India's first official "Heritage Village," this tiny hamlet was founded as a memorial to a brave warrior princess who led a resistance against invaders in the 17th century. Pragpur is wonderful for exploring, a veritable warren of tiny lanes and old, atmospheric buildings. The surrounding landscape offers opportunities for nature walks, cycling, bird-watching, and fishing. Upper Pragpur is known for its home weaving industry, so this is the place to look for good deals on local crafts. Spend the night in Pragpur's beautiful **Judge's Court,** one of Himachal's most enchanting hotels (reviewed below).

WHERE TO STAY

The Judge's Court ⚜⚜⚜   This atmospheric Indo-European haveli, architecturally detailed with domes, galleries, terraces, and porticoes, is filled with the sort of tranquil charm that whisks guests straight back into a bygone age. Set in a magnificent property with orchards of mango, lychee, plum, persimmon, and citrus fruit trees, the main manor house was built in 1918 by a descendant of Pragpur's founders as a gift for his son, a well-known judge of the Punjab High Court. Gorgeously maintained, the hotel offers a variety of accommodations; the very best guest room is the spookily romantic Judge's Suite, which has its own sitting room and two plush armchairs strategically placed in front of the fireplace. All of the rooms have their charms, however, including ancient bathrooms and original beds. Staff can assist you with exploring the village or finding adventure in the Kangra Valley.

Note: If you want to stay in the heart of the medieval village, look into the availability of one of the two Judge's Court annex buildings: two semi-detached 17th-century houses in Pragpur's highly atmospheric Kuthiala Courtyard. Visitors can rent these to experience life along the narrow lanes and cobbled walkways of the village—perfect for families, and ideal for romance. Marble floors are offset by mud-themed walls, an ancient gas-powered kitchen, and big bedrooms with tiny shuttered windows.

Heritage Village Pragpur, Tehsil Dehra, District Kangra 177 107. © **01970/45035** or 01970/45335. Reservations: 3/44, Shanti Niketan, New Delhi 110 021. © 011/2467-4135. Fax 011/2688-5970. www.judgescourt.com. 10 units. Doubles: Rs 2,300 ($50); Rs 2,400 ($53) heritage cottage; Rs 500 ($11) extra bed. AE, MC, V. **Amenities:** Restaurant; cultural performances; local sightseeing, taxi, and travel arrangements. *In room:* A/C, tea- and coffee-making facilities, torch.

Taragarh Palace Hotel 🏨🏨   A pleasant change from more commercial hill-station retreats such as Shimla and Mussourie, the Kangra Valley attracts travelers seeking peace and tranquillity. At this 6-hectare (15-acre) forested estate, a touch of pre-independence class is thrown in for good measure. Once known as Al Hilal ("the land of the crescent moon"), this Art Deco mansion was built in the 1930s as the summer resort of the Nawab of Bahawalpur until he fled to Pakistan after Partition (see the appendix). One of the least-visited destinations in the heart of the scenic and serene Kangra Valley, Taragarh is surrounded by thick vegetation, moss-covered walls, and gorgeous grounds, making it particularly popular with meditation groups who come here for the clean air and idyllic environment. Reminiscent of the setting for a brooding Agatha Christie whodunit, the mansion is all high ceilings, broad staircases, chandeliers, and long passages. Book the characterful Maharajah, Maharani, or Rajmata suites—smart, spacious, and elegantly decorated with charming touches entirely absent from the rather dull double rooms, which are more reminiscent of English country-hotel rooms than royal retiring quarters (and which are also a tad on the small side). Better doubles are nos. 106 and 107 downstairs, which have larger bathrooms; and upstairs room nos. 210 and 211, which have small dressing room/studies. Traditional Indian, Kashmiri, and local dishes are served in the charming wood-paneled dining room dominated by a near-psychedelic red chandelier.

Taragarh Palace, Taragarh, District Kangra 176 081. © and fax **01894/42034** or 01894/43077. www.taragarh. com. www.welcomheritage.com. reservations@taragarh.com. Reservations: 15 Institutional Area, Lodhi Rd., New Delhi 110 003. © 011/2464-3046. Fax 011/2469-2317. 16 units. Doubles: Rs 1,200 ($26) cabin; Rs 2,200 ($48) deluxe; Rs 2,800 ($60) suite; Rs 500 ($11) extra bed. AE, MC, V. **Amenities:** Restaurant; pool; tennis court; badminton court; children's park; sightseeing, taxi, and travel arrangements; limited room service (snacks and tea). *In room:* TV. 2 suites have water cooler.

7 Leh & Environs 🔶🔶

Leh is 475km (295 miles) from Manali

Leh is little touched by rain, but the extreme cold during the long winter season means that this remote region remains isolated for much of the year. Come June, however, when the tourists begin to trickle into Leh, the sober, somber slumber of this remote high-altitude town lifts along with the temperatures. Situated in a fertile valley at the foot of the Namgyal Tsemo peak, 8km (5 miles) northeast of the Indus River, Leh is deeply reliant during this short, intense tourist season. From June to September the surrounding barren mountains and distant snowcapped peaks are the perfect natural backdrop for the verdant fields and avenues of trees which cluster around the whitewashed, flat-roofed buildings.

Developed as a market for traders from across the North India belt, Leh was an important stop for travelers traversing the challenging caravan routes to Yarkand and Kashgar. The Silk Road brought Buddhist travelers, and today the population remains predominantly Buddhist. You can spend up to a week exploring the town and the numerous Buddhist monuments within a 2- or 3-hour drive of Leh. Adventure-seekers can get caught up in river-rafting on the Indus, high-level mountain-climbing, or treks into remote, barren wilderness regions, which can easily extend your stay by an additional week.

ESSENTIALS

GETTING THERE   By Air   If you'd rather save time and get to Leh without the arduous cliff-hanging road journey, **Jet Airways** (Dreamland Complex, Main Bazaar; ✆ **01982/250999;** daily 9am–1pm and 2–4pm) now offers daily flights between New Delhi and Leh in the summer. The disadvantage of flying in is that you may need to spend up to 48 hours acclimatizing anyway, whereas the road journey might have already put you through your paces. Flying out of Leh is definitely a good idea; reserve a window seat. Indian Airlines also flies to Leh, but these flights are often booked up by military personnel.

By Road   Two rather tiring days are required to get from Manali to Leh. For those seeking an adventurous road trip coupled with exquisite, endlessly changing scenery, the journey—by off-road vehicle or bus—is highly recommended. See "Negotiating the Manali–Leh Highway," below.

VISITOR INFORMATION   Leh has a Tourist Information Center, but you are advised not to waste your time there. Speak to your hotel manager or any of the many tour operators who offer various services throughout Ladakh.

GETTING AROUND   By Car   Thanks to a strong military presence in the region, Ladakh's roads are excellent and the network of accessible destinations extensive.

By Taxi   Although Leh has but one auto-rickshaw, it has as many as 1,500 taxis, but the fixed rates to practically any place in the state are high. Unless you've rented a vehicle outside Leh, you will have little choice but to cough up the dough. Your best bet is to share a jeep with fellow travelers interested in visiting similar destinations. For taxi rates and bookings, call the **Leh Taxi Stand** (✆ **01982/252723**).

GUIDED TOURS, ADVENTURE & TREKKING COMPANIES   It's easy to plan your own outings and simply give instructions to your jeep or taxi driver. If you want to deal with an outfitter, refer to the "Staying Active" section earlier in this chapter. If you are very keen on receiving expert information as you explore monasteries and other sights, then a licensed operator may be useful. Speak to Ghulam Mohiuddin at **Adventure North** (Hotel Dragon; ✆ **01982/ 252139** or 01982/252720; fax 01982/252720; advnorth@vsnl.com) about organizing treks and adventures throughout Ladakh.

WHAT TO SEE & DO

Leh's wide street **bazaar** runs east-west. Together with the labyrinth of adjoining side streets and alleys, the bazaar is the center of business and shopping—particularly for visitors who find the plethora of antiques (and not-antiques) shops worth checking out. Locals tend to visit the alternative market nearer the Leh **polo**

Negotiating the Manali–Leh Highway

Nearly 500km (310 miles) of tricky roads, mountain passes, and exceptional roller-coaster scenery separates Leh from Manali. For most of the year, this spectacular stretch of road is closed to traffic, covered by thick snow. Even when the road is officially open in late June and early July, the danger of unexpected snowfall looms, bringing with it various risks associated with getting stuck in the middle of vast unpopulated areas with only freezing cold nights for company. Once summer has set in, a variety of makeshift *dhabas* and *chai* stalls are gathered in mini-colonies along the way. You'll need your passport for a string of checkpoints, the first of which is just beyond the Rohtang Pass at the head of the Kullu Valley. Beyond this, you enter **Lahaul,** a vast Trans-Himalayan landscape dotted with flat-roofed, whitewashed houses built from sun-dried bricks. **Sarchu,** a motley collection of tented camps, is where you'll probably bed down for the night; you'll be too cold to complain about the limited facilities. You reach the world's second-highest motorable road at the summit of the Taklang-La Pass (5,241m/17,469 ft.); here you will find a small multifaith shrine adorned by images of gurus, deities, and religious icons. Beyond the pass, exquisite mountains in a host of unbelievable colors compete with charming villages for your attention.

Your cheapest viable option is an ostensibly "luxury" bus operated by HPTDC (© **0177/225-2561;** www.hptdc.nic.in). For Rs 1,150 ($25) you get an ass-numbing 2-day trip with spartan tented accommodations and dinner en route near Sarchu. Occasional stops for *chai* and photographs are obligatory, but bring plenty of camera film and refreshments. Bottled water is particularly important because dehydration is one of the symptoms of altitude sickness. Jeeps and minivan taxis are pricier but represent relative luxury and the opportunity to explore villages and off-road sites along the way. Hiring your own vehicle and driver is an even better way to go, of course, if you don't mind paying between Rs 6,000 and Rs 12,000 ($130 and $260). Bernard Lazarevitch is an adventurous European who offers "motorbike safaris" to fascinating destinations throughout northern India. When the Manali-Leh highway opens in late June, you can experience this legendary route by hopping onto the back of Bernard's bike or by joining one of his expeditions. For details, contact **AventureMoto** (Blazarevitch@hotmail.com; www.AventureMoto.com).

ground, east of the center. For a truly exotic and atmospheric experience, visit the **Old Village** ❀, a disorganized cluster of cobblestone lanes, ancient homes, and low-vaulted tunnels. It's well worth an exploratory jaunt, during which you should sample the freshly baked breads sold by local bakers. Walking northwest of the city (beyond the **Women's Alliance of Ladakh** headquarters, where you can shop for traditional Ladakhi handicrafts), you will quickly discover a **rural farmlike community.** Gone are the shops and eager sellers—here you'll find only fields of green sprinkled with bright-yellow blossoms, gentle streams trickling past squat stone walls, and small Ladakhi houses with little vegetable gardens. To the west are the cobbled streets of the popular **Changspa** neighborhood, characterized by the number of guesthouses and laid-back marijuana-smoking travelers who come here for the pastoral atmosphere. To the west of Changspa lies **Shanti Stupa**, a Buddhist monument most easily reached by motorable road. Inaugurated by the Dalai Lama in the 1980s, the large white *stupa* (commemorative cairn) was conceived as part of a Japanese-inspired peace movement to spread Buddhism throughout the world. From the vast courtyard at the base of the stupa you can enjoy matchless **panoramic views** ⛰⛰⛰ of Leh and the rugged beauty of the surrounding mountains, which seem to stretch on forever.

WHERE TO STAY

With tourism the single most important industry in town, Leh is inundated with accommodations options, but don't expect luxury. Hotels are priced according to unfathomable government regulations, so despite mediocre facilities, you may be paying unreasonable rates based on the fact that you, theoretically, have hot running water. **Shambha-La Hotel** is a little out of the center of things, but this is by far the most comfortable accommodations option (reviewed below). Another worth considering is the spacious new suite (no. 15)—which includes a glassed-in deck with striking views of Leh Palace and the surrounding mountainscape—at the **Lotus Hotel** (✆ **01982/250265;** fax 01982/252414; double: Rs 2,270/$50; all meals included).

Hotel Dragon   In its price range, Dragon offers the best stay in Leh. Owned by Ghulam Mustafa and his brother Mohiuddin since 1976, this popular establishment has shown consistent improvements over the years. Each floor of the squat, traditionally styled building has its own terrace, and you can catch fantastic 360-degree views of Leh from the rooftop. The limited number of suites are well worth the extra $6—they're considerably better than the doubles with their kitschy shiny bedcovers; the suites also have tubs (although you should think twice before filling a bathtub in this water-strapped region). Upstairs room nos. 131 through 133 are more spacious than the other, typically small—but neat and cozy—doubles. At night, when a campfire is lit, the small garden courtyard becomes an ideal spot to wind down the day. Delicious Ladakhi and Tibetan meals are served in the dining room, which is decorated with gorgeous paintings by one of the owners.

Leh 194 101. ✆ 01982/252139 or 01982/252720. Fax 01982/252720. www.indiamartadvnorth.com. 32 units. Doubles: Rs 1,575 ($35) standard; Rs 1,875 ($41) suite. Rates include all meals. No credit cards. **Amenities:** Restaurant; tours and sightseeing; conferencing; foreign exchange; shop; 24-hr. room service; doctor-on-call.

Omasila   Built in the early 1980s, this intimate hotel occupying a pleasant Ladakhi-style building and offering an array of accommodations is adored by film crews. But Omasila enjoys a peaceful setting despite the occasional presence of an overbearing Bollywood director and its proximity to the backpackers' haven of Changspa. Fresh vegetables, apricots, and apples are grown in an adjoining garden, and the stream alongside is a natural aural tonic during laid-back afternoons on the terrace (shame about the plastic garden chairs, though). In summer the mountains surrounding Leh provide the perfect backdrop to magnificent sweeps of colorful flora perfectly visible from each room in the hotel. The suites offer the most comfortable stay, with larger and better bathrooms (at least the showers are curtained) and a faint Tibetan-design aesthetic. For views to match the price, ask for room no. 21, 23, or 26. Buffet meals are served in the relatively stylish "Ladakhi-Tibetan" restaurant, which features colorful murals.

Overnighting in a Ladakhi Yurt

If you don't mind being a short way out of Leh, reserve a yurt (a canvas and bamboo tentlike structure modeled on a Mongolian *akoi*) at **Ladakh Sarai** 🐾🐾 and have all your treks and sightseeing outings expertly arranged for you. Each of the 14 circular tents is large and has twin beds, warm bedding, and an attached bathroom with hot water by the bucket and a Western toilet. Located among willow trees, the camp has a pleasant Ladakhi-style dining hall where traditional meals are served, and during the day you can laze in a hammock and gaze at the surrounding mountains. Ladakh Sarai is 6km (4 miles) from Leh, in the peaceful hamlet of Sabu. Reservations are through **Tiger Mountain India** (3 Rani Jhansi Rd., New Delhi 110 055; ✆ **011/2777-1055** or 011/2367-1035; www.tigermountain india.com). Packages inclusive of meals and sightseeing start at $100 per person sharing.

Karzoo-Changspa, Leh 194 101. ✆ **01982/252119**, 01982/251178, or 01982/250207. www.omasila.com. 32 units. Doubles: Rs 2,400 ($53) standard; Rs 3,000 ($65) deluxe; Rs 3,800 ($82) suite. Rates include all meals. No credit cards. **Amenities:** Restaurant; tour and travel arrangements; room service; laundry; doctor-on-call; oxygen facilities. *In room:* Suites and deluxe rooms have telephone and TV; heaters on request.

Shambha-La Hotel 🐾   This hotel was once a part of the excellent Oberoi chain; now only the bathroom towels suggest that former pedigree. Nevertheless, Shambha-La remains the best hotel in Leh, offering straightforward but dignified accommodations in a flat-roofed Ladakhi-style lodge with fluttering prayer flags and comfortable hammocks in the neat garden. Public areas—including a colorful Tibetan lounge area—are attractive, and the views from the upstairs terrace are mesmerizing. As with all of Leh's hotels, the bathroom facilities are merely adequate. Guest rooms are far from lavish, but you get a warm bed and you can book a stove-heated unit in the colder months. Power outages can be a serious problem this far from the town center, so have your hot shower early, just in case. A hotel jeep is on hand to drop you in town whenever you require a lift, and the helpful manager is a mine of useful information. The hotel also organizes tours to any destination in Ladakh; ask about their campsites in the Nubra Valley.

Note: Often considered in the same category as Shambha-La, the rather disappointing **Lha-Ri-Mo** (P.O. Leh 194 101; ✆ **01982/252101**) is Ladakh's largest, slightly weathered hotel. Despite its relatively central location, beautiful views, and excellent Ladakhi building, service is stodgy, the public spaces are ugly, and the smallish rooms are musty.

South of the bazaar, Leh 194 101. ✆ **01982/251100**, 01982/252607, or 01982/253500. Fax 01982/251100. www.welcomheritage.com. 27 units. Doubles: Rs 2,500 ($55); Rs 500 ($11) extra bed. Rates include all meals. AE, MC, V. **Amenities:** Restaurant; TV lounge; billiards; travel assistance, tours, treks, sightseeing, and taxi arrangements; laundry; doctor-on-call; library.

WHERE TO DINE

For the best Tibetan dishes in Leh, dinner at **The Tibetan Kitchen** (reviewed below) is highly recommended. In the Main Street Bazaar, you might be forgiven for not even noticing the very reliable **Himalaya Café** (✆ **01982/ 250144;** summer 9am–11pm, winter 10am–8pm; Rs 30–Rs 90/60¢–$1.90; no credit cards), where marvelous Tibetan and Chinese dishes are served in the Ladakhi version of a dimly lit bistro—one of the few eating establishments in

Leh where you'll experience some sort of atmosphere. At first glance it would appear that the only real attraction at **Ibex Bar & Restaurant** (Fort Rd.; Ⓒ **01982/252281;** daily 8am–11pm; everything under $10) is the fact that you can order beer with your meal. While locals flock here to get loud and raucous, the extensive Indian menu is well worth perusing; the *sikh* kebabs are served with a delicious mint sauce (or *podina*), and mutton and chicken curries are exceptional—perfect with steaming-hot *naan* bread.

For a continental fix of filter coffee and croissants, a disproportionate number of German bakeries are scattered around the town. For a spacious, outdoorsy cafe experience, head to **Penguin Garden Restaurant & Bar & German Bakery** (Fort Rd.; daily 7am–11pm; Rs 95–Rs 138/$2–$3), a laid-back hangout set in a large leafy courtyard with seating under a couple of apple trees decorated with speakers from which cool lounge tunes resonate. The confectionery is equally delicious and is a lovely place to chill out with the locals, who gather here to play cards and catch up on the latest Leh gossip; there's the added advantage of being able to order liquor with your meal. If you're looking for a great Indian lunch or dinner, be prepared to wait 30 minutes for the highly recommended Resmi Kebab, a melt-in-the-mouth blend of minced chicken, mixed spices, and fresh herbs. While you wait, try a piece of delicious *kulcha,* which is similar to *naan* bread but comes filled with onion or a blend of spices. Penguin is also great for health food and salads and the ideal spot to kick off your day with a filling breakfast. *Note:* On request, the Penguin staff will happily prepare special meals for road journeys or trekking trips. Their long-lasting trekking bread made from specially prepared sour dough lasts up to a week.

The Tibetan Kitchen 🏮🏮 *Value* TIBETAN   Tibetan fare is de rigueur in Leh, and after more than a decade, the town's best restaurant does not disappoint. Pre-order the traditional Tibetan hot pot, or *giyacko,* suitable for four fairly hungry diners: A brass pot with a communal broth is heated at the table, while salads, *papads,* fine noodles, rice, and mutton are served in abundance for you to cook at will. Note that the restaurant has only one pot, so be sure to book well ahead. If you'd prefer to have your food cooked for you by skilled Tibetan and Nepalese chefs, there's plenty to choose from. Try wanton *pe shee* soup, Tibetan salad (avocado, tomato, and mint), or delicious *shavaglee* (a freshly baked meat- or vegetable-filled bun). The steamed mutton *momos* (dumplings), prepared with garlic and onion and served with a salad, are the probably best you'll find this side of the Indo-Tibetan border.

Hotel Tso-Kar, Lud Tok Rd. Ⓒ **01982/253071.** Main courses Rs 45–Rs 220 (95¢–$4.80); Tibetan hot pot for 4 Rs 1,200 ($26). No credit cards. Daily 8am–11pm; last orders 10:30pm.

DISCOVERING LADAKHI GOMPAS & OTHER DIVERSIONS
NORTH OF LEH

There are enough Buddhist *gompas* within easy reach of Leh to keep enthusiasts busy for several days. North along the road to Srinigar are **Phyang Gompa** 🏮🏮 (16km/10 miles from Leh), and the 15th-century **Spituk Gompa** 🏮🏮 (8km/5 miles from Leh), which sits atop a lone rocky hill. If you're prepared to spend some time on the road (a scintillating journey), **Alchi** 🏮🏮🏮 (along the left bank of the Indus around 70km/43 miles northwest of Leh, a short way off the Srinigar–Leh Rd.) is highly recommended. One of the oldest monasteries in the region, it dates back to the 11th century. Situated in a quiet hamlet with a handful of souvenir and snack stalls and some very modest budget accommodations, Alchi is centered around its inactive five-temple *gompa* complex, administered by the yellow-hat Gelugpa monks of Likir Monastery 30km (18 miles) across the river. You'll need a flashlight or torch to explore the temple interiors, which are covered with vibrant, colorful, detailed murals. A courtyard leads to the *dukhang,* or assembly hall, where the statue of Avalokiteswara is believed to be of pure gold.

On the way to Alchi, stop at **Basgo** 🌟🌟, where a hillside citadel consists of several Buddhist temples attached to a ruined castle. A two-story-high golden statue of the future Buddha is housed in the Maitreya temple, which has fantastic murals of fierce divinities that were the guardian deities of the royal family once resident here.

SOUTH OF LEH

Venturing south of Leh along the same road that goes all the way to Manali, you can take in a number of monasteries, and one or two Ladakhi palaces. Located across from Choglamsar on the opposite side of the Indus, **Stok Palace** 🌟🌟 (May–Oct 8am–7pm; Rs 25/50¢) is the only inhabited palace in Ladakh, home to the 74th generation of the Namgyal dynasty. The land-holding rights of Stok were granted to the royal family by Gen. Zorawar Singh in 1834 when he deposed Tshe-spal-Namgyal, the *Gyalpo* (king) of Ladakh. It's an imposing complex, with around 80 rooms, only a few of which are still used by the current widowed *Gyalmo* (queen), who is sometimes in residence with her immediate family. Several rooms are taken up by the modest museum housed in one section. Museum highlights include a vast *thangka* collection, weapons, jewels and, of special note, the queen's *perak,* a turquoise-studded headdress. The ghostly Buddhist shrine is an experience not to be missed.

Fifteen kilometers (9 miles) from Leh, **Shey Palace and Monastery** 🌟🌟 (May–Oct, daily 8am–7pm; Rs 20/40¢) is worthwhile for the *gompa,* but the palace is little more than crumbling ruins. **Thikse Gompa** 🌟🌟🌟 (daily 6am–6pm), 25km (16 miles) south of Leh, is a striking 12-story edifice with tapering walls that sits atop a craggy peak. From here you get magnificent views of the valley, strewn with whitewashed *stupas.*

Hidden from the world on a remote verdant hillock, **Hemis Gompa** 🌟🌟🌟 (45km/28 miles from Leh) is considered the wealthiest Ladakhi monastery, its atmospheric prayer and assembly halls rich with ancient relics and ritual symbols. During the summer season in June and July, the monastery comes alive for the annual **Hemis Tsechu** 🌟🌟🌟, a festival commemorating Guru Padmasambhava's birth. Masked dancing by the lamas and ritual dramas are played out in the courtyard, and the locals sell Ladakhi handicrafts and jewelry. Every 12 years, a magnificent embroidered silk *thangka* (tantric wall hanging) is displayed to the public; the next such unveiling takes place in June 2004.

NUBRA VALLEY

A 5-hour jeep drive over the world's highest motorable pass, the **Khardung-La** (5,578m/18,000 ft.), leads to northern Ladakh's lush **Nubra Valley** 🌟🌟🌟, a fertile region with *gompas,* hot sulphurous springs (at Panamik), and rare camels. Deep within the breathtaking Karakoram mountain range, the valley combines terrific desertscapes and fertile fields watered by the Siachen and Shayok rivers.

For centuries, the route into Nubra was part of the legendary Silk Route used by caravans of traders operating between the Punjab and various regions within central Asia. The valley is dotted with peaceful, pleasant, sparsely populated villages, but its landscape is little explored and the ultimate getaway for the traveler in search of escape; rent a bike and take time to explore. You need to arrange an Inner-Line Permit in Leh (which can be done through any travel agent or through your hotel), and technically you must be traveling in a group of at least four people. Hire a jeep with driver (count on spending Rs 6,000/$130 for 3 days), and set off early in the day. **Shamba-La Hotel** (reviewed earlier) offers all-inclusive tours to the Nubra Valley, with accommodations at their own camping site. Otherwise, your best option for a comfortable night's stay is probably the village of Tegar, where **Hotel Yarah Tso** (✆ **01982/220008;** doubles $50) has clean accommodations with attached Western bathrooms.

11

Uttaranchal: Sacred Source of the Ganges

For devout Hindus, a trip into the Himalayan ranges of Uttaranchal—source of the sacred **Ganges**—is no mere journey, but a *yatra,* or spiritual pilgrimage. For the city-smothered traveler, it's balm for the soul. Comprising the territories of Garhwal (west) and Kumaon (east), tiny Uttaranchal is one of India's newest states, carved from Uttar Pradesh in 2000. Besides Hindu pilgrims and adventurous trekkers and river rafters, Garhwal attracts New Age Westerners who flock to the ashrams of **Rishikesh,** situated on the banks of the holy river Ganges, and to nearby **Ananda-in-the-Himalayas,** one of the top spa destinations in the world. For visitors looking for a gentle road trip, the picturesque lower-altitude **hill stations of the Kumaon** offer glorious views of panoramic snowcapped mountains and a chance to spot tigers in one of the country's best-known wildlife sanctuaries, **Corbett National Park,** which vies with Rajasthan's Ranthambore National Park in terms of accessibility—it's some 264km (164 miles) from Delhi.

1 Garhwal

Sacred source of the Ganges, the western part of Uttaranchal is where Hindu devotees come on mountain *yatras* (pilgrimages) to Badrinath, Kedarnath, Gangotri, and Yamunotri. Westerners tend to head for **Rishikesh,** said to be the birthplace of yoga. Today scores of garish concrete ashrams and temples draw visitors who seek out yogis and tantric enlightenment, as well as hippies and backpackers keen to contemplate life, the universe, and everything else through an edifying cloud of hash smoke. Up in the hills, with staggering views of the vast Doon Valley and western Garhwal's Himalayan peaks, **Mussoorie** is the quintessential Raj-era hill station, but it gets crowded and detestable in summer (and on weekends), packed with honeymooning and vacationing domestic tourists who send the decibel level skyrocketing. In winter, however, much of its charm returns.

ESSENTIALS

GETTING THERE & AWAY   By Air   Dehra Dun's **Jolly Grant Airport** is a 50-minute flight from Delhi. From there, catch a taxi to either Mussoorie or Rishikesh, or have your hotel pick you up.

By Train   Dehra Dun is the terminus of the Northern Railway, and is the jumping-off point for Mussoorie. For Rishikesh, Haridwar is the most convenient terminal, 30 minutes away by taxi. There are several good connections between the capital and both Dehra Dun and Haridwar, including the **Dehra Dun Shatabdi** and the **Dehra Dun Janshatabdi,** which both stop at Haridwar. An overnight alternative is the **Mussoorie Express.**

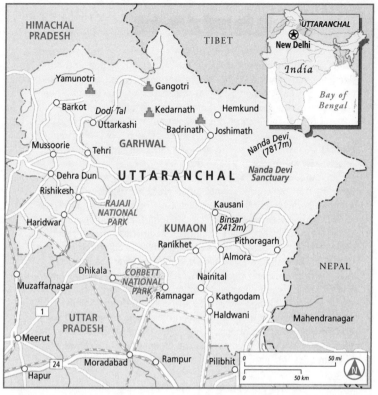

By Road   The drive from Delhi to Rishikesh (250km/155 miles) takes between 5 and 6 hours. If you're at Corbett, the drive to Rishikesh takes around 4 hours. There are regular buses from Deli to Haridwar and Rishikesh. Mussoorie is 280km (173 miles) from Delhi, including a final 33km (20 miles) from Dehra Dun, along a steeply ascending series of troublesome hairpin bends.

VISITOR INFORMATION   In Mussoorie, the **Uttaranchal Tourist Bureau** (© **0135/263-2863;** www.uttaranchaltourism.gov.in) is located near the ropeway, on the Mall. In Rishikesh, visit the **Garhwal Mandal Vikas Nigam Tourist Office** (Muni-ki Reti; © **0135/243-0799,** -2648, or -5174; www. gmvnl.com) or the **Tourist Information Centre** (Ambedkar Chowk, Railway Rd.; © **0135/243-0209**).

GETTING AROUND   Hire the services of a car and driver for the duration of your visit, unless you plan on trekking. In Mussoorie, the taxi union frowns upon outside taxis.

MUSSOORIE
278km (172 miles) NE of Delhi; 35km (22 miles) N of Dehra Dun; 110km (68 miles) NW of Rishikesh

Smaller than Shimla and some 450m (1,500 ft.) lower, this hill station enjoys a more spectacular setting but has rather gone to seed, its regal colonial mansions all peeling plaster and overgrown hedges. It was once a favorite summer refuge of the Raj, but these days the strutting *sahibs* and *memsahibs* have been replaced by

Trekking through the Land of the Gods

Below are some of the best treks in Uttaranchal. You're strongly urged to engage the services of a guide for any of the routes, and don't skimp on equipment. Bring clothes and footwear to withstand extreme weather conditions. Note that certain treks in Garhwal require a **permit;** your trekking company can arrange this for you.

From Uttarkashi, a short drive takes you to Kalyani, which is the starting point for one of Garhwal's most popular treks—to fabulous **Dodital** ⭐, a striking lake surrounded by fantastic alpine forests. A relatively easy trek lasting 3 days, the 23km (14-mile) route takes you through the Asi Ganga river valley. Several treks with varying levels of difficulty start out from **Gangotri** (at an altitude of 3,000m/10,000 ft.), a small pilgrim town at the confluence of the rivers Bhagirathi and Kedar Ganga, in the shadow of Mount Sudarshan (6,500m/2,980 ft.), some 98km (60 miles) from Uttarkashi. From Gangotri, a beautiful 26km (16-mile) hike takes you along a gradual ascent along the Bhagirathi to **Gaumukh** ⭐⭐⭐, which is where the river has its source in the Gangotri Glacier—here the water gushes out from a small amphitheater carved out of the 15m to 20m (50-ft.–65-ft.) ice walls. En route, you pass through scenic valleys and alpine forests, following an ancient pilgrimage route; a panorama of towering snowcapped peaks accompanies you throughout. At night, you camp on the banks of the embryonic Ganges, known here as the **Bhagirathi.** Beyond Gaumukh, you can cross the glacier to reach the high-altitude meadows of **Tapovan** and **Nandanvan,** although the route to Tapovan varies with the constant downward movement of the glacier. You can schedule the trek to last anywhere between 6 and 9 days, even longer if you wish to explore the meadows and glaciers at the foot of Hinduism's center of the universe, **Mount Meru.** A popular alternative trek takes you along the **Kedar Ganga Valley,** from **Gangotri** to **Kedartal,** a gorgeous lake surrounded by mountain peaks.

One of the best-known routes in the Kumaon is the **Pindari Glacier Trek** ⭐, a fairly moderate trek that lasts up to 8 or 9 days and can be combined with a tour of Corbett National Park. A shorter trek takes you on a 20km (12-mile) climb through the **Valley of Flowers National Park** ⭐, high up in the Himalayas. Between June and September, hundreds of species of flowers—many of them rare alpine varieties—fill the valley floor, through which the Pushpawati River flows. Nainital's **Parbat Tours** (☎ 05942/23-5656) organizes treks in the Kumaon. Operators in Rishikesh that organize treks in Garhwal include **Garhwal Tours and Trekking** (☎ 0135/265-3005) and **Garhwal Himalayan Explorations** (☎ 0135/243-1654). For equipment rentals and assistance, contact the local tourism office (see "Visitor Information,"above).

hordes of visitors escaping Delhi's blistering summer heat (when Mussoorie is best avoided). Until recently, Mussoorie's historical ambience was also overwhelmed by unchecked urban development; the government has now intervened (but it's a little too late, it must be said).

Whitewater Adventures

Rafting the Ganges or the border-hugging Kali River is best undertaken when you have several days at hand, allowing time for transfers and a variety of rapids, gorges, and the occasional shallow waterfall. Contact **Himalayan River Runners** ⚘ (N-8 Green Park, 1st Floor, New Delhi 110 016; ⓒ **011/2696-6981** or -8169; fax 011/2686-5604; www.hrrindia.com), which provides overnight eco-friendly camping on the Ganges river beach. Or contact **Mercury Himalayan Explorations** ⚘ (ⓒ **011/2334-0033** or -6209; www. himalayanadventure.com) for an all-inclusive experience that includes luxury tents and Western-style toilets. You'll have incredible experiences with **Outdoor Adventures India** ⚘⚘ (S-234 Panchsheel Park, 2nd Floor; New Delhi 110 017; ⓒ **011/2601-3571** or -3572; fax 011/2601-4230; www.outdoor adventuresindia.com) or **Aquaterra Adventures India** ⚘⚘ (S-507, ground floor, Greater Kailash 2; New Delhi 110 048; ⓒ **011/2623-2641**; www. treknraft.com), both good for lighthearted adventuring coupled with excellent food. Most important, the guides are adept at negotiating the rivers.

Unlike Shimla, Mussoorie in its glory days was pleasantly free of administrators, with plenty of nocturnal cavorting between young men and the wives of the hardworking bureaucrats who had remained back in the plains—it is said that a bell was rung at predawn at the famous **Savoy Hotel** to encourage impious lovers to get back to their own beds. The quintessential crumbling relic, the Savoy has been visited by Indira Gandhi, the Dalai Lama, Jawaharlal Nehru, Haile Selassie, the king of Nepal, and Queen Mary, but it now tries to push barren, moldy rooms on unsuspecting travelers seeking Raj-era glory. Still in residence behind the ancient brass reception grilles is Mr. Negi, who has been working at the hotel since 1931 and still enjoys taking visitors on a tour of the "best" rooms. The Savoy's melancholic **Writers' Bar** has hosted Rudyard Kipling, Pearl S. Buck, and Arthur Conan Doyle, but you'd better rush to pay your respects before the whole thing collapses.

The town's lifeline is the **Mall,** a stretch of pedestrian road that links its two centers, **Library Bazaar** and **Kulri Bazaar.** You can walk the entire length of the ridge, from the bandstand at the western end of the Mall to the old churches and cemeteries at the quieter end of Kulri. Above the town is **Gun Hill,** from where the British punctually fired their noonday guns. Today, visitors reach the summit by means of a ropeway, or rent horses for a 15-minute ride from the central police station. Along Mussoorie's upper ridge, **Camel's Back Road** is another fine place for a stroll. Farther east of Kulri Bazaar is **Landour,** which is quieter and better-preserved than touristy Mussoorie. Continue on foot for an hour beyond Kulri Bazaar and you'll reach **Lal Tibba,** where the lookout point provides sensational views of the Himalayas. Farther still is **Sisters' Bazaar,** a wooded area named for the nurses who attended to convalescing soldiers, and where you can explore an empty colonial mansion, said to be haunted.

WHERE TO STAY & DINE

The two best places to stay are **Kasmanda Palace Hotel** and **Claridges Nabha Retreat.** Located in the heart of town, Kasmanda is a stately, airy mansion where you can negotiate a double room for as little as Rs 800 ($18) in the low season. This well-preserved former holiday palace of the Maharajah of Kasmanda is packed with hunting trophies, animal skins, and antique furniture, including an elephant's-foot piano stool. Book a suite (Rs 2,300/$40), which has exceptional views of the Doon Valley even though it features stuffed animal heads mounted on the walls and a liberal use of gaudy floral fabrics (© **0135/263-2424** or -3949; www.heritagehotels.com/kasmanda; doubles from Rs 1,700/$37). Set on the outskirts of town, Claridges Nabha is a serene and lovely estate (ca. 1845), once used by the Maharajah of Nabha for his summer escapades; in the surrounding canopy of trees, langur monkeys perform daredevil acrobatic feats while you lounge on the terrace. The best accommodations are room nos. 110 through 115; these enjoy attractive forest views (no. 114 is the biggest). Disappointingly, guest-room fireplaces are no longer in use. The hotel conducts courtesy pickups from the Mall throughout the day (© **0135/263-1426** or -1427, or 011/2301-0211; fax: 011/ 2379-2388; doubles from Rs 3,250/$70).

RISHIKESH

It was The Beatles—who came here during the 1960s to visit the maharishi (a visit that inspired much of *Sgt. Pepper*)—who put Rishikesh on the map, and today the town is full of ashrams and yoga schools catering to Westerners keen to fine-tune their spiritual tool kits. Sadhus (holy men) in ginger robes, hippies in tie-dyed cheesecloth, and backpackers with plenty of time (and plenty of First World credit) gather here on the banks of the Ganga to talk about the evils of the West and the failure of communism. By day, it's like a spiritual Disneyland, where the commercial excesses of packaged meditation hang heavily about the concrete ashrams, bedecked with gaudy statues of Vishnu and Shiva. But at night, to the accompaniment of hypnotic prayers and harmonious singing, Rishikesh undergoes a magical transformation. Thousands of golden marigolds and devotional candles mounted on banana leaves are set adrift upon the river, a gloriously simple spectacle, reminding all that this really is a spiritual retreat.

WHERE TO STAY & DINE

In a town full of ashrams and sadhus, you might very well expect Rishikesh luxury to involve a bed of sharpened stainless-steel nails. Fortunately, you can indulge in the unadulterated luxury of one of the country's finest spa resorts: **Ananda-in-the-Himalayas** (reviewed below). Of course, you won't be in Rishikesh itself (potentially a very good thing). For a truly unusual place to stay, don't miss the **Glasshouse on the Ganges** (also reviewed below), a work of remarkable design where you can hear the waters roaring by from the comfort of your four-poster bed. There are also several clean and convenient options that won't unsettle your budget (or your stomach). **High Banks Peasant Cottage** (Tapovan; © **0135/243-1167;** fax 01364/243-1654; hmalayas@vsnl.com) has four spartan guest rooms and serves healthy vegetarian meals on request; its big claim to fame is that Kate Winslet stayed here. Strange, as the proprietor is a touch irritating, and there's a dearth of views. In the same cluster of guesthouses is **New Bhandari Swiss Cottage** (P.O. Shivananda Nagar, P.O. no. 12, Tapovan 249 192; © **0135/243-5322**), which has a range of accommodations—opt for the rooftop suite (around Rs 1,200/$26) with air-conditioning, TV, and bathtub.

Ananda-in-the-Himalayas ✦✦✦　At this destination spa, high-class pampering is definitely the order of the day. The resort's immaculate, palatial reception rooms are located in the restored Viceregal Palace, added to the palace of the Maharaja of Tehri Garhwal in 1910 to accommodate the likes of Lord Mountbatten. Now the grounds have been fabulously landscaped, enhanced with flower beds and water features, and primped to satisfy Western tastes. Some distance from the palace, in a dull five-story block (entirely out of synch with the historical appeal of the Viceregal Palace), guest accommodations are elegant, with chic-modern decor, teak parquet wood flooring, coir mats, ultra-comfortable beds, and balconies (the more expensive "valley view" is the category to go for). Personal yoga mats are placed in each room, and there are comfortable, light-fitting *kurta* pajamas for you to wear throughout your stay; these are ideal if you're going to spend lots of time receiving treatments in the 1,951-sq.-m (21,000-sq.-ft.) Wellness Center—choose between Thai, Ayurvedic, or Swedish massage, or lie back for an Ananda royal facial, seaweed body wrap, or ancient Indian body mask. From the moment you wake in the morning (to a steaming cup of honey, lemon, and ginger) until you retire to a bath (for which a candle is lit to heat fragrant essential oils) and bed (warmed by a hot-water bottle), you're totally pampered.

The Palace Estate, Narendra Nagar, Tehri Garhwal 249 175. © **01378/22-7500.** Fax 01378/22-7550 or 01378/22-7555. www.anandaspa.com. anandaspa@vsnl.com. 75 units. Doubles: $300 deluxe palace-view room; $350 deluxe valley-view room; $550–$1,100 suite. AE, DC, MC, V. **Amenities:** Restaurant; spa; pool; tennis court; squash court; bicycles; jogging track; safaris; trekking; kayaking; fishing; whitewater rafting; daily health and relaxation program; limousine service; room service; laundry and dry-cleaning service; in-house doctor; ashram; library. *In room:* A/C, TV, dataport, minibar, tea- and coffee-making facilities, hair dryer, scale, electronic safe.

The Glasshouse on the Ganges 🌟🌟🌟

Spectacularly situated on the banks of the Ganges, 23km (16 miles) north of Rishikesh, this former garden-retreat of the maharajahs of Tehri Garhwal is—quite correctly—billed as a "non-hotel." Extraordinary, design-conscious refurbishment has produced a series of individual accommodations, of which you have two general choices, either in the main block, fronted by a pillared veranda with relaxing planters' chairs, or cottages in the lush gardens of hammock-strung mango, lychee, and citrus trees and tropical plants. The best of the lot (book now!) is the Gangeshwari (one of the cottages)—immaculately laid out and spacious, with its own lounge area and balcony, and a bathroom partially open to the elements where a sunken tub is carved from rock, and greenery spills down the walls. If it's not available, ask about the Yamuna room, where simple antique furnishings (four-poster bed), a working fireplace, and soft white linen provide superb comfort. The cheaper rooms are quite a bit smaller, but ask for Gomti or the unit above it, and you'll enjoy views through large windows in a spacious environment. Ask for your breakfast or lunch to be served on the rock terrace perched over the Ganges.

23rd Milestone, Rishikesh-Badrinath Rd., Village and P.O. Gular-Dogi, Tehri-Garhwal District 249 303. © **01378/26-9224** or -9218. Reservations: Neemrana Hotels Pvt. Ltd., A-58 Nizamuddin E., New Delhi 110 013. © **011/2461-6145,** 011/2461-8962, or 011/2462-5214. Fax: 011/2462-1112. www.neemrana.com. sales@neemrana.com. 16 units. Doubles: Rs 2,000–Rs 2,500 ($44–$55) standard; Rs 2,500–Rs 3,000 ($55–$65) double and deluxe suites; Rs 6,500 ($140) triple suite; Rs 300 ($6.50) extra bed. AE, MC, V. **Amenities:** Restaurant; travel assistance; laundry; doctor-on-call. *In room:* TV in some.

2 Kumaon

The British Raj claimed this eastern pocket of Himalayan India from Nepal in 1815. Free of the hustle and bustle of urban India and blessed with a gentle, laid-back quality, the Kumaon is great for viewing breathtaking scenery, breathing in restorative oxygen-rich air, taking wonderful walks, and seeing decaying reminders of the British preoccupation with transforming remote villages into proper English towns. Prominent among these are **Nainital** and **Ranikhet.** Both are surrounded by pine forests and good for catching your breath; the latter is arguably the most evocative former British hill station in India. A good route is to set off from Nainital or Mukteshwar, overnight at Binsar before heading to Ranikhet for a night, and end your journey at Corbett National Park. Wherever you overnight, the road journeys between these destinations are the real joy of the Kumaon; when you're this close to gorgeous Himalayan mountain ranges, you simply cannot escape breathtaking views.

ESSENTIALS

GETTING THERE & AROUND   There are many trains heading out of both Delhi and Lucknow towards Kathgodam, 35km (28 miles) from Nainital. The overnight Ranikhet Express leaves Old Delhi at 10:45pm and arrives at 6:15am. There are always taxis and share-taxis available, or you can avoid the haggle and have your hotel pick you up from the station. Ranikhet is an extra 60km (37 miles) from Nainital, or a 3½-hour journey from the Kathgodam railway station. Once you've found your bearings, hire a car (preferably a four-wheel-drive) and driver for the duration of your stay in Uttaranchal. You can expect to pay around Rs 4 (8¢) per kilometer, plus an additional fee per day and a reasonable contribution towards the driver's overnight expenses.

VISITOR INFORMATION   While in Delhi, you can visit the **KMVN Tourist Information Office** (103 Indraprakash Building, 21 Barakhamba Rd.; ✆ **011/2371-2246;** fax 011/2331-9835; www.kmvn.org). In Nainital, the KMVN is at Oak Park House, Mallital (✆ **05942/23-6356**).

A ROAD TRIP THROUGH KUMAON

Your first stop, Nainital, is set around the ebony-emerald **Naini Tal** (Lake)—according to Hindu mythology, one of the eyes of Shiva's wife, Sati. The **Naina Devi Temple** is said to be the precise spot where Sati's eye fell when her body parts were scattered throughout the country in a bid to stop Shiva's "dance of cosmic destruction." High above the town, at 2,235m (7,450 ft.), is the aptly named **Snow View,** a hilltop viewing area from where you can see Nanda Devi, India's second-highest peak. Make use of the Aerial Express ropeway;

⟨Tips   **A Good Reason to Drive from Delhi**

Recent bypass extensions to National Highway 24 linking Delhi with popular weekend destinations mean that it's no longer a hellish struggle to drive from the capital to any of the popular resort areas in Uttaranchal's Kumaon region. Be sure to plan departure times carefully, in conjunction with your driver, however. We highly recommend that you overnight en route to either Corbett National Park or Nainital (320km/198 miles from Delhi), however, even if only to stay at the **Mud Fort, Kuchesar** ★★ (Village Kuchesar, via B.B. Nagar, District Bulandshahr 245 402; ✆ **098370/22-3730;** www.neemrana.com), which is just less than 80km (50 miles) from Delhi. Built in the mid–18th century, the turreted, fortified citadel of the Kuchesar Jats overlooks fantastic gardens. Beautifully restored with tasteful, design-conscious interiors, the "hotel" is ideal for those with a yen for personal attention (there are only 10 guest rooms) and a unique setting devoid of things like phones and televisions. Besides exploring the historic fortress, you can spend time wandering through the local villages, far from tourist traps, touts, and civilization.

round-trips cost Rs 50 ($1.05). You can overnight here, but we recommend you opt for **Mountain Quail Camp** just outside Nainital, one of the two gorgeous **Ramgarh Bungalows,** or **Mountain Trail** in remote and lovely Mukteshwar (all are reviewed below).

Perched on a ridge some 2,254m (7,513 ft.) above sea level, where you are surrounded by little more than dramatic views of the Himalayas, conifer forests, fruit orchards, and fresh, clean air, Mukteshwar is easily the most charming setting in the Kumaon. At the edge of town, atop a cliff, is the century-old **Mukteshwar Temple,** dedicated to Lord Shiva. On the same hill is an ashram administered by a hermit whose disciples come from around the world. Behind the temple, a rocky cliff juts out of the hillside at Chauthi Jaali; take an early-morning walk here for stunning views.

The next day, set off for Binsar, for the best view in motorable Kumaon; here you can watch the sunrise over Nepal and the sunset on Garhwal. Time allowing, visit the **Binsar Sanctuary** to view Himalayan wildlife (Rs 225/$4.80, including guide) before you set off for Ranikhet.

Even more than Nainital, Ranikhet—surrounded by slopes draped with forests of thick pine and deodar and impeccable views of Nanda Devi—exudes the ambience of a haunted English Gothic township, forever waiting for a cloak of thick mist and the echoes of a long-lost era to descend.

Whether you arrive from Nainital (60km/37 miles away) or Binsar, you'll first encounter the typically Indian **Sadar Bazaar,** an unappealing town center that is entirely avoidable. Take the turnoff for the **Mall,** and head into the peaceful Cantonment area. Ranikhet is occupied by the army's Kumaon Regiment, which maintains a strict code that seems to have had a positive impact on the Sleepy Hollow serenity evident here. You'll encounter an abundance of flagstone colonial buildings topped by tin roofs, many used by the military and in fairly attractive condition, surrounded by hedges and greenery. **Lower Mall Road,** as you head farther south, is good for walks, with only ancient trees for company. Continue on, past the 14th-century **Jhula Devi Temple,** and 10km (6¼ miles) south you'll come upon the state-run **Chaubatia Orchards,** a great place for a picnic (ask your hotel to pack one).

From here it's an easy drive to Corbett, reviewed below.

WHERE TO STAY & DINE
NAINITAL TO MUKTESHWAR

The best place to stay in Nainital itself is the **Palace Belvedere** ✦ (© 05942/23-7434; www.welcomheritage.com). Built in 1897, this former summer palace is a lovely way to experience a casual historic ambience with personal, attentive service. Book a lake-facing room (Rs 2,700/$60), which has an enclosed porch-cum-study (no. 19 is particularly large) from where the view of the sun rising over Nainital Lake is simply exquisite; even the bathrooms have views of the lake. Other than this, you could consider **Claridges Naini Retreat** (© 05942/23-5105 or -5108; www.corbetthideaway.com; doubles from Rs 2,200/$48). The gabled bluestone summer retreat of the Maharajah of Pilibeet, situated above Naini Lake, underwent a major overhaul early in 2003 but retains much of its charm. Standard rooms are neat but a tad cramped (book nos. 304–311). It's best to reserve one of three garden suites, which share a common balcony. Nainital is in fact overrun with accommodations possibilities, but note that a visit during peak season is likely to be accompanied by crowds, noise, and irritation.

Mountain Quail Camp ⭐ The drive from Nainital to this out-of-the-way mountainside resort provides jaw-dropping views back down over the town and lake, as well as entrancing vistas of the Himalayan range—particularly gorgeous just after sunrise, when a striking color palette whips over mountain peaks. The hill-hugging half-hour journey brings you to a remote and exquisitely peaceful site with deluxe tents and a lodge in a clearing between forested hills and terraced farmland. Opt for the tented accommodations, which feature fully tiled attached bathrooms with basin, shower (with running hot water), and Western toilet. The bedroom interiors have patterned "walls," pitched roofs, carpets, and thick but uneven mattresses. The resort is ideal for scenic walks and easy treks, and even more perfect for simply doing nothing. There's a mobile phone for emergencies.

Pangot 263 001. ⓒ **05942/23-5493.** Reservations: Meander Holidays, Delhi, ⓒ and fax 011/2632-7731, -7732, or -0822. info@meanderholiday.com. 10 tents and 2 units in the lodge. Doubles: Rs 2,500 ($55) tent; Rs 3,400 ($74) lodge unit. Rates include all meals. No credit cards. **Amenities:** Restaurant; trekking; fishing; camping; white-water rafting; doctor-on-call.

Mountain Trail This is the best place to overnight if you want to stay in Mukteshwar itself. Mountain Trail is well-maintained and is situated on a terraced slope with a lovely rose garden and direct views of the Himalayas. Accommodations are large, neat, and simple. Ask for a deluxe double room; each has high-pitched ceilings, enclosed porch with exquisite views, and large tiled shower. A tad rustic, perhaps, but guest rooms are comfortable and spotless, and the pleasant restaurant has a working fireplace. There's no bar, but most other facilities are available, and there's a game room with a small library.

P.O. Sargakhet, Mukteshwar 263 132. ⓒ **05942/28-8040** or -8240. www.mountaintrail.com. Reservations: Mountain Trail Holidays Pvt. Ltd., 224 Vardhaman Plaza, 9 Local Shopping Centre, I.P. Extension, Delhi 110 092. ⓒ 011/2765-2024, -4053, or -0008. 12 units. Doubles: Rs 2,500 ($55) superior; Rs 1,950 ($42) deluxe; Rs 1,550 ($34) comfort; Rs 2,500 ($55) 4-bed deluxe family room; Rs 3,800 ($83) 2-bedroom combination for 4 adults; Rs 500 ($11) extra adult. AE, MC, V. **Amenities:** Restaurant; river rafting; adventure activities; game room; room service; laundry; doctor-on-call; library. *In room:* TV, minibar.

The Ramgarh Bungalows ⭐⭐ An ideal and lovely base from which to explore the tranquil Kumaon Hills, these two 19th-century British bungalows feature deep verandas, bay windows, and dainty gardens. The Writers' Bungalow was built in 1860, while the Old Bungalow dates back to 1830; both have been given a bright, homey atmosphere with colorful floral fabrics. Ramgarh is 24km (15 miles) from Mukteshwar. Because of the remote location, you must make arrangements and reservations in advance.

Ramgarh (Malla), Kumaon Hills, Nainital District 263 137. ⓒ 05942/28-156 or -137. Reservations: Neemrana Hotels Pvt. Ltd., A-58 Nizamuddin E., New Delhi 110 013. ⓒ 011/2461-6145, -8962, or -5214. Fax 011/2462-1112. www.neemrana.com. 7 units. Doubles: Rs 800–Rs 1,750 ($18–$38) Old Bungalow; Rs 1,000–Rs 2,500 ($22–$55) Writers' Bungalow. AE, MC, V. **Amenities:** Restaurant; trekking; volleyball; basketball; room service; laundry; doctor-on-call; mobile phone.

BINSAR

High on the hill within Binsar Wildlife Sanctuary, the **forest rest house** is characterized by long, musty rooms, high ceilings, old-fashioned furnishings, a lack of electricity, and ridiculously low room rent. The rest house is looked after by a *chowkidar* (caretaker), who may even prepare meals for you if you bring your own supplies. Book a room through the Almora Forest Office. Near Almora, within a forest, the **Deodars** (Papparsalle; ⓒ **05962/23-3025;** rwheeler@rediffmail.com) is a family-run lodging option with three guest rooms in an old stone cottage; solitude is guaranteed.

> ## Golf Anyone?
> Play golf at what must be one of the most gorgeously scenic courses in India: The Kumaon Regiment's **Upat Kalika** in Ranikhet is set in pine forests and features a natural hazard—a 300m (1,000-ft.) cliff. Even if signboards threaten all nonmilitary personnel who attempt to play here, visitors are welcome (Mon, Tues, and Fri 7am–6pm; Wed, Thurs, and Sat 7am–12:30pm; 9 holes Rs 200/$4.30, clubs Rs 100/$2.10, caddy Rs 50/$1.05).

Club Mahindra Valley Resort Binsar ⚔   The appearance of this lovely luxury hideaway resort in October 2002 indicates the escalating interest in upmarket tourism in Uttaranchal. Stone pathways and slate stairways run between the various studios and one-bedroom apartments in smart mushroom-colored blocks spread across a terraced hillside. The apartments (club suites) are huge, with kitchenette, separate dining and sitting areas, Zen-style bedroom with rugs, and private balcony. Upbeat decor includes dark cream floor tiles, wood and cane furniture, and dark red rugs and ochre cushions offset by sandy-orange curtains and pale-yellow fabrics. Bathrooms are large and have a curtained drench shower. Deluxe accommodations are smaller but have the same well-considered, warm, contemporary decor. The management organizes a range of activities and excursions, primarily aimed at keeping well-heeled Indian guests busy. You can also chill out in the beer garden, and at night a bonfire warms guests in the icy air.

Bhainsori P.O., Binsar, Almora 263 684. ℂ 05962/25-3028, -3062, or -3174. Fax 05962/25-3035. www.club mahindra.com. resv.binsar@clubmahindra.com. 32 units. Doubles (July 16–Sept 30/Oct 1–Dec 20/Apr 1–July 15 and Dec 21–Jan 5): $70/$80/$90 deluxe suite; $80/$90/$110 club suite; children under 12 free. Rates include all meals, less $20 for room only. AE, DC, MC, V. **Amenities:** Restaurant; beer garden; cultural performances; table tennis; sightseeing excursions and adventure activities; camping; children's activity room; limited room service; laundry; doctor-on-call. *In room:* Heater, TV, minibar, microwave, tea- and coffee-making facilities.

RANIKHET

A charming alternative to the hotel reviewed below is **Chevron Rosemount** (ℂ **05966/22-1391** or -0989; www.chevronhotels.com), a century-old two-story colonial bungalow set in a forest clearing that's showing its age in a charmingly dilapidated way. Reserve room no. 202, the Nirvana Suite (Rs 3,000/$65). Unwind on the armchairs, chaise lounge, or large comfortable bed; the large bathroom has plenty of natural light. Another option worth considering is **Holm Farm** ⚔, the first bungalow in Ranikhet, with rooms from Rs 2,500 ($55). This is ideal if you're up for adventure, with arranged activities including trekking and rock climbing (ℂ **05966/22-0891** or -0831; www.holmfarm heritage.com).

West View Hotel ⚔   This stone brick colonial mansion—an atmospheric relic of the Raj set in a lovely garden—offers large accommodations with carpeted bedrooms, old dark wooden furniture, upholstered armchairs, hard mattresses on big beds, and massive bathrooms with drench showers and natural light. Deluxe guest rooms have a working stone fireplace, half-canopied two-poster beds, and floral blinds and bed frill. Ask for room no. 21, which is the best room in the house and has a view. Suites feature four-poster beds and a separate lounge. Some of the rooms are only accessible via creaking wooden stairways. There's a quaint, old-fashioned lounge and a homey dining room with a log fire and blue-patterned porcelain plates decorating the wallpapered walls. Note that hot water is only available in mornings and evenings.

Mahatma Gandhi Rd., Ranikhet 263 645. Ⓒ **05966/22-0261** or -1075. Fax 05966/22-0396. www.west viewhotel.com. info@westviewhotel.com. Reservations: C-16 Greater Kailash 1, New Delhi 110 048. Ⓒ 011/ 2648-5981. Fax 011/2648-5981. 19 units. Doubles: Rs 1,800 ($37); Rs 2,400 ($52) deluxe room; Rs 3,500 ($76) luxury suite; 2 children under 12 free; Rs 500 ($11) extra bed. Rates include breakfast and 1 other meal. Taxes extra. No credit cards. **Amenities:** Restaurant; badminton; table tennis; horseback riding in season (May/June); indoor games; limited transport assistance; limited room service; laundry; doctor-on-call. *In room:* TV; suites have a minibar.

3 Corbett National Park ★★★

264km (164 miles) NE of Delhi; 436km (279 miles) NW of Lucknow

Covering 1,319 sq. km, Corbett became India's first national park on August 8, 1936. When renowned conservationist Jim Corbett passed away in Kenya in 1955, it was renamed to honor his efforts to establish the park in the first place.

The biggest draw of the park, of course, is the possibility of spotting a tiger in the wild. Project Tiger, a government undertaking aimed at saving India's dwindling tiger population, was first launched here in 1973. Despite the fact that 140 or so tigers are currently found here, sightings are not to be taken for granted, and your chances of an encounter are far better at Ranthambore (Rajasthan) and Bandavgarh (Madhya Pradesh). The advantage of Corbett, however, is that you can overnight within the park itself. The landscape consists of Sal forests and bamboo trees, with an abundance of other wildlife, including leopards, herds of wild elephant, wild boars, black bears, sambar, spotted deer, four-horned antelope *(chausingha),* monkeys, hundreds of bird species, and a reptile population that includes pythons and the endangered gharial crocodile.

VISITING THE PARK

Hours   Corbett is open from November 15 through June 15, closing when the monsoon causes rivers to flood their banks. Sightings are best between March and June.

Entering the Park   Access to the park is via the town of Ramnagar, where the **Park Office** (opposite the Ramnagar bus stand; Ⓒ **05947/25-1489;** daily 8:30am–1pm and 3–5pm) processes and issues the required permits, and handles all park accommodations as well as jeep safaris. There are direct trains from Delhi to Ramnagar; driving takes 6 to 8 hours (around 300km/186 miles). Corbett is divided into five mutually exclusive tourist zones, and you can visit only

The Hunter-Turned-Conservationist

Born in Nainital, Jim Corbett was a reformed hunter who, in his pre-conservationist years, hunted large animals for pleasure, killing his first leopard at the age of 8. During the 1920s, he gave up his bloody hobby but regularly shot vicious man-eating tigers or cats believed to be threats to humans. To get yourself in the mood for your visit, pick up an omnibus of Corbett's fearsome hunting tales, or a copy of his first book, *Man-Eaters of the Kumaon,* which recounts how he hunted and killed the Champawat tigress that was responsible for the death of 434 people.

one zone at a time. If you do not have your own vehicle, hire one in Ramnagar or at the Dhangari gate. It's best to undertake jeep safaris early in the morning. You are not permitted to enter the park more than 30 minutes before the sun descends, and nighttime driving within Corbett is not allowed. Don't make the mistake of arriving in Ramnagar too late in the day; you will have to fill out forms, pay for permits and accommodations, and still get to the gate 30 minutes before sunset. Corbett is extremely popular and likely to be fully booked, so don't arrive unannounced.

Exploring the Park   Perhaps the most visually attractive area of the park is **Jhirna,** which incidentally does not close during the monsoon season. Try to visit the **Ramganga Reservoir,** where endangered gharial crocodiles bask on the banks and a sign warning against swimming proclaims that SURVIVORS WILL BE PROSECUTED. Surrounded by vast elephant grassland savannahs, **Dhikala** has the greatest selection of accommodations, and substitutes solitude for access to facilities like restaurants, a library, and wildlife film screenings. Dhikala is reached via **Dhangarhi Gate** (16km/10 miles north of Ramnagar); it's open daily 7am to 5pm in winter, and 6am to 6pm when the days are longer. **Elephant rides,** available from Dhikala and Bijrani, are the most promising and nature-friendly way of tracking tigers through the *chaur.* Departing at sun-up and sunset, each 2-hour ride through the forests and across the plains costs just Rs 100 ($2.10). You need to book your place well in advance (a full day is recommended), and reward your *mahout* (elephant handler) with a tip if you do, indeed, spot a tiger.

Tip: If you don't plan on staying in the park, it's far easier (particularly if you're staying at one of the resorts reviewed below) to have your hotel management make all your safari arrangements; the bureaucracy and form-filling that go with acquiring the necessary permits can be exasperating.

WHERE TO STAY & DINE
INSIDE THE PARK

We recommend that you stay outside the park—Corbett Ramganga and Solluna are located some distance from the entrance, while Claridges Corbett Hideaway and Infinity are much closer. Although overnighting within the park itself has many advantages, comfort and service are not among them. The commercially popular and often crowded **Dikhala** camp is the only place where you can find food inside the park; it has two vegetarian restaurants. Dikhala's accommodations include cabins and three-bed "hutments" with attached bathrooms, and dorms that sleep 12 and are serviced by a separate washroom. **Forest bungalows** are scattered throughout the reserve and are best booked at least 1 month in advance; they offer seclusion and complete privacy, but—as with all of the rest houses outside Dikhala—you'll have to bring your own supplies. (Beware of leaving food lying around—there are reports of elephants ripping out the screen windows of forest rest houses in attempts to get to the provisions inside.) One of the best bungalows is at **Gairal,** near the Ramganga River and close to a hide bank. **Kandha rest house** is situated on the highest point within the park. If you're up for a little more style, ask about **lodges** that were once used by British hunters; these have such unexpected luxuries as attached bathrooms, fireplaces, and carpets. For reservations for any of these camps, contact the Director, Corbett Reserve Reception Centre, Ramnagar 244 715 (© **05947/25-1489,** 05947/25-1362, or 05947/25-1376; Dhikala tariffs: cabins Rs 1,000/$22 per foreigner; log huts Rs 500/$11 per foreigner; dorms Rs 300/$6.50 per foreigner; forest bungalows Rs 1,000/$22 per foreigner; no credit cards; ask about hiring guides and elephant and jeep safaris).

OUTSIDE THE PARK

Claridges Corbett Hideaway ★★ Pebbled pathways interweave between the pretty gardens and cozy mustard-colored cottages set in a mango orchard. The older, jungle-themed cottages have thatched, pitched ceilings, stone-tile flooring, comfortable beds, and separate sitting area with fireplace. Luxury Swiss tents are also available; carpeted with coir, they are furnished and have attached shower-toilets, heater, telephone, and terrace. A lovely place to relax is the newly refurbished thatched-roof bar, with its distinguished air. There's a well-stocked library with a selection of Jim Corbett's books to get you in the mood for tiger-spotting safaris. If you don't feel like lazing, and you're not on the back of a pachyderm, it's possible to organize river rafting on the Kosi River. Or check out the resort's own herd of water buffalo.

Zero Garjia, Dhikuli 224 715. ℂ **05947/28-4132** or -4134. Fax 05947/28-4133. www.corbetthideaway.com. corbett@ndf.vsnl.net.in. 39 cottages and 14 tents. Rs 4,950 ($110) double. AE, DC, MC, V. **Amenities:** 2 restaurants; bar; pool; kids' pool; jeep, elephant, and coach safaris; river rafting; fishing; archery; table tennis; badminton; bird-watching; indoor games; billiards; nature shop; laundry; doctor-on-call. *In room:* Tea- and coffee-making facilities.

Corbett Ramganga Resort ★ Tiger-spotting is not the only reason to venture into the lower Kumaon Mountains. Die-hard anglers head here in hope of bagging India's ultimate big game fishing trophy: the mighty *mahseer*. This decade-old resort, situated on the banks of the Ramganga River, is not as attractive as its riverfront neighbor Solluna, but it draws an interesting mix of people, many here only to fish—the world record for the heaviest *mahseer* ever caught was bagged just 500m (1,600 ft.) from the Corbett resort. Guest rooms are large and simple, in semi-circular brick cabins with stone tile floors. We prefer the tented accommodations—each large, army-style structure is encased in a thatch shell, with a tiny dressing room and a small shower room attached; best of all, the mattresses are a great deal more comfortable. Around the resort, green forests and mountain peaks provide the ultimate getaway. The resort now draws diplomats representing every corner of the globe. At night, guests—mostly moneyed Indians—gather around a shallow bonfire and share rum-induced fishing tales told by faux-modest industrialists from the plains; in the background, the gurgling Ramganga reminds you that you're miles away from the pollution, congestion, and ceaseless traffic of the cities. You might also like to ask the manager about a rainy night when he witnessed a standoff between a tiger and a boar, just outside his office. The resort also organizes night safaris through the surrounding valleys, providing an opportunity for potential tiger and leopard sightings. Buffet meals, served in a high-ceiling, circular restaurant, are wonderful. Although it has no liquor license, alcohol is available.

Village Jhamaria, P.O. Sankar, Marchula. ℂ **05947/25-3357.** Reservations: Surbhi Adventures, 5 Sainik Farms, New Delhi 110 062. ℂ 011/2652-2955. Fax 011/2685-5428. www.welcomheritage.com. 16 units and 10 deluxe tents. Doubles: Rs 3,550 ($77) tent; Rs 4,100 ($89) room; Rs 5,000 ($110) suite. Rates include all meals. AE, DC, MC, V. **Amenities:** Restaurant; bar service; pool; snacks-only room service; fishing; night safaris; river-rafting; rappelling and other adventure activities; badminton; cycling; indoor and outdoor games; day excursions; laundry; doctor-on-call. *In room:* Suites have kitchenettes and tea- and coffee-making facilities.

Infinity Resorts ★ Activities at this pleasant riverside hotel center around a huge enclosed octagonal building with a terrace and indoor bonfire; this is where meals are served, wildlife movies are shown, and cultural performances are held. It's worthwhile to pay a little more for the deluxe guest rooms, which lead off open corridors on the floor above the standard units. They're spacious (though not particularly tasteful), and each one has a large terrace with a river view. From your room, you can hear the river and enjoy great bird-watching. The setting is peaceful, perhaps more so than at Claridges Corbett Hideaway. There's a relaxing swimming pool, and a terraced rock embankment leads down to a riverside pond filled with *mahseer* and a nearby shrine to Ganesha. Hammocks are strung up between the *aam* trees and rhododendrons, and the idyllic setting is wonderful for stretching out with a copy of Jim Corbett's memoirs.

P.O. Dhikuli, Ramnagar 244 715. ℂ **05947/25-1279**, -1280, or 05947/28-7957. Fax 05947/25-1880. www. infinityresorts.com. Reservations: A3 Geetanjali Enclave, New Delhi 110 017. ℂ 011/2669-1209. Fax 011/ 2669-1219. 24 units. Doubles (Apr 16–Nov 14/Nov 15–Apr 15): $130/$160 standard; $150/$190 deluxe; $10 extra bed. Rates include all meals and 1 safari per day. AE, DC, MC, V. **Amenities:** Restaurant; bar; cultural events; pool; health club; fishing; park jeep safaris, elephant safaris; nature walks; wildlife film shows; conference hall; souvenir shop; room service on request; laundry; medical center. *In room:* A/C, heater.

The Solluna Resort 🔒 Not as well-known as its older neighbor, Corbett Ramganga, this resort—named for the sun and the moon—has better rooms (gorgeous cottages, each with comfortable mattress, bay window seats, a skylight that allows you to watch the stars from your bed, a good tiled shower room, cupboard space, working surfaces, and two small private verandas with wicker chairs and a cane swing), but it's not as popular and therefore not as convivial. Above the reception area (where there's a small dining area), a lovely viewing terrace with comfortable wicker chairs is great for lazing and drinking in the natural spectacle that's all around you. Expansive lawns surround the cottages, with bougainvillea and mango and cherry trees scattered here and there. At night pathways are lit up with storm lanterns, and a bonfire is lit for a communal chinwag. Alcohol isn't available, but you're welcome to bring your own.

Marchula 244 715. Reservations: ℂ **011/2332-0264**, 011/2335-0040, or 011/2331-0227. www.indiamart. com/sollunaresort. spime_solluna@rediffmail.com. 18 cottages and 5 tents. Doubles: Rs 4,500 ($98); 2 children under 7 stay free; Rs 1,800 ($40) extra person. Rates include all meals. Expect discounts of up to 50% during the off season mid-June to mid-Nov. No credit cards. **Amenities:** 2 dining areas; pool; safaris; sightseeing; limited room service; laundry; doctor-on-call. *In room:* Air-cooler.

12

Kolkata (Calcutta) & East India

The image most people have of Calcutta is one of abject poverty and misery—mostly the result of media focus on Mother Teresa's good work. Despite this unfortunate perception, Kolkata (as the Communist-ruled West Bengal capital became known in 2001) attracts its fare share of visitors, most of whom are taken aback by the seductive charms of this intoxicating city. Believed to be the ethereal abode of the goddess Kali, who embodies *shakti*—fortitude and strength—it is home to a joyous, cerebral, and sophisticated community, some of the best Raj-era architecture in India, many of the country's best artists, a thriving film and fashion industry, five-star hotels, and a host of superb restaurants. Kolkata is also the natural starting point for a trip to the Himalayan mountains of the north, where you can drink in the crystal-clear air of **Darjeeling,** India's

most famous hill station, imbibing in the "champagne of teas" before picking up a permit to hike the tiny state of **Sikkim.** One of the least explored regions of India, Sikkim is a world apart, surrounded by jagged peaks, and home to serene snow-fed lakes, remote Buddhist monasteries, yak-herding Tibetans, high-altitude forests, and some 4,000 varieties of wildflowers (including 600 varieties of orchid). South of West Bengal, in the coastal state of **Orissa**—often called the "soul of India"—you can join the pilgrims who gather in the thousands to pay homage to the Lord of the Universe, who resides at the seaside town of Puri; within easy striking distance from here is Konark's **Sun Temple,** a World Heritage Site, a testament to the technical and artistic brilliance of Orissa in the 13th century, and unreservedly one of India's top attractions.

1 Kolkata

1,310km (812 miles) SE of Delhi

Once the proud capital of the British Raj, Kolkata is deeply evocative of an era and sensibility lost in time. Established as the trading post for the East India Company on the banks of the River Hooghly by Job Charnock in 1690, it grew to be the biggest colonial trade center in Asia, earning it the moniker "Jewel of the East." With its splendid Victorian buildings, ornamental pools, stone-paved footpaths, figured lampposts, and sweeping esplanade, it was entirely European in its architecture and sensibilities, and the burgeoning city became the stomping ground of a new breed of *sahibs* and *memsahibs* who wore their white skins and British manners as though they were royal insignias. But Kolkata was effectively built on a disease-breeding swamp—the marshy delta of the Ganges and Brahmaputra rivers—and this, combined with the heat, humidity, and the Bengalis' prominence in the struggle for independence, finally persuaded the British to transfer the capital. In 1911 they left for Delhi, leaving Calcutta to rot.

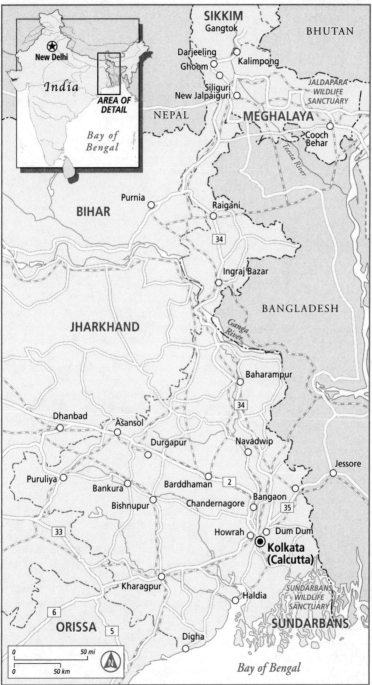

Kolkata (Calcutta)

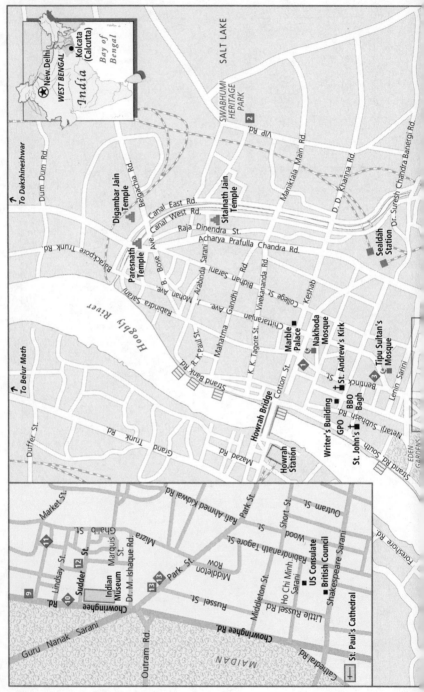

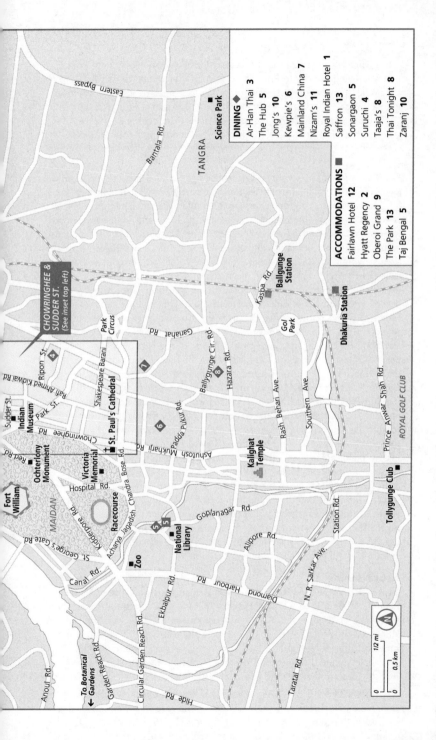

DINING ◆
Ar-Han Thai **3**
The Hub **5**
Jong's **10**
Kewpie's **6**
Mainland China **7**
Nizam's **11**
Royal Indian Hotel **1**
Saffron **13**
Sonargaon **5**
Suruchi **4**
Taaja's **8**
Thai Tonight **8**
Zaranj **10**

ACCOMMODATIONS ■
Fairlawn Hotel **12**
Hyatt Regency **2**
Oberoi Grand **9**
The Park **13**
Taj Bengal **5**

CHOWRINGHEE & SUDDER ST.
(See inset top left)

TANGRA

Science Park

Eastern Bypass

Bantala Rd.

Ballygunge Station

Kasba Rd.

Gol Park

Dhakuria Station

Park Circus

Garihat Rd.

Ballygunge Cir. Rd.

Hazara Rd.

Southern Ave.

Rash Behari Ave.

ROYAL GOLF CLUB

Prince Anwar Shah Rd.

Shakespeare Sarani

Ripon St.

Rafi Ahmed Kidwai Rd.

Park St.

Chowringhee Rd.

St. Paul's Cathedral

Padda Pukur Rd.

Ashutosh Mukherji Rd.

Kalighat Temple

Sudder St.

Indian Museum

Ochterlony Monument

Red Rd.

Fort William

MAIDAN

Victoria Memorial

Hospital Rd.

Racecourse

Kidderpore Rd.

St. George's Gate Rd.

Acharya Jagadish Chandra Bose Rd.

Goplanagar Rd.

National Library

Zoo

Alipore Rd.

Station Rd.

Tollygunge Club

N. R. Sarkar Ave.

Diamond Harbour Rd.

Ekbalpur Rd.

Canal Rd.

Circular Garden Reach Rd.

Garden Reach Rd.

Anqul Rd.

Hide Rd.

Taratal Rd.

To Botanical Gardens

N

1/2 mi
0.5 km

Tips **Exploring East India**

To cover all of the three Eastern states, you will need a minimum of 9 days, ideally flying directly to Bhubaneswar, capital of Orissa, to visit **Puri** and **Konark,** then heading northward to **West Bengal** to visit the capital, Kolkata, and the state's idyllic hill station, **Darjeeling.** End your tour in laid-back **Sikkim** before flying back to Delhi from nearby Bagdogra Airport. Set aside extra time for trekking in Sikkim or tribal tours in Orissa.

Today much of the city's architectural heritage stands crumbling and in ruins, its monumental colonial structures nowhere nearly as well maintained as those of Mumbai. Moss and grime cover tattered buildings that should be celebrated as the city's finest—the collapsing masonry, peeling paint, and sun-scorched woodwork testaments to the indifference of time. Unable to stem the long-term industrial and commercial decline of the city or the flood of refugees that have been arriving from Bangladesh since the first days of Partition, the Communist ruling party (CPI) struggles to adequately provide for the city's 14 million inhabitants. The second-largest city on the subcontinent (after Mumbai), it is packed to capacity, politically beleaguered and heavily polluted, an *entrêpote* of India's sorriest social woes. Yet the charms of Kolkata are fiercely touted by its proud citizens, who speak rapturously of its benefits over the other big Indian metropolises. In fact, meeting Bengalis is one of the best aspects of traveling here—Kolkata is the self-proclaimed capital of India's intellectuals, home to three Nobel Prize laureates (including the revered Rabindranath Tagore, who became Asia's first Nobel laureate in 1913) and an Oscar-winning film director (Satyajit Ray). Warm, helpful, and imbued with a great sense of humor (not to mention a famously keen appreciation for dining), the Bengalis live by the maxim that "what Bengal does today, India will do tomorrow." Engaging in some lively discussion on the benefits or drawbacks of Communism or the original recipe for *mishti doi* (milk-based sweets, the Bengali specialty) is likely to be one of your more memorable experiences in India.

In some ways, the city is as frightening as one fears, a degraded mess where squalor, filth, and the ubiquitous *bustees* (slums) can overwhelm the senses. If you're in India to enjoy the country's softer side, then don't tarry here long; head for the Himalayan mountainscapes of Sikkim or Darjeeling, or the temples and beaches of Orissa, farther south. But if you delight in eclectic city culture, spend at least 2 or 3 nights in this thrilling city.

ESSENTIALS

VISITOR INFORMATION   The **West Bengal Tourism Centre** (3/2 B.B.D. Bagh E.; © 033/2248-8271, -8272, or -8273) is good for up-to-date information (pick up a copy of *Kolkata This Fortnight,* a leaflet with information about current events); you can also arrange city tours here. Visit the **Government of India Regional Tourist Office** (4 Shakespeare Sarani; © 033/2282-5813) for (limited) information on the entire subcontinent. *Cal Calling* is a monthly catalog of events and general information.

GETTING THERE & AWAY   By Air   Kolkata is served by domestic flights from most major destinations in India. **Dum Dum Airport** (renamed Netaji Subbash Chandra Bose International Airport; © 033/2511-8070 or -8079) lies 15km (9 miles) northeast. You can exchange currency and get tourist information from two separate booths here. Use the prepaid taxi stand; the 40-minute trip should cost Rs 150 to Rs 180 ($3.15–$4).

By Train   Kolkata's **Howrah Junction** (✆ **033/2220-4025** or -3545), just south of Howrah Bridge, connects the city with most other parts of the country. It's made up of the adjoining Old and New Howrah stations. You're advised to purchase tickets through your hotel or a travel agent, but there is a section specifically for foreigners in the main **reservations office** (daily 9am–1pm and 1:30–4pm). For general inquiries, call ✆ **1310;** for prerecorded information, call ✆ 1331. Trains to destinations farther east and to the northern areas of West Bengal often depart from **Sealdah Station** (Bepin Behari Ganguly St.; ✆ **033/2350-3535** or -3496); check your ticket to confirm which station you need to be at. Also arrive with time to spare so that you can navigate through the crowds and find out about any changes to the schedule.

By Road   Don't consider getting to or from Kolkata by motor vehicle; you'll find yourself wasting a great deal of vacation time; this includes traveling by bus.

GETTING AROUND   By Taxi & Auto-Rickshaw   The full-to-capacity streets of Kolkata can be the very devil to get around, but a jaunt in a Morris Oxford is a good way to experience the city. Taxi drivers here are notoriously keen on ripping you off even after you've negotiated a fare. Ask your hotel concierge for an approximate idea of the fare given your route, check that the meter is reset, and make sure that your driver knows where you're going (use a street map to ensure you aren't taken on a detour). You can hire a good car and driver through **Wenz** (Oberoi Grand; ✆ **033/2249-2323,** ext. 6247). **Hertz** has an office at the New Kenilworth Hotel (Little Russel St.; ✆ **033/2242-8394**); see "Car Rentals" under "Fast Facts," below, for other companies. Note that rickshaws are outlawed from entering many of the city's major streets. You may feel too guilty to engage the services of a hand-pulled rickshaw, but you're helping cut down on pollution and feed a family; tip generously.

The Metro   India's first underground railway was started in Calcutta in 1984; it currently connects Tollygunge in the south with Dum Dum Station in the

---

The Dance of Destruction

For Hindus, India is a Holy Land, with thousands of *tirthas*—celestial "cross over" points where mortals can access the world of the gods. Legend has it that these were created after Lord Shiva's wife, Sati, jumped into a fire in an act of shame because her father, Raja Daksha, had neglected to invite Shiva to an important ritual. Unable to bear the loss, the grief-struck Shiva—carrying Sati's body—began to pace India in a *tandava nritya,* or "dance of destruction." Terrified that his fury and pain would destroy the universe, Brahma, Vishnu, and Shani dispersed her body across the vast plains and peaks of India, and wherever a body part fell, this became a *tirtha.* Many of these are important pilgrimage sites Hindu believers must visit at least once in their lifetime, such as those at Varanasi (see chapter 8). One of Sati's toes also fell in a dense forest in southwest Bengal. Today, this site—now the **Kalighat Temple**—is one of India's most important pilgrimage centers, where the goddess is worshipped as Kali. The toe is supposedly housed in a chamber of the temple. Every year in June, as part of a secretive ritual, the toe is bathed.

north. It's a reliable, clean, and surprisingly uncrowded transport option, and tickets are cheap. The Metro operates Monday through Saturday from 7am to 9:45pm, and on Sunday from 3 to 9:45pm. For information, contact the **Metro Rail Bhavan** (33/1 Jawaharlal Nehru Rd.; ✆ **033/2226-1053** or -7280).

By Bus or Tram If you're keen to experience India at its most confusing, claustrophobic, and unpredictable, by all means hop aboard one of Kolkata's battered buses or road-clogging trams.

On Foot Early morning is the best time to get out and stroll through the streets; it's still relatively quiet, and the air is cooler and less choked by pollution. Pick up a cup of tea from the *chai-wallahs* who serve their sweet brew in tiny unfired clay cups—India's answer to the polystyrene cup, these are simply discarded after use.

GUIDED TOURS The following two are worth booking before arriving: **Shanti Bhattacharjee** is a retired history teacher with a profound knowledge of his city, who provides in-depth tours of Kolkata (✆ **033/350-1576**); and architect **Manish Chakrabovti** conducts **heritage walks** 🎯🎯 of northern Kolkata on behalf of Action Research in Conservation of Heritage (✆ **033/2337-5757** or 033/2355-0915). **The Tourism Centre** (3/2 B.B.D. Bagh E.; ✆ **033/248-8271** or -8272) conducts two different daily sightseeing tours of the city; these inevitably involve a great deal of bus travel and little sightseeing. In the same center, the **West Bengal Tourist Development Corporation** (✆ **033/210-3199** or 033/248-5917) organizes short and long-distance tours of the state and selected destinations around the country.

FAST FACTS: Kolkata

Airlines **Jet Airways:** ✆ **033/229-2227,** -2237, -2214; or 033/229-2084 or 033/229-2813. **Air Sahara:** ✆ **033/282-6118** through -6122. **Indian Airlines:** ✆ **033/211-0810,** -0730, or -0870.

American Express 21 Old Court House St., near Raj Bhavan; ✆ **033/2248-2133.** Open Monday to Friday 9:30am to 5:30pm and Saturday 9:30am to 2pm.

Area Code The area code for **Kolkata** is **033.**

ATMs There are plenty of 24-hour ATMs where you can draw money against your credit card: **UTI Bank** (7/1 Lord Sinha Rd.; ✆ **033/2282-2933**), **HDFC Bank** (Stephen House, 4 B.B.D. Bagh E.; ✆ **033/2243-5813,** -5814, or -5819), **Standard Chartered Grindlays Bank** (41 J. L. Nehru Rd.; ✆ **033/2246-5000**), **HSBC Bank** (8 Netaji Subhash Rd., 31 B.B.D. Bagh; ✆ **033/2248-6363**).

Banks Most banks are open Monday to Friday 10am to 2 or 3pm, and Saturday 10am to noon.

Bookstores One of India's best, **Oxford Bookstore** (17 Park St., Kolkata 700 016; ✆ **033/2229-7662;** oxfordcal@apeejaygroup.com) carries a good range of local and imported periodicals, books on India and Calcutta, and fiction. Another shop worth investigating is **Family Book Shop** (1A Park St.; ✆ **033/ 2229-3486**); it's tiny, but there's an interesting upstairs section.

Car Rentals **Avis Rent-A-Car** is situated at the Oberoi Grand (15 Jawaharlal Nehru Rd.; ✆ **033/2249-2323** or -6181). Upmarket cars are available from **Car-Cab** (2 Manook Lane, off Ezra St., Kolkata 1; ✆ **033/2235-3535;** vayuseva@cal.vsnl.net.in).

Changed Telephone Number Announcement Dial **1952** for computerized English information if you encounter a wrong number announcement.

Consulates **United States:** 5/1 Ho Chi Minh Sarani; ✆ **033/2242-3611;** Monday to Friday 8:30am to 12:30pm and 2 to 4pm. **United Kingdom:** 1 Ho Chi Minh Sarani; ✆ **033/2242-5171;** Monday to Friday 9am to noon. **Canada:** Duncan House, 31 N.S. Rd.; ✆ **033/2225-0163;** call for hours.

Currency Exchange **Thomas Cook** is at 230 A.J.C. Bose Rd. (✆ **033/2247-5378);** hours are Monday to Saturday 9:30am to 1pm and 1:45 to 6pm.

Drugstores Twenty-four-hour chemists include **AMRI Apollo Hospital Pharmacy** (P4 Gariahat Rd., Block A-29; ✆ **033/2440-3675),** **Dhanwantary** (65 Diamond Harbour Rd.; ✆ **033/2449-3204), Jeevan Deep** (114B Hazra Rd.; ✆ **033/2455-0926),** and **Life Care** (1/2A Hazra Rd.; ✆ **033/2475-4628).**

Emergencies For fire brigade, dial ✆ **101** or 033/2244-0101.

Hospitals **Belle Vue Clinic** (9 U.N. Brahmachari St.; ✆ **033/2247-2321,** -6921, -6925, or -7473) has ambulances on standby round-the-clock, and there's a blood bank. There are English-speaking doctors at the 24-hour **B. M. Birla Heart Research Center** (1/1A National Library Ave.; ✆ **033/2479-4003** or -4024).

Newspapers/Magazines Peruse the pages of *The Statesman,* one of India's oldest English dailies, for information about special events.

Police Dial ✆ **100** or **033/2215-5000.** Police headquarters are in Lal Bazaar (✆ **033/2479-1311,** -1312, -1313, -1314, or -1315).

Post Office B.B.D. Bagh (✆ **033/2220-1451** or -1601); Monday to Saturday 8am to 8:30pm and Sunday 8am to 3:30pm.

ORIENTATION

Kolkata is a huge, sprawling city, divided into **north** and **south,** both spread along the eastern bank of the Hooghly River, which divides it from the vast suburb of **Howrah,** located on the western bank. Howrah is where you'll be deposited if you arrive by train; the main station is close to the Howrah Bridge, which connects with the city proper. Just east and south of Howrah Bridge are Kolkata's commercial and tourist hubs, centered around **B.B.D. Bagh,** formerly known as Dalhousie Square, and the long stretch of road once known as **Chowringhee** (now Jawaharlal Nehru Rd.) that runs southward, alongside the Maidan, Kolkata's vast urban park. Many visitors base themselves around Chowringhee; nearby Sudder Street teems with budget accommodations, while Park Street has plenty of boutiques and fine restaurants.

To the northeast is the rapidly expanding business district of **Salt Lake City,** which has few historical sites but is steadily developing a reputation for its upscale business hotels and high-tech entertainment facilities. It's the closest district to the airport.

WHAT TO SEE & DO

You need at least 2 full days to cover Kolkata. Spend the first exploring central and south Kolkata, and the second covering the sites in the north, for which you should hire a car and driver.

Hurray for Tollywood

Kolkata has its own film industry, known throughout the Bengali world as Tollywood. In fact, it was this city that gave birth to India's finest filmmaker, Satyajit Ray, who died in 1992—the same year he received a Lifetime Achievement Oscar. While Bollywood was churning out dazzling choreographic daydreams, Ray made classic films that filled arthouse cinemas around the world. For more on Ray, go to the appendix.

DAY ONE (CENTRAL & SOUTH KOLKATA)

Start by catching a taxi south, to visit the city's most famous temple, **Kalighat Kali** (reviewed below). After this, either visit Mother Teresa's **Nirmal Hirday** home for the destitute and dying, right next door; or, if you're a bookworm, check out the **National Library** (located in the 300-year-old former summer residence of Prince Azim-us-Shan, the grandson of Emperor Aurangzeb, it has a catalog of over two million books). Our recommendation is to enjoy the relaxing, tranquil atmosphere of **South Park Street Cemetery** instead (see below) before you head into the chaos of central Kolkata. If you're feeling hungry, nearby **Suruchi** (© 033/2229-1763; 89 Elliot Rd., near Mallik Bazaar) is probably Kolkata's most authentic Bengali restaurant, with a real no-frills homegrown atmosphere. It's closed on Friday and Saturday and takes no credit cards.

You can save time by using a car to move on to central Kolkata, or enjoy the walk along Park Street to **Chowringhee Road,** taking in the upmarket shops and boutiques and perhaps stopping at **Flury's** for tea and a sandwich. Now officially know as Jawaharlal Nehru Road, Chowringhee is Kolkata's main beat, with less human excrement along its sidewalks than almost anywhere else in the city. It is lined with colonial Victoriana—including the monumental **Indian Museum** (see below) and that pinnacle of Calcutta's society life, the **Oberoi Grand.** Continue north along Chowringhee into the heart of the city, where you can explore the roads around **B.B.D. Bagh** (see below).

When you've had your fill of life on the sidewalks, make your way south again, along Government Place East. You'll soon find yourself in the green expanse that is the **Maidan**—the world's largest urban park—where the Ochterlony Monument, or **Shahid Minar (Martyr's Tower),** is worth noting. Walking west through the Maidan will bring you to **Eden Gardens,** often crowded with others seeking refuge from the city, while much farther south is the imperious **Victoria Memorial** (see below). It's worth buying a ticket and venturing in if you are keen to broaden your knowledge of the city's history. But don't feel guilty if you just want to lie on the lawn and watch Bengalis socializing. Otherwise, brave the traffic and catch a cab to Howrah to explore the 18th-century **Indian Botanical Gardens** (Shibpur; © 033/2660-3235; closes an hour before sunset), said to house the largest banyan tree on earth.

TOP ATTRACTIONS

B.B.D. Bagh ✦✦✦ For those interested in colonial architecture, this part of central Kolkata makes for very worthwhile exploration on foot. Once called Dalhousie Square, B.B.D. refers to the names of three Indian freedom fighters (Benoy, Badal, and Dinesh) who shot a British police inspector-general in 1930. At the center of the square *(bagh)* is the Lal Dighi Tank, where locals wade and bathe in the dodgy-looking spring-fed water. Most impressive of the surrounding monuments is the **Writers' Building,** which stretches along B.B.D. Bagh

North Road; it was built to house the British bachelors imported to serve the East India Company. Across the road is the early-19th-century **St. Andrew's Kirk,** recognizable by its tall white steeple. At the other end of B.B.D. Bagh North is the **General Post Office,** with a monumental rotunda; it's thought to be the site of the notorious Black Hole of Calcutta incident (see the appendix). Southwest of the tank is the St. Martin-in-the-Fields–inspired **St. John's Church** and, within the grounds, the tomb of Calcutta's founding father, Job Charnock. East of B.B.D. Bagh, to the south of Lal Bazaar, you'll find numerous tea merchants, where teas from Darjeeling, the Dooars, and Assam are packed and exported. **Nilhat House,** located behind the Old Mission Church, is the oldest tea auction house in India—join the action on Monday and Tuesday mornings.

Central Kolkata, south of Howrah Bridge, and north of Jawaharlal Nehru Rd.

Indian Museum ✸✸✸ If you're at all impressed by things beautiful, unusual, and ancient, you'll understand why the museum is known to locals as *Jadu Ghar,* the House of Magic. The oldest institution of its kind in the Asia–Pacific region, it holds the country's largest repository of artifacts (over 100,000 exhibits). Among the dinosaur and mammoth skeletons and the 4,000-year-old Egyptian mummy are extraordinary Indian cultural items, including Shah Jahan's emerald goblet, and an urn said to contain the Buddha's ashes. Don't miss the cultural anthropology section—accompanied by good explanations—if you are interested in India's many tribal groups. The textiles-and-decorative-arts gallery is most impressive. It can be difficult to find, however—ask for assistance.

27 Jawaharlal Nehru Rd., at the corner of Sudder St. ✆ **033/2249-9853.** Rs 150 ($3.15). Mar–Nov, Tues–Sun 10am-5pm; Dec–Feb, Tues–Sun 10am–4:30pm.

South Park Street Cemetery ✸✸ This is Kolkata's most famous cemetery, where monumental gravestones and lichen- and moss-covered tombstones to large numbers of ill-fated Brits buried on Indian soil provide a tranquil retreat. It's a really atmospheric place to wander around, and worth reading the headstones that bear unlikely epitaphs like MAJ. GEN. C. GREEN DIED 51TH OF JULY.

Park St. and southeast end of Cemetery Rd. Free admission. Daily 7:30am–4:30pm.

Victoria Memorial ✸ Conceived by Lord Curzon as a monument to his queen 4 years after her death, this domed structure is Kolkata's most recognizable landmark. It's billed as one of the city's top attractions, but with portraits of fairly boring-looking individuals filling many of the walls, it's more likely to excite Rajophiles. There are 25 galleries in the central hall, and around 3,500 articles relating to the Raj are on display, including the queen's rosewood piano. Exhibits are not restricted to Raj-artifacts; the black marble throne that belonged to Siraj-ud-Daulah is impressive, as is a gigantic painting of a Jaipur royal procession, said to be one of the largest paintings in Asia.

Queen's Way. ✆ **033/2223-1889,** -1890, or -1891. www.victoriamemorial-cal.org. Rs 150 ($3.15). Tues–Sun 10am–4:30pm. Sound-and-light show: Tues–Sun at 7:15pm and 8:15pm.

Kalighat Kali Temple ✸✸ Violent, vengeful Kali is the patron goddess of Kolkata, and this temple complex—believed to be the site where the toe of Shiva's wife fell when her body was scattered across the earth by the gods anxious to stop Lord Shiva's dance of destruction (see "The Dance of Destruction," earlier in this chapter)—is a major pilgrimage center, drawing some 20,000 visitors each day. If you're a non-Hindu, you cannot enter the inner sanctum, but it's worth exploring the courtyards and the various stalls selling flowers, fruit,

The Miracle of Mother Teresa & the "Pure Hearts"

Mother Teresa's **Missions of Charity (MOC)** is now headed by Sister Nirmala, a converted Brahmin. There are around 3,500 MOC sisters around the world, working in 569 centers in 120 countries, but their selfless efforts are not without controversy. Even during Mother Teresa's time, tales of pecuniary troubles and controversies over the way in which the poor and dying were being treated (and converted) beleaguered the MOC. There have always been plenty of cynics, despite the Vatican's confirmation of Mother Teresa's "miraculous" healing of a young woman's malignant tumor (the woman claims to have been cured after seeing Mother Teresa in her dreams), a move that has irritated rationalists and the medical profession. Still, in Kolkata alone, more than 50,000 destitute sick and dying are looked after by the blue-and-white sari-wearing nuns of the MOC, a demonstration of selflessness that you might deem miraculous in itself. Adjacent the Kali Temple is "Pure Heart," or **Nirmal Hirday** (251 Kalighat Rd.; ℗ **033/2464-4223;** Fri–Wed 8:30–11:30am and 3–5pm), the very first MOC center. **Mother House** (54A A.J.C. Bose Rd.; ℗ **033/2249-7115;** Fri–Wed 8:30–11:30am and 3–5pm) is the MOC headquarters, where Mother Teresa is buried. Nearby is **Shishu Bhawan** (78 A.J.C. Bose Rd.; Fri–Wed 8:30–11:30am and 3–5pm), where some 250 orphans are cared for.

and religious paraphernalia. Beware the sticky floors throughout the complex; they're sticky with the blood of sacrificed goats (replacing the human victims who were sacrificed up to the 19th century). Be equally aware of the so-called priests—temple "guides" who usher you into the complex and conduct a whirlwind tour of the facilities only to present you with a donation book that records the radically generous donations of other foreigners.

Kalighat Rd., Kalighat. Daily 5am–2pm and 4:30–11pm.

DAY TWO (NORTH KOLKATA)

Early in the morning, head toward **Howrah Bridge,** where you can witness people bathing at the *ghats* or the pandemonium at the colorful **flower market** (you need to arrive before 7am). There you can sip *chai* and watch the stall holders deftly thread marigold garlands for the gods and bridal headgear from tuberoses and dahlias. Crossing over Howrah Bridge, head toward the **Belur Math Shrine** (see below). From here you can either incorporate a short stop at the popular **Dakshineshwar Temple** (crossing the Vivekananda Bridge) or take a look at the potters' village at **Kumartuli** (N. Chitpur Rd.), a warren of alleys where clay deities and images of Mother Teresa are produced by the thousands. If you prefer to slow the pace, however, skip these and head south to the beautiful **Paresnath Temple** (see below)—not as famous as the Kali temple, but certainly Kolkata's prettiest, and north Kolkata's star attraction. From here, you can head east to shop and eat at the **Swabhumi Heritage Plaza,** a mall that covers 2.4 hectares (6 acres) and packs in a great many shopping, dining, and entertainment diversions; or head south to **Rabindra Bharati University Museum** to visit the **Rabindranath Tagore house museum.** Born to a wealthy entrepreneurial family in 1861, Tagore remains Bengal's best-loved artist and intellectual, and his home is filled with artworks and collectibles (closed Sun, and only open until 1:30pm on Sat). Move on to the nearby **Marble Palace** (see below).

By now, you may be in serious need of sustenance, which you'll find in the vicinity of the enormous **Nakhoda,** Calcutta's largest mosque (Rabindra Sarani and M.G. Rd.). The mosque is closed to non-Muslims during prayers, but is set within a busy bazaar area where Muslim tradespeople sell all sorts of goods, as well as a range of breads, sweetmeats, and snacks. Alternatively, enjoy a cheap, substantial Kolkata-Mughlai meal at the 99-year-old **Royal Indian Hotel** (147 Rabindra Sarani; ☎ **033/248-1073;** daily 10am–11:30pm). Finish with coffee at the **Indian Coffee House** (see below), after browsing through the thousands of bookstalls along **College Street.**

Belur Math Shrine ★★   The headquarters of the international Ramakrishna Order, Belur Math combines the architectural elements of a church, a mosque, and a temple, symbolically embodying the embracing teachings of the monk and seer Sri Ramakrishna Paramahansa. It was established in 1897, and the ashes of Sri Ramakrishna were placed here by his most prominent disciple, Swami Vivekananda, who also set up the Order. The location is quite lovely, with smaller shrines along the riverbank and earnest devotees and seekers of spiritual peace roaming the grounds. Within the immaculate main shrine, activity is enlivened by evening *aarti* (musical prayers sung to the movement of a ghee lamp).

Belur Rd., Howrah. Daily 6:30am–noon and 3:30–7:30pm.

College Street ★★   This stretch of road, deep in the heart of the university quarter, is famous for its 5,000 or so secondhand bookstalls, and for the renowned Presidency College, where India's greatest filmmaker, Satyajit Ray, studied. Many of the booksellers here are semi-literate, but remarkably, each is able to recall the title and price of thousands of academic and technical books, the volumes typically piled meters high. Look for the bust commemorating the father of Bengali prose literature, the reformer and philanthropist Pandit Iswar Chandra Vidyasagar, who also introduced a ban on forced marriages.

Bidhan Sarani, N. Kolkata.

Marble Palace ★★   Up a back street, in what was once known as Black Town, stands a vast mansion—a wonder to behold—sporting a plush Romanesque veneer that incorporates at least 90 different varieties of marble. Built in 1835 by the wealthy *zamindar* (landowner) Raja Rajendra Mullick Bahadur, this palatial family home has seen better days, and is now the center of

---

⌐Moments Meeting Bengalis

For men, the **Indian Coffee House** (1st Floor, 15 Bankin Chatterjee St.), where the Young Bengal Movement started, is the quintessential College Street haunt. A lone photograph of Rabindranath Tagore looks across a vast former 1930s dance hall with sagging ceiling fans and scattered tables around which men, young and old, demonstratively argue the debates of the day. The surly waiters plod around rather aimlessly, so be patient while waiting for your greasy *pakora* and a strong Coorg. Meals are slight, but the coffee and conversation will get you buzzing.

a bitter feud between relatives, some of whom have been accused of sneaking off with the more valuable displays. But several works attributed to Titian and Renoir remain, while Venetian chandeliers; Ming vases; Egyptian statuary; and paintings, sculptures, furniture, and antique vases accumulated from 90 countries crowd the enormous, dimly lit rooms that open off deep verandas around an inner courtyard. Get there soon, since the feuding of the Mullicks makes it uncertain which prized item might next disappear.

46 Muktaram Basu St., off Chittaranjan Ave. Admission is free, but pass must be collected from the West Bengal Tourist Office at least a day in advance; alternatively, offer the gate guard a bribe. You are expected to tip your guide. Tues–Wed and Fri–Sun 10am–4pm.

Paresnath Temple ★★★ Jain temples are generally the most beautifully adorned in India, and Paresnath, dedicated to Sithalnath—one of the 24 perfect souls (*tirthankaras*) of the Jain religion—is no exception. Built in 1867 by a jeweler whose love of intricate designs, mirrors, and colored glass is evident everywhere, it boasts lavishly adorned patterned marble, beautiful European chandeliers, and stained-glass windows. A quiet garden is dotted with silver statues, and the temple houses an eternal flame that's apparently never gone out.

Badridas Temple St. Free admission. Daily 6am–noon and 3–7pm.

WHERE TO STAY

Note: The prices below are sometimes given in rupees, with U.S. dollar conversions. Others are stated in U.S. dollars only, which is how many hotels targeting foreign markets quote their rates.

Fairlawn Hotel ★ Hollywood's production of *City of Joy* made use of this small, popular heritage hotel and its neoclassical facade for several days of shooting, and it's also played host to ace British playwright Tom Stoppard and actress Felicity Kendal. Established by Armenian refugees who escaped Eastern Europe in 1917, the hotel remains a family enterprise run by the extremely enthusiastic Mrs. Violet Smith and her rather hapless staff. News clippings, hotel awards, and copious family and celebrity photographs cover the walls, while old wicker chairs, vases, decorative plates, and even Buddhas and Ganeshas are used to create a homey atmosphere. Guest rooms (book nos. 16–21) are quite cozy, if simply furnished. Bathrooms are lovely, with red polished floors, old-fashioned bathtubs, and white wooden towel racks. In the kitchen, a wood and coal fire stove is still used to prepare wholesome home-style meals from a menu that changes daily. There's a pleasant garden terrace, which has abundant greenery and is packed every night with Rajophiles and beer-swilling travelers.

13/A Sudder S., Kolkata 700 016. ⓒ 033/2252-1510 or -8766. Fax 033/2252-1835. www.fairlawnhotel.com. fairlawn@cal.vsnl.net.in. 20 units. Doubles: $50. Rate includes all meals. AE, MC, V. **Amenities:** Restaurant; bar; travel assistance; limited room service; laundry; small library. *In room:* A/C, TV, tea-making facility. 1st-floor rooms have fridges.

Hyatt Regency ★★ *Value* If it's a design-conscious luxury hotel you're after, absolutely nothing in Kolkata compares with the Hyatt, which opened in 2002 right next door to Swabhumi Heritage Park in the rapidly expanding business district of Salt Lake City. At press time, introductory tariffs were also extremely competitive, with accommodations in the exclusive Regency Club priced at a mere $70 per night—this buys you an evening spent in the most comfortable king-size bed (with thick custom-made mattress). There's a large pool backed by tall trees, while inside, a trendy cigar lounge appears suspended in mid-air.

JA-1, Sector III, Salt Lake City, Kolkata 700 098. ℂ **033/2335-1234.** Fax 033/2335-1235. www.hyatt.com. Toll-free reservations from within India: ℂ 1-600-118-001. 235 units. $70 double; check the website for most recent tariffs. AE, DC, MC, V. **Amenities:** 2 restaurants; bar; pool; tennis; squash; fitness center and spa; concierge; salon; 24-hr. room service; babysitting; laundry and valet service; doctor-on-call. *In room:* A/C, TV, dataport, tea- and coffee-making facilities, hair dryer, electronic safe.

Oberoi Grand ⚜⚜⚜   This quintessential Kolkata monument is the city's top accommodations option and one of the best hotels in all of India. Elegant, with regal old-world charm, its guest rooms draw ambassadors, diplomats, heads of state, and royalty (although the Hollywood charity crowd head for The Park). Superior guest rooms (city or garden view) are marvelous; ask for room no. 432 if you want the biggest of the lot. If you want a private balcony, book one on the third floor. In the central courtyard, you can sip gin and tonics around the best pool in town. And for inspiration about what to do when you run out of sights and restaurants, speak to the head concierge, Amitava Sarkar, whose knowledge and enthusiasm will deepen your appreciation of the city.

15 Jawaharlal Nehru Rd., Kolkata 700 013. ℂ 033/2249-2323. Fax 033/2249-1217. www.oberoihotels.com. 219 units. Doubles: $225 superior city-view rooms; $240 premium garden-view rooms; $285 deluxe garden-view rooms; $500–$600 suites; check the website for online discounts. AE, DC, MC, V. **Amenities:** 4 restaurants; 2 bars; pool; health club and spa; 24-hr. room service; babysitting; laundry and dry cleaning; doctor-on-call. *In room:* A/C, TV, DVD player, minibar, tea- and coffee-making facilities, hair dryer. Fax machines in deluxe rooms.

The Park ⚜⚜⚜   Space is something of a premium in Calcutta, and a stylish overhaul has transformed this tiny slither of Park Street into a fantastic model of urban chic, the abode of choice for the likes of Penelope Cruz and Melanie Griffith. Guest rooms may be small, but they're neat, functional, and bright, with Art Deco elements, antique tribal artworks, and bold color combinations. Book a Residence room and you get a private lounge, slightly larger bedroom with walk-in dressing room, stylish furniture, thick mattresses on queen-size beds, a floor butler, and a Jacuzzi in the bathroom. The Park also houses the city's hippest, most happening nightclub.

17 Park St., Kolkata 700 016. ℂ 033/2249-3121 or -7336. City toll-free 1-600-33-3411. Fax 033/249-7343 or -9457. www.theparkhotels.com/calcutta_home.htm. 150 units. Doubles: $250 superior; $275 residence/deluxeroom; suite from $300; $25 extra bed. AE, DC, MC, V. **Amenities:** 3 restaurants; pub; disco; pool; golf on request; health club/fitness center; travel desk; doctor-on-call. *In room:* A/C, TV.

Taj Bengal ⚜⚜   This smart hotel, popular with businesspeople, is a good choice if you want to stay south of the city, enjoy views of the Maidan, and dine in-house—Taj Bengal boasts some of Calcutta's most impressive restaurants. Besides **Sonargaon** and **The Hub,** both reviewed below, it houses one of India's best Chinese restaurants, **Chinoiserie.** Guest rooms on the third and fourth floors have recently been refurbished and feature dark teakwood parquet floors, rugs, shimmering olive curtains, and wall paintings depicting Calcuttan city scenes. Club Rooms (top floor) have added space (thanks to a window alcove) and access to posh lounges and exclusive restaurants where the city's elite plot and play. The "gentlemen's club" ambience at the exclusive residents' lounge goes down well with a game of pool, a book from the small library, or time at the Internet bar.

34B Belvedere Rd., Alipore, Kolkata 700 027. ℂ **033/2223-3939.** Fax 033/2223-1766. www.tajhotels.com. 229 units. Doubles: $104–$150 superior; $160–$208 Taj Club; $370 executive. Rates include breakfast. AE, DC, MC, V. **Amenities:** 3 restaurants; bar; nightclub; tea lounge; patisserie; pool; health club; travel desk; concierge; salon; 24-hr. room service; laundry. *In room:* A/C, TV, tea- and coffee-making facilities, hair dryer, electronic safe.

WHERE TO DINE

Bengalis are known for their fine palates and love of dining out, and a wide range of cuisines are theirs to choose from. Make sure to sample **Kolkata-Mughlai food**—blending the best of the Bengali *nawabs'* cuisine with influences from the Deccan, Awadh, and North India—at least once. **Nizam's** (1 Corporation Rd.; ✆ **033/2216-7517;** call for hours) claims to be the place where the *kathi* kebab roll (kebab wrapped in dough) was invented. The food is legendary, and the prices unbeatable—the owners plan to open franchises of the Kolkatan institution around the city in the next year. Another popular Bengali-Muslim joint is **Shiraz** (56 Park St., at the intersection of Park St. and A.J.C. Bose Rd.; ✆ **033/ 247-7702** or 033/280-5006; daily 6am–11pm), which has a "men only" section on the ground level. Go to the first floor for air-conditioned comfort, or to the rooftop. The menu is extensive and includes numerous exotic-sounding Kolkata-Mughlai items, as well as a range of kebabs. If you're in the vicinity of the Nakhoda Mosque, try the **Royal Indian Hotel** (147 Rabindra Sarani; ✆ **033/ 248-1073;** daily 10am–11:30pm), which opened in 1905 and is the oldest restaurant of its kind. On Thursday or Sunday, you can order *murgh mussalam* (lamb), while the mutton *chanmps tikiya* is legendary.

Chinese cuisine is very popular with Kolkatans—**Mainland China** ★★ (Uniworth House, 3A Gurusadary Rd.; ✆ **033/287-2006,** -2007, -2008, or -2009; daily noon–3pm and 7–11pm) is currently considered the best place in town (vying with the Taj Bengal's in-house Chinese restaurant). It serves sugar-cane chicken, Hublai lobster, Hunan-style prawns, and Szechuan chili crab. Be sure to reserve a table.

Ar-Han Thai ★ *Finds* THAI/ASIAN   Owner Prabhakar Singh has a long association with Thailand and, unable to live without the cuisine, imported a Thai chef. Come for tasty portions of stir-fried chicken made with fresh chilies, garlic, and basil, or delicious broiled jumbo prawns in a tamarind sauce. The menu offers a range of noodle combinations; try yellow curry noodles with your choice of vegetables, chicken, prawns, or an eclectic combo. It's worth coming to this intimate restaurant hungry, because the portions are huge.

31 Bentick St. ✆ **033/2243-7857** or 033/2243-6766. Reservations essential Fri–Sun. Main courses Rs 70– Rs 395 ($1.50–$8.75). AE, MC, V. Daily 11am–11:30pm.

The Hub ★★ ECLECTIC   The Italian chef at this bright restaurant in the lobby of the Taj Bengal likes to experiment. The fare includes burgers, pastas, thin-crusted pizzas (try the spicy *alla Indiana*), grills, and griddles. The highlight is the "food theater" experience, where guests can watch a five-course meal being prepared, and then dig into the results. Definitely try the *ajwaini jhinga,* fresh Chilka prawns flavored with *ajwain* (thyme-like spice) and grilled in the tandoor

---

Moments **Fast Food, Kolkata Style**

At almost any time of the day you'll see expectant customers standing outside a small booth at 17 Park St. (✆ **033/2229-7662**) marked by a prominent sign advertising HOT KATI ROLL. They're waiting for one of Kolkata's favorite lunchtime snacks, a pizza-style roll filled with chicken, mutton, or egg *paneer* (Indian cheese). The meat is prepared kebab-style and topped off with onion and lemon juice—simply delicious.

oven; or the *gamberoni all' anice,* king prawns cooked in a heavenly Sambuca sauce. Or sample an Italian take on a local fish by ordering *beckti Mediterraneo.*

Taj Bengal, 34B Belvedere Rd., Alipore. ℭ **033/2223-3939**. Main courses Rs 220–Rs 620 ($4.70–$13). Food theater Rs 595–Rs 645 ($13–$14) per performance. AE, DC, MC, V. Open 24 hr.

Jong's ✹✹✹ CHINESE/JAPANESE/THAI Sharing an entrance with the equally excellent Indian restaurant **Zaranj** (see below), this stylish spot is our choice for top Asian restaurant in West Bengal. On offer is an eclectic and wildly exciting selection of well-considered dishes. Start with traditional *tom yam kai,* a spicy hot-and-sour chicken broth flavored with kafir lime leaves, lemon grass, and chili paste. Nonmeat eaters should opt for *kaeng phak,* a Thai preparation of seasonal veggies cooked in a spicy curry with galangal, lemon grass, and kafir lime leaves, topped off with coconut milk. For your main course, favorites include ginger chicken, Shanghai-style tangerine chicken, coconut prawns with bamboo shoots, crab in a zesty Penang curry, and drunken fish made with Bay of Bengal *bekti* grilled in red wine.

26 J.L. Nehru Rd., Kolkata 700 087. ℭ **033/2249-5572**, -9744, -0369, or -0370. Reservations highly recommended; essential at weekends. Main courses: Rs 105–Rs 305 ($2.10–$6.50). AE, DC, MC, V. Daily 12:30–3pm and 7:30–11pm.

Kewpie's ✹ BENGALI Popular with local celebrities and bigwig visitors to the city, this tiny family kitchen has been very well marketed but is not necessarily the most authentic (for that you're better off visiting **Suruchi,** ideally combined with a visit to South Park Cemetery). The menu changes daily, but the highlight is Kewpie's *thali* (multicourse platter)—various fish, vegetable, and meat items (or strictly vegetarian), served with different breads.

2 Elgin Lane, off Heysham Rd., behind Netaji Bhavan. ℭ **033/2475-9880** or 033/2476-9929. kewpies_k@ yahoo.com. Reservations essential. Minimum charge Rs 150 ($3.15) per person. MC, V. Tues–Sun 12:30–2:30pm and 7:30–10:30pm.

Saffron ✹✹✹ NORTH-WEST FRONTIER/LUCKNOWI/INDIAN The Qureshi brothers, celebrity chefs of famed Lucknowi parentage, have been wowing a distinguished clientele here since 2002. In the *kadai* (wok), they use coarsely ground spices to prepare exquisite masala chops, while on the griddle, they use Australian corn, green peppers, and tomatoes to make wonderful *makai khumb tak a tuk,* named for the sound made during preparation. Simmered overnight on a slow fire, their perfect *dal bukhari* is finished with cream and white butter. But perhaps the best item on the menu is the kebab—try the *kakori* kebab, skewered balls of minced mutton, cloves, and cinnamon, grilled and drizzled with saffron; or the prawn kebab, also served with a fragrant saffron sauce. If you're in the mood for a rich rice dish, have the lamb biryani, made with dried plums and apricot and baby potatoes. Leave space for *jamun,* a dessert based on an old family recipe (topped with honey and stuffed with saffron and nuts)—divine. Note that the Park has a second restaurant, **Zen House** ✹✹, where Bangkok-born master chef Nut Kunlert serves Asian specialties like prawns, barbecued whole with a chili sauce; sweet-and-sour chicken prepared with a hint of ginger and jalapeño; or lemon-grass soufflé. Prices are similar to those of Saffron.

The Park, 17 Park St. ℭ **033/2249-3121**. Main courses Rs 195–Rs 545 ($4.25–$12). AE, DC, MC, V. Daily 12:45–2:45pm and 7:30–11:45pm (last orders).

Sonargaon ✹✹✹ BENGALI/INDIAN Exposed stone masonry and Mediterranean-style whitewashed walls, wooden tables, tribal wall hangings, and enormous storm lanterns set the right atmosphere for this upmarket take on village-style Bengali dining. Order a traditional Bengali thali, served on a silver platter, and give yourself plenty of time to recover; diners tend to leave with very full stomachs. Bengali specialties include a rich and spicy prawn curry *(chingri malai)*, and *paturi maach*, sliced *beckti* fish coated with a paste of mustard and green chili, wrapped in a banana leaf, and steamed. Leave space for *rossogollar payesh*, a typical Bengali dessert made from lightly thickened sweet milk.

Taj Bengal, 34B Belvedere Rd., Alipore. © 033/2223-3939. Main courses Rs 115–Rs 650 ($2.40–$14). AE, DC, MC, V. Daily 12:30–2:45pm and 7:30–11:30pm.

Taaja's ⋆ ECLECTIC/INTERNATIONAL   For a wild variety of dishes from the world's kitchens and a dynamic, upbeat crowd, this charming, casual restaurant is a winner. Don't miss barbecued pork ribs, hot Singaporean prawns, Goan prawn *vindaloo*, Hungarian goulash, or the local *bekti* fish prepared with a Creole sauce. There are also dishes from Vietnam and Burma, and a selection of Indian specialties. A bar has recently been added, which means it's even more necessary to reserve ahead.

29/1A Ballygunge Circular Rd. © 033/2476-7334. Reservations for Sat and Sun evening essential. Main courses Rs 95–Rs 265 ($2.05–$5.60). AE, MC, V. Tues–Sun noon–4:30pm and 7pm–midnight.

Thai Tonight ⋆ *Value* THAI/FUSION   The Bangkok chef at this minimalist-chic restaurant has tweaked his Thai roots to cater to local palates— among the tasty dishes here are crispy *bekti* in a tangy sauce *(pla rad prik);* prawns sautéed in coriander, garlic, and lemon; stir-fried lamb with long beans; and deep-fried crabmeat prepared in a hot chili sauce and served in the shell.

29/1A Ballygunge Circular Rd. © 033/2454-2034 or -2036. Weekend reservations recommended. Main courses Rs 100–Rs 350 ($2.10–$7.60). AE, DC. MC, V. Daily 12:30–3:30pm and 7–11:30pm; closed Tues lunch.

Zaranj ⋆⋆⋆ NORTH-WEST FRONTIER   Named for a hamlet in Afghanistan, this upmarket restaurant is one of the city's most opulent dining options, where miniature waterfalls and plush seating provide a warm, luxurious atmosphere. The **Raphael Lounge** is an ideal spot to kick off the evening in style, and a fine selection of imported wines and champagnes are on offer. Popular dishes include tandoori prawns *(jhinga)* and *dahi ka* kebab, which are prepared in the display kitchen behind a wall of glass. For dinner, be sure to reserve a table, or you'll be watching the city's movers and groovers feasting while you wait.

26 Jawaharlal Nehru Rd. © 033/2249-5572, -9744, -0369, or -0370. Reservations essential. Main courses Rs 150–Rs 375 ($3.15–$8). AE, DC, MC, V. Daily 12:30–3pm and 7:30–11pm.

SHOPPING

Kolkata is also renowned for its fashion designers. Look for garments by promising local **Sabyasachi Mukherjee,** who is taking Kolkata's fashion industry to new heights (there's an outlet at 86C Jatin Das Rd., but make an appointment first; © 033/2466-5026). Other names to be on the lookout for are **Kiran Uttan Ghosh** and **Shabari Datta.** For more contemporary Bengali fashion, pop in at **Mithai** (433 Syed Amir Ali Ave.). For Bengali handicrafts, visit **Bengal Home Industries** (1 A.J.C. Bose Rd.; © 033/2242-1562) or **Sasha** (27 Mirza Ghalib St.; © 033/2245-1586). You can pick up a wide range of Indian curios, along with everything from saris to silk carpets, from the government-operated **Central Cottage Industries Emporium** in Chowringhee (7 Jawaharlal Nehru Rd.; © 033/2228-4139 or -3205; Mon–Fri 10am–7pm, Sat 10am–2pm).

KOLKATA AFTER DARK
DRINKING & PARTYING

Kolkata is officially dry on Thursday, but this doesn't affect the upscale hotels. Local laws supposedly prohibit the sale of alcohol after 10:30pm, so if you're keen for an all-nighter, be sure to ask the exact time for last rounds at any bar you decide to visit. In the budget-oriented Sudder Street precinct, the open-air bar at the **Fairlawn Hotel** (13/A Sudder St.; ✆ 033/2252-1510) is wonderful for sun-downers and early-evening drinks. It's not for nothing that **the Park** (✆ 033/2249-3121 or -7336) is the place to hang out after hours—despite a postage stamp–size dance floor, **Someplace Else** rocks all night long. Together with **Tantra** ₰ (also at the Park; 8pm–4am; Rs 350/$7.60), it attracts the city's hippest crowd.

LIVE PERFORMANCE

Theater, music, dance, and poetry recitals all thrive here. Check out the listings in *Kolkata This Fortnight* (free from tourist offices) or in the "Bulletin Board" section of *The Times of India*. Upscale hotels also carry the useful monthly booklet *Cal Calling*. The **Rabindra Sadan** concert hall (A.J.C. Bose Rd. and Cathedral Rd.; ✆ 033/2223-9936 or -9917) hosts regular theater and musical events, as well as dance-drama performances and local-flavored Bengali poetry evenings. Cultural events also take place at the **Academy of Fine Arts** (2 Cathedral Rd.; ✆ 033/2223-4302). The **British Council** (5 Shakespeare Sarani; ✆ 033/2242-5478) is often responsible for staging plays and performances in English. Bengali and English dramas are often performed at the **Kala Mandir** (48 Shakespeare Sarani; ✆ 033/2247-9086). For musical programs, contact **Sisir Mancha** (1/1 A.J.C. Bose Rd.; ✆ 033/2223-2451). Indo-German productions are occasionally held at **Max Meuller Bhavan** (8 Pramathesh Barua Sarani; ✆ 033/2475-9398).

CINEMA, GALLERIES & EXHIBITIONS

Considered the art capital of India, Kolkata hosts an unimaginable number of art exhibitions. Scan the newspapers for information about what's on while you're in town. Or check out the **Birla Academy of Art and Culture** (108–109 Southern Ave.; ✆ 033/2466-2843) or the **Centre for International Modern Art** (Sunny Towers, 43 Ashutosh Chowdhari Ave.; ✆ 033/2478-8717; Tues–Sun 2–8pm). The **Academy of Fine Arts** (2 Cathedral Rd.; ✆ 033/2223-4302) has art galleries (daily 3–8pm) and a museum (Tues–Sun noon–6:30pm; admission Rs 2/4¢), where you can see works by Rabindranath Tagore.

The best cinema complex in the city is **Nandan** (A.J.C. Bose Rd.; ✆ 033/2223-1310 or -1777), with excellent screens and a fantastic sound system. Nandan also regularly hosts art-film screenings and retrospectives. There are a number of cinemas in Chowringhee where you can watch movies in the company of feverishly excitable Indian audiences.

2 Orissa's Golden Temple Triangle

The tropical state that flourished during the 13th century on India's central eastern seaboard, Orissa is famous for its temples, which draw thousands of pilgrims here throughout the year, predominantly to the **Jagannath Temple** in the coastal town of **Puri,** to worship Vishnu in his avatar as the Lord of the Universe. Architecturally, the **Sun Temple** at **Konark** is of even greater significance, with its massive stone-carved chariot adorned with sculptures, rising up to carry Surya, the sun god, to the heavens. Even Orissa's capital, **Bhubaneswar** (the 3rd point of Orissa's Golden Triangle), is more important for its enormous collection of Hindu temples—at one time 7,000—than it is as an administrative or industrial center.

Orissa remains largely tribal, with many villages still completely off-limits to outsiders, and the state is therefore also well-known for its "Tribal Tourism"— for the truly adventurous, or the anthropologically inclined, these offer a chance to get completely off the beaten track and meet people who have seldom, if ever, encountered a foreign face. The state is also a good place to pick up crafts, particularly textiles and paintings—even when tending to the rice paddies, the women of Orissa are dressed in glamorous saris. Cottage textile industries are the mainstays for entire villages, which produce beautiful *ikat* (patterned) textiles, palm-leaf paintings, and bright *patachitra* (cloth) paintings (the best-known of Orissa's handicrafts). *Note:* Although Orissa has long, golden beaches that curve around the Bay of Bengal, the infrastructure here is limited and the sea can be treacherous; beach lovers are best off heading for Kerala or Goa.

BHUBANESWAR
485km (300 miles) SW of Kolkata

Orissa's capital emerged in the 7th century as a center of prolific and accomplished temple building, and by the 11th century the city of Bhubaneswar (derived from Shiva's incarnation as Tribhubaneswar, Lord of the Three Worlds) had become a significant religious hub, with an estimated 7,000 temples. Of these, only several hundred remain today, but those that survive reveal the evolution over time of the Nagara style into an architectural form unique to Orissa. You won't need to stay here beyond a day—Konark's Sun Temple, one of India's top attractions, is just under an hour's drive away.

ESSENTIALS
VISITOR INFORMATION   If you're fortunate, the **Government of Orissa Tourist Office** (5 Jaydev Nagar; ✆ **0674/243-1299;** Mon–Sat 10am–5pm, closed on the 2nd Sat of each month) will be manned by Kamal Mohanty, who is passionate about his state and about improving the lot of tourism in the region.

GETTING THERE   By Air   Jet Airways has a 55-minute daily flight from Kolkata. **Indian Airlines** operates regular flights to and from Delhi (2 hr.), Kolkata, Mumbai (3 hr.), and several destinations in South India, including Chennai and Hyderabad. **Bhubaneswar Airport** (✆ **0674/253-4472** or -4084) is around 4km (2½ miles) from the center, in the southwest. The airport has a tourist information counter, as well as a prepaid taxi service; transfers into the city should cost around Rs 150 ($3.15).

By Train   The best train from Delhi is the **Rajdhani Express,** but the trip is still lengthy—25 hours—and departures are only 2 days per week; other trains may take up to 42 hours. From Kolkata, the **Howrah-Puri Express** is most convenient (it's overnight); alternatively, the quickest is the **Dhauli Express** (under 8 hr.). Puri is 2½ hours from Bhubaneswar, and there is regular train service between the two cities. For inquiries and reservations, call (daily 8am–7:30pm) ✆ **131,** 0674/240-1084, or -6472.

By Road   If you want to drive or bus it here from Kolkata (500km/310 miles away), count on spending 13 hours propped up in your seat.

GETTING AROUND   By Taxi & Auto-Rickshaw   Auto-rickshaws in Bhubaneswar are unusually comfortable and well maintained. Drivers are genuinely helpful, if often unable to understand you. Taxis from Bhubaneswar to

Puri or Konark are readily available; for taxi excursions, be clear about the duration of your journey, and the sights you wish to cover. Hiring a car and driver is a good way to save time; try the ever-reliable **Sita World Travels** (14A Bapuji Nagar, Janpath; © **0674/253-1408**), **Mercury Travels** at The Trident (Nayapalli; © **0674/244-0890**), or **Swosti Travels** (103 Janpath; © **0674/253-5773, -4058, or -6228**)—each of which handles flights, car rentals, and tours of the state, including tribal tours (see "Tribal Tours in Orissa," later in this chapter). Inexpensive full-day coach tours of the city and the entire Golden Triangle region are administered by **O.T.D.C. Head Office** (© **0674/243-2382;** www.orissa-tourism.com/otdc.htm), but these are targeted at domestic visitors.

Tip: **Heritage Tours** is a reputable outfit with years of experience; located at the entrance of the Mayfair Beach Resort, it specializes in "Lifestyle Tours" and tribal excursions. Besides organizing every aspect of trips lasting anything from 1 to 20 days, Heritage Tours also deals with ticketing and transportation matters.

BHUBANESWAR'S TOP ATTRACTIONS

In the heart of Bhubaneswar's Old Town, the most important temples—almost all Shiavite—are clustered around the **Bindusagar** lake, a holy reservoir that is believed to hold water from each and every holy river and lake in India. Of the 7,000 temples that are said to have once surrounded the tank, only around 500 remain. Traditionally, pilgrims perform their ablutions in the lake before heading into the temples to perform *puja* (a ritual of respect, such as prayer). The best are easily visited in a morning (more than three or four is overkill), leaving you time to explore some of the outlying sights during the course of the afternoon.

The best of the city's Nagara-style temples (built during the 7th c. and the 12th c. A.D.) are testament to both a radical resurgence of Hinduism and Buddhist defeat—frequently represented in temple sculptures by the image of a lion lunging down upon an elephant. With the exception of the wonderful **Rajarani Temple** (see below), all of those worth visiting are living temples. The best are the magnificently carved **Mukteshwar Temple**—the 10th-century "Gem of Orissan Architecture," where a squat, cobra-protected lingam stands in the sanctum sanctorum—and the **Lingaraj Temple;** although the complex is off-limits to non-Hindus, you can admire it from a well-known vantage point, a raised platform built by the British, where you'll be harassed by a hood with a phony register of donations from other foreigners (simply ignore his advances and mention the police). If you have time, also make a stop at the well-preserved 7th-century **Parasurameswar Temple** (or **Brahmeswar**), for its lavish carvings, including a number of amorous couples. For something more "exotic," visit **Vaital Temple** ⭐ and view its creepy tantric carvings; you'll need a torch to see the images of humans being put to death while the goddess Chamunda looks on.

Rajarani Temple ⭐⭐   Surrounded by open space and paddy fields, this 11th-century temple—maintained by the Archaeological Survey of India—glimmers in the light of day, built as it was using a superior-quality burgundy-gold sandstone. Unusual for Orissan temples, the tower *(shikhara)* features miniature versions of itself. Sculptural representations of lotus flowers with the guardians of the eight cardinal directions are a standout feature of the temple walls, which also feature delightful female figures engaged in mundane (but beautiful) daily activities.
Tankapani Rd. Rs 100 ($2.10). Daily 6am–6pm.

Museum of Tribal Art and Artefacts ⭐   Anything and everything connected with the life of Orissa's tribal people is on display in the exhibition rooms at this newly built museum decorated with primitive murals. Traditional costumes, jewelry, household appliances, and hunting equipment such as bows and arrows, axes, and traps for birds and fish give an indication of the way of life of the numerous tribal peoples of Orissa.

Near C.R.P. Sq., NH 5. © **0674/256-1635** or -3649. Free admission. Mon–Sat 10am–5pm; closed 2nd Sat of each month.

Orissa State Museum ⊛ This collection does a convincing job of explaining the religious context of Hindu sculptures, but you may be more fascinated by some of the erotic friezes that date back as far as the 7th century A.D. Upstairs, the **Manuscript Gallery** includes early examples of the type of work you'll encounter in some Orissan crafts villages. Along with a collection of folk musical instruments, a number of dioramas depict different Orissan tribes, and next door is a collection of *patachitra* (cloth) paintings dealing primarily with the Jagannath cult and tales from the *Ramayana*.

Puri Rd., near Kalpana Sq. Rs 2 (4¢). Tues–Sun 10am–1pm and 2–4pm.

Dhauli ⊛ The glistening white-domed *Shanti Stupa* (Peace Pagoda) at the top of Dhauli Hill is clearly visible from the main road as you head toward this site where historic Ashokan rock edicts are carved. Guarded by pale yellow Ashokan lions, the Kalinga World Peace Pagoda is a celebration of Ashoka's decision, 2,300 years ago, to renounce violence and war and embrace Buddhism —a decision made in the wake of his massacre against the local Kalinga people, then rulers of Orissa. A plaque here notes that Ashoka built 84,000 *stupas* (commemorative cairns), some as far away as Greece.

Free admission. Daily 5am–8pm.

WHERE TO STAY

The Trident ⊛⊛ Situated some distance out of the city center, this classy low-rise hotel is surrounded by 5.6 hectares (14 acres) of exquisite lawns, mango groves, and rockeries. Drawing businesspeople, travelers, and even the English cricket team, this is Bhubaneswar's most fabulous, and expensive, hotel. Stepping inside the lobby is like entering a temple, but sans the chaos brought by masses of worshippers. The space has been carefully designed with stone columns, beautiful brickwork, and trellised railings enhanced by concealed lighting and spectacular brass-bell lighting features. Mythical lions perch above, looking down on guests as they arrive. In the evenings, live Indian music is played here. Guest rooms are smart, stylish, and well laid out, with pale parquet floors and sleek furniture, marble-topped surfaces, blue and mushroom-beige fabrics, and scatter cushions. Individually lit gilt-framed color photographs of Orissan temple art and elegant stone reproductions of temple friezes decorate the walls. Deluxe units are larger in all respects and worth the extra $10. Suites have dressing rooms, marble chandeliers, and separate dining areas. Bird-watchers should ask for a room facing the rose garden. Best of all, gastronomes can have the chef conjure up special meals. The kitchen will also prepare a picnic hamper for you should you be heading out on a long day of temple-spotting.

C.B.-1, Nayapalli, Bhubaneswar 751 013. © **0674/230-1010**. Fax 0674/230-1302. www.oberoihotels.com. 62 units. Doubles: $150 superior; $160 deluxe; $200 executive suite; $250 deluxe suite. AE, DC, MC, V. **Amenities:** Restaurant; bar; pool; 2 tennis courts; badminton court; jogging track; travel agency; business center; secretarial services; 24-hr. room service; babysitting; laundry; dry cleaning; doctor-on-call. *In room:* A/C, TV, dataport, minibar, tea- and coffee-making facilities, hair dryer. DVD player in suites.

WHERE TO DINE

Ignore the seedy neighborhood and dour look of the lodge where this upstairs eatery, **Venus Inn** (217 Bapuji Nagar; *©* **0674/253-1908;** daily 6:30am–10pm), is good for a quick South Indian *dosa* (filled pancake). Soft Hindi music fills the neat, clean interior as you dine on butter paper *masala dosa,* the onion *rawa masala dosa,* a *dosa* stuffed full of *paneer,* or an *uttapam* (rice pancake) with coconut. For the best chicken in town, **Cook's Kitchen** (260 Bapuji Nagar; *©* **0674/253-0025;** daily 10:30am–10:30pm) is the place to be—chicken *tikka* butter masala is for those who can handle their spices. Order an Orissan thali at Swosti Plaza's **Chandan** *✦* (*©* **0674/230-1936,** -1937, -1938, or 1939), where waiters in gold-trimmed red jackets (all part of the kitschy decor) keenly talk you through the evening's selection while Fat Boy Slim provides prerecorded entertainment. The menu changes daily, but a typical selection might include fragrant dry Oriya mutton *(mangsha kasha);* Rohu fish (beware of the fine bones) cooked in a mustard sauce *(sorisa machha);* traditionally prepared mixed vegetables *(santula);* and soft *paneer* (Indian cheese) cooked under charcoal and then caramelized *(chhena poda)*—all served with breads and condiments on a brass platter.

Hare Krishna *✦* PURE VEGETARIAN   You won't find garlic or onion in the vegetarian dishes served at this surreally decorated restaurant reached via a series of Art Deco linoleum steps. The food is rich and flavorful, so don't over-order. Lord Krishna's favorite is apparently Govinda's Pasanda, a *paneer*-based dish that's heavy on the spices and includes cashew nuts, tomato, and fresh vegetables. Also spicy, but with an added hint of sour, is Chaitanya's Pasanda, also made with *paneer.* We can also heartily recommend Nanda Moharaja's *palak paneer,* which makes good use of mineral-rich spinach and is accompanied by thick, warm, fresh *naan.* The steaming-hot vegetable biryani is known as Bhaktivinod's Delight, and it's good.

1st floor, Lalchand Market, Jan Path. *©* 0674/253-4188. Main courses Rs 45–Rs 80 (95¢–$1.70). No credit cards. Daily 11am–3pm and 6:30–10:30pm.

SHOPPING

Sixteen kilometers (10 miles) north of Puri, **Raghurajpur Crafts Village,** a quaint rural village of thatched-roof houses, offers a variety of traditional Oriya crafts. Craftspeople will meet you as you emerge from your taxi or auto-rickshaw and lead you to their homes, which double as production centers for specific art forms. Along with a cup of *chai,* you'll be given a thorough account of the creative process. *Patachitra* paintings, the best known of Orissa's handicrafts, fetch up to Rs 15,000 ($325) and are created on a cloth canvas, using a brush made from mouse hair. Vibrant colors are used to create extraordinarily detailed depictions of mythological events—most of these revolve around the life of Krishna. Also impressive are traditional palm-leaf drawings made with an iron pen. These are typically presented as a concertina-style fold-up poster made from palm fronds and featuring concealed erotic images and Sanskrit inscriptions. *Note:* Although prices are reasonable, they are slightly inflated, and you shouldn't feel pressured to buy something you don't want.

EXPLORING PURI & THE SUN TEMPLE AT KONARK

Puri is 65km (40 miles) S of Bhubaneswar. Konark is 35km (28 miles) NE of Puri.

Puri is considered one of the four holiest places in all of India, home to the magnificent 15th-century **Sri Jagannath Temple,** where pilgrims throng to be absolved of past sins by the Lord of the Universe. But given that this is off-limits to non-Hindus, the real highlight lies farther up the coast, in the mellow town of Konark, site of the legendary 13th-century **Sun Temple.**

Sri Jagannath Temple ⚹ Topped by Vishnu's wheel and flag, the 64m (215-ft.) *shikhara* (spire) of the Jagannath Temple dominates Puri's skyline, and it's possible to circumambulate the entire complex by wandering through the market streets around the periphery walls. However, for non-Hindus, the best view of this mighty Kalinga temple is from the balcony of **Raghunandan Library,** across the street. From here, you not only get a glimpse of tremendously active temple life, but you'll be privy to the colorful activity around the souvenir stalls that spread around the temple in every direction. From this viewing point, both the size of the temple and the sheer numbers of swarming people are impressive; the temple buildings themselves are filthy with mildew. Incidentally, you will find images of Lord Jagannath and his siblings everywhere in this part of India. Pitch-black with squat physiques and exaggerated features, they could well have been inspiration for the animation technique used by the creators of *South Park:* The crude, flat-featured, raccoon-eyed faces have thin red curling grins.

Raghunandan Library is open daily 7am–noon and 4–8pm. All rickshaw drivers can show you the way.

Sun Temple ⚹⚹⚹ Visualized as the gigantic chariot of Surya, the sun god, emerging from the ocean, the Sun Temple at Konark was built (though not completed) at the zenith of Orissan architectural development, right at the edge of a 483km (300-mile) beach. Guarded by stone elephants and mythical lions, the immense structure was carved from rock so as to look like an enormous war chariot (originally drawn by seven galloping horses), and was covered with detailed sculpted scenes depicting everyday facets of life. Even the spokes of the 24 giant wheels that adorn the base of the temple are intricately carved. The temple was at some point submerged by sand; when the ocean retreated just over a century ago, the temple that had been lost to the world was excavated by the British. The entire complex is surrounded by a periphery wall. To first get an idea of the enormity of the project, circumnavigate the temple by slowly skirting this outer wall. The sanctum, or *deul,* has collapsed inward, so it is no longer possible to enter the temple building, but you can clamber over most of the exterior for close-up views of the various scenes of love and war, trade and commerce, sports and mythical figures. Among the friezes are those depicting amorous dalliances between entwined couples—these provide stiff competition for the world-renowned sculpted erotica at Khajuraho, including spokes with miniature examples of the erotic carvings found all over the rest of the temple.

As is the case elsewhere, the earlier you arrive, the better your chances of enjoying this World Heritage Site in peace. And definitely avoid visiting the temple on the weekend, when day-tripping domestic visitors swarm to Konark as part of a high-paced pilgrimage around Orissa's golden circuit.

If you're here in early December, you may be able to catch the 5-day **Konark Dance Festival** ⚹⚹⚹, which attracts performances by some of the country's most sought-after dancers. The striking monument forms a remarkable backdrop to traditional dance styles accompanied by music created on classical Indian instruments.

64km (40 miles) southeast of Bhubaneswar; 35km (21 miles) northeast of Puri. Rs 250 ($5.35). Open sunrise– sunset. For information on the Konark Dance Festival, contact O.T.D.C. in Bhubaneswar (✆ **0674/43-2699**).

WHERE TO STAY

Small, intimate, peaceful, and close to the beach, **Z Hotel**—the former seaside residence of the Raja of Serampore—is the best budget lodging in the state, offering huge guest rooms, simply furnished, with sea views. Reserve room no. 25, 26, or 27 (© **06752/22-2554;** www.zhotelindia.com; Rs 500/$11; no credit cards) well in advance to secure an upstairs unit with attached bathroom (drench shower only). Don't miss the beach view from the rooftop which, unfortunately, also reveals Puri's unchecked development. Alternatively, try **Toshali Sands,** en route to Konark (© **06752/25-0571,** -0572, -0573, or -0574; www.toshali international.com; doubles from Rs 2,450/$54). Though it's certainly never going to win any design awards, this is the closest acceptable accommodations option to the Sun Temple. A beach is nearby, and the restaurant's not bad. "Villa" units are best, with small sitting rooms, a porch, shared kitchenette, and big bathrooms with tubs.

Mayfair Beach Resort   This is the best place in the vicinity of the Sun Temple by a long shot, popular with middle-class Indian families who come to strut their stuff on the wide expanse of beach, a short walk from the resort; service can be pretty surly, however. Disinterested staff members wear bright Hawaiian shirts, and the entrance and lobby areas are equally colorful, playing off the Jagannath Temple theme. The rough-hewn redbrick resort makes the most of its limited space, its gardens profuse with lovely trees, potted plants, and stone statues of various deities. Unless you can afford the presidential suite, book a garden cottage; it has a small sitting area, a semi-private veranda, and a small shower room. Beyond the crow-infested pool, which is neatly lined with white wood loungers, a nicely maintained stretch of beach is constantly watched by the resort's lifeguards, although hawkers still ply their trades. The major drawback here is an inconvenient 8am checkout, but if this doesn't suit you, say so, and the management may be able to accommodate you with a later checkout.

Chakratirtha Rd., Puri 752 002. © 06752/22-7800. Fax 06752/22-4242. www.mayfairhotel.com. 34 units. Doubles: Rs 3,000 ($65) deluxe room; Rs 3,300 ($72) cottage; Rs 4,300 ($94) presidential suite; Rs 400 ($8.75) extra person. AE, MC, V. **Amenities:** 2 restaurants; 2 bars; pool; table tennis; pool table; health club; steam; Jacuzzi; indoor games; travel desk; currency exchange; boutique; 24-hr. room service; doctor-on-call. *In room:* A/C, TV, minibar.

WHERE TO DINE

Besides the **Mayfair's Aquarium & Veranda** (© **06752/27-800**), where you can sample Orissan seafood specialties (*chingudi tarkari,* prawn prepared in a traditional Orissan gravy, is delicious), you can choose to dine at **Wild Grass** (V.I.P. Rd.; © **06752/22-9293;** daily 11am–11pm; no credit cards), a self-consciously eco-friendly open-air restaurant set in a lush garden with stone and slate pathways and tables arranged in various nooks at different levels. Come for the delightful ambience, but don't expect the most spectacular food or service. One of the highlights here is an Orissan thali, but it must be ordered a full day in advance (well worth it, though). Grilled *brinjal* (eggplant, known as *baigan poda*) is another favorite; or try tandoori prawns, *nargisi* fish kebab, very affordable lobster, or prawn *malai* curry. For dessert, try the local cheesecake, *chhena poda.* **Restaurant Peace** is an utterly laid-back cafe-style eatery with plastic chairs under thatched roofing. Owner-manager Velu serves fresh locally caught fish and shellfish at ridiculously low prices: 10 grilled prawns cost around $2. If you like things spicy, ask for the masala option, or try prawns *tikka.* Restaurant Peace opens early and serves the best bowl of muesli in India, a genuinely huge portion of fresh fruit, mixed nuts, curd, and honey, a perfect way to start the day (C.T. Rd., © **06752/ 22-6642;** daily 6:30am–11pm; no credit cards).

TRIBAL TOURS IN ORISSA

Venturing into Orissa's tribal heartland is a true off-the-beaten-track adventure, allowing you to meet people with social, cultural, and agricultural practices that have remained unchanged for centuries. Many of Orissa's tribal people are still hunter-gatherers, and are physically distinct from any other ethnic group on the subcontinent. Opportunities for travelers to interact with members of these unique societies are generally limited to weekly markets held at various tribal centers. Visitors with an especially strong interest in anthropology can arrange to spend a night or two in a traditional village, but expect plenty of walking— and forget any modern conveniences. In Puri, your best option for a responsibly organized tribal tour is **Heritage Tours** (see earlier in this chapter); to ensure that a suitable trip is planned around your specific interests, e-mail the highly knowledgeable Bubu in advance (namaskar@heritagetours.org). A typical tribal tour for two persons will cost in the vicinity of $40 per person per day, for a minimum of 5 or 6 days. The fee factors in the services of a guide, an Ambassador car and driver, food, and (ultra-basic) accommodations.

3 Darjeeling

500km (310 miles) N of Kolkata

Darjeeling, "Land of the Celestial Thunderbolt," was given to the British as a "gift" from the once-independent kingdom of Sikkim. Situated in the Himalayan foothills and entirely surrounded by snowcapped vistas, Darjeeling soon became the favorite summer resort of the British Raj during the heyday of Calcutta—when Mark Twain visited, he exclaimed it was "the one land that all men desire to see, and having seen once by even a glimpse would not give that glimpse for the shows of the rest of the world combined." Today, the incredible view of the world's third-highest mountain, Mount Kanchenjunga (8,598m/27,400 ft.), is undoubtedly Darjeeling's best-loved attraction, though the town has of course also acquired a global reputation for producing the "champagne of teas," and retains some of its haunting Gothic Victorian ambience. Most visitors are here to pick up a permit and acclimatize for hikes through the mountainous state of Sikkim. It's worth noting that if you want an even sleepier colonial hill-station environment, with splendid flower-filled walks, head for nearby **Kalimpong,** which is blessed with a number of charming old-world accommodations options.

Two nights in Darjeeling should be more than enough, particularly if you're moving on to other Himalayan foothill towns. As with most hill stations, Darjeeling involves a considerable amount of climbing, and you'll do well to avoid the ugly mess of lower Darjeeling, which is typically congested, with suspicious odors, confusing back alleys, and a jumble of paths and stairways. Stick to The Mall and Chowrasta (crossroads) in upper Darjeeling, where life proceeds at a polite pace, and you can enjoy leisurely walks, stopping here and there for a cup of tea or to browse shops stuffed full of trinkets and artifacts.

ESSENTIALS

VISITOR INFORMATION Darjeeling's **Tourist Information Centre** (The Mall; © **0354/25-4050;** daily 10am–4:30pm) is helpful and can sell you a Rs 3 (6¢) map of the area.

ACQUIRING YOUR SIKKIM PERMIT IN DARJEELING Be warned: Getting your Sikkim permit is a laborious process that will take at least an hour. Take your passport to the **District Magistrate's Office** (off Hill Cart Rd.; Mon–Fri 11am–1pm and 2:30–4pm). Fill in a permit application form (remember to have it stamped), then go to the **Foreigners' Registration Office** (Laden La Rd.; © 0354/54-203; Mon–Fri 10am–4pm), where a policeman will endorse your form. Finally, head back to the District Magistrate's Office, making sure you arrive before closing time, and your passport will be stamped and the permit issued. It's valid for 15 days, is free of charge, and states clearly which areas you may enter. (Permits also available from the Ministry of Home Affairs in New Delhi.)

GETTING THERE **By Road** Darjeeling is 80km (50 miles) from Siliguri, which is the nearest main transit point. Buses from Darjeeling usually leave from the Bazaar bus stand on Hill Cart Road. Darjeeling is connected by road with Siliguri, Bagdogra, Gangtok, and Kathmandu across the Nepali border.

By Air The nearest airport is at Bagdogra (near Siliguri), 90km (56 miles) away. Jet Airways and Indian Airlines both have flights to Bagdogra from Kolkata and Delhi. Catch the **toy train** (8 hr.; see below) or a **taxi** (2–3 hr.) to get to Darjeeling.

By Train From Kolkata, the best option is to take the overnight N.J.P. Express, which arrives at the New Jalpaiguri railway station at 7:45am, in time to connect with the Darjeeling Himalayan Railway's famous **toy train.** It departs at 9am for the scenic 8-hour journey (see "The Most Spectacular Train Journey," below). Or you can either hire a taxi or share a jeep (readily available), directly from the station, for the 88km (54-mile) journey to Darjeeling. Although the toy train runs daily, bad weather may disrupt services. If you intend to catch the toy train out of Darjeeling at the end of your stay, and wish to travel in first class, you need to book your ticket in advance at the counter at New Jalpaiguri station. You can reserve other tickets for major trains out of New Jalpaiguri at the Darjeeling railway station between 10am and 4pm daily (closed 1–2 pm).

GETTING AROUND It's best to explore Darjeeling on foot, and if you need to haul luggage, ask for a porter and pay him well. Taxis are overpriced and unnecessary (with the exception of excursions to places some distance from the town). For local sightseeing tours or even jeep trips to Gangtok and other mid-distance destinations, contact the helpful **Darjeeling Transport Corporation** (30 Laden La Rd., opposite Apsara Hotel; © 0354/25-2074). It's open from 8am until 8pm and can advise you on alternatives if they're unable to accommodate you.

TREKKING & ADVENTURE ACTIVITIES Darjeeling is a good base for various "acclimatization treks" at lower altitudes than those you're going to come up against if you intend to trek in Sikkim. **Himalayan Travels** (18 Gandhi Rd.; © 0354/25-5405; kkgurung@cal.vsnl.net.in) undertakes sightseeing as well as trekking tours around Darjeeling and western Sikkim; all you need to bring are sleeping bags and adequate clothing and footwear. For white-water rafting, kayaking, canoeing, rock climbing, and mountain-biking, contact **D.G.H.C. Tourism** (Silver Fir Building, The Mall; © 0354/25-4214).

SIGHTS TO SEE

Darjeeling is the type of place where you might easily find yourself wanting to do very little other than drink in the restorative climate and tea. There are over

---

Moments The Most Spectacular Train Journey

A polite voice at New Jalpaiguri railway station frequently announces that " . . . the train is running 30 minutes late, the inconvenience caused is deeply regretted. . . . " It's a small price to pay for what must be one of the slowest, most spectacular train journeys in the world. Since July 4, 1881, Darjeeling's aptly named **toy trains**—including the world's oldest functioning steam locomotive—have puffed and wheezed their way between the hill station and the plains. In December 1999, the railway became India's 22nd World Heritage Site, only the second railway in the world to be so recognized. The trip between New Jalpaiguri and Darjeeling covers a mere 87km (54 miles) but takes almost an entire day to transport passengers up 2,055m (6,850 ft.). En route, with rhododendron slopes, rolling hills, and Kanchenjunga in almost constant view, you pass through villages with names like Margaret's Hope, and often drift right past the front doors of homes that range from shacks to quaint red-tiled cottages surrounded by potted flowers. You also traverse a total of 498 bridges and 153 unmanned level crossings. The final stop before Darjeeling is **Ghum (Ghoom)**, the second-highest railway station in the world. For details see "Getting There by Train," above, or contact Mr. Sidheque, PRO Indian Railways (© 011/2338-5072).

---

70 different tea plantations in the area, and a typical tour (**Happy Valley Tea Estate** will usually accommodate visitors) demonstrates everything from harvesting to how different varieties of tea are sorted and prepared for export around the globe. For the finest selection of organic and non-organic teas—20 to 30 plantations are represented—pay a visit to **Nathmulls** (© 0354/25-6437; Mon–Sat 9am–1pm and 2–7pm), a family business that's been selling tea since 1931. For a good vantage, climb **Observatory Hill**, held sacred by Hindus and Buddhists; there's also a Kali shrine guarded by foul-tempered monkeys that play on the colorful Buddhist prayer flags strung between the pine trees.

Darjeeling has a sizeable Tibetan presence and a number of Buddhist monasteries you can visit. Set against the backdrop of Kanchenjunga, the colorful **Bhutia Busty Gompa**, near Chowrasta, is famous for the contents of its upstairs Buddhist library—one of the esteemed texts kept there is the original *Tibetan Book of the Dead*. On Tenzing Norgay Road, **Aloobari Monastery** is where you may be able to buy Tibetan and Sikkimese handicrafts.

A GLORIOUS SUNRISE

Watching the sun rise from **Tiger Hill**, near the sleepy town of Ghoom, is one of the best things to do in the area (11km/7 miles from Darjeeling): The sight of the first rays of dawn carving a dramatic, golden silhouette around the not-too-distant eastern Himalayan peaks is quite brilliant. Occasionally, Mount Everest is also visible, just 225km (140 miles) away. Come armed with spare film and warm clothing—at an altitude of 2,550m (8,160 ft.), predawn Tiger Hill is bone-jarringly cold, and if you want to join the crowds who flock there each morning, you have to be up before dawn. The entry fee is Rs 5 (10¢), but you can pay a little extra for VIP treatment inside a special observation tower (Rs 20/40¢), where heating is accompanied by soothing Darjeeling tea. On the way back, visit the Ghoom *(Liga Choling)* Gompa; possibly the best-known Buddhist monastery around Darjeeling, it was founded in the late 1800s and enshrines a 5m (16-ft.) high clay statue of the Maitreya Buddha. In the early morning light, the colorfully painted figures over the facade and rooftops—intended to scare away evil spirits—are quite radiant. Along the exterior walls are prayer wheels that are spun in order to send countless prayers to the heavens, while inside, butter lamps are lit in offering to the deity.

WHERE TO STAY

Darjeeling is a great place to experience some real colonial coziness, with several charming heritage hotels. In this category our preference is for **Mayfair Hill,** but **Windamere Hotel** (© 0354/25-4041 or -4042; www.windamerehotel.com; doubles from $120), originally a Victorian boardinghouse for English teaplanters located on Observatory Hill, has atmospheric public spaces (you can almost hear some wealthy *memsahib* tinkling away at one of the pianos, while guests celebrate another summer in the hills) and huge heritage rooms with immense charm. However, the hotel is showing signs of wear and tear (as you'd expect from a place built in 1889); sadly, this includes the service. Another good heritage property, the **New Elgin Hotel** (© 0354/25-4114; www.elginhotels. com; doubles from $91) is one of Darjeeling's oldest hotels, and with the air of a country manor is frequented by an upmarket foreign crowd looking to relive the splendor of the British Raj. Like Windamere, the public spaces are filled with oldworld charm—old-fashioned sofas, deep armchairs, fireplaces, and beautiful rugs—but some of the rooms aren't quite as grand (some odd color combinations, too), and the bathrooms are small. The best views are from room nos. 21 to 23, 31 to 33, and 51 to 53.

Finally, if you want to be assured of absolute peace and quiet, head for the nearby hill station of Kalimpong (see "Looking for Orchids in Kalimpong," below).

Dekeling Hotel ✶ (Value) Some of the cedar-paneled guest rooms at this charming hotel (the best choice if you're on a tight budget) have the very best views in town. Spotlessly clean and simple, this is the place to go for Tibetan hospitality (run by the wonderfully warm Norbu and Sangay Dekeva) rather than Raj-style sophistication. An old iron chimney heater keeps the lounge/library (stone tile floors, Tibetan sofas, *thangkas,* Tibetan paintings) cozy and warm; it's a wonderful place to kick back with a book, watched by the family dog, Doma. Guest rooms are basic, and although the bathrooms are a little small (with shower only), they're immaculately clean. On cold nights, a hot-water bottle is usually

---

Looking for Orchids in Kalimpong

For even more peace and quiet, head for this nearby hill station. Situated at 1,250m (4,000 ft.), Kalimpong is a truly restorative destination, with magnificent views, relaxing walks, and an abundance of wild orchids. You'll find a variety of places to stay, including several charming hotels that will delight Raj-ophiles. **Silver Oaks** (Rinkingpong Rd.; © 03552/25-5296, -5766, or -5767; www.elginhotels.com) has excellent views and terrific old-world ambience; luxurious doubles go for $84 including all meals. Representing real heritage, the **Himalayan Hotel** (Upper Cart Rd.; © 03552/25-5248) feels like the setting for a Sherlock Holmes mystery. It's crammed full of history, and has a wonderful hilltop location (full-board doubles from Rs 3,400/$74).

tucked into your bed. On the attic floor, room no. 3 has a 180-degree view that takes in Darjeeling town and Mount Kachenchunga in all its snowcapped magnificence. One drawback is that the hotel, located high above Dekevas Restaurant, is locked up quite early at night.

51 Gandhi Rd., Darjeeling 734 101. ℂ **0354/25-3298** or -4159. Fax 0354/25-3298. www.dekeling.com. 22 units. Doubles: Rs 650 ($14) back-facing; Rs 850 ($19) standard; Rs 1,150 ($25) deluxe; Rs 650–Rs 1,150 attic ($14–$25); Rs 2,450 ($54) deluxe with all meals included; Rs 250 ($5.35) extra bed. Discounts of up to 50% available off season. MC, V. **Amenities:** Restaurant; travel, sightseeing, and car rental assistance; limited room service; laundry; library. *In room:* Electric heater on request, TV.

Dekeling Resort ⋆ *Value* This guesthouse (resort is an ill-chosen descriptor) is the best value-for-money deal in town. A stiff, athletic climb leads you to "Hawke's Nest," the colonial bungalow with a commanding situation high above the town, now re-dubbed Dekeling Resort. Prayer flags flutter around this 120-year-old green-roofed, bay-windowed, two-leveled, all-suite cottage offering simple comfort, effortless charm, and complete privacy. There's a small, one-table dining room where breakfasts and home-cooked meals are served; or you can be served in bed, which the obliging staff of two will arrange. Ask for a double bed in an upstairs room; accommodations there are huge and charming, with wood floors, carved antique dressers, Tibetan rugs, pale floral fabrics, and lovely fireplaces. Bathrooms have large drench showers and plenty of natural light. This is a true haven if you don't mind the 20-minute walk to The Mall.

2 A.J.C. Bose Rd., Darjeeling 734 101. ℂ **0354/25-3092** or -3347. Fax 0354/25-3298. www.dekeling.com. 4 units. Doubles: Rs 2,000 ($44) suite; Rs 3,300 ($72) suite with all meals included; up to 40% discount off season. MC, V. **Amenities:** Dining room; lounge; assistance with travel; sightseeing; car rental; room service; laundry.

Mayfair Hill Resort ⋆⋆ Once the summer palace of the Maharajah of Nazargung, this class act has warmer staff and better ambience than popular New Elgin, and the views are far superior. Two copper elephants guard the entrance of the main building, and a signboard informs guests of daily weather conditions. It's set in a lovely garden with potted plants, sculpted deities, and its own temple. The partially wood-paneled guest rooms—in ivy-covered buildings, which feel more like cozy cottages—are a tad feminine (floral fabrics, predominantly pink) but lovely, featuring Tibetan rugs, fireplaces, fine wooden furnishings, a bay window with a seat, and an entrance/dressing room. They also receive plenty of natural light and enjoy superb views of the town, the mountains, and the valley below. There are tubs in the tiled, well-spaced bathrooms, which have good shelving and vintage-style free-standing wooden towel racks.

Opposite Governor's House, The Mall, Darjeeling 734 101. ℂ **0354/25-6376** or -6476. Fax 0354/25-2674. Mayfair@cal2.vsnl.net.in. 31 units. Doubles: Rs 5,500 ($120); Rs 1,000 ($22) extra bed. Rates include all meals. AE, MC, V. **Amenities:** Restaurant; bar; health club and tennis privileges; pool table; billiards; squash; ice-skating; travel assistance; car rental; currency exchange; babysitting; laundry; doctor-on-call; library. *In room:* Heater, TV, hair dryer.

Early to Bed, Early to Rise

Life kicks off early here, and fades very early at night. By 8:30pm, you'd best be in your hotel, or perched at the bar at **Joey's Pub** (ℂ **0354/52-748**), which has an authentic British pub atmosphere and a well-stocked bar. Out of season, even restaurants close a touch earlier than seems appropriate, and darkness creeps quickly over the streets, sidewalks, and alleys. You'll need a flashlight to find your way back to your hotel at night.

WHERE TO DINE

The following recommendations are all within walking distance of each other; ask for directions before you set out. For Tibetan food, **Dekevas Restaurant** has some delicious favorites, including *momos* (dumplings) and wonton soup, with a choice of chicken, pork, or vegetable as a base. Try a delicious *shabalay,* Tibetan pie filled with mince, onion, and spring onion; spice it up with a hint of chili sauce. Also sample the awesome *tsampa*—roasted barley served with cheese, butter, and a glass of milk. For those extra-cold days, it has a selection of soups. Also available are Chinese dishes, pizzas, and burgers (© **0354/25-4159;** no credit cards). At **Lemon Grass** (also known as The Park) you can order from the Thai or Indian menu—the Indian tandoori chicken is a stand-out favorite (© **0354/25-4989;** no credit cards). Part of a three-floor food center, with a delicatessen and Internet cafe one floor below and an American diner at the basement level, **Glenary's** has been serving guests since 1938. Although staff may boast about the Continental cuisine, the best options are Indian—try *mahi tikka* (spicy fish tandoori) or *bhuna gosht,* a mutton curry cooked with ginger, garlic, and masala in its own juices (© **0354/25-4122**). Spectacular views of Mount Kachenjunga make **Keventer's Snack Bar** (1 Nehru Rd.; © **0354/25-6542** or -4026) something of a Darjeeling institution, even if the food is nothing to write home about. Sit upstairs on the terrace for breakfast served by disaffected waiters in maroon jackets. For more views that help mediocre food go down, the **Windamere Hotel Restaurant** (Observatory Hill; © **0354/25-4041** or -4042) is open for all meals and a good place to soak up Raj-era ambience.

4 Sikkim

Sikkim's original inhabitants are the Rongtub (literally "the dearest people of Mother Earth"), who named their home *Ley Mayal Lyang,* or "heaven." And how. Crammed in between Tibet, Nepal, Bhutan, and West Bengal, this tiny, mountainous state is as pristine a pocket of India as you are likely to encounter, with some 4,000 varieties of wildflowers (including 600 varieties of orchids), snow-fed lakes, high-altitude mountain forests, and hidden Buddhist monasteries. Some travelers come simply to enjoy the refreshing views and clean air, but most are here to tackle the fantastic treks through western Sikkim, exploring remote valleys and villages of yak-herding Tibetans. Ideally, you should spend a day or two in the state capital, **Gangtok,** to organize permits and transport/trekking arrangements, then head to **Pelling** before undertaking a demanding high-altitude trek for several days. Or you can skip Gangtok, either hiring a jeep that goes directly from Siliguri (near the railway station at New Jalpaiguri) to Pelling, or travel from Bagdogra, the nearest airport; both are about 6 hours away by road.

ESSENTIALS

PERMITS   In addition to the standard visa, foreign visitors must be in possession of an **Inner Line Permit** (see "Acquiring your Sikkim Permit in Darjeeling," above). This, together with your passport, must be carried at all times. If you wish to travel north of Gangtok or Pelling, you will require an additional endorsement or **Protected Area Permit** from Sikkim Tourism in Gangtok.

VISITOR INFORMATION   **Sikkim Tourism** (Mahatma Gandhi Marg; © **03592/22-3425** or -2064; www.sikkimindia.com) is open May through August 10am to 4pm; March through April and September through October 9am to 7pm. The center has a computerized touch-screen kiosk that will provide more-or-less up-to-date tourist information (when it's working). This is where you can

---

View from the Sky

An alternative way to experience Sikkim is from the air. **Sikkim Helicopter Service** operates a five-seater throughout the year, closing only for repairs and maintenance. Bookings are taken at **Sikkim Tourism** in Gangtok (M.G. Marg; ✆ 03592/22-3425 or -2064). A 60-minute flight over western Sikkim costs Rs 3,250 ($70) per person, while the spectacular 90-minute Kanchenjunga flight costs Rs 6,250 ($135). Flights must be confirmed the previous day. **Burtuk Helipad** (✆ 03592/22-5277) is 3km (2 miles) out of town; a free pickup is available.

---

book highly recommended scenic helicopter rides. The office downstairs is where you must have your Sikkim permit endorsed if you intend to visit certain restricted areas in the state. There's also an **Information Counter** at Bagdogra Airport.

GETTING THERE   For the time being, **Bagdogra** in neighboring West Bengal is the closest airport, and is served by flights from major cities like Kolkata and Delhi. From Bagdogra, Sikkim Helicopter Service runs daily 30-minute flights to Gangtok for around Rs 1,500 ($33), well worth it just for the views. Alternatively, taxis (4 hr.) and buses are available. Shared jeep services are also available from Darjeeling, Siliguri, and Kalimpong, all in West Bengal. These are highly affordable; book more than one seat for yourself, preferably the two front seats for the best views. If you're coming from Kathmandu, fly to **Bhadrapur** in east Nepal, and head to Gangtok via Kakarbhitta (on the Nepalese-Indian border) and Siliguri in West Bengal.

GETTING AROUND SIKKIM   Unless you pick up a helicopter from Bagdogra airport, you will travel in Sikkim by road. Use either a private or shared jeep. Although roads are open throughout the year, bear in mind that all of Sikkim is mountainous and routes inevitably take far longer than they appear on maps. The shared taxi and jeep services from Gangtok to Pelling (Rs 120/$2.50) are served by **Nam Nam taxi stand** (✆ 03595/22-6763); book your seat in advance. Again, book both front seats, for the views. Sikkim's roads invariably traverse steep mountains and deep valleys, so travel can be exhausting (the journey to Pelling, via Ravangla, takes 5 hr.), but the scenery is spectacular. Within **Gangtok,** you're best off doing most of your wandering on foot; because of one-way roads, taxis are frequently required to skirt much of the city. To get to the Tibetology Institute and to Rumtek Monastery, you'll have to use a taxi.

GUIDED TOURS & TRAVEL AGENTS   **Blue Sky Tours & Travel** (Tourism Building, Mahatma Gandhi Marg; ✆ 03592/22-5113) specializes in a jeep tour of northern Sikkim. They can also help you with local sightseeing, and have an exhaustive 10-day Monastery Tour that takes in all the Buddhist monasteries in the state. Like all tour operators in Gangtok, rates depend on numbers. For trekking arrangements, try **Sikkim Tours & Travels** (GPO 155, Church St.; ✆ 03592/22-2188; www.sikkimtours.com). **Tashila Tours & Travels** (✆ 03592/22-2978 or -9842; www.tashila.com) undertakes a range of services, including trekking, rafting, and specialist tours. **Modern Tours and Treks** (Mahatma Gandhi Rd., Gangtok; ✆ 03592/22-7319) organizes well-priced all-inclusive treks and tours of Sikkim. **Yeti Tours and Treks** is based in Gangtok and undertakes a wide range of spectacular treks in various regions of Sikkim. These include outings to Dzongri (6 days), Goechala (9 days), Singaleela and Versay in the west, Greenlake in the north, and Kedi (3 days) and Teenjure in the east. Most treks cost in the vicinity of $40 per person per day, and include tents, food, porters, yaks, and guides.

GANGTOK & ENVIRONS

Sikkim's capital sits at an altitude of 1,780m (5,800 ft.), straddling a high ridge where houses and concrete blocks spill down the hillside; below is the Ranipul River. With only 50,000 inhabitants, it's relatively laid-back and generally free from the malaise that stalks India's many overpopulated towns and cities. For visitors, the most noble of Gangtok's charms is its proximity to marvelous mountain vistas; the town itself is threatened by unchecked construction. A base for visitors who come to organize treks or wind down after a high-altitude experience, it's pleasant to roam around but certainly not packed with attractions. The town's most significant drawing card is the **Nyamgal Research Institute of Tibetology** ⚝ (Rs 5/10¢; Mon–Sat 10am–4pm), which houses a collection of Tibetan, Sanskrit, and Lepcha manuscripts, as well as statues, Buddhist icons, masks, scrolls, musical instruments, jewelry, ornaments, incense burners, and beautiful *thangkas* (painted or embroidered tapestry wall hangings).

Rumtek Monastery ⚝⚝   The region's top attraction lies 24km (15 miles) from Gangtok. It was established in 1959 after the Chinese invaded Tibet by Ringpe Dorjee, the "supreme head" of the one of Tibetan Buddhism's four major sects—the Kagyu, or "Black Hat" order. Regarded as the richest Buddhist monastic center in India, Rumtek houses some of the word's rarest and most unique religious artifacts; its design is said to replicate that of the original Kagyu headquarters in Tibet. Try to get here during prayer times, when the red-carpeted benches are occupied by the Vajra chant and disciplinary master, who leads the chanting of prayers. The venerated part of the complex is the **Golden Stupa,** a 4m (13-ft.) high *chorten* in which the mortal remains of the 16th Gyalwa Karmapa (founder of the Black Hat order; see below) are enshrined. Gold-plated and embedded with jewels, turquoise, and coral, the *stupa* is kept in a locked shrine room, which must be specially unlocked for visitors. Ask a monk to help you find the way; he may help you track down the keeper of the key.

Fun Fact **Who Will Rule the Black Hat Order?**

In September 1992, an 8-year-old Tibetan boy named Ugen Thinley Dorjee was officially sanctified as the 17th Gyalwa Karmapa and new head of the "Black Hat" order, and recognized by the Dalai Lama as the true reincarnation of the 16th Karmapa. But controversy has surrounded Dorjee ever since his coronation at Tibet's Tshurpu monastery. Chinese authorities, welcoming him as a state guest, have been intent on using him as a political puppet, while a group of rival lamas have identified another candidate as the true reincarnation. In January 2000, Dorjee undertook a grueling 1,400km (858-mile) trek and escaped from Chinese-controlled Tibet in order to join the Dalai Lama in Dharamsala. There he waits for the dispute over his identity to be settled, hoping to take his place at Rumtek Monastery, which has been without a head since 1981.

Himalayan Brew

Chang, made from fermented millet, is the brew of choice in Sikkim. It's usually served in a wooden tumbler (called a *tomba*) with a bamboo straw and should look like a small mountain of chestnut-colored caviar sprinkled with a few grains of rice. Believed to aid sleep, it supposedly never causes hangovers. Many Western travelers would disagree.

WHERE TO STAY & DINE

If you're traveling on a budget, **Mintokling Guest House** (✆ 03592/22-4226; mintokling@hotmail.com; doubles from Rs 600/$13) is a 20-year-old Sikkimese home with fairly spacious, clean guest rooms; book no. 304. The owner is a fantastic source of information on Sikkimese history, especially if you're interested in the political lowdown; his mother was the niece of the last king of Sikkim.

Sikkim's smartest hotel, **Nor-Khill** (see below), also hosts its best restaurant, **Shangri-La** (✆ 03592/22-5637). Splurge on an all-inclusive full-course Sikkimese meal or find out if fried fiddlehead ferns are available, and do try their juicy chicken *momos* (Tibetan dumplings). Book a table at the window. Nor-Khill also has the best pub in town, the cozy **Dragon Bar. Snowlion** (✆ 03592/22-2523) is also good for Tibetan fare, including chicken *sha-dre* (rice noodles with a curry sauce) and *sumei,* or open *momos.* Adventurous diners can sample traditional *dre-thuk,* a thick, porridge-like rice soup topped with a mountain of finely grated cheese. They also serve delicious body-warming beverages—try the hot brandy toddy with brandy, rum, and cloves, or the hot whiskey lemonade.

Netuk House ✦✦ *(Value* Buddhist prayer flags flutter above this gorgeously situated and well-run family guesthouse with real Sikkimese flavor. It's owned by the warmly aristocratic Denzong family, who are always pleased to introduce guests to local culture. All accommodations are unique; four guest rooms are in the main house and six are in the colorful annex, with its traditional rainbow-hued Sikkimese-style facade. Guest rooms are simple but lovely, and have good, comfortable mattresses covered in crisp white linen. Carefully prepared traditional four-course Sikkimese meals are served in the dining room; just below is a charming Sikkimese-style living room with an old-fashioned wood-burning heater. There's also a lovely bar.

Tibet Rd., Gangtok 737 101. ✆ 03592/22-2374 or -6778. Fax 03592/22-6778. slg_netuk@sancharnet.in. 10 units. Doubles: Rs 3,600 ($78); Rs 1,200 ($26) extra person; Rs 725 ($16) children 8–12; Rs 375 ($8) children 4–7; children under 4 free. Rates include all meals. No credit cards. **Amenities:** Restaurant; bar; TV lounge; travel assistance; sightseeing; car hire; laundry; doctor-on-call.

Nor-Khill ✦✦✦ This stylish hotel offers the priciest and most luxurious accommodations in the state of Sikkim, fronted by a lovely lawn (sadly, overlooking Gangtok's new sports stadium). The deluxe units are like suites, with a large bedroom area extending off a comfortable and beautiful living area; views are excellent. There are huge floral rugs on wood tile floors and carved and painted Sikkimese-style furnishings and fittings. Beds are a little narrow and slightly soft, however, but have lovely fabrics and scatter cushions. Bathrooms are spacious, with tubs and natural light. Standard doubles are spacious and equally beautiful; reserve room no. 43, which is large and well-positioned. The room rent includes all meals, served in the formal **Shangri-La Restaurant.**

Paljor Stadium Rd., Gangtok 737 101. ✆ 03592/22-5637. Fax 03592/22-5639. Reservations: 5 Park Row, 47 Park St., Kolkata 700 016. ✆ 033/2226-9878. Fax 033/2246-6388. www.elginhotels.com. 25 units.

Doubles: Rs 4,800 ($105) standard; Rs 5,500 ($121) super deluxe; Rs 2,000 ($44) extra bed. Rates include all meals. AE, DC, MC, V. **Amenities:** Restaurant; bar; travel assistance; currency exchange; gift shop; room service; laundry; doctor-on-call. *In room:* Heater, TV.

NEAR RUMTEK
Where to Stay

Shambhala Mountain Resort ★★ *Value*   Occupying the side of a ridge, this pretty ivy-covered hotel is surrounded by rhododendrons in a peaceful setting. It has wonderful, good-value accommodations and a genuinely Sikkimese ambience, with smart, clean, bright public areas. Each deluxe room has a small private balcony overlooking a terraced valley slope, distant mountains, and the nearby Rumtek complex. For a good view, reserve room nos. 201 to 204. Alternatively, opt for one of two rather unique cottages—reached via a small footbridge. The all-wood bedrooms are filled with brightly painted Sikkimese tables, chairs, and cupboards, offset by pale-colored or white fabrics; a small private patio has its own collection of fluttering prayer flags. Meals are taken in the beautiful wood-floor dining hall furnished with dark rattan chairs and decorated with Buddhist paintings, fans, and umbrellas.

Rumtek 737 135. (℗ **03592/25-2240** or -2243. Fax 03592/25-2275. sikkim@ahmedindia.com. 12 units. Doubles: Rs 1,650 ($36) deluxe; Rs 1,700 ($38) super deluxe (cottage); Rs 660–Rs 880 ($14–$19) extra person; children under 4 free. Rates include breakfast. Excellent meal plans available. AE, DC, MC, V. **Amenities:** Restaurant; bar; CD/video lounge; indoor games; travel desk; laundry; doctor-on-call; library. *In room:* Heater.

PELLING & ENVIRONS

Traditionally a stopover for trekkers headed for Yoksum, Dzongri, and similar high-altitude spots in western Sikkim, Pelling has begun to establish itself as a tourist destination in its own right, and as a result concrete lodges have sprung up indiscriminately to cash in on the passing trade. Nevertheless, the surrounding scenery is spectacular, and the sunrise behind snow-clad Khangchendzonga will leave you breathless. Besides hiking or rafting, the top attractions are the nearby monasteries. From Pelling, a pleasant 30-minute walk along the main road toward Geyzing, will lead you to one of Sikkim's oldest and most revered monasteries, **Pemayangtse** ★ (daily 7am–4pm), situated at 2,085m (6,672 ft.) in a cliff-top forest clearing. Set up as a monastery for *Ta-Sang,* or "pure monks" of the Nyingmapa order, Pemayangtse was established in 1705 by Lhatsun Chempo, one of the lamas who performed the consecration ritual of Sikkim's first king. Its prized treasure is a 7m (22-ft.) tall wooden depiction of Guru Rinpoche's *Sang-tok-palri,* or "heavenly palace," encased in glass in the monastery's upper room. Note that it's worth trying to contact Yapo S. Yongda (℗ **03595/25-0760**), who resides here—he's a fascinating source of information on Sikkimese history. Southeast of Pemayangste, on a lower hillock, are the ruins of the late-17th-century **Rabdentse Palace,** from where you can see the **Tashiding monastery** ★★, one of the most idyllic, peaceful, and sublime monasteries in India. Hire a jeep from Pelling to get here (Rs 1,200/$26 round-trip). A mere glance at Tashiding's **Thongwa Rangdol,** Sikkim's most venerated *chorten,* will (if Buddhist legends are to be believed) absolve you of all your sins. Also of special significance is the *bhumpa,* a copper vase that contains the holy water used each year during the *Bhumchu* festival, when a sacred ritual reveals Sikkim's fate for the upcoming year. It's a somewhat stiff 50-minute hike in the opposite direction to the hilltop **Sanga Choling monastery** ★—but it's worth it, for the most panoramic views around. Constructed in 1697, this is believed to be the second-oldest Buddhist monastery in Sikkim. Go when morning or evening prayers are held.

Husbands, Inc.

Part of Sikkim's unique high-altitude culture is the continued existence—typically in remote regions—of polyandrous communities, where one woman is married to a number of men. In some cases, a woman marries all the brothers from a single family.

WHERE TO STAY & DINE

A cheaper option to Norbu Ghang, **Hotel Mount Pandim** is set atop a hill a 10-minute walk from Pemayangtse Monastery. Guest rooms and facilities are spartan, but they're generally clean, and the views over the surrounding valleys and expansive mountainside are awesome. Try to reserve deluxe room no. 203 (© **03595/25-0756;** www.sikkiminfo.com; doubles Rs 650–Rs 850/$14–$19). In Pelling itself, the best budget accommodations are at **Hotel Phamrong** (Upper Pelling; © **03595/25-8218** or -0660; hotelphamrong@hotmail.com; doubles from Rs 600/$13), which has large en-suite rooms that generally come with fantastic views. Don't expect luxury, but the sunrises are brilliant. Pelling's best dining is at the Norbu Ghang Resort (see below), but the restaurant at the tiny **Garuda** guest lodge (next door to Hotel Phamrong) serves a variety of dishes, including Tibetan and Sikkimese specialties.

Norbu Ghang Resort ★ Norbu Ghang (which means "Jewel on the Hilltop") is the most tasteful accommodation in western Sikkim. It's built on four levels over a 2-hectare (5-acre) stretch of flower-speckled terraced hillside. The corrugated-roof cottages are fairly decent in size. All the best rooms and cottages have views of mighty Khangchendzonga (book cottage no. 601). The resort also has Pelling's best restaurant, serving traditional Sikkimese cuisine.

Pelling 737 113. © **03595/25-8245,** -8272, or -0566. Fax 03595/25-8271. www.sikkiminfo.com/ norbughang. 28 units. Doubles: Rs 2,000 ($44); Rs 3,000 ($65) Denzong suite; Rs 450 ($9.80) extra bed. No credit cards. **Amenities:** Restaurant; bar; travel assistance; currency exchange; shop; room service; doctor-on-call. *In room:* TV.

TREKS THROUGH WESTERN SIKKIM ★★★

Treks around western Sikkim are justifiably popular because of the spectacular views afforded throughout. If you want something relatively short and undemanding, the 4-day trek from Pelling to Tashiding and back is ideal, covering both cultural sights and majestic scenery. Far more challenging, and requiring more time and extra stamina, are the high-altitude treks to **Dzongri** (4,024m/12,870 ft.) and **Goeche La** (4,940m/15,800 ft.). Trekking here is only allowed with a recognized trekking operator in Gangtok; a daily fee of $30 to $45 will include guides, porters, yaks, tents, and food. March through May, the fabulous—and less strenuous—5-day **Rhododendron trek** through the exotic forests of the Singalila Range, near the border with Nepal, become possible. The much longer **Singalila Trek,** occasionally taking you across the border into Nepal and ending in Dzongri, is now also possible if you have 2 to 3 weeks to spare; Nepalese visas aren't required. For trek operators, see "Essentials: Guided Tours & Travel Agents," above.

Appendix:
India in Depth

A great triangle of land thrusting out of Asia, past the Bay of Bengal and the Arabian Sea, and deep into the Indian Ocean, India is a vast country (similar in size to Europe) and home to an ancient culture with a host of historic and architectural treasures unparalleled in the world. But more than anything else, it is India's enigmatic "otherness" that so fascinates the first-time visitor, for perhaps no other country on earth can offer so much contrast—traveling within the subcontinent feels at times like traveling through time. From the snowy peaks of the Himalayas, where prayer flags flutter against an impossibly blue sky, to the golden deserts of Rajasthan and Gujarat, where women wear saris saturated in fuchsias and saffron; from the vast plains of Madhya Pradesh, dotted with ruins and tiger parks, to the lush tropical mountains and paradisiacal beaches off the Malabar Coast, the spectrum of images and experiences is stupendous. Perhaps one of the most heterogeneous cultures in the world, with a mosaic of languages, dialects, religions, races, customs, and cuisines, India and its people cannot be defined, labeled, or pigeonholed—only experienced. Whether you're planning your trip to do a spiritual pilgrimage, view (or shop for) its myriad treasures, live like royalty in medieval palaces, unwind on unspoiled beaches, or simply indulge in the most holistic spa therapies known to man, India will leave an indelible impression on you. The following essays are merely a backdrop; to get to grips with the strange and fascinating world that is India, you will need to immerse yourself in some of the reading suggested at the end of this chapter. And travel to India again. And again. And again.

1 India Today

by Anita Pratap

Former CNN bureau chief for South Asia, freelance journalist,
and columnist for *Outlook,* India's weekly newsmagazine

There are many ways to describe "modern" India, but perhaps the most fitting is "Land of Paradoxes." For whatever your understanding of India today, the exact opposite is probably equally true. Life has changed dramatically in the last decade, when India began to liberalize its economy, and yet it remains a land where several centuries exist simultaneously. If you visit one of its scientific centers, you could well believe you are at NASA, but walk to a village that still has no connection to a driveable road (and there are thousands of them), and you will find people living exactly as they did 2,000 years ago. More than 25% of the world's software engineers are Indian, but another 25% of the Indian population go to bed hungry every night. Women have risen to top positions of power and authority, yet millions struggle without the most basic human rights. India has the world's highest number of malnourished children, yet obesity in urban children is a new and menacing problem. The country has armed itself with nuclear weapons, but has difficulty providing drinking water to millions of its citizens. It ranks extremely low in the United Nations' Human Development

Index, which measures quality of life (124th out of 173 countries), but in terms of purchasing parity, India is the fourth-biggest economy in the world after the United States, China, and Japan. No wonder India is confusing, confounding, incomprehensible. How can you make sense of this land? It's like emptying an ocean with a spoon.

All through the 1970s and even 1980s, Western diplomats and journalists predicted the "Balkanization" of India. It didn't happen. They predicted India would be a basket case. It didn't happen. In 1991, India's foreign exchange reserves plunged to a catastrophic $1 billion, barely sufficient to service 2 weeks of imports. India was forced to embark on a liberalization program, reducing aspects of government control such as high import tariffs and privatizing key sectors. Since then, India's economy has grown by an average of 6% annually, and today the reserves have reached a staggering $80 billion. According to statistics, the overall standard of living has improved since liberalization, but no doubt it has also aggravated disparity—India still has the world's largest concentration of poor. Nearly 300 million people live without the basic necessities of life: water, food, roads, education, medical care, and jobs. These are the Indians living on the outer edges of the nation's consciousness, far away in remote tribal areas, barren wastelands, and dirty slums, totally outside the market economy. Their tragedy is that they lack the basic skills needed to gain entry into the marketplace. And no one is even trying to equip them.

This brings us to the inherent weakness of Indian politics. India is the world's largest democracy. Every national election is the biggest spectacle of fair and peaceful democracy that humankind has ever witnessed. And yet, increasingly one cannot deny that democracy is often a masquerade for a modern version of feudalism. Clan loyalties propel electoral victories. The victor rules his or her province like a medieval tribal chieftain, showing scant respect for merit or rule of law. Cronies are handpicked for jobs, rivals are attacked or harassed, public funds are misused to promote personal agendas. Modern-day versions of Marie Antoinette abound in Indian democracy—during the acute summer water scarcity of 2003, the chief minister of Delhi, Sheila Dixit, actually urged her citizens not to bathe in tubs! Not only do a mere few thousand of Delhi's 12 million have access to tubs, but taps are perpetually dry in summer. And while the poor were dying of cold in January 2003 in nearby Uttar Pradesh, its chief minister, Mayawati, was strutting around in diamonds and celebrating her birthday with a cake the size of a minibus. One assumes that the withering media criticism that came her way would have wilted her arrogance but, far from being humbled, the lady turned her wrath on the media, countering that her low caste was the real reason for their criticism. Surprisingly, many low-caste people, whose cause she is supposed to champion, support her reasoning, marveling that she too can celebrate her birthday like India's rich. Never mind the waste of public funds that could have been used to buy blankets to save many people from freezing to death—Mayawati's outrageous behavior only filled them with pride and nationalistic fervor.

In fact, nationalism is one of the biggest growth industries in India, one that is guaranteed to stymie, if not wreck, genuine economic progress. In the last decade, the rise of Hindu nationalism has become a growing nightmare for India's Muslims and Christians. At the heart of this ideology is the belief that today's Muslims should be punished for historical wrongs perpetrated by medieval Muslim invaders and conquerors. The worst Hindu-Muslim rioting and looting happened in the western state of Gujarat in 2002, when Hindu mobs killed and maimed thousands of innocent Muslim civilians, including pregnant women and children, avenging another ghastly incident in which Muslim criminals roasted alive 58 Hindu pilgrims in a train. If unchecked, nationalism will also take its toll on the dangerous Kashmir dispute that bedevils relations between the nuclear-capable neighbors India and Pakistan. The two countries have fought two of their three wars over Kashmir, engaged in another low-level conflict in 1998, and come to the brink of another in 2002, prevented mainly through diplomatic intervention by the U.S. The situation is exacerbated by politicians who polarize Hindus and Muslims before elections in order to garner Hindu or Muslim votes—with Hindus constituting 82% of the population, Hindu nationalism clearly has a better chance of winning the electoral stakes. The battle for votes may be won through this diabolical strategy of dividing communities, but the opportunity for India to achieve her true destiny as a stable, prosperous giant in the 21st century will be lost.

Bill Clinton once said: "India remains a battleground for every single conflict the world has to win." Certainly India copes with massive problems—mounting corruption, joblessness, judicial bottlenecks with few convictions and delays of up to 20 years for delivering justice, AIDS, acute water shortages, poverty, disease, environmental degradation, unbearable overcrowding in metropolitan cities, crises of governance, sectarian violence, and terrorism. India adds one Australia to itself every year—*18 million people.* The rural poor (who form the majority) see children as an economic resource, the only security net for old age, and high child-mortality rates necessitate the need for more than one or two. Apart from India's huge natural growth rate, an estimated one to two million poor Bangladeshis slip into India every year in search of work.

It is really a miracle that India has not collapsed, but this is a country of remarkable stamina. The trouble is, India does not act until a crisis is full-blown. Indians are terrible at prevention, but terrific in crisis management. As it looms closer—like the imminent judicial collapse—it is exasperating and frightening to see citizens and authorities insouciantly lurch towards the abyss. But once they reach the precipice, Indians are adept at pulling back quickly and effectively. They don't descend into chaos because they are adaptable and resilient. For if disparity is India's weakness, diversity and courage are her strengths. India has a strong network of grass-roots-level institutions, NGOs, and activists that form a kind of coral reef, erecting little barriers on which political and economic onslaughts falter, such as the recent attempts to build an industrial belt around the Taj Mahal that, once exposed in the media, were shelved. These onslaughts come from an array of "threats"—from local politicians to multinational corporations. Nobody can ride roughshod over India. Nobody can fool Indians. Foreigners may be smooth-talking, willing to bribe, have fancy degrees, and speak English with a beautiful accent. But they can neither arm-twist nor hoodwink Indians. The shenanigans of Enron were exposed first in India. India stood firm amid the Enron-orchestrated swirl of accusations of being difficult, corrupt, untrustworthy. All of which is true. But it was equally true of Enron. Eventually, it was Enron that went bust.

When they cannot do it their way and according to their schedule, politicians rail against the bureaucrats, trade unionists, judges, journalists, and NGOs. But this defensive "coral reef" is what has saved India from sliding precipitously to economic ruin. The pace of Indian economic reforms was widely attacked as too slow by the IMF and World Bank. And yet Joseph Stiglitz, winner of the Nobel Prize for Economics in 2001 and a former chief economist for the World Bank,

Impressions

Who is an authentic Indian and who isn't? Is India Indian? Does it matter? Let's just say we're an ancient people learning to live in a recent nation . . .

—Arundhati Roy, *The Algebra of Injustice*

now admits that India's caution and slow, deliberate steps are precisely what saved the nation from the catastrophic meltdowns and flights of capital that befell Asian and Latin American countries.

India has always been a giant and will continue to be a giant. But she will move at her own pace. She is not an Asian tiger. She is more like a stately Indian elephant. No one can whip or crack her into a run. If you try, the stubborn elephant will dig in her heels and refuse to budge. No power on earth can then force her to move. The desire for change and movement must come from within. India will move, but she will be slow, ponderous, circuitous. Progress will come, but it will come in measured steps, not in leaps and bounds. There is no point arguing whether this is good or bad. It is good and bad. And it is many things in between.

After all, this is India.

2 India Past to Present

by Nigel Worden

A professor of history specializing in Indian Ocean history

No visitor to India can fail to be overwhelmed by the combination of a bustling, modernizing nation and an ancient but omnipresent past. India's history is everywhere, in its temples and mosques, forts and palaces, tombs and monuments, but it has only recently become a single country, which makes its history a complex one. Successions of kingdoms and empires have controlled parts of the subcontinent, but none unified the whole—even the British Raj's "Jewel in the Crown of the Empire" excluded large swaths of territory ruled by independent princes. Thus the accounts of history vary, and competing versions have often been the cause of bitter conflict. Given the tensions between Hindu and Muslim in South Asia, it is hardly surprising that the Islamic era in particular is highly controversial. Were the Muslims invaders and pillagers of an ancient Indian tradition, as Hindu nationalist historians claim? Or were

Dateline

- Circa 3000–1700 B.C. Harappan civilization of the Indus valley marks earliest farming communities in the region.
- 1500–600 B.C. Vedic states in the north establish the basis of Hinduism and the caste system.
- 326 B.C. Alexander the Great's army halts at the Indus.
- 322–185 B.C. Mauryan state in North India; conversions to Buddhism under Asoka (reigned 272–232 B.C.).
- A.D. 319–540 Gupta empire reunites northern India.
- 300–900 Pallava empire in Dravidian southern India.
- 900–1300 Chola empire in southern India.
- 1206–1400s Islamic Delhi sultanates established in north.
- 1510 Portuguese establish first European coastal settlement in India.
- 1526 Mughal conquest of Delhi (returned permanently in 1555).
- 1556–1605 Akbar extends Mughal power.

they Indians who created a distinctive culture of architecture, painting, and literature by blending indigenous forms with Islamic influences? Is the Taj Mahal a uniquely Indian master-piece, or a symbol of the Islamic oppressor? As is usually the case with history, it all depends on where you are, and who you're talking to.

ANCIENT   INDIA Historical accounts of India usually begin with the **Harappan civilization** of the Indus Valley, a sophisticated agricul-tural and urban society that flourished from 3000–1700 B.C. (about the same time as the earliest Egyptian civiliza-tion); although many of its sites are now located in latter-day Pakistan, you can view Harappan artifacts in places like the National Museum in New Delhi. Not much is known about the people, not least because their writing system has yet to be deci-phered, but their active trade with the civilizations of the Euphrates (con-temporary Iran and Iraq) show that northern India had links from very early on with the rest of Asia.

A more recognizably and distinctive "Indian" culture developed from around 1500 B.C in the northern part of the subcontinent, spreading steadily eastward in the 1st millennium B.C, although never penetrating to the far south. This is usually referred to as the **Vedic period.** The ancient written Vedas provide a rich record of this era, led by a Sanskrit-speaking elite, which embedded into India Hinduism, the caste system (led by a Brahmin priest-hood), and the dichotomy between a rural farming majority and an urban-ized merchant class, all ruled by local kings and princes. A series of Vedic kingdoms rose and fell, each centered on a city, of which Varanasi is today the oldest-living and best-known example. Much controversy surrounds the inter-pretation of the "Aryans," as the Vedic culture is known—some claim that they originated as invaders from the

- **1600** Founding of British East India Company.
- **1658–1707** Aurangzab conquers south for Mughal empire.
- **1739** Persian sack of Delhi and removal of the Peacock Throne accelerates Mughal decline.
- **1757** Clive defeats *nawab* of Bengal at Battle of Plassey, establishing British rule in Bengal.
- **1790s–1820s** British extend power in southern, western, and central India.
- **1856–7** Indian "Mutiny": uprising against British. British sack of Delhi and expulsion of Mughals.
- **1858** Dissolution of East India Company; India to be ruled directly from London.
- **1877** Queen Victoria declared Queen-Empress of India.
- **1885** Foundation of the Indian National Congress.
- **1890s** Bengal famine and plague epidemics.
- **1903** British capital moved from Calcutta to Delhi.
- **1905** Division of Bengal provokes boycott campaigns against British.
- **1906** Muslim League founded.
- **1915** Gandhi returns to India.
- **1919** Amritsar massacre galvanizes Indian nationalist opposition to British.
- **1930** Gandhi leads salt march to protest British taxation policies.
- **1935** Government of India Act gives measure of local self-government to India, but retains British power at the center.
- **1939–45** World War II: India threatened by Japanese advance in Southeast Asia.
- **1942** Gandhi announces "Quit India" campaign and is imprisoned.
- **1946** Labor government in Britain announces future independence for India, with Mountbatten as new viceroy.
- **1947** British leave India. Partitioning into the separate states of India and Pakistan. Massacres of refugees across new frontiers. Nehru becomes independent India's first prime minister.
- **1948** Gandhi assassinated by a Hindu fundamentalist.

continues

north who conquered and subjugated the local population, while Hindu nationalists today see them as the archetypal indigenous Indian—a controversy that makes Indian archaeology a tempestuous field of study. Whichever interpretation you buy into, the influence of the Vedic era is all-pervasive in modern Indian life, and the historical focus of a modern Hindu identity.

From the 6th century B.C., the Aryan states were themselves subject to invasions from the north, in a cycle of incursion and subsequent local adaptation that was to dominate much of India's history. Even Alexander the Great, hearing of the wealth and fertility of the area, tried to invade, but his army apparently refused to cross the Indus River and instead made their way back to Macedonia. Other invaders (or settlers, depending on your preference) of Greek, Persian, and central Asian origin moved in, challenging some of the indigenous states, such as Shakas of western India and the Magadha state of the northeast, and, in time, all of

- 1964 Death of Nehru.
- 1966 Nehru's daughter, Indira Gandhi, becomes prime minister.
- 1975 Indira Gandhi declares State of Emergency but is ousted from power in the 1977 elections.
- 1980 Indira Gandhi regains power.
- 1984 Indian army besieges Sikh temple at Amritsar. Indira Gandhi assassinated by Sikh bodyguards in revenge.
- 1984–89 Indira Gandhi's son Rajiv is prime minister.
- 1991 Assassination of Rajiv Gandhi by a Tamil separatist. Liberalization of the economy by reducing government controls, privatizing, and drastically reducing import tariffs and taxes.
- 1992 BJP-led attack on mosque at Ayodhya.
- 1996 BJP Hindu fundamentalist party wins electoral majority and forms coalition government.
- 2002 Threat of nuclear war with Pakistan over Kashmir averted by international mediation. Gujarat sees tensions between Hindu and Muslim nationalists inflamed.
- 2004 National elections held; BJP expected to win again.

these newcomers were absorbed into the local population. It was during this period that Siddhartha Gautama (Buddha) was born in latter-day Nepal; he later moved to India, where he sought—and found—enlightenment at Bodghaya, and starting teaching at Sarnath, just outside Varanasi.

The first large state to emerge in this region was under the **Mauryan rulers** (322 B.C.–185 B.C.), who incorporated much of northern India, including the region west of the Indus; at its largest, it even reached south to Karnataka. The most famous of these rulers was **Asoka,** who converted to Buddhism after a particularly murderous episode of conquest pricked his conscience; he spread the Buddha's teachings throughout northern India, particularly at Sarnath and Sanchi, where you can still view the *stupas* (commemorative cairns) he built. Asoka's decrees, which were inscribed onto rock (literally), carved his reputation throughout the region, while his emblem of four back-to-back lion heads (which you can also view at Sarnath) has been adopted as the modern symbol of India.

Asoka's empire barely survived his death in 232 B.C., however, and in the subsequent centuries local states rose and fell in the north with alacrity. The **Gupta empire** emerged in A.D. 319 to A.D. 540 under Sumadra Gupta, who conquered the small kingdoms of much of northern India and Bengal, while his son extended its range to the west. This loose confederacy was marked by a reinvigoration of Hinduism and the power of the Brahmins, which reduced the influence of Buddhism in the subcontinent (though it had taken strong root in Sri Lanka and Southeast Asia). But Hun invasions from the north in turn destroyed Gupta power, and northern India was again split into numerous small kingdoms.

It should be noted that the southern part of India remained unaffected by these developments. With the exception of Asoka's Mauryan empire, none of the northern states of the north extended their influence beyond the central plains, and South India developed its own economic systems, trading with Southeast Asia and across the western Indian Ocean as far afield as the Roman Empire. Dravidian kingdoms emerged, some of which established sizable empires such as the **Pallava** (A.D. 300–A.D. 900) and **Chola** (A.D. 900–A.D. 1300). Hinduism flourished, evident in the rich legacy of Dravidian temple architecture (notably at Thanjavur).

THE ISLAMIC ERA   Even Indian historians refer to the period from the 10th to the 16th centuries as "medieval," but a more accurate characterization of it relates to the impact of Islam. Muslim influence from the northwest was evident in northern India from at least A.D. 1000, but it was only with the arrival of Islamic forces from the 13th century onward that its presence became dominant. A succession of fragmented and unstable Moslem states emerged around new centers such as Lahore (Pakistan), Delhi, and Agra, collectively known as the Delhi Sultanates. Conversions to Islam were made among the local population, mainly from the lower castes or where Hinduism was weaker, like in Bengal, but the majority of the population remained Hindu. In most areas the Muslim rulers and their administrators were but a thin layer, ruling societies that followed earlier traditions and practices.

In the south, Muslims made much less impact. Muslim raids in the 14th century instead led to unified Hindu resistance by the Vijayanagar empire centered in Hampi, which flourished in the south as one of the strongest Hindu states in Indian history, surviving until the 16th century.

By this stage a more vigorous wave of Islamization had emerged in the form of the **Mughals,** a dynasty that originated from the Persian borderlands (and possibly driven south by the opposing might of Genghis Khan in central Asia). The Mughals established themselves initially in Kabul, then the Punjab, and in 1555 they finally conquered Delhi, which became their capital. Under **Akbar** (1556–1605) and **Aurangzab** (1658–1707), the Mughals extended their empire south into the Deccan and, after defeating the Vijayanagar state, deep into the south, although their ambitions to conquer the entire subcontinent were stymied by the opposition of the Hindu Maratha states in the southwest.

Rulers such as Aurangzeb were not slow to show merciless terror against those who opposed them, but previous images of the Mughal empire's ruthless despotism have now been challenged by many historians, who point out that, other than Aurangzeb, the Mughal emperors were happy to allow local rulers to continue in power, provided they regularly sent tribute to Delhi and provided troops and cavalry when needed. Close to Delhi, the fiercely independent Hindu princes of Rajasthan retained their authority so long as they did not openly flout Mughal rule. Taxes were levied on landowners, but the levels were in general no higher than before. Trade and local textile production flourished in many regions, notably in Bengal and Gujarat. Muslim law, Persian language, and administrative structures were introduced, although in many outlying parts of the empire, local customs continued.

But by the 18th century, the Mughal empire was in decline. Some of this was the result of direct opposition, especially from the Marathas, who were consolidating their power in the southwest, but in other respects, decline might have been a product of the Mughal empire's own prosperity. Local regions such as Bengal, Oudh, and the Punjab began to benefit from economic growth and to assert their independence. When Delhi was attacked by yet more incursions from the north, culminating in the sack of the city by Persians in 1739 and the hauling off of the fabulously valuable Peacock Throne, symbol of Mughal power, local regions went their own way. In Bengal, the local ruler made an agreement with foreign merchants who had appeared along the coast in the 17th century, allowing them to built a small settlement at the mouth of the Hooghly River (later to become Calcutta) and to trade in cotton and cloth in return for tribute. These foreign merchants were members of the British East India Company, formed in 1600, which had failed to establish a niche in the more lucrative spice trade of Southeast Asia, and was thus forced to settle for less-plum pickings along the Indian coastline: They obtained permission from locals to set up stations at Surat and what were to become the cities of Madras and Bombay. They were not the only Europeans to settle in India; the Portuguese had first established a base in Goa in 1510, and in the 17th century the Dutch made similar agreements with local rulers in Bengal, Nagapatnam, and the Malabar coast, while the French set up shop in Pondicherry. Even the Belgians, Danes, and Swedes formed trading companies, but unlike the others, they had little impact on the indigenous culture.

As was the case elsewhere, it was the British who moved from trade to empire in India. In part this was the outcome of inter-European rivalries: The English grabbed French ships and produce in India (along with French Canada) in the **Seven Years War** (1756–63), then moved on Dutch posts in India and Sri Lanka after the Napoleonic wars. But the main impetus came from their dealings with Indian rulers. In Bengal, English traders were making a killing, often marrying local women and living the high life. Frustrated by their continued and unwelcome presence, the local *nawab* attacked the English settlement at Calcutta in 1756, imprisoning a number of people in a cramped cell, where some suffocated. The "Black Hole of Calcutta" martyrs became a rallying cry to justify further incursions by the British: Troops were shipped to Calcutta, which defeated the *nawab* at Plassey the following year and again in 1764. The British East India Company filled the local power vacuum—and although nominal vassals of the Mughals still lived in the Red Fort in Delhi, the East India Company was effectively the local government.

In the course of the late 18th and early 19th centuries, the Company's area of influence grew apace. Presenting itself as the "defenders of Bengal," it forged alliances and provided military support for local rulers in areas such as Bihar and the northwestern regions, then moved in when they defaulted on repayments. By the mid–19th century, English armies (manned overwhelmingly by Indian troops) overran Oudh and the Punjab. In the south the Company moved inland from Madras to the Carnatic and across to Malabar. It inherited the Mughals' rivalry with the Marathas (the region around latter-day Mumbai), which erupted into open warfare in 1810 and led to the Company's conquest of the western coast and its hinterland.

While extending their power base, the Company still claimed allegiance to the Mughals, whose emperor retained nominal control in Delhi. But this, too, was to end. In 1856 and 1857, following decades of resentment against British policies and their impact, an army mutiny (caused by the use of animal fat on bullet cartridges, which affronted the Hindus) triggered uprisings against the British across northern and central India. Despite claims by later nationalist historians that this was a united revolt against the foreign oppressor, most of the violence in the "Indian Mutiny" of 1856 to 1857 was by Indians against other Indians, in which old scores of class, religious, or regional rivalries were festering. Nonetheless, epic stories abounded of Indian valor or British heroism and martyrdom (depending, again, on which side told them). The British, taken by surprise, only regained control by the skin of their teeth—and by ruthless retaliation. Some of the resisters had appealed to the Mughal emperor to reassert control over India, which in an unwise moment he had agreed to do. The British army sacked Delhi, forced the emperor into exile, and declared the end of the Mughal empire. But London was unimpressed by the chaos that the East India Company rule and policies had brought, and moved to abolish the Company's charter, effectively establishing direct rule from London. The pretence was over. India was now to be ruled by a new foreign power.

THE RAJ   The East India Company was replaced by a new system of government. The British Crown was represented in India by a viceroy sent out from London who presided over a professional class of British-born and (mainly) Oxbridge-educated administrators appointed through the Indian Civil Service. Most Indians never saw this relatively small body of men (never exceeding 5,000 at any one time), and they in turn were dependent on the military (still primarily composed of Indian troops, or *sepoys,* lorded over by a British officer class) and on another army of Indian lesser-ranking administrators, lawyers, and civil servants, who were prevented by race from rising to the upper ranks. For India, unlike British Africa and Australasia, was not to be a settler colony. The British initially played on the fiction that they were the legitimate successors to the Mughals, mounting spectacular *durbars* (receptions) to demonstrate their power and the loyalty of India's princes–in 1877 the occasion was used to declare an absent Victoria "Queen-Empress of India"; it was only in 1911 that the reigning British monarch finally attended a durbar. The British built a set of administrative buildings in "New Delhi," declared the capital in 1903, that today are considered the finest architectural achievements of the empire.

In many ways British rule was a new experience for India. For one thing, the entire subcontinent was viewed as a single whole, despite the continuation of nominally independent princely states in much of its central regions. With a mania characteristic of the Victorian, the British mapped the landscape; surveyed the diverse systems of landholding; separated its inhabitants by race, language, and caste (for census purposes); and built the huge railway network that connects the country today. Much of this had the practical purpose of raising revenues from trade and taxation, since the British were determined that the Raj should be self-financing. But it also created a body of knowledge that was to shape many of their political and social policies, and to solidify categories of race and caste that had earlier been somewhat more permeable.

The Indian economy in the era of the Raj became closely dependent on British and other imperial markets, with promotion of the export of raw materials rather than internal industrialization, although by the early 20th century, parts of Bengal and the region around Bombay were starting to manufacture for local purchasers. It was from the "new" Indian administrative and mercantile classes that the first stirrings of opposition to British rule came. The local modernizers demanded equal access to economic and political opportunities, rather than a return to India's precolonial past. Thus the first **Indian National Congress (INC)** was formed in 1885, with members primarily from Bengal, Bombay Presidency, and Madras. The INC carried out its proceedings in English, and called for access to the higher ranks of the civil service (with examinations for entry held in India, not in Britain) and for relief of the heavy levies on Indian-produced local textiles. By the turn of the century, after the disastrous famine and plague epidemic that broke out in Bengal in the 1890s, more extremist members of the INC were demanding *swaraj,* or "self-rule," although what they had in mind was a degree of self-government akin to the British dominions in Canada, Australia, or South Africa, rather than total independence. An unpopular administrative division of Bengal in 1905 led to a boycott of British imports, and some Bengali intellectuals began to evoke Hindu notions of a free Indian nation. The British conceded limited electoral reform, granting a local franchise to a tiny percentage of the propertied, but they ominously listed voters in separate voter rolls according to whether they were Muslim or Hindu; a separate **Muslim League (ML)** was formed in 1906.

World War I, in which large numbers of Indian troops served the British cause, dampened anti-British protests and saw a pact between the ML and the INC, not least because of vague British promises of meaningful change once the war was won. But in 1919, British General Dwyer opened fire on a demonstration held in the enclosed space of the Jallianwala Bagh in Amritsar, killing and wounding over 2,000. This gave Indian nationalism its first clear martyrs, and the callousness with which Dwyer's actions were applauded by the British general public enflamed matters further.

The period between the two World Wars saw a seismic transformation of Indian nationalism, growing from the protests of a small elite to a mass-based movement that overwhelmed the British. The figure with whom Indian nationalism is most associated is **Mohandas Karamchand Gandhi,** the "Mahatma." After an early career in law, he developed his concepts of *satyagraha* (nonviolent protest) and passive resistance in defending Indian interests in colonial South Africa before he returned to his native India in 1915. Gandhi persuaded the INC to embrace a concept of a united India that belonged to all Indians, irrespective of religion or caste. Mass support for Congress campaigns of non-cooperation with the colonial state was ensured by well-publicized and symbolic campaigns such as the 1930 march from Ahmedabad to the Gujarat coast to defy a salt tax by making salt from sea water. Membership of the INC soared to over two million. But not all of Gandhi's ideas were triumphs—he was much criticized by some for his failure to support the socialist leanings of Bombay factory workers, while others took little interest in his appeal for religious tolerance or equal acceptance of the outcast *dalits.* The British granted a degree of self-government to India in 1935, although only at the provincial level. Another group that did not accept INC's call for unity was the Muslim League. Fearing Hindu domination in a united India (revealed by the 1935 elections), they began, under their leader Mohammed Ali Jinnah, to call for a separatist Islamic state named "Pakistan" (after the initials of areas they claimed: Punjab, the Afghan states, Kashmir, and Sind). At first, few took this seriously, although Gandhi was alarmed at the divisive trends.

World War II was to change everything. Gandhi and INC leaders called in 1942 for the British to "quit India" and were imprisoned. Although many Indian regiments in the British army supported the Allies, a number of other Indians joined the Japanese-trained Indian National Army under the INC leader Subhas Chandra Bose. After 1945, Muslim and Hindu violence broke out, with each side claiming power. The new Labor government in Britain was now anxious to divest itself of its troublesome Raj and sent Lord Mountbatten as a new viceroy to oversee the process. Mountbatten's decision that the British should cut their losses as quickly as possible by leaving in August 1947 took everyone by surprise. More seriously, he agreed to partition the country to appease Jinnah and the Muslim League rather than risk continuing civil war in the new state. In a frenzy of activity, "Partition" became official, and the boundaries of the new Pakistan were summarily drawn across the map, splitting the Punjab into two and dividing communities. Millions of refugees spent Independence Day desperately trying to get to the "right" side of the border, amid murderous attacks in which well over a million lost their lives. The trauma of these months still casts a deep shadow over the subcontinent. While the British Raj in India lasted less than a hundred years, the processes that led the British to divide the country into two states, India and Pakistan, have fundamentally shaped the modern nation state.

INDEPENDENT INDIA   For almost 4 decades, independent India was to be governed by the INC, initially under its leader Jawaharlal Nehru, who had led Congress in the negotiations of 1946 and 1947. Gandhi was bitterly disillusioned by Partition, even proposing at one stage that Jinnah be made prime minister of India to restore unity. This was enough to alienate him from some Hindu nationalists, one of whom assassinated the Mahatma in 1948. Such rival visions of the Indian nation were to plague the new country.

The most pressing political issues centered around India's relations with Pakistan. The Indian government was (rightly) accused of fomenting dissent in East Pakistan in the late 1960s, leading to war in 1971. Continued conflict has centered around Kashmir, an independent princely state with a predominantly Muslim population but whose Hindu ruler, under threat from Muslim forces from Pakistan, placed it under Indian rule in 1948. Pakistani and Indian troops have tensely faced each other in the territory ever since. With the development of nuclear weapons by both states, and a militant Kashmiri independence movement, the area is a potential powder keg of international concern.

Under Nehru, internal stability was obtained, remarkable considering the circumstances of India's independence, and until his death in 1964, he established India as the world's leading postcolonial democracy, a key player (along with Sukarno's Indonesia) in the non-alignment movement that avoided Cold War conflicts. Communal rivalries were downplayed by a focus on India's secular status. Regional separatism continued to threaten unity, especially Tamil opposition to Hindi linguistic domination from Delhi, but this was resolved by a reorganization of local states along linguistic lines.

Nonetheless, Congress never obtained more than 45% of the national vote and only held power because of the division of its political opponents. After Nehru's death, its attraction weakened. In an attempt to restore its popularity, his daughter, Indira Gandhi (no relation to the Mahatma), became prime minister in 1966. From 1969, she implemented a more populist program of social change, including land reform and a planned economy—a program that was to alienate some of the richer landowners and regional party leaders. Economic

Impressions

'And do thy duty, even if it be humble,' says the Aryan Gita, 'rather than another's, even if it be great. To die in one's duty is life; to live in another's is death' . . . Indian poverty is more dehumanizing than any machine . . . men in India are units, locked up in the straitest obedience by their idea of their dharma. The blight of caste is not only untouchability; it is the overall obedience it imposes.

—V.S. Naipaul, *India: A Wounded Civilization*

restructuring led to strikes and civil opposition in the cities, and in 1975, a State of Emergency was declared that lasted 2 years. Believing that she had reasserted control, Indira Gandhi held elections in 1977. The result was the first defeat for Congress, although no party was able to form a united government to replace it, and by 1980 Gandhi was back in power.

The INC never regained its previous level of control, however. Resentment by Sikhs at their failure to secure autonomy in the Punjab culminated in 1984 with the Indian army's siege and capture of the main Sikh temple at Amritsar with thousands of casualties, and Indira Gandhi was assassinated by her Sikh bodyguards. Her son, Rajiv Gandhi, succeeded her, and instituted new programs of economic liberalization, but he also embroiled India unsuccessfully in the ongoing civil war in Sri Lanka, leading to his assassination in 1991 by a Tamil activist. Although his widow, the Italian-born Sonia Gandhi, inherited leadership of Congress, the era of the Nehru family's domination of Indian politics (which has been compared to the Kennedy family's political impact in the U.S.) was over.

In 1989, Congress was again defeated at the polls, this time led by the Hindu nationalist **Bharatiya Janata Party (BJP).** Although the BJP initially failed to hold together a coalition government, its strength grew. It accused Congress of allowing India to be dominated by outside interests, including globalized economic forces, but more specifically by Indian Muslims who it considered to be unduly tolerated under Congress's secular state policies. In 1992, a BJP–led campaign led to the destruction of the mosque at Ayodhya, believed to be the birthplace of the Hindu god Ram.

In the 1996 elections the BJP defeated a Congress government plagued by accusations of corruption and emerged as the leading group in the coalition governments that have ruled India since. Under the BJP Prime Minister Atal Behari Vajpayee, tensions with Muslim Pakistan have increased, with both sides testing and threatening the use of nuclear weapons, especially in conflicts over Kashmir. Fortunately, 2003 saw a welcome cooling. The general perception is that the next elections, tentatively scheduled for September/October 2004, will again be won by the BJP.

3 The Religions of India

The diversity of religious belief and practice in India is both unique and somewhat confounding. What follows is a very brief introduction to the religions that took root in India; this will hopefully provide some insight into the patterns and diversity that exist. Tribal religions, ostensibly pagan, still exist in isolated pockets but are declining rapidly and are not covered here.

HINDUISM   To begin the unending journey of studying India, you need to take the first step toward understanding Hinduism, the religion of some 80% of India's population. It can only be a "first step" for, like India itself, Hinduism defies attempts to clearly define or categorize, and what may be described as universal Hindu religious practice in one place may very well be contradicted by others elsewhere.

Hinduism has no ecclesiastical order, nor is there a central religious book. (While many religious texts like the ancient Upanishads and Bhagavad-Gita exist, they are not the "word of god" like the Bible or Koran.) It is not possible to convert to Hinduism; you are born Hindu, usually into one of the four main hierarchical castes (Brahmin, or "priest"; Kshatriya, or "warrior"; Vaisya, or "merchant"; Sudra, or "peasant") or—at the very bottom of the social order—as a Dalit, better known as the "untouchables." Unlike organized religions such as Christianity or Islam where truth is specified, categorical, linear, and unidimensional, truth in Hinduism is in fact extremely multidimensional—contradictions are not bad, but inevitable. Unlike Christianity and Islam, which say there is one true path that leads to one God, Hinduism says there are many paths that lead to many gods (some say—probably hyperbolically—330 million gods, who epitomize a host of human qualities, from gluttony to vengefulness). This intrinsic Hindu acceptance of diversity and multiplicity has defined India's history, allowing it to successfully adapt by absorbing the beliefs of successive invaders. Even today it is not difficult for Hindus to look upon Allah or Jesus as deities worthy of veneration—more than half the devotees who flock to pray at the famous Muslim shrine in Ajmer city in North India or at the fabled Velankanni church in South India are Hindus.

Rather than a formal religion, Hinduism is considered a way of life, or *Sanatan Dharma* (an eternal path), in which the universe is part of an endless cycle of creation, preservation, and dissolution. The human soul is also part of this cycle, endlessly reincarnated, and seeking freedom. According to Hindu philosophy, we determine our destiny by our actions. *Karma* is the law of cause and effect through which individuals create their own destiny by virtuous thoughts, words, and deeds. One can control the nature and experiences of the next life *(karma)* by "living right" or *dharma*—through *dharma* (a righteous pattern of conduct), individuals determine their *karma*. By resolving all *karmas,* the soul can finally attain *moksha,* an escape from the cycle of life.

There are many sects and denominations within Hinduism, and priests, *sadhus* (holy men), and other spiritually enlightened individuals are important parts of the religious process: *Bhakti* is devotion to and communication with the gods, which devotees express in the performance of *puja* (religious ritual-like prayer), *bhajan* (devotional singing), and meditation. *Puja* may be performed at home or in a temple in front of an idol(s) of god(s). It involves some kind of offering to the gods (flowers being the most common) and is an essential part of the practice of Hindu faith. For Hindus the physical symbol or idol of god is the material form through which god appears in this world. Hindu devotees may worship Shiva, Kali, Ganesha, or any one of thousands of gods and manifestations of gods in the Hindu pantheon, and may believe in a Supreme Being who is either their chosen deity or some unnamed force even higher than the gods. Hinduism believes in the existence of three worlds: The material universe we live in, the astral plane where angels and spirits live and, finally, the spiritual world of the gods.

BUDDHISM   Though Buddhism originated in India around 500 B.C., when the Indian prince Siddhartha Gautama attained enlightenment and became the Buddha (Enlightened One) at Bodhgaya, only some six million still practice the belief in India, the majority of them from Tibet or Nepal or converted during the mass conversion of lower castes by the anti-caste leader Dr. Ambedkar in 1956. (The Buddhist following is of course far higher outside India, particularly in the rest of Asia; even in the West, Buddhism appears to be on the rise.)

Unlike any other religion, Buddhism does not advocate belief in a godhead; it instead expects the individual to seek truth within his own experience and control his dharma and karma without relying on divine intervention. Buddhist philosophy is based on the idea that life is riddled with conflict and pain caused by desire (or craving) and ignorance, and to escape from this suffering you need to follow the Eight-Fold Path to gain Enlightenment, or *nirvana.* The Eight-Fold Path advocates Right Understanding, Right Thought, Right Speech, Right Action, Right Mode of Living, Right Endeavor, Right Mindfulness, and Right Concentration. As is the case in Hinduism, one carries one's karma through a cycle of rebirths until the attainment of nirvana. Meditation, chanting, counting beads, and lighting lamps are some of the ways in which Buddhists pursue their spiritual goal of enlightenment.

JAINISM   This began as a reform movement and became a religion under the 24th Jain *trithankara* (prophet) Vardhaman, later called Mahavira (incidentally, a contemporary of Buddha), in the 6th century B.C. Though it never spread beyond India, today some four million Jains live here, predominantly in Gujarat. The principles of Jainism include strict vegetarianism and extreme reverence for all forms of life—even insects and plants are believed to have *jives,* or souls. Jains believe in reincarnation and salvation (or *moksha*), which can be achieved through respect for and consideration of all forms of life, and living a life of asceticism, meditation, fasting, and pilgrimage to holy places. According to Jain philosophy, the soul journeys through 14 stages before the final burning up of all karma and freedom from bondage.

There are two sects of Jains—Shvetambara and Digambara. Shvetambara vow to avoid intentional injury to others and to lead a life of honesty and detachment from worldly passions. The Digambaras are even more strict in their beliefs and practices—as a symbol of their complete detachment from material possessions, the highest monks of this sect wear no clothes. Their temples are among the finest in India: Karnataka's famous Shravanbelagola Temple is a Digambara temple, while the celebrated Dilwara (Mount Abu, Rajasthan) and Shatrunjaya (Palitana, Gujarat) temples are important Svetambara places of pilgrimage.

SIKHISM   This religion emerged in the 15th century out of a rejection of caste distinctions and idolatry under the founder, Guru Nanak, who wanted to bring together the best of Hinduism and Islam. Nine gurus, all of whom are equally revered by Sikhs, followed him, and today there are over 16 million Sikhs in India. Like Hinduism, Sikhism accepts the doctrine of reincarnation, but worship is based on meditation and not ritual or asceticism. Like Muslims, Sikhs believe in one omnipresent universal God; worship takes place in *gurdwaras,* and the holy book is the *Granth Sahib.* The 16th-century Golden Temple at Amritsar is the holiest Sikh place of worship (and has a truly sacred atmosphere).

Charity is an important aspect of the religion, and the gurdwaras always run community kitchens where anyone can eat free. Sikhs are expected to never cut their hair—which makes Sikh men, who wind their long hair under large turbans and sport large beards, one of the most easily recognized male communities in India.

OTHER RELIGIONS   **Zoroastrianism, Judaism, Islam,** and **Christianity** did not originate in India, but are all represented, with Islam and Christianity (which, incidentally, originated within 600 years of each other) the second- and third-largest religious groups, respectively, in India. Muslims (who comprise about 10% of the population) tend to be concentrated in the north, Christians in the south. Every major Christian and Muslim sect and denomination is represented, and the beliefs and practices of each group vary accordingly, some with indigenous nuances. But overall they tend to follow the main tenets of these religions as practiced worldwide. It is estimated that only some 15,000 Jews still live in India, mostly in Cochin, Kerala, and these numbers continue to dwindle. Zoroastrianism, one of the world's oldest religions, dating back to the 7th or 6th century B.C., arrived in India in the 10th century A.D. with refugees fleeing religious persecution in Persia (latter-day Iran). Though numerically they are a tiny religious minority, the descendents of these refugees (called **Parsis**) have made a distinctive mark as a social and economic group in India. Followers believe in a single God, Ahura Mazda, whose prophet Zarathustra is their guide, and fire is considered sacred and symbolic of God. Parsis therefore worship in a Fire Temple (closed to non-Parsis), and Zoroastrian philosophy regards life as an eternal battle of the forces good and evil. Again, the path to overcome evil is through good thoughts, words, and deeds. Where possible, their dead are placed in dry wells at a Tower of Silence to be consumed by vultures. This practice is based on the belief that since dead matter pollutes, cremation and burial would pollute the respective elements. Today's Parsis regard this unique method of disposing of the dead as being useful to the cycle of life even after one's death.

4 Indian Cuisine

by Niloufer Venkatraman
Anthropologist, writer, and dedicated foodie

Indian cooking is one of the great cuisines of the world. Like the country itself, however, it varies greatly from region to region, and you'll discover a great deal more to savor than the ubiquitous *kormas* and *tikka* masalas (known to the naive simply as "curry") that most Westerners are familiar with. Not only does each Indian community and ethnic and regional group have a distinct cuisine, but there is a great deal of fusion within the country—subtle variations and combinations you're only likely to pick up once you are familiar with the basics. A good way to sample a variety of dishes in a particular region is to order a *thali* meal, in which an assortment of items is served. Basic staples served with every meal throughout the subcontinent are rice, *dal* (lentils), and/or some form of *roti* (breads). The following is a brief summary of regional variations and general dining tips.

SOUTHERN STATES   Food from the coastal areas of India almost always contains a generous quantity of coconut—besides using it in cooking, most Maharashtrian homes offer grated coconut as a garnish to every dish. Rice also dominates the food of southern India, as do their "breads," which are more like pancakes and made of a rice (and/or dal) batter—these *appams, idiapams,* and *dosas* are found throughout the south. *Dosas* are in fact a South Indian "breakfast" favorite (consumed anytime), as are *idlis* and *vadas,* all of which have become part of mainstream cooking in many parts of India. *Idli* is a steamed rice and lentil dumpling, *dosa* a pancake (similar batter), and *vada* a deep-fried donut-shaped snack. All should be eaten fresh and hot with a coconut chutney and *sambar,* which is a specially seasoned *dal* (lentils), also eaten with steamed rice. In Tamil Nadu a large number of people are vegetarian, but in Kerala, Goa, and Mumbai, you must sample the fresh fish! Delicious kebabs and slow-cooked meals are what you'll find in Hyderabadi cuisine; inspired by the courts of the *nawabs* (nobles), it's similar to Mughlai cooking, but stronger in flavor.

NORTHERN STATES   India's great meat-eating tradition comes from the Mughals and Kashmiris, whose *rogan josh* and creamy *korma* dishes, along with kebabs and biryanis, have become the backbone of Indian restaurants overseas. The most popular tradition—tandoor (clay oven) cooking—is part of India's Mughal gastronomic heritage. Tandoor dishes are effectively "barbecued" vegetables, *paneer* (Indian cheese), or meat that has been marinated and tenderized in spiced yogurt, cooked over coals, and then either served "dry" as a kebab or in a rich spiced gravy like the *korma.* Recently revived is the tradition of *dum pukht,* enjoyed by the erstwhile *nawabs* of Awadh in Lucknow and surrounds, where all the ingredients are sealed and slow-cooked in a pot, around which coals are placed. Nothing escapes the sealed pot, preserving the flavors.

NORTH-WEST (PUNJAB) SPECIALS   Besides trying the various tandoor dishes, you should order *parathas:* A Punjabi specialty, this thick version of the traditional *chapati* is stuffed with potatoes, cabbage, radish, or a variety of other fillings. Be aware that many North Indians love their ghee (clarified butter); sensitive stomachs (or those watching their weight) should simply specify that they would prefer their *paratha* without ghee. A general note of caution when dining in North India: If the menu specifies a choice between oil and ghee as a cooking method, you should probably specify the former. And keep in mind that if you exclusively eat oily, highly pungent, so-called Punjabi fare, you are bound to feel ill, so make sure you vary your meals by dining at South Indian restaurants, which combine a healthy balance of carbohydrate and protein (rice and dal); in northern states you will find *rotis* (breads) combined with *rajma* (kidney beans), *puris* (bread), *chole* (chickpeas), and so on.

EASTERN STATES   Freshwater fish (such as *hilsa, bekti,* and *rohu*) take pride of place at the Bengali table, which incidentally considers itself to be the apotheosis of Indian cooking. In Bengal, mustard oil (which has its own powerful flavor) is the preferred cooking oil. Sweets are another Bengali gift to the world; these are made from milk that has been split and converted to *paneer* (Indian cheese) and that has names like *rosogolla* (or *rasgulla*) and *sandesh.*

SPICES   Literally hundreds of spices (masalas) and spice combinations form the culinary backdrop to India, but a few are used so often that they are considered indispensable. Turmeric *(haldi)*—in its common form a yellow powder with a slightly bitter flavor—is the foremost, not least for its antiseptic properties. Mustard seeds are also very important, particularly in the South. Cumin seeds and coriander seeds and their powders are widely used in different forms—whether you powder, roast, or fry a spice, and how you do so, makes a big difference in determining the flavors of a dish. Chili powder is another common ingredient, available in umpteen different varieties and potencies. Then there are the vital "sweet" spices—cardamom *(elaichi),* clove *(lavang),* cinnamon *(dalchini),* and black pepper *(kali miri)* are key ingredients in the making of the spice combination known as *garam masala.* Though tolerance to spicy food is extremely subjective, let your preference be known by asking whether the item is spicy-hot *(tikha hai)* and indicating no-chili, medium-spicy, and so on. "Curry powder" as it is merchandised in the West is rarely found or used in India. "Curry" more or less defines the complex and very diverse combination of spices freshly ground together, often to create a spicy sauce-like liquid that comes in varying degrees of pungency and varies in texture and consistency, from thin and smooth to thick and grainy, ideally accompanied by rice or breads.

STAPLES & ACCOMPANIMENTS   All over the country, Indian food is served with either the staple of rice or bread—the most popular being unleavened (pan-roasted) breads (called *rotis*); tandoor-baked breads; deep-fried breads *(puris and bhaturas)* or pancake-style ones. *Chapatis,* thin whole-wheat breads fried in a flat iron pan *(tava),* are the most common bread eaten in Indian homes, though these are not as widely available as restaurant breads. The thicker version of *chapatis* are called *parathas,* which can be stuffed with an assortment of vegetables or even ground meat. Tandoor-roasted breads are made with a more refined flour and include *naans,* tandoori *rotis,* and the super-thin *roomali* (handkerchief) *rotis.* Tandoor breads turn a little leathery when cold and are best eaten fresh.

Dal, made of lentils (any of a huge variety) and seasoned with mustard, cumin, chilies, and/or other spices, is another Indian staple eaten throughout the country. *Khichdi,* a mixture of rice, lentils, and spices, is a great meal by itself and considered comfort food. In some parts it's served with *kadhi*—a savory sour yogurt-based stew to which chickpea flour dumplings may be added. You'll usually be served accompaniments in the form of onion and lime, chutneys, pickles, relishes, and a variety of yogurt-based salads called *raita. Papads* (roasted or fried crisps) are another favorite food accompaniment that arrive with your meal in a variety of shapes, sizes, and flavors.

MEAT   A large number of Indians are vegetarian for religious reasons, with entire towns serving only vegetarian meals, but these are so delicious that meat lovers are unlikely to feel put out. Elsewhere, meat lovers should probably (unless you're dining in a top-end big-city restaurant) opt for the chicken and fish dishes—not only are these usually very tender and succulent, but the "mutton" or "lamb" promised on the menu is more often than not goat, while "beef" (seldom on the menu—beef is taboo for most Hindus, and the ban on cow slaughter continues to be a raging national debate) is usually water buffalo. Again, there are regional differences, like in "Portuguese" Goa, where pork is common.

SWEETS   Indians love sweets (called *mithais, mishtaan,* or "sweet meats'"), and they love them very sweet. In fact, Western palates often find Indian sweets *too* sweet; if this is the case, sample some of the dry-fruit-based sweets. Any occasion for celebration necessitates distributing a round of sweets as a symbol of spreading sweetness (happiness) around. Every region of the country has a variety of specialty dishes made from an array of ingredients, but largely milk-based. This includes *pedas* and *laddus* (soft, circular), *barfis* (brownie-like), *halwas* (sticky or wet), *kheer* (rice pudding-like), and so on. Whatever you do, don't miss the Indian *kulfi,* a creamy, rich ice cream flavored with saffron, nuts, or seasonal fruit.

FRUITS   If the spiciness of the meals unsettles your stomach, try living on fruit for a day. You'll get a whole range of delicious tropical varieties (with any luck, in a basket in your hotel room) ranging from guavas and jackfruit to lychees and the most coveted fruit of them all, the mango. More than 200 varieties of mangoes are grown in India, but the most popular ones (Alphonso or *aphoos*) come from Maharashtra; try to taste one when you're in Mumbai.

BEVERAGES   *Chai* (tea) is India's national drink. Normally served in small quantities, it is hot, made with milk that is usually flavored with ginger or cardamom, and rather sweet unless you request otherwise. Instant coffee is widely available (and may be mixed in your five-star hotel's "filter coffee" pot), but in South India you'll get excellent fresh brews. Another drink worth trying is *lassi,* liquefied sweetened yogurt. ***Note:*** The yogurt is sometimes thinned with water, so you're only safe consuming *lassis* in places where they can assure you no water was added at all, or where they will make it with bottled water (that you purchase separately). *Lassi*'s close companion is *chaas,* a savory version that is very thin and served with Gujarati meals. With southern food, it is served with a flavorful assortment of herbs and spices. In general, you should avoid ice in any beverage unless you are satisfied that it is made from boiled water.

EATING ETIQUETTE   **Eating with your hands:** Indians generally eat with their hands, and although very few do so in five-star Westernized restaurants, the majority will in most other places. Even the simplest restaurant will be able to provide a spoon as cutlery, but if you really want to experience your meal in an authentic manner, follow suit. Note that you should ideally only use your right hand (though in places where tourists go, people are unlikely to be offended if you use your left). In the North, where the food is "drier," you are traditionally not supposed to dirty more than the first two digits of your hand. In the South, where the food is much "wetter," you may use the whole hand to eat.

Sharing your food: It is typically Indian to share food or drinks, even if you don't really want to. On long train journeys, you're likely to meet Indian families carrying a lot of food, which they will invite you to share—do sample some, if only to get a taste of home cooking. In return, you can buy them a round of tea or cold drinks when the vendors come by.

Sharing food at a restaurant is another Indian norm; menus are set up to cater to this style of dining. So, for example, if two or more of you go to a Mughlai restaurant, you would order perhaps two kinds of kebabs, two kinds of meat/vegetable entrees, one rice, and several breads *(rotis)*. It's a good way to try a range of items.

The hygiene of *jootha:* While sharing is good manners, *jootha* is considered offensive in many parts. This refers to drinking from the same glass, eating with the same spoon, taking a bite out of someone's sandwich, or "double dipping." To share a bread or snack, break off a piece; when sharing a bottle of water, don't put your mouth to it but tilt your head back and pour. Although there are no definite rules about what is permissible or not, just make sure that you use common courtesy when sharing a meal with others.

SALADS   The practice of eating Western-style salads (except raw onion) is unusual, but some restaurants do have them on the menu. Beware that it is only advisable to eat these in top-end restaurants, and make sure that the vegetables have been freshly cut and washed in boiled water.

STREET FOOD   Even in smaller cities like Indore and Jaipur, street food has a fantastic tradition and following. *Samosas, vadas, bhelpuri, sev, bhajias,* and a host of deep-fried foods are all delicious, and you should try them on your trip. It's not easy for the first-time visitor to figure out which street foods are safe to eat, however—best to look for an outlet that has loads of people lining up; this means that neither the food nor the oil have been around long. Alternatively, ask your hotel for suggestions.

5 Reading India

by Lynne Aschman
Indiaphile

More than almost any other destination, India demands that you immerse yourself in the local culture to make sense of all you see and experience.

LITERATURE/FICTION   Note that while E. M. Forster's classic, *A Passage to India,* remains a wonderful read, as does the lengthy *Jewel in the Crown* series by Anthony Powell, these are mainly told from the perspective of English colonizers and won't give you much insight into India today. All of the books listed below are set in India.

A highly recommended start is ***The Circle of Reason*** (Viking), written by Amitav Ghosh, an anthropologist by training and a born writer; his book gives a brilliant description of village life. Alternatively, pick up a copy of ***The Calcutta Chromosome*** (HarperCollins), a slyly subversive take on Western science that reads almost like a Victorian thriller. And of course, Arundhati Roy's Booker Prize–winner ***The God of Small Things*** (HarperCollins) will make you want to travel the waterways of Kerala to see the village life she describes so vividly.

Another Booker Prize–winner, Salman Rushdie, is a controversial, challenging, and richly rewarding writer whose work is impossible to categorize easily; suffice it to say that he is incapable of writing a boring sentence. The first long section of ***The Moor's Last Sigh*** (Knopf) is located in the old town of Cochin; read this book while you're in Kerala and visiting some of the sites about which Rushdie writes. ***Midnight's Children*** tells of two babies swapped at birth, one Hindu and one Muslim, one rich and one poor, born on the stroke of midnight at India's independence. ***The Satanic Verses*** is his most difficult read, but worth dipping into if you want to see why a *fatwa* was issued against him and the book banned in many countries.

Vikram Seth's ***A Suitable Boy*** (HarperCollins) is a huge (1,475 pages), enjoyable novel set in several cities. If you drive from Varanasi to Agra, you will pass by the scene, described by Seth, of a disaster that befell pilgrims there in the 1980s. (You may also find yourself incorporating the phrase "a tight slap" into your speech; don't ask—just read.) Like Rohinton Mistry's novels, it has been compared with novels by Dickens. Rohinton Mistry's own ***A Fine Balance*** and ***Such a Long Journey*** (Faber & Faber) both won several prizes. The latter, set in Bombay, is documentary realism at its finest and describes the lives of ordinary people against a political background. *A Fine Balance* is a political novel with unforgettable characters and appalling horrors, set during 1975's State of Emergency. The central characters will stay with you for a long time.

Aniruddha Bahal is a journalist whose government exposés led to the toppling of several top ministers. His first novel, ***Bunker 13*** (Farrar, Straus & Giroux), is set in modern Kashmir and has been described as "dirty realism." **Note:** *Bunker 13* might be a good companion piece to Arundhati Roy's lengthy essay on nuclear nonproliferation, the main ideas of which appear in a shortened form as an ***Introduction to India: A Mosaic*** (edited by Robert B. Silvers and Barbara Epstein; NYRB). This is a book of writings that formerly appeared in the *New*

Bollywood & Beyond: India on the Big Screen

Bollywood (the word used to denominate most Hindi cinema) is the biggest producer of films in the world, churning out hundreds of movies annually, all of which feature super-kitschy images of buxom, bee-stung-lipped heroines gyrating to high-pitched melodies while strapping studs thrust their groins in time to lip-synched banal-and-breezy lyrics. These are wonderful, predictable melodramas in which the hero is always valiant and virile, the girl always voluptuous and virtuous. The battle between good and evil (a bankable hero and a recognizably nasty villain) must be intense, long-winded, and ultimately unsurprising—audiences do not pay good money to be challenged, but to be entertained. These are not only the dreams of popular imagination, but dependable workings and reworkings of the myths and epic legends that Hindus learn from early childhood. And while 2002 was heralded as the worst year ever for Bollywood, the rest of the world has finally begun to sit up and take notice with Ashutosh Gowariker's **Lagaan** (2001), which was nominated for an Oscar. A wonderful tale of heroism (with the requisite song and dance) about a group of peasants who take on their British rulers in a game of cricket, it should top your list. Another movie well worth seeking out is **Devdas** (2002), the most expensive Hindu movie ever made. This popular tale of a man frustrated by his quest for love and money has been remade eight times; the most recent stars Bollywood biggies: Shah Rukh Khan, Madhuri Dixit, and the beautiful Aishwarya Rai, a former Miss Universe. Another worthwhile watch is **Asoka**, an epic Indian film about the powerful warrior king (see "India Past to Present," earlier in this chapter) who turned to Buddhism. Big on action and romance, it's saturated with images that call up India's legend-soaked history.

But to view Bollywood movies as the be-all and end-all of India's film industry would be akin to thinking that big-budget blockbusters are the

York Review of Books and cover a wide spectrum of topics from literature, politics, and nuclear power to personal memoirs set in Varanasi and Srinagar.

Many Indians' favorite writer is Khushwant Singh, India's best-known journalist. *Train to Pakistan* in *The Collected Novels* (Penguin Books) is his best-known novella and deals with the pain of Partition and its cruel consequences.

NONFICTION   Essential nonfiction includes Nobel Prize–winner V. S. Naipaul's *India, A Million Mutinies Now* (Vintage), which shows Naipaul's brilliance at evoking a complex society through listening sympathetically to ordinary Indians and interpreting the country through their stories. The section on Bangalore, where most of India's young software writers live, is particularly interesting, as is the section on Bombay, where he visits parts of the city few tourists will venture. His *India: A Wounded Civilization,* written several years earlier, gives a darker view of the country and its politics.

There are several good recent histories of India, of which *A New History of India* by Stanley Wolpert (OUP) is very readable, as is the heavily illustrated

only movies the U.S. film industry make. In fact, the first Indian director who made international art audiences sit up and take notice was Satyajit Ray, who received a Lifetime Achievement Oscar for his prolific body of work in 1992. Operating out of West Bengal's "Tollywood," Ray made movies that were the antithesis of Bollywood's; he was the director who stated that "the man in the street is a more challenging subject for exploration than people in the heroic mold" and that he found "muted emotions more interesting and challenging." Ray directed some 40 feature films, documentaries, and short subjects, of which *Pather Panchali (Song of the Little Road)* in 1955, *Aparajito (The Unvanquished)* in1956, *Apur Sansar (The World of Apu)* in 1959, and *Goopy Gyne Bagha Byne (The Adventures of Goopy and Bagha)* in 1968 were the most internationally acclaimed.

For those interested in classic dramas dealing with India's history under the Raj, the classic dramas include David Lean's atmospheric *A Passage to India* (which will make you squirm at Western cultural arrogance) and Richard Attenborough's *Gandhi* (1982). But to gain an insight into contemporary India, you need to delve into Mira Nair; her *Salaam Bombay* (1988) will give you a taste of what life is like for the homeless on Mumbai's streets, seen through the eyes of a filmmaker with a deep sense of empathy. More recently, Nair's award-winning *Monsoon Wedding* (2002), a joyous celebration of India's wet season, will introduce you to the Indian experience of love, romance, and family gatherings; it's uproarious good fun and a wonderful exposé of local middle-class issues. Last, but not least, *Fire, Earth,* and *Water*—a trilogy of powerful films by Deepa Mehta—examine burning social and political issues from a feminine perspective. Banned in India, *Fire* is a poignant tale about a pair of sisters-in-law who long to be loved and ultimately find comfort in one another's arms.

A Concise History of India by Francis Watson. Also recommended are *Modern South Asia: History, Culture, Political Economy,* by Sugata Bose and Ayesha Jalal (Routledge); *A History of India,* by Peter Robb (Palgrave); and *A Concise History of India* by Barbara Metcalf and Thomas Metcalf (Cambridge University Press). If you are interested in Indian politics, *The Idea of India,* by Sunil Khilnani (Farrar Strauss & Giroux) is a challenging look at contemporary India and its notion of nationhood and democracy.

For a spiritual view, try the beautifully illustrated *A Spiritual Journal,* by Osho (St. Martin's Press). If the Bhagavad-Gita interests you, Ranchor Prime's *The Illustrated Bhagavad Gita* (Barron's) is a good edition.

This is just a start. But be warned—the writing of India is as seductive as the place of its origin. Once hooked, you'll want more.

Index

Ruthlessly Honest Destination Guides with an Attitude

- Irreverent Guide to Amsterdam
- Irreverent Guide to Boston
- Irreverent Guide to Chicago
- Irreverent Guide to Las Vegas
- Irreverent Guide to London
- Irreverent Guide to Los Angeles
- Irreverent Guide to Manhattan
- Irreverent Guide to New Orleans

- Irreverent Guide to Paris
- Irreverent Guide to Rome
- Irreverent Guide to San Francisco
- Irreverent Guide to Seattle & Portland
- Irreverent Guide to Vancouver
- Irreverent Guide to Walt Disney World®
- Irreverent Guide to Washington, D.C.

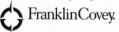

Booked aisle seat.

Reserved room with a view.

With a queen – no, make that a king-size bed.

With Travelocity, you can book your flights and hotels together, so you can get even better deals than if you booked them separately. You'll save time and money without compromising the quality of your trip. Choose your airline seat, search for alternate airports, pick your hotel room type, even choose the neighborhood you'd like to stay in

Travelocity

Visit www.travelocity.com
or call 1-888-TRAVELOCITY